OCP

Oracle® Certified Professional Java® SE 11 Programmer II

Study Guide

Exam 1Z0-816 and Exam 1Z0-817

Scott Selikoff

Jeanne Boyarsky

SYBEX®
A Wiley Brand

For my daughter, Sophia, you're the best combination of super silly and super serious. You always know exactly what you want. May you never lose that trait as you grow into a strong woman.
—Scott

Happy 20th anniversary to NYC FIRST and StuyPulse FRC Team 694.
—Jeanne

Acknowledgments

Scott and Jeanne would like to thank numerous individuals for their contribution to this book. Thank you to Kathryn Duggan for guiding us through the process and making the book better in so many ways. Thank you to Janeice DelVecchio for being our technical editor as we wrote this book. Janeice pointed out many subtle errors in addition to the big ones. And thank you to Elena Felder for being our technical proofreader and finding the errors that we managed to sneak by Janeice. This book also wouldn't be possible without many people at Wiley, including Kenyon Brown, Pete Gaughan, Christine O'Connor, Kim Wimpsett, Johnna VanHoose Dinse and so many others.

Scott could not have reached this point without his wife, Patti, and family, whose love and support makes this book possible. He would like to thank his twin daughters, Olivia and Sophia, and youngest daughter, Elysia, for their patience and understanding especially when it was "time for Daddy to work in his office!" Scott would like to extend his gratitude to his wonderfully patient co-author, Jeanne, on this, their fifth book. He doesn't know how she puts up with him, but he's glad she does and thrilled at the quality of books we produce. A big thanks to Matt Dalen, who has been a great friend, sounding board, and caring father to Olivia, Adeline, and newborn Henry. Finally, Scott would like to thank his mother and retired teacher, Barbara Selikoff, for teaching him the value of education, and his father, Mark Selikoff, for instilling in him the benefits of working hard.

Jeanne would personally like to thank Chris Kreussling for knowing more than a decade ago that she would someday write a book. He was a great mentor for many years and definitely shaped her career. Sibon Barman was helpful in getting feedback on the modules chapter, and Susanta Chattopadhyay provided real-life use cases for both service locator and serialization. Stuart Dabbs Halloway's 2001 book provided examples of `serialPeristentFields`. Scott was a great co-author, improving everything Jeanne wrote while writing his own chapters. A big thank-you to everyone at `CodeRanch.com` who asked and responded to questions and comments about our books. Finally, Jeanne would like to thank all of the new programmers at `CodeRanch.com` and FIRST robotics teams FRC 694, FTC 310, and FTC 479 for the constant reminders of how new programmers think.

We'd both like to thank Marcus Biel for providing a European's take on our localization content. Last but not least, both Scott and Jeanne would like to give a big thank-you to the readers of all our books. Hearing from all of you who enjoyed the book and passed the exam is a great feeling. We'd also like to thank those who pointed out errors and made suggestions for improvements in the 1Z0-815 Java 11 book. As of April 2020, the top two were Nikolai Vinoku and Edmond Yong. Also, an honorable mention to Jakub Chrobak.

About the Authors

Scott Selikoff is a professional software consultant, author, and owner of Selikoff Solutions, LLC, which provides software development solutions to businesses in the tri-state New York City area. Skilled in a plethora of software languages and platforms, Scott specializes in full-stack database-driven systems, cloud-based applications, microservice architectures, and service-oriented architectures.

A native of Toms River, New Jersey, Scott achieved his Bachelor of Arts degree from Cornell University in Mathematics and Computer Science in 2002, after three years of study. In 2003, he received his Master of Engineering degree in Computer Science, also from Cornell University.

As someone with a deep love of education, Scott has always enjoyed teaching others new concepts. He's given lectures at Cornell University and Rutgers University, as well as conferences including Oracle Code One and The Server Side Java Symposium. Scott lives in New Jersey with his loving wife, Patti; three amazing daughters, twins Olivia and Sophia and little Elysia; and two very playful dogs, Webby and Georgette. You can find out more about Scott at www.linkedin.com/in/selikoff or follow him on Twitter @ScottSelikoff.

Jeanne Boyarsky was selected as a Java Champion in 2019. She has worked as a Java developer for more than 18 years at a bank in New York City where she develops, mentors, and conducts training. Besides being a senior moderator at CodeRanch.com in her free time, she works on the forum code base. Jeanne also mentors the programming division of a FIRST robotics team where she works with students just getting started with Java. She also speaks at several conferences each year.

Jeanne got her Bachelor of Arts degree in 2002 and her Master in Computer Information Technology degree in 2005. She enjoyed getting her Master's degree in an online program while working full-time. This was before online education was cool! Jeanne is also a Distinguished Toastmaster and a Scrum Master. You can find out more about Jeanne at www.jeanneboyarsky.com or follow her on Twitter at @JeanneBoyarsky.

Scott and Jeanne are both moderators on the CodeRanch.com forums and can be reached there for question and comments. They also co-author a technical blog called Down Home Country Coding at www.selikoff.net.

In addition to this book, Scott and Jeanne are also authors of the following best-selling Java 8 certification books: *OCA Oracle Certified Associate Java SE 8 Programmer I Study Guide* (Sybex, 2015) and *OCP Oracle Certified Professional Java SE 8 Programmer II Study Guide* (Sybex, 2016). These two books have been combined into the single release: *OCA/OCP Java SE 8 Programmer Certification Kit: Exam 1Z0-808 and Exam 1Z0-809* (Sybex 2016). They have also written a book of practice test questions for the Java 8 certification exams: *OCA/OCP Java SE 8 Programmer Practice Tests* (Sybex, 2017). Their most recent book is *OCP Oracle Certified Professional Java SE 11 Programmer I Study Guide: Exam 1Z0-815* (Sybex, 2019).

Contents at a Glance

Contents

Introduction

Congratulations! If you are reading this, you've likely passed the 1Z0-815 Programmer I exam, and you are now ready to start your journey through the 1Z0-816 (Java SE Programmer II) exam. Or perhaps you came here from an older version of the certification and are now taking the IZ0-817 (Upgrade OCP Java 6, 7 & 8 to Java SE 11 Developer) exam. In either case, this book will guide you on your path to becoming a Java 11 Oracle Certified Professional.

The Programmer II exam builds upon the Programmer I exam. You are expected to know all of Programmer I material when taking the second exam. Some objectives on the 1Z0-816 exam are the same as those on the 1Z0-815 exam, such as the `final` modifier. Most are implied. For example, the 1Z0-816 exam objectives don't mention `if` statements, loops, and constructors. Clearly, you still need to know these. We will also point out differences in Java 11 to help those of you new to Java 11.

If you didn't score well on the 1Z0-815 exam or if it has been a while since you took it, we recommend reviewing the book you used to study for it. You really need to know the fundamentals well. If you've misplaced your study materials, feel free to check out our 1Z0-815 book, *OCP Oracle Certified Professional Java SE 11 Programmer I Study Guide: Exam 1Z0-815* (Sybex, 2019).

In the introduction, we will cover important information about the exam before moving on to information about this book. Finally, this introduction ends with an assessment test so you can see how much studying lays ahead of you.

Understanding the Exam

At the end of the day, the exam is a list of questions. The more you know about the structure of the exam, the better you are likely to do. For example, knowing how many questions the exam contains allows you to manage your progress and time remaining better. In this section, we discuss the details of the exam, along with some history of previous certification exams.

Broader Objectives

In previous certification exams, the list of exam objectives tended to include specific topics, classes, and APIs that you needed to know for the exam. For example, take a look at an objective for the 1Z0-809 (OCP 8) exam:

- Use BufferedReader, BufferedWriter, File, FileReader, FileWriter, FileInputStream, FileOutputStream, ObjectOutputStream, ObjectInputStream, and PrintWriter in the java.io package.

Now compare it with the equivalent objective for the 1Z0-816 (OCP 11) exam:

- Use I/O Streams to read and write files

Notice the difference? The older version is more detailed and describes specific classes you will need to understand. The newer version is a lot vaguer. It also gives the exam writers a lot more freedom to insert a new feature, for example, without having to update the list of objectives.

So how do you know what to study? By reading this study guide of course! We've spent years studying the certification exams, in all of their forms, and have carefully cultivated topics, material, and practice questions that we are confident can lead to successfully passing the exam.

Choosing Which Exam to Take

Java is now 25 years old, celebrating being "born" in 1995. As with anything 25 years old, there is a good amount of history and variation between different versions of Java. Over the years, the certification exams have changed to cover different topics. The names of the exams have even changed. This book covers the Java 11 exam.

Those with more recent certifications might remember that Oracle released two exams each for Java 7 and Java 8. The first exam tended to be easier, and completing it granted you the title of Oracle Certified Associate (OCA). The second exam was a lot more difficult, with much longer questions, and completing it granted you the title of Oracle Certified Professional (OCP).

Oracle did not release an exam for Java 9 or Java 10, probably because neither of these is a Long Term Support (LTS) release. With Java 11, Oracle decided to discontinue both the OCA certification and its associated exam. You still have to take two exams to earn an OCP title. The difference is that now you do not obtain a certification title from completing the first exam.

Figure I.1 shows these past and current Java certifications. This image is helpful if you run into material online that references older exams. It is also helpful if you have an older certification and are trying to determine where it fits in.

FIGURE I.1   Past and current Java certifications

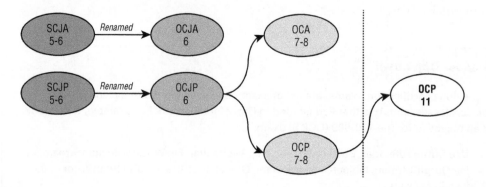

Figure I.2 shows the exams you need to take in order to earn the latest Java certification if you don't have any existing Java certifications. If you haven't taken the 1Z0-815 exam yet, see our *OCP Oracle Certified Professional Java SE 11 Programmer I Study Guide: Exam 1Z0-815* (Sybex, 2019).

FIGURE I.2   Latest Java certification exams

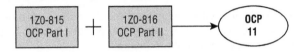

If you already hold a Java certification, you need to decide which exam you can take to earn the Java 11 OCP title. Besides the 1Z0-816 Programmer II exam, there is also a 1Z0-817 Upgrade exam. Oracle has defined a number of upgrade paths to achieve the OCP title, shown in Figure I.3.

FIGURE I.3   Exam prerequisites

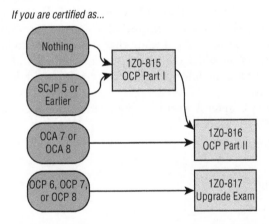

In a nutshell, you can take the 1Z0-816 exam if you passed the 1Z0-815 exam or hold the OCA 7 or 8 title. Oracle's goal here is to help people get to Java 11 OCP certification if they are halfway through the journey to OCP certification.

If you hold a recent OCP 6, 7, or 8 certification title (or even the older Sun Certified Programmer 6 title), then you can take the 1Z0-817 exam to obtain the Java 11 OCP title with just one exam. Those with a Java certification older than this will have to start over and take the 1Z0-815 exam, followed by the 1Z0-816 exam.

What if you hold both OCA and OCP Java 7 or 8 certifications? Well, in that case you have a decision to make. Passing either the 1Z0-816 or 1Z0-817 exam will grant you the Java 11 OCP title. We recommend reviewing the objectives between the two exams and deciding which one you feel more comfortable with.

There are also two edge cases. Those who passed the OCA 6 exam must still take the 1Z0-815 exam. The OCA 6 exam covered far less material than the OCA 7 or 8.

Additionally, those who passed the OCP 7 or 8 exam but never received the OCP title because they didn't pass the OCA exam, need to take the 1Z0-815 exam. After that, you have a choice of the 1Z0-816 exam or the 1Z0-817 exam.

> If you're not sure which exam you should take, you can post questions on CodeRanch.com, and the community will be happy to help. You might even get a response from Scott or Jeanne!

Taking the Upgrade Exam

The chapters of this book are structured for those taking the 1Z0-816 Programmer II exam. As we said earlier, though, you can easily rely on this book to prepare for the 1Z0-817 exam. If, after reading the previous section, you decide to take the 1Z0-817 exam, then you should be aware that the objectives between the two exams are not the same.

To help support those taking the 1Z0-817 exam, we include Appendix A, "The Upgrade Exam," as part of this book. This appendix includes material you would have learned when taking the 1Z0-815 Programmer I exam that you will need to know for the 1Z0-817 exam. Because of this, you should actually read this appendix first. For example, you need to first know how to create a module before you can create a module service in Chapter 6, "Modular Applications."

While we think every chapter is worth reading, here are some chapters you can skip if you are taking the 1Z0-817 exam:

- Chapter 2, "Annotations"
- Chapter 8, "I/O"
- Chapter 10, "JDBC"
- Chapter 11, "Security"

For other chapters, the 1Z0-817 exam may involve understanding the entire chapter or select portions of the chapter. We've included a mapping of all of the upgrade exam objectives and their associated chapters in the "Reviewing Exam Objectives" section of this introduction.

Changes to the Exam

At the time of this book being published, all OCP 11 certification exams contain 80 questions and have a duration of 3 hours. The 1Z0-816 exam requires a passing score of 63 percent, while the 1Z0-817 exam requires a passing score of 61 percent.

Oracle has a tendency to fiddle with the length of the exam and the passing score once it comes out. Oracle also likes to "tweak" the exam topics over time. It wouldn't be a surprise for Oracle to make minor changes to the exam objectives, the number of questions, or the passing score after this book goes to print.

If there are any changes to the exam after this book is published, we will note them on the book page of our blog.

www.selikoff.net/ocp11-2

Exam Questions

The exams consist entirely of multiple-choice questions. There are between four and seven possible answers. If a question has more than one answer, the question specifically states exactly how many correct answers there are. This book does not do that. We say "Choose all that apply" to make the questions harder. This means the questions in this book are generally harder than those on the exam. The idea is to give you more practice so you can spot the correct answer more easily on the real exam.

If you read about older versions of the exam online, you might see references to drag-and-drop questions. These questions had you do a puzzle on how to complete a piece of code. Luckily, these are no longer on the exam.

Many of the questions on the exam are code snippets rather than full classes. Saving space by not including imports and/or class definitions leaves room for lots of other code. For example, it is common to come across classes on the exam with portions omitted, like so:

```java
public class Zoo {
   String name;
   // Getters/Setters/Constructors omitted
}
```

In this case, you would assume methods like getName() and setName(), as well as related constructors, exist. For example, we would expect this code to compile:

```java
var name = new Zoo("Java Zoo").getName();
```

Out-of-Scope Material

When you take the exam, you may see some questions that appear to be out of scope. *Don't panic!* Often, these questions do not require knowing anything about the topic to answer the question. For example, after reading this book, you should be able to spot that the following does not compile, even if you've never heard of LocalDate and ChronoUnit:

```java
final LocalDate holiday = LocalDate.now();
holiday = LocalDate.now().plus(5, ChronoUnit.HOURS);
```

The classes and enums used in this question are not in scope for the exam, but the reason it does not compile is in scope. In particular, you should know that you cannot reassign a variable marked `final`.

See, not so scary is it? Expect to see at least a few structures on the exam that you are not familiar with. If they aren't part of your exam preparation material, then you don't need to understand them to answer the question.

Question Topic Tips

The following list of topics is meant to give you an idea of the types of questions and oddities that you might come across on the exam. Being aware of these categories of such questions will help you get a higher score on the exam.

Questions with Extra Information Provided   Imagine the question includes a statement that `XMLParseException` is a checked exception. It's fine if you don't know what an `XMLParseException` is or what XML is for that matter. (If you are wondering, it is a format for data.) This question is a gift. You know the question is about checked and unchecked exceptions.

Questions with Embedded Questions   To answer some questions on the exam, you may have to actually answer two or three subquestions. For example, the question may contain two blank lines, and the question may ask you to choose the two answers that fill in each blank. In some cases, the two answer choices are not related, which means you're really answering multiple questions, not just one! These questions are among the most difficult and time-consuming on the exam because they contain multiple, often independent, questions to answer. Unfortunately, the exam does not give partial credit, so take care when answering questions like these.

Questions with Unfamiliar APIs   If you see a class or method that wasn't covered in this book, assume it works as you would expect. Some of these APIs you might come across, such as `LocalDate`, were on the Java 8 exam and are not part of the Java 11 exams. Assume that the part of the code using that API is correct and look very hard for other errors.

Questions with Made-Up or Incorrect Concepts   In the context of a word problem, the exam may bring up a term or concept that does not make any sense such as saying an interface inherits from a class, which is not a correct statement. In other cases, they may use a keyword that does not exist in Java, like `struct`. For these, you just have to read them carefully and recognize when the exam is using invalid terminology.

Questions That Are Really Out of Scope   When introducing new questions, Oracle includes them as unscored questions at first. This allows them to see how real exam takers do without impacting your score. You will still receive the number of questions as the exam lists. However, a few of them may not count. These unscored questions may contain out-of-scope material or even errors. They will not be marked as unscored, so you still have to do your best to answer them. Follow the previous advice to assume that anything you haven't seen before is correct. That will cover you if the question is being counted!

Reading This Book

It might help to have some idea about how this book has been written. This section contains details about some of the common structures and features you will find in this book, where to go for additional help, and how to obtain bonus material for this book.

Who Should Buy This Book

If you want to obtain the OCP 11 Java programmer certification, this book is definitely for you. If you want to acquire a solid foundation in Java and your goal is to prepare for the exam, then this book is also for you. You'll find clear explanations of the concepts you need to grasp and plenty of help to achieve the high level of professional competency you need in order to succeed in your chosen field.

Since both the 1Z0-816 and 1Z0-817 exams have prerequisites, we assume you have taken at least one Java certification exam prior to reading this book. To help ease the transition, though, we provide refresher material throughout this book. For example, before covering advanced exception handling topics, we review the core exception classes. Likewise, we review how to create functional interfaces and lambda expressions from scratch since this topic is the foundation for a lot of other topics.

How This Book Is Organized

This book consists of this introduction, 11 chapters, and two appendixes. You might have noticed that there are more than 11 exam objectives. We organized what you need to know to make it easy to learn and remember. Each chapter begins with a list of the objectives that are covered in that chapter.

The chapters and appendixes are organized as follows:

- **Chapter 1: Java Fundamentals** covers core Java topics including enums, the `final` modifier, inner classes, and interfaces. There are now many types of interface methods that you need to know for the exam. It also includes an introduction to creating functional interfaces and lambda expressions.

- **Chapter 2: Annotations** describes how to define and apply your own custom annotations, as well as how to use the common built-in ones.

- **Chapter 3: Generics and Collections** goes beyond the basics and demonstrates method references, generics with wildcards, and Collections. The Collections portion covers many common interfaces, classes, and methods that are useful for the exam and in everyday software development.

- **Chapter 4: Functional Programming** explains lambdas and stream pipelines in detail. It also covers the built-in functional interfaces and the Optional class. If you want to become skilled at creating streams, read this chapter more than once!

- **Chapter 5: Exceptions, Assertions, and Localization** shows advanced exception handling topics including creating custom exceptions, try-with-resources statements, and suppressed exceptions. It also covers how to use assertions to validate your program. It concludes with localization and formatting, which allows your program to gracefully support multiple countries or languages.

- **Chapter 6: Modular Applications** shows advanced modularization concepts including services and how to migrate an application to a modular infrastructure.

- **Chapter 7: Concurrency** introduces the concept of thread management and teaches you how to build multithreaded programs using the concurrency API and parallel streams.

- **Chapter 8: I/O** introduces you to managing files and directories using the java.io API. It covers a number of I/O stream classes, teaches you how to serialize data, and shows how to interact with a user.

- **Chapter 9: NIO.2** shows you how to manage files and directories using the newer NIO.2 API. It includes techniques for using streams to traverse and search the file system.

- **Chapter 10: JDBC** provides the basics of working with databases in Java including working with stored procedures.

- **Chapter 11: Security** describes how to securely build your program and protect against common malicious attacks.

- **Appendix A: The Upgrade Exam** covers topics from the 1Z0-815 Programmer I exam that are on the 1Z0-817 Upgrade exam but not on the 1Z0-816 Programmer II exam.

- **Appendix B: Answers to Review Questions** lists the answers to the review questions that are at the end of each chapter.

At the end of each chapter, you'll find a few elements you can use to prepare for the exam:

Summary   This section reviews the most important topics that were covered in the chapter and serves as a good review.

Exam Essentials   This section summarizes highlights that were covered in the chapter. You should be able to convey the information described.

Review Questions   Each chapter concludes with at least 20 review questions. You should answer these questions and check your answers against the ones provided in Appendix B. If you can't answer at least 80 percent of these questions correctly, go back and review the chapter, or at least those sections that seem to be giving you difficulty.

The review questions, assessment test, and other testing elements included in this book are *not* derived from the real exam questions, so don't memorize the answers to these questions and assume that doing so will enable you to pass the exam. You should focus on understanding the topic, as described in the text of the book. This will let you answer the questions provided with this book *and* pass the exam. Learning the underlying topic is also the approach that will serve you best in the workplace—the ultimate goal of a certification.

To get the most out of this book, you should read each chapter from start to finish before going to the chapter-end elements. They are most useful for checking and reinforcing your understanding. Even if you're already familiar with a topic, you should skim the chapter. There are a number of subtleties to Java that you could easily not encounter even when working with Java for years.

If you've taken the OCP 8 Programmer II certification exam, then you'll likely notice that annotations, modular applications, and security are new topics. The exam writers have made changes to all the objectives, though, so make sure you review all of the Java 11 objectives and study the material carefully.

Conventions Used in This Book

This book uses certain typographic styles to help you quickly identify important information and to avoid confusion over the meaning of words such as on-screen prompts. In particular, look for the following styles:

- *Italicized text* indicates key terms that are described at length for the first time in a chapter. (Italics are also used for emphasis.)
- A `monospaced font` indicates code or command-line text.
- *`Italicized monospaced text`* indicates a variable.

In addition to these text conventions, which can apply to individual words or entire paragraphs, a few conventions highlight segments of text.

A tip is something to call particular attention to an aspect of working with a language feature or API.

A note indicates information that's useful or interesting. It is often something to pay special attention to for the exam.

Sidebars

A sidebar is like a note but longer. The information in a sidebar is useful, but it doesn't fit into the main flow of the text.

 Real World Scenario

Real-World Scenario

A real-world scenario is a type of sidebar that describes a task or an example that's particularly grounded in the real world. This is something that is useful in the real world but is not going to show up on the exam.

Getting Help

Both of the authors are moderators at CodeRanch.com. This site is a quite large and active programming forum that is friendly toward Java beginners. It has a forum just for this exam called Programmer Certification. It also has a forum called Java in General for non-exam-specific questions. As you read the book, feel free to ask your questions in either of those forums. It could be you are having trouble compiling a class or that you are just plain confused about something. You'll get an answer from a knowledgeable Java programmer. It might even be one of us.

Interactive Online Learning Environment and Test Bank

We've put together some really great online tools to help you pass the IZ0-816 exam. The interactive online learning environment that accompanies this study guide provides a test bank and study tools to help you prepare for the exam. By using these tools, you can dramatically increase your chances of passing the exam on your first try.

The online test bank includes the following:

Practice Exams   Many sample tests are provided throughout this book and online, including the assessment test, which you'll find at the end of this introduction, and the chapter tests that include the review questions at the end of each chapter. In addition, there are two bonus practice exams. Use these questions to test your knowledge of the study guide material. The online test bank runs on multiple devices.

Flashcards   The online text bank includes two sets of flashcards specifically written to hit you hard, so don't get discouraged if you don't ace your way through them at first! They're there to ensure that you're really ready for the exam. And no worries—armed with the review questions, practice exams, and flashcards, you'll be more than prepared when exam day comes! Questions are provided in digital flashcard format (a question followed by a single correct answer). You can use the flashcards to reinforce your learning and provide last-minute test prep before the exam.

Resources   A glossary of key terms from this book and their definitions is available as a fully searchable PDF.

To register and gain access to this interactive online learning environment, please visit this URL:

www.wiley.com/go/Sybextestprep

Preparing for the Exam

This section includes suggestions and recommendations for how you should prepare for the certification exam. If you're an experienced test taker or you've taken a certification test before, most of this should be common knowledge. For those who are taking the exam for the first time, don't worry! We'll present a number of tips and strategies to help you prepare for the exam.

Creating a Study Plan

Rome wasn't built in a day, so you shouldn't attempt to study for the exam in only one day. Even if you have been certified with a previous version of Java, the new test includes features and components unique to Java 9, 10, and 11 that are covered in this text.

Once you have decided to take the test, you should construct a study plan that fits with your schedule. We recommend that you set aside some amount of time each day, even if it's just a few minutes during lunch, to read or practice for the exam. The idea is to keep your momentum going throughout the exam preparation process. The more consistent you are in how you study, the better prepared you will be for the exam. Try to avoid taking a few days or weeks off from studying, or you're likely to spend a lot of time relearning existing material instead of moving on to new material.

Creating and Running the Code

Although some people can learn Java just by reading a textbook, that's not how we recommend that you study for a certification exam. We want you to be writing your own Java sample applications throughout this book so that you don't just learn the material but that you understand the material as well. For example, it may not be obvious why the following line of code does not compile, but if you try to compile it yourself, the Java compiler will tell you the problem:

```
Predicate pred = String::compareTo // DOES NOT COMPILE
```

 A lot of people post the question "Why does this code not compile?" on the CodeRanch.com forum. If you're stuck or just curious about a behavior in Java, we encourage you to post to the forum. There are a lot of nice people in the Java community standing by to help you.

Sample Test Class

Throughout this book, we present numerous code snippets and ask you whether they'll compile or not and what their output will be. You will place these snippets inside a simple Java application that starts, executes the code, and terminates. You can accomplish this by compiling and running a public class containing a `public static void main(String[] args)` method and adding the necessary import statements, such as the following:

```
// Add any necessary import statements here
public class TestClass {
    public static void main(String[] args) {
        // Add test code here

        // Add any print statements here
        System.out.println("Hello World!");
    }
}
```

This application isn't particularly interesting—it just outputs Hello World! and exits. That said, you could insert many of the code snippets presented in this book in the main() method to determine whether the code compiles, as well as what the code outputs when it does compile.

 Real World Scenario

IDE Software

While studying for the exam, you should develop code using a text editor and command-line Java compiler. Some of you may have prior experience with integrated development environments (IDEs), such as Eclipse, IntelliJ, or Visual Studio Code. An IDE is a software application that facilitates software development for computer programmers. Although such tools are extremely valuable in developing software, they can interfere with your ability to spot problems readily on the exam.

Identifying Your Weakest Link

The review questions in each chapter are designed to help you hone in on those features of the Java language where you may be weak and that are required knowledge for the exam. For each chapter, you should note which questions you got wrong, understand why you got them wrong, and study those areas even more. After you've reread the chapter and written lots of code, you can do the review questions again. In fact, you can take the review questions over and over to reinforce your learning as long as you explain to yourself why it is correct.

"Overstudying" the Online Practice Exam

Although we recommend reading this book and writing your own sample applications multiple times, redoing the online practice exam over and over can have a negative impact in the long run. For example, some individuals study the practice exam so much that they end up memorizing the answers. In this scenario, they can easily become overconfident; that is, they can achieve perfect scores on the practice exams but may fail the actual exam.

Understanding the Question

The majority of questions on the exam will contain code snippets and ask you to answer questions about them. For those items containing code snippets, the number-one question we recommend that you answer before attempting to solve the question is this:

Does the code compile?

It sounds simple, but many people dive into answering the question without checking whether the code actually compiles. If you can determine whether a particular set of code compiles and what line or lines cause it to not compile, answering the question often becomes easy.

Applying the Process of Elimination

Although you might not immediately know the correct answer to a question, if you can reduce the question from five answers to three, your odds of guessing the correct answer will be markedly improved. Moreover, if you can reduce a question from four answers to two, you'll double your chances of guessing the correct answer!

The exam software allows you to eliminate answer choices by right-clicking an answer choice, which causes the text to be struck through, as shown in the following example:

A. ~~123~~

B. Elephant

C. ~~Vulture~~

D. The code does not compile due to line n1.

Even better, the exam software remembers which answer choices you have eliminated anytime you go back to the question. You can undo the crossed-out answer simply by right-clicking the choice again.

Sometimes you can eliminate answer choices quickly without reading the entire question. In some cases, you may even be able to solve the question based solely on the answer choices. If you come across such questions on the exam, consider it a gift. Can you correctly answer the following question in which the application code has been left out?

5.   Which line, when inserted independently at line m1, allows the code to compile?

```
- Code Omitted -
```

   A. `public abstract final int swim();`

   B. `public abstract void swim();`

   C. `public abstract swim();`

   D. `public abstract void swim() {}`

   E. `public void swim() {}`

Without reading the code or knowing what line m1 is, we can actually eliminate three of the five answer choices. Options A, C, and D contain invalid declarations, leaving us with options B and E as the only possible correct answers.

Skipping Difficult Questions

The exam software also includes an option to "mark" a question and review all marked questions at the end of the exam. If you are pressed for time, answer a question as best you can and then mark it to come back to later.

All questions are weighted equally, so spending 10 minutes answering five questions correctly is a lot better use of your time than spending 10 minutes on a single question. If you finish the exam early, you have the option of reviewing the marked questions, as well as all of the questions on the exam if you so choose.

Being Suspicious of Strong Words

Many questions on the exam include answer choices with descriptive sentences rather than lines of code. When you see such questions, be wary of any answer choice that includes strong words such as "must," "all," or "cannot." If you think about the complexities of programming languages, it is rare for a rule to have no exceptions or special cases. Therefore, if you are stuck between two answers and one of them uses "must" while the other uses "can" or "may," you are better off picking the one with the weaker word since it is a more ambiguous statement.

Using the Provided Writing Material

Depending on your particular testing center, you will be provided with a sheet of blank paper or a whiteboard to use to help you answer questions. In our experience, a whiteboard with a marker and an eraser are more commonly handed out. If you sit down and you are not provided with anything, make sure to ask for such materials.

On the 1Z0-815 exam, you were more likely to be presented with questions where you had to trace many variables. This is less likely on the 1Z0-816 and 1Z0-817 exams. There are other good uses of writing material. For example, you could write down facts you have difficulty memorizing the second the exam starts. For example, you could write down the difference between `Comparable` and `Comparator` at the start of the exam. Alternatively, you could write down facts you are unsure of. Sometimes information from another question will help you out.

Choosing the Best Answer

Sometimes you read a question and immediately spot a compiler error that tells you exactly what the question is asking. Other times, though, you may stare at a method declaration for a couple of minutes and have no idea what the question is asking. While you might not know for sure which answer is correct in these situations, there are some test-taking tips that can improve the probability that you will pick the correct answer.

Unlike some other standardized tests, there's no penalty for answering a question incorrectly versus leaving it blank. If you're nearly out of time or you just can't decide on an answer, select a random answer and move on. If you've been able to eliminate even one answer, then your guess will be better than blind luck.

Answer All Questions!

You should set a hard stop at five minutes of time remaining on the exam to ensure that you've answered each and every question. Remember, if you fail to answer a question, you'll definitely get it wrong and lose points, but if you guess, there's at least a chance that you'll be correct. There's no harm in guessing!

When in doubt, we generally recommend picking a random answer that includes "Does not compile" if available, although which choice you select is not nearly as important as making sure that you do not leave any questions unanswered on the exam!

Getting a Good Night's Rest

Although a lot of people are inclined to cram as much material as they can in the hours leading up to the exam, most studies have shown that this is a poor test-taking strategy. The best thing we can recommend that you do before the exam is to get a good night's rest!

Given the length of the exam and number of questions, the exam can be quite draining, especially if this is your first time taking a certification exam. You might come in expecting to be done 30 minutes early, only to discover that you are only a quarter of the way through the exam with half the time remaining. At some point, you may begin to panic, and it is in these moments that these test-taking skills are most important. Just remember to take a deep breath, stay calm, eliminate as many wrong answers as you can, and make sure to answer each and every question. It is for stressful moments like these that being well rested with a good night's sleep will be most beneficial!

Taking the Exam

So you've decided to take the exam? We hope so if you've bought this book! In this section, we discuss the process of scheduling and taking the exam, along with various options for each.

Scheduling the Exam

The exam is administered by Pearson VUE and can be taken at any Pearson VUE testing center. To find a testing center or register for the exam, go to:

```
www.pearsonvue.com
```

Next, search for *Oracle* as the exam provider. If you haven't been to the test center before, we recommend visiting in advance. Some testing centers are nice and professionally run. Others stick you in a closet with lots of people talking around you. You don't want to be taking the test with people complaining about their broken laptops nearby!

At this time, you can reschedule the exam without penalty until up to 24 hours before. This means you can register for a convenient time slot well in advance, knowing that you can delay if you aren't ready by that time. Rescheduling is easy and can be done completely on the Pearson VUE website. This may change, so check the rules before paying.

The At-Home Online Option

Oracle now offers online-proctored exams that can be taken in the comfort of your own home. You choose a specific date and time, like a proctored exam, and take it at your computer.

While this option may be appealing for a lot of people, especially if you live far away from a testing center, there are a number of restrictions.

- Your session will be closely monitored by another individual from a remote location.

- You must set up a camera and microphone, and they must be on for the entire exam. At the start, you will also need to turn the camera around the room to show your workspace to prove you are not in reach of exam material.

- The exam software will also monitor your facial expressions and track eye movement. We've heard reports that it will warn you if you are looking away from the screen too much.

- You must be alone in a completely isolated space for the duration of the test. If someone comes in during your test, your test will be invalidated.

- You cannot have any papers, material, or items in your immediate vicinity.

- Unlike exam centers that provide writing material, writing down any notes or the use of scratch paper is prohibited. You do get to make notes on a digital whiteboard within the exam software.

- Stopping for any reason, including a restroom break, is prohibited.

With so many rules, you want to think carefully before taking the test at home. If you do plan to go this route, please visit Oracle's website for a complete set of rules and requirements.

The Day of the Exam

When you go to take the exam, remember to bring two forms of ID including one that is government issued. See Pearson's list of acceptable IDs here:

www.pearsonvue.com/policies/1S.pdf

Try not to bring too much extra with you as it will not be allowed into the exam room. While you will be allowed to check your belongings, it is better to leave extra items at home or in the car.

You will not be allowed to bring paper, your phone, and the like into the exam room with you. Some centers are stricter than others. At one center, tissues were even taken away from us! Most centers allow keeping your ID and money. They watch you taking the exam, though, so don't even think about writing notes on money.

As we mentioned earlier, the exam center will give you writing materials to use during the exam, either scratch paper or a whiteboard. If you aren't given these materials, remember to ask. These items will be collected at the end of the exam.

Finding Out Your Score

In the past, you would find out right after finishing the exam if you passed. Now you have to wait nervously until you can check your score online. Many test takers check their score from a mobile device as they are walking out of the test center.

If you go onto the Pearson VUE website, it will just have a status of "Taken" rather than your result. Oracle uses a separate system for scores. You'll need to go to Oracle's CertView website to find out whether you passed and your score.

certview.oracle.com

It usually updates shortly after you finish your exam but can take up to an hour in some cases. In addition to your score, you'll also see objectives for which you got a question wrong. Once you have passed the exam, the OCP title will be granted within a few days.

Oracle has partnered with Acclaim, which is an Open Badge platform. Upon obtaining a certification from Oracle, you also receive a "badge" that you can choose to share publicly with current or prospective employers.

Objective Map

Before starting out, you should review the list of exam objectives, especially if you still need to decide between taking the 1Z0-816 exam or the 1Z0-817 exam. You should also review the objectives when you think you are ready to take the exam to make sure you understand each topic.

Java SE 11 Programmer II (1Z0–816) Exam

The following table provides a breakdown of this book's exam coverage for the Java SE 11 Programmer II (1Z0–816) exam, showing you the chapter where each objective or subobjective is covered.

Exam Objective	Chapter
Java Fundamentals	
Create and use final classes	1
Create and use inner, nested and anonymous classes	1
Create and use enumerations	1
Exception Handling and Assertions	
Use the try-with-resources construct	5
Create and use custom exception classes	5
Test invariants by using assertions	5
Java Interfaces	
Create and use interfaces with default methods	1
Create and use interfaces with private methods	1
Generics and Collections	
Use wrapper classes, autoboxing and autounboxing	3
Create and use generic classes, methods with diamond notation and wildcards	3

Exam Objective	Chapter
Securely constructing sensitive objects	11
Secure Serialization and Deserialization	11
Database Applications with JDBC	
Connect to databases using JDBC URLs and DriverManager	10
Use PreparedStatement to perform CRUD operations	10
Use PreparedStatement and CallableStatement APIs to perform database operations	10
Localization	
Use the Locale class	5
Use resource bundles	5
Format messages, dates, and numbers with Java	5
Annotations	
Describe the purpose of annotations and typical usage patterns	2
Apply annotations to classes and methods	2
Describe commonly used annotations in the JDK	2
Declare custom annotations	2

Upgrade OCP Java 6, 7 & 8 to Java SE 11 Developer (1Z0–817) Exam

The following table provides a breakdown of this book's exam coverage for the Upgrade OCP Java 6, 7 & 8 to Java SE 11 Developer (1Z0–817) exam, showing you the chapter where each objective or sub-objective is covered. Remember, if you are taking the upgrade exam, you should start with Appendix A.

Exam Objective	Chapter/Appendix
Understanding Modules	
Describe the Modular JDK	A
Declare modules and enable access between modules	A
Describe how a modular project is compiled and run	A
Migration to a Modular Application	

Taking the Assessment Test

Use the following assessment test to gauge your current level of skill in Java. This test is designed to highlight some topics for your strengths and weaknesses so that you know which chapters you might want to read multiple times. Even if you do well on the assessment test, you should still read the book from cover to cover, as the real exam is quite challenging.

Assessment Test

1. Which operations in the CRUD acronym are not allowed in an `executeUpdate()` call? (Choose all that apply.)

   A. Delete

   B. Deletion

   C. Disable

   D. Read

   E. Reading

   F. Select

   G. None of the above. All operations are allowed.

2. Assume the current directory is /bats/day and all of the files and directories referenced exist. What is the result of executing the following code?

   ```
   var path1 = Path.of("/bats/night","..")
       .resolve(Paths.get( "./sleep.txt")).normalize();
   var path2 = new File("../sleep.txt").toPath().toRealPath();
   System.out.print(Files.isSameFile(path1,path2));
   System.out.print(" " + path1.equals(path2));
   ```

   A. `true true`

   B. `true false`

   C. `false true`

   D. `false false`

   E. The code does not compile.

   F. The code compiles but throws an exception at runtime.

3. A(n) _____ module always contains a `module-info` file, while a(n) _____ module always exports all its packages to other modules.

   A. automatic, named

   B. automatic, unnamed

C. named, automatic

D. named, unnamed

E. unnamed, automatic

F. unnamed, named

G. None of the above

4. Which of the following lines of code do not compile? (Choose all that apply.)

```
1:  import java.lang.annotation.*;
2:  class IsAware {}
3:  enum Mode {AUTONOMOUS,DEPENDENT}
4:  @interface CleaningProgram {
5:      Mode mode();
6:  }
7:  @Documented public @interface Robot {
8:      CleaningProgram cp()
9:          default @CleaningProgram(Mode.AUTONOMOUS);
10:     final int MAX_CYCLES = 10;
11:     IsAware aware();
12:     String name() = 10;
13: }
```

A. Line 5

B. Line 7

C. Line 8

D. Line 9

E. Line 10

F. Line 11

G. Line 12

H. All of the lines compile.

5. What is the result of executing the following application?

```
final var cb = new CyclicBarrier(3,
    () -> System.out.println("Clean!"));  // u1
ExecutorService service = Executors.newSingleThreadExecutor();
try {
  IntStream.generate(() -> 1)
      .limit(12)
      .parallel()
      .forEach(i -> service.submit(
```

```
                    () -> cb.await())); // u2
       } finally {
          if (service != null) service.shutdown();
       }
```

A. It outputs Clean! at least once.

B. It outputs Clean! exactly four times.

C. The code will not compile because of line u1.

D. The code will not compile because of line u2.

E. It compiles but throws an exception at runtime.

F. It compiles but waits forever at runtime.

6. What modifiers must be used with the serialPersistentFields field in a class? (Choose all that apply.)

A. final

B. private

C. protected

D. public

E. transient

F. static

7. What is the output of the following code?

```
import java.io.*;
public class RaceCar {
    static class Door implements AutoCloseable {
        public void close() { System.out.print("D"); }
    }
    static class Window implements Closeable {
        public void close() { System.out.print("W"); }
    }
    public static void main(String[] args) {
        Window w = new Window() {};
        Door d = new Door();
        try (w; d) {
            System.out.print("T");
        } catch (Exception e) {
            System.out.print("E");
        } finally {
            System.out.print("F");
        }
    }
```

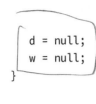

```
        d = null;
        w = null;
      }
  }
```

A. TF

B. TEF

C. TDWF

D. TWDF

E. A compilation error occurs.

8. What are possible results of executing the following code snippet? (Choose all that apply.)

```
String line;
Console c = System.console();
if ((line = c.readLine()) != null)
    System.out.print("Your requested meal: "+line);
```

A. Nothing is printed.

B. A message followed by the text the user entered is printed.

C. An `ArrayIndexOutOfBoundsException` is thrown.

D. A `NullPointerException` is thrown.

E. An `IOException` is thrown.

F. None of the above, as the code does not compile

9. Suppose you have separate modules for a service provider interface, service provider, service locator, and consumer. If you add a new `abstract` method to the service provider interface and call it from the consumer module, how many of these modules do you need to re-compile?

A. Zero

B. One

C. Two

D. Three

E. Four

10. Which of the following statements can fill in the blank to make the code compile successfully? (Choose all that apply.)

```
Set<? extends RuntimeException> mySet = new _____ ();
```

A. `HashSet<? extends RuntimeException>`

B. `HashSet<Exception>`

C. `TreeSet<RuntimeException>`

D. `TreeSet<NullPointerException>`

E. None of the above

11. Suppose that we have the following property files and code. Which bundle is used on lines 8 and 9, respectively?

Dolphins.properties
```
name=The Dolphin
age=0
```

Dolphins_de.properties
```
name=Dolly
age=4
```

Dolphins_en.properties
```
name=Dolly
```

```
5: Locale fr = new Locale("fr");
6: Locale.setDefault(new Locale("en", "US"));
7: var b = ResourceBundle.getBundle("Dolphins", fr);
8: b.getString("name");
9: b.getString("age");
```

A. Dolphins.properties and Dolphins.properties are used.

B. Dolphins.properties and Dolphins_en.properties are used.

C. Dolphins_en.properties and Dolphins.properties are used.

D. Dolphins_en.properties and Dolphins_en.properties are used.

E. Dolphins_de.properties and Dolphins_en.properties are used.

F. The code does not compile.

12. Given the following program, what can be inserted into the blank line that would allow it to compile and print Poof! at runtime? (Choose all that apply.)

```
class Wizard {
    private enum Hat {
        BIG, SMALL
    }
    protected class MagicWand {
        void abracadabra() {
            System.out.print("Poof!");
        }
    }
}
public class CastSpells {
    public static void main(String[] args) {
        var w = new Wizard();
```

```
                   _____.abracadabra();
              }
         }
```

A. class DarkWizard extends Wizard {}.new MagicWand()

B. new Wizard().new MagicWand()

C. Wizard.new MagicWand()

D. w.new MagicWand(){
```
       void abracadabra(int spell) {
          System.out.print("Oops!"); } }
```

E. new MagicWand()

F. w.new MagicWand()

G. None of the above, as the code does not compile.

13. Assume birds.dat exists, is accessible, and contains data for a Bird object. What is the result of executing the following code? (Choose all that apply.)

```
1:  import java.io.*;
2:  public class Bird {
3:      private String name;
4:      private transient Integer age;
5:
6:      // Getters/setters omitted
7:
8:      public static void main(String[] args) {
9:          try(var is = new ObjectInputStream(
10:                 new BufferedInputStream(
11:                 new FileInputStream("birds.dat")))) {
12:             Bird b = is.readObject();
13:             System.out.println(b.age);
14:          } } }
```

A. It compiles and prints 0 at runtime.

B. It compiles and prints null at runtime.

C. It compiles and prints a number at runtime.

D. The code will not compile because of lines 9–11.

E. The code will not compile because of line 12.

F. It compiles but throws an exception at runtime.

14. Which of the following are true? (Choose all that apply.)

```
private static void magic(Stream<Integer> s) {
   Optional o = s
```

```
        .filter(x -> x < 5)
        .limit(3)
        .max((x, y) -> x-y);
    System.out.println(o.get());
}
```

A. `magic(Stream.empty());` runs infinitely.

B. `magic(Stream.empty());` throws an exception.

C. `magic(Stream.iterate(1, x -> x++));` runs infinitely.

D. `magic(Stream.iterate(1, x -> x++));` throws an exception.

E. `magic(Stream.of(5, 10));` runs infinitely.

F. `magic(Stream.of(5, 10));` throws an exception.

G. The method does not compile.

15. Assume the file `/gorilla/signs.txt` exists within the file system. Which statements about the following code snippet are correct? (Choose all that apply.)

```
var x = Path.of("/gorilla/signs.txt");
Files.find(x.getParent(), 10.0, // k1
    (Path p) -> p.toString().endsWith(".txt")) // k2
    .collect(Collectors.toList())
    .forEach(System.out::println);

Files.readAllLines(x) // k3
    .flatMap(p -> Stream.of(p.split(" "))) // k4
    .map(s -> s.toLowerCase())
    .forEach(System.out::println);
```

A. Nothing is printed.

B. All of the .txt files and directories in the directory tree are printed.

C. All of the words in `signs.txt` are printed.

D. Line k1 contains a compiler error.

E. Line k2 contains a compiler error.

F. Line k3 contains a compiler error.

G. Line k4 contains a compiler error.

16. Which interface is used to run stored procedures?

A. `Callable`

B. `CallableStatement`

C. `PreparedStatement`

D. `ProceduralStatement`

E. Statement

F. StoredStatement

17. What is the result of the following class?

```
1:  public class Box<T> {
2:      T value;
3:
4:      public Box(T value) {
5:          this.value = value;
6:      }
7:      public T getValue() {
8:          return value;
9:      }
10:     public static void main(String[] args) {
11:         var one = new Box<String>("a string");
12:         var two = new Box<Integer>(123);
13:         System.out.print(one.getValue());
14:         System.out.print(two.getValue());
15: } }
```

A. Compiler error on line 1

B. Compiler error on line 2

C. Compiler error on line 11

D. Compiler error on line 12

E. a string123

F. An exception is thrown.

18. Which changes, when made independently, guarantee the following code snippet prints 100 at runtime? (Choose all that apply.)

```
List<Integer> data = new ArrayList<>();
IntStream.range(0,100).parallel().forEach(s -> data.add(s));
System.out.println(data.size());
```

A. Change the data implementation class to a CopyOnWriteArrayList.

B. Remove parallel() in the stream operation.

C. Change forEach() to forEachOrdered() in the stream operation.

D. Change parallel() to serial() in the stream operation.

E. Wrap the data implementation class with a call to Collections.synchronizedList().

F. The code snippet will always print 100 as is.

19. Fill in the blanks: The _____ annotation can be used to indicate a method may be removed in a future version, while the _____ annotation can be used to ignore it.

  A. @Ignore, @Suppress

  B. @Retention, @SuppressWarnings

  C. @Deprecated, @Suppress

  D. @ForRemoval, @Ignore

  E. @Deprecated, @SuppressWarnings

  F. @Deprecated, @Ignore

20. What is the output of this code?

```
20: Predicate<String> empty = String::isEmpty;
21: Predicate<String> notEmpty = empty.negate();
22:
23: var result = Stream.generate(() -> "")
24:     .filter(notEmpty)
25:     .collect(Collectors.groupingBy(k -> k))
26:     .entrySet()
27:     .stream()
28:     .map(Entry::getValue)
29:     .flatMap(Collection::stream)
30:     .collect(Collectors.partitioningBy(notEmpty));
31: System.out.println(result);
```

  A. It outputs: {}

  B. It outputs: {false=[], true=[]}

  C. The code does not compile.

  D. The code does not terminate.

21. Which attack could exploit this code?

```
public boolean isValid(String hashedPassword)
      throws SQLException {

    var sql = "SELECT * FROM users WHERE password = '"
       + hashedPassword +"'";
    try (var stmt = conn.prepareStatement(sql);
       var rs = stmt.executeQuery(sql)) {
       return rs.next();
    }
}
```

A. Command injection
B. Confidential data exposure
C. Denial of service
D. SQL injection
E. SQL stealing
F. None of the above

22. Which lines of the following interface do not compile? (Choose all that apply.)

```
1: @FunctionalInterface
2: public interface PlayDnD {
3:     public static void roll() { roll(); }
4:     private int takeBreak() { roll(); return 1; }
5:     void startGame();
6:     default void win();
7:     static void end() { win(); }
8:     boolean equals(Object o);
9: }
```

A. Line 1
B. Line 3
C. Line 4
D. Line 5
E. Line 6
F. Line 7
G. Line 8
H. All of the lines compile.

Answers to Assessment Test

1. D. CRUD stands for Create Read Update Delete, making options B, C, E, and F incorrect. The executeUpdate() method is not allowed to make read operations. Option F is tricky, but incorrect, because it is a SQL keyword and not part of the CRUD acronym. Option D is the correct answer since it is a read operation. For more information, see Chapter 10.

2. A. The code compiles and runs without issue, so options E and F are incorrect. First, path1 simplifies to /bats/sleep.txt after the path symbols have been removed and the normalize() method applied. The path2 variable using the current directory of /bats/ day is assigned a path value of /bats/sleep.txt. The toRealPath() method will also remove path symbols. Since the file Path objects represent the same path within the file system, they will return true for both equals() and isSameFile(), making option A correct. For more information, see Chapter 9.

3. C. Only named modules are required to have a module-info file, ruling out options A, B, E, and F. Unnamed modules are not readable by any other types of modules, ruling out option D. Automatic modules always export all packages to other modules, making the answer option C. For more information, see Chapter 6.

4. D, F, G. Line 9 does not compile because the use of @CleaningProgram is missing the element name mode. The element name can be dropped only if the element is named value() in the annotation type declaration. Line 11 does not compile because an annotation element must be a primitive, String, Class, enum, another annotation, or an array of these types. Line 12 does not compile because an element uses the keyword default to assign a default value, not the equal (=) sign. For more information, see Chapter 2.

5. F. The code compiles without issue, so options C and D are incorrect. The key to understanding this code is to notice that our thread executor contains only one thread, but our CyclicBarrier limit is 3. Even though 12 tasks are all successfully submitted to the service, the first task will block forever on the call to await(). Since the barrier is never reached, nothing is printed, and the program hangs, making option F correct. For more information, see Chapter 7.

6. A, B, F. The serialPersistentFields field is used to specify which fields should be used in serialization. It must be declared private static final, or it will be ignored. Therefore, options A, B, and F are correct. For more information, see Chapter 11.

7. E. A resource must be marked final or be effectively final to be used in a try-with-resources statement. Since the variables d and w are reassigned after the try-with-resources statement, they are not effectively final. Therefore, the code does not compile, making option E correct. If those two lines were removed, then the program would compile and print TDWF at runtime. Remember that resources in a try-with-resources statement are closed in the reverse order in which they are declared. For more information, see Chapter 5.

8. B, D. If the console is not available, System.console() returns null, making option D correct. On the other hand, if the console is available, it will read the user input and print the result, making option B correct. For more information, see Chapter 8.

9. D. Since you are changing the service provider interface, you have to re-compile it. Similarly, you need to re-compile the service provider because it now needs to implement the new method. The consumer module needs to be re-compiled as well since the code has changed to call the new method. Therefore, three modules need to be re-compiled, and option D is correct. The service locator does not need to be re-compiled since it simply looks up the interface. For more information, see Chapter 6.

10. C, D. The mySet declaration defines an upper bound of type RuntimeException. This means that classes may specify RuntimeException or any subclass of RuntimeException as the type parameter. Option B is incorrect because Exception is a superclass, not a subclass, of RuntimeException. Option A is incorrect because the wildcard cannot occur on the right side of the assignment. Options C and D compile and are the answers. For more information, see Chapter 3.

11. C. Java will use Dolphins_en.properties as the matching resource bundle on line 7. Since there is no match for French, the default locale is used. Line 8 finds a matching key in this file. Line 9 does not find a match in that file; therefore, it has to look higher up in the hierarchy. For more information, see Chapter 5.

12. B, D, F. The MagicWand class is an inner class that requires an instance of the outer class Wizard to instantiate. Option A is incorrect, as DarkWizard declares a local class but does not create an instance of the local class. Options B and F both correctly create an inner class instance from an outer class instance, printing Poof! at runtime. Options C and E are incorrect, as they each require an instance of the outer class. Remember, MagicWand is not a static nested class. Finally, option D is correct, as it creates an anonymous class of MagicWand. The method declared in the anonymous class is never called, though, since it is an overload of the original method with a different signature, not an override. In this manner, Poof! is still printed at runtime. For more information, see Chapter 1.

13. D, E. Line 10 includes an unhandled checked IOException, while line 11 includes an unhandled checked FileNotFoundException, making option D correct. Line 12 does not compile because is.readObject() must be cast to a Bird object to be assigned to b. It also does not compile because it includes two unhandled checked exceptions, IOException and ClassNotFoundException, making option E correct. If a cast operation were added on line 13 and the main() method were updated on line 8 to declare the various checked exceptions, then the code would compile but throw an exception at runtime since Bird does not implement Serializable. Finally, if the class did implement Serializable, then the program would print null at runtime, as that is the default value for the transient field age. For more information, see Chapter 8.

14. B, F. Calling get() on an empty Optional causes an exception to be thrown, making option B correct. Option F is also correct because filter() makes the Optional empty before it calls get(). Option C is incorrect because the infinite stream is made finite by the intermediate limit() operation. Options A and E are incorrect because the source streams are not infinite. Therefore, the call to max() sees only three elements and terminates. For more information, see Chapter 4.

15. D, E, G. The code contains multiple compiler errors. First, the second parameter of Files.find() takes an int depth limit, not double, so line k1 does not compile. Next, the lambda expression on line k2 does not compile. The parameter must be of type

BiPredicate<Path, BasicFileAttributes>. Finally, readAllLines() on line k3 returns a List<String>, not a Stream<String>, resulting in line k4 not compiling. For this code to compile, the Files.lines() method should be used. If the code was corrected, then the first stream operation would print all of the files and directories that end with .txt in the directory tree up to a depth limit of 10. The second stream operation would print each word in the sign.txt as lowercase on a separate line. For more information, see Chapter 9.

16. B. Option A is incorrect because Callable is used for concurrency rather than JDBC code. Option B is the correct answer as CallableStatement is used to run a stored procedure. Option C is incorrect because PreparedStatement is used for SQL specified in your application. Option E is incorrect because Statement is the generic interface and does not have functionality specific to stored procedures. Options D and F are incorrect because they are not interfaces in the JDK. For more information, see Chapter 10.

17. E. This class is a proper use of generics. Box uses a generic type named T. On line 11, the generic type is String. On line 12, the generic type is Integer. Both lines 11 and 12 use var for local variables to represent the types, so you have to keep track of them yourself. For more information, see Chapter 3.

18. A, B, C, E. The code may print 100 without any changes, but since the data class is not thread-safe, the code may print other values. For this reason, option F is incorrect. Options A and E both change the data class to a thread-safe class and guarantee 100 will be printed at runtime. Options B and C are also correct, as they both cause the stream to apply the add() operation in a serial manner. Option D is incorrect, as serial() is not a stream method. For more information, see Chapter 7.

19. E. The @Deprecated annotation can be used to indicate that a method or class may be removed in a future version. The @SuppressWarnings with the "deprecation" value can be used to ignore deprecated warnings. For these reasons, option E is correct. The @Retention annotation is used to specify when/if the annotation information should be discarded. The other options are not built-in Java annotations. For more information, see Chapter 2.

20. D. First, this mess of code does compile. However, the source is an infinite stream. The filter operation will check each element in turn to see whether any are not empty. While nothing passes the filter, the code does not terminate. Therefore, option D is correct. For more information, see Chapter 4.

21. D. Option E is incorrect because SQL stealing is not the name of an attack. Option C is incorrect because the PreparedStatement and ResultSet are closed in a try-with-resources block. While we do not see the Connection closed, we also don't see it opened. The exam allows us to assume code that we can't see is correct.

Option D is the answer because bind variables are not used. The potentially unsafe provided method parameter hashedPassword is passed directly to the SQL statement. Remember that using a PreparedStatement is a necessary, but not sufficient, step to prevent SQL injection. For more information, see Chapter 11.

22. E, F. Line 1 compiles, as this is a functional interface and contains exactly one abstract method: `startGame()`. Note that `equals(Object)` on line 8 does not contribute to the abstract method count, as it is always provided by `java.lang.Object`. Line 3 compiles, although if executed, it would generate an infinite recursive call at runtime. Line 4 compiles since `private` interface methods can call `static` interface methods. Line 6 does not compile because the `default` interface methods must include a body. Line 7 also does not compile, as static interface methods are not permitted to call `default`, `abstract`, or non-`static` `private` interface methods. For these reasons, options E and F are correct. For more information, see Chapter 1.

Chapter

1

Java Fundamentals

OCP EXAM OBJECTIVES COVERED IN THIS CHAPTER:

✓ **Java Fundamentals**

- Create and use final classes

- Create and use inner, nested and anonymous classes

- Create and use enumerations

✓ **Java Interfaces**

- Create and use interfaces with default methods

- Create and use interfaces with private methods

✓ **Functional Interface and Lambda Expressions**

- Define and write functional interfaces

- Create and use lambda expressions including statement lambdas, local-variable for lambda parameters

Welcome to the first chapter on your road to taking the 1Z0-816 Programmer II exam! If you've recently taken the 1Z0-815 Programmer I exam, then you should be well versed in class structure, inheritance, scope, abstract types, etc. If not, you might want to review your previous study materials. The exam expects you to have a solid foundation on these topics. You can also read our 1Z0-815 exam book, *OCP Oracle Certified Professional Java SE 11 Programmer I Study Guide: Exam 1Z0-815* (Sybex, 2019).

In this chapter, we are going to expand your understanding of Java fundamentals including enums and nested classes, various interface members, functional interfaces, and lambda expressions. Pay attention in this chapter, as many of these topics will be used throughout the rest of this book. Even if you use them all the time, there are subtle rules you might not be aware of.

Finally, we want to wish you a hearty congratulations on beginning your journey to prepare for the 1Z0-816 Programmer II exam!

Taking the Upgrade Exam?

If you're studying for the 1Z0-817 Upgrade Exam, please consult the list of objectives in the introduction to know which topics to study. For these readers, we have also written a specialized Appendix A, "The Upgrade Exam," which covers additional objectives that are not part of the 1Z0-816 exam, such as var and module creation. If you're taking the 1Z0-817 exam, you should read Appendix A before reading this chapter.

Applying the *final* Modifier

From your previous study material, you should remember the final modifier can be applied to variables, methods, and classes. Marking a variable final means the value cannot be changed after it is assigned. Marking a method or class final means it cannot be overridden or extended, respectively. In this section, we will review the rules for using the final modifier.

NOTE If you studied `final` classes for the 1Z0-815 exam recently, then you can probably skip this section and go straight to enums.

Declaring *final* Local Variables

Let's start by taking a look at some local variables marked with the `final` modifier:

```
private void printZooInfo(boolean isWeekend) {
    final int giraffe = 5;
    final long lemur;
    if(isWeekend) lemur = 5;
    else lemur = 10;
    System.out.println(giraffe+" "+lemur);
}
```

As shown with the `lemur` variable, we don't need to assign a value when a `final` variable is declared. The rule is only that it must be assigned a value before it can be used. Contrast this with the following example:

```
private void printZooInfo(boolean isWeekend) {
    final int giraffe = 5;
    final long lemur;
    if(isWeekend) lemur = 5;
    giraffe = 3;                              // DOES NOT COMPILE
    System.out.println(giraffe+" "+lemur);   // DOES NOT COMPILE
}
```

This snippet contains two compilation errors. The `giraffe` variable is already assigned a value, so attempting to assign it a new value is not permitted. The second compilation error is from attempting to use the `lemur` variable, which would not be assigned a value if `isWeekend` is `false`. The compiler does not allow the use of local variables that may not have been assigned a value, whether they are marked `final` or not.

Just because a variable reference is marked `final` does not mean the object associated with it cannot be modified. Consider the following code snippet:

```
final StringBuilder cobra = new StringBuilder();
cobra.append("Hssssss");
cobra.append("Hssssss!!!");
```

In the `cobra` example, the object reference is constant, but that doesn't mean the data in the class is constant.

Throughout this book, you'll see a lot of examples involving zoos and animals. We chose this topic because it is a fruitful topic for data modeling. There are a wide variety of species, with very interesting attributes, relationships, and hierarchies. In addition, there are a lot of complex tasks involved in managing a zoo. Ideally, you enjoy the topic and learn about animals along the way!

Adding *final* to Instance and *static* Variables

Instance and static class variables can also be marked final. If an instance variable is marked final, then it must be assigned a value when it is declared or when the object is instantiated. Like a local final variable, it cannot be assigned a value more than once, though. The following PolarBear class demonstrates these properties:

```
public class PolarBear {
   final int age = 10;
   final int fishEaten;
   final String name;

   { fishEaten = 10; }

   public PolarBear() {
      name = "Robert";
   }
   public PolarBear(int height) {
      this();
   }
}
```

The age variable is given a value when it is declared, while the fishEaten variable is assigned a value in an instance initializer. The name variable is given a value in the no-argument constructor. Notice that the second constructor does not assign a value to name, but since it calls the no-argument constructor first, name is guaranteed to be assigned a value in the first line of this constructor.

The rules for static final variables are similar to instance final variables, except they do not use static constructors (there is no such thing!) and use static initializers instead of instance initializers.

```
public class Panda {
   final static String name = "Ronda";
   static final int bamboo;
   static final double height; // DOES NOT COMPILE
   static { bamboo = 5;}
}
```

The name variable is assigned a value when it is declared, while the bamboo variable is assigned a value in a static initializer. The height variable is not assigned a value anywhere in the class definition, so that line does not compile.

Writing *final* Methods

Methods marked final cannot be overridden by a subclass. This essentially prevents any polymorphic behavior on the method call and ensures that a specific version of the method is always called.

Remember that methods can be assigned an abstract or final modifier. An abstract method is one that does not define a method body and can appear only inside an abstract class or interface. A final method is one that cannot be overridden by a subclass. Let's take a look at an example:

```
public abstract class Animal {
    abstract void chew();
}

public class Hippo extends Animal {
    final void chew() {}
}

public class PygmyHippo extends Hippo {
    void chew() {}  // DOES NOT COMPILE
}
```

The chew() method is declared abstract in the Animal class. It is then implemented in the concrete Hippo class, where it is marked final, thereby preventing a subclass of Hippo from overriding it. For this reason, the chew() method in PygmyHippo does not compile since it is inherited as final.

What happens if a method is marked both abstract and final? Well, that's like saying, "I want to declare a method that someone else will provide an implementation for, while also telling that person that they are not allowed to provide an implementation." For this reason, the compiler does not allow it.

```
abstract class ZooKeeper {
    public abstract final void openZoo();  // DOES NOT COMPILE
}
```

Marking Classes *final*

Lastly, the final modifier can be applied to class declarations as well. A final class is one that cannot be extended. For example, the following does not compile:

```
public final class Reptile {}

public class Snake extends Reptile {}  // DOES NOT COMPILE
```

Like we saw with final methods, classes cannot be marked both abstract and final. For example, the following two declarations do not compile:

```
public abstract final class Eagle {}  // DOES NOT COMPILE
```

```
public final interface Hawk {}        // DOES NOT COMPILE
```

It is not possible to write a class that provides a concrete implementation of the abstract Eagle class, as it is marked final and cannot be extended. The Hawk interface also does not compile, although the reason is subtler. The compiler automatically applies the implicit abstract modifier to each interface declaration. Just like abstract classes, interfaces cannot be marked final.

From your 1Z0-815 exam studies, a modifier that is inserted automatically by the compiler is referred to as an *implicit modifier*. Think of an implicit modifier as being present, even if it is not written out. For example, a method that is implicitly public cannot be marked private. Implicit modifiers are common in interface members, as we will see later in this chapter.

Working with Enums

In programming, it is common to have a type that can only have a finite set of values, such as days of the week, seasons of the year, primary colors, etc. An *enumeration* is like a fixed set of constants. In Java, an *enum*, short for "enumerated type," can be a top-level type like a class or interface, as well as a nested type like an inner class.

Using an enum is much better than using a bunch of constants because it provides type-safe checking. With numeric or String constants, you can pass an invalid value and not find out until runtime. With enums, it is impossible to create an invalid enum value without introducing a compiler error.

Enumerations show up whenever you have a set of items whose types are known at compile time. Common examples include the compass directions, the months of the year, the planets in the solar system, or the cards in a deck (well, maybe not the planets in a solar system, given that Pluto had its planetary status revoked).

Creating Simple Enums

To create an enum, use the enum keyword instead of the class or interface keyword. Then list all of the valid types for that enum.

```
public enum Season {
    WINTER, SPRING, SUMMER, FALL
}
```

Keep the Season enum handy, as we will be using it throughout this section.

Enum values are considered constants and are commonly written using snake case, often stylized as snake_case. This style uses an underscore (_) to separate words with constant values commonly written in all uppercase. For example, an enum declaring a list of ice cream flavors might include values like VANILLA, ROCKY_ROAD, MINT_CHOCOLATE_CHIP, and so on.

Behind the scenes, an enum is a type of class that mainly contains static members. It also includes some helper methods like name(). Using an enum is easy.

```
Season s = Season.SUMMER;
System.out.println(Season.SUMMER);      // SUMMER
System.out.println(s == Season.SUMMER); // true
```

As you can see, enums print the name of the enum when toString() is called. They can be compared using == because they are like static final constants. In other words, you can use equals() or == to compare enums, since each enum value is initialized only once in the Java Virtual Machine (JVM).

An enum provides a values() method to get an array of all of the values. You can use this like any normal array, including in an enhanced for loop, often called a *for-each loop*.

```
for(Season season: Season.values()) {
    System.out.println(season.name() + " " + season.ordinal());
}
```

The output shows that each enum value has a corresponding int value, and the values are listed in the order in which they are declared.

```
WINTER 0
SPRING 1
SUMMER 2
FALL 3
```

The int value will remain the same during your program, but the program is easier to read if you stick to the human-readable enum value.

You can't compare an int and enum value directly anyway since an enum is a type, like a Java class, and *not* a primitive int.

```
if ( Season.SUMMER == 2) {} // DOES NOT COMPILE
```

Another useful feature is retrieving an enum value from a String using the valueOf() method. This is helpful when working with older code. The String passed in must match the enum value exactly, though.

```
Season s = Season.valueOf("SUMMER"); // SUMMER
```

```
Season t = Season.valueOf("summer"); // Throws an exception at runtime
```

The first statement works and assigns the proper enum value to s. Note that this line is not creating an enum value, at least not directly. Each enum value is created once when the enum is first loaded. Once the enum has been loaded, it retrieves the single enum value with the matching name.

The second statement encounters a problem. There is no enum value with the lowercase name summer. Java throws up its hands in defeat and throws an IllegalArgumentException.

```
Exception in thread "main" java.lang.IllegalArgumentException:
   No enum constant enums.Season.summer
```

One thing that you can't do is extend an enum.

```
public enum ExtendedSeason extends Season { } // DOES NOT COMPILE
```

The values in an enum are all that are allowed. You cannot add more by extending the enum.

Using Enums in *Switch* Statements

Enums can be used in switch statements. Pay attention to the case values in this code:

```
Season summer = Season.SUMMER;
switch (summer) {
  case WINTER:
      System.out.println("Get out the sled!");
      break;
  case SUMMER:
      System.out.println("Time for the pool!");
      break;
  default:
      System.out.println("Is it summer yet?");
}
```

The code prints "Time for the pool!" since it matches SUMMER. In each case statement, we just typed the value of the enum rather than writing Season.WINTER. After all, the compiler already knows that the only possible matches can be enum values. Java treats the enum type as implicit. In fact, if you were to type case Season.WINTER, it would not compile. Don't believe us? Take a look at the following example:

```
switch (summer) {
  case Season.FALL:   // DOES NOT COMPILE
      System.out.println("Rake some leaves!");
      break;
  case 0:             // DOES NOT COMPILE
      System.out.println("Get out the sled!");
      break;
}
```

The first case statement does not compile because Season is used in the case value. If we changed Season.FALL to just FALL, then the line would compile. What about the second case statement? Just as earlier we said that you can't compare enums with int values, you cannot use them in a switch statement with int values either. On the exam, pay special attention when working with enums that they are used only as enums.

Adding Constructors, Fields, and Methods

Enums can have more in them than just a list of values. Let's say our zoo wants to keep track of traffic patterns for which seasons get the most visitors.

```
1: public enum Season {
2:     WINTER("Low"), SPRING("Medium"), SUMMER("High"), FALL("Medium");
3:     private final String expectedVisitors;
4:     private Season(String expectedVisitors) {
5:         this.expectedVisitors = expectedVisitors;
6:     }
7:     public void printExpectedVisitors() {
8:         System.out.println(expectedVisitors);
9:     } }
```

There are a few things to notice here. On line 2, the list of enum values ends with a semicolon (;). While this is optional when our enum is composed solely of a list of values, it is required if there is anything in the enum besides the values.

Lines 3–9 are regular Java code. We have an instance variable, a constructor, and a method. We mark the instance variable final on line 3 so that our enum values are considered immutable. Although this is certainly not required, it is considered a good coding practice to do so. Since enum values are shared by all processes in the JVM, it would be problematic if one of them could change the value inside an enum.

 Real World Scenario

Creating Immutable Objects

The *immutable objects pattern* is an object-oriented design pattern in which an object cannot be modified after it is created. Instead of modifying an immutable object, you create a new object that contains any properties from the original object you want copied over.

Many Java libraries contain immutable objects, including String and classes in the java.time package, just to name a few. Immutable objects are invaluable in concurrent applications since the state of the object cannot change or be corrupted by a rogue thread. You'll learn more about threads in Chapter 7, "Concurrency."

All enum constructors are implicitly `private`, with the modifier being optional. This is reasonable since you can't extend an enum and the constructors can be called only within the enum itself. An enum constructor will not compile if it contains a `public` or `protected` modifier.

How do we call an enum method? It's easy.

```
Season.SUMMER.printExpectedVisitors();
```

Notice how we don't appear to call the constructor. We just say that we want the enum value. The first time that we ask for any of the enum values, Java constructs all of the enum values. After that, Java just returns the already constructed enum values. Given that explanation, you can see why this calls the constructor only once:

```
public enum OnlyOne {
   ONCE(true);
   private OnlyOne(boolean b) {
      System.out.print("constructing,");
   }
}


public class PrintTheOne {
   public static void main(String[] args) {
      System.out.print("begin,");
      OnlyOne firstCall = OnlyOne.ONCE;   // prints constructing,
      OnlyOne secondCall = OnlyOne.ONCE;  // doesn't print anything
      System.out.print("end");
   }
}
```

This class prints the following:

```
begin,constructing,end
```

If the `OnlyOne` enum was used earlier, and therefore initialized sooner, then the line that declares the `firstCall` variable would not print anything.

This technique of a constructor and state allows you to combine logic with the benefit of a list of values. Sometimes, you want to do more. For example, our zoo has different seasonal hours. It is cold and gets dark early in the winter. We could keep track of the hours through instance variables, or we can let each enum value manage hours itself.

```
public enum Season {
   WINTER {
      public String getHours() { return "10am-3pm"; }
   },
   SPRING {
      public String getHours() { return "9am-5pm"; }
   },
```

```
SUMMER {
    public String getHours() { return "9am-7pm"; }
},
FALL {
    public String getHours() { return "9am-5pm"; }
};
public abstract String getHours();
}
```

What's going on here? It looks like we created an abstract class and a bunch of tiny subclasses. In a way we did. The enum itself has an abstract method. This means that each and every enum value is required to implement this method. If we forget to implement the method for one of the values, then we get a compiler error.

```
The enum constant WINTER must implement the abstract method getHours()
```

If we don't want each and every enum value to have a method, we can create a default implementation and override it only for the special cases.

```
public enum Season {
    WINTER {
        public String getHours() { return "10am-3pm"; }
    },
    SUMMER {
        public String getHours() { return "9am-7pm"; }
    },
    SPRING, FALL;
    public String getHours() { return "9am-5pm"; }
}
```

This one looks better. We only code the special cases and let the others use the enum-provided implementation. Of course, overriding getHours() is possible only if it is not marked final.

Just because an enum can have lots of methods doesn't mean that it should. Try to keep your enums simple. If your enum is more than a page or two, it is way too long. Most enums are just a handful of lines. The main reason they get long is that when you start with a one- or two-line method and then declare it for each of your dozen enum types, it grows long. When they get too long or too complex, it makes the enum hard to read.

You might have noticed that in each of these enum examples, the list of values came first. This was not an accident. Whether the enum is simple or contains a ton of methods, constructors, and variables, the compiler requires that the list of values always be declared first.

Creating Nested Classes

A *nested class* is a class that is defined within another class. A nested class can come in one of four flavors.

- *Inner class*: A non-static type defined at the member level of a class
- *Static nested class*: A static type defined at the member level of a class
- *Local class*: A class defined within a method body
- *Anonymous class*: A special case of a local class that does not have a name

There are many benefits of using nested classes. They can encapsulate helper classes by restricting them to the containing class. They can make it easy to create a class that will be used in only one place. They can make the code cleaner and easier to read. This section covers all four types of nested classes.

By convention and throughout this chapter, we often use the term *inner* or *nested class* to apply to other Java types, including interfaces and enums. Although you are unlikely to encounter this on the exam, interfaces and enums can be declared as both inner classes and static nested classes, but not as local or anonymous classes.

When used improperly, though, nested classes can sometimes make the code harder to read. They also tend to tightly couple the enclosing and inner class, whereas there may be cases where you want to use the inner class by itself. In this case, you should move the inner class out into a separate top-level class.

Unfortunately, the exam tests these edge cases where programmers wouldn't typically use a nested class. For example, the exam might have an inner class within another inner class. This tends to create code that is difficult to read, so please never do this in practice!

Declaring an Inner Class

An *inner class*, also called a *member inner class*, is a non-static type defined at the member level of a class (the same level as the methods, instance variables, and constructors). Inner classes have the following properties:

- Can be declared public, protected, package-private (default), or private
- Can extend any class and implement interfaces
- Can be marked abstract or final
- Cannot declare static fields or methods, except for static final fields
- Can access members of the outer class including private members

The last property is actually pretty cool. It means that the inner class can access variables in the outer class without doing anything special. Ready for a complicated way to print Hi three times?

```java
1:  public class Outer {
2:      private String greeting = "Hi";
3:
4:      protected class Inner {
5:          public int repeat = 3;
6:          public void go() {
7:              for (int i = 0; i < repeat; i++)
8:                  System.out.println(greeting);
9:          }
10:     }
11:
12:     public void callInner() {
13:         Inner inner = new Inner();
14:         inner.go();
15:     }
16:     public static void main(String[] args) {
17:         Outer outer = new Outer();
18:         outer.callInner();
19: } }
```

An inner class declaration looks just like a stand-alone class declaration except that it happens to be located inside another class. Line 8 shows that the inner class just refers to greeting as if it were available. This works because it is in fact available. Even though the variable is private, it is within that same class.

Since an inner class is not static, it has to be used with an instance of the outer class. Line 13 shows that an instance of the outer class can instantiate Inner normally. This works because callInner() is an instance method on Outer. Both Inner and callInner() are members of Outer. Since they are peers, they just write the name.

There is another way to instantiate Inner that looks odd at first. OK, well maybe not just at first. This syntax isn't used often enough to get used to it:

```java
20:     public static void main(String[] args) {
21:         Outer outer = new Outer();
22:         Inner inner = outer.new Inner(); // create the inner class
23:         inner.go();
24:     }
```

Let's take a closer look at line 22. We need an instance of Outer to create Inner. We can't just call new Inner() because Java won't know with which instance of Outer it is associated. Java solves this by calling new as if it were a method on the outer variable.

.class Files for Inner Classes

Compiling the Outer.java class with which we have been working creates two class files. Outer.class you should be expecting. For the inner class, the compiler creates Outer$Inner.class. You don't need to know this syntax for the exam. We mention it so that you aren't surprised to see files with $ appearing in your directories. You do need to understand that multiple class files are created.

Inner classes can have the same variable names as outer classes, making scope a little tricky. There is a special way of calling this to say which variable you want to access. This is something you might see on the exam but ideally not in the real world.

In fact, you aren't limited to just one inner class. Please never do this in code you write. Here is how to nest multiple classes and access a variable with the same name in each:

```
1:  public class A {
2:      private int x = 10;
3:      class B {
4:          private int x = 20;
5:          class C {
6:              private int x = 30;
7:              public void allTheX() {
8:                  System.out.println(x);         // 30
9:                  System.out.println(this.x);    // 30
10:                 System.out.println(B.this.x);  // 20
11:                 System.out.println(A.this.x);  // 10
12:     } } }
13:     public static void main(String[] args) {
14:         A a = new A();
15:         A.B b = a.new B();
16:         A.B.C c = b.new C();
17:         c.allTheX();
18: }}
```

Yes, this code makes us cringe too. It has two nested classes. Line 14 instantiates the outermost one. Line 15 uses the awkward syntax to instantiate a B. Notice the type is A.B. We could have written B as the type because that is available at the member level of B. Java knows where to look for it. On line 16, we instantiate a C. This time, the A.B.C type is necessary to specify. C is too deep for Java to know where to look. Then line 17 calls a method on c.

Lines 8 and 9 are the type of code that we are used to seeing. They refer to the instance variable on the current class—the one declared on line 6 to be precise. Line 10 uses this in a special way. We still want an instance variable. But this time we want the one on the B class, which is the variable on line 4. Line 11 does the same thing for class A, getting the variable from line 2.

Inner Classes Require an Instance

Take a look at the following and see whether you can figure out why two of the three constructor calls do not compile:

```java
public class Fox {
    private class Den {}
    public void goHome() {
        new Den();
    }
    public static void visitFriend() {
        new Den();   // DOES NOT COMPILE
    }
}

public class Squirrel {
    public void visitFox() {
        new Den();   // DOES NOT COMPILE
    }
}
```

The first constructor call compiles because goHome() is an instance method, and therefore the call is associated with the this instance. The second call does not compile because it is called inside a static method. You can still call the constructor, but you have to explicitly give it a reference to a Fox instance.

The last constructor call does not compile for two reasons. Even though it is an instance method, it is not an instance method inside the Fox class. Adding a Fox reference would not fix the problem entirely, though. Den is private and not accessible in the Squirrel class.

Creating a *static* Nested Class

A *static nested class* is a static type defined at the member level. Unlike an inner class, a static nested class can be instantiated without an instance of the enclosing class. The trade-off, though, is it can't access instance variables or methods in the outer class directly. It can be done but requires an explicit reference to an outer class variable.

In other words, it is like a top-level class except for the following:

- The nesting creates a namespace because the enclosing class name must be used to refer to it.

- It can be made `private` or use one of the other access modifiers to encapsulate it.

- The enclosing class can refer to the fields and methods of the `static` nested class.

Let's take a look at an example:

```
1: public class Enclosing {
2:    static class Nested {
3:        private int price = 6;
4:    }
5:    public static void main(String[] args) {
6:        Nested nested = new Nested();
7:        System.out.println(nested.price);
8: } }
```

Line 6 instantiates the nested class. Since the class is `static`, you do not need an instance of Enclosing to use it. You are allowed to access `private` instance variables, which is shown on line 7.

Importing a *static* Nested Class

Importing a `static` nested class is interesting. You can import it using a regular import.

```
// Toucan.java
package bird;
public class Toucan {
    public static class Beak {}
}
```

```
// BirdWatcher.java
package watcher;
import bird.Toucan.Beak; // regular import ok
public class BirdWatcher {
    Beak beak;
}
```

Since it is `static`, you can also use a `static` import.

```
import static bird.Toucan.Beak;
```

Either one will compile. Surprising, isn't it? Remember, Java treats the enclosing class as if it were a namespace.

Writing a Local Class

A *local class* is a nested class defined within a method. Like local variables, a local class declaration does not exist until the method is invoked, and it goes out of scope when the method returns. This means you can create instances only from within the method. Those instances can still be returned from the method. This is just how local variables work.

> Local classes are not limited to being declared only inside methods. They can be declared inside constructors and initializers too. For simplicity, we limit our discussion to methods in this chapter.

Local classes have the following properties:

- They do not have an access modifier.
- They cannot be declared static and cannot declare static fields or methods, except for static final fields.
- They have access to all fields and methods of the enclosing class (when defined in an instance method).
- They can access local variables if the variables are final or effectively final.

> From your 1Z0-815 exam studies, remember that *effectively final* refers to a local variable whose value does not change after it is set. A simple test for effectively final is to add the final modifier to the local variable declaration. If it still compiles, then the local variable is effectively final.

Ready for an example? Here's a complicated way to multiply two numbers:

```
1:  public class PrintNumbers {
2:      private int length = 5;
3:      public void calculate() {
4:          final int width = 20;
5:          class MyLocalClass {
6:              public void multiply() {
7:                  System.out.print(length * width);
8:              }
9:          }
10:         MyLocalClass local = new MyLocalClass();
11:         local.multiply();
12:     }
13:     public static void main(String[] args) {
14:         PrintNumbers outer = new PrintNumbers();
15:         outer.calculate();
16:     }
17: }
```

Lines 5 through 9 are the local class. That class's scope ends on line 12 where the method ends. Line 7 refers to an instance variable and a final local variable, so both variable references are allowed from within the local class.

Earlier, we made the statement that local variable references are allowed if they are final or effectively final. Let's talk about that now. The compiler is generating a .class file from your local class. A separate class has no way to refer to local variables. If the local variable is final, Java can handle it by passing it to the constructor of the local class or by storing it in the .class file. If it weren't effectively final, these tricks wouldn't work because the value could change after the copy was made.

As an illustrative example, consider the following:

```java
public void processData() {
    final int length = 5;
    int width = 10;
    int height = 2;
    class VolumeCalculator {
        public int multiply() {
            return length * width * height; // DOES NOT COMPILE
        }
    }
    width = 2;
}
```

The length and height variables are final and effectively final, respectively, so neither causes a compilation issue. On the other hand, the width variable is reassigned during the method so it cannot be effectively final. For this reason, the local class declaration does not compile.

Defining an Anonymous Class

An *anonymous class* is a specialized form of a local class that does not have a name. It is declared and instantiated all in one statement using the new keyword, a type name with parentheses, and a set of braces {}. Anonymous classes are required to extend an existing class or implement an existing interface. They are useful when you have a short implementation that will not be used anywhere else. Here's an example:

```java
1:  public class ZooGiftShop {
2:      abstract class SaleTodayOnly {
3:          abstract int dollarsOff();
4:      }
5:      public int admission(int basePrice) {
6:          SaleTodayOnly sale = new SaleTodayOnly() {
7:              int dollarsOff() { return 3; }
8:          };  // Don't forget the semicolon!
9:          return basePrice - sale.dollarsOff();
10: } }
```

Lines 2 through 4 define an abstract class. Lines 6 through 8 define the anonymous class. Notice how this anonymous class does not have a name. The code says to instantiate a new SaleTodayOnly object. But wait, SaleTodayOnly is abstract. This is OK because we provide the class body right there—anonymously. In this example, writing an anonymous class is equivalent to writing a local class with an unspecified name that extends SaleTodayOnly and then immediately using it.

Pay special attention to the semicolon on line 8. We are declaring a local variable on these lines. Local variable declarations are required to end with semicolons, just like other Java statements—even if they are long and happen to contain an anonymous class.

Now we convert this same example to implement an interface instead of extending an abstract class.

```
1:  public class ZooGiftShop {
2:      interface SaleTodayOnly {
3:          int dollarsOff();
4:      }
5:      public int admission(int basePrice) {
6:          SaleTodayOnly sale = new SaleTodayOnly() {
7:              public int dollarsOff() { return 3; }
8:          };
9:          return basePrice - sale.dollarsOff();
10: } }
```

The most interesting thing here is how little has changed. Lines 2 through 4 declare an interface instead of an abstract class. Line 7 is public instead of using default access since interfaces require public methods. And that is it. The anonymous class is the same whether you implement an interface or extend a class! Java figures out which one you want automatically. Just remember that in this second example, an instance of a class is created on line 6, not an interface.

But what if we want to implement both an interface and extend a class? You can't with an anonymous class, unless the class to extend is java.lang.Object. The Object class doesn't count in the rule. Remember that an anonymous class is just an unnamed local class. You can write a local class and give it a name if you have this problem. Then you can extend a class and implement as many interfaces as you like. If your code is this complex, a local class probably isn't the most readable option anyway.

There is one more thing that you can do with anonymous classes. You can define them right where they are needed, even if that is an argument to another method.

```
1:  public class ZooGiftShop {
2:      interface SaleTodayOnly {
3:          int dollarsOff();
4:      }
5:      public int pay() {
```

```
6:          return admission(5, new SaleTodayOnly() {
7:              public int dollarsOff() { return 3; }
8:          });
9:      }
10:     public int admission(int basePrice, SaleTodayOnly sale) {
11:         return basePrice - sale.dollarsOff();
12: }}
```

Lines 6 through 8 are the anonymous class. We don't even store it in a local variable. Instead, we pass it directly to the method that needs it. Reading this style of code does take some getting used to. But it is a concise way to create a class that you will use only once.

You can even define anonymous classes outside a method body. The following may look like we are instantiating an interface as an instance variable, but the {} after the interface name indicates that this is an anonymous inner class implementing the interface.

```
public class Gorilla {
    interface Climb {}
    Climb climbing = new Climb() {};
}
```

 Real World Scenario

Anonymous Classes and Lambda Expressions

Prior to Java 8, anonymous classes were frequently used for asynchronous tasks and event handlers. For example, the following shows an anonymous class used as an event handler in a JavaFX application:

```
Button redButton = new Button();
redButton.setOnAction(new EventHandler<ActionEvent>() {
    public void handle(ActionEvent e) {
        System.out.println("Red button pressed!");
    }
});
```

Since Java 8, though, lambda expressions are a much more concise way of expressing the same thing.

```
Button redButton = new Button();
redButton.setOnAction(e -> System.out.println("Red button pressed!"));
```

The only restriction is that the variable type must be a functional interface. If you haven't worked with functional interfaces and lambda expressions before, don't worry. We'll be reviewing them in this chapter.

Reviewing Nested Classes

For the exam, make sure that you know the information in Table 1.1 and Table 1.2 about which syntax rules are permitted in Java.

TABLE 1.1   Modifiers in nested classes

Permitted Modifiers	Inner class	static nested class	Local class	Anonymous class
Access modifiers	All	All	None	None
abstract	Yes	Yes	Yes	No
Final	Yes	Yes	Yes	No

TABLE 1.2   Members in nested classes

Permitted Members	Inner class	static nested class	Local class	Anonymous class
Instance methods	Yes	Yes	Yes	Yes
Instance variables	Yes	Yes	Yes	Yes
static methods	No	Yes	No	No
static variables	Yes (if final)	Yes	Yes (if final)	Yes (if final)

You should also know the information in Table 1.3 about types of access. For example, the exam might try to trick you by having a static class access an outer class instance variable without a reference to the outer class.

TABLE 1.3   Nested class access rules

	Inner class	static nested class	Local class	Anonymous class
Can extend any class or implement any number of interfaces	Yes	Yes	Yes	No—must have exactly one superclass or one interface
Can access instance members of enclosing class without a reference	Yes	No	Yes (if declared in an instance method)	Yes (if declared in an instance method)
Can access local variables of enclosing method	N/A	N/A	Yes (if final or effectively final)	Yes (if final or effectively final)

Understanding Interface Members

When Java was first released, there were only two types of members an interface declaration could include: abstract methods and constant (`static final`) variables. Since Java 8 and 9 were released, four new method types have been added that we will cover in this section. Keep Table 1.4 handy as we discuss the various interface types in this section.

TABLE 1.4   Interface member types

	Since Java version	Membership type	Required modifiers	Implicit modifiers	Has value or body?
Constant variable	1.0	Class	—	public static final	Yes
Abstract method	1.0	Instance	—	public abstract	No
Default method	8	Instance	default	public	Yes
Static method	8	Class	static	public	Yes

	Since Java version	Membership type	Required modifiers	Implicit modifiers	Has value or body?
Private method	9	Instance	`private`	—	Yes
Private static method	9	Class	`private static`	—	Yes

We assume from your previous studies that you know how to define a constant variable and abstract method, so we'll move on to the newer interface member types.

Relying on a *default* Interface Method

A *default method* is a method defined in an interface with the `default` keyword and includes a method body. Contrast `default` methods with abstract methods in an interface, which do not define a method body.

A `default` method may be overridden by a class implementing the interface. The name *default* comes from the concept that it is viewed as an abstract interface method with a default implementation. The class has the option of overriding the `default` method, but if it does not, then the default implementation will be used.

Purpose of *default* Methods

One motivation for adding `default` methods to the Java language was for backward compatibility. A `default` method allows you to add a new method to an existing interface, without the need to modify older code that implements the interface.

Another motivation for adding `default` methods to Java is for convenience. For instance, the `Comparator` interface includes a `default reversed()` method that returns a new `Comparator` in the order reversed. While these can be written in every class implementing the interface, having it defined in the interface as a `default` method is quite useful.

The following is an example of a `default` method defined in an interface:

```
public interface IsWarmBlooded {
    boolean hasScales();
```

```
    default double getTemperature() {
        return 10.0;
    }
}
```

This example defines two interface methods: one is the abstract hasScales()method, and the other is the default getTemperature()method. Any class that implements IsWarmBlooded may rely on the default implementation of getTemperature() or override the method with its own version. Both of these methods include the implicit public modifier, so overriding them with a different access modifier is not allowed.

 Note that the default interface method modifier is not the same as the default label used in switch statements. Likewise, although package-private access is commonly referred to as default access, that feature is implemented by omitting an access modifier. Sorry if this is confusing! We agree Java has overused the word *default* over the years.

For the exam, you should be familiar with various rules for declaring default methods.

Default Interface Method Definition Rules

1. A default method may be declared only within an interface.
2. A default method must be marked with the default keyword and include a method body.
3. A default method is assumed to be public.
4. A default method cannot be marked abstract, final, or static.
5. A default method may be overridden by a class that implements the interface.
6. If a class inherits two or more default methods with the same method signature, then the class must override the method.

The first rule should give you some comfort in that you'll only see default methods in interfaces. If you see them in a class or enum on the exam, something is wrong. The second rule just denotes syntax, as default methods must use the default keyword. For example, the following code snippets will not compile:

```
public interface Carnivore {
    public default void eatMeat();          // DOES NOT COMPILE
    public int getRequiredFoodAmount() {    // DOES NOT COMPILE
        return 13;
    }
}
```

The first method, eatMeat(), doesn't compile because it is marked as default but doesn't provide a method body. The second method, getRequiredFoodAmount(), also doesn't compile because it provides a method body but is not marked with the default keyword.

What about our third, fourth, and fifth rules? Like abstract interface methods, default methods are implicitly public. Unlike abstract methods, though, default interface methods cannot be marked abstract and must provide a body. They also cannot be marked as final, because they can always be overridden in classes implementing the interface. Finally, they cannot be marked static since they are associated with the instance of the class implementing the interface.

Inheriting Duplicate *default* Methods

We have one last rule for default methods that warrants some discussion. You may have realized that by allowing default methods in interfaces, coupled with the fact that a class may implement multiple interfaces, Java has essentially opened the door to multiple inheritance problems. For example, what value would the following code output?

```
public interface Walk {
    public default int getSpeed() { return 5; }
}
```

```
public interface Run {
    public default int getSpeed() { return 10; }
}
```

```
public class Cat implements Walk, Run {   // DOES NOT COMPILE
    public static void main(String[] args) {
        System.out.println(new Cat().getSpeed());
    }
}
```

In this example, Cat inherits the two default methods for getSpeed(), so which does it use? Since Walk and Run are considered siblings in terms of how they are used in the Cat class, it is not clear whether the code should output 5 or 10. In this case, Java throws up its hands and says "Too hard, I give up!" and fails to compile.

If a class implements two interfaces that have default methods with the same method signature, the compiler will report an error. This rule holds true even for abstract classes because the duplicate method could be called within a concrete method within the abstract class. All is not lost, though. If the class implementing the interfaces *overrides* the duplicate default method, then the code will compile without issue.

By overriding the conflicting method, the ambiguity about which version of the method to call has been removed. For example, the following modified implementation of Cat will compile and output 1:

```
public class Cat implements Walk, Run {
    public int getSpeed() { return 1; }
```

```
public static void main(String[] args) {
    System.out.println(new Cat().getSpeed());
}
}
```

> In this section, all of our conflicting methods had identical declarations. These rules also apply to methods with the same signature but different return types or declared exceptions. If a default method is overridden in the concrete class, then it must use a declaration that is compatible, following the rules for overriding methods you learned about when studying for the 1Z0-815 exam.

Calling a Hidden *default* Method

Let's conclude our discussion of default methods by revisiting the Cat example, with two inherited default getSpeed() methods. Given our corrected implementation of Cat that overrides the getSpeed() method and returns 1, how would you call the version of the default method in the Walk interface? Take a few minutes to think about the following incomplete code:

```
public class Cat implements Walk, Run {
    public int getSpeed() { return 1; }

    public int getWalkSpeed() {
        return _____; // TODO: Call Walk's version of getSpeed()
    }

    public static void main(String[] args) {
        System.out.println(new Cat().getWalkSpeed());
    }
}
```

This is an area where a default method exhibits properties of both a static and instance method. Ready for the answer? Well, first off, you definitely can't call Walk.getSpeed(). A default method is treated as part of the instance since they can be overridden, so they cannot be called like a static method.

What about calling super.getSpeed()? That gets us a little closer, but which of the two inherited default methods is called? It's ambiguous and therefore not allowed. In fact, the compiler won't allow this even if there is only one inherited default method, as an interface is not part of the class hierarchy.

The solution is a combination of both of these answers. Take a look at the getWalkSpeed() method in this implementation of the Cat class:

```java
public class Cat implements Walk, Run {
   public int getSpeed() {
      return 1;
   }

   public int getWalkSpeed() {
      return Walk.super.getSpeed();
   }

   public static void main(String[] args) {
      System.out.println(new Cat().getWalkSpeed());
   }
}
```

In this example, we first use the interface name, followed by the super keyword, followed by the default method we want to call. We also put the call to the inherited default method inside the instance method getWalkSpeed(), as super is not accessible in the main() method.

Congratulations—if you understood this section, then you are prepared for the most complicated thing the exam can throw at you on default methods!

Using *static* Interface Methods

If you've been using an older version of Java, you might not be aware that Java now supports static interface methods. These methods are defined explicitly with the static keyword and for the most part behave just like static methods defined in classes.

Static Interface Method Definition Rules

1. A static method must be marked with the static keyword and include a method body.

2. A static method without an access modifier is assumed to be public.

3. A static method cannot be marked abstract or final.

4. A static method is not inherited and cannot be accessed in a class implementing the interface without a reference to the interface name.

These rules should follow from what you know so far of classes, interfaces, and static methods. For example, you can't declare static methods without a body in classes either. Like default and abstract interface methods, static interface methods are implicitly public if they are declared without an access modifier. As we'll see shortly, you can use the private access modifier with static methods.

Let's take a look at a static interface method.

```java
public interface Hop {
    static int getJumpHeight() {
        return 8;
    }
}
```

The method getJumpHeight() works just like a static method as defined in a class. In other words, it can be accessed without an instance of a class using the Hop.getJumpHeight() syntax. Since the method was defined without an access modifier, the compiler will automatically insert the public access modifier.

The fourth rule about inheritance might be a little confusing, so let's look at an example. The following is an example of a class Bunny that implements Hop and does not compile:

```java
public class Bunny implements Hop {
    public void printDetails() {
        System.out.println(getJumpHeight());  // DOES NOT COMPILE
    }
}
```

Without an explicit reference to the name of the interface, the code will not compile, even though Bunny implements Hop. In this manner, the static interface methods are not inherited by a class implementing the interface, as they would if the method were defined in a parent class. Because static methods do not require an instance of the class, the problem can be easily fixed by using the interface name and calling the public static method.

```java
public class Bunny implements Hop {
    public void printDetails() {
        System.out.println(Hop.getJumpHeight());
    }
}
```

Java "solved" the multiple inheritance problem of static interface methods by not allowing them to be inherited. This applies to both subinterfaces and classes that implement the interface. For example, a class that implements two interfaces containing static methods with the same signature will still compile. Contrast this with the behavior you saw for default interface methods in the previous section.

Introducing *private* Interface Methods

New to Java 9, interfaces may now include private interface methods. Putting on our thinking cap for a minute, what do you think private interface methods are useful for? Since they are private, they cannot be used outside the interface definition. They also cannot be used in `static` interface methods without a `static` method modifier, as we'll see in the next section. With all these restrictions, why were they added to the Java language?

Give up? The answer is that `private` interface methods can be used to reduce code duplication. For example, let's say we had a `Schedule` interface with a bunch of `default` methods. In each `default` method, we want to check some value and log some information based on the hour value. We could copy and paste the same code into each method, or we could use a `private` interface method. Take a look at the following example:

```java
public interface Schedule {
    default void wakeUp()       { checkTime(7);  }
    default void haveBreakfast() { checkTime(9);  }
    default void haveLunch()    { checkTime(12); }
    default void workOut()      { checkTime(18); }
    private void checkTime(int hour) {
        if (hour > 17) {
            System.out.println("You're late!");
        } else {
            System.out.println("You have "+(17-hour)+" hours left "
                + "to make the appointment");
        }
    }
}
```

While you can write this code without using a `private` interface method by copying the contents of the `checkTime()` method into every `default` method, it's a lot shorter and easier to read if we don't. Since the authors of Java were nice enough to add this feature for our convenience, we might as well make use of it!

The rules for `private` interface methods are pretty straightforward.

Private Interface Method Definition Rules

1. A `private` interface method must be marked with the `private` modifier and include a method body.

2. A `private` interface method may be called only by `default` and `private` (non-static) methods within the interface definition.

Private interface methods behave a lot like instance methods within a class. Like `private` methods in a class, they cannot be declared `abstract` since they are not inherited.

Introducing *private static* Interface Methods

Alongside `private` interface methods, Java 9 added `private static` interface methods. As you might have already guessed, the purpose of `private static` interface methods is to reduce code duplication in `static` methods within the interface declaration. Furthermore, because instance methods can access `static` methods within a class, they can also be accessed by `default` and `private` methods.

The following is an example of a Swim interface that uses a private static method to reduce code duplication within other methods declared in the interface:

```
public interface Swim {
    private static void breathe(String type) {
        System.out.println("Inhale");
        System.out.println("Performing stroke: " + type);
        System.out.println("Exhale");
    }
    static void butterfly()       { breathe("butterfly");   }
    public static void freestyle() { breathe("freestyle");   }
    default void backstroke()     { breathe("backstroke"); }
    private void breaststroke()    { breathe("breaststroke"); }
}
```

The breathe() method is able to be called in the static butterfly() and freestyle() methods, as well as the default backstroke() and private breaststroke() methods. Also, notice that butterfly() is assumed to be public static without any access modifier. The rules for private static interface methods are nearly the same as the rules for private interface methods.

Private Static Interface Method Definition Rules

1. A private static method must be marked with the private and static modifiers and include a method body.

2. A private static interface method may be called only by other methods within the interface definition.

Both private and private static methods can be called from default and private methods. This is equivalent to how an instance method is able to call both static and instance methods. On the other hand, a private method cannot be called from a private static method. This would be like trying to access an instance method from a static method in a class.

Why Mark Interface Methods *private*?

Instead of private and private static methods, we could have created default and public static methods, respectively. The code would have compiled just the same, so why mark them private at all?

The answer is to improve encapsulation, as we might not want these methods exposed outside the interface declaration. Encapsulation and security work best when the outside caller knows as little as possible about the internal implementation of a class or an interface. Using private interface methods doesn't just provide a way to reduce code duplication, but also a way to hide some of the underlying implementation details from users of the interface.

Reviewing Interface Members

We conclude our discussion of interface members with Table 1.5.

TABLE 1.5   Interface member access

	Accessible from default and private methods within the interface definition?	Accessible from static methods within the interface definition?	Accessible from instance methods implementing or extending the interface?	Accessible outside the interface without an instance of interface?
Constant variable	Yes	Yes	Yes	Yes
abstract method	Yes	No	Yes	No
default method	Yes	No	Yes	No
private method	Yes	No	No	No
static method	Yes	Yes	Yes	Yes
private static method	Yes	Yes	No	No

The first two data columns of Table 1.5 refer to access within the same interface definition. For example, a private method can access other private and private static methods defined within the same interface declaration.

When working with interfaces, we consider abstract, default, and private interface methods as instance methods. With that thought in mind, the last two columns of Table 1.5 should follow from what you know about class access modifiers and private members. Recall that instance methods can access static members within the class, but static members cannot access instance methods without a reference to the instance. Also, private members are never inherited, so they are never accessible directly by a class implementing an interface.

Real World Scenario

Abstract Classes vs. Interfaces

By introducing six different interface member types, Java has certainly blurred the lines between an abstract class and an interface. A key distinction, though, is that interfaces do not implement constructors and are not part of the class hierarchy. While a class can implement multiple interfaces, it can only directly extend a single class.

In fact, a common interview question is to ask an interviewee to describe the difference between an abstract class and an interface. These days, the question is more useful in determining which version of Java the candidate has most recently worked with. If you do happen to get this question on an interview, an appropriate tongue-in-cheek response would be, "How much time have you got?"

Introducing Functional Programming

Functional interfaces are used as the basis for lambda expressions in functional programming. A *functional interface* is an interface that contains a single abstract method. Your friend Sam can help you remember this because it is officially known as a *single abstract method (SAM)* rule.

A *lambda expression* is a block of code that gets passed around, sort of like an anonymous class that defines one method. As you'll see in this section, it can be written in a variety of short or long forms.

> Since lambdas were part of the 1Z0-815 exam, some of this you should already know. Considering how important functional interfaces and lambda expressions are to passing the exam, you should read this section carefully, even if some of it is review.

Defining a Functional Interface

Let's take a look at an example of a functional interface and a class that implements it:

```
@FunctionalInterface
public interface Sprint {
    public void sprint(int speed);
}
```

```java
public class Tiger implements Sprint {
    public void sprint(int speed) {
        System.out.println("Animal is sprinting fast! " + speed);
    }
}
```

In this example, the Sprint interface is a functional interface, because it contains exactly one abstract method, and the Tiger class is a valid class that implements the interface.

 We'll cover the meaning of the @FunctionalInterface annotation in Chapter 2, "Annotations." For now, you just need to know that adding the annotation to a functional interface is optional.

Consider the following four interfaces. Given our previous Sprint functional interface, which of the following are functional interfaces?

```java
public interface Dash extends Sprint {}
```

```java
public interface Skip extends Sprint {
    void skip();
}
```

```java
public interface Sleep {
    private void snore() {}
    default int getZzz() { return 1; }
}
```

```java
public interface Climb {
    void reach();
    default void fall() {}
    static int getBackUp() { return 100; }
    private static boolean checkHeight() { return true; }
}
```

All four of these are valid interfaces, but not all of them are functional interfaces. The Dash interface is a functional interface because it extends the Sprint interface and inherits the single abstract method sprint(). The Skip interface is not a valid functional interface because it has two abstract methods: the inherited sprint() method and the declared skip() method.

The Sleep interface is also not a valid functional interface. Neither snore() nor getZzz() meet the criteria of a single abstract method. Even though default methods function like abstract methods, in that they can be overridden in a class implementing the interface, they are insufficient for satisfying the single abstract method requirement.

Finally, the Climb interface is a functional interface. Despite defining a slew of methods, it contains only one abstract method: reach().

Declaring a Functional Interface with *Object* Methods

As you may remember from your previous studies, all classes inherit certain methods from Object. For the exam, you should be familiar with the following Object method declarations:

- `String toString()`
- `boolean equals(Object)`
- `int hashCode()`

We bring this up now because there is one exception to the single abstract method rule that you should be familiar with. If a functional interface includes an abstract method with the same signature as a public method found in Object, then those methods do not count toward the single abstract method test. The motivation behind this rule is that any class that implements the interface will inherit from Object, as all classes do, and therefore always implement these methods.

 Since Java assumes all classes extend from Object, you also cannot declare an interface method that is incompatible with Object. For example, declaring an abstract method int toString() in an interface would not compile since Object's version of the method returns a String.

Let's take a look at an example. Is the Soar class a functional interface?

```
public interface Soar {
    abstract String toString();
}
```

It is not. Since toString() is a public method implemented in Object, it does not count toward the single abstract method test.

On the other hand, the following implementation of Dive is a functional interface:

```
public interface Dive {
    String toString();
    public boolean equals(Object o);
    public abstract int hashCode();
    public void dive();
}
```

The dive() method is the single abstract method, while the others are not counted since they are public methods defined in the Object class.

Be wary of examples that resemble methods in the Object class but are not actually defined in the Object class. Do you see why the following is not a valid functional interface?

```
public interface Hibernate {
    String toString();
    public boolean equals(Hibernate o);
    public abstract int hashCode();
    public void rest();
}
```

Despite looking a lot like our Dive interface, the Hibernate interface uses equals(Hibernate) instead of equals(Object). Because this does not match the method signature of the equals(Object) method defined in the Object class, this interface is counted as containing two abstract methods: equals(Hibernate) and rest().

 Real World Scenario

Overriding *toString()*, *equals(Object)*, and *hashCode()*

While knowing how to properly override toString(), equals(Object), and hashCode() was part of Java certification exams prior to Java 11, this requirement was removed on all of the Java 11 exams. As a professional Java developer, it is important for you to know at least the basic rules for overriding each of these methods.

- toString(): The toString() method is called when you try to print an object or concatenate the object with a String. It is commonly overridden with a version that prints a unique description of the instance using its instance fields.

- equals(Object): The equals(Object) method is used to compare objects, with the default implementation just using the == operator. You should override the equals(Object) method anytime you want to conveniently compare elements for equality, especially if this requires checking numerous fields.

- hashCode(): Any time you override equals(Object), you must override hash Code() to be consistent. This means that for any two objects, if a.equals(b) is true, then a.hashCode()==b.hashCode() must also be true. If they are not consistent, then this could lead to invalid data and side effects in hash-based collections such as HashMap and HashSet.

All of these methods provide a default implementation in Object, but if you want to make intelligent use out of them, then you should override them.

Implementing Functional Interfaces with Lambdas

In addition to functional interfaces you write yourself, Java provides a number of pre-defined ones. You'll learn about many of these in Chapter 4, "Functional Programming." For now, let's work with the Predicate interface. Excluding any static or default methods defined in the interface, we have the following:

```
public interface Predicate<T> {
    boolean test(T t);
}
```

We'll review generics in Chapter 3, "Generics and Collections," but for now you just need to know that <T> allows the interface to take an object of a specified type. Now that we have a functional interface, we'll show you how to implement it using a lambda expression. The relationship between functional interfaces and lambda expressions is as follows: *any functional interface can be implemented as a lambda expression.*

Even older Java interfaces that pass the single abstract method test are functional interfaces, which can be implemented with lambda expressions.

Let's try an illustrative example. Our goal is to print out all the animals in a list according to some criteria. We start out with the Animal class.

```
public class Animal {
    private String species;
    private boolean canHop;
    private boolean canSwim;
    public Animal(String speciesName, boolean hopper, boolean swimmer) {
        species = speciesName;
        canHop = hopper;
        canSwim = swimmer;
    }
    public boolean canHop()  { return canHop; }
    public boolean canSwim() { return canSwim; }
    public String toString() { return species; }
}
```

The Animal class has three instance variables, which are set in the constructor. It has two methods that get the state of whether the animal can hop or swim. It also has a toString() method so we can easily identify the Animal in programs.

Now we have everything that we need to write our code to find each Animal that hops.

```
1:  import java.util.*;
2:  import java.util.function.Predicate;
3:  public class TraditionalSearch {
4:      public static void main(String[] args) {
5:
```

```
6:          // list of animals
7:          var animals = new ArrayList<Animal>();
8:          animals.add(new Animal("fish",     false, true));
9:          animals.add(new Animal("kangaroo", true,  true));
10:         animals.add(new Animal("rabbit",   true,  false));
11:         animals.add(new Animal("turtle",   false, true));
12:
13:         // Pass lambda that does check
14:         print(animals, a -> a.canHop());
15:     }
16:     private static void print(List<Animal> animals,
17:         Predicate<Animal> checker) {
18:         for (Animal animal : animals) {
19:             if (checker.test(animal))
20:                 System.out.print(animal + " ");
21:         }
22:     }
23: }
```

This program compiles and prints kangaroo rabbit at runtime. The print()
method on line 14 method is very general—it can check for any trait. This is good design.
It shouldn't need to know what specifically we are searching for in order to print a list
of animals.

 You may have noticed we used var in the last class. If you have already
taken the 1Z0-815 exam, then you should have learned all about local variable type inference using var. If not, you should review the var section in
Appendix A before continuing. Like the exam, we will be using var a lot in
this book!

Now what happens if we want to print the Animals that swim? We only have to add one
line of code—no need for an extra class to do something simple. Here's that other line:

```
14:         print(animals, a -> a.canSwim());
```

This prints fish kangaroo turtle at runtime. How about Animals that
cannot swim?

```
14:         print(animals, a -> !a.canSwim());
```

This prints rabbit by itself. The point here is that it is really easy to write code that
uses lambdas once you get the basics in place.

Lambda expressions rely on the notion of deferred execution. *Deferred execution* means that code is specified now but runs later. In this case, *later* is when the `print()` method calls it. Even though the execution is deferred, the compiler will still validate that the code syntax is correct.

Writing Lambda Expressions

The syntax of lambda expressions is tricky because many parts are optional. Despite this, the overall structure is the same. The left side of the lambda expression lists the variables. It must be compatible with the type and number of input parameters of the functional interface's single abstract method.

The right side of the lambda expression represents the body of the expression. It must be compatible with the return type of the functional interface's abstract method. For example, if the abstract method returns `int`, then the lambda expression must return an `int`, a value that can be implicitly cast to an `int`, or throw an exception.

Let's take a look at a functional interface in both its short and long forms. Figure 1.1 shows the short form of this functional interface and has three parts:

- A single parameter specified with the name a

- The arrow operator to separate the parameter and body

- A body that calls a single method and returns the result of that method

FIGURE 1.1   Lambda syntax omitting optional parts

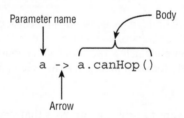

Now let's look at a more verbose version of this lambda expression, shown in Figure 1.2. It also contains three parts.

- A single parameter specified with the name a and stating the type is `Animal`

- The arrow operator to separate the parameter and body

- A body that has one or more lines of code, including a semicolon and a `return` statement

FIGURE 1.2   Lambda syntax, including optional parts

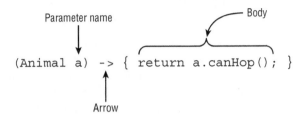

Parameter name

Body

(Animal a) -> { return a.canHop(); }

Arrow

The parentheses can be omitted only if there is a single parameter and its type is not explicitly stated. Java does this because developers commonly use lambda expressions this way so they can do as little typing as possible.

It shouldn't be news to you that we can omit braces when we have only a single statement. We did this with if statements and loops already. What is different here is that the rules change when you omit the braces. Java doesn't require you to type return or use a semicolon when no braces are used. This special shortcut doesn't work when we have two or more statements. At least this is consistent with using {} to create blocks of code elsewhere.

As a fun fact, s -> {} is a valid lambda. If the return type of the functional interface method is void, then you don't need the semicolon or return statement.

Let's take a look at some examples. The following are all valid lambda expressions, assuming that there are functional interfaces that can consume them:

```
() -> new Duck()
d -> {return d.quack();}
(Duck d) -> d.quack()
(Animal a, Duck d) -> d.quack()
```

The first lambda expression could be used by a functional interface containing a method that takes no arguments and returns a Duck object. The second and third lambda expressions both can be used by a functional interface that takes a Duck as input and returns whatever the return type of quack() is. The last lambda expression can be used by a functional interface that takes as input Animal and Duck objects and returns whatever the return type of quack() is.

Now let's make sure you can identify invalid syntax. Let's assume we needed a lambda that returns a boolean value. Do you see what's wrong with each of these?

```
3: a, b -> a.startsWith("test")        // DOES NOT COMPILE
4: Duck d -> d.canQuack();             // DOES NOT COMPILE
```

```
5: a -> { a.startsWith("test"); }       // DOES NOT COMPILE
6: a -> { return a.startsWith("test") } // DOES NOT COMPILE
7: (Swan s, t) -> s.compareTo(t) != 0   // DOES NOT COMPILE
```

Lines 3 and 4 require parentheses around each parameter list. Remember that the parentheses are optional *only* when there is one parameter and it doesn't have a type declared. Line 5 is missing the return keyword, which is required since we said the lambda must return a boolean. Line 6 is missing the semicolon inside of the braces, {}. Finally, line 7 is missing the parameter type for t. If the parameter type is specified for one of the parameters, then it must be specified for all of them.

Working with Lambda Variables

Variables can appear in three places with respect to lambdas: the parameter list, local variables declared inside the lambda body, and variables referenced from the lambda body. All three of these are opportunities for the exam to trick you.

Parameter List

Earlier you learned that specifying the type of parameters is optional. Now var can be used in a lambda parameter list. That means that all three of these statements are interchangeable:

```
Predicate<String> p = x -> true;
Predicate<String> p = (var x) -> true;
Predicate<String> p = (String x) -> true;
```

The exam might ask you to identify the type of the lambda parameter. In the previous example, the answer is String. OK, but how did we figure that out? A lambda infers the types from the surrounding context. That means you get to do the same!

In this case, the lambda is being assigned to a Predicate that takes a String. Another place to look for the type is in a method signature. Let's try another example. Can you figure out the type of x?

```
public void whatAmI() {
    test((var x) -> x>2, 123);
}

public void test(Predicate<Integer> c, int num) {
    c.test(num);
}
```

If you guessed Integer, you were right. The whatAmI() method creates a lambda to be passed to the test() method. Since the test() method expects an Integer as the generic, we know that is what the inferred type of x will be.

But wait, there's more! In some cases, you can determine the type without even seeing the method signature. What do you think the type of x is here?

```java
public void counts(List<Integer> list) {
    list.sort((var x, var y) -> x.compareTo(y));
}
```

The answer is again Integer. Since we are sorting a list, we can use the type of the list to determine the type of the lambda parameter.

Restrictions on Using *var* in the Parameter List

While you can use var inside a lambda parameter list, there is a rule you need to be aware of. If var is used for one of the types in the parameter list, then it must be used for all parameters in the list. Given this rule, which of the following lambda expressions do not compile if they were assigned to a variable?

```java
3: (var num) -> 1
4: var w -> 99
5: (var a, var b) -> "Hello"
6: (var a, Integer b) -> true
7: (String x, var y, Integer z) -> true
8: (var b, var k, var m) -> 3.14159
9: (var x, y) -> "goodbye"
```

Line 3 compiles and is similar to our previous examples. Line 4 does not compile because parentheses, (), are required when using the parameter name. Lines 5 and 8 compile because all of the parameters in the list use var. Lines 6 and 7 do not compile, though, because the parameter types include a mix of var and type names. Finally, line 9 does not compile because the parameter type is missing for the second parameter, y. Even when using var for all the parameter types, each parameter type must be written out.

Local Variables Inside the Lambda Body

While it is most common for a lambda body to be a single expression, it is legal to define a block. That block can have anything that is valid in a normal Java block, including local variable declarations.

The following code does just that. It creates a local variable named c that is scoped to the lambda block.

```java
(a, b) -> { int c = 0; return 5;}
```

When writing your own code, a lambda block with a local variable is a good hint that you should extract that code into a method.

Now let's try another one. Do you see what's wrong here?

```
(a, b) -> { int a = 0; return 5;}      // DOES NOT COMPILE
```

We tried to redeclare a, which is not allowed. Java doesn't let you create a local variable with the same name as one already declared in that scope. Now let's try a hard one. How many syntax errors do you see in this method?

```
11: public void variables(int a) {
12:     int b = 1;
13:     Predicate<Integer> p1 = a -> {
14:         int b = 0;
15:         int c = 0;
16:         return b == c;}
17: }
```

There are actually three syntax errors. The first is on line 13. The variable a was already used in this scope as a method parameter, so it cannot be reused. The next syntax error comes on line 14 where the code attempts to redeclare local variable b. The third syntax error is quite subtle and on line 16. See it? Look really closely.

The variable p1 is missing a semicolon at the end. There is a semicolon before the }, but that is inside the block. While you don't normally have to look for missing semicolons, lambdas are tricky in this space, so beware!

Variables Referenced from the Lambda Body

Lambda bodies are allowed to use static variables, instance variables, and local variables if they are final or effectively final. Sound familiar? Lambdas follow the same rules for access as local and anonymous classes! This is not a coincidence, as behind the scenes, anonymous classes are used for lambda expressions. Let's take a look at an example:

```
4:  public class Crow {
5:      private String color;
6:      public void caw(String name) {
7:          String volume = "loudly";
8:          Predicate<String> p = s -> (name+volume+color).length()==10;
9:      }
10: }
```

On the other hand, if the local variable is not final or effectively final, then the code does not compile.

```
4:  public class Crow {
5:      private String color;
6:      public void caw(String name) {
7:          String volume = "loudly";
8:          color = "allowed";
```

```
9:          name = "not allowed";
10:         volume = "not allowed";
11:         Predicate<String> p =
12:             s -> (name+volume+color).length()==9; // DOES NOT COMPILE
13:     }
14: }
```

In this example, the values of name and volume are assigned new values on lines 9 and 10. For this reason, the lambda expression declared on lines 11 and 12 does not compile since it references local variables that are not final or effectively final. If lines 9 and 10 were removed, then the class would compile.

Summary

This chapter focused on core fundamentals of the Java language that you will use throughout this book. We started with the final modifier and showed how it could be applied to local, instance, and static variables, as well as methods and classes.

We next moved on to enumerated types, which define a list of fixed values. Like boolean values, enums are not integers and cannot be compared this way. Enums can be used in switch statements. Besides the list of values, enums can include instance variables, constructors, and methods. Methods can even be abstract, in which case all enum values must provide an implementation. Alternatively, if an enum method is not marked final, then it can be overridden by one of its value declarations.

There are four types of nested classes. An inner class requires an instance of the outer class to use, while a static nested class does not. A local class is one defined within a method. Local classes can access final and effectively final local variables. Anonymous classes are a special type of local class that does not have a name. Anonymous classes are required to extend exactly one class by name or implement exactly one interface. Inner, local, and anonymous classes can access private members of the class in which they are defined, provided the latter two are used inside an instance method.

As of Java 9, interfaces now support six different members. Constant variables (static final) and abstract methods should have been familiar to you. Newer member types include default, static, private, and private static methods. While interfaces now contain a lot of member types, they are still distinct from abstract classes and do not participate in the class instantiation.

Last but certainly not least, this chapter included an introduction to functional interfaces and lambda expressions. A functional interface is an interface that contains exactly one abstract method. Any functional interface can be implemented with a lambda expression. A lambda expression can be written in a number of different forms, since many of the parts are optional. Make sure you understand the basics of writing lambda expressions as you will be using them throughout the book.

Exam Essentials

Be able to correctly apply the *final* modifier.   Applying the final modifier to a variable means its value cannot change after it has been assigned, although its contents can be modified. An instance final variable must be assigned a value when it is declared, in an instance initializer, or in a constructor at most once. A static final variable must be assigned a value when it is declared or in a static initializer. A final method is one that cannot be overridden by a subclass, while a final class is one that cannot be extended.

Be able to create and use enum types.   An enum is a data structure that defines a list of values. If the enum does not contain any other elements, then the semicolon (;) after the values is optional. An enum can have instance variables, constructors, and methods. Enum constructors are implicitly private. Enums can include methods, both as members or within individual enum values. If the enum declares an abstract method, each enum value must implement it.

Identify and distinguish between types of nested classes.   There are four types of nested types: inner classes, static classes, local classes, and anonymous classes. The first two are defined as part of a class declaration. Local classes are used inside method bodies and scoped to the end of the current block of code. Anonymous classes are created and used once, often on the fly. More recently, they are commonly implemented as lambda expressions.

Be able to declare and use nested classes.   Instantiating an inner class requires an instance of the outer class, such as calling new Outer.new Inner(). On the other hand, static nested classes can be created without a reference to the outer class, although they cannot access instance members of the outer class without a reference. Local and anonymous classes cannot be declared with an access modifier. Anonymous classes are limited to extending a single class or implementing one interface.

Be able to create *default, static, private*, and *private static* interface methods.   A default interface method is a public interface that contains a body, which can be overridden by a class implementing the interface. If a class inherits two default methods with the same signature, then the class must override the default method with its own implementation. An interface can include public static and private static methods, the latter of which can be accessed only by methods declared within the interface. An interface can also include private methods, which can be called only by default and other private methods in the interface declaration.

Determine whether an interface is a functional interface.   Use the single abstract method (SAM) rule to determine whether an interface is a functional interface. Other interface method types (default, private, static, and private static) do not count toward the single abstract method count, nor do any public methods with signatures found in Object.

Write simple lambda expressions.   Look for the presence or absence of optional elements in lambda code. Parameter types are optional. Braces and the `return` keyword are optional when the body is a single statement. Parentheses are optional when only one parameter is specified and the type is implicit. If one of the parameters is a `var`, then they all must use `var`.

Determine whether a variable can be used in a lambda body.   Local variables and method parameters must be `final` or effectively final to be referenced in a lambda expression. Class variables are always allowed. Instance variables are allowed if the lambda is used inside an instance method.

Review Questions

The answers to the chapter review questions can be found in Appendix B.

1. Which statements about the `final` modifier are correct? (Choose all that apply.)

    A. Instance and static variables can be marked `final`.

    B. A variable is effectively final if it is marked `final`.

    C. The `final` modifier can be applied to classes and interfaces.

    D. A `final` class cannot be extended.

    E. An object that is marked `final` cannot be modified.

    F. Local variables cannot be declared with type `var` and the `final` modifier.

2. What is the result of the following program?

    ```java
    public class FlavorsEnum {
        enum Flavors {
            VANILLA, CHOCOLATE, STRAWBERRY
            static final Flavors DEFAULT = STRAWBERRY;
        }
        public static void main(String[] args) {
            for(final var e : Flavors.values())
                System.out.print(e.ordinal()+" ");
        }
    }
    ```

    A. 0 1 2

    B. 1 2 3

    C. Exactly one line of code does not compile.

    D. More than one line of code does not compile.

    E. The code compiles but produces an exception at runtime.

    F. None of the above

3. What is the result of the following code? (Choose all that apply.)

    ```java
    1: public class Movie {
    2:     private int butter = 5;
    3:     private Movie() {}
    4:     protected class Popcorn {
    5:         private Popcorn() {}
    6:         public static int butter = 10;
    7:         public void startMovie() {
    8:             System.out.println(butter);
    ```

```
9:          }
10:     }
11:     public static void main(String[] args) {
12:         var movie = new Movie();
13:         Movie.Popcorn in = new Movie().new Popcorn();
14:         in.startMovie();
15:     } }
```

A. The output is 5.

B. The output is 10.

C. Line 6 generates a compiler error.

D. Line 12 generates a compiler error.

E. Line 13 generates a compiler error.

F. The code compiles but produces an exception at runtime.

4. Which statements about `default` and `private` interface methods are correct? (Choose all that apply.)

A. A `default` interface method can be declared `private`.

B. A `default` interface method can be declared `public`.

C. A `default` interface method can be declared `static`.

D. A `private` interface method can be declared `abstract`.

E. A `private` interface method can be declared `protected`.

F. A `private` interface method can be declared `static`.

5. Which of the following are valid lambda expressions? (Choose all that apply.)

A. `(Wolf w, var c) -> 39`

B. `(final Camel c) -> {}`

C. `(a,b,c) -> {int b = 3; return 2;}`

D. `(x,y) -> new RuntimeException()`

E. `(var y) -> return 0;`

F. `() -> {float r}`

G. `(Cat a, b) -> {}`

6. What are some advantages of using `private` interface methods? (Choose all that apply.)

A. Improve polymorphism

B. Improve performance at runtime

C. Reduce code duplication

D. Backward compatibility

E. Encapsulate interface implementation

F. Portability

7. What is the result of the following program?

```java
public class IceCream {
    enum Flavors {
        CHOCOLATE, STRAWBERRY, VANILLA
    }

    public static void main(String[] args) {
        Flavors STRAWBERRY = null;
        switch (STRAWBERRY) {
            case Flavors.VANILLA: System.out.print("v");
            case Flavors.CHOCOLATE: System.out.print("c");
            case Flavors.STRAWBERRY: System.out.print("s");
            break;
            default: System.out.println("missing flavor"); }
    }
}
```

A. v

B. vc

C. s

D. `missing flavor`

E. Exactly one line of code does not compile.

F. More than one line of code does not compile.

G. The code compiles but produces an exception at runtime.

8. Which statements about functional interfaces are true? (Choose all that apply.)

A. A functional interface can contain `default` and `private` methods.

B. A functional interface can be defined by a class or interface.

C. Abstract methods with signatures that are contained in `public` methods of `java.lang.Object` do not count toward the abstract method count for a functional interface.

D. A functional interface cannot contain `static` or `private static` methods.

E. A functional interface contains at least one abstract method.

F. A functional interface must be marked with the `@FunctionalInterface` annotation.

9. Which lines, when entered independently into the blank, allow the code to print `Not scared` at runtime? (Choose all that apply.)

```java
public class Ghost {
    public static void boo() {
        System.out.println("Not scared");
    }
}
```

```
        protected final class Spirit {
            public void boo() {
                System.out.println("Booo!!!");
            }
        }
        public static void main(String... haunt) {
            var g = new Ghost().new Spirit() {};
            _____;
        }
    }
```

A. g.boo()

B. g.super.boo()

C. new Ghost().boo()

D. g.Ghost.boo()

E. new Spirit().boo()

F. Ghost.boo()

G. None of the above

10. The following code appears in a file named Ostrich.java. What is the result of compiling the source file?

```
1: public class Ostrich {
2:     private int count;
3:     private interface Wild {}
4:     static class OstrichWrangler implements Wild {
5:         public int stampede() {
6:             return count;
7:     } } }
```

A. The code compiles successfully, and one bytecode file is generated: Ostrich.class.

B. The code compiles successfully, and two bytecode files are generated: Ostrich.class and OstrichWrangler.class.

C. The code compiles successfully, and two bytecode files are generated: Ostrich.class and Ostrich$OstrichWrangler.class.

D. A compiler error occurs on line 4.

E. A compiler error occurs on line 6.

11. What is the result of the following code?

```
1:  public interface CanWalk {
2:      default void walk() { System.out.print("Walking"); }
3:      private void testWalk() {}
4:  }
5:  public interface CanRun {
6:      abstract public void run();
7:      private void testWalk() {}
8:      default void walk() { System.out.print("Running"); }
9:  }
10: public interface CanSprint extends CanWalk, CanRun {
11:     void sprint();
12:     default void walk(int speed) {
13:        System.out.print("Sprinting");
14:     }
15:     private void testWalk() {}
16: }
```

A. The code compiles without issue.
B. The code will not compile because of line 6.
C. The code will not compile because of line 8.
D. The code will not compile because of line 10.
E. The code will not compile because of line 12.
F. None of the above

12. What is the result of executing the following program?

```
interface Sing {
   boolean isTooLoud(int volume, int limit);
}
public class OperaSinger {
   public static void main(String[] args) {
      check((h, l) -> h.toString(), 5);   // m1
   }
   private static void check(Sing sing, int volume) {
      if (sing.isTooLoud(volume, 10))    // m2
         System.out.println("not so great");
      else System.out.println("great");
   }
}
```

A. great
B. not so great

C. Compiler error on line m1

D. Compiler error on line m2

E. Compiler error on a different line

F. A runtime exception is thrown.

13. Which lines of the following interface declaration do not compile? (Choose all that apply.)

```
1: public interface Herbivore {
2:     int amount = 10;
3:     static boolean gather = true;
4:     static void eatGrass() {}
5:     int findMore() { return 2; }
6:     default float rest() { return 2; }
7:     protected int chew() { return 13; }
8:     private static void eatLeaves() {}
9: }
```

A. All of the lines compile without issue.

B. Line 2

C. Line 3

D. Line 4

E. Line 5

F. Line 6

G. Line 7

H. Line 8

14. What is printed by the following program?

```
public class Deer {
    enum Food {APPLES, BERRIES, GRASS}
    protected class Diet {
        private Food getFavorite() {
            return Food.BERRIES;
        }
    }
    public static void main(String[] seasons) {
        switch(new Diet().getFavorite()) {
            case APPLES: System.out.print("a");
            case BERRIES: System.out.print("b");
            default: System.out.print("c");
        }
    }
}
```

A. b

B. bc

C. abc

D. The code declaration of the Diet class does not compile.

E. The main() method does not compile.

F. The code compiles but produces an exception at runtime.

G. None of the above

15. Which of the following are printed by the Bear program? (Choose all that apply.)

```java
public class Bear {
    enum FOOD {
        BERRIES, INSECTS {
            public boolean isHealthy() { return true; }},
        FISH, ROOTS, COOKIES, HONEY;
        public abstract boolean isHealthy();
    }
    public static void main(String[] args) {
        System.out.print(FOOD.INSECTS);
        System.out.print(FOOD.INSECTS.ordinal());
        System.out.print(FOOD.INSECTS.isHealthy());
        System.out.print(FOOD.COOKIES.isHealthy());
    }
}
```

A. insects

B. INSECTS

C. 0

D. 1

E. false

F. true

G. The code does not compile.

16. Which of the following are valid functional interfaces? (Choose all that apply.)

```java
public interface Transport {
    public int go();
    public boolean equals(Object o);
}
```

```
public abstract class Car {
    public abstract Object swim(double speed, int duration);
}

public interface Locomotive extends Train {
    public int getSpeed();
}

public interface Train extends Transport {}

abstract interface Spaceship extends Transport {
    default int blastOff();
}

public interface Boat {
    int hashCode();
    int hashCode(String input);
}
```

A. Boat
B. Car
C. Locomotive
D. Tranport
E. Train
F. Spaceship
G. None of these is a valid functional interface.

17. Which lambda expression when entered into the blank line in the following code causes the program to print hahaha? (Choose all that apply.)

```
import java.util.function.Predicate;
public class Hyena {
    private int age = 1;
    public static void main(String[] args) {
        var p = new Hyena();
        double height = 10;
        int age = 1;
        testLaugh(p, _____ );
        age = 2;
    }
```

```
static void testLaugh(Hyena panda, Predicate<Hyena> joke) {
    var r = joke.test(panda) ? "hahaha" : "silence";
    System.out.print(r);
}
}
```

A. var -> p.age <= 10

B. shenzi -> age==1

C. p -> true

D. age==1

E. shenzi -> age==2

F. h -> h.age < 5

G. None of the above, as the code does not compile.

18. Which of the following can be inserted in the rest() method? (Choose all that apply.)

```
public class Lion {
    class Cub {}
    static class Den {}
    static void rest() {
        _____;
    } }
```

A. Cub a = Lion.new Cub()

B. Lion.Cub b = new Lion().Cub()

C. Lion.Cub c = new Lion().new Cub()

D. var d = new Den()

E. var e = Lion.new Cub()

F. Lion.Den f = Lion.new Den()

G. Lion.Den g = new Lion.Den()

H. var h = new Cub()

19. Given the following program, what can be inserted into the blank line that would allow it to print Swim! at runtime?

```
interface Swim {
    default void perform() { System.out.print("Swim!"); }
}
interface Dance {
    default void perform() { System.out.print("Dance!"); }
}
public class Penguin implements Swim, Dance {
```

```
public void perform() { System.out.print("Smile!"); }
private void doShow() {

    _____

}
public static void main(String[] eggs) {
    new Penguin().doShow();
}
}
```

A. super.perform();

B. Swim.perform();

C. super.Swim.perform();

D. Swim.super.perform();

E. The code does not compile regardless of what is inserted into the blank.

F. The code compiles, but due to polymorphism, it is not possible to produce the requested output without creating a new object.

20. Which statements about effectively final variables are true? (Choose all that apply.)

A. The value of an effectively final variable is not modified after it is set.

B. A lambda expression can reference effectively final variables.

C. A lambda expression can reference final variables.

D. If the final modifier is added, the code still compiles.

E. Instance variables can be effectively final.

F. Static variables can be effectively final.

21. Which lines of the following interface do not compile? (Choose all that apply.)

```
1: public interface BigCat {
2:     abstract String getName();
3:     static int hunt() { getName(); return 5; }
4:     default void climb() { rest(); }
5:     private void roar() { getName();  climb(); hunt(); }
6:     private static boolean sneak() { roar(); return true; }
7:     private int rest() { return 2; };
8: }
```

A. Line 2

B. Line 3

C. Line 4

D. Line 5

E. Line 6

F. Line 7

G. None of the above

22. What are some advantages of using `default` interface methods? (Choose all that apply.)

A. Automatic resource management

B. Improve performance at runtime

C. Better exception handling

D. Backward compatibility

E. Highly concurrent execution

F. Convenience in classes implementing the interface

23. Which statements about the following enum are true? (Choose all that apply.)

```
1:  public enum AnimalClasses {
2:      MAMMAL(true), INVERTIBRATE(Boolean.FALSE), BIRD(false),
3:      REPTILE(false), AMPHIBIAN(false), FISH(false) {
4:          public int swim() { return 4; }
5:      }
6:      final boolean hasHair;
7:      public AnimalClasses(boolean hasHair) {
8:          this.hasHair = hasHair;
9:      }
10:     public boolean hasHair() { return hasHair; }
11:     public int swim() { return 0; }
12: }
```

A. Compiler error on line 2

B. Compiler error on line 3

C. Compiler error on line 7

D. Compiler error on line 8

E. Compiler error on line 10

F. Compiler error on another line

G. The code compiles successfully.

24. Which lambdas can replace the `new Sloth()` call in the `main()` method and produce the same output at runtime? (Choose all that apply.)

```
import java.util.List;
interface Yawn {
    String yawn(double d, List<Integer> time);
}
```

```
class Sloth implements Yawn {
    public String yawn(double zzz, List<Integer> time) {
        return "Sleep: " + zzz;
    }
}
public class Vet {
    public static String takeNap(Yawn y) {
        return y.yawn(10, null);
    }
    public static void main(String... unused) {
        System.out.print(takeNap(new Sloth()));
    }
}
```

A. (z,f) -> { String x = ""; return "Sleep: " + x }

B. (t,s) -> { String t = ""; return "Sleep: " + t; }

C. (w,q) -> {"Sleep: " + w}

D. (e,u) -> { String g = ""; "Sleep: " + e }

E. (a,b) -> "Sleep: " + (double)(b==null ? a : a)

F. (r,k) -> { String g = ""; return "Sleep:"; }

G. None of the above, as the program does not compile.

25. What does the following program print?

```
1:  public class Zebra {
2:      private int x = 24;
3:      public int hunt() {
4:          String message = "x is ";
5:          abstract class Stripes {
6:              private int x = 0;
7:              public void print() {
8:                  System.out.print(message + Zebra.this.x);
9:              }
10:         }
11:         var s = new Stripes() {};
12:         s.print();
13:         return x;
14:     }
```

```
15:     public static void main(String[] args) {
16:        new Zebra().hunt();
17:     } }
```

A. x is 0

 B. x is 24

C. Line 6 generates a compiler error.

D. Line 8 generates a compiler error.

E. Line 11 generates a compiler error.

F. None of the above

Chapter

2

Annotations

OCP EXAM OBJECTIVES COVERED IN THIS CHAPTER:

✓ Annotations

- Describe the purpose of annotations and typical usage patterns

- Apply annotations to classes and methods

- Describe commonly used annotations in the JDK

- Declare custom annotations

There are some topics you need to know to pass the exam, some that are important in your daily development experience, and some that are important for both. Annotations definitely fall into this last category. Annotations were added to the Java language to make a developer's life a lot easier.

Prior to annotations, adding extra information about a class or method was often cumbersome and required a lot of extra classes and configuration files. Annotations solved this by having the data and the information about the data defined in the same location.

In this chapter, we define what an annotation is, how to create a custom annotation, and how to properly apply annotations. We will also teach you about built-in annotations that you will need to learn for the exam. We hope this chapter increases your understanding and usage of annotations in your professional development experience.

Introducing Annotations

Annotations are all about metadata. That might not sound very exciting at first, but they add a lot of value to the Java language. Or perhaps, better said, they allow you to add a lot of value to your code.

Understanding Metadata

What exactly is metadata? *Metadata* is data that provides information about other data. Imagine our zoo is having a sale on tickets. The *attribute data* includes the price, the expiration date, and the number of tickets purchased. In other words, the attribute data is the transactional information that makes up the ticket sale and its contents.

On the other hand, the *metadata* includes the rules, properties, or relationships surrounding the ticket sales. Patrons must buy at least one ticket, as a sale of zero or negative tickets is silly. Maybe the zoo is having a problem with scalpers, so they add a rule that each person can buy a maximum of five tickets a day. These metadata rules describe information about the ticket sale but are not part of the ticket sale.

As you'll learn in this chapter, annotations provide an easy and convenient way to insert metadata like this into your applications.

While annotations allow you to insert rules around data, it does not mean the values for these rules need to be defined in the code, aka "hard-coded." In many frameworks, you can define the rules and relationships in the code but read the values from elsewhere. In the previous example, you could define an annotation specifying a maximum number of tickets but load the value of 5 from a config file or database. For this chapter, though, you can assume the values are defined in the code.

Purpose of Annotations

The purpose of an *annotation* is to assign metadata attributes to classes, methods, variables, and other Java types. Let's start with a simple annotation for our zoo: @ZooAnimal. Don't worry about how this annotation is defined or the syntax of how to call it just yet; we'll delve into that shortly. For now, you just need to know that annotations start with the at (@) symbol and can contain attribute/value pairs called *elements*.

```
public class Mammal {}
public class Bird {}

@ZooAnimal public class Lion extends Mammal {}

@ZooAnimal public class Peacock extends Bird {}
```

In this case, the annotation is applied to the Lion and Peacock classes. We could have also had them extend a class called ZooAnimal, but then we have to change the class hierarchy. By using an annotation, we leave the class structure intact.

That brings us to our first rule about annotations: *annotations function a lot like interfaces*. In this example, annotations allow us to *mark* a class as a ZooAnimal without changing its inheritance structure.

So if annotations function like interfaces, why don't we just use interfaces? While interfaces can be applied only to classes, annotations can be applied to any declaration including classes, methods, expressions, and even other annotations. Also, unlike interfaces, annotations allow us to pass a set of values where they are applied.

Consider the following Veterinarian class:

```
public class Veterinarian {
    @ZooAnimal(habitat="Infirmary") private Lion sickLion;

    @ZooAnimal(habitat="Safari") private Lion healthyLion;

    @ZooAnimal(habitat="Special Enclosure") private Lion blindLion;
}
```

This class defines three variables, each with an associated habitat value. The habitat value is part of the type declaration of each variable, not an individual object. For example, the healthyLion may change the object it points to, but the value of the annotation does not. Without annotations, we'd have to define a new Lion type for each habitat value, which could become cumbersome given a large enough application.

That brings us to our second rule about annotations: *annotations establish relationships that make it easier to manage data about our application.*

Sure, we could write applications without annotations, but that often requires creating a lot of extra classes, interfaces, or data files (XML, JSON, etc.) to manage these complex relationships. Worse yet, because these extra classes or files may be defined outside the class where they are being used, we have to do a lot of work to keep the data and the relationships in sync.

 Real World Scenario

External Metadata Files

Prior to annotations, many early Java enterprise frameworks relied on external XML files to store metadata about an application. Imagine managing an application with dozens of services, hundreds of objects, and thousands of attributes. The data would be stored in numerous Java files alongside a large, ever-growing XML file. And a change to one often required a change to the other.

As you can probably imagine, this becomes untenable very quickly! Many of these frameworks were abandoned or rewritten to use annotations. These days, XML files are still used with Java projects but often serve to provide minimal configuration information, rather than low-level metadata.

Consider the following methods that use a hypothetical @ZooSchedule annotation to indicate when a task should be performed.

```java
// Lion.java
public class Lion {
    @ZooSchedule(hours={"9am","5pm","10pm"}) void feedLions() {
        System.out.print("Time to feed the lions!");
    }
}
```

```java
// Peacock.java
public class Peacock {
    @ZooSchedule(hours={"4am","5pm"}) void cleanPeacocksPen() {
        System.out.print("Time to sweep up!");
    }
}
```

These methods are defined in completely different classes, but the interpretation of the annotation is the same. With this approach, the task and its schedule are defined right next to each other. This brings us to our third rule about annotations: *an annotation ascribes custom information on the declaration where it is defined.* This turns out to be a powerful tool, as the same annotation can often be applied to completely unrelated classes or variables.

There's one final rule about annotations you should be familiar with: *annotations are optional metadata and by themselves do not do anything.* This means you can take a project filled with thousands of annotations and remove all of them, and it will still compile and run, albeit with potentially different behavior at runtime.

This last rule might seem a little counterintuitive at first, but it refers to the fact that annotations aren't utilized where they are defined. It's up to the rest of the application, or more likely the underlying framework, to enforce or use annotations to accomplish tasks. For instance, marking a method with @SafeVarargs informs other developers and development tools that no unsafe operations are present in the method body. It does not actually prevent unsafe operations from occurring!

 While an annotation can be removed from a class and it will still compile, the opposite is not true; adding an annotation can trigger a compiler error. As we will see this in chapter, the compiler validates annotations are properly used and include all required fields.

For the exam, you need to know how to define your own custom annotations, how to apply annotations properly, and how to use common annotations. Writing code that processes or enforces annotations is not required for the exam.

🌐 Real World Scenario

The Spring Framework

While there are many platforms that rely on annotations, one of the most recognized and one of the first to popularize using annotations is the Spring Framework, or Spring for short. Spring uses annotations for many purposes, including dependency injection, which is a common technique of decoupling a service and the clients that use it.

In Chapter 6, "Modular Applications," you'll learn all about Java's built-in service implementation, which uses module-info files rather than annotations to manage services. While modules and Spring are both providing dependencies dynamically, they are implemented in a very different manner.

Spring, along with the well-known convention over configuration Spring Boot framework, isn't on the exam, but we recommend professional Java developers be familiar with both of them.

Creating Custom Annotations

Creating your own annotation is surprisingly easy. You just give it a name, define a list of optional and required elements, and specify its usage. In this section, we'll start with the simplest possible annotation and work our way up from there.

Creating an Annotation

Let's say our zoo wants to specify the exercise metadata for various zoo inhabitants using annotations. We use the @interface annotation (all lowercase) to declare an annotation. Like classes and interfaces, they are commonly defined in their own file as a top-level type, although they can be defined inside a class declaration like an inner class.

```
public @interface Exercise {}
```

Yes, we use an annotation to create an annotation! The Exercise annotation is referred to as a *marker annotation,* since it does not contain any elements. In Chapter 8, "I/O," you'll actually learn about something called a marker interface, which shares a lot of similarities with annotations.

How do we use our new annotation? It's easy. We use the at (@) symbol, followed by the type name. In this case, the annotation is @Exercise. Then, we apply the annotation to other Java code, such as a class.

Let's apply @Exercise to some classes.

```
@Exercise() public class Cheetah {}
```

```
@Exercise public class Sloth {}
```

```
@Exercise
public class ZooEmployee {}
```

Oh no, we've mixed animals and zoo employees! That's perfectly fine. There's no rule that our @Exercise annotation has to be applied to animals. Like interfaces, annotations can be applied to unrelated classes.

You might have noticed that Cheetah and Sloth differ on their usage of the annotation. One uses parentheses, (), while the other does not. When using a marker annotation, parentheses are optional. Once we start adding elements, though, they are required if the annotation includes any values.

We also see ZooEmployee is not declared on the same line as its annotation. If an annotation is declared on a line by itself, then it applies to the next nonannotation type found on the proceeding lines. In fact, this applies when there are multiple annotations present.

```
@Scaley        @Flexible
   @Food("insect") @Food("rodent")        @FriendlyPet
@Limbless public class Snake {}
```

Some annotations are on the same line, some are on their own line, and some are on the line with the declaration of Snake. Regardless, all of the annotations apply to Snake. As with other declarations in Java, spaces and tabs between elements are ignored.

 Whether you put annotations on the same line as the type they apply to or on separate lines is a matter of style. Either is acceptable.

In this example, some annotations are all lowercase, while others are mixed case. Annotation names are case sensitive. Like class and interface names, it is common practice to have them start with an uppercase letter, although it is not required.

Finally, some annotations, like @Food, can be applied more than once. We'll cover repeatable annotations later in this chapter.

Specifying a Required Element

An *annotation element* is an attribute that stores values about the particular usage of an annotation. To make our previous example more useful, let's change @Exercise from a marker annotation to one that includes an element.

```
public @interface Exercise {
    int hoursPerDay();
}
```

The syntax for the hoursPerDay() element may seem a little strange at first. It looks a lot like an abstract method, although we're calling it an element (or attribute). Remember, annotations have their roots in interfaces. Behind the scenes, the JVM is creating elements as interface methods and annotations as implementations of these interfaces. Luckily, you don't need to worry about those details; the compiler does that for you.

Let's see how this new element changes our usage:

```
@Exercise(hoursPerDay=3) public class Cheetah {}

@Exercise hoursPerDay=0 public class Sloth {}       // DOES NOT COMPILE

@Exercise public class ZooEmployee {}               // DOES NOT COMPILE
```

The Cheetah class compiles and correctly uses the annotation, providing a value for the element. The Sloth class does not compile because it is missing parentheses around the annotation parameters. Remember, parentheses are optional only if no values are included.

What about ZooEmployee? This class does not compile because the hoursPerDay field is required. Remember earlier when we said annotations are optional metadata? While the annotation itself is optional, the compiler still cares that they are used correctly.

Wait a second, when did we mark hoursPerDay() as required? We didn't. But we also didn't specify a default value either. *When declaring an annotation, any element without a default value is considered required.* We'll show you how to declare an optional element next.

Providing an Optional Element

For an element to be optional, rather than required, it must include a default value. Let's update our annotation to include an optional value.

```
public @interface Exercise {
   int hoursPerDay();
   int startHour() default 6;
}
```

 In Chapter 1, "Java Fundamentals," we mentioned that the default key-word can be used in switch statements and interface methods. Yep, they did it again. There is yet another use of the default keyword that is unre-lated to any of the usages you were previously familiar with. And don't forget package-private access is commonly referred to as default access without any modifiers. Good grief!

Next, let's apply the updated annotation to our classes.

```
@Exercise(startHour=5, hoursPerDay=3) public class Cheetah {}

@Exercise(hoursPerDay=0) public class Sloth {}

@Exercise(hoursPerDay=7, startHour="8")   // DOES NOT COMPILE
public class ZooEmployee {}
```

There are a few things to unpack here. First, when we have more than one element value within an annotation, we separate them by a comma (,). Next, each element is written using the syntax *elementName=elementValue*. It's like a shorthand for a Map. Also, the order of each element does not matter. Cheetah could have listed hoursPerDay first.

We also see that Sloth does not specify a value for startHour, meaning it will be instantiated with the default value of 6.

In this version, the ZooEmployee class does not compile because it defines a value that is incompatible with the int type of startHour. The compiler is doing its duty validating the type!

Defining a Default Element Value

The default value of an annotation cannot be just any value. Similar to case statement values, *the default value of an annotation must be a non-null constant expression.*

```
public @interface BadAnnotation {
   String name() default new String("");  // DOES NOT COMPILE
   String address() default "";
   String title() default null;           // DOES NOT COMPILE
}
```

In this example, name() does not compile because it is not a constant expression, while title() does not compile because it is null. Only address() compiles. Notice that while null is not permitted as a default value, the empty String "" is.

Selecting an Element Type

Similar to a default element value, an annotation element cannot be declared with just any type. It must be a primitive type, a String, a Class, an enum, another annotation, or an array of any of these types.

Given this information and our previous Exercise annotation, which of the following elements compile?

```
public class Bear {}

public enum Size {SMALL, MEDIUM, LARGE}

public @interface Panda {
   Integer height();
   String[][] generalInfo();
   Size size() default Size.SMALL;
   Bear friendlyBear();
   Exercise exercise() default @Exercise(hoursPerDay=2);
}
```

The height() element does not compile. While primitive types like int and long are supported, wrapper classes like Integer and Long are not. The generalInfo() element also does not compile. The type String[] is supported, as it is an array of String values, but String[][] is not.

The size() and exercise() elements both compile, with one being an enum and the other being an annotation. To set a default value for exercise(), we use the @Exercise annotation. Remember, this is the only way to create an annotation value. Unlike instantiating a class, the new keyword is never used to create an annotation.

Finally, the friendlyBear() element does not compile. The type of friendlyBear() is Bear (not Class). Even if Bear were changed to an interface, the friendlyBear() element would still not compile since it is not one of the supported types.

Applying Element Modifiers

Like abstract interface methods, annotation elements are implicitly abstract and public, whether you declare them that way or not.

```
public @interface Material {}

public @interface Fluffy {
   int cuteness();
   public abstract int softness() default 11;
   protected Material material();   // DOES NOT COMPILE
   private String friendly();       // DOES NOT COMPILE
   final boolean isBunny();         // DOES NOT COMPILE
}
```

The elements cuteness() and softness() are both considered abstract and public, even though only one of them is marked as such. The elements material() and friendly() do not compile because the access modifier conflicts with the elements being implicitly public. The element isBunny() does not compile because, like abstract methods, it cannot be marked final.

Adding a Constant Variable

Annotations can include constant variables that can be accessed by other classes without actually creating the annotation.

```
public @interface ElectricitySource {
   public int voltage();
   int MIN_VOLTAGE = 2;
   public static final int MAX_VOLTAGE = 18;
}
```

Yep, just like interface variables, annotation variables are implicitly public, static, and final. These constant variables are not considered elements, though. For example, marker annotations can contain constants.

Reviewing Annotation Rules

We conclude creating custom annotations with Figure 2.1, which summarizes many of the syntax rules that you have learned thus far.

Figure 2.2 shows how to apply this annotation to a Java class. For contrast, it also includes a simple marker annotation @Alert. Remember, a marker annotation is one that does not contain any elements.

If you understand all of the parts of these two figures, then you are well on your way to understanding annotations. If not, then we suggest rereading this section. The rest of the chapter will build on this foundation; you will see more advanced usage, apply annotations to other annotations, and learn the built-in annotations that you will need to know for the exam.

FIGURE 2.1   Annotation declaration

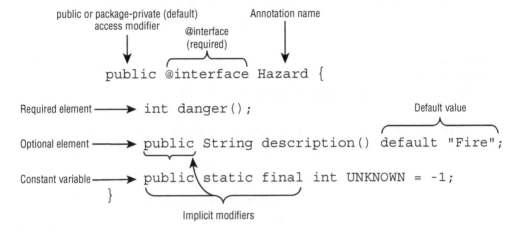

FIGURE 2.2   Using an annotation

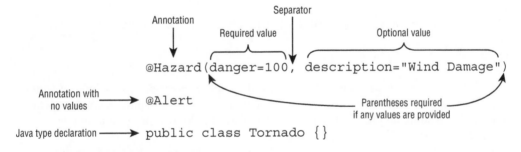

Applying Annotations

Now that we have described how to create and use simple annotations, it's time to discuss other ways to apply annotations.

Using Annotations in Declarations

Up until now, we've only been applying annotations to classes and methods, but they can be applied to any Java declaration including the following:

- Classes, interfaces, enums, and modules
- Variables (`static`, instance, local)
- Methods and constructors
- Method, constructor, and lambda parameters
- Cast expressions
- Other annotations

The following compiles, assuming the annotations referenced in it exist:

```
1:  @FunctionalInterface interface Speedster {
2:      void go(String name);
3:  }
4:  @LongEars
5:  @Soft @Cuddly public class Rabbit {
6:      @Deprecated public Rabbit(@NotNull Integer size) {}
7:
8:      @Speed(velocity="fast") public void eat(@Edible String input) {
9:          @Food(vegetarian=true) String m = (@Tasty String) "carrots";
10:
11:         Speedster s1 = new @Racer Speedster() {
12:             public void go(@FirstName @NotEmpty String name) {
13:                 System.out.print("Start! "+name);
14:             }
15:         };
16:
17:         Speedster s2 = (@Valid String n) -> System.out.print(n);
18:     }
19: }
```

It's a little contrived, we know. Lines 1, 4, and 5 apply annotations to the interface and class declarations. Some of the annotations, like @Cuddly, do not require any values, while others, like @Speed, do provide values. You would need to look at the annotation declaration to know if these values are optional or required.

Lines 6 and 8 contain annotations applied to constructor and method declarations. These lines also contain annotations applied to their parameters.

Line 9 contains the annotation @Food applied to a local variable, along with the annotation @Tasty applied to a cast expression.

 When applying an annotation to an expression, a cast operation including the Java type is required. On line 9, the expression was cast to String, and the annotation @Tasty was applied to the type.

Line 11 applies an annotation to the type in the anonymous class declaration, and line 17 shows an annotation in a lambda expression parameter. Both of these examples may look a little odd at first, but they are allowed. In fact, you're more likely to see examples like this on the exam than you are in real life.

In this example, we applied annotations to various declarations, but this isn't always permitted. An annotation can specify which declaration type they can be applied to using the @Target annotation. We'll cover this, along with other annotation-specific annotations, in the next part of the chapter.

Mixing Required and Optional Elements

One of the most important rules when applying annotations is the following: *to use an annotation, all required values must be provided.* While an annotation may have many elements, values are required only for ones without default values.

Let's try this. Given the following annotation:

```
public @interface Swimmer {
    int armLength = 10;
    String stroke();
    String name();
    String favoriteStroke() default "Backstroke";
}
```

which of the following compile?

```
@Swimmer class Amphibian {}

@Swimmer(favoriteStroke="Breaststroke", name="Sally") class Tadpole {}

@Swimmer(stroke="FrogKick", name="Kermit") class Frog {}

@Swimmer(stroke="Butterfly", name="Kip", armLength=1) class Reptile {}

@Swimmer(stroke="", name="", favoriteStroke="") class Snake {}
```

Amphibian does not compile, because it is missing the required elements stroke() and name(). Likewise, Tadpole does not compile, because it is missing the required element stroke().

Frog provides all of the required elements and none of the optional ones, so it compiles. Reptile does not compile since armLength is a constant, not an element, and cannot be included in an annotation. Finally, Snake does compile, providing all required and optional values.

Creating a *value()* Element

In your development experience, you may have seen an annotation with a value, written without the *elementName*. For example, the following is valid syntax under the right condition:

```
@Injured("Broken Tail") public class Monkey {}
```

This is considered a shorthand or abbreviated annotation notation. What qualifies as *the right condition*? An annotation must adhere to the following rules to be used without a name:

- The annotation declaration must contain an element named value(), which may be optional or required.

- The annotation declaration must not contain any other elements that are required.
- The annotation usage must not provide values for any other elements.

Let's create an annotation that meets these requirements.

```
public @interface Injured {
    String veterinarian() default "unassigned";
    String value() default "foot";
    int age() default 1;
}
```

This annotation is composed of multiple optional elements. In this example, we gave `value()` a default value, but we could have also made it required. Using this declaration, the following annotations are valid:

```
public abstract class Elephant {
    @Injured("Legs") public void fallDown() {}
    @Injured(value="Legs") public abstract int trip();
    @Injured String injuries[];
}
```

The usage in the first two annotations are equivalent, as the compiler will convert the shorthand form to the long form with the `value()` element name. The last annotation with no values is permitted because `@Injured` does not have any required elements.

 Typically, the `value()` of an annotation should be related to the name of the annotation. In our previous example, `@Injured` was the annotation name, and the `value()` referred to the item that was impacted. This is especially important since all shorthand elements use the same element name, `value()`.

For the exam, make sure that if the shorthand notation is used, then there is an element named `value()`. Also, check that there are no other required elements. For example, the following annotation declarations cannot be used with a shorthand annotation:

```
public @interface Sleep {
    int value();
    String hours();
}
```

```
public @interface Wake {
    String hours();
}
```

The first declaration contains two required elements, while the second annotation does not include an element named `value()`.

Likewise, the following annotation is not valid as it provides more than one value:

```
@Injured("Fur",age=2) public class Bear {}  // DOES NOT COMPILE
```

Passing an Array of Values

Annotations support a shorthand notation for providing an array that contains a single element. Let's say we have an annotation Music defined as follows:

```
public @interface Music {
    String[] genres();
}
```

If we want to provide only one value to the array, we have a choice of two ways to write the annotation. Either of the following is correct:

```
public class Giraffe {
    @Music(genres={"Rock and roll"}) String mostDisliked;
    @Music(genres="Classical") String favorite;
}
```

The first annotation is considered the regular form, as it is clear the usage is for an array. The second annotation is the shorthand notation, where the array braces ({}) are dropped for convenience. Keep in mind that this is still providing a value for an array element; the compiler is just inserting the missing array braces for you.

This notation can be used only if the array is composed of a single element. For example, only one of the following annotations compiles:

```
public class Reindeer {
    @Music(genres="Blues","Jazz") String favorite;     // DOES NOT COMPILE
    @Music(genres=) String mostDisliked;                // DOES NOT COMPILE
    @Music(genres=null) String other;                   // DOES NOT COMPILE
    @Music(genres={}) String alternate;
}
```

The first provides more than one value, while the next two do not provide any values. The last one does compile, as an array with no elements is still a valid array.

While this shorthand notation can be used for arrays, it does not work for List or Collection. As mentioned earlier, they are not in the list of supported element types for annotations.

Combining Shorthand Notations

It might not surprise you that we can combine both of our recent rules for shorthand notations. Consider this annotation:

(Continued)

```
public @interface Rhythm {
    String[] value();
}
```

Each of the following four annotations is valid:

```
public class Capybara {
    @Rhythm(value={"Swing"}) String favorite;
    @Rhythm(value="R&B") String secondFavorite;
    @Rhythm({"Classical"}) String mostDisliked;
    @Rhythm("Country") String lastDisliked;
}
```

The first annotation provides all of the details, while the last one applies both short-hand rules.

Declaring Annotation-Specific Annotations

Congratulations—if you've gotten this far, then you've learned all of the general rules for annotations we have to teach you! From this point on, you'll need to learn about specific annotations and their associated rules for the exam. Many of these rules are straightforward, although some will require memorization.

In this section, we'll cover built-in annotations applied to other annotations. Yes, metadata about metadata! Since these annotations are built into Java, they primarily impact the compiler. In the final section, we'll cover built-in annotations applied to various Java data types.

Limiting Usage with @*Target*

Earlier, we showed you examples of annotations applied to various Java types, such as classes, methods, and expressions. When defining your own annotation, you might want to limit it to a particular type or set of types. After all, it may not make sense for a particular annotation to be applied to a method parameter or local variable.

Many annotation declarations include @Target annotation, which limits the types the annotation can be applied to. More specifically, the @Target annotation takes an array of ElementType enum values as its value() element.

Learning the *ElementType* Values

Table 2.1 shows all of the values available for the @Target annotation.

TABLE 2.1   Values for the `@Target` annotation

ElementType value	Applies to
TYPE	Classes, interfaces, enums, annotations
FIELD	Instance and static variables, enum values
METHOD	Method declarations
PARAMETER	Constructor, method, and lambda parameters
CONSTRUCTOR	Constructor declarations
LOCAL_VARIABLE	Local variables
ANNOTATION_TYPE	Annotations
PACKAGE*	Packages declared in package-info.java
TYPE_PARAMETER*	Parameterized types, generic declarations
TYPE_USE	Able to be applied anywhere there is a Java type declared or used
MODULE*	Modules

*Applying these with annotations is out of scope for the exam.

You might notice that some of the `ElementType` applications overlap. For example, to create an annotation usable on other annotations, you could declare an `@Target` with `ANNOTATION_TYPE` or `TYPE`. Either will work for annotations, although the second option opens the annotation usage to other types like classes and interfaces.

While you are not likely to be tested on all of these types, you may see a few on the exam. Make sure you can recognize proper usage of them. Most are pretty self-explanatory.

 You can't add a package annotation to just any package declaration, only those defined in a special file, which must be named package-info.java. This file stores documentation metadata about a package. Don't worry, though, this isn't on the exam.

Consider the following annotation:

```
import java.lang.annotation.ElementType;
import java.lang.annotation.Target;

@Target({ElementType.METHOD,ElementType.CONSTRUCTOR})
public @interface ZooAttraction {}
```

Even though the java.lang package is imported automatically by the compiler, the java.lang.annotation package is not. Therefore, import statements are required for many of the examples in the remainder of this chapter.

Based on this annotation, which of the following lines of code will compile?

```
1: @ZooAttraction class RollerCoaster {}
2: class Events {
3:    @ZooAttraction String rideTrain() {
4:        return (@ZooAttraction String) "Fun!";
5:    }
6:    @ZooAttraction Events(@ZooAttraction String description) {
7:        super();
8:    }
9:    @ZooAttraction int numPassengers; }
```

This example contains six uses of @ZooAttraction with only two of them being valid. Line 1 does not compile, because the annotation is applied to a class type. Line 3 compiles, because it is permitted on a method declaration. Line 4 does not compile, because it is not permitted on a cast operation.

Line 6 is tricky. The first annotation is permitted, because it is applied to the constructor declaration. The second annotation is not, as the annotation is not marked for use in a constructor parameter. Finally, line 9 is not permitted, because it cannot be applied to fields or variables.

Understanding the *TYPE_USE* Value

While most of the values in Table 2.1 are straightforward, TYPE_USE is without a doubt the most complex. The TYPE_USE parameter *can be used anywhere there is a Java type*. By including it in @Target, it actually includes nearly all the values in Table 2.1 including classes, interfaces, constructors, parameters, and more. There are a few exceptions; for example, it can be used only on a method that returns a value. Methods that return void would still need the METHOD value defined in the annotation.

It also allows annotations in places where types are *used*, such as cast operations, object creation with new, inside type declarations, etc. These might seem a little strange at first, but the following are valid TYPE_USE applications:

```
// Technical.java
import java.lang.annotation.ElementType;
import java.lang.annotation.Target;

@Target(ElementType.TYPE_USE)
@interface Technical {}
```

```java
// NetworkRepair.java
import java.util.function.Predicate;
public class NetworkRepair {
    class OutSrc extends @Technical NetworkRepair {}
    public void repair() {
        var repairSubclass = new @Technical NetworkRepair() {};

        var o = new @Technical NetworkRepair().new @Technical OutSrc();

        int remaining = (@Technical int)10.0;
    }
}
```

For the exam, you don't need to know all of the places TYPE_USE can be used, nor what applying it to these locations actually does, but you do need to recognize that they can be applied in this manner if TYPE_USE is one of the @Target options.

Storing Annotations with *@Retention*

As you might have learned when studying for the 1Z0-815 exam, the compiler discards certain types of information when converting your source code into a .class file. With generics, this is known as *type erasure*.

In a similar vein, annotations *may* be discarded by the compiler or at runtime. We say "may," because we can actually specify how they are handled using the @Retention annotation. This annotation takes a value() of the enum RetentionPolicy. Table 2.2 shows the possible values, in increasing order of retention.

TABLE 2.2   Values for the @Retention annotation

RetentionPolicy value	Description
SOURCE	Used only in the source file, discarded by the compiler
CLASS	Stored in the .class file but not available at runtime (default compiler behavior)
RUNTIME	Stored in the .class file and available at runtime

Using it is pretty easy.

```java
import java.lang.annotation.Retention;
import java.lang.annotation.RetentionPolicy;
```

```
@Retention(RetentionPolicy.CLASS) @interface Flier {}
@Retention(RetentionPolicy.RUNTIME) @interface Swimmer {}
```

In this example, both annotations will retain the annotation information in their .class files, although only Swimmer will be available (via reflection) at runtime.

Generating Javadoc with @*Documented*

When trying to determine what methods or classes are available in Java or a third-party library, you've undoubtedly relied on web pages built with Javadoc. Javadoc is a built-in standard within Java that generates documentation for a class or API.

In fact, you can generate Javadoc files for any class you write! Better yet, you can add additional metadata, including comments and annotations, that have no impact on your code but provide more detailed and user-friendly Javadoc files.

For the exam, you should be familiar with the marker annotation @Documented. If present, then the generated Javadoc will include annotation information defined on Java types. Because it is a marker annotation, it doesn't take any values; therefore, using it is pretty easy.

```
// Hunter.java
import java.lang.annotation.Documented;
@Documented public @interface Hunter {}


// Lion.java
@Hunter public class Lion {}
```

In this example, the @Hunter annotation would be published with the Lion Javadoc information because it's marked with the @Documented annotation.

Java vs. Javadoc Annotations

Javadoc has its own annotations that are used solely in generating data within a Javadoc file.

```
public class ZooLightShow {

    /**
     * Performs a light show at the zoo.
     *
     * @param     distance    length the light needs to travel.
     * @return     the result of the light show operation.
     * @author     Grace Hopper
     * @since      1.5
```

```
     * @deprecated Use EnhancedZooLightShow.lights() instead.
     */
    @Deprecated(since="1.5") public static String perform(int distance) {
        return "Beginning light show!";
    }
}
```

Be careful not to confuse Javadoc annotations with the Java annotations. Take a look at the @deprecated and @Deprecated annotations in this example. The first, @deprecated, is a Javadoc annotation used inside a comment, while @Deprecated is a Java annotation applied to a class. Traditionally, Javadoc annotations are all lowercase, while Java annotations start with an uppercase letter.

Inheriting Annotations with *@Inherited*

Another marker annotation you should know for the exam is @Inherited. When this annotation is applied to a class, subclasses will inherit the annotation information found in the parent class.

// Vertebrate.java
```
import java.lang.annotation.Inherited;
@Inherited public @interface Vertebrate {}
```

// Mammal.java
```
@Vertebrate public class Mammal {}
```

// Dolphin.java
```
public class Dolphin extends Mammal {}
```

In this example, the @Vertebrate annotation will be applied to both Mammal and Dolphin objects. Without the @Inherited annotation, @Vertebrate would apply only to Mammal instances.

Supporting Duplicates with *@Repeatable*

The last annotation-specific annotation you need to know for the exam is arguably the most complicated to use, as it actually requires creating two annotations. The @Repeatable annotation is used when you want to specify an annotation more than once on a type.

Why would you want to specify twice? Well, if it's a marker annotation with no elements, you probably wouldn't. Generally, you use repeatable annotations when you want to apply the same annotation with different values.

Let's assume we have a repeatable annotation @Risk, which assigns a set of risk values to a zoo animal. We'll show how it is used and then work backward to create it.

```
public class Zoo {
   public static class Monkey {}

   @Risk(danger="Silly")
   @Risk(danger="Aggressive",level=5)
   @Risk(danger="Violent",level=10)
   private Monkey monkey;
}
```

Next, let's define a simple annotation that implements these elements:

```
public @interface Risk {
   String danger();
   int level() default 1;
}
```

Now, as written, the Zoo class does not compile. Why? Well, the Risk annotation is missing the @Repeatable annotation! That brings us to our first rule: *without the @Repeatable annotation, an annotation can be applied only once*. So, let's add the @Repeatable annotation.

```
import java.lang.annotation.Repeatable;

@Repeatable   // DOES NOT COMPILE
public @interface Risk {
   String danger();
   int level() default 1;
}
```

This code also does not compile, but this time because the @Repeatable annotation is not declared correctly. It requires a reference to a second annotation. That brings us to our next rule: *to declare a @Repeatable annotation, you must define a containing annotation type value*.

A *containing annotation type* is a separate annotation that defines a value() array element. The type of this array is the particular annotation you want to repeat. By convention, the name of the annotation is often the plural form of the repeatable annotation.

Putting all of this together, the following Risks declaration is a containing annotation type for our Risk annotation:

```
public @interface Risks {
   Risk[] value();
}
```

Finally, we go back to our original Risk annotation and specify the containing annotation class:

```
import java.lang.annotation.Repeatable;

@Repeatable(Risks.class)
public @interface Risk {
   String danger();
   int level() default 1;
}
```

With these two annotations, our original Zoo class will now compile. Notice that we never actually use @Risks in our Zoo class. Given the declaration of the Risk and Risks annotations, the compiler takes care of applying the annotations for us.

The following summarizes the rules for declaring a repeatable annotation, along with its associated containing type annotation:

- The repeatable annotation must be declared with @Repeatable and contain a value that refers to the containing type annotation.

- The containing type annotation must include an element named value(), which is a primitive array of the repeatable annotation type.

Once you understand the basic structure of declaring a repeatable annotation, it's all pretty convenient.

Repeatable Annotations vs. an Array of Annotations

Repeatable annotations were added in Java 8. Prior to this, you would have had to use the @Risks containing annotation type directly:

```
@Risks({
   @Risk(danger="Silly"),
   @Risk(danger="Aggressive",level=5),
   @Risk(danger="Violent",level=10)
})
private Monkey monkey;
```

With this implementation, @Repeatable is not required in the Risk annotation declaration. The @Repeatable annotation is the preferred approach now, as it is easier than working with multiple nested statements.

Reviewing Annotation-Specific Annotations

We conclude this part of the chapter with Table 2.3, which shows the annotations that can be applied to other annotations that might appear on the exam.

TABLE 2.3   Annotation-specific annotations

Annotation	Marker annotation	Type of value()	Default compiler behavior (if annotation not present)
@Target	No	Array of ElementType	Annotation able to be applied to all locations except TYPE_USE and TYPE_PARAMETER
@Retention	No	RetentionPolicy	RetentionPolicy.CLASS
@Documented	Yes	—	Annotations are not included in the generated Javadoc.
@Inherited	Yes	—	Annotations in supertypes are not inherited.
@Repeatable	No	Annotation	Annotation cannot be repeated.

Prior to this section, we created numerous annotations, and we never used any of the annotations in Table 2.3. So, what did the compiler do? Like implicit modifiers and default no-arg constructors, the compiler auto-inserted information based on the lack of data.

The default behavior for most of the annotations in Table 2.3 is often intuitive. For example, without the @Documented or @Inherited annotation, these features are not supported. Likewise, the compiler will report an error if you try to use an annotation more than once without the @Repeatable annotation.

The @Target annotation is a bit of a special case. When @Target is not present, an annotation can be used in any place except TYPE_USE or TYPE_PARAMETER scenarios (cast operations, object creation, generic declarations, etc.).

Why Doesn't *@Target*'s Default Behavior Apply to All Types?

We learn from Table 2.3 that to use an annotation in a type use or type parameter location, such as a lambda expression or generic declaration, you must explicitly set the @Target to include these values. If an annotation is declared without the @Target annotation that includes these values, then these locations are prohibited.

One possible explanation for this behavior is backward compatibility. When these values were added to Java 8, it was decided that they would have to be explicitly declared to be used in these locations.

That said, when the authors of Java added the MODULE value in Java 9, they did not make this same decision. If @Target is absent, the annotation is permitted in a module declaration by default.

Using Common Annotations

For the exam, you'll need to know about a set of built-in annotations, which apply to various types and methods. Unlike custom annotations that you might author, many of these annotations have special rules. In fact, if they are used incorrectly, the compiler will report an error.

Some of these annotations (like @Override) are quite useful, and we recommend using them in practice. Others (like @SafeVarargs), you are likely to see only on a certification exam. For each annotation, you'll need to understand its purposes, identify when to use it (or not to use it), and know what elements it takes (if any).

Marking Methods with *@Override*

The @Override is a marker annotation that is used to indicate a method is overriding an inherited method, whether it be inherited from an interface or parent class. From your 1Z0-815 studies, you should know that the overriding method must have the same signature, the same or broader access modifier, and a covariant return type, and not declare any new or broader checked exceptions.

Let's take a look at an example:

```java
public interface Intelligence {
    int cunning();
}
public class Canine implements Intelligence {
    @Override public int cunning() { return 500; }
    void howl() { System.out.print("Woof!"); }
}
public class Wolf extends Canine {
    @Override
    public int cunning() { return Integer.MAX_VALUE; }
    @Override void howl() { System.out.print("Howl!"); }
}
```

In this example, the @Override annotation is applied to three methods that it inherits from the parent class or interface.

During the exam, you should be able to identify anywhere this annotation is used incorrectly. For example, using the same Canine class, this Dog class does not compile:

```java
public class Dog extends Canine {
    @Override
    public boolean playFetch() { return true; }   // DOES NOT COMPILE
    @Override void howl(int timeOfDay) {}          // DOES NOT COMPILE
}
```

The playFetch() method does not compile, because there is no inherited method with that name. In the Dog class, howl() is an overloaded method, not an overridden one. While there is a howl() method defined in the parent class, it does not have the same signature. It is a method overload, not a method override.

Removing both uses of the @Override annotation in the Dog class would allow the class to compile. Using these annotations is not required, but using them incorrectly is prohibited.

> The annotations in this section are entirely optional but help improve the quality of the code. By adding these annotations, though, you help take the guesswork away from someone reading your code. It also enlists the compiler to help you spot errors. For example, applying @Override on a method that is not overriding another triggers a compilation error and could help you spot problems if a class or interface is later changed.

Declaring Interfaces with @*FunctionalInterface*

In Chapter 1, we showed you how to create and identify functional interfaces, which are interfaces with exactly one abstract method. The @FunctionalInterface marker annotation can be applied to any valid functional interface. For example, our previous Intelligence example was actually a functional interface.

```
@FunctionalInterface public interface Intelligence {
    int cunning();
}
```

The compiler will report an error, though, if applied to anything other than a valid functional interface. From what you learned in Chapter 1, which of the following declarations compile?

```
@FunctionalInterface abstract class Reptile {
    abstract String getName();
}
```

```
@FunctionalInterface interface Slimy {}
```

```
@FunctionalInterface interface Scaley {
    boolean isSnake();
}
```

```
@FunctionalInterface interface Rough extends Scaley {
    void checkType();
}
```

```
@FunctionalInterface interface Smooth extends Scaley {
    boolean equals(Object unused);
}
```

The `Reptile` declaration does not compile, because the `@FunctionalInterface` annotation can be applied only to interfaces. The `Slimy` interface does not compile, because it does not contain any abstract methods. The `Scaley` interface compiles, as it contains exactly one abstract method.

The `Rough` interface does not compile, because it contains two abstract methods, one of which it inherits from `Scaley`. Finally, the `Smooth` interface contains two abstract methods, although since one matches the signature of a method in `java.lang.Object`, it does compile.

Like we saw with the `@Override` annotation, removing the `@FunctionalInterface` annotation in the invalid declarations would allow the code to compile. Review functional interfaces in Chapter 1 if you had any trouble with these examples.

If you are declaring a complex interface, perhaps one that contains `static`, `private`, and `default` methods, there's a simple test you can perform to determine whether it is a valid functional interface. Just add the `@FunctionalInterface` annotation to it! If it compiles, it is a functional interface and can be used with lambda expressions.

Retiring Code with *@Deprecated*

In professional software development, you rarely write a library once and never go back to it. More likely, libraries are developed and maintained over a period of years. Libraries change for external reasons, like new business requirements or new versions of Java, or internal reasons, like a bug is found and corrected.

Sometimes a method changes so much that we need to create a new version of it entirely with a completely different signature. We don't want to necessarily remove the old version of the method, though, as this could cause a lot of compilation headaches for our users if the method suddenly disappears. What we want is a way to notify our users that a new version of the method is available and give them time to migrate their code to the new version before we finally remove the old version.

With those ideas in mind, Java includes the `@Deprecated` annotation. The `@Deprecated` annotation is similar to a marker annotation, in that it can be used without any values, but it includes some optional elements. The `@Deprecated` annotation can be applied to nearly any Java declaration, such as classes, methods, or variables.

Let's say we have an older class `ZooPlanner`, and we've written a replacement `ParkPlanner`. We want to notify all users of the older class to switch to the new version.

```
/**
 * Design and plan a zoo.
 * @deprecated Use ParkPlanner instead.
 */
@Deprecated
public class ZooPlanner { ... }
```

That's it! The users of the ZooPlanner class will now receive a compiler warning if they are using ZooPlanner. In the next section, we'll show how they can use another annotation to ignore these warnings.

Always Document the Reason for Deprecation

Earlier, we discussed @Deprecated and @deprecated, the former being a Java annotation and the latter being a Javadoc annotation. Whenever you deprecate a method, you should add a Javadoc annotation to instruct users on how they should update their code.

For the exam, you should know that it is good practice to document why a type is being deprecated and be able to suggest possible alternatives.

While this may or may not appear on the exam, the @Deprecated annotation does support two optional values: String since() and boolean forRemoval(). They provide additional information about when the deprecation occurred in the past and whether or not the type is expected to be removed entirely in the future.

```
/**
 * Method to formulate a zoo layout.
 * @deprecated Use ParkPlanner.planPark(String... data) instead.
 */
@Deprecated(since="1.8", forRemoval=true)
public void plan() {}
```

Note that the @Deprecated annotation does not allow you to provide any suggested alternatives. For that, you should use the Javadoc annotation.

When reviewing the Java JDK, you may encounter classes or methods that are marked deprecated, with the purpose that developers migrate to a new implementation. For example, the constructors of the wrapper classes (like Integer or Double) were recently marked @Deprecated, with the Javadoc note that you should use the factory method valueOf() instead. In this case, the advantage is that an immutable value from a pool can be reused, rather than creating a new object. This saves memory and improves performance.

Ignoring Warnings with *@SuppressWarnings*

One size does not fit all. While the compiler can be helpful in warning you of potential coding problems, sometimes you need to perform a particular operation, and you don't care whether or not it is a potential programming problem.

Enter @SuppressWarnings. Applying this annotation to a class, method, or type basically tells the compiler, "I know what I am doing; do not warn me about this." Unlike the previous annotations, it requires a `String[] value()` parameter. Table 2.4 lists some of the values available for this annotation.

TABLE 2.4 Common *@SuppressWarnings* values

Value	Description
"deprecation"	Ignore warnings related to types or methods marked with the @Deprecated annotation.
"unchecked"	Ignore warnings related to the use of raw types, such as List instead of List<String>.

The annotation actually supports a lot of other values, but for the exam, you only need to know the ones listed in this table. Let's try an example:

```
import java.util.*;

class SongBird {
    @Deprecated static void sing(int volume) {}
    static Object chirp(List<String> data) { return data.size(); }
}

public class Nightingale {
    public void wakeUp() {
        SongBird.sing(10);
    }
    public void goToBed() {
        SongBird.chirp(new ArrayList());
    }
    public static void main(String[] args) {
        var birdy = new Nightingale();
        birdy.wakeUp();
        birdy.goToBed();
    }
}
```

This code compiles and runs but produces two compiler warnings.

```
Nightingale.java uses or overrides a deprecated API.
Nightingale.java uses unchecked or unsafe operations.
```

The first warning is because we are using a method SongBird.sing() that is dep-recated. The second warning is triggered by the call to new ArrayList(), which does not define a generic type. An improved implementation would be to use new ArrayList<String>().

Let's say we are absolutely sure that we don't want to change our Nightingale imple-mentation, and we don't want the compiler to bother us anymore about these warnings. Adding the @SuppressWarnings annotation, with the correct values, accomplishes this.

```
@SuppressWarnings("deprecation") public void wakeUp() {
    SongBird.sing(10);
}


@SuppressWarnings("unchecked") public void goToBed() {
    SongBird.chirp(new ArrayList());
}
```

Now our code compiles, and no warnings are generated.

You should use the @SuppressWarnings annotation sparingly. Oftentimes, the compiler is correct in alerting you to potential coding problems. In some cases, a developer may use this annotation as a way to ignore a problem, rather than refactoring code to solve it.

Protecting Arguments with @*SafeVarargs*

The @SafeVargs marker annotation indicates that a method does not perform any potential unsafe operations on its varargs parameter. It can be applied only to constructors or methods that cannot be overridden (aka methods marked private, static, or final).

Let's review varargs for a minute. A varargs parameter is used to indicate the method may be passed zero or more values of the same type, by providing an ellipsis (...). In addition, a method can have at most one varargs parameter, and it must be listed last.

Returning to @SafeVargs, the annotation is used to indicate to other developers that your method does not perform any unsafe operations. It basically tells other developers, "Don't worry about the varargs parameter; I promise this method won't do anything bad with it!" It also suppresses unchecked compiler warnings for the varargs parameter.

In the following example, thisIsUnsafe() performs an unsafe operation using its varargs parameter:

```
1:   import java.util.*;
2:
3:   public class NeverDoThis {
4:       final int thisIsUnsafe(List<Integer>... carrot) {
5:           Object[] stick = carrot;
```

```
6:         stick[0] = Arrays.asList("nope!");
7:         return carrot[0].get(0);  // ClassCastException at runtime
8:     }
9:     public static void main(String[] a) {
10:        var carrot = new ArrayList<Integer>();
11:        new NeverDoThis().thisIsUnsafe(carrot);
12:    }
13: }
```

This code compiles, although it generates two compiler warnings. Both are related to type safety.

```
[Line 4]  Type safety: Potential heap pollution via varargs
   parameter carrot
[Line 11] Type safety: A generic array of List<Integer> is created
   for a varargs parameter
```

We can remove both compiler warnings by adding the @SafeVarargs annotation to line 4.

```
3:     @SafeVarargs final int thisIsUnsafe(List<Integer>... carrot) {
```

Did we actually fix the unsafe operation? No! It still throws a ClassCastException at runtime on line 7. However, we made it so the compiler won't warn us about it anymore.

For the exam you don't need to know how to create or resolve unsafe operations, as that can be complex. You just need to be able to identify unsafe operations and know they often involve generics.

You should also know the annotation can be applied only to methods that contain a varargs parameter and are not able to be overridden. For example, the following do not compile:

```
@SafeVarargs
public static void eat(int meal) {}        // DOES NOT COMPILE

@SafeVarargs
protected void drink(String... cup) {}      // DOES NOT COMPILE

@SafeVarargs void chew(boolean... food) {}  // DOES NOT COMPILE
```

The eat() method is missing a varargs parameter, while the drink() and chew() methods are not marked static, final, or private.

Reviewing Common Annotations

Table 2.5 lists the common annotations that you will need to know for the exam along with how they are structured.

TABLE 2.5   Understanding common annotations

Annotation	Marker annotation	Type of value()	Optional members
@Override	Yes	—	—
@FunctionalInterface	Yes	—	—
@Deprecated	No	—	String since() boolean forRemoval()
@SuppressWarnings	No	String[]	—
@SafeVarargs	Yes	—	—

Some of these annotations have special rules that will trigger a compiler error if used incorrectly, as shown in Table 2.6.

TABLE 2.6   Applying common annotations

Annotation	Applies to	Compiler error when
@Override	Methods	Method signature does not match the signature of an inherited method
@FunctionalInterface	Interfaces	Interface does not contain a single abstract method
@Deprecated	Most Java declarations	—
@SuppressWarnings	Most Java declarations	—
@SafeVarargs	Methods, constructors	Method or constructor does not contain a varargs parameter or is applied to a method not marked private, static, or final

While none of these annotations is required, they do improve the quality of your code. They also help prevent you from making a mistake.

Let's say you override a method but accidentally alter the signature so that the compiler considers it an overload. If you use the @Override annotation, then the compiler will immediately report the error, rather than finding it later during testing.

🌐 Real World Scenario

JavaBean Validation

This chapter covered only the annotations you need to know for the exam, but there are many incredibly useful annotations available.

If you've ever used JavaBeans to transmit data, then you've probably written code to validate it. While this can be cumbersome for large data structures, annotations allow you to mark `private` fields directly. The following are some useful `javax.validation` annotations:

- `@NotNull`: Object cannot be `null`

- `@NotEmpty`: Object cannot be `null` or have size of 0

- `@Size(min=5,max=10)`: Sets minimum and/or maximum sizes

- `@Max(600)` and `@Min(-5)`: Sets the maximum or minimum numeric values

- `@Email`: Validates that the email is in a valid format

These annotations can be applied to a variety of data types. For example, when `@Size` is applied to a `String`, it checks the number of characters in the `String`. When applied to an array or `Collection`, it checks the number of elements present.

Of course, using the annotations is only half the story. The service receiving or processing the data needs to perform the validation step. In some frameworks like Spring Boot, this can be performed automatically by adding the `@Valid` annotation to a service parameter.

Summary

In this chapter, we taught you everything you need to know about annotations for the exam. Ideally, we also taught you how to create and use custom annotations in your daily programming life. As we mentioned early on, annotations are one of the most convenient tools available in the Java language.

For the exam, you need to know the structure of an annotation declaration, including how to declare required elements, optional elements, and constant variables. You also need to know how to apply an annotation properly and ensure required elements have values. You should also be familiar with the two shorthand notations we discussed in this chapter. The first allows you to drop the *elementName* under certain conditions. The second allows you to specify a single value for an array element without the array braces ({}).

You need to know about the various built-in annotations available in the Java language. We sorted these into two groups: annotations that apply to other annotations and common annotations. The annotation-specific annotations provide rules for how annotations are handled by the compiler, such as specifying an inheritance or retention policy. They can also be used to disallow certain usage, such as using a method-targeted annotation applied to a class declaration.

The second set of annotations are common ones that you should know for the exam. Many, like @Override and @FunctionalInterface, are quite useful and provide other developers with additional information about your application.

Exam Essentials

Be able to declare annotations with required elements, optional elements, and variables.   An annotation is declared with the @interface type. It may include elements and public static final constant variables. If it does not include any elements, then it is a marker annotation. Optional elements are specified with a default keyword and value, while required elements are those specified without one.

Be able to identify where annotations can be applied.   An annotation is applied using the at (@) symbol, followed by the annotation name. Annotations must include a value for each required element and can be applied to types, methods, constructors, and variables. They can also be used in cast operations, lambda expressions, or inside type declarations.

Understand how to apply an annotation without an element name.   If an annotation contains an element named value() and does not contain any other elements that are required, then it can be used without the *elementName*. For it to be used properly, no other values may be passed.

Understand how to apply an annotation with a single-element array.   If one of the annotation elements is a primitive array and the array is passed a single value, then the annotation value may be written without the array braces ({}).

Apply built-in annotations to other annotations.   Java includes a number of annotations that apply to annotation declarations. The @Target annotation allows you to specify where an annotation can and cannot be used. The @Retention annotation allows you to specify at what level the annotation metadata is kept or discarded. @Documented is a marker annotation that allows you to specify whether annotation information is included in the generated documentation. @Inherited is another marker annotation that determines whether annotations are inherited from super types. The @Repeatable annotation allows you to list an annotation more than once on a single declaration. It requires a second containing type annotation to be declared.

Apply common annotations to various Java types.   Java includes many built-in annotations that apply to classes, methods, variables, and expressions. The @Override annotation is used to indicate that a method is overriding an inherited method. The @FunctionalInterface annotation confirms that an interface contains exactly one abstract method. Marking a type @Deprecated means that the compiler will generate a depreciation warning when it is referenced. Adding @SuppressWarnings with a set of values to a declaration causes the compiler to ignore the set of specified warnings. Adding @SafeVarargs on a constructor or private, static, or final method instructs other developers that no unsafe operations will be performed on its varargs parameter. While all of these annotations are optional, they are quite useful and improve the quality of code when used.

Review Questions

The answers to the chapter review questions can be found in Appendix B.

1. What modifier is used to mark that an annotation element is required?

    A. optional

    B. default

    C. required

    D. *

    E. None of the above

2. Which of the following lines of code do not compile? (Choose all that apply.)

```
1: import java.lang.annotation.Documented;
2: enum Color {GREY, BROWN}
3: @Documented public @interface Dirt {
4:     boolean wet();
5:     String type() = "unknown";
6:     public Color color();
7:     private static final int slippery = 5;
8: }
```

    A. Line 2

    B. Line 3

    C. Line 4

    D. Line 5

    E. Line 6

    F. Line 7

    G. All of the lines compile.

3. Which built-in annotations can be applied to an annotation declaration? (Choose all that apply.)

    A. @Override

    B. @Deprecated

    C. @Document

    D. @Target

    E. @Repeatable

    F. @Functional

4. Given an automobile sales system, which of the following information is best stored using an annotation?

   A. The price of the vehicle

   B. A list of people who purchased the vehicle

   C. The sales tax of the vehicle

   D. The number of passengers a vehicle is rated for

   E. The quantity of models in stock

5. Which of the following lines of code do not compile? (Choose all that apply.)

```
1: import java.lang.annotation.*;
2: class Food {}
3: @Inherited public @interface Unexpected {
4:    public String rsvp() default null;
5:    Food food();
6:    public String[] dessert();
7:    final int numberOfGuests = 5;
8:    long startTime() default 0L;
9: }
```

   A. Line 3

   B. Line 4

   C. Line 5

   D. Line 6

   E. Line 7

   F. Line 8

   G. All of the lines compile.

6. Which annotations, when applied independently, allow the following program to compile? (Choose all that apply.)

```
import java.lang.annotation.*;
@Documented @Deprecated
public @interface Driver {
   int[] directions();
   String name() default "";
}
_____ class Taxi {}
```

A. @Driver

B. @Driver(1)

C. @Driver(3,4)

D. @Driver({5,6})

E. @Driver(directions=7)

F. @Driver(directions=8,9)

G. @Driver(directions={0,1})

H. None of the above

7. Annotations can be applied to which of the following? (Choose all that apply.)

A. Class declarations

B. Constructor parameters

C. Local variable declarations

D. Cast operations

E. Lambda expression parameters

F. Interface declarations

G. None of the above

8. Fill in the blanks with the correct answers that allow the entire program to compile. (Choose all that apply.)

```
@interface FerociousPack {
    _____;              // m1
}


@Repeatable(_____)  // m2
public @interface Ferocious {}


@Ferocious @Ferocious class Lion {}
```

A. Ferocious value() on line m1.

B. Ferocious[] value() on line m1.

C. Object[] value() on line m1.

D. @FerociousPack on line m2.

E. FerociousPack on line m2.

F. FerociousPack.class on line m2.

G. None of the above. The code will not compile due to its use of the Lion class.

9. What properties must be true to use an annotation with an element value, but no element name? (Choose all that apply.)

  A. The element must be named values().

  B. The element must be required.

  C. The annotation declaration must not contain any other elements.

  D. The annotation must not contain any other values.

  E. The element value must not be array.

  F. None of the above

10. Which statement about the following code is correct?

```
import java.lang.annotation.*;
@Target(ElementType.TYPE) public @interface Furry {
    public String[] value();
    boolean cute() default true;
}
class Bunny {
    @Furry("Soft") public static int hop() {
        return 1;
    }
}
```

  A. The code compiles without any changes.

  B. The code compiles only if the type of value() is changed to a String in the annotation declaration.

  C. The code compiles only if cute() is removed from the annotation declaration.

  D. The code compiles only if @Furry includes a value for cute().

  E. The code compiles only if @Furry includes the element name for value.

  F. The code compiles only if the value in @Furry is changed to an array.

  G. None of the above

11. What properties of applying @SafeVarargs are correct? (Choose all that apply.)

  A. By applying the annotation, the compiler verifies that all operations on parameters are safe.

  B. The annotation can be applied to abstract methods.

  C. The annotation can be applied to method and constructor declarations.

  D. When the annotation is applied to a method, the method must contain a varargs parameter.

  E. The annotation can be applied to method and constructor parameters.

  F. The annotation can be applied to static methods.

12. Which of the following lines of code do not compile? (Choose all that apply.)

```
1: import java.lang.annotation.*;
2: enum UnitOfTemp { C, F }
3: @interface Snow { boolean value(); }
4: @Target(ElementType.METHOD) public @interface Cold {
5:    private Cold() {}
6:    int temperature;
7:    UnitOfTemp unit default UnitOfTemp.C;
8:    Snow snow() default @Snow(true);
9: }
```

- **A.** Line 4
- **B.** Line 5
- **C.** Line 6
- **D.** Line 7
- **E.** Line 8
- **F.** All of the lines compile.

13. Which statements about an optional annotation are correct? (Choose all that apply.)

- **A.** The annotation declaration always includes a default value.
- **B.** The annotation declaration may include a default value.
- **C.** The annotation always includes a value.
- **D.** The annotation may include a value.
- **E.** The annotation must not include a value.
- **F.** None of the above

14. Fill in the blanks: The _____ annotation determines whether annotations are discarded at runtime, while the _____ annotation determines whether they are discarded in generated Javadoc.

- **A.** @Target, @Deprecated
- **B.** @Discard, @SuppressWarnings
- **C.** @Retention, @Generated
- **D.** @Retention, @Documented
- **E.** @Inherited, @Retention
- **F.** @Target, @Repeatable
- **G.** None of the above

15. What statement about marker annotations is correct?

   A. A marker annotation does not contain any elements or constant variables.

   B. A marker annotation does not contain any elements but may contain constant variables.

   C. A marker annotation does not contain any required elements but may include optional elements.

   D. A marker annotation does not contain any optional elements but may include required elements.

   E. A marker annotation can be extended.

16. Which options, when inserted into the blank in the code, allow the code to compile without any warnings? (Choose all that apply.)

```
import java.util.*;
import java.lang.annotation.*;
public class Donkey {

    _____
    public String kick(List... t) {
        t[0] = new ArrayList();
        t[0].add(1);
        return (String)t[0].get(0);
    }
}
```

   A. @SafeVarargs

   B. @SafeVarargs("unchecked")

   C. @Inherited

   D. @SuppressWarnings

   E. @SuppressWarnings("ignore")

   F. @SuppressWarnings("unchecked")

   G. None of the above

17. What motivations would a developer have for applying the @FunctionalInterface annotation to an interface? (Choose all that apply.)

   A. To allow the interface to be used in a lambda expression

   B. To provide documentation to other developers

   C. To allow the interface to be used as a method reference

   D. There is no reason to use this annotation.

   E. To trigger a compiler error if the annotation is used incorrectly

18. Which of the following lines of code do not compile? (Choose all that apply.)

```
1: @interface Strong {
2:    int force(); }
3: @interface Wind {
4:    public static final int temperature = 20;
5:    Boolean storm() default true;
6:    public void kiteFlying();
7:    protected String gusts();
8:    Strong power() default @Strong(10);
9: }
```

- **A.** Line 2
- **B.** Line 4
- **C.** Line 5
- **D.** Line 6
- **E.** Line 7
- **F.** Line 8
- **G.** All of the lines compile.

19. Which annotations can be added to an existing method declaration but could cause a compiler error depending on the method signature? (Choose all that apply.)

- **A.** @Override
- **B.** @Deprecated
- **C.** @FunctionalInterface
- **D.** @Repeatable
- **E.** @Retention
- **F.** @SafeVarargs

20. Given the Floats annotation declaration, which lines in the Birch class contain compiler errors? (Choose all that apply.)

```
// Floats.java
import java.lang.annotation.*;
@Target(ElementType.TYPE_USE)
public @interface Floats {
    int buoyancy() default 2;
}
```

```
// Birch.java
1: import java.util.function.Predicate;
2: interface Wood {}
```

```
3: @Floats class Duck {}
4: @Floats
5: public class Birch implements @Floats Wood {
6:     @Floats(10) boolean mill() {
7:         Predicate<Integer> t = (@Floats Integer a) -> a > 10;
8:         return (@Floats) t.test(12);
9:     } }
```

- **A.** Line 3
- **B.** Line 4
- **C.** Line 5
- **D.** Line 6
- **E.** Line 7
- **F.** Line 8
- **G.** None of the above. All of the lines compile without issue.

21. Fill in the blanks: The _____ @Inherited _____ annotation determines what annotations from a super-class or interface are applied, while the _____ @Target _____ annotation determines what declarations an annotation can be applied to.

- **A.** @Target, @Retention
- **B.** @Inherited, @ElementType
- **C.** @Documented, @Deprecated
- **D.** @Target, @Generated
- **E.** @Repeatable, @Element
- **F.** @Inherited, @Retention
- **G.** None of the above

22. Which annotation can cancel out a warning on a method using the @Deprecated API at compile time?

- **A.** @FunctionalInterface
- **B.** @Ignore
- **C.** @IgnoreDeprecated
- **D.** @Retention
- **E.** @SafeVarargs
- **F.** @SuppressWarnings
- **G.** None of the above

23. The `main()` method in the following program reads the annotation `value()` of `Plumber` at runtime on each member of `Team`. It compiles and runs without any errors. Based on this, how many times is `Mario` printed at runtime?

```
import java.lang.annotation.*;
import java.lang.reflect.Field;
@interface Plumber {
    String value() default "Mario";
}

public class Team {
    @Plumber("") private String foreman = "Mario";
    @Plumber private String worker = "Kelly";
    @Plumber("Kelly") private String trainee;

    public static void main(String[] args) {
        var t = new Team();
        var fields = t.getClass().getDeclaredFields();
        for (Field field : fields)
           if(field.isAnnotationPresent(Plumber.class))
               System.out.print(field.getAnnotation(Plumber.class)
                   .value());
    }
}
```

A. Zero

B. One

C. Two

D. Three

E. The answer cannot be determined until runtime.

24. Which annotations, when applied independently, allow the following program to compile? (Choose all that apply.)

```
public @interface Dance {
    long rhythm() default 66;
    int[] value();
    String track() default "";
    final boolean fast = true;
}
class Sing {
    _____ String album;
}
```

- **A.** @Dance(77)
- **B.** @Dance(33, 10)
- **C.** @Dance(value=5, rhythm=2, fast=false)
- **D.** @Dance(5, rhythm=9)
- **E.** @Dance(value=5, rhythm=2, track="Samba")
- **F.** @Dance()
- **G.** None of the above

25. When using the @Deprecated annotation, what other annotation should be used and why?

- **A.** @repeatable, along with a containing type annotation
- **B.** @retention, along with a location where the value should be discarded
- **C.** @deprecated, along with a reason why and a suggested alternative
- **D.** @SuppressWarnings, along with a cause
- **E.** @Override, along with an inherited reference

Chapter 3

Generics and Collections

THE OCP EXAM TOPICS COVERED IN THIS CHAPTER INCLUDE THE FOLLOWING:

✓ **Generics and Collections**

- Use wrapper classes, autoboxing and autounboxing
- Create and use generic classes, methods with diamond notation and wildcards
- Describe the Collections Framework and use key collection interfaces
- Use Comparator and Comparable interfaces
- Create and use convenience methods for collections

✓ **Java Stream API**

- Use lambda expressions and method references

You learned the basics of the Java Collections Framework when studying for the 1Z0-815 exam, along with generics and the basics of sorting. We will review these topics while diving into them more deeply.

First, we will cover how to use method references. After a review of autoboxing and unboxing, we will explore more classes and APIs in the Java Collections Framework. The thread-safe collection types will be discussed in Chapter 7, "Concurrency."

Next, we will cover details about Comparator and Comparable. Finally, we will discuss how to create your own classes and methods that use generics so that the same class can be used with many types.

In Chapter 1, "Java Fundamentals," we presented the functional interface Predicate and showed how to use it. When studying for the 1Z0-815 exam, you should have studied other functional interfaces like Consumer, Function, and Supplier. We will review all of these functional interfaces in Chapter 4, "Functional Programming," but since some will be used in this chapter, we provide Table 3.1 as a handy reference. The letters (R, T, and U) are generics that you can pass any type to when using these functional interfaces.

TABLE 3.1   Functional interfaces used in this chapter

Functional interfaces	Return type	Method name	# parameters
Supplier<T>	T	get()	0
Consumer<T>	void	accept(T)	1 (T)
BiConsumer<T, U>	void	accept(T,U)	2 (T, U)
Predicate<T>	boolean	test(T)	1 (T)
BiPredicate<T, U>	boolean	test(T, U)	2 (T, U)
Function<T, R>	R	apply(T)	1 (T)
BiFunction<T, U, R>	R	apply(T,U)	2 (T, U)
UnaryOperator<T>	T	apply(T)	1 (T)

For this chapter, you can just use these functional interfaces as is. In the next chapter, though, we'll be presenting and testing your knowledge of them.

Using Method References

In Chapter 1, we went over lambdas and showed how they make code shorter. *Method references* are another way to make the code easier to read, such as simply mentioning the name of the method. Like lambdas, it takes time to get used to the new syntax.

In this section, we will show the syntax along with the four types of method references. We will also mix in lambdas with method references. If you'd like to review using lambdas, see Chapter 1. This will prepare you well for the next chapter, which uses both heavily.

Suppose we are coding a duckling who is trying to learn how to quack. First, we have a functional interface. As you'll recall from Chapter 1, this is an interface with exactly one abstract method.

```
@FunctionalInterface
public interface LearnToSpeak {
    void speak(String sound);
}
```

Next, we discover that our duckling is lucky. There is a helper class that the duckling can work with. We've omitted the details of teaching the duckling how to quack and left the part that calls the functional interface.

```
public class DuckHelper {
    public static void teacher(String name, LearnToSpeak trainer) {

        // exercise patience

        trainer.speak(name);
    }
}
```

Finally, it is time to put it all together and meet our little Duckling. This code implements the functional interface using a lambda:

```
public class Duckling {
    public static void makeSound(String sound) {
        LearnToSpeak learner = s -> System.out.println(s);
        DuckHelper.teacher(sound, learner);
    }
}
```

Not bad. There's a bit of redundancy, though. The lambda declares one parameter named s. However, it does nothing other than pass that parameter to another method. A method reference lets us remove that redundancy and instead write this:

LearnToSpeak learner = **System.out::println**;

The :: operator tells Java to call the println() method later. It will take a little while to get used to the syntax. Once you do, you may find your code is shorter and less distracting without writing as many lambdas.

> Remember that :: is like a lambda, and it is used for deferred execution with a functional interface.

A method reference and a lambda behave the same way at runtime. You can pretend the compiler turns your method references into lambdas for you.

There are four formats for method references:

- Static methods
- Instance methods on a particular instance
- Instance methods on a parameter to be determined at runtime
- Constructors

Let's take a brief look at each of these in turn. In each example, we will show the method reference and its lambda equivalent. We are going to use some built-in functional interfaces in these examples. We will remind you what they do right before each example. In Chapter 4, we will cover many such interfaces.

Calling Static Methods

The Collections class has a static method that can be used for sorting. Per Table 3.1, the Consumer functional interface takes one parameter and does not return anything. Here we will assign a method reference and a lambda to this functional interface:

```
14: Consumer<List<Integer>> methodRef = Collections::sort;
15: Consumer<List<Integer>> lambda = x -> Collections.sort(x);
```

On line 14, we reference a method with one parameter, and Java knows that it's like a lambda with one parameter. Additionally, Java knows to pass that parameter to the method.

Wait a minute. You might be aware that the sort() method is overloaded. How does Java know that we want to call the version with only one parameter? With both lambdas and method references, Java is inferring information from the context. In this case, we said that we were declaring a Consumer, which takes only one parameter. Java looks for a method that matches that description. If it can't find it or it finds multiple ones that could match multiple methods, then the compiler will report an error. The latter is sometimes called an *ambiguous* type error.

Calling Instance Methods on a Particular Object

The String class has a startsWith() method that takes one parameter and returns a boolean. Conveniently, a Predicate is a functional interface that takes one parameter and returns a boolean. Let's look at how to use method references with this code:

```
18: var str = "abc";
19: Predicate<String> methodRef = str::startsWith;
20: Predicate<String> lambda = s -> str.startsWith(s);
```

Line 19 shows that we want to call str.startsWith() and pass a single parameter to be supplied at runtime. This would be a nice way of filtering the data in a list. In fact, we will do that later in the chapter.

A method reference doesn't have to take any parameters. In this example, we use a Supplier, which takes zero parameters and returns a value:

```
var random = new Random();
Supplier<Integer> methodRef = random::nextInt;
Supplier<Integer> lambda = () -> random.nextInt();
```

Since the methods on Random are instance methods, we call the method reference on an instance of the Random class.

Calling Instance Methods on a Parameter

This time, we are going to call an instance method that doesn't take any parameters. The trick is that we will do so without knowing the instance in advance.

```
23: Predicate<String> methodRef = String::isEmpty;
24: Predicate<String> lambda = s -> s.isEmpty();
```

Line 23 says the method that we want to call is declared in String. It looks like a static method, but it isn't. Instead, Java knows that isEmpty() is an instance method that does not take any parameters. Java uses the parameter supplied at runtime as the instance on which the method is called.

Compare lines 23 and 24 with lines 19 and 20 of our instance example. They look similar, although one references a local variable named str, while the other only references the functional interface parameters.

You can even combine the two types of instance method references. We are going to use a functional interface called a BiPredicate, which takes two parameters and returns a boolean.

```
26: BiPredicate<String, String> methodRef = String::startsWith;
27: BiPredicate<String, String> lambda = (s, p) -> s.startsWith(p);
```

Since the functional interface takes two parameters, Java has to figure out what they represent. The first one will always be the instance of the object for instance methods. Any others are to be method parameters.

Remember that line 26 may look like a `static` method, but it is really a method reference declaring that the instance of the object will be specified later. Line 27 shows some of the power of a method reference. We were able to replace two lambda parameters this time.

Calling Constructors

A *constructor reference* is a special type of method reference that uses new instead of a method, and it instantiates an object. It is common for a constructor reference to use a `Supplier` as shown here:

```
30: Supplier<List<String>> methodRef = ArrayList::new;
31: Supplier<List<String>> lambda = () -> new ArrayList();
```

It expands like the method references you have seen so far. In the previous example, the lambda doesn't have any parameters.

Method references can be tricky. In our next example, we will use the `Function` functional interface, which takes one parameter and returns a result. Notice that line 32 in the following example has the same method reference as line 30 in the previous example:

```
32: Function<Integer, List<String>> methodRef = ArrayList::new;
33: Function<Integer, List<String>> lambda = x -> new ArrayList(x);
```

This means you can't always determine which method can be called by looking at the method reference. Instead, you have to look at the context to see what parameters are used and if there is a return type. In this example, Java sees that we are passing an `Integer` parameter and calls the constructor of `ArrayList` that takes a parameter.

Reviewing Method References

Reading method references is helpful in understanding the code. Table 3.2 shows the four types of method references. If this table doesn't make sense, please reread the previous section. It can take a few tries before method references start to make sense.

TABLE 3.2 Method references

Type	Before colon	After colon	Example
Static methods	Class name	Method name	`Collections::sort`
Instance methods on a particular object	Instance variable name	Method name	`str::startsWith`
Instance methods on a parameter	Class name	Method name	`String::isEmpty`
Constructor	Class name	new	`ArrayList::new`

Number of Parameters in a Method Reference

We mentioned that a method reference can look the same even when it will behave differently based on the surrounding context. For example, given the following method:

```java
public class Penguin {
    public static Integer countBabies(Penguin... cuties) {
        return cuties.length;
    }
}
```

we show three ways that Penguin::countBabies can be interpreted. This method allows you to pass zero or more values and creates an array with those values.

```java
10: Supplier<Integer> methodRef1 = Penguin::countBabies;
11: Supplier<Integer> lambda1 = () -> Penguin.countBabies();
12:
13: Function<Penguin, Integer> methodRef2 = Penguin::countBabies;
14: Function<Penguin, Integer> lambda2 = (x) -> Penguin.countBabies(x);
15:
16: BiFunction<Penguin, Penguin, Integer> methodRef3 = Penguin::countBabies;
17: BiFunction<Penguin, Penguin, Integer> lambda3 =
18:    (x, y) -> Penguin.countBabies(x, y);
```

Lines 10 and 11 do not take any parameters because the functional interface is a Supplier. Lines 13 and 14 take one parameter. Lines 16 and 17 take two parameters. All six lines return an Integer from the method reference or lambda.

There's nothing special about zero, one, and two parameters. If we had a functional interface with 100 parameters of type Penguin and the final one of Integer, we could still implement it with Penguin::countBabies.

Using Wrapper Classes

From your 1Z0-815 studies, you should remember that each Java primitive has a corresponding wrapper class, shown in Table 3.3. With *autoboxing*, the compiler automatically converts a primitive to the corresponding wrapper. Unsurprisingly, *unboxing* is the process in which the compiler automatically converts a wrapper class back to a primitive.

TABLE 3.3   Wrapper classes

Primitive type	Wrapper class	Example of initializing
boolean	Boolean	Boolean.valueOf(true)
byte	Byte	Byte.valueOf((byte) 1)
short	Short	Short.valueOf((short) 1)
int	Integer	Integer.valueOf(1)
long	Long	Long.valueOf(1)
float	Float	Float.valueOf((float) 1.0)
double	Double	Double.valueOf(1.0)
char	Character	Character.valueOf('c')

Can you spot the autoboxing and unboxing in this example?

```
12: Integer pounds = 120;
13: Character letter = "robot".charAt(0);
14: char r = letter;
```

Line 12 is an example of autoboxing as the int primitive is autoboxed into an Integer object. Line 13 demonstrates that autoboxing can involve methods. The charAt() method returns a primitive char. It is then autoboxed into the wrapper object Character. Finally, line 14 shows an example of unboxing. The Character object is unboxed into a primitive char.

There are two tricks in the space of autoboxing and unboxing. The first has to do with null values. This innocuous-looking code throws an exception:

```
15: var heights = new ArrayList<Integer>();
16: heights.add(null);
17: int h = heights.get(0); // NullPointerException
```

On line 16, we add a null to the list. This is legal because a null reference can be assigned to any reference variable. On line 17, we try to unbox that null to an int primitive. This is a problem. Java tries to get the int value of null. Since calling any method on null gives a NullPointerException, that is just what we get. Be careful when you see null in relation to autoboxing.

Wrapper Classes and *null*

Speaking of null, one advantage of a wrapper class over a primitive is that it can hold a null value. While null values aren't particularly useful for numeric calculations, they are quite useful in data-based services. For example, if you are storing a user's location data using (latitude, longitude), it would be a bad idea to store a missing point as (0,0) since that refers to an actual location off the cost of Africa where the user could theoretically be.

Also, be careful when autoboxing into Integer. What do you think this code outputs?

```
23: List<Integer> numbers = new ArrayList<Integer>();
24: numbers.add(1);
25: numbers.add(Integer.valueOf(3));
26: numbers.add(Integer.valueOf(5));
27: numbers.remove(1);
28: numbers.remove(Integer.valueOf(5));
29: System.out.println(numbers);
```

It actually outputs [1]. Let's walk through why that is. On lines 24 through 26, we add three Integer objects to numbers. The one on line 24 relies on autoboxing to do so, but it gets added just fine. At this point, numbers contains [1, 3, 5].

Line 27 contains the second trick. The remove() method is overloaded. One signature takes an int as the index of the element to remove. The other takes an Object that should be removed. On line 27, Java sees a matching signature for int, so it doesn't need to autobox the call to the method. Now numbers contains [1, 5]. Line 28 calls the other remove() method, and it removes the matching object, which leaves us with just [1].

Using the Diamond Operator

In the past, we would write code using generics like the following:

```
List<Integer> list = new ArrayList<Integer>();
Map<String,Integer> map = new HashMap<String,Integer>();
```

You might even have generics that contain other generics, such as this:

```
Map<Long,List<Integer>> mapLists = new HashMap<Long,List<Integer>>();
```

That's a lot of duplicate code to write! We'll cover expressions later in this chapter where the generic types might not be the same, but often the generic types for both sides of the expression are identical.

Luckily, the diamond operator, <>, was added to the language. The diamond operator is a shorthand notation that allows you to omit the generic type from the right side of a statement when the type can be inferred. It is called the *diamond operator* because <> looks like a diamond. Compare the previous declarations with these new, much shorter versions:

```java
List<Integer> list = new ArrayList<>();
Map<String,Integer> map = new HashMap<>();
Map<Long,List<Integer>> mapOfLists = new HashMap<>();
```

The first is the variable declaration and fully specifies the generic type. The second is an expression that infers the type from the assignment operator, using the diamond operator. To the compiler, both these declarations and our previous ones are equivalent. To us, though, the latter is a lot shorter and easier to read.

The diamond operator cannot be used as the type in a variable declaration. It can be used only on the right side of an assignment operation. For example, none of the following compiles:

```java
List<> list = new ArrayList<Integer>();    // DOES NOT COMPILE
Map<> map = new HashMap<String, Integer>(); // DOES NOT COMPILE
class InvalidUse {
    void use(List<> data) {}                // DOES NOT COMPILE
}
```

Since var is new to Java, let's look at the impact of using var with the diamond operator. Do you think these two statements compile and are equivalent?

```java
var list = new ArrayList<Integer>();
var list = new ArrayList<>();
```

While they both compile, they are not equivalent. The first one creates an ArrayList<Integer> just like the prior set of examples. The second one creates an ArrayList<Object>. Since there is no generic type specified, it cannot be inferred. Java happily assumes you wanted Object in this scenario.

Using Lists, Sets, Maps, and Queues

A *collection* is a group of objects contained in a single object. The *Java Collections Framework* is a set of classes in java.util for storing collections. There are four main interfaces in the Java Collections Framework.

- **List:** A *list* is an ordered collection of elements that allows duplicate entries. Elements in a list can be accessed by an int index.

- **Set:** A *set* is a collection that does not allow duplicate entries.

- **Queue:** A *queue* is a collection that orders its elements in a specific order for processing. A typical queue processes its elements in a first-in, first-out order, but other orderings are possible.

- **Map:** A *map* is a collection that maps keys to values, with no duplicate keys allowed. The elements in a map are key/value pairs.

Figure 3.1 shows the `Collection` interface, its subinterfaces, and some classes that implement the interfaces that you should know for the exam. The interfaces are shown in rectangles, with the classes in rounded boxes.

FIGURE 3.1   The `Collection` interface is the root of all collections except maps.

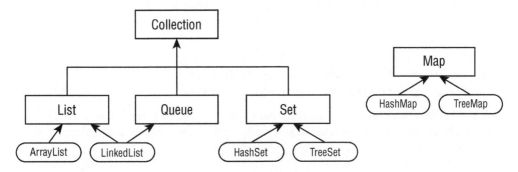

Notice that `Map` doesn't implement the `Collection` interface. It is considered part of the Java Collections Framework, even though it isn't technically a `Collection`. It is a collection (note the lowercase), though, in that it contains a group of objects. The reason why maps are treated differently is that they need different methods due to being key/value pairs.

We will first discuss the methods `Collection` provides to all implementing classes. Then we will cover the different types of collections, including when to use each one and the concrete subclasses. Then we will compare the different types.

Common Collections Methods

The `Collection` interface contains useful methods for working with lists, sets, and queues. In the following sections, we will discuss the most common ones. We will cover streams in the next chapter. Many of these methods are *convenience methods* that could be implemented in other ways but make your code easier to write and read. This is why they are convenient.

In this section, we use `ArrayList` and `HashSet` as our implementation classes, but they can apply to any class that inherits the `Collection` interface. We'll cover the specific properties of each `Collection` class in the next section.

add()

The add() method inserts a new element into the Collection and returns whether it was successful. The method signature is as follows:

```
boolean add(E element)
```

Remember that the Collections Framework uses generics. You will see E appear frequently. It means the generic type that was used to create the collection. For some Collection types, add() always returns true. For other types, there is logic as to whether the add() call was successful. The following shows how to use this method:

```
3: Collection<String> list = new ArrayList<>();
4: System.out.println(list.add("Sparrow")); // true
5: System.out.println(list.add("Sparrow")); // true
6:
7: Collection<String> set = new HashSet<>();
8: System.out.println(set.add("Sparrow")); // true
9: System.out.println(set.add("Sparrow")); // false
```

A List allows duplicates, making the return value true each time. A Set does not allow duplicates. On line 9, we tried to add a duplicate so that Java returns false from the add() method.

remove()

The remove() method removes a single matching value in the Collection and returns whether it was successful. The method signature is as follows:

```
boolean remove(Object object)
```

This time, the boolean return value tells us whether a match was removed. The following shows how to use this method:

```
3: Collection<String> birds = new ArrayList<>();
4: birds.add("hawk");                              // [hawk]
5: birds.add("hawk");                              // [hawk, hawk]
6: System.out.println(birds.remove("cardinal")); // false
7: System.out.println(birds.remove("hawk"));     // true
8: System.out.println(birds);                     // [hawk]
```

Line 6 tries to remove an element that is not in birds. It returns false because no such element is found. Line 7 tries to remove an element that is in birds, so it returns true. Notice that it removes only one match.

Since calling remove() on a List with an int uses the index, an index that doesn't exist will throw an exception. For example, birds.remove(100); throws an IndexOutOfBoundsException. Remember that there are overloaded remove() methods. One takes the element to remove. The other takes the index of the element to remove. The latter is being called here.

Deleting while Looping

Java does not allow removing elements from a list while using the enhanced for loop.

```
Collection<String> birds = new ArrayList<>();
birds.add("hawk");
birds.add("hawk");
birds.add("hawk");

for (String bird : birds) // ConcurrentModificationException
    birds.remove(bird);
```

Wait a minute. Concurrent modification? We don't get to concurrency until Chapter 7. That's right. It is possible to get a ConcurrentModificationException without threads. This is Java's way of complaining that you are trying to modify the list while looping through it. In Chapter 7, we'll return to this example and show how to fix it with the CopyOnWriteArrayList class.

isEmpty() and size()

The isEmpty() and size() methods look at how many elements are in the Collection. The method signatures are as follows:

```
boolean isEmpty()
int size()
```

The following shows how to use these methods:

```
Collection<String> birds = new ArrayList<>();
System.out.println(birds.isEmpty()); // true
System.out.println(birds.size());    // 0
birds.add("hawk");                    // [hawk]
birds.add("hawk");                    // [hawk, hawk]
System.out.println(birds.isEmpty()); // false
System.out.println(birds.size());    // 2
```

At the beginning, birds has a size of 0 and is empty. It has a capacity that is greater than 0. After we add elements, the size becomes positive, and it is no longer empty.

clear()

The clear() method provides an easy way to discard all elements of the Collection. The method signature is as follows:

```
void clear()
```

The following shows how to use this method:

```
Collection<String> birds = new ArrayList<>();
birds.add("hawk");                      // [hawk]
birds.add("hawk");                      // [hawk, hawk]
System.out.println(birds.isEmpty()); // false
System.out.println(birds.size());    // 2
birds.clear();                          // []
System.out.println(birds.isEmpty()); // true
System.out.println(birds.size());    // 0
```

After calling clear(), birds is back to being an empty ArrayList of size 0.

contains()

The contains() method checks whether a certain value is in the Collection. The method signature is as follows:

```
boolean contains(Object object)
```

The following shows how to use this method:

```
Collection<String> birds = new ArrayList<>();
birds.add("hawk"); // [hawk]
System.out.println(birds.contains("hawk"));  // true
System.out.println(birds.contains("robin")); // false
```

The contains() method calls equals() on elements of the ArrayList to see whether there are any matches.

removeIf()

The removeIf() method removes all elements that match a condition. We can specify what should be deleted using a block of code or even a method reference.

The method signature looks like the following. (We will explain what the ? super means in the "Working with Generics" section later in this chapter.)

```
boolean removeIf(Predicate<? super E> filter)
```

It uses a Predicate, which takes one parameter and returns a boolean. Let's take a look at an example:

```
4: Collection<String> list = new ArrayList<>();
5: list.add("Magician");
6: list.add("Assistant");
7: System.out.println(list);     // [Magician, Assistant]
8: list.removeIf(s -> s.startsWith("A"));
9: System.out.println(list);     // [Magician]
```

Line 8 shows how to remove all of the String values that begin with the letter A. This allows us to make the Assistant disappear.

How would you replace line 8 with a method reference? Trick question—you can't. The removeIf() method takes a Predicate. We can pass only one value with this method reference. Since startsWith takes a literal, it needs to be specified "the long way."

Let's try one more example that does use a method reference.

```
11: Collection<String> set = new HashSet<>();
12: set.add("Wand");
13: set.add("");
14: set.removeIf(String::isEmpty); // s -> s.isEmpty()
15: System.out.println(set);       // [Wand]
```

On line 14, we remove any empty String objects from the set. The comment on that line shows the lambda equivalent of the method reference. Line 15 shows that the removeIf() method successfully removed one element from the list.

forEach()

Looping through a Collection is common. On the 1Z0-815 exam, you wrote lots of loops. There's also a forEach() method that you can call on a Collection. It uses a Consumer that takes a single parameter and doesn't return anything. The method signature is as follows:

```
void forEach(Consumer<? super T> action)
```

Cats like to explore, so let's print out two of them using both method references and streams.

```
Collection<String> cats = Arrays.asList("Annie", "Ripley");
cats.forEach(System.out::println);
cats.forEach(c -> System.out.println(c));
```

The cats have discovered how to print their names. Now they have more time to play (as do we)!

Using the *List* Interface

Now that you're familiar with some common Collection interface methods, let's move on to specific classes. You use a list when you want an ordered collection that can contain duplicate entries. Items can be retrieved and inserted at specific positions in the list based on an int index much like an array. Unlike an array, though, many List implementations can change in size after they are declared.

Lists are commonly used because there are many situations in programming where you need to keep track of a list of objects.

For example, you might make a list of what you want to see at the zoo: First, see the lions because they go to sleep early. Second, see the pandas because there is a long line later in the day. And so forth.

Figure 3.2 shows how you can envision a List. Each element of the List has an index, and the indexes begin with zero.

FIGURE 3.2 Example of a List

List

Ordered Index	Data
0	lions
1	pandas
2	zebras
...	...

Sometimes, you don't actually care about the order of elements in a list. List is like the "go to" data type. When we make a shopping list before going to the store, the order of the list happens to be the order in which we thought of the items. We probably aren't attached to that particular order, but it isn't hurting anything.

While the classes implementing the List interface have many methods, you need to know only the most common ones. Conveniently, these methods are the same for all of the implementations that might show up on the exam.

The main thing that all List implementations have in common is that they are ordered and allow duplicates. Beyond that, they each offer different functionality. We will look at the implementations that you need to know and the available methods.

Pay special attention to which names are classes and which are interfaces. The exam may ask you which is the best class or which is the best interface for a scenario.

Comparing *List* Implementations

An ArrayList is like a resizable array. When elements are added, the ArrayList automatically grows. When you aren't sure which collection to use, use an ArrayList.

The main benefit of an ArrayList is that you can look up any element in constant time. Adding or removing an element is slower than accessing an element. This makes an ArrayList a good choice when you are reading more often than (or the same amount as) writing to the ArrayList.

A LinkedList is special because it implements both List and Queue. It has all the methods of a List. It also has additional methods to facilitate adding or removing from the beginning and/or end of the list.

The main benefits of a LinkedList are that you can access, add, and remove from the beginning and end of the list in constant time. The trade-off is that dealing with an arbitrary index takes linear time. This makes a LinkedList a good choice when you'll be using it as Queue. As you saw in Figure 3.1, a LinkedList implements both the List and Queue interface.

Creating a *List* with a Factory

When you create a List of type ArrayList or LinkedList, you know the type. There are a few special methods where you get a List back but don't know the type. These methods let you create a List including data in one line using a factory method. This is convenient, especially when testing. Some of these methods return an immutable object. As we saw in Chapter 1, an immutable object cannot be changed or modified. Table 3.4 summarizes these three lists.

TABLE 3.4   Factory methods to create a List

Method	Description	Can add elements?	Can replace element?	Can delete elements?
Arrays .asList(varargs)	Returns fixed size list backed by an array	No	Yes	No
List.of(varargs)	Returns immutable list	No	No	No
List .copyOf(collection)	Returns immutable list with copy of original collection's values	No	No	No

Let's take a look at an example of these three methods.

```
16: String[] array = new String[] {"a", "b", "c"};
17: List<String> asList = Arrays.asList(array); // [a, b, c]
18: List<String> of = List.of(array);          // [a, b, c]
19: List<String> copy = List.copyOf(asList);    // [a, b, c]
20:
21: array[0] = "z";
22:
23: System.out.println(asList); // [z, b, c]
24: System.out.println(of);     // [a, b, c]
25: System.out.println(copy);   // [a, b, c]
26:
27: asList.set(0, "x");
28: System.out.println(Arrays.toString(array)); // [x, b, c]
29:
30: copy.add("y");  // throws UnsupportedOperationException
```

Line 17 creates a List that is backed by an array. Line 21 changes the array, and line 23 reflects that change. Lines 27 and 28 show the other direction where changing the List updates the underlying array. Lines 18 and 19 create an immutable List. Line 30 shows it is immutable by throwing an exception when trying to add a value. All three lists would throw an exception when adding or removing a value. The of and copy lists would also throw one on trying to update a reference.

Working with *List* Methods

The methods in the List interface are for working with indexes. In addition to the inherited Collection methods, the method signatures that you need to know are in Table 3.5.

TABLE 3.5   List methods

Method	Description
boolean add(E element)	Adds element to end (available on all Collection APIs)
void add(int index, E element)	Adds element at index and moves the rest toward the end
E get(int index)	Returns element at index
E remove(int index)	Removes element at index and moves the rest toward the front
void replaceAll (UnaryOperator<E> op)	Replaces each element in the list with the result of the operator
E set(int index, E e)	Replaces element at index and returns original. Throws IndexOutOfBoundsException if the index is larger than the maximum one set

The following statements demonstrate most of these methods for working with a List:

```
3:  List<String> list = new ArrayList<>();
4:  list.add("SD");                    // [SD]
5:  list.add(0, "NY");                 // [NY,SD]
6:  list.set(1, "FL");                 // [NY,FL]
7:  System.out.println(list.get(0));   // NY
8:  list.remove("NY");                 // [FL]
9:  list.remove(0);                    // []
10: list.set(0, "?");                  // IndexOutOfBoundsException
```

On line 3, list starts out empty. Line 4 adds an element to the end of the list. Line 5 adds an element at index 0 that bumps the original index 0 to index 1. Notice how the ArrayList is now automatically one larger. Line 6 replaces the element at index 1 with a new value.

Line 7 uses the get() method to print the element at a specific index. Line 8 removes the element matching NY. Finally, line 9 removes the element at index 0, and list is empty again.

Line 10 throws an IndexOutOfBoundsException because there are no elements in the List. Since there are no elements to replace, even index 0 isn't allowed. If line 10 were moved up between lines 4 and 5, the call would have succeeded.

The output would be the same if you tried these examples with LinkedList. Although the code would be less efficient, it wouldn't be noticeable until you have very large lists.

Now, let's look at using the replaceAll() method. It takes a UnaryOperator that takes one parameter and returns a value of the same type.

```
List<Integer> numbers = Arrays.asList(1, 2, 3);
numbers.replaceAll(x -> x*2);
System.out.println(numbers);    // [2, 4, 6]
```

This lambda doubles the value of each element in the list. The replaceAll() method calls the lambda on each element of the list and replaces the value at that index.

Iterating through a List

There are many ways to iterate through a list. For example, when studying for the 1Z0-815 exam, you saw how to loop through a list using an enhanced for loop.

```
for (String string: list) {
    System.out.println(string);
}
```

You may see another approach used.

```
Iterator<String> iter = list.iterator();
while(iter.hasNext()) {
    String string = iter.next();
    System.out.println(string);
}
```

Pay attention to the difference between these techniques. The hasNext() method checks whether there is a next value. In other words, it tells you whether next() will execute without throwing an exception. The next() method actually moves the Iterator to the next element.

Using the *Set* Interface

You use a set when you don't want to allow duplicate entries. For example, you might want to keep track of the unique animals that you want to see at the zoo. You aren't concerned with the order in which you see these animals, but there isn't time to see them more than once. You just want to make sure you see the ones that are important to you and remove them from the set of outstanding animals to see after you see them.

Figure 3.3 shows how you can envision a Set. The main thing that all Set implementations have in common is that they do not allow duplicates. We will look at each implementation that you need to know for the exam and how to write code using Set.

FIGURE 3.3   Example of a Set

Comparing *Set* Implementations

A HashSet stores its elements in a *hash table*, which means the keys are a hash and the values are an Object. This means that it uses the hashCode() method of the objects to retrieve them more efficiently.

The main benefit is that adding elements and checking whether an element is in the set both have constant time. The trade-off is that you lose the order in which you inserted the elements. Most of the time, you aren't concerned with this in a set anyway, making HashSet the most common set.

A TreeSet stores its elements in a sorted tree structure. The main benefit is that the set is always in sorted order. The trade-off is that adding and checking whether an element exists take longer than with a HashSet, especially as the tree grows larger.

Figure 3.4 shows how you can envision HashSet and TreeSet being stored. HashSet is more complicated in reality, but this is fine for the purpose of the exam.

Working with *Set* Methods

Like List, you can create an immutable Set in one line or make a copy of an existing one.

```
Set<Character> letters = Set.of('z', 'o', 'o');
Set<Character> copy = Set.copyOf(letters);
```

FIGURE 3.4   Examples of a HashSet and TreeSet

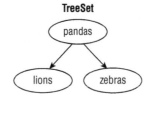

hashCode() Value	Data
−995544615	pandas
...	
−705903059	zebras
...	
102978519	lions

Those are the only extra methods you need to know for the Set interface for the exam! You do have to know how sets behave with respect to the traditional Collection methods. You also have to know the differences between the types of sets. Let's start with HashSet:

```
3: Set<Integer> set = new HashSet<>();
4: boolean b1 = set.add(66);     // true
5: boolean b2 = set.add(10);     // true
6: boolean b3 = set.add(66);     // false
7: boolean b4 = set.add(8);      // true
8: set.forEach(System.out::println);
```

This code prints three lines:

```
66
8
10
```

The add() methods should be straightforward. They return true unless the Integer is already in the set. Line 6 returns false, because we already have 66 in the set and a set must preserve uniqueness. Line 8 prints the elements of the set in an arbitrary order. In this case, it happens not to be sorted order, or the order in which we added the elements.

Remember that the equals() method is used to determine equality. The hashCode() method is used to know which bucket to look in so that Java doesn't have to look through the whole set to find out whether an object is there. The best case is that hash codes are unique, and Java has to call equals() on only one object. The worst case is that all implementations return the same hashCode(), and Java has to call equals() on every element of the set anyway.

Now let's look at the same example with TreeSet.

```
3: Set<Integer> set = new TreeSet<>();
4: boolean b1 = set.add(66); // true
5: boolean b2 = set.add(10); // true
```

```
6: boolean b3 = set.add(66); // false
7: boolean b4 = set.add(8);  // true
8: set.forEach(System.out::println);
```

This time, the code prints the following:

```
8
10
66
```

The elements are printed out in their natural sorted order. Numbers implement the Comparable interface in Java, which is used for sorting. Later in the chapter, you will learn how to create your own Comparable objects.

Using the *Queue* Interface

You use a queue when elements are added and removed in a specific order. Queues are typically used for sorting elements prior to processing them. For example, when you want to buy a ticket and someone is waiting in line, you get in line behind that person. And if you are British, you get in the queue behind that person, making this really easy to remember!

Unless stated otherwise, a queue is assumed to be *FIFO* (first-in, first-out). Some queue implementations change this to use a different order. You can envision a FIFO queue as shown in Figure 3.5. The other format is *LIFO* (last-in, first-out), which is commonly referred to as a *stack*. In Java, though, both can be implemented with the Queue interface.

FIGURE 3.5   Example of a Queue

Since this is a FIFO queue, Rover is first, which means he was the first one to arrive. Bella is last, which means she was last to arrive and has the longest wait remaining. All queues have specific requirements for adding and removing the next element. Beyond that, they each offer different functionality. We will look at the implementations that you need to know and the available methods.

Comparing *Queue* Implementations

You saw LinkedList earlier in the List section. In addition to being a list, it is a double-ended queue. A double-ended queue is different from a regular queue in that you can insert and remove elements from both the front and back of the queue. Think, "Mr. Woodie Flowers, come right to the front. You are the only one who gets this special treatment. Everyone else will have to start at the back of the line."

The main benefit of a `LinkedList` is that it implements both the `List` and `Queue` interfaces. The trade-off is that it isn't as efficient as a "pure" queue. You can use the `ArrayDeque` class (short for double-ended queue) if you need a more efficient queue. However, `ArrayDeque` is not in scope for the exam.

Working with *Queue* Methods

The Queue interface contains many methods. Luckily, there are only six methods that you need to focus on. These methods are shown in Table 3.6.

TABLE 3.6   Queue methods

Method	Description	Throws exception on failure
boolean add(E e)	Adds an element to the back of the queue and returns `true` or throws an exception	Yes
E element()	Returns next element or throws an exception if empty queue	Yes
boolean offer(E e)	Adds an element to the back of the queue and returns whether successful	No
E remove()	Removes and returns next element or throws an exception if empty queue	Yes
E poll()	Removes and returns next element or returns null if empty queue	No
E peek()	Returns next element or returns null if empty queue	No

As you can see, there are basically two sets of methods. One set throws an exception when something goes wrong. The other uses a different return value when something goes wrong. The `offer()`/`poll()`/`peek()` methods are more common. This is the standard language people use when working with queues.

Let's look at an example that uses some of these methods.

```
12: Queue<Integer> queue = new LinkedList<>();
13: System.out.println(queue.offer(10)); // true
14: System.out.println(queue.offer(4));  // true
15: System.out.println(queue.peek());    // 10
```

```
16: System.out.println(queue.poll());    // 10
17: System.out.println(queue.poll());    // 4
18: System.out.println(queue.peek());    // null
```

Figure 3.6 shows what the queue looks like at each step of the code. Lines 13 and 14 successfully add an element to the end of the queue. Some queues are limited in size, which would cause offering an element to the queue to fail. You won't encounter a scenario like that on the exam. Line 15 looks at the first element in the queue, but it does not remove it. Lines 16 and 17 actually remove the elements from the queue, which results in an empty queue. Line 18 tries to look at the first element of a queue, which results in null.

FIGURE 3.6   Working with a queue

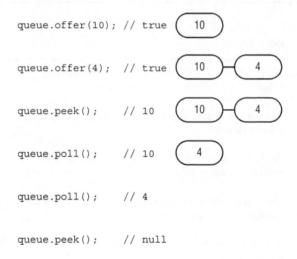

Using the *Map* Interface

You use a map when you want to identify values by a key. For example, when you use the contact list in your phone, you look up "George" rather than looking through each phone number in turn.

You can envision a Map as shown in Figure 3.7. You don't need to know the names of the specific interfaces that the different maps implement, but you do need to know that TreeMap is sorted.

The main thing that all Map classes have in common is that they all have keys and values. Beyond that, they each offer different functionality. We will look at the implementations that you need to know and the available methods.

FIGURE 3.7   Example of a Map

Map

Key	Value
George	555-555-5555
May	777-777-7777

Map.of() and *Map.copyOf()*

Just like List and Set, there is a helper method to create a Map. You pass any number of pairs of keys and values.

```
Map.of("key1", "value1", "key2", "value2");
```

Unlike List and Set, this is less than ideal. Suppose you miscount and leave out a value.

```
Map.of("key1", "value1", "key2"); // INCORRECT
```

This code compiles but throws an error at runtime. Passing keys and values is also harder to read because you have to keep track of which parameter is which. Luckily, there is a better way. Map also provides a method that lets you supply key/value pairs.

```
Map.ofEntries(
    Map.entry("key1", "value1"),
    Map.entry("key1", "value1"));
```

Now we can't forget to pass a value. If we leave out a parameter, the entry() method won't compile. Conveniently, Map.copyOf(map) works just like the List and Set interface copyOf() methods.

Comparing *Map* Implementations

A HashMap stores the keys in a hash table. This means that it uses the hashCode() method of the keys to retrieve their values more efficiently.

The main benefit is that adding elements and retrieving the element by key both have constant time. The trade-off is that you lose the order in which you inserted the elements. Most of the time, you aren't concerned with this in a map anyway. If you were, you could use LinkedHashMap, but that's not in scope for the exam.

A TreeMap stores the keys in a sorted tree structure. The main benefit is that the keys are always in sorted order. Like a TreeSet, the trade-off is that adding and checking whether a key is present takes longer as the tree grows larger.

Working with *Map* Methods

Given that Map doesn't extend Collection, there are more methods specified on the Map interface. Since there are both keys and values, we need generic type parameters for both. The class uses K for key and V for value. The methods you need to know for the exam are in Table 3.7. Some of the method signatures are simplified to make them easier to understand.

TABLE 3.7   Map methods

Method	Description
void clear()	Removes all keys and values from the map.
boolean containsKey (Object key)	Returns whether key is in map.
boolean containsValue (Object value)	Returns whether value is in map.
Set<Map.Entry<K,V>> entrySet()	Returns a Set of key/value pairs.
void forEach(BiConsumer(K key, V value))	Loop through each key/value pair.
V get(Object key)	Returns the value mapped by key or null if none is mapped.
V getOrDefault(Object key, V defaultValue)	Returns the value mapped by the key or the default value if none is mapped.
boolean isEmpty()	Returns whether the map is empty.
Set<K> keySet()	Returns set of all keys.
V merge(K key, V value, Function(<V, V, V> func))	Sets value if key not set. Runs the function if the key is set to determine the new value. Removes if null.
V put(K key, V value)	Adds or replaces key/value pair. Returns previous value or null.
V putIfAbsent(K key, V value)	Adds value if key not present and returns null. Otherwise, returns existing value.
V remove(Object key)	Removes and returns value mapped to key. Returns null if none.

Method	Description
`V replace(K key, V value)`	Replaces the value for a given key if the key is set. Returns the original value or `null` if none.
`void replaceAll (BiFunction<K, V, V> func)`	Replaces each value with the results of the function.
`int size()`	Returns the number of entries (key/value pairs) in the map.
`Collection<V> values()`	Returns `Collection` of all values.

Basic Methods

Let's start out by comparing the same code with two Map types. First up is HashMap.

```java
Map<String, String> map = new HashMap<>();
map.put("koala", "bamboo");
map.put("lion", "meat");
map.put("giraffe", "leaf");
String food = map.get("koala"); // bamboo
for (String key: map.keySet())
    System.out.print(key + ","); // koala,giraffe,lion,
```

Here we set the `put()` method to add key/value pairs to the map and `get()` to get a value given a key. We also use the `keySet()` method to get all the keys.

Java uses the `hashCode()` of the key to determine the order. The order here happens to not be sorted order, or the order in which we typed the values. Now let's look at TreeMap.

```java
Map<String, String> map = new TreeMap<>();
map.put("koala", "bamboo");
map.put("lion", "meat");
map.put("giraffe", "leaf");
String food = map.get("koala"); // bamboo
for (String key: map.keySet())
    System.out.print(key + ","); // giraffe,koala,lion,
```

TreeMap sorts the keys as we would expect. If we were to have called `values()` instead of `keySet()`, the order of the values would correspond to the order of the keys.

With our same map, we can try some boolean checks.

```
System.out.println(map.contains("lion")); // DOES NOT COMPILE
System.out.println(map.containsKey("lion")); // true
System.out.println(map.containsValue("lion")); // false
System.out.println(map.size()); // 3
map.clear();
System.out.println(map.size()); // 0
System.out.println(map.isEmpty()); // true
```

The first line is a little tricky. The contains() method is on the Collection interface but not the Map interface. The next two lines show that keys and values are checked separately. We can see that there are three key/value pairs in our map. Then we clear out the contents of the map and see there are zero elements and it is empty.

In the following sections, we show Map methods you might not be as familiar with.

forEach() and entrySet()

You saw the forEach() method earlier in the chapter. Note that it works a little differently on a Map. This time, the lambda used by the forEach() method has two parameters; the key and the value. Let's look at an example, shown here:

```
Map<Integer, Character> map = new HashMap<>();
map.put(1, 'a');
map.put(2, 'b');
map.put(3, 'c');
map.forEach((k, v) -> System.out.println(v));
```

The lambda has both the key and value as the parameters. It happens to print out the value but could do anything with the key and/or value. Interestingly, if you don't care about the key, this particular code could have been written with the values() method and a method reference instead.

```
map.values().forEach(System.out::println);
```

Another way of going through all the data in a map is to get the key/value pairs in a Set. Java has a static interface inside Map called Entry. It provides methods to get the key and value of each pair.

```
map.entrySet().forEach(e ->
    System.out.println(e.getKey() + e.getValue()));
```

getOrDefault()

The get() method returns null if the requested key is not in map. Sometimes you prefer to have a different value returned. Luckily, the getOrDefault() method makes this easy. Let's compare the two methods.

```
3: Map<Character, String> map = new HashMap<>();
4: map.put('x', "spot");
```

```
5: System.out.println("X marks the " + map.get('x'));
6: System.out.println("X marks the " + map.getOrDefault('x', ""));
7: System.out.println("Y marks the " + map.get('y'));
8: System.out.println("Y marks the " + map.getOrDefault('y', ""));
```

This code prints the following:

```
X marks the spot
X marks the spot
Y marks the null
Y marks the
```

As you can see, lines 5 and 6 have the same output because get() and getOrDefault() behave the same way when the key is present. They return the value mapped by that key. Lines 7 and 8 give different output, showing that get() returns null when the key is not present. By contrast, getOrDefault() returns the empty string we passed as a parameter.

replace() and replaceAll()

These methods are similar to the Collection version except a key is involved.

```
21: Map<Integer, Integer> map = new HashMap<>();
22: map.put(1, 2);
23: map.put(2, 4);
24: Integer original = map.replace(2, 10); // 4
25: System.out.println(map);      // {1=2, 2=10}
26: map.replaceAll((k, v) -> k + v);
27: System.out.println(map);      // {1=3, 2=12}
```

Line 24 replaces the value for key 2 and returns the original value. Line 26 calls a function and sets the value of each element of the map to the result of that function. In our case, we added the key and value together.

putIfAbsent()

The putIfAbsent() method sets a value in the map but skips it if the value is already set to a non-null value.

```
Map<String, String> favorites = new HashMap<>();
favorites.put("Jenny", "Bus Tour");
favorites.put("Tom", null);
favorites.putIfAbsent("Jenny", "Tram");
favorites.putIfAbsent("Sam", "Tram");
favorites.putIfAbsent("Tom", "Tram");
System.out.println(favorites); // {Tom=Tram, Jenny=Bus Tour, Sam=Tram}
```

As you can see, Jenny's value is not updated because one was already present. Sam wasn't there at all, so he was added. Tom was present as a key but had a null value. Therefore, he was added as well.

merge()

The merge() method adds logic of what to choose. Suppose we want to choose the ride with the longest name. We can write code to express this by passing a mapping function to the merge() method.

```
11: BiFunction<String, String, String> mapper = (v1, v2)
12:    -> v1.length() > v2.length() ? v1: v2;
13:
14: Map<String, String> favorites = new HashMap<>();
15: favorites.put("Jenny", "Bus Tour");
16: favorites.put("Tom", "Tram");
17:
18: String jenny = favorites.merge("Jenny", "Skyride", mapper);
19: String tom = favorites.merge("Tom", "Skyride", mapper);
20:
21: System.out.println(favorites); // {Tom=Skyride, Jenny=Bus Tour}
22: System.out.println(jenny);     // Bus Tour
23: System.out.println(tom);       // Skyride
```

The code on lines 11 and 12 take two parameters and returns a value. Our implementation returns the one with the longest name. Line 18 calls this mapping function, and it sees that Bus Tour is longer than Skyride, so it leaves the value as Bus Tour. Line 19 calls this mapping function again. This time, Tram is not longer than Skyride, so the map is updated. Line 21 prints out the new map contents. Lines 22 and 23 show that the result gets returned from merge().

The merge() method also has logic for what happens if null values or missing keys are involved. In this case, it doesn't call the BiFunction at all, and it simply uses the new value.

```
BiFunction<String, String, String> mapper =
   (v1, v2) -> v1.length() > v2.length() ? v1 : v2;
Map<String, String> favorites = new HashMap<>();
favorites.put("Sam", null);
favorites.merge("Tom", "Skyride", mapper);
favorites.merge("Sam", "Skyride", mapper);
System.out.println(favorites);   // {Tom=Skyride, Sam=Skyride}
```

Notice that the mapping function isn't called. If it were, we'd have a NullPointerException. The mapping function is used only when there are two actual values to decide between.

The final thing to know about merge() is what happens when the mapping function is called and returns null. The key is removed from the map when this happens:

```
BiFunction<String, String, String> mapper = (v1, v2) -> null;
Map<String, String> favorites = new HashMap<>();
favorites.put("Jenny", "Bus Tour");
favorites.put("Tom", "Bus Tour");
```

```
favorites.merge("Jenny", "Skyride", mapper);
favorites.merge("Sam", "Skyride", mapper);
System.out.println(favorites);   // {Tom=Bus Tour, Sam=Skyride}
```

Tom was left alone since there was no merge() call for that key. Sam was added since that key was not in the original list. Jenny was removed because the mapping function returned null.

Table 3.8 shows all of these scenarios as a reference.

TABLE 3.8 Behavior of the merge() method

If the requested key _____	And mapping function returns _____	Then:
Has a null value in map	N/A (mapping function not called)	Update key's value in map with value parameter.
Has a non-null value in map	null	Remove key from map.
Has a non-null value in map	A non-null value	Set key to mapping function result.
Is not in map	N/A (mapping function not called)	Add key with value parameter to map directly without calling mapping function.

Comparing Collection Types

We conclude this section with a review of all the collection classes. Make sure that you can fill in Table 3.9 to compare the four collections types from memory.

TABLE 3.9 Java Collections Framework types

Type	Can contain duplicate elements?	Elements always ordered?	Has keys and values?	Must add/remove in specific order?
List	Yes	Yes (by index)	No	No
Map	Yes (for values)	No	Yes	No
Queue	Yes	Yes (retrieved in defined order)	No	Yes
Set	No	No	No	No

Additionally, make sure you can fill in Table 3.10 to describe the types on the exam.

TABLE 3.10   Collection attributes

Type	Java Collections Framework interface	Sorted?	Calls hashCode?	Calls compareTo?
ArrayList	List	No	No	No
HashMap	Map	No	Yes	No
HashSet	Set	No	Yes	No
LinkedList	List, Queue	No	No	No
TreeMap	Map	Yes	No	Yes
TreeSet	Set	Yes	No	Yes

Next, the exam expects you to know which data structures allow null values. The data structures that involve sorting do not allow null values.

Finally, the exam expects you to be able to choose the right collection type given a description of a problem. We recommend first identifying which type of collection the question is asking about. Figure out whether you are looking for a list, map, queue, or set. This lets you eliminate a number of answers. Then you can figure out which of the remaining choices is the best answer.

 Real World Scenario

Older Collections

There are a few collections that are no longer on the exam that you might come across in older code. All three were early Java data structures you could use with threads. In Chapter 7, you'll learn about modern alternatives if you need a concurrent collection.

- **Vector**: Implements List. If you don't need concurrency, use ArrayList instead.

- **Hashtable**: Implements Map. If you don't need concurrency, use HashMap instead.

- **Stack**: Implements Queue. If you don't need concurrency, use a LinkedList instead.

Sorting Data

We discussed "order" for the TreeSet and TreeMap classes. For numbers, order is obvious—it is numerical order. For String objects, order is defined according to the Unicode character mapping. As far as the exam is concerned, that means numbers sort before letters, and uppercase letters sort before lowercase letters.

Remember that numbers sort before letters, and uppercase letters sort before lowercase letters.

We will be using Collections.sort() in many of these examples. To review from your 1Z0-815 studies, this method sorts a list. It returns void because the method parameter is what gets sorted.

You can also sort objects that you create yourself. Java provides an interface called Comparable. If your class implements Comparable, it can be used in these data structures that require comparison. There is also a class called Comparator, which is used to specify that you want to use a different order than the object itself provides.

Comparable and Comparator are similar enough to be tricky. The exam likes to see if it can trick you into mixing up the two. Don't be confused! In this section, we will discuss Comparable first. Then, as we go through Comparator, we will point out all of the differences.

Creating a *Comparable* Class

The Comparable interface has only one method. In fact, this is the entire interface:

```java
public interface Comparable<T> {
    int compareTo(T o);
}
```

The generic T lets you implement this method and specify the type of your object. This lets you avoid a cast when implementing compareTo(). Any object can be Comparable. For example, we have a bunch of ducks and want to sort them by name. First, we update the class declaration to inherit Comparable<Duck>, and then we implement the compareTo() method.

```java
import java.util.*;
public class Duck implements Comparable<Duck> {
    private String name;
    public Duck(String name) {
        this.name = name;
    }
```

```
    public String toString() { // use readable output
        return name;
    }
    public int compareTo(Duck d) {
        return name.compareTo(d.name); // sorts ascendingly by name
    }
    public static void main(String[] args) {
        var ducks = new ArrayList<Duck>();
        ducks.add(new Duck("Quack"));
        ducks.add(new Duck("Puddles"));
        Collections.sort(ducks);    // sort by name
        System.out.println(ducks); // [Puddles, Quack]
}}
```

Without implementing that interface, all we have is a method named compareTo(), but it wouldn't be a Comparable object. We could also implement Comparable<Object> or some other class for T, but this wouldn't be as useful for sorting a group of Duck objects with each other.

 The Duck class overrides the toString() method from Object, which we described in Chapter 1. This override provides useful output when printing out ducks. Without this override, the output would be something like [Duck@70dea4e, Duck@5c647e05]—hardly useful in seeing which duck's name comes first.

Finally, the Duck class implements compareTo(). Since Duck is comparing objects of type String and the String class already has a compareTo() method, it can just delegate.

We still need to know what the compareTo() method returns so that we can write our own. There are three rules to know.

- The number 0 is returned when the current object is equivalent to the argument to compareTo().

- A negative number (less than 0) is returned when the current object is smaller than the argument to compareTo().

- A positive number (greater than 0) is returned when the current object is larger than the argument to compareTo().

Let's look at an implementation of compareTo() that compares numbers instead of String objects.

```
1:  public class Animal implements Comparable<Animal> {
2:      private int id;
3:      public int compareTo(Animal a) {
4:          return id - a.id; // sorts ascending by id
```

```
5:      }
6:      public static void main(String[] args) {
7:          var a1 = new Animal();
8:          var a2 = new Animal();
9:          a1.id = 5;
10:         a2.id = 7;
11:         System.out.println(a1.compareTo(a2)); // -2
12:         System.out.println(a1.compareTo(a1)); // 0
13:         System.out.println(a2.compareTo(a1)); // 2
14:     } }
```

Lines 7 and 8 create two Animal objects. Lines 9 and 10 set their id values. This is not a good way to set instance variables. It would be better to use a constructor or setter method. Since the exam shows nontraditional code to make sure that you understand the rules, we throw in some non-traditional code as well.

Lines 3-5 show one way to compare two int values. We could have used Integer.compare(id, a.id) instead. Be sure to be able to recognize both approaches.

Remember that id - a.id sorts in ascending order, and a.id - id sorts in descending order.

Lines 11 through 13 confirm that we've implemented compareTo() correctly. Line 11 compares a smaller id to a larger one, and therefore it prints a negative number. Line 12 compares animals with the same id, and therefore it prints 0. Line 13 compares a larger id to a smaller one, and therefore it returns a positive number.

Casting the *compareTo()* Argument

When dealing with legacy code or code that does not use generics, the compareTo() method requires a cast since it is passed an Object.

```
public class LegacyDuck implements Comparable {
    private String name;
    public int compareTo(Object obj) {
        LegacyDuck d = (LegacyDuck) obj; // cast because no generics
        return name.compareTo(d.name);
    }
}
```

Since we don't specify a generic type for Comparable, Java assumes that we want an Object, which means that we have to cast to LegacyDuck before accessing instance variables on it.

Checking for *null*

When working with Comparable and Comparator in this chapter, we tend to assume the data has values, but this is not always the case. When writing your own compare methods, you should check the data before comparing it if is not validated ahead of time.

```java
public class MissingDuck implements Comparable<MissingDuck> {
   private String name;
   public int compareTo(MissingDuck quack) {
      if (quack == null)
         throw new IllegalArgumentException("Poorly formed duck!");
      if (this.name == null && quack.name == null)
         return 0;
      else if (this.name == null) return -1;
      else if (quack.name == null) return 1;
      else return name.compareTo(quack.name);
   }
}
```

This method throws an exception if it is passed a null MissingDuck object. What about the ordering? If the name of a duck is null, then it's sorted first.

Keeping *compareTo()* and *equals()* Consistent

If you write a class that implements Comparable, you introduce new business logic for determining equality. The compareTo() method returns 0 if two objects are equal, while your equals() method returns true if two objects are equal. A *natural ordering* that uses compareTo() is said to be *consistent with equals* if, and only if, x.equals(y) is true whenever x.compareTo(y) equals 0.

Similarly, x.equals(y) must be false whenever x.compareTo(y) is not 0. You are strongly encouraged to make your Comparable classes consistent with equals because not all collection classes behave predictably if the compareTo() and equals() methods are not consistent.

For example, the following Product class defines a compareTo() method that is not consistent with equals:

```java
public class Product implements Comparable<Product> {
   private int id;
   private String name;

   public int hashCode() { return id; }
   public boolean equals(Object obj) {
      if(!(obj instanceof Product)) return false;
      var other = (Product) obj;
      return this.id == other.id;
   }
```

```
      public int compareTo(Product obj) {
         return this.name.compareTo(obj.name);
   } }
```

You might be sorting Product objects by name, but names are not unique. Therefore, the return value of compareTo() might not be 0 when comparing two equal Product objects, so this compareTo() method is not consistent with equals. One way to fix that is to use a Comparator to define the sort elsewhere.

Now that you know how to implement Comparable objects, you get to look at Comparators and focus on the differences.

Comparing Data with a *Comparator*

Sometimes you want to sort an object that did not implement Comparable, or you want to sort objects in different ways at different times. Suppose that we add weight to our Duck class. We now have the following:

```
1:   import java.util.ArrayList;
2:   import java.util.Collections;
3:   import java.util.Comparator;
4:
5:   public class Duck implements Comparable<Duck> {
6:       private String name;
7:       private int weight;
8:
9:       // Assume getters/setters/constructors provided
10:
11:      public String toString() { return name; }
12:
13:      public int compareTo(Duck d) {
14:          return name.compareTo(d.name);
15:      }
16:
17:      public static void main(String[] args) {
18:          Comparator<Duck> byWeight = new Comparator<Duck>() {
19:              public int compare(Duck d1, Duck d2) {
20:                  return d1.getWeight()-d2.getWeight();
21:              }
22:          };
23:          var ducks = new ArrayList<Duck>();
24:          ducks.add(new Duck("Quack", 7));
25:          ducks.add(new Duck("Puddles", 10));
```

```
26:        Collections.sort(ducks);
27:        System.out.println(ducks); // [Puddles, Quack]
28:        Collections.sort(ducks, byWeight);
29:        System.out.println(ducks); // [Quack, Puddles]
30:    }
31: }
```

First, notice that this program imports java.util.Comparator on line 3. We don't always show imports since you can assume they are present if not shown. Here, we do show the import to call attention to the fact that Comparable and Comparator are in different packages, namely, java.lang versus java.util, respectively. That means Comparable can be used without an import statement, while Comparator cannot.

The Duck class itself can define only one compareTo() method. In this case, name was chosen. If we want to sort by something else, we have to define that sort order outside the compareTo() method using a separate class or lambda expression.

Lines 18-22 of the main() method show how to define a Comparator using an inner class. On lines 26-29, we sort without the comparator and then with the comparator to see the difference in output.

Comparator is a functional interface since there is only one abstract method to implement. This means that we can rewrite the comparator on lines 18-22 using a lambda expression, as shown here:

```
Comparator<Duck> byWeight = (d1, d2) -> d1.getWeight()-d2.getWeight();
```

Alternatively, we can use a method reference and a helper method to specify we want to sort by weight.

```
Comparator<Duck> byWeight = Comparator.comparing(Duck::getWeight);
```

In this example, Comparator.comparing() is a static interface method that creates a Comparator given a lambda expression or method reference. Convenient, isn't it?

Is *Comparable* a Functional Interface?

We said that Comparator is a functional interface because it has a single abstract method. Comparable is also a functional interface since it also has a single abstract method. However, using a lambda for Comparable would be silly. The point of Comparable is to implement it inside the object being compared.

Comparing *Comparable* and *Comparator*

There are a good number of differences between Comparable and Comparator. We've listed them for you in Table 3.11.

TABLE 3.11 Comparison of Comparable and Comparator

Difference	Comparable	Comparator
Package name	`java.lang`	`java.util`
Interface must be implemented by class comparing?	Yes	No
Method name in interface	`compareTo()`	`compare()`
Number of parameters	1	2
Common to declare using a lambda	No	Yes

Memorize this table—really. The exam will try to trick you by mixing up the two and seeing if you can catch it. Do you see why this one doesn't compile?

```
var byWeight = new Comparator<Duck>() { // DOES NOT COMPILE
   public int compareTo(Duck d1, Duck d2) {
      return d1.getWeight()-d2.getWeight();
   }
};
```

The method name is wrong. A `Comparator` must implement a method named `compare()`. Pay special attention to method names and the number of parameters when you see `Comparator` and `Comparable` in questions.

Comparing Multiple Fields

When writing a `Comparator` that compares multiple instance variables, the code gets a little messy. Suppose that we have a `Squirrel` class, as shown here:

```
public class Squirrel {
   private int weight;
   private String species;
   // Assume getters/setters/constructors provided
}
```

We want to write a `Comparator` to sort by species name. If two squirrels are from the same species, we want to sort the one that weighs the least first. We could do this with code that looks like this:

```
public class MultiFieldComparator implements Comparator<Squirrel> {
   public int compare(Squirrel s1, Squirrel s2) {
      int result = s1.getSpecies().compareTo(s2.getSpecies());
```

```
    if (result != 0) return result;
    return s1.getWeight()-s2.getWeight();
}}
```

This works assuming no species names are null. It checks one field. If they don't match, we are finished sorting. If they do match, it looks at the next field. This isn't that easy to read, though. It is also easy to get wrong. Changing != to == breaks the sort completely.

Alternatively, we can use method references and build the comparator. This code represents logic for the same comparison.

```
Comparator<Squirrel> c = Comparator.comparing(Squirrel::getSpecies)
    .thenComparingInt(Squirrel::getWeight);
```

This time, we chain the methods. First, we create a comparator on species ascending. Then, if there is a tie, we sort by weight. We can also sort in descending order. Some methods on Comparator, like thenComparingInt(), are default methods. As discussed in Chapter 1, default methods were introduced in Java 8 as a way of expanding APIs.

Suppose we want to sort in descending order by species.

```
var c = Comparator.comparing(Squirrel::getSpecies).reversed();
```

Table 3.12 shows the helper methods you should know for building Comparator. We've omitted the parameter types to keep you focused on the methods. They use many of the functional interfaces you'll be learning about in the next chapter.

TABLE 3.12   Helper static methods for building a Comparator

Method	Description
comparing(function)	Compare by the results of a function that returns any Object (or object autoboxed into an Object).
comparingDouble(function)	Compare by the results of a function that returns a double.
comparingInt(function)	Compare by the results of a function that returns an int.
comparingLong(function)	Compare by the results of a function that returns a long.
naturalOrder()	Sort using the order specified by the Comparable implementation on the object itself.
reverseOrder()	Sort using the reverse of the order specified by the Comparable implementation on the object itself.

Table 3.13 shows the methods that you can chain to a Comparator to further specify its behavior.

TABLE 3.13   Helper default methods for building a Comparator

Method	Description
reversed()	Reverse the order of the chained Comparator.
thenComparing(function)	If the previous Comparator returns 0, use this comparator that returns an Object or can be autoboxed into one.
thenComparingDouble(function)	If the previous Comparator returns 0, use this comparator that returns a double. Otherwise, return the value from the previous Comparator.
thenComparingInt(function)	If the previous Comparator returns 0, use this comparator that returns an int. Otherwise, return the value from the previous Comparator.
thenComparingLong(function)	If the previous Comparator returns 0, use this comparator that returns a long. Otherwise, return the value from the previous Comparator.

You've probably noticed by now that we often ignore null values in checking equality and comparing objects. This works fine for the exam. In the real world, though, things aren't so neat. You will have to decide how to handle null values or prevent them from being in your object.

Sorting and Searching

Now that you've learned all about Comparable and Comparator, we can finally do something useful with it, like sorting. The Collections.sort() method uses the compareTo() method to sort. It expects the objects to be sorted to be Comparable.

```
2: public class SortRabbits {
3:    static class Rabbit{ int id; }
4:    public static void main(String[] args) {
5:       List<Rabbit> rabbits = new ArrayList<>();
6:       rabbits.add(new Rabbit());
7:       Collections.sort(rabbits); // DOES NOT COMPILE
8:    } }
```

Java knows that the Rabbit class is not Comparable. It knows sorting will fail, so it doesn't even let the code compile. You can fix this by passing a Comparator to sort(). Remember that a Comparator is useful when you want to specify sort order without using a compareTo() method.

```
2: public class SortRabbits {
3:     static class Rabbit{ int id; }
4:     public static void main(String[] args) {
5:         List<Rabbit> rabbits = new ArrayList<>();
6:         rabbits.add(new Rabbit());
7:         Comparator<Rabbit> c = (r1, r2) -> r1.id - r2.id;
8:         Collections.sort(rabbits, c);
9:     } }
```

The sort() and binarySearch() methods allow you to pass in a Comparator object when you don't want to use the natural order.

Reviewing *binarySearch()*

The binarySearch() method requires a sorted List.

```
11: List<Integer> list = Arrays.asList(6,9,1,8);
12: Collections.sort(list); // [1, 6, 8, 9]
13: System.out.println(Collections.binarySearch(list, 6)); // 1
14: System.out.println(Collections.binarySearch(list, 3)); // -2
```

Line 12 sorts the List so we can call binary search properly. Line 13 prints the index at which a match is found. Line 14 prints one less than the negated index of where the requested value would need to be inserted. The number 3 would need to be inserted at index 1 (after the number 1 but before the number 6). Negating that gives us −1, and subtracting 1 gives us −2.

There is a trick in working with binarySearch(). What do you think the following outputs?

```
3: var names = Arrays.asList("Fluffy", "Hoppy");
4: Comparator<String> c = Comparator.reverseOrder();
5: var index = Collections.binarySearch(names, "Hoppy", c);
6: System.out.println(index);
```

The correct answer is −1. Before you panic, you don't need to know that the answer is −1. You do need to know that the answer is not defined. Line 3 creates a list, [Fluffy, Hoppy]. This list happens to be sorted in ascending order. Line 4 creates a Comparator that reverses the natural order. Line 5 requests a binary search in descending order. Since the list is in ascending order, we don't meet the precondition for doing a search.

Earlier in the chapter, we talked about collections that require classes to implement Comparable. Unlike sorting, they don't check that you have actually implemented Comparable at compile time.

Going back to our Rabbit that does not implement Comparable, we try to add it to a TreeSet.

```
2:  public class UseTreeSet {
3:      static class Rabbit{ int id; }
4:      public static void main(String[] args) {
5:          Set<Duck> ducks = new TreeSet<>();
6:          ducks.add(new Duck("Puddles"));
7:
8:          Set<Rabbit> rabbits = new TreeSet<>();
9:          rabbits.add(new Rabbit());  // ClassCastException
10: } }
```

Line 6 is fine. Duck does implement Comparable. TreeSet is able to sort it into the proper position in the set. Line 9 is a problem. When TreeSet tries to sort it, Java discovers the fact that Rabbit does not implement Comparable. Java throws an exception that looks like this:

```
Exception in thread "main" java.lang.ClassCastException:
   class Duck cannot be cast to class java.lang.Comparable
```

It may seem weird for this exception to be thrown when the first object is added to the set. After all, there is nothing to compare yet. Java works this way for consistency.

Just like searching and sorting, you can tell collections that require sorting that you want to use a specific Comparator, for example:

```
8: Set<Rabbit> rabbits = new TreeSet<>((r1, r2) -> r1.id-r2.id);
9: rabbits.add(new Rabbit());
```

Now Java knows that you want to sort by id and all is well. Comparators are helpful objects. They let you separate sort order from the object to be sorted. Notice that line 9 in both of the previous examples is the same. It's the declaration of the TreeSet that has changed.

Working with Generics

We conclude this chapter with one of the most useful, and at times most confusing, feature in the Java language: generics. Why do we need generics? Well, remember when we said that we had to hope the caller didn't put something in the list that we didn't expect? The following does just that:

```
14: static void printNames(List list) {
15:     for (int i = 0; i < list.size(); i++) {
16:         String name = (String) list.get(i); // ClassCastException
17:         System.out.println(name);
18:     }
19: }
20: public static void main(String[] args) {
21:     List names = new ArrayList();
22:     names.add(new StringBuilder("Webby"));
23:     printNames(names);
24: }
```

This code throws a `ClassCastException`. Line 22 adds a `StringBuilder` to `list`. This is legal because a nongeneric list can contain anything. However, line 16 is written to expect a specific class to be in there. It casts to a `String`, reflecting this assumption. Since the assumption is incorrect, the code throws a `ClassCastException` that `java.lang.StringBuilder` cannot be cast to `java.lang.String`.

Generics fix this by allowing you to write and use parameterized types. You specify that you want an `ArrayList` of `String` objects. Now the compiler has enough information to prevent you from causing this problem in the first place.

```
List<String> names = new ArrayList<String>();
names.add(new StringBuilder("Webby")); // DOES NOT COMPILE
```

Getting a compiler error is good. You'll know right away that something is wrong rather than hoping to discover it later.

Generic Classes

You can introduce generics into your own classes. The syntax for introducing a generic is to declare a *formal type parameter* in angle brackets. For example, the following class named `Crate` has a generic type variable declared after the name of the class.

```
public class Crate<T> {
    private T contents;
    public T emptyCrate() {
        return contents;
    }
    public void packCrate(T contents) {
        this.contents = contents;
    }
}
```

The generic type T is available anywhere within the Crate class. When you instantiate the class, you tell the compiler what T should be for that particular instance.

Naming Conventions for Generics

A type parameter can be named anything you want. The convention is to use single uppercase letters to make it obvious that they aren't real class names. The following are common letters to use:

- E for an element

- K for a map key

- V for a map value

- N for a number

- T for a generic data type

- S, U, V, and so forth for multiple generic types

For example, suppose an Elephant class exists, and we are moving our elephant to a new and larger enclosure in our zoo. (The San Diego Zoo did this in 2009. It was interesting seeing the large metal crate.)

```
Elephant elephant = new Elephant();
Crate<Elephant> crateForElephant = new Crate<>();
crateForElephant.packCrate(elephant);
Elephant inNewHome = crateForElephant.emptyCrate();
```

To be fair, we didn't pack the crate so much as the elephant walked into it. However, you can see that the Crate class is able to deal with an Elephant without knowing anything about it.

This probably doesn't seem particularly impressive yet. We could have just typed in Elephant instead of T when coding Crate. What if we wanted to create a Crate for another animal?

```
Crate<Zebra> crateForZebra = new Crate<>();
```

Now we couldn't have simply hard-coded Elephant in the Crate class since a Zebra is not an Elephant. However, we could have created an Animal superclass or interface and used that in Crate.

Generic classes become useful when the classes used as the type parameter can have absolutely nothing to do with each other. For example, we need to ship our 120-pound robot to another city.

```
Robot joeBot = new Robot();
Crate<Robot> robotCrate = new Crate<>();
robotCrate.packCrate(joeBot);
```

```
// ship to St. Louis
Robot atDestination = robotCrate.emptyCrate();
```

Now it is starting to get interesting. The Crate class works with any type of class. Before generics, we would have needed Crate to use the Object class for its instance variable, which would have put the burden on the caller of needing to cast the object it receives on emptying the crate.

In addition to Crate not needing to know about the objects that go into it, those objects don't need to know about Crate either. We aren't requiring the objects to implement an interface named Crateable or the like. A class can be put in the Crate without any changes at all.

Don't worry if you can't think of a use for generic classes of your own. Unless you are writing a library for others to reuse, generics hardly show up in the class definitions you write. They do show up frequently in the code you call, such as the Java Collections Framework.

Generic classes aren't limited to having a single type parameter. This class shows two generic parameters.

```
public class SizeLimitedCrate<T, U> {
   private T contents;
   private U sizeLimit;
   public SizeLimitedCrate(T contents, U sizeLimit) {
      this.contents = contents;
      this.sizeLimit = sizeLimit;
   } }
```

T represents the type that we are putting in the crate. U represents the unit that we are using to measure the maximum size for the crate. To use this generic class, we can write the following:

```
Elephant elephant = new Elephant();
Integer numPounds = 15_000;
SizeLimitedCrate<Elephant, Integer> c1
   = new SizeLimiteCrate<>(elephant, numPounds);
```

Here we specify that the type is Elephant, and the unit is Integer. We also throw in a reminder that numeric literals can contain underscores.

What Is Type Erasure?

Specifying a generic type allows the compiler to enforce proper use of the generic type. For example, specifying the generic type of Crate as Robot is like replacing the T in the Crate class with Robot. However, this is just for compile time.

Behind the scenes, the compiler replaces all references to T in Crate with Object. In other words, after the code compiles, your generics are actually just Object types. The Crate class looks like the following at runtime:

```
public class Crate {
    private Object contents;
    public Object emptyCrate() {
        return contents;
    }
    public void packCrate(Object contents) {
        this.contents = contents;
    }
}
```

This means there is only one class file. There aren't different copies for different parameterized types. (Some other languages work that way.)

This process of removing the generics syntax from your code is referred to as *type erasure*. Type erasure allows your code to be compatible with older versions of Java that do not contain generics.

The compiler adds the relevant casts for your code to work with this type of erased class. For example, you type the following:

```
Robot r = crate.emptyCrate();
```

The compiler turns it into the following:

```
Robot r = (Robot) crate.emptyCrate();
```

Generic Interfaces

Just like a class, an interface can declare a formal type parameter. For example, the following Shippable interface uses a generic type as the argument to its ship() method:

```
public interface Shippable<T> {
    void ship(T t);
}
```

There are three ways a class can approach implementing this interface. The first is to specify the generic type in the class. The following concrete class says that it deals only with robots. This lets it declare the ship() method with a Robot parameter.

```
class ShippableRobotCrate implements Shippable<Robot> {
    public void ship(Robot t) { }
}
```

The next way is to create a generic class. The following concrete class allows the caller to specify the type of the generic:

```
class ShippableAbstractCrate<U> implements Shippable<U> {
   public void ship(U t) { }
}
```

In this example, the type parameter could have been named anything, including T. We used U in the example so that it isn't confusing as to what T refers to. The exam won't mind trying to confuse you by using the same type parameter name.

Raw Types

The final way is to not use generics at all. This is the old way of writing code. It generates a compiler warning about Shippable being a *raw type*, but it does compile. Here the ship() method has an Object parameter since the generic type is not defined:

```
class ShippableCrate implements Shippable {
   public void ship(Object t) { }
}
```

 Real World Scenario

What You Can't Do with Generic Types

There are some limitations on what you can do with a generic type. These aren't on the exam, but it will be helpful to refer to this scenario when you are writing practice programs and run into one of these situations.

Most of the limitations are due to type erasure. Oracle refers to types whose information is fully available at runtime as *reifiable*. Reifiable types can do anything that Java allows. Nonreifiable types have some limitations.

Here are the things that you can't do with generics (and by "can't," we mean without resorting to contortions like passing in a class object):

- **Calling a constructor:** Writing new T() is not allowed because at runtime it would be new Object().

- **Creating an array of that generic type:** This one is the most annoying, but it makes sense because you'd be creating an array of Object values.

- **Calling instanceof:** This is not allowed because at runtime List<Integer> and List<String> look the same to Java thanks to type erasure.

- **Using a primitive type as a generic type parameter**: This isn't a big deal because you can use the wrapper class instead. If you want a type of `int`, just use `Integer`.

- **Creating a static variable as a generic type parameter**: This is not allowed because the type is linked to the instance of the class.

Generic Methods

Up until this point, you've seen formal type parameters declared on the class or interface level. It is also possible to declare them on the method level. This is often useful for `static` methods since they aren't part of an instance that can declare the type. However, it is also allowed on non-`static` methods.

In this example, both methods use a generic parameter:

```
public class Handler {
   public static <T> void prepare(T t) {
      System.out.println("Preparing " + t);
   }
   public static <T> Crate<T> ship(T t) {
      System.out.println("Shipping " + t);
      return new Crate<T>();
   }
}
```

The method parameter is the generic type T. Before the return type, we declare the formal type parameter of <T>. In the `ship()` method, we show how you can use the generic parameter in the return type, Crate<T>, for the method.

Unless a method is obtaining the generic formal type parameter from the class/interface, it is specified immediately before the return type of the method. This can lead to some interesting-looking code!

```
2: public class More {
3:    public static <T> void sink(T t) { }
4:    public static <T> T identity(T t) { return t; }
5:    public static T noGood(T t) { return t; } // DOES NOT COMPILE
6: }
```

Line 3 shows the formal parameter type immediately before the return type of void. Line 4 shows the return type being the formal parameter type. It looks weird, but it is correct. Line 5 omits the formal parameter type, and therefore it does not compile.

 **Real World Scenario**

Optional Syntax for Invoking a Generic Method

You can call a generic method normally, and the compiler will try to figure out which one you want. Alternatively, you can specify the type explicitly to make it obvious what the type is.

```
Box.<String>ship("package");
Box.<String[]>ship(args);
```

As to whether this makes things clearer, it is up to you. You should at least be aware that this syntax exists.

When you have a method declare a generic parameter type, it is independent of the class generics. Take a look at this class that declares a generic T at both levels:

```
1: public class Crate<T> {
2:    public <T> T tricky(T t) {
3:       return t;
4:    }
5: }
```

See if you can figure out the type of T on lines 1 and 2 when we call the code as follows:

```
10: public static String createName() {
11:    Crate<Robot> crate = new Crate<>();
12:    return crate.tricky("bot");
13: }
```

Clearly, "T is for tricky." Let's see what is happening. On line 1, T is Robot because that is what gets referenced when constructing a Crate. On line 2, T is String because that is what is passed to the method. When you see code like this, take a deep breath and write down what is happening so you don't get confused.

Bounding Generic Types

By now, you might have noticed that generics don't seem particularly useful since they are treated as an Object and therefore don't have many methods available. Bounded wildcards solve this by restricting what types can be used in a wildcard. A *bounded parameter type* is a generic type that specifies a bound for the generic. Be warned that this is the hardest section in the chapter, so don't feel bad if you have to read it more than once.

A *wildcard generic type* is an unknown generic type represented with a question mark (?). You can use generic wildcards in three ways, as shown in Table 3.14. This section looks at each of these three wildcard types.

TABLE 3.14   Types of bounds

Type of bound	Syntax	Example
Unbounded wildcard	?	List<?> a = new ArrayList<String>();
Wildcard with an upper bound	? extends type	List<? extends Exception> a = new ArrayList<RuntimeException>();
Wildcard with a lower bound	? super type	List<? super Exception> a = new ArrayList<Object>();

Unbounded Wildcards

An unbounded wildcard represents any data type. You use ? when you want to specify that any type is okay with you. Let's suppose that we want to write a method that looks through a list of any type.

```
public static void printList(List<Object> list) {
for (Object x: list)
   System.out.println(x);
}
public static void main(String[] args) {
   List<String> keywords = new ArrayList<>();
   keywords.add("java");
   printList(keywords); // DOES NOT COMPILE
}
```

Wait. What's wrong? A String is a subclass of an Object. This is true. However, List<String> cannot be assigned to List<Object>. We know, it doesn't sound logical. Java is trying to protect us from ourselves with this one. Imagine if we could write code like this:

```
4: List<Integer> numbers = new ArrayList<>();
5: numbers.add(new Integer(42));
6: List<Object> objects = numbers; // DOES NOT COMPILE
7: objects.add("forty two");
8: System.out.println(numbers.get(1));
```

On line 4, the compiler promises us that only Integer objects will appear in numbers. If line 6 were to have compiled, line 7 would break that promise by putting a String in there since numbers and objects are references to the same object. Good thing that the compiler prevents this.

Going back to printing a list, we cannot assign a List<String> to a List<Object>. That's fine; we don't really need a List<Object>. What we really need is a List of "whatever." That's what List<?> is. The following code does what we expect:

```
public static void printList(List<?> list) {
for (Object x: list)
   System.out.println(x);
}
public static void main(String[] args) {
   List<String> keywords = new ArrayList<>();
   keywords.add("java");
   printList(keywords);
}
```

The printList() method takes any type of list as a parameter. The keywords variable is of type List<String>. We have a match! List<String> is a list of anything. "Anything" just happens to be a String here.

Finally, let's look at the impact of var. Do you think these two statements are equivalent?

```
List<?> x1 = new ArrayList<>();
var x2 = new ArrayList<>();
```

They are not. There are two key differences. First, x1 is of type List, while x2 is of type ArrayList. Additionally, we can only assign x2 to a List<Object>. These two variables do have one thing in common. Both return type Object when calling the get() method.

Upper-Bounded Wildcards

Let's try to write a method that adds up the total of a list of numbers. We've established that a generic type can't just use a subclass.

```
ArrayList<Number> list = new ArrayList<Integer>(); // DOES NOT COMPILE
```

Instead, we need to use a wildcard.

```
List<? extends Number> list = new ArrayList<Integer>();
```

The upper-bounded wildcard says that any class that extends Number or Number itself can be used as the formal parameter type:

```
public static long total(List<? extends Number> list) {
   long count = 0;
   for (Number number: list)
      count += number.longValue();
   return count;
}
```

Remember how we kept saying that type erasure makes Java think that a generic type is an Object? That is still happening here. Java converts the previous code to something equivalent to the following:

```
public static long total(List list) {
    long count = 0;
    for (Object obj: list) {
        Number number = (Number) obj;
        count += number.longValue();
    }
    return count;
}
```

Something interesting happens when we work with upper bounds or unbounded wildcards. The list becomes logically immutable and therefore cannot be modified. Technically, you can remove elements from the list, but the exam won't ask about this.

```
2: static class Sparrow extends Bird { }
3: static class Bird { }
4:
5: public static void main(String[] args) {
6:     List<? extends Bird> birds = new ArrayList<Bird>();
7:     birds.add(new Sparrow()); // DOES NOT COMPILE
8:     birds.add(new Bird());    // DOES NOT COMPILE
9: }
```

The problem stems from the fact that Java doesn't know what type List<? extends Bird> really is. It could be List<Bird> or List<Sparrow> or some other generic type that hasn't even been written yet. Line 7 doesn't compile because we can't add a Sparrow to List<? extends Bird>, and line 8 doesn't compile because we can't add a Bird to List<Sparrow>. From Java's point of view, both scenarios are equally possible, so neither is allowed.

Now let's try an example with an interface. We have an interface and two classes that implement it.

```
interface Flyer { void fly(); }
class HangGlider implements Flyer { public void fly() {} }
class Goose implements Flyer { public void fly() {} }
```

We also have two methods that use it. One just lists the interface, and the other uses an upper bound.

```
private void anyFlyer(List<Flyer> flyer) {}
private void groupOfFlyers(List<? extends Flyer> flyer) {}
```

Note that we used the keyword extends rather than implements. Upper bounds are like anonymous classes in that they use extends regardless of whether we are working with a class or an interface.

You already learned that a variable of type List<Flyer> can be passed to either method. A variable of type List<Goose> can be passed only to the one with the upper bound. This shows one of the benefits of generics. Random flyers don't fly together. We want our groupOfFlyers() method to be called only with the same type. Geese fly together but don't fly with hang gliders.

Lower-Bounded Wildcards

Let's try to write a method that adds a string "quack" to two lists.

```
List<String> strings = new ArrayList<String>();
strings.add("tweet");

List<Object> objects = new ArrayList<Object>(strings);
addSound(strings);
addSound(objects);
```

The problem is that we want to pass a List<String> and a List<Object> to the same method. First, make sure that you understand why the first three examples in Table 3.15 do *not* solve this problem.

TABLE 3.15   Why we need a lower bound

public static void addSound(_____list) {list.add("quack");}	Method compiles	Can pass a List<String>	Can pass a List<Object>
List<?>	No (unbounded generics are immutable)	Yes	Yes
List<? extends Object>	No (upper-bounded generics are immutable)	Yes	Yes
List<Object>	Yes	No (with generics, must pass exact match)	Yes
List<? super String>	Yes	Yes	Yes

To solve this problem, we need to use a lower bound.

```java
public static void addSound(List<? super String> list) {
    list.add("quack");
}
```

With a lower bound, we are telling Java that the list will be a list of String objects or a list of some objects that are a superclass of String. Either way, it is safe to add a String to that list.

Just like generic classes, you probably won't use this in your code unless you are writing code for others to reuse. Even then it would be rare. But it's on the exam, so now is the time to learn it!

Understand Generic Supertypes

When you have subclasses and superclasses, lower bounds can get tricky.

```java
3: List<? super IOException> exceptions = new ArrayList<Exception>();
4: exceptions.add(new Exception()); // DOES NOT COMPILE
5: exceptions.add(new IOException());
6: exceptions.add(new FileNotFoundException());
```

Line 3 references a List that could be List<IOException> or List<Exception> or List<Object>. Line 4 does not compile because we could have a List<IOException> and an Exception object wouldn't fit in there.

Line 5 is fine. IOException can be added to any of those types. Line 6 is also fine. FileNotFoundException can also be added to any of those three types. This is tricky because FileNotFoundException is a subclass of IOException, and the keyword says super. What happens is that Java says, "Well, FileNotFoundException also happens to be an IOException, so everything is fine."

Putting It All Together

At this point, you know everything that you need to know to ace the exam questions on generics. It is possible to put these concepts together to write some *really* confusing code, which the exam likes to do.

This section is going to be difficult to read. It contains the hardest questions that you could possibly be asked about generics. The exam questions will probably be easier to read than these. We want you to encounter the really tough ones here so that you are ready for the exam. In other words, don't panic. Take it slow, and reread the code a few times. You'll get it.

Combining Generic Declarations

Let's try an example. First, we declare three classes that the example will use.

```
class A {}
class B extends A {}
class C extends B {}
```

Ready? Can you figure out why these do or don't compile? Also, try to figure out what they do.

```
6: List<?> list1 = new ArrayList<A>();
7: List<? extends A> list2 = new ArrayList<A>();
8: List<? super A> list3 = new ArrayList<A>();
```

Line 6 creates an `ArrayList` that can hold instances of class A. It is stored in a variable with an unbounded wildcard. Any generic type can be referenced from an unbounded wildcard, making this okay.

Line 7 tries to store a list in a variable declaration with an upper-bounded wildcard. This is okay. You can have `ArrayList<A>`, `ArrayList<B>`, or `ArrayList<C>` stored in that reference. Line 8 is also okay. This time, you have a lower-bounded wildcard. The lowest type you can reference is A. Since that is what you have, it compiles.

Did you get those right? Let's try a few more.

```
9:  List<? extends B> list4 = new ArrayList<A>(); // DOES NOT COMPILE
10: List<? super B> list5 = new ArrayList<A>();
11: List<?> list6 = new ArrayList<? extends A>(); // DOES NOT COMPILE
```

Line 9 has an upper-bounded wildcard that allows `ArrayList<B>` or `ArrayList<C>` to be referenced. Since you have `ArrayList<A>` that is trying to be referenced, the code does not compile. Line 10 has a lower-bounded wildcard, which allows a reference to `ArrayList<A>`, `ArrayList<B>`, or `ArrayList<Object>`.

Finally, line 11 allows a reference to any generic type since it is an unbounded wildcard. The problem is that you need to know what that type will be when instantiating the `ArrayList`. It wouldn't be useful anyway, because you can't add any elements to that `ArrayList`.

Passing Generic Arguments

Now on to the methods. Same question: try to figure out why they don't compile or what they do. We will present the methods one at a time because there is more to think about.

```
<T> T first(List<? extends T> list) {
   return list.get(0);
}
```

The first method, `first()`, is a perfectly normal use of generics. It uses a method-specific type parameter, T. It takes a parameter of `List<T>`, or some subclass of T, and it returns a single object of that T type. For example, you could call it with a `List<String>`

parameter and have it return a String. Or you could call it with a List<Number> parameter and have it return a Number. Or ... well, you get the idea.

Given that, you should be able to see what is wrong with this one:

```
<T> <? extends T> second(List<? extends T> list) { // DOES NOT COMPILE
  return list.get(0);
}
```

The next method, second(), does not compile because the return type isn't actually a type. You are writing the method. You know what type it is supposed to return. You don't get to specify this as a wildcard.

Now be careful—this one is extra tricky:

```
<B extends A> B third(List<B> list) {
  return new B(); // DOES NOT COMPILE
}
```

This method, third(), does not compile. <B extends A> says that you want to use B as a type parameter just for this method and that it needs to extend the A class. Coincidentally, B is also the name of a class. It isn't a coincidence. It's an evil trick. Within the scope of the method, B can represent class A, B, or C, because all extend the A class. Since B no longer refers to the B class in the method, you can't instantiate it.

After that, it would be nice to get something straightforward.

```
void fourth(List<? super B> list) {}
```

We finally get a method, fourth(), which is a normal use of generics. You can pass the types List<B>, List<A>, or List<Object>.

Finally, can you figure out why this example does not compile?

```
<X> void fifth(List<X super B> list) { // DOES NOT COMPILE
}
```

This last method, fifth(), does not compile because it tries to mix a method-specific type parameter with a wildcard. A wildcard must have a ? in it.

Phew. You made it through generics. That's the hardest topic in this chapter (and why we covered it last!). Remember that it's okay if you need to go over this material a few times to get your head around it.

Summary

A method reference is a compact syntax for writing lambdas that refer to methods. There are four types: static methods, instance methods on a particular object, instance methods on a parameter, and constructor references.

Each primitive class has a corresponding wrapper class. For example, `long`'s wrapper class is `Long`. Java can automatically convert between primitive and wrapper classes when needed. This is called autoboxing and unboxing. Java will use autoboxing only if it doesn't find a matching method signature with the primitive. For example, `remove(int n)` will be called rather than `remove(Object o)` when called with an `int`.

The diamond operator (`<>`) is used to tell Java that the generic type matches the declaration without specifying it again. The diamond operator can be used for local variables or instance variables as well as one-line declarations.

The Java Collections Framework includes four main types of data structures: lists, sets, queues, and maps. The `Collection` interface is the parent interface of `List`, `Set`, and `Queue`. The `Map` interface does not extend `Collection`. You need to recognize the following:

- **List**: An ordered collection of elements that allows duplicate entries
  - **ArrayList**: Standard resizable list
  - **LinkedList**: Can easily add/remove from beginning or end

- **Set**: Does not allow duplicates
  - **HashSet**: Uses `hashCode()` to find unordered elements
  - **TreeSet**: Sorted. Does not allow null values

- **Queue**: Orders elements for processing
  - **LinkedList**: Can easily add/remove from beginning or end

- **Map**: Maps unique keys to values
  - **HashMap**: Uses `hashCode()` to find keys
  - **TreeMap**: Sorted map. Does not allow null keys

The `Comparable` interface declares the `compareTo()` method. This method returns a negative number if the object is smaller than its argument, 0 if the two objects are equal, and a positive number otherwise. The `compareTo()` method is declared on the object that is being compared, and it takes one parameter. The `Comparator` interface defines the `compare()` method. A negative number is returned if the first argument is smaller, zero if they are equal, and a positive number otherwise. The `compare()` method can be declared in any code, and it takes two parameters. `Comparator` is often implemented using a lambda.

The `Arrays` and `Collections` classes have methods for `sort()` and `binarySearch()`. Both take an optional `Comparator` parameter. It is necessary to use the same sort order for both sorting and searching, so the result is not undefined.

Generics are type parameters for code. To create a class with a generic parameter, add `<T>` after the class name. You can use any name you want for the type parameter. Single uppercase letters are common choices.

Generics allow you to specify wildcards. `<?>` is an unbounded wildcard that means any type. `<? extends Object>` is an upper bound that means any type that is `Object` or extends it. `<? extends MyInterface>` means any type that implements `MyInterface`.

<? super Number> is a lower bound that means any type that is Number or a superclass. A compiler error results from code that attempts to add an item in a list with an unbounded or upper-bounded wildcard.

Exam Essentials

Translate method references to the "long form" lambda.   Be able to convert method references into regular lambda expressions and vice versa. For example, System.out::print and x -> System.out.print(x) are equivalent. Remember that the order of method parameters is inferred for both based on usage.

Use autoboxing and unboxing.   Autoboxing converts a primitive into an Object. For example, int is autoboxed into Integer. Unboxing converts an Object into a primitive. For example, Character is autoboxed into char.

Pick the correct type of collection from a description.   A List allows duplicates and orders the elements. A Set does not allow duplicates. A Queue orders its elements to facilitate retrievals. A Map maps keys to values. Be familiar with the differences of implementations of these interfaces.

Work with convenience methods.   The Collections Framework contains many methods such as contains(), forEach(), and removeIf() that you need to know for the exam. There are too many to list in this paragraph for review, so please do review the tables in this chapter.

Differentiate between Comparable and Comparator.   Classes that implement Comparable are said to have a natural ordering and implement the compareTo() method. A class is allowed to have only one natural ordering. A Comparator takes two objects in the compare() method. Different Comparators can have different sort orders. A Comparator is often implemented using a lambda such as (a, b) -> a.num - b.num.

Write code using the diamond operator.   The diamond operator (<>) is used to write more concise code. The type of the generic parameter is inferred from the surrounding code. For example, in List<String> c = new ArrayList<>(), the type of the diamond operator is inferred to be String.

Identify valid and invalid uses of generics and wildcards.   <T> represents a type parameter. Any name can be used, but a single uppercase letter is the convention. <?> is an unbounded wildcard. <? extends X> is an upper-bounded wildcard and applies to both classes and interfaces. <? super X> is a lower-bounded wildcard.

Review Questions

The answers to the chapter review questions can be found in Appendix B.

1. Suppose that you have a collection of products for sale in a database and you need to display those products. The products are not unique. Which of the following collections classes in the `java.util` package best suits your needs for this scenario?

    A. Arrays

    B. ArrayList

    C. HashMap

    D. HashSet

    E. LinkedList

2. Suppose that you need to work with a collection of elements that need to be sorted in their natural order, and each element has a unique text `id` that you want to use to store and retrieve the record. Which of the following collections classes in the `java.util` package best suits your needs for this scenario?

    A. ArrayList

    B. HashMap

    C. HashSet

    D. TreeMap

    E. TreeSet

    F. None of the above

3. Which of the following are true? (Choose all that apply.)

    ```
    12: List<?> q = List.of("mouse", "parrot");
    13: var v = List.of("mouse", "parrot");
    14:
    15: q.removeIf(String::isEmpty);
    16: q.removeIf(s -> s.length() == 4);
    17: v.removeIf(String::isEmpty);
    18: v.removeIf(s -> s.length() == 4);
    ```

    A. This code compiles and runs without error.

    B. Exactly one of these lines contains a compiler error.

    C. Exactly two of these lines contain a compiler error.

    D. Exactly three of these lines contain a compiler error.

    E. Exactly four of these lines contain a compiler error.

    F. If any lines with compiler errors are removed, this code runs without throwing an exception.

    G. If all lines with compiler errors are removed, this code throws an exception.

4. What is the result of the following statements?

```
3:   var greetings = new LinkedList<String>();
4:   greetings.offer("hello");
5:   greetings.offer("hi");
6:   greetings.offer("ola");
7:   greetings.pop();
8:   greetings.peek();
9:   while (greetings.peek() != null)
10:      System.out.print(greetings.pop());
```

   A. hello

   B. hellohi

   C. hellohiola

   D. hiola

   E. ola

   F. The code does not compile.

   G. An exception is thrown.

5. Which of these statements compile? (Choose all that apply.)

   A. HashSet<Number> hs = new HashSet<Integer>();

   B. HashSet<? super ClassCastException> set = new
       HashSet<Exception>();

   C. List<> list = new ArrayList<String>();

   D. List<Object> values = new HashSet<Object>();

   E. List<Object> objects = new ArrayList<? extends Object>();

   F. Map<String, ? extends Number> hm = new
       HashMap<String, Integer>();

6. What is the result of the following code?

```
1:   public class Hello<T> {
2:      T t;
3:      public Hello(T t) { this.t = t; }
4:      public String toString() { return t.toString(); }
5:      private <T> void println(T message) {
6:         System.out.print(t + "-" + message);
7:      }
8:      public static void main(String[] args) {
9:         new Hello<String>("hi").println(1);
10:        new Hello("hola").println(true);
11:   } }
```

A. hi followed by a runtime exception

B. hi-1hola-true

C. The first compiler error is on line 1.

D. The first compiler error is on line 4.

E. The first compiler error is on line 5.

F. The first compiler error is on line 9.

G. The first compiler error is on line 10.

7. Which of the following statements are true? (Choose all that apply.)

```
3:  var numbers = new HashSet<Number>();
4:  numbers.add(Integer.valueOf(86));
5:  numbers.add(75);
6:  numbers.add(Integer.valueOf(86));
7:  numbers.add(null);
8:  numbers.add(309L);
9:  Iterator iter = numbers.iterator();
10: while (iter.hasNext())
11:     System.out.print(iter.next());
```

A. The code compiles successfully.

B. The output is 8675null309.

C. The output is 867586null309.

D. The output is indeterminate.

E. There is a compiler error on line 3.

F. There is a compiler error on line 9.

G. An exception is thrown.

8. Which of the following can fill in the blank to print [7, 5, 3]? (Choose all that apply.)

```
3:  public class Platypus {
4:      String name;
5:      int beakLength;
6:
7:      // Assume getters/setters/constructors provided
8:
9:      public String toString() {return "" + beakLength;}
10:
11:     public static void main(String[] args) {
12:         Platypus p1 = new Platypus("Paula", 3);
13:         Platypus p2 = new Platypus("Peter", 5);
14:         Platypus p3 = new Platypus("Peter", 7);
```

```
15:
16:          List<Platypus> list = Arrays.asList(p1, p2, p3);
17:
18:          Collections.sort(list, Comparator.comparing_____);
19:
20:          System.out.println(list);
21:     }
22: }
```

A.

```
(Platypus::getBeakLength)
```

B.

```
(Platypus::getBeakLength).reversed()
```

C.

```
(Platypus::getName)
    .thenComparing(Platypus::getBeakLength)
```

D.

```
(Platypus::getName)
    .thenComparing(
        Comparator.comparing(Platypus::getBeakLength)
    .reversed())
```

E.

```
(Platypus::getName)
    .thenComparingNumber(Platypus::getBeakLength)
    .reversed()
```

F.

```
(Platypus::getName)
    .thenComparingInt(Platypus::getBeakLength)
    .reversed()
```

G. None of the above

9. Which of the answer choices are valid given the following code? (Choose all that apply.)

```
Map<String, Double> map = new HashMap<>();
```

A. `map.add("pi", 3.14159);`

B. `map.add("e", 2L);`

C. `map.add("log(1)", new Double(0.0));`

D. `map.add('x', new Double(123.4));`

E. None of the above

10. What is the result of the following program?

```
3:   public class MyComparator implements Comparator<String> {
4:       public int compare(String a, String b) {
5:           return b.toLowerCase().compareTo(a.toLowerCase());
6:       }
7:       public static void main(String[] args) {
8:           String[] values = { "123", "Abb", "aab" };
9:           Arrays.sort(values, new MyComparator());
10:          for (var s: values)
11:              System.out.print(s + " ");
12:      }
13: }
```

   A. Abb aab 123
   B. aab Abb 123
   C. 123 Abb aab
   D. 123 aab Abb
   E. The code does not compile.
   F. A runtime exception is thrown.

11. What is the result of the following code?

```
3: var map = new HashMap<Integer, Integer>(10);
4: for (int i = 1; i <= 10; i++) {
5:     map.put(i, i * i);
6: }
7: System.out.println(map.get(4));
```

   A. 16
   B. 25
   C. Compiler error on line 3.
   D. Compiler error on line 5.
   E. Compiler error on line 7.
   F. A runtime exception is thrown.

12. Which of these statements can fill in the blank so that the Helper class compiles successfully? (Choose all that apply.)

```
2:   public class Helper {
3:       public static <U extends Exception>
4:           void printException(U u) {
5:
```

```
6:          System.out.println(u.getMessage());
7:       }
8:       public static void main(String[] args) {
9:          Helper._____ ;
10:     } }
```

A. printException(new FileNotFoundException("A"))

B. printException(new Exception("B"))

C. <Throwable>printException(new Exception("C"))

D. <NullPointerException>printException
     (new NullPointerException ("D"))

E. printException(new Throwable("E"))

13. Which of these statements can fill in the blank so that the Wildcard class compiles successfully? (Choose all that apply.)

```
3:  public class Wildcard {
4:      public void showSize(List<?> list) {
5:          System.out.println(list.size());
6:      }
7:      public static void main(String[] args) {
8:          Wildcard card = new Wildcard();
9:          _____;
10:         card.showSize(list);
11:     } }
```

A. List<?> list = new HashSet <String>()

B. ArrayList<? super Date> list = new ArrayList<Date>()

C. List<?> list = new ArrayList<?>()

D. List<Exception> list = new LinkedList<java.io.IOException>()

E. ArrayList <? extends Number> list = new ArrayList <Integer>()

F. None of the above

14. What is the result of the following program?

```
3:  public class Sorted
4:      implements Comparable<Sorted>, Comparator<Sorted> {
5:
6:      private int num;
7:      private String text;
8:
9:      // Assume getters/setters/constructors provided
10:
```

```
11:    public String toString() { return "" + num; }
12:    public int compareTo(Sorted s) {
13:        return text.compareTo(s.text);
14:    }
15:    public int compare(Sorted s1, Sorted s2) {
16:        return s1.num - s2.num;
17:    }
18:    public static void main(String[] args) {
19:        var s1 = new Sorted(88, "a");
20:        var s2 = new Sorted(55, "b");
21:        var t1 = new TreeSet<Sorted>();
22:        t1.add(s1); t1.add(s2);
23:        var t2 = new TreeSet<Sorted>(s1);
24:        t2.add(s1); t2.add(s2);
25:        System.out.println(t1 + " " + t2);
26:    } }
```

A. [55, 88] [55, 88]

B. [55, 88] [88, 55]

C. [88, 55] [55, 88]

D. [88, 55] [88, 55]

E. The code does not compile.

F. A runtime exception is thrown.

15. What is the result of the following code? (Choose all that apply.)

```
Comparator<Integer> c1 = (o1, o2) -> o2 - o1;
Comparator<Integer> c2 = Comparator.naturalOrder();
Comparator<Integer> c3 = Comparator.reverseOrder();

var list = Arrays.asList(5, 4, 7, 2);
Collections.sort(list, _____);
System.out.println(Collections.binarySearch(list, 2));
```

A. One or more of the comparators can fill in the blank so that the code prints 0.

B. One or more of the comparators can fill in the blank so that the code prints 1.

C. One or more of the comparators can fill in the blank so that the code prints 2.

D. The result is undefined regardless of which comparator is used.

E. A runtime exception is thrown regardless of which comparator is used.

F. The code does not compile.

16. Which of the following statements are true? (Choose all that apply.)

A. Comparable is in the java.util package.

B. Comparator is in the java.util package.

C. compare() is in the Comparable interface.

D. compare() is in the Comparator interface.

E. compare() takes one method parameter.

F. compare() takes two method parameters.

17. Which options can fill in the blanks to make this code compile? (Choose all that apply.)

```
1: public class Generic_____  {
2:    public static void main(String[] args) {
3:        Generic<String> g = new Generic_____();
4:        Generic<Object> g2 = new Generic();
5:    }
6: }
```

A. On line 1, fill in with <>.

B. On line 1, fill in with <T>.

C. On line 1, fill in with <?>.

D. On line 3, fill in with <>.

E. On line 3, fill in with <T>.

F. On line 3, fill in with <?>.

18. Which of the following lines can be inserted to make the code compile? (Choose all that apply.)

```
class W {}
class X extends W {}
class Y extends X {}
class Z<Y> {
// INSERT CODE HERE
}
```

A. W w1 = new W();

B. W w2 = new X();

C. W w3 = new Y();

D. Y y1 = new W();

E. Y y2 = new X();

F. Y y1 = new Y();

19. Which options are true of the following code? (Choose all that apply.)

```
3: _____<Integer> q = new LinkedList<>();
4: q.add(10);
5: q.add(12);
6: q.remove(1);
7: System.out.print(q);
```

A. If we fill in the blank with List, the output is [10].

B. If we fill in the blank with List, the output is [10, 12].

C. If we fill in the blank with Queue, the output is [10].

D. If we fill in the blank with Queue, the output is [10, 12].

E. The code does not compile in either scenario.

F. A runtime exception is thrown.

20. What is the result of the following code?

```
4: Map m = new HashMap();
5: m.put(123, "456");
6: m.put("abc", "def");
7: System.out.println(m.contains("123"));
```

A. false

B. true

C. Compiler error on line 4

D. Compiler error on line 5

E. Compiler error on line 7

F. A runtime exception is thrown.

21. What is the result of the following code? (Choose all that apply.)

```
48: var map = Map.of(1,2, 3, 6);
49: var list = List.copyOf(map.entrySet());
50:
51: List<Integer> one = List.of(8, 16, 2);
52: var copy = List.copyOf(one);
53: var copyOfCopy = List.copyOf(copy);
54: var thirdCopy = new ArrayList<>(copyOfCopy);
55:
56: list.replaceAll(x -> x * 2);
57: one.replaceAll(x -> x * 2);
58: thirdCopy.replaceAll(x -> x * 2);
59:
60: System.out.println(thirdCopy);
```

A. One line fails to compile.

B. Two lines fail to compile.

C. Three lines fail to compile.

D. The code compiles but throws an exception at runtime.

E. If any lines with compiler errors are removed, the code throws an exception at runtime.

F. If any lines with compiler errors are removed, the code prints [16, 32, 4].

G. The code compiles and prints [16, 32, 4] without any changes.

22. What code change is needed to make the method compile assuming there is no class named T?

```
public static T identity(T t) {
   return t;
}
```

A. Add <T> after the public keyword.

B. Add <T> after the static keyword.

C. Add <T> after T.

D. Add <?> after the public keyword.

E. Add <?> after the static keyword.

F. No change required. The code already compiles.

23. Which of the answer choices make sense to implement with a lambda? (Choose all that apply.)

A. Comparable interface

B. Comparator interface

C. remove method on a Collection

D. removeAll method on a Collection

E. removeIf method on a Collection

24. Which of the following compiles and prints out the entire set? (Choose all that apply.)

```
Set<?> set = Set.of("lion", "tiger", "bear");
var s = Set.copyOf(set);
s.forEach(_____);
```

A. () -> System.out.println(s)

B. s -> System.out.println(s)

C. (s) -> System.out.println(s)

D. System.out.println(s)

E. System::out::println

F. System.out::println

G. None of the above

25. What is the result of the following?

```
var map = new HashMap<Integer, Integer>();
map.put(1, 10);
map.put(2, 20);
map.put(3, null);
map.merge(1, 3, (a,b) -> a + b);
map.merge(3, 3, (a,b) -> a + b);
System.out.println(map);
```

  A. {1=10, 2=20}

  B. {1=10, 2=20, 3=null}

  C. {1=10, 2=20, 3=3}

  D. {1=13, 2=20}

  E. {1=13, 2=20, 3=null}

  F. {1=13, 2=20, 3=3}

  G. The code does not compile.

  H. An exception is thrown.

Chapter

4

Functional Programming

THE OCP EXAM TOPICS COVERED IN THIS CHAPTER INCLUDE THE FOLLOWING:

✓ **Java Stream API**

- Describe the Stream interface and pipelines
- Use lambda expressions and method references

✓ **Built-in Functional Interfaces**

- Use interfaces from the java.util.function package
- Use core functional interfaces including Predicate, Consumer, Function and Supplier
- Use primitive and binary variations of base interfaces of java.util.function package

✓ **Lambda Operations on Streams**

- Extract stream data using map, peek and flatMap methods
- Search stream data using search findFirst, findAny, anyMatch, allMatch and noneMatch methods
- Use the Optional class
- Perform calculations using count, max, min, average and sum stream operations
- Sort a collection using lambda expressions
- Use Collectors with streams, including the groupingBy and partitioningBy operations

By now, you should be comfortable with the lambda and method reference syntax. Both are used when implementing functional interfaces. If you need more practice, you may want to go back and review Chapter 1, "Java Fundamentals," and Chapter 3, "Generics and Collections." You even used methods like forEach() and merge() in Chapter 3. In this chapter, we'll add actual functional programming to that, focusing on the Streams API.

Note that the Streams API in this chapter is used for functional programming. By contrast, there are also java.io streams, which we will talk about in Chapter 8, "I/O." Despite both using the word *stream*, they are nothing alike.

In this chapter, we will introduce many more functional interfaces and Optional classes. Then we will introduce the Stream pipeline and tie it all together. You might have noticed that this chapter covers a long list of objectives. Don't worry if you find the list daunting. By the time you finish the chapter, you'll see that many of the objectives cover similar topics. You might even want to read this chapter twice before doing the review questions so that you really get the hang of it. Functional programming tends to have a steep learning curve but can be really exciting once you get the hang of it.

Working with Built-in Functional Interfaces

In Table 3.1, we introduced some basic functional interfaces that we used with the Collections Framework. Now, we will learn them in more detail and more thoroughly. As discussed in Chapter 1, a functional interface has exactly one abstract method. We will focus on that method here.

All of the functional interfaces in Table 4.1 are provided in the java.util.function package. The convention here is to use the generic type T for the type parameter. If a second type parameter is needed, the next letter, U, is used. If a distinct return type is needed, R for *return* is used for the generic type.

TABLE 4.1   Common functional interfaces

Functional interface	Return type	Method name	# of parameters
Supplier<T>	T	get()	0
Consumer<T>	void	accept(T)	1 (T)
BiConsumer<T, U>	void	accept(T,U)	2 (T, U)
Predicate<T>	boolean	test(T)	1 (T)
BiPredicate<T, U>	boolean	test(T,U)	2 (T, U)
Function<T, R>	R	apply(T)	1 (T)
BiFunction<T, U, R>	R	apply(T,U)	2 (T, U)
UnaryOperator<T>	T	apply(T)	1 (T)
BinaryOperator<T>	T	apply(T,T)	2 (T, T)

There is one functional interface here that was not in Table 3.1 (BinaryOperator.) We introduced only what you needed in Chapter 3 at that point. Even Table 4.1 is a subset of what you need to know. Many functional interfaces are defined in the java.util .function package. There are even functional interfaces for handling primitives, which you'll see later in the chapter.

While you need to know a lot of functional interfaces for the exam, luckily many share names with the ones in Table 4.1. With that in mind, you need to memorize Table 4.1. We will give you lots of practice in this section to help make this memorable. Before you ask, most of the time we don't actually assign the implementation of the interface to a variable. The interface name is implied, and it gets passed directly to the method that needs it. We are introducing the names so that you can better understand and remember what is going on. Once we get to the streams part of the chapter, we will assume that you have this down and stop creating the intermediate variable.

As you saw in Chapter 1, you can name a functional interface anything you want. The only requirements are that it must be a valid interface name and contain a single abstract method. Table 4.1 is significant because these interfaces are often used in streams and other classes that come with Java, which is why you need to memorize them for the exam.

As you'll learn in Chapter 7, "Concurrency," there are two more functional interfaces called Runnable and Callable, which you need to know for the exam. They are used for concurrency the majority of the time. However, they may show up on the exam when you are asked to recognize which functional interface to use. All you need to know is that Runnable and Callable don't take any parameters, with Runnable returning void and Callable returning a generic type.

Let's look at how to implement each of these interfaces. Since both lambdas and method references show up all over the exam, we show an implementation using both where possible. After introducing the interfaces, we will also cover some convenience methods available on these interfaces.

Implementing *Supplier*

A Supplier is used when you want to generate or supply values without taking any input. The Supplier interface is defined as follows:

```
@FunctionalInterface
public interface Supplier<T> {
   T get();
}
```

You can create a LocalDate object using the factory method now(). This example shows how to use a Supplier to call this factory:

```
Supplier<LocalDate> s1 = LocalDate::now;
Supplier<LocalDate> s2 = () -> LocalDate.now();

LocalDate d1 = s1.get();
LocalDate d2 = s2.get();

System.out.println(d1);
System.out.println(d2);
```

This example prints a date such as 2020–02–20 twice. It's also a good opportunity to review static method references. The LocalDate::now method reference is used to create a Supplier to assign to an intermediate variable s1. A Supplier is often used when constructing new objects. For example, we can print two empty StringBuilder objects.

```
Supplier<StringBuilder> s1 = StringBuilder::new;
Supplier<StringBuilder> s2 = () -> new StringBuilder();

System.out.println(s1.get());
System.out.println(s2.get());
```

This time, we used a constructor reference to create the object. We've been using generics to declare what type of Supplier we are using. This can get a little long to read. Can you figure out what the following does? Just take it one step at a time.

```
Supplier<ArrayList<String>> s3 = ArrayList<String>::new;
ArrayList<String> a1 = s3.get();
System.out.println(a1);
```

We have a Supplier of a certain type. That type happens to be ArrayList<String>. Then calling get() creates a new instance of ArrayList<String>, which is the generic type of the Supplier—in other words, a generic that contains another generic. It's not hard to understand, so just look at the code carefully when this type of thing comes up.

Notice how we called get() on the functional interface. What would happen if we tried to print out s3 itself?

```
System.out.println(s3);
```

The code prints something like this:

```
functionalinterface.BuiltIns$$Lambda$1/0x0000000800066840@4909b8da
```

That's the result of calling toString() on a lambda. Yuck. This actually does mean something. Our test class is named BuiltIns, and it is in a package that we created named functionalinterface. Then comes $$, which means that the class doesn't exist in a class file on the file system. It exists only in memory. You don't need to worry about the rest.

Implementing *Consumer* and *BiConsumer*

You use a Consumer when you want to do something with a parameter but not return anything. BiConsumer does the same thing except that it takes two parameters. The interfaces are defined as follows:

```
@FunctionalInterface
public interface Consumer<T> {
    void accept(T t);
    // omitted default method
}

@FunctionalInterface
public interface BiConsumer<T, U> {
    void accept(T t, U u);
    // omitted default method
}
```

You'll notice this pattern. *Bi* means two. It comes from Latin, but you can remember it from English words like *binary* (0 or 1) or *bicycle* (two wheels). Always add another parameter when you see *Bi* show up.

You used a Consumer in Chapter 3 with forEach(). Here's that example actually being assigned to the Consumer interface:

```java
Consumer<String> c1 = System.out::println;
Consumer<String> c2 = x -> System.out.println(x);

c1.accept("Annie");
c2.accept("Annie");
```

This example prints Annie twice. BiConsumer is called with two parameters. They don't have to be the same type. For example, we can put a key and a value in a map using this interface:

```java
var map = new HashMap<String, Integer>();
BiConsumer<String, Integer> b1 = map::put;
BiConsumer<String, Integer> b2 = (k, v) -> map.put(k, v);

b1.accept("chicken", 7);
b2.accept("chick", 1);

System.out.println(map);
```

The output is {chicken=7, chick=1}, which shows that both BiConsumer implementations did get called. When declaring b1, we used an instance method reference on an object since we want to call a method on the local variable map. The code to instantiate b1 is a good bit shorter than the code for b2. This is probably why the exam is so fond of method references.

As another example, we use the same type for both generic parameters.

```java
var map = new HashMap<String, String>();
BiConsumer<String, String> b1 = map::put;
BiConsumer<String, String> b2 = (k, v) -> map.put(k, v);

b1.accept("chicken", "Cluck");
b2.accept("chick", "Tweep");

System.out.println(map);
```

The output is {chicken=Cluck, chick=Tweep}, which shows that a BiConsumer can use the same type for both the T and U generic parameters.

Implementing *Predicate* and *BiPredicate*

You've been using Predicate since the 1Z0-815 exam, and you saw it again more recently with removeIf() in Chapter 3. Predicate is often used when filtering or matching. Both are common operations. A BiPredicate is just like a Predicate except that it takes two parameters instead of one. The interfaces are defined as follows:

```
@FunctionalInterface
public interface Predicate<T> {
    boolean test(T t);
    // omitted default and static methods
}


@FunctionalInterface
public interface BiPredicate<T, U> {
    boolean test(T t, U u);
    // omitted default methods
}
```

It should be old news by now that you can use a Predicate to test a condition.

```
Predicate<String> p1 = String::isEmpty;
Predicate<String> p2 = x -> x.isEmpty();

System.out.println(p1.test(""));  // true
System.out.println(p2.test(""));  // true
```

This prints true twice. More interesting is a BiPredicate. This example also prints true twice:

```
BiPredicate<String, String> b1 = String::startsWith;
BiPredicate<String, String> b2 =
    (string, prefix) -> string.startsWith(prefix);

System.out.println(b1.test("chicken", "chick"));  // true
System.out.println(b2.test("chicken", "chick"));  // true
```

The method reference includes both the instance variable and parameter for startsWith(). This is a good example of how method references save a good bit of typing. The downside is that they are less explicit, and you really have to understand what is going on!

Implementing *Function* and *BiFunction*

In Chapter 3, we used Function with the merge() method. A Function is responsible for turning one parameter into a value of a potentially different type and returning it. Similarly, a BiFunction is responsible for turning two parameters into a value and returning it. The interfaces are defined as follows:

```
@FunctionalInterface
public interface Function<T, R> {
```

```
   R apply(T t);
   // omitted default and static methods
}

@FunctionalInterface
public interface BiFunction<T, U, R> {
   R apply(T t, U u);
   // omitted default method
}
```

For example, this function converts a `String` to the length of the `String`:

```
Function<String, Integer> f1 = String::length;
Function<String, Integer> f2 = x -> x.length();

System.out.println(f1.apply("cluck")); // 5
System.out.println(f2.apply("cluck")); // 5
```

This function turns a `String` into an `Integer`. Well, technically it turns the `String` into an `int`, which is autoboxed into an `Integer`. The types don't have to be different. The following combines two `String` objects and produces another `String`:

```
BiFunction<String, String, String> b1 = String::concat;
BiFunction<String, String, String> b2 =
   (string, toAdd) -> string.concat(toAdd);

System.out.println(b1.apply("baby ", "chick")); // baby chick
System.out.println(b2.apply("baby ", "chick")); // baby chick
```

The first two types in the `BiFunction` are the input types. The third is the result type. For the method reference, the first parameter is the instance that `concat()` is called on, and the second is passed to `concat()`.

Creating Your Own Functional Interfaces

Java provides a built-in interface for functions with one or two parameters. What if you need more? No problem. Suppose that you want to create a functional interface for the wheel speed of each wheel on a tricycle. You could create a functional interface such as this:

```
@FunctionalInterface
interface TriFunction<T,U,V,R> {
   R apply(T t, U u, V v);
}
```

There are four type parameters. The first three supply the types of the three wheel speeds. The fourth is the return type. Now suppose that you want to create a function to determine how fast your quad-copter is going given the power of the four motors. You could create a functional interface such as the following:

```
@FunctionalInterface
interface QuadFunction<T,U,V,W,R> {
    R apply(T t, U u, V v, W w);
}
```

There are five type parameters here. The first four supply the types of the four motors. Ideally these would be the same type, but you never know. The fifth is the return type in this example.

Java's built-in interfaces are meant to facilitate the most common functional interfaces that you'll need. It is by no means an exhaustive list. Remember that you can add any functional interfaces you'd like, and Java matches them when you use lambdas or method references.

Implementing *UnaryOperator* and *BinaryOperator*

UnaryOperator and BinaryOperator are a special case of a Function. They require all type parameters to be the same type. A UnaryOperator transforms its value into one of the same type. For example, incrementing by one is a unary operation. In fact, UnaryOperator extends Function. A BinaryOperator merges two values into one of the same type. Adding two numbers is a binary operation. Similarly, BinaryOperator extends BiFunction. The interfaces are defined as follows:

```
@FunctionalInterface
public interface UnaryOperator<T> extends Function<T, T> { }
```

```
@FunctionalInterface
public interface BinaryOperator<T> extends BiFunction<T, T, T> {
    // omitted static methods
}
```

This means that method signatures look like this:

```
T apply(T t);          // UnaryOperator
```

```
T apply(T t1, T t2);  // BinaryOperator
```

In the Javadoc, you'll notice that these methods are actually inherited from the Function/BiFunction superclass. The generic declarations on the subclass are what force the type to be the same. For the unary example, notice how the return type is the same type as the parameter.

```
UnaryOperator<String> u1 = String::toUpperCase;
UnaryOperator<String> u2 = x -> x.toUpperCase();

System.out.println(u1.apply("chirp"));  // CHIRP
System.out.println(u2.apply("chirp"));  // CHIRP
```

This prints CHIRP twice. We don't need to specify the return type in the generics because UnaryOperator requires it to be the same as the parameter. And now here's the binary example:

```
BinaryOperator<String> b1 = String::concat;
BinaryOperator<String> b2 = (string, toAdd) -> string.concat(toAdd);

System.out.println(b1.apply("baby ", "chick")); // baby chick
System.out.println(b2.apply("baby ", "chick")); // baby chick
```

Notice that this does the same thing as the BiFunction example. The code is more succinct, which shows the importance of using the correct functional interface. It's nice to have one generic type specified instead of three.

Checking Functional Interfaces

It's really important to know the number of parameters, types, return value, and method name for each of the functional interfaces. Now would be a good time to memorize Table 4.1 if you haven't done so already. Let's do some examples to practice.

What functional interface would you use in these three situations?

- Returns a String without taking any parameters
- Returns a Boolean and takes a String
- Returns an Integer and takes two Integers

Ready? Think about what your answer is before continuing. Really. You have to know this cold. OK. The first one is a Supplier<String> because it generates an object and takes zero parameters. The second one is a Function<String,Boolean> because it takes one parameter and returns another type. It's a little tricky. You might think it is a Predicate<String>. Note that a Predicate returns a boolean primitive and not a Boolean object. Finally, the third one is either a BinaryOperator<Integer> or a BiFunction<Integer,Integer,Integer>. Since BinaryOperator is a special case of BiFunction, either is a correct answer. BinaryOperator<Integer> is the better answer of the two since it is more specific.

Let's try this exercise again but with code. It's harder with code. With code, the first thing you do is look at how many parameters the lambda takes and whether there is a return value. What functional interface would you use to fill in the blank for these?

```
6: _____<List> ex1 = x -> "".equals(x.get(0));
7: _____<Long> ex2 = (Long l) -> System.out.println(l);
8: _____<String, String> ex3 = (s1, s2) -> false;
```

Again, think about the answers before continuing. Ready? Line 6 passes one List parameter to the lambda and returns a boolean. This tells us that it is a Predicate or Function. Since the generic declaration has only one parameter, it is a Predicate.

Line 7 passes one Long parameter to the lambda and doesn't return anything. This tells us that it is a Consumer. Line 8 takes two parameters and returns a boolean. When you see a boolean returned, think Predicate unless the generics specify a Boolean return type. In this case, there are two parameters, so it is a BiPredicate.

Are you finding these easy? If not, review Table 4.1 again. We aren't kidding. You need to know the table really well. Now that you are fresh from studying the table, we are going to play "identify the error." These are meant to be tricky:

```
6: Function<List<String>> ex1 = x -> x.get(0);    // DOES NOT COMPILE
7: UnaryOperator<Long> ex2 = (Long l) -> 3.14;     // DOES NOT COMIPLE
8: Predicate ex4 = String::isEmpty;                // DOES NOT COMPILE
```

Line 6 claims to be a Function. A Function needs to specify two generics—the input parameter type and the return value type. The return value type is missing from line 6, causing the code not to compile. Line 7 is a UnaryOperator, which returns the same type as it is passed in. The example returns a double rather than a Long, causing the code not to compile.

Line 8 is missing the generic for Predicate. This makes the parameter that was passed an Object rather than a String. The lambda expects a String because it calls a method that exists on String rather than Object. Therefore, it doesn't compile.

Convenience Methods on Functional Interfaces

By definition, all functional interfaces have a single abstract method. This doesn't mean they can have only one method, though. Several of the common functional interfaces provide a number of helpful default methods.

Table 4.2 shows the convenience methods on the built-in functional interfaces that you need to know for the exam. All of these facilitate modifying or combining functional interfaces of the same type. Note that Table 4.2 shows only the main interfaces. The BiConsumer, BiFunction, and BiPredicate interfaces have similar methods available.

Let's start with these two Predicate variables.

```
Predicate<String> egg = s -> s.contains("egg");
Predicate<String> brown = s -> s.contains("brown");
```

TABLE 4.2   Convenience methods

Interface instance	Method return type	Method name	Method parameters
Consumer	Consumer	andThen()	Consumer
Function	Function	andThen()	Function
Function	Function	compose()	Function
Predicate	Predicate	and()	Predicate
Predicate	Predicate	negate()	—
Predicate	Predicate	or()	Predicate

Now we want a `Predicate` for brown eggs and another for all other colors of eggs. We could write this by hand, as shown here:

```
Predicate<String> brownEggs =
   s -> s.contains("egg") && s.contains("brown");
Predicate<String> otherEggs =
   s -> s.contains("egg") && ! s.contains("brown");
```

This works, but it's not great. It's a bit long to read, and it contains duplication. What if we decide the letter *e* should be capitalized in *egg*? We'd have to change it in three variables: egg, brownEggs, and otherEggs. A better way to deal with this situation is to use two of the `default` methods on `Predicate`.

```
Predicate<String> brownEggs = egg.and(brown);
Predicate<String> otherEggs = egg.and(brown.negate());
```

Neat! Now we are reusing the logic in the original `Predicate` variables to build two new ones. It's shorter and clearer what the relationship is between variables. We can also change the spelling of *egg* in one place, and the other two objects will have new logic because they reference it.

Moving on to `Consumer`, let's take a look at the andThen() method, which runs two functional interfaces in sequence.

```
Consumer<String> c1 = x -> System.out.print("1: " + x);
Consumer<String> c2 = x -> System.out.print(",2: " + x);

Consumer<String> combined = c1.andThen(c2);
combined.accept("Annie");              // 1: Annie,2: Annie
```

Notice how the same parameter gets passed to both c1 and c2. This shows that the Consumer instances are run in sequence and are independent of each other. By contrast, the compose() method on Function chains functional interfaces. However, it passes along the output of one to the input of another.

```
Function<Integer, Integer> before = x -> x + 1;
Function<Integer, Integer> after = x -> x * 2;

Function<Integer, Integer> combined = after.compose(before);
System.out.println(combined.apply(3));   // 8
```

This time the before runs first, turning the 3 into a 4. Then the after runs, doubling the 4 to 8. All of the methods in this section are helpful in simplifying your code as you work with functional interfaces.

Returning an *Optional*

Suppose that you are taking an introductory Java class and receive scores of 90 and 100 on the first two exams. Now, we ask you what your average is. An average is calculated by adding the scores and dividing by the number of scores, so you have (90+100)/2. This gives 190/2, so you answer with 95. Great!

Now suppose that you are taking your second class on Java, and it is the first day of class. We ask you what your average is in this class that just started. You haven't taken any exams yet, so you don't have anything to average. It wouldn't be accurate to say that your average is zero. That sounds bad, and it isn't true. There simply isn't any data, so you don't have an average yet.

How do we express this "we don't know" or "not applicable" answer in Java? We use the Optional type. An Optional is created using a factory. You can either request an empty Optional or pass a value for the Optional to wrap. Think of an Optional as a box that might have something in it or might instead be empty. Figure 4.1 shows both options.

FIGURE 4.1   Optional

Optional.empty()

Optional.of(95)

Creating an *Optional*

Here's how to code our average method:

```
10: public static Optional<Double> average(int... scores) {
11:     if (scores.length == 0) return Optional.empty();
12:     int sum = 0;
13:     for (int score: scores) sum += score;
14:     return Optional.of((double) sum / scores.length);
15: }
```

Line 11 returns an empty Optional when we can't calculate an average. Lines 12 and 13 add up the scores. There is a functional programming way of doing this math, but we will get to that later in the chapter. In fact, the entire method could be written in one line, but that wouldn't teach you how Optional works! Line 14 creates an Optional to wrap the average.

Calling the method shows what is in our two boxes.

```
System.out.println(average(90, 100)); // Optional[95.0]
System.out.println(average());        // Optional.empty
```

You can see that one Optional contains a value and the other is empty. Normally, we want to check whether a value is there and/or get it out of the box. Here's one way to do that:

```
20: Optional<Double> opt = average(90, 100);
21: if (opt.isPresent())
22:     System.out.println(opt.get()); // 95.0
```

Line 21 checks whether the Optional actually contains a value. Line 22 prints it out. What if we didn't do the check and the Optional was empty?

```
26: Optional<Double> opt = average();
27: System.out.println(opt.get()); // NoSuchElementException
```

We'd get an exception since there is no value inside the Optional.

```
java.util.NoSuchElementException: No value present
```

When creating an Optional, it is common to want to use empty() when the value is null. You can do this with an if statement or ternary operator. We use the ternary operator (? :) to simplify the code. You should have learned about this operator, along with many other operators, when studying for the 1Z0-815 exam.

```
Optional o = (value == null) ? Optional.empty() : Optional.of(value);
```

If value is null, o is assigned the empty Optional. Otherwise, we wrap the value. Since this is such a common pattern, Java provides a factory method to do the same thing.

```
Optional o = Optional.ofNullable(value);
```

That covers the `static` methods you need to know about `Optional`. Table 4.3 summarizes most of the instance methods on `Optional` that you need to know for the exam. There are a few others that involve chaining. We will cover those later in the chapter.

TABLE 4.3 Optional instance methods

Method	When `Optional` is empty	When `Optional` contains a value
`get()`	Throws an exception	Returns value
`ifPresent(Consumer c)`	Does nothing	Calls Consumer with value
`isPresent()`	Returns false	Returns true
`orElse(T other)`	Returns other parameter	Returns value
`orElseGet(Supplier s)`	Returns result of calling Supplier	Returns value
`orElseThrow()`	Throws NoSuchElementException	Returns value
`orElseThrow (Supplier s)`	Throws exception created by calling Supplier	Returns value

You've already seen `get()` and `isPresent()`. The other methods allow you to write code that uses an `Optional` in one line without having to use the ternary operator. This makes the code easier to read. Instead of using an `if` statement, which we used when checking the average earlier, we can specify a `Consumer` to be run when there is a value inside the `Optional`. When there isn't, the method simply skips running the `Consumer`.

```
Optional<Double> opt = average(90, 100);
opt.ifPresent(System.out::println);
```

Using `ifPresent()` better expresses our intent. We want something done if a value is present. You can think of it as an `if` statement with no `else`.

Dealing with an Empty *Optional*

The remaining methods allow you to specify what to do if a value isn't present. There are a few choices. The first two allow you to specify a return value either directly or using a `Supplier`.

```
30: Optional<Double> opt = average();
31: System.out.println(opt.orElse(Double.NaN));
32: System.out.println(opt.orElseGet(() -> Math.random()));
```

This prints something like the following:

```
NaN
0.49775932295380165
```

Line 31 shows that you can return a specific value or variable. In our case, we print the "not a number" value. Line 32 shows using a Supplier to generate a value at runtime to return instead. I'm glad our professors didn't give us a random average, though!

Alternatively, we can have the code throw an exception if the Optional is empty.

```
30: Optional<Double> opt = average();
31: System.out.println(opt.orElseThrow());
```

This prints something like the following:

```
Exception in thread "main" java.util.NoSuchElementException:
  No value present
    at java.base/java.util.Optional.orElseThrow(Optional.java:382)
```

Without specifying a Supplier for the exception, Java will throw a NoSuchElementException. This method was added in Java 10. Remember that the stack trace looks weird because the lambdas are generated rather than named classes. Alternatively, we can have the code throw a custom exception if the Optional is empty.

```
30: Optional<Double> opt = average();
31: System.out.println(opt.orElseThrow(
32:     () -> new IllegalStateException()));
```

This prints something like the following:

```
Exception in thread "main" java.lang.IllegalStateException
    at optionals.Methods.lambda$orElse$1(Methods.java:30)
    at java.base/java.util.Optional.orElseThrow(Optional.java:408)
```

Line 32 shows using a Supplier to create an exception that should be thrown. Notice that we do not write throw new IllegalStateException(). The orElseThrow() method takes care of actually throwing the exception when we run it.

The two methods that take a Supplier have different names. Do you see why this code does not compile?

```
System.out.println(opt.orElseGet(
    () -> new IllegalStateException())); // DOES NOT COMPILE
```

The opt variable is an Optional<Double>. This means the Supplier must return a Double. Since this supplier returns an exception, the type does not match.

The last example with Optional is really easy. What do you think this does?

```
Optional<Double> opt = average(90, 100);
System.out.println(opt.orElse(Double.NaN));
System.out.println(opt.orElseGet(() -> Math.random()));
System.out.println(opt.orElseThrow());
```

It prints out 95.0 three times. Since the value does exist, there is no need to use the "or else" logic.

Is *Optional* the Same as *null?*

Before Java 8, programmers would return null instead of Optional. There were a few shortcomings with this approach. One was that there wasn't a clear way to express that null might be a special value. By contrast, returning an Optional is a clear statement in the API that there might not be a value in there.

Another advantage of Optional is that you can use a functional programming style with ifPresent() and the other methods rather than needing an if statement. Finally, you'll see toward the end of the chapter that you can chain Optional calls.

Using Streams

A *stream* in Java is a sequence of data. A *stream pipeline* consists of the operations that run on a stream to produce a result. First we will look at the flow of pipelines conceptually. After that, we will actually get into code.

Understanding the Pipeline Flow

Think of a stream pipeline as an assembly line in a factory. Suppose that we were running an assembly line to make signs for the animal exhibits at the zoo. We have a number of jobs. It is one person's job to take signs out of a box. It is a second person's job to paint the sign. It is a third person's job to stencil the name of the animal on the sign. It's the last person's job to put the completed sign in a box to be carried to the proper exhibit.

Notice that the second person can't do anything until one sign has been taken out of the box by the first person. Similarly, the third person can't do anything until one sign has been painted, and the last person can't do anything until it is stenciled.

The assembly line for making signs is finite. Once we process the contents of our box of signs, we are finished. *Finite* streams have a limit. Other assembly lines essentially run forever, like one for food production. Of course, they do stop at some point when the factory closes down, but pretend that doesn't happen. Or think of a sunrise/sunset cycle as *infinite*, since it doesn't end for an inordinately large period of time.

Another important feature of an assembly line is that each person touches each element to do their operation and then that piece of data is gone. It doesn't come back. The next person deals with it at that point. This is different than the lists and queues that you saw in the previous chapter. With a list, you can access any element at any time. With a queue, you are limited in which elements you can access, but all of the elements are there. With streams, the data isn't generated up front—it is created when needed. This is an example of *lazy evaluation*, which delays execution until necessary.

Many things can happen in the assembly line stations along the way. In functional programming, these are called *stream operations*. Just like with the assembly line, operations occur in a pipeline. Someone has to start and end the work, and there can be any number of stations in between. After all, a job with one person isn't an assembly line! There are three parts to a stream pipeline, as shown in Figure 4.2.

- **Source:** Where the stream comes from
- **Intermediate operations:** Transforms the stream into another one. There can be as few or as many intermediate operations as you'd like. Since streams use lazy evaluation, the intermediate operations do not run until the terminal operation runs.
- **Terminal operation:** Actually produces a result. Since streams can be used only once, the stream is no longer valid after a terminal operation completes.

FIGURE 4.2 Stream pipeline

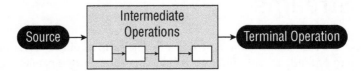

Notice that the operations are unknown to us. When viewing the assembly line from the outside, you care only about what comes in and goes out. What happens in between is an implementation detail.

You will need to know the differences between intermediate and terminal operations well. Make sure you can fill in Table 4.4.

TABLE 4.4 Intermediate vs. terminal operations

Scenario	Intermediate operation	Terminal operation
Required part of a useful pipeline?	No	Yes
Can exist multiple times in a pipeline?	Yes	No
Return type is a stream type?	Yes	No
Executed upon method call?	No	Yes
Stream valid after call?	Yes	No

A factory typically has a foreman who oversees the work. Java serves as the foreman when working with stream pipelines. This is a really important role, especially when dealing with lazy evaluation and infinite streams. Think of declaring the stream as giving instructions to the foreman. As the foreman finds out what needs to be done, he sets up the stations and tells the workers what their duties will be. However, the workers do not start until the foreman tells them to begin. The foreman waits until he sees the terminal operation to actually kick off the work. He also watches the work and stops the line as soon as work is complete.

Let's look at a few examples of this. We aren't using code in these examples because it is really important to understand the stream pipeline concept before starting to write the code. Figure 4.3 shows a stream pipeline with one intermediate operation.

FIGURE 4.3   Steps in running a stream pipeline

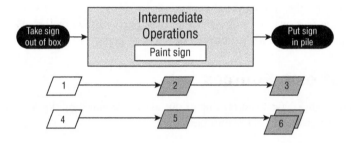

Let's take a look at what happens from the point of the view of the foreman. First, he sees that the source is taking signs out of the box. The foreman sets up a worker at the table to unpack the box and says to await a signal to start. Then the foreman sees the intermediate operation to paint the sign. He sets up a worker with paint and says to await a signal to start. Finally, the foreman sees the terminal operation to put the signs into a pile. He sets up a worker to do this and yells out that all three workers should start.

Suppose that there are two signs in the box. Step 1 is the first worker taking one sign out of the box and handing it to the second worker. Step 2 is the second worker painting it and handing it to the third worker. Step 3 is the third worker putting it in the pile. Steps 4–6 are this same process for the other sign. Then the foreman sees that there are no more signs left and shuts down the entire enterprise.

The foreman is smart. He can make decisions about how to best do the work based on what is needed. As an example, let's explore the stream pipeline in Figure 4.4.

The foreman still sees a source of taking signs out of the box and assigns a worker to do that on command. He still sees an intermediate operation to paint and sets up another worker with instructions to wait and then paint. Then he sees an intermediate step that we need only two signs. He sets up a worker to count the signs that go by and notify him when the worker has seen two. Finally, he sets up a worker for the terminal operation to put the signs in a pile.

FIGURE 4.4   A stream pipeline with a limit

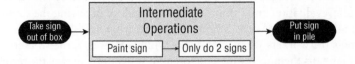

This time, suppose that there are 10 signs in the box. We start out like last time. The first sign makes its way down the pipeline. The second sign also makes its way down the pipeline. When the worker in charge of counting sees the second sign, she tells the foreman. The foreman lets the terminal operation worker finish her task and then yells out "stop the line." It doesn't matter that there are eight more signs in the box. We don't need them, so it would be unnecessary work to paint them. And we all want to avoid unnecessary work!

Similarly, the foreman would have stopped the line after the first sign if the terminal operation was to find the first sign that gets created.

In the following sections, we will cover the three parts of the pipeline. We will also discuss special types of streams for primitives and how to print a stream.

Creating Stream Sources

In Java, the streams we have been talking about are represented by the Stream<T> interface, defined in the java.util.stream package.

Creating Finite Streams

For simplicity, we'll start with finite streams. There are a few ways to create them.

```
11: Stream<String> empty = Stream.empty();              // count = 0
12: Stream<Integer> singleElement = Stream.of(1);    // count = 1
13: Stream<Integer> fromArray = Stream.of(1, 2, 3); // count = 3
```

Line 11 shows how to create an empty stream. Line 12 shows how to create a stream with a single element. Line 13 shows how to create a stream from a varargs. You've undoubtedly noticed that there isn't an array on line 13. The method signature uses varargs, which let you specify an array or individual elements.

Java also provides a convenient way of converting a Collection to a stream.

```
14: var list = List.of("a", "b", "c");
15: Stream<String> fromList = list.stream();
```

Line 15 shows that it is a simple method call to create a stream from a list. This is helpful since such conversions are common.

Creating a Parallel Stream

It is just as easy to create a parallel stream from a list.

```
24: var list = List.of("a", "b", "c");
25: Stream<String> fromListParallel = list.parallelStream();
```

This is a great feature because you can write code that uses concurrency before even learning what a thread is. Using parallel streams is like setting up multiple tables of workers who are able to do the same task. Painting would be a lot faster if we could have five painters painting signs instead of just one. Just keep in mind some tasks cannot be done in parallel, such as putting the signs away in the order that they were created in the stream. Also be aware that there is a cost in coordinating the work, so for smaller streams, it might be faster to do it sequentially. You'll learn much more about running tasks concurrently in Chapter 7.

Creating Infinite Streams

So far, this isn't particularly impressive. We could do all this with lists. We can't create an infinite list, though, which makes streams more powerful.

```
17: Stream<Double> randoms = Stream.generate(Math::random);
18: Stream<Integer> oddNumbers = Stream.iterate(1, n -> n + 2);
```

Line 17 generates a stream of random numbers. How many random numbers? However many you need. If you call randoms.forEach(System.out::println), the program will print random numbers until you kill it. Later in the chapter, you'll learn about operations like limit() to turn the infinite stream into a finite stream.

Line 18 gives you more control. The iterate() method takes a seed or starting value as the first parameter. This is the first element that will be part of the stream. The other parameter is a lambda expression that gets passed the previous value and generates the next value. As with the random numbers example, it will keep on producing odd numbers as long as you need them.

If you try to call System.out.print(stream), you'll get something like the following:

    java.util.stream.ReferencePipeline$3@4517d9a3

This is different from a Collection where you see the contents. You don't need to know this for the exam. We mention it so that you aren't caught by surprise when writing code for practice.

What if you wanted just odd numbers less than 100? Java 9 introduced an overloaded version of `iterate()` that helps with just that.

```
19: Stream<Integer> oddNumberUnder100 = Stream.iterate(
20:    1,                 // seed
21:    n -> n < 100,      // Predicate to specify when done
22:    n -> n + 2);       // UnaryOperator to get next value
```

This method takes three parameters. Notice how they are separated by commas (,) just like all other methods. The exam may try to trick you by using semicolons since it is similar to a `for` loop. Similar to a `for` loop, you have to take care that you aren't accidentally creating an infinite stream.

Reviewing Stream Creation Methods

To review, make sure you know all the methods in Table 4.5. These are the ways of creating a source for streams, given a `Collection` instance `coll`.

TABLE 4.5   Creating a source

Method	Finite or infinite?	Notes
Stream.empty()	Finite	Creates Stream with zero elements
Stream.of(varargs)	Finite	Creates Stream with elements listed
coll.stream()	Finite	Creates Stream from a Collection
coll. parallelStream()	Finite	Creates Stream from a Collection where the stream can run in parallel
Stream. generate(supplier)	Infinite	Creates Stream by calling the Supplier for each element upon request
Stream.iterate(seed, unaryOperator)	Infinite	Creates Stream by using the seed for the first element and then calling the UnaryOperator for each subsequent element upon request
Stream.iterate(seed, predicate, unaryOperator)	Finite or infinite	Creates Stream by using the seed for the first element and then calling the UnaryOperator for each subsequent element upon request. Stops if the Predicate returns false

Using Common Terminal Operations

You can perform a terminal operation without any intermediate operations but not the other way around. This is why we will talk about terminal operations first. *Reductions* are a special type of terminal operation where all of the contents of the stream are combined into a single primitive or Object. For example, you might have an int or a Collection.

Table 4.6 summarizes this section. Feel free to use it as a guide to remember the most important points as we go through each one individually. We explain them from simplest to most complex rather than alphabetically.

TABLE 4.6   Terminal stream operations

Method	What happens for infinite streams	Return value	Reduction
count()	Does not terminate	long	Yes
min() max()	Does not terminate	Optional<T>	Yes
findAny() findFirst()	Terminates	Optional<T>	No
allMatch() anyMatch() noneMatch()	Sometimes terminates	boolean	No
forEach()	Does not terminate	void	No
reduce()	Does not terminate	Varies	Yes
collect()	Does not terminate	Varies	Yes

count()

The count() method determines the number of elements in a finite stream. For an infinite stream, it never terminates. Why? Count from 1 to infinity and let us know when you are finished. Or rather, don't do that because we'd rather you study for the exam than spend the rest of your life counting. The count() method is a reduction because it looks at each element in the stream and returns a single value. The method signature is as follows:

```
long count()
```

This example shows calling count() on a finite stream:

```
Stream<String> s = Stream.of("monkey", "gorilla", "bonobo");
System.out.println(s.count());    // 3
```

min() and max()

The min() and max() methods allow you to pass a custom comparator and find the smallest or largest value in a finite stream according to that sort order. Like the count() method, min() and max() hang on an infinite stream because they cannot be sure that a smaller or larger value isn't coming later in the stream. Both methods are reductions because they return a single value after looking at the entire stream. The method signatures are as follows:

```
Optional<T> min(Comparator<? super T> comparator)
Optional<T> max(Comparator<? super T> comparator)
```

This example finds the animal with the fewest letters in its name:

```
Stream<String> s = Stream.of("monkey", "ape", "bonobo");
Optional<String> min = s.min((s1, s2) -> s1.length()-s2.length());
min.ifPresent(System.out::println); // ape
```

Notice that the code returns an Optional rather than the value. This allows the method to specify that no minimum or maximum was found. We use the Optional method ifPresent() and a method reference to print out the minimum only if one is found. As an example of where there isn't a minimum, let's look at an empty stream.

```
Optional<?> minEmpty = Stream.empty().min((s1, s2) -> 0);
System.out.println(minEmpty.isPresent()); // false
```

Since the stream is empty, the comparator is never called, and no value is present in the Optional.

> What if you need both the min() and max() values of the same stream? For now, you can't have both, at least not using these methods. Remember, a stream can have only one terminal operation. Once a terminal operation has been run, the stream cannot be used again. As we'll see later in this chapter, there are built-in summary methods for some numeric streams that will calculate a set of values for you.

findAny() and findFirst()

The findAny() and findFirst() methods return an element of the stream unless the stream is empty. If the stream is empty, they return an empty Optional. This is the first method you've seen that can terminate with an infinite stream. Since Java generates only the amount of stream you need, the infinite stream needs to generate only one element.

As its name implies, the findAny() method can return any element of the stream. When called on the streams you've seen up until now, it commonly returns the first element, although this behavior is not guaranteed. As you'll see in Chapter 7, the findAny() method is more likely to return a random element when working with parallel streams.

These methods are terminal operations but not reductions. The reason is that they sometimes return without processing all of the elements. This means that they return a value based on the stream but do not reduce the entire stream into one value.

The method signatures are as follows:

```
Optional<T> findAny()
Optional<T> findFirst()
```

This example finds an animal:

```
Stream<String> s = Stream.of("monkey", "gorilla", "bonobo");
Stream<String> infinite = Stream.generate(() -> "chimp");


s.findAny().ifPresent(System.out::println);         // monkey (usually)
infinite.findAny().ifPresent(System.out::println); // chimp
```

Finding any one match is more useful than it sounds. Sometimes we just want to sample the results and get a representative element, but we don't need to waste the processing generating them all. After all, if we plan to work with only one element, why bother looking at more?

allMatch(), anyMatch(), and noneMatch()

The allMatch(), anyMatch(), and noneMatch() methods search a stream and return information about how the stream pertains to the predicate. These may or may not terminate for infinite streams. It depends on the data. Like the find methods, they are not reductions because they do not necessarily look at all of the elements.

The method signatures are as follows:

```
boolean anyMatch(Predicate <? super T> predicate)
boolean allMatch(Predicate <? super T> predicate)
boolean noneMatch(Predicate <? super T> predicate)
```

This example checks whether animal names begin with letters:

```
var list = List.of("monkey", "2", "chimp");
Stream<String> infinite = Stream.generate(() -> "chimp");
Predicate<String> pred = x -> Character.isLetter(x.charAt(0));


System.out.println(list.stream().anyMatch(pred));  // true
System.out.println(list.stream().allMatch(pred));  // false
System.out.println(list.stream().noneMatch(pred)); // false
System.out.println(infinite.anyMatch(pred));       // true
```

This shows that we can reuse the same predicate, but we need a different stream each time. The `anyMatch()` method returns `true` because two of the three elements match. The `allMatch()` method returns `false` because one doesn't match. The `noneMatch()` method also returns `false` because one matches. On the infinite stream, one match is found, so the call terminates. If we called `allMatch()`, it would run until we killed the program.

> Remember that `allMatch()`, `anyMatch()`, and `noneMatch()` return a `boolean`. By contrast, the find methods return an `Optional` because they return an element of the stream.

forEach()

Like in the Java Collections Framework, it is common to iterate over the elements of a stream. As expected, calling `forEach()` on an infinite stream does not terminate. Since there is no return value, it is not a reduction.

Before you use it, consider if another approach would be better. Developers who learned to write loops first tend to use them for everything. For example, a loop with an `if` statement could be written with a filter. You will learn about filters in the intermediate operations section.

The method signature is as follows:

```
void forEach(Consumer<? super T> action)
```

Notice that this is the only terminal operation with a return type of `void`. If you want something to happen, you have to make it happen in the `Consumer`. Here's one way to print the elements in the stream (there are other ways, which we cover later in the chapter):

```
Stream<String> s = Stream.of("Monkey", "Gorilla", "Bonobo");
s.forEach(System.out::print); // MonkeyGorillaBonobo
```

> Remember that you can call `forEach()` directly on a `Collection` or on a `Stream`. Don't get confused on the exam when you see both approaches.

Notice that you can't use a traditional `for` loop on a stream.

```
Stream<Integer> s = Stream.of(1);
for (Integer i  : s) {} // DOES NOT COMPILE
```

While `forEach()` sounds like a loop, it is really a terminal operator for streams. Streams cannot be used as the source in a `for-each` loop to run because they don't implement the `Iterable` interface.

reduce()

The reduce() method combines a stream into a single object. It is a reduction, which means it processes all elements. The three method signatures are these:

```
T reduce(T identity, BinaryOperator<T> accumulator)

Optional<T> reduce(BinaryOperator<T> accumulator)

<U> U reduce(U identity,
    BiFunction<U,? super T,U> accumulator,
    BinaryOperator<U> combiner)
```

Let's take them one at a time. The most common way of doing a reduction is to start with an initial value and keep merging it with the next value. Think about how you would concatenate an array of String objects into a single String without functional programming. It might look something like this:

```
var array = new String[] { "w", "o", "l", "f" };
var result = "";
for (var s: array) result = result + s;
System.out.println(result); // wolf
```

The *identity* is the initial value of the reduction, in this case an empty String. The *accumulator* combines the current result with the current value in the stream. With lambdas, we can do the same thing with a stream and reduction:

```
Stream<String> stream = Stream.of("w", "o", "l", "f");
String word = stream.reduce("", (s, c) -> s + c);
System.out.println(word); // wolf
```

Notice how we still have the empty String as the identity. We also still concatenate the String objects to get the next value. We can even rewrite this with a method reference.

```
Stream<String> stream = Stream.of("w", "o", "l", "f");
String word = stream.reduce("", String::concat);
System.out.println(word); // wolf
```

Let's try another one. Can you write a reduction to multiply all of the Integer objects in a stream? Try it. Our solution is shown here:

```
Stream<Integer> stream = Stream.of(3, 5, 6);
System.out.println(stream.reduce(1, (a, b) -> a*b));  // 90
```

We set the identity to 1 and the accumulator to multiplication. In many cases, the identity isn't really necessary, so Java lets us omit it. When you don't specify an identity, an Optional is returned because there might not be any data. There are three choices for what is in the Optional.

- If the stream is empty, an empty Optional is returned.
- If the stream has one element, it is returned.
- If the stream has multiple elements, the accumulator is applied to combine them.

The following illustrates each of these scenarios:

```
BinaryOperator<Integer> op = (a, b) -> a * b;
Stream<Integer> empty = Stream.empty();
Stream<Integer> oneElement = Stream.of(3);
Stream<Integer> threeElements = Stream.of(3, 5, 6);

empty.reduce(op).ifPresent(System.out::println);         // no output
oneElement.reduce(op).ifPresent(System.out::println);    // 3
threeElements.reduce(op).ifPresent(System.out::println); // 90
```

Why are there two similar methods? Why not just always require the identity? Java could have done that. However, sometimes it is nice to differentiate the case where the stream is empty rather than the case where there is a value that happens to match the identity being returned from calculation. The signature returning an Optional lets us differentiate these cases. For example, we might return Optional.empty() when the stream is empty and Optional.of(3) when there is a value.

The third method signature is used when we are dealing with different types. It allows Java to create intermediate reductions and then combine them at the end. Let's take a look at an example that counts the number of characters in each String:

```
Stream<String> stream = Stream.of("w", "o", "l", "f!");
int length = stream.reduce(0, (i, s) -> i+s.length(), (a, b) -> a+b);
System.out.println(length); // 5
```

The first parameter (0) is the value for the initializer. If we had an empty stream, this would be the answer. The second parameter is the *accumulator*. Unlike the accumulators you saw previously, this one handles mixed data types. In this example, the first argument, i, is an Integer, while the second argument, s, is a String. It adds the length of the current String to our running total. The third parameter is called the *combiner*, which combines any intermediate totals. In this case, a and b are both Integer values.

The three-argument reduce() operation is useful when working with parallel streams because it allows the stream to be decomposed and reassembled by separate threads. For example, if we needed to count the length of four 100-character strings, the first two values and the last two values could be computed independently. The intermediate result (200 + 200) would then be combined into the final value.

collect()

The collect() method is a special type of reduction called a *mutable reduction*. It is more efficient than a regular reduction because we use the same mutable object while accumulating. Common mutable objects include StringBuilder and ArrayList. This is a really useful method, because it lets us get data out of streams and into another form. The method signatures are as follows:

```
<R> R collect(Supplier<R> supplier,
    BiConsumer<R, ? super T> accumulator,
    BiConsumer<R, R> combiner)

<R,A> R collect(Collector<? super T, A,R> collector)
```

Let's start with the first signature, which is used when we want to code specifically how collecting should work. Our wolf example from reduce can be converted to use collect().

```
Stream<String> stream = Stream.of("w", "o", "l", "f");

StringBuilder word = stream.collect(
    StringBuilder::new,
    StringBuilder::append,
    StringBuilder::append)

System.out.println(word); // wolf
```

The first parameter is the *supplier,* which creates the object that will store the results as we collect data. Remember that a Supplier doesn't take any parameters and returns a value. In this case, it constructs a new StringBuilder.

The second parameter is the *accumulator,* which is a BiConsumer that takes two parameters and doesn't return anything. It is responsible for adding one more element to the data collection. In this example, it appends the next String to the StringBuilder.

The final parameter is the *combiner,* which is another BiConsumer. It is responsible for taking two data collections and merging them. This is useful when we are processing in parallel. Two smaller collections are formed and then merged into one. This would work with StringBuilder only if we didn't care about the order of the letters. In this case, the accumulator and combiner have similar logic.

Now let's look at an example where the logic is different in the accumulator and combiner.

```
Stream<String> stream = Stream.of("w", "o", "l", "f");

TreeSet<String> set = stream.collect(
    TreeSet::new,
    TreeSet::add,
    TreeSet::addAll);

System.out.println(set); // [f, l, o, w]
```

The collector has three parts as before. The supplier creates an empty `TreeSet`. The accumulator adds a single `String` from the `Stream` to the `TreeSet`. The combiner adds all of the elements of one `TreeSet` to another in case the operations were done in parallel and need to be merged.

We started with the long signature because that's how you implement your own collector. It is important to know how to do this for the exam and to understand how collectors work. In practice, there are many common collectors that come up over and over. Rather than making developers keep reimplementing the same ones, Java provides a class with common collectors cleverly named `Collectors`. This approach also makes the code easier to read because it is more expressive. For example, we could rewrite the previous example as follows:

```
Stream<String> stream = Stream.of("w", "o", "l", "f");
TreeSet<String> set =
  stream.collect(Collectors.toCollection(TreeSet::new));
System.out.println(set); // [f, l, o, w]
```

If we didn't need the set to be sorted, we could make the code even shorter:

```
Stream<String> stream = Stream.of("w", "o", "l", "f");
Set<String> set = stream.collect(Collectors.toSet());
System.out.println(set); // [f, w, l, o]
```

You might get different output for this last one since `toSet()` makes no guarantees as to which implementation of `Set` you'll get. It is likely to be a `HashSet`, but you shouldn't expect or rely on that.

The exam expects you to know about common predefined collectors in addition to being able to write your own by passing a supplier, accumulator, and combiner.

Later in this chapter, we will show many `Collectors` that are used for grouping data. It's a big topic, so it's best to master how streams work before adding too many `Collectors` into the mix.

Using Common Intermediate Operations

Unlike a terminal operation, an intermediate operation produces a stream as its result. An intermediate operation can also deal with an infinite stream simply by returning another infinite stream. Since elements are produced only as needed, this works fine. The assembly line worker doesn't need to worry about how many more elements are coming through and instead can focus on the current element.

filter()

The filter() method returns a Stream with elements that match a given expression. Here is the method signature:

```
Stream<T> filter(Predicate<? super T> predicate)
```

This operation is easy to remember and powerful because we can pass any Predicate to it. For example, this filters all elements that begin with the letter *m*:

```
Stream<String> s = Stream.of("monkey", "gorilla", "bonobo");
s.filter(x -> x.startsWith("m"))
    .forEach(System.out::print); // monkey
```

distinct()

The distinct() method returns a stream with duplicate values removed. The duplicates do not need to be adjacent to be removed. As you might imagine, Java calls equals() to determine whether the objects are the same. The method signature is as follows:

```
Stream<T> distinct()
```

Here's an example:

```
Stream<String> s = Stream.of("duck", "duck", "duck", "goose");
s.distinct()
    .forEach(System.out::print); // duckgoose
```

limit() and skip()

The limit() and skip() methods can make a Stream smaller, or they could make a finite stream out of an infinite stream. The method signatures are shown here:

```
Stream<T> limit(long maxSize)
Stream<T> skip(long n)
```

The following code creates an infinite stream of numbers counting from 1. The skip() operation returns an infinite stream starting with the numbers counting from 6, since it skips the first five elements. The limit() call takes the first two of those. Now we have a finite stream with two elements, which we can then print with the forEach() method.

```
Stream<Integer> s = Stream.iterate(1, n -> n + 1);
s.skip(5)
    .limit(2)
    .forEach(System.out::print); // 67
```

map()

The map() method creates a one-to-one mapping from the elements in the stream to the elements of the next step in the stream. The method signature is as follows:

```
<R> Stream<R> map(Function<? super T, ? extends R> mapper)
```

This one looks more complicated than the others you have seen. It uses the lambda expression to figure out the type passed to that function and the one returned. The return type is the stream that gets returned.

 The map() method on streams is for transforming data. Don't confuse it with the Map interface, which maps keys to values.

As an example, this code converts a list of String objects to a list of Integer objects representing their lengths.

```
Stream<String> s = Stream.of("monkey", "gorilla", "bonobo");
s.map(String::length)
    .forEach(System.out::print); // 676
```

Remember that String::length is shorthand for the lambda x -> x.length(), which clearly shows it is a function that turns a String into an Integer.

flatMap()

The flatMap() method takes each element in the stream and makes any elements it contains top-level elements in a single stream. This is helpful when you want to remove empty elements from a stream or you want to combine a stream of lists. We are showing you the method signature for consistency with the other methods, just so you don't think we are hiding anything. You aren't expected to be able to read this:

```
<R> Stream<R> flatMap(
    Function<? super T, ? extends Stream<? extends R>> mapper)
```

This gibberish basically says that it returns a Stream of the type that the function contains at a lower level. Don't worry about the signature. It's a headache.

What you should understand is the example. This gets all of the animals into the same level along with getting rid of the empty list.

```
List<String> zero = List.of();
var one = List.of("Bonobo");
var two = List.of("Mama Gorilla", "Baby Gorilla");
Stream<List<String>> animals = Stream.of(zero, one, two);

animals.flatMap(m -> m.stream())
    .forEach(System.out::println);
```

Here's the output:

```
Bonobo
Mama Gorilla
Baby Gorilla
```

As you can see, it removed the empty list completely and changed all elements of each list to be at the top level of the stream.

sorted()

The sorted() method returns a stream with the elements sorted. Just like sorting arrays, Java uses natural ordering unless we specify a comparator. The method signatures are these:

```
Stream<T> sorted()
Stream<T> sorted(Comparator<? super T> comparator)
```

Calling the first signature uses the default sort order.

```
Stream<String> s = Stream.of("brown-", "bear-");
s.sorted()
   .forEach(System.out::print); // bear-brown-
```

We can optionally use a Comparator implementation via a method or a lambda. In this example, we are using a method:

```
Stream<String> s = Stream.of("brown bear-", "grizzly-");
s.sorted(**Comparator.reverseOrder**())
   .forEach(System.out::print); // grizzly-brown bear-
```

Here we passed a Comparator to specify that we want to sort in the reverse of natural sort order. Ready for a tricky one? Do you see why this doesn't compile?

```
s.sorted(Comparator::reverseOrder); // DOES NOT COMPILE
```

Take a look at the method signatures again. Comparator is a functional interface. This means that we can use method references or lambdas to implement it. The Comparator interface implements one method that takes two String parameters and returns an int. However, Comparator::reverseOrder doesn't do that. It is a reference to a function that takes zero parameters and returns a Comparator. This is not compatible with the interface. This means that we have to use a method and not a method reference. We bring this up to remind you that you really do need to know method references well.

peek()

The peek() method is our final intermediate operation. It is useful for debugging because it allows us to perform a stream operation without actually changing the stream. The method signature is as follows:

```
Stream<T> peek(Consumer<? super T> action)
```

You might notice the intermediate peek() operation takes the same argument as the terminal forEach() operation Think of peek() as an intermediate version of forEach() that returns the original stream back to you.

The most common use for peek() is to output the contents of the stream as it goes by. Suppose that we made a typo and counted bears beginning with the letter *g* instead of *b*. We are puzzled why the count is 1 instead of 2. We can add a peek() method to find out why.

```java
var stream = Stream.of("black bear", "brown bear", "grizzly");
long count = stream.filter(s -> s.startsWith("g"))
    .peek(System.out::println).count();           // grizzly
System.out.println(count);                         // 1
```

In Chapter 3, you saw that peek() looks only at the first element when working with a Queue. In a stream, peek() looks at each element that goes through that part of the stream pipeline. It's like having a worker take notes on how a particular step of the process is doing.

Danger: Changing State with *peek()*

Remember that peek() is intended to perform an operation without changing the result. Here's a straightforward stream pipeline that doesn't use peek():

```java
var numbers = new ArrayList<>();
var letters = new ArrayList<>();
numbers.add(1);
letters.add('a');

Stream<List<?>> stream = Stream.of(numbers, letters);
stream.map(List::size).forEach(System.out::print); // 11
```

Now we add a peek() call and note that Java doesn't prevent us from writing bad peek code.

```java
Stream<List<?>> bad = Stream.of(numbers, letters);
bad.peek(x -> x.remove(0))
    .map(List::size)
    .forEach(System.out::print); // 00
```

This example is bad because peek() is modifying the data structure that is used in the stream, which causes the result of the stream pipeline to be different than if the peek wasn't present.

Putting Together the Pipeline

Streams allow you to use chaining and express what you want to accomplish rather than how to do so. Let's say that we wanted to get the first two names of our friends alphabetically that are four characters long. Without streams, we'd have to write something like the following:

```
var list = List.of("Toby", "Anna", "Leroy", "Alex");
List<String> filtered = new ArrayList<>();
for (String name: list)
    if (name.length() == 4) filtered.add(name);


Collections.sort(filtered);
var iter = filtered.iterator();
if (iter.hasNext()) System.out.println(iter.next());
if (iter.hasNext()) System.out.println(iter.next());
```

This works. It takes some reading and thinking to figure out what is going on. The problem we are trying to solve gets lost in the implementation. It is also very focused on the how rather than on the what. With streams, the equivalent code is as follows:

```
var list = List.of("Toby", "Anna", "Leroy", "Alex");
list.stream().filter(n -> n.length() == 4).sorted()
    .limit(2).forEach(System.out::println);
```

Before you say that it is harder to read, we can format it.

```
var list = List.of("Toby", "Anna", "Leroy", "Alex");
list.stream()
    .filter(n -> n.length() == 4)
    .sorted()
    .limit(2)
    .forEach(System.out::println);
```

The difference is that we express what is going on. We care about String objects of length 4. Then we want them sorted. Then we want the first two. Then we want to print them out. It maps better to the problem that we are trying to solve, and it is simpler.

Once you start using streams in your code, you may find yourself using them in many places. Having shorter, briefer, and clearer code is definitely a good thing!

In this example, you see all three parts of the pipeline. Figure 4.5 shows how each intermediate operation in the pipeline feeds into the next.

FIGURE 4.5   Stream pipeline with multiple intermediate operations

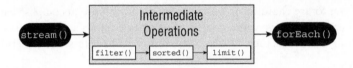

Remember that the assembly line foreman is figuring out how to best implement the stream pipeline. He sets up all of the tables with instructions to wait before starting. He tells the limit() worker to inform him when two elements go by. He tells the sorted() worker that she should just collect all of the elements as they come in and sort them all at once. After sorting, she should start passing them to the limit() worker one at a time. The data flow looks like this:

1. The stream() method sends Toby to filter(). The filter() method sees that the length is good and sends Toby to sorted(). The sorted() method can't sort yet because it needs all of the data, so it holds Toby.

2. The stream() method sends Anna to filter(). The filter() method sees that the length is good and sends Anna to sorted(). The sorted() method can't sort yet because it needs all of the data, so it holds Anna.

3. The stream() method sends Leroy to filter(). The filter() method sees that the length is not a match, and it takes Leroy out of the assembly line processing.

4. The stream() method sends Alex to filter(). The filter() method sees that the length is good and sends Alex to sorted(). The sorted() method can't sort yet because it needs all of the data, so it holds Alex. It turns out sorted() does have all of the required data, but it doesn't know it yet.

5. The foreman lets sorted() know that it is time to sort and the sort occurs.

6. The sorted() method sends Alex to limit(). The limit() method remembers that it has seen one element and sends Alex to forEach(), printing Alex.

7. The sorted() method sends Anna to limit(). The limit() method remembers that it has seen two elements and sends Anna to forEach(), printing Anna.

8. The limit() method has now seen all of the elements that are needed and tells the foreman. The foreman stops the line, and no more processing occurs in the pipeline.

Make sense? Let's try a few more examples to make sure that you understand this well. What do you think the following does?

```
Stream.generate(() -> "Elsa")
    .filter(n -> n.length() == 4)
    .sorted()
    .limit(2)
    .forEach(System.out::println);
```

It actually hangs until you kill the program or it throws an exception after running out of memory. The foreman has instructed `sorted()` to wait until everything to sort is present. That never happens because there is an infinite stream. What about this example?

```
Stream.generate(() -> "Elsa")
   .filter(n -> n.length() == 4)
   .limit(2)
   .sorted()
   .forEach(System.out::println);
```

This one prints `Elsa` twice. The filter lets elements through, and `limit()` stops the earlier operations after two elements. Now `sorted()` can sort because we have a finite list. Finally, what do you think this does?

```
Stream.generate(() -> "Olaf Lazisson")
   .filter(n -> n.length() == 4)
   .limit(2)
   .sorted()
   .forEach(System.out::println);
```

This one hangs as well until we kill the program. The filter doesn't allow anything through, so `limit()` never sees two elements. This means we have to keep waiting and hope that they show up.

You can even chain two pipelines together. See if you can identify the two sources and two terminal operations in this code.

```
30: long count =  Stream.of("goldfish", "finch")
31:     .filter(s -> s.length() > 5)
32:     .collect(Collectors.toList())
33:     .stream()
34:     .count();
35: System.out.println(count);     // 1
```

Lines 30–32 are one pipeline, and lines 33 and 34 are another. For the first pipeline, line 30 is the source, and line 32 is the terminal operation. For the second pipeline, line 33 is the source, and line 34 is the terminal operation. Now that's a complicated way of outputting the number 1!

On the exam, you might see long or complex pipelines as answer choices. If this happens, focus on the differences between the answers. Those will be your clues to the correct answer. This approach will also save you time from not having to study the whole pipeline on each option.

When you see chained pipelines, note where the source and terminal operations are. This will help you keep track of what is going on. You can even rewrite the code in your head to have a variable in between so it isn't as long and complicated. Our prior example can be written as follows:

```
List<String> helper =  Stream.of("goldfish", "finch")
    .filter(s -> s.length() > 5)
    .collect(Collectors.toList());
long count = helper.stream()
    .count();
System.out.println(count);
```

Which style you use is up to you. However, you need to be able to read both styles before you take the exam.

 Real World Scenario

Peeking behind the Scenes

The peek() method is useful for seeing how a stream pipeline works behind the scenes. Remember that the methods run against each element one at a time until processing is done. Suppose that we have this code:

```
var infinite = Stream.iterate(1, x -> x + 1);
infinite.limit(5)
    .filter(x -> x % 2 == 1)
    .forEach(System.out::print); // 135
```

The source is an infinite stream of numbers. Only the first five elements are allowed through before the foreman instructs work to stop. The filter() operation is limited to seeing whether these five numbers from 1 to 5 are odd. Only three are, and those are the ones that get printed, giving 135.

Now what do you think this prints?

```
var infinite = Stream.iterate(1, x -> x + 1);
infinite.limit(5)
    .peek(System.out::print)
    .filter(x -> x % 2 == 1)
    .forEach(System.out::print);
```

The correct answer is 11233455. As the first element passes through, 1 shows up in the peek() and print(). The second element makes it past limit() and peek(), but it gets caught in filter(). The third and fifth elements behave like the first element. The fourth behaves like the second.

Reversing the order of the intermediate operations changes the result.

```
var infinite = Stream.iterate(1, x -> x + 1);
infinite.filter(x -> x % 2 == 1)
    .limit(5)
    .forEach(System.out::print); // 13579
```

The source is still an infinite stream of numbers. The first element still flows through the entire pipeline, and `limit()` remembers that it allows one element through. The second element doesn't make it past `filter()`. The third element flows through the entire pipeline, and `limit()` allows its second element. This proceeds until the ninth element flows through and `limit()` has allowed its fifth element through.

Finally, what do you think this prints?

```
var infinite = Stream.iterate(1, x -> x + 1);
infinite.filter(x -> x % 2 == 1)
    .peek(System.out::print)
    .limit(5)
    .forEach(System.out::print);
```

The answer is 1133557799. Since `filter()` is before `peek()`, we see only the odd numbers.

Working with Primitive Streams

Up until now, all of the streams we've created used the `Stream` class with a generic type, like `Stream<String>`, `Stream<Integer>`, etc. For numeric values, we have been using the wrapper classes you learned about in Chapter 3. We did this with the `Collections` API so it would feel natural.

Java actually includes other stream classes besides `Stream` that you can use to work with select primitives: `int`, `double`, and `long`. Let's take a look at why this is needed. Suppose that we want to calculate the sum of numbers in a finite stream.

```
Stream<Integer> stream = Stream.of(1, 2, 3);
System.out.println(stream.reduce(0, (s, n) -> s + n));  // 6
```

Not bad. It wasn't hard to write a reduction. We started the accumulator with zero. We then added each number to that running total as it came up in the stream. There is another way of doing that, shown here:

```
Stream<Integer> stream = Stream.of(1, 2, 3);
System.out.println(stream.mapToInt(x -> x).sum());  // 6
```

This time, we converted our Stream<Integer> to an IntStream and asked the IntStream to calculate the sum for us. An IntStream has many of the same intermediate and terminal methods as a Stream but includes specialized methods for working with numeric data. The primitive streams know how to perform certain common operations automatically.

So far, this seems like a nice convenience but not terribly important. Now think about how you would compute an average. You need to divide the sum by the number of elements. The problem is that streams allow only one pass. Java recognizes that calculating an average is a common thing to do, and it provides a method to calculate the average on the stream classes for primitives.

```
IntStream intStream = IntStream.of(1, 2, 3);
OptionalDouble avg = intStream.average();
System.out.println(avg.getAsDouble());  // 2.0
```

Not only is it possible to calculate the average, but it is also easy to do so. Clearly primitive streams are important. We will look at creating and using such streams, including optionals and functional interfaces.

Creating Primitive Streams

Here are three types of primitive streams.

- **IntStream:** Used for the primitive types int, short, byte, and char
- **LongStream:** Used for the primitive type long
- **DoubleStream:** Used for the primitive types double and float

Why doesn't each primitive type have its own primitive stream? These three are the most common, so the API designers went with them.

 When you see the word *stream* on the exam, pay attention to the case. With a capital *S* or in code, Stream is the name of a class that contains an Object type. With a lowercase *s*, a stream is a concept that might be a Stream, DoubleStream, IntStream, or LongStream.

Table 4.7 shows some of the methods that are unique to primitive streams. Notice that we don't include methods in the table like empty() that you already know from the Stream interface.

TABLE 4.7   Common primitive stream methods

Method	Primitive stream	Description
OptionalDouble average()	IntStream LongStream DoubleStream	The arithmetic mean of the elements

TABLE 4.7   Common primitive stream methods *(continued)*

Method	Primitive stream	Description
Stream<T> boxed()	IntStream LongStream DoubleStream	A Stream<T> where T is the wrapper class associated with the primitive value
OptionalInt max() OptionalLong max() OptionalDouble max()	IntStream LongStream DoubleStream	The maximum element of the stream
OptionalInt min() OptionalLong min() OptionalDouble min()	IntStream LongStream DoubleStream	The minimum element of the stream
IntStream range(int a, int b) LongStream range(long a, long b)	IntStream LongStream	Returns a primitive stream from a (inclusive) to b (exclusive)
IntStream rangeClosed(int a, int b) LongStream rangeClosed(long a, long b)	IntStream LongStream	Returns a primitive stream from a (inclusive) to b (inclusive)
int sum() long sum() double sum()	IntStream LongStream DoubleStream	Returns the sum of the elements in the stream
IntSummaryStatistics summaryStatistics() LongSummaryStatistics summaryStatistics() DoubleSummaryStatistics summaryStatistics()	IntStream LongStream DoubleStream	Returns an object containing numerous stream statistics such as the average, min, max, etc.

Some of the methods for creating a primitive stream are equivalent to how we created the source for a regular `Stream`. You can create an empty stream with this:

```
DoubleStream empty = DoubleStream.empty();
```

Another way is to use the of() factory method from a single value or by using the varargs overload.

```
DoubleStream oneValue = DoubleStream.of(3.14);
oneValue.forEach(System.out::println);

DoubleStream varargs = DoubleStream.of(1.0, 1.1, 1.2);
varargs.forEach(System.out::println);
```

This code outputs the following:

```
3.14
1.0
1.1
1.2
```

You can also use the two methods for creating infinite streams, just like we did with `Stream`.

```
var random = DoubleStream.generate(Math::random);
var fractions = DoubleStream.iterate(.5, d -> d / 2);
random.limit(3).forEach(System.out::println);
fractions.limit(3).forEach(System.out::println);
```

Since the streams are infinite, we added a limit intermediate operation so that the output doesn't print values forever. The first stream calls a `static` method on `Math` to get a random double. Since the numbers are random, your output will obviously be different. The second stream keeps creating smaller numbers, dividing the previous value by two each time. The output from when we ran this code was as follows:

```
0.07890654781186413
0.28564363465842346
0.6311403511266134
0.5
0.25
0.125
```

You don't need to know this for the exam, but the `Random` class provides a method to get primitives streams of random numbers directly. Fun fact! For example, `ints()` generates an infinite `IntStream` of primitives.

It works the same way for each type of primitive stream. When dealing with `int` or `long` primitives, it is common to count. Suppose that we wanted a stream with the numbers from 1 through 5. We could write this using what we've explained so far:

```
IntStream count = IntStream.iterate(1, n -> n+1).limit(5);
count.forEach(System.out::println);
```

This code does print out the numbers 1–5, one per line. However, it is a lot of code to do something so simple. Java provides a method that can generate a range of numbers.

```
IntStream range = IntStream.range(1, 6);
range.forEach(System.out::println);
```

This is better. If we wanted numbers 1–5, why did we pass 1–6? The first parameter to the `range()` method is *inclusive*, which means it includes the number. The second parameter to the `range()` method is *exclusive*, which means it stops right before that number. However, it still could be clearer. We want the numbers 1–5 inclusive. Luckily, there's another method, `rangeClosed()`, which is inclusive on both parameters.

```
IntStream rangeClosed = IntStream.rangeClosed(1, 5);
rangeClosed.forEach(System.out::println);
```

Even better. This time we expressed that we want a closed range, or an inclusive range. This method better matches how we express a range of numbers in plain English.

Mapping Streams

Another way to create a primitive stream is by mapping from another stream type. Table 4.8 shows that there is a method for mapping between any stream types.

TABLE 4.8   Mapping methods between types of streams

Source stream class	To create Stream	To create DoubleStream	To create IntStream	To create LongStream
Stream<T>	map()	mapToDouble()	mapToInt()	mapToLong()
DoubleStream	mapToObj()	map()	mapToInt()	mapToLong()
IntStream	mapToObj()	mapToDouble()	map()	mapToLong()
LongStream	mapToObj()	mapToDouble()	mapToInt()	map()

Obviously, they have to be compatible types for this to work. Java requires a mapping function to be provided as a parameter, for example:

```
Stream<String> objStream = Stream.of("penguin", "fish");
IntStream intStream = objStream.mapToInt(s -> s.length());
```

This function takes an `Object`, which is a `String` in this case. The function returns an `int`. The function mappings are intuitive here. They take the source type and return the target type. In this example, the actual function type is `ToIntFunction`. Table 4.9 shows the mapping function names. As you can see, they do what you might expect.

TABLE 4.9   Function parameters when mapping between types of streams

Source stream class	To create `Stream`	To create `DoubleStream`	To create `IntStream`	To create `LongStream`
`Stream<T>`	`Function<T,R>`	`ToDouble Function<T>`	`ToInt Function<T>`	`ToLong Function<T>`
`DoubleStream`	`Double Function<R>`	`DoubleUnary Operator`	`DoubleToInt Function`	`DoubleToLong Function`
`IntStream`	`IntFunction<R>`	`IntToDouble Function`	`IntUnary Operator`	`IntToLong Function`
`LongStream`	`Long Function<R>`	`LongToDouble Function`	`LongToInt Function`	`LongUnary Operator`

You do have to memorize Table 4.8 and Table 4.9. It's not as hard as it might seem. There are patterns in the names if you remember a few rules. For Table 4.8, mapping to the same type you started with is just called `map()`. When returning an object stream, the method is `mapToObj()`. Beyond that, it's the name of the primitive type in the map method name.

For Table 4.9, you can start by thinking about the source and target types. When the target type is an object, you drop the To from the name. When the mapping is to the same type you started with, you use a unary operator instead of a function for the primitive streams.

Using *flatMap()*

The `flatMap()` method exists on primitive streams as well. It works the same way as on a regular `Stream` except the method name is different. Here's an example:

```
var integerList = new ArrayList<Integer>();
IntStream ints = integerList.stream()
  .flatMapToInt(x -> IntStream.of(x));
DoubleStream doubles = integerList.stream()
  .flatMapToDouble(x -> DoubleStream.of(x));
LongStream longs = integerList.stream()
  .flatMapToLong(x -> LongStream.of(x));
```

Additionally, you can create a Stream from a primitive stream. These methods show two ways of accomplishing this:

```
private static Stream<Integer> mapping(IntStream stream) {
   return stream.mapToObj(x -> x);
}


private static Stream<Integer> boxing(IntStream stream) {
   return stream.boxed();
}
```

The first one uses the mapToObj() method we saw earlier. The second one is more succinct. It does not require a mapping function because all it does is autobox each primitive to the corresponding wrapper object. The boxed() method exists on all three types of primitive streams.

Using *Optional* with Primitive Streams

Earlier in the chapter, we wrote a method to calculate the average of an int[] and promised a better way later. Now that you know about primitive streams, you can calculate the average in one line.

```
var stream = IntStream.rangeClosed(1,10);
OptionalDouble optional = stream.average();
```

The return type is not the Optional you have become accustomed to using. It is a new type called OptionalDouble. Why do we have a separate type, you might wonder? Why not just use Optional<Double>? The difference is that OptionalDouble is for a primitive and Optional<Double> is for the Double wrapper class. Working with the primitive optional class looks similar to working with the Optional class itself.

```
optional.ifPresent(System.out::println);                  // 5.5
System.out.println(optional.getAsDouble());               // 5.5
System.out.println(optional.orElseGet(() -> Double.NaN)); // 5.5
```

The only noticeable difference is that we called getAsDouble() rather than get(). This makes it clear that we are working with a primitive. Also, orElseGet() takes a DoubleSupplier instead of a Supplier.

As with the primitive streams, there are three type-specific classes for primitives. Table 4.10 shows the minor differences among the three. You probably won't be surprised that you have to memorize it as well. This is really easy to remember since the primitive name is the only change. As you should remember from the terminal operations section, a number of stream methods return an optional such as min() or findAny(). These each return the corresponding optional type. The primitive stream implementations also add two new methods that you need to know. The sum() method does not return an optional. If you try to add up an empty stream, you simply get zero. The average() method always returns an OptionalDouble since an average can potentially have fractional data for any type.

TABLE 4.10   Optional types for primitives

	OptionalDouble	OptionalInt	OptionalLong
Getting as a primitive	getAsDouble()	getAsInt()	getAsLong()
orElseGet() parameter type	DoubleSupplier	IntSupplier	LongSupplier
Return type of max() and min()	OptionalDouble	OptionalInt	OptionalLong
Return type of sum()	double	int	long
Return type of average()	OptionalDouble	OptionalDouble	OptionalDouble

Let's try an example to make sure that you understand this.

```
5: LongStream longs = LongStream.of(5, 10);
6: long sum = longs.sum();
7: System.out.println(sum);       // 15
8: DoubleStream doubles = DoubleStream.generate(() -> Math.PI);
9: OptionalDouble min = doubles.min(); // runs infinitely
```

Line 5 creates a stream of long primitives with two elements. Line 6 shows that we don't use an optional to calculate a sum. Line 8 creates an infinite stream of double primitives. Line 9 is there to remind you that a question about code that runs infinitely can appear with primitive streams as well.

Summarizing Statistics

You've learned enough to be able to get the maximum value from a stream of int primitives. If the stream is empty, we want to throw an exception.

```
private static int max(IntStream ints) {
    OptionalInt optional = ints.max();
    return optional.orElseThrow(RuntimeException::new);
}
```

This should be old hat by now. We got an OptionalInt because we have an IntStream. If the optional contains a value, we return it. Otherwise, we throw a new RuntimeException.

Now we want to change the method to take an IntStream and return a range. The range is the minimum value subtracted from the maximum value. Uh-oh. Both min() and max() are terminal operations, which means that they use up the stream when they are run. We can't run two terminal operations against the same stream. Luckily, this is a common problem and the primitive streams solve it for us with summary statistics. *Statistic* is just a big word for a number that was calculated from data.

```
private static int range(IntStream ints) {
   IntSummaryStatistics stats = ints.summaryStatistics();
   if (stats.getCount() == 0) throw new RuntimeException();
   return stats.getMax()-stats.getMin();
}
```

Here we asked Java to perform many calculations about the stream. Summary statistics include the following:

- Smallest number (minimum): getMin()
- Largest number (maximum): getMax()
- Average: getAverage()
- Sum: getSum()
- Number of values: getCount()

If the stream were empty, we'd have a count and sum of zero. The other methods would return an empty optional.

Learning the Functional Interfaces for Primitives

Remember when we told you to memorize Table 4.1, with the common functional interfaces, at the beginning of the chapter? Did you? If you didn't, go do it now. We are about to make it more involved. Just as there are special streams and optional classes for primitives, there are also special functional interfaces.

Luckily, most of them are for the double, int, and long types that you saw for streams and optionals. There is one exception, which is BooleanSupplier. We will cover that before introducing the ones for double, int, and long.

Functional Interfaces for *boolean*

BooleanSupplier is a separate type. It has one method to implement:

```
boolean getAsBoolean()
```

It works just as you've come to expect from functional interfaces. Here's an example:

```
12: BooleanSupplier b1 = () -> true;
13: BooleanSupplier b2 = () -> Math.random() > .5;
14: System.out.println(b1.getAsBoolean());  // true
15: System.out.println(b2.getAsBoolean());  // false
```

Lines 12 and 13 each create a BooleanSupplier, which is the only functional interface for boolean. Line 14 prints true, since it is the result of b1. Line 15 prints out true or false, depending on the random value generated.

Functional Interfaces for *double, int,* and *long*

Most of the functional interfaces are for double, int, and long to match the streams and optionals that we've been using for primitives. Table 4.11 shows the equivalent of Table 4.1 for these primitives. You probably won't be surprised that you have to memorize it. Luckily, you've memorized Table 4.1 by now and can apply what you've learned to Table 4.11.

TABLE 4.11   Common functional interfaces for primitives

Functional interfaces	# parameters	Return type	Single abstract method
DoubleSupplier	0	double	getAsDouble
IntSupplier		int	getAsInt
LongSupplier		long	getAsLong
DoubleConsumer	1 (double)	void	accept
IntConsumer	1 (int)		
LongConsumer	1 (long)		
DoublePredicate	1 (double)	boolean	test
IntPredicate	1 (int)		
LongPredicate	1 (long)		
DoubleFunction<R>	1 (double)	R	apply
IntFunction<R>	1 (int)		
LongFunction<R>	1 (long)		
DoubleUnaryOperator	1 (double)	double	applyAsDouble
IntUnaryOperator	1 (int)	int	applyAsInt
LongUnaryOperator	1 (long)	long	applyAsLong
DoubleBinaryOperator	2 (double, double)	double	applyAsDouble
IntBinaryOperator	2 (int, int)	int	applyAsInt
LongBinaryOperator	2 (long, long)	long	applyAsLong

There are a few things to notice that are different between Table 4.1 and Table 4.11.

- Generics are gone from some of the interfaces, and instead the type name tells us what primitive type is involved. In other cases, such as IntFunction, only the return type generic is needed because we're converting a primitive int into an object.

- The single abstract method is often renamed when a primitive type is returned.

In addition to Table 4.1 equivalents, some interfaces are specific to primitives. Table 4.12 lists these.

TABLE 4.12   Primitive-specific functional interfaces

Functional interfaces	# parameters	Return type	Single abstract method
ToDoubleFunction<T>	1 (T)	double	applyAsDouble
ToIntFunction<T>		int	applyAsInt
ToLongFunction<T>		long	applyAsLong
ToDoubleBiFunction<T, U>	2 (T, U)	double	applyAsDouble
ToIntBiFunction<T, U>		int	applyAsInt
ToLongBiFunction<T, U>		long	applyAsLong
DoubleToIntFunction	1 (double)	int	applyAsInt
DoubleToLongFunction	1 (double)	long	applyAsLong
IntToDoubleFunction	1 (int)	double	applyAsDouble
IntToLongFunction	1 (int)	long	applyAsLong
LongToDoubleFunction	1 (long)	double	applyAsDouble
LongToIntFunction	1 (long)	int	applyAsInt
ObjDoubleConsumer<T>	2 (T, double)	void	accept
ObjIntConsumer<T>	2 (T, int)		
ObjLongConsumer<T>	2 (T, long)		

We've been using functional interfaces all chapter long, so you should have a good grasp of how to read the table by now. Let's do one example just to be sure. Which functional interface would you use to fill in the blank to make the following code compile?

```
var d = 1.0;
_____ f1 = x -> 1;
f1.applyAsInt(d);
```

When you see a question like this, look for clues. You can see that the functional interface in question takes a double parameter and returns an int. You can also see that it has a single abstract method named applyAsInt. The DoubleToIntFunction and ToIntFunction meet all three of those criteria.

Working with Advanced Stream Pipeline Concepts

You've almost reached the end of learning about streams. We have only a few more topics left. You'll see the relationship between streams and the underlying data, chaining Optional and grouping collectors.

Linking Streams to the Underlying Data

What do you think this outputs?

```
25: var cats = new ArrayList<String>();
26: cats.add("Annie");
27: cats.add("Ripley");
28: var stream = cats.stream();
29: cats.add("KC");
30: System.out.println(stream.count());
```

The correct answer is 3. Lines 25–27 create a List with two elements. Line 28 requests that a stream be created from that List. Remember that streams are lazily evaluated. This means that the stream isn't actually created on line 28. An object is created that knows where to look for the data when it is needed. On line 29, the List gets a new element. On line 30, the stream pipeline actually runs. The stream pipeline runs first, looking at the source and seeing three elements.

Chaining Optionals

By now, you are familiar with the benefits of chaining operations in a stream pipeline. A few of the intermediate operations for streams are available for Optional.

Suppose that you are given an Optional<Integer> and asked to print the value, but only if it is a three-digit number. Without functional programming, you could write the following:

```
private static void threeDigit(Optional<Integer> optional) {
    if (optional.isPresent()) {  // outer if
        var num = optional.get();
        var string = "" + num;
        if (string.length() == 3) // inner if
            System.out.println(string);
    }
}
```

It works, but it contains nested `if` statements. That's extra complexity. Let's try this again with functional programming.

```java
private static void threeDigit(Optional<Integer> optional) {
    optional.map(n -> "" + n)              // part 1
        .filter(s -> s.length() == 3)      // part 2
        .ifPresent(System.out::println);   // part 3
}
```

This is much shorter and more expressive. With lambdas, the exam is fond of carving up a single statement and identifying the pieces with a comment. We've done that here to show what happens with both the functional programming and nonfunctional programming approaches.

Suppose that we are given an empty `Optional`. The first approach returns `false` for the outer `if` statement. The second approach sees an empty `Optional` and has both `map()` and `filter()` pass it through. Then `ifPresent()` sees an empty `Optional` and doesn't call the Consumer parameter.

The next case is where we are given an `Optional.of(4)`. The first approach returns `false` for the inner `if` statement. The second approach maps the number 4 to `"4"`. The `filter()` then returns an empty `Optional` since the filter doesn't match, and `ifPresent()` doesn't call the Consumer parameter.

The final case is where we are given an `Optional.of(123)`. The first approach returns `true` for both `if` statements. The second approach maps the number 123 to `"123"`. The `filter()` then returns the same `Optional`, and `ifPresent()` now does call the Consumer parameter.

Now suppose that we wanted to get an `Optional<Integer>` representing the length of the `String` contained in another `Optional`. Easy enough.

```java
Optional<Integer> result = optional.map(String::length);
```

What if we had a helper method that did the logic of calculating something for us that returns `Optional<Integer>`? Using map doesn't work.

```java
Optional<Integer> result = optional
    .map(ChainingOptionals::calculator); // DOES NOT COMPILE
```

The problem is that calculator returns `Optional<Integer>`. The `map()` method adds another `Optional`, giving us `Optional<Optional<Integer>>`. Well, that's no good. The solution is to call `flatMap()` instead.

```java
Optional<Integer> result = optional
    .flatMap(ChainingOptionals::calculator);
```

This one works because `flatMap` removes the unnecessary layer. In other words, it flattens the result. Chaining calls to `flatMap()` is useful when you want to transform one `Optional` type to another.

 **Real World Scenario**

Checked Exceptions and Functional Interfaces

You might have noticed by now that most functional interfaces do not declare checked exceptions. This is normally OK. However, it is a problem when working with methods that declare checked exceptions. Suppose that we have a class with a method that throws a checked exception.

```java
import java.io.*;
import java.util.*;
public class ExceptionCaseStudy {
    private static List<String> create() throws IOException {
        throw new IOException();
    }
}
```

Now we use it in a stream.

```java
public void good() throws IOException {
    ExceptionCaseStudy.create().stream().count();
}
```

Nothing new here. The create() method throws a checked exception. The calling method handles or declares it. Now what about this one?

```java
public void bad() throws IOException {
    Supplier<List<String>> s = ExceptionCaseStudy::create; // DOES NOT COMPILE
}
```

The actual compiler error is as follows:

```
unhandled exception type IOException
```

Say what now? The problem is that the lambda to which this method reference expands does not declare an exception. The Supplier interface does not allow checked exceptions. There are two approaches to get around this problem. One is to catch the exception and turn it into an unchecked exception.

```java
public void ugly() {
    Supplier<List<String>> s = () -> {
        try {
            return ExceptionCaseStudy.create();
        } catch (IOException e) {
```

```
            throw new RuntimeException(e);
        }
    };
}
```

This works. But the code is ugly. One of the benefits of functional programming is that the code is supposed to be easy to read and concise. Another alternative is to create a wrapper method with the try/catch.

```
private static List<String> createSafe() {
    try {
        return ExceptionCaseStudy.create();
    } catch (IOException e) {
        throw new RuntimeException(e);
    } }
```

Now we can use the safe wrapper in our Supplier without issue.

```
public void wrapped() {
    Supplier<List<String>> s2 = ExceptionCaseStudy::createSafe;
}
```

Collecting Results

You're almost finished learning about streams. The last topic builds on what you've learned so far to group the results. Early in the chapter, you saw the collect() terminal operation. There are many predefined collectors, including those shown in Table 4.13. These collectors are available via static methods on the Collectors interface. We will look at the different types of collectors in the following sections.

TABLE 4.13 Examples of grouping/partitioning collectors

Collector	Description	Return value when passed to collect
averagingDouble(ToDoubleFunction f) averagingInt(ToIntFunction f) averagingLong(ToLongFunction f)	Calculates the average for our three core primitive types	Double
counting()	Counts the number of elements	Long

TABLE 4.13   Examples of grouping/partitioning collectors *(continued)*

Collector	Description	Return value when passed to collect
groupingBy(Function f) groupingBy(Function f, Collector dc) groupingBy(Function f, Supplier s, Collector dc)	Creates a map grouping by the specified function with the optional map type supplier and optional downstream collector	Map<K, List<T>>
joining(CharSequence cs)	Creates a single String using cs as a delimiter between elements if one is specified	String
maxBy(Comparator c) minBy(Comparator c)	Finds the largest/smallest elements	Optional<T>
mapping(Function f, Collector dc)	Adds another level of collectors	Collector
partitioningBy(Predicate p) partitioningBy(Predicate p, Collector dc)	Creates a map grouping by the specified predicate with the optional further downstream collector	Map<Boolean, List<T>>
summarizingDouble(ToDoubleFunction f) summarizingInt(ToIntFunction f) summarizingLong(ToLongFunction f)	Calculates average, min, max, and so on	DoubleSummary Statistics IntSummary Statistics LongSummary Statistics
summingDouble(ToDoubleFunction f) summingInt(ToIntFunction f) summingLong(ToLongFunction f)	Calculates the sum for our three core primitive types	Double Integer Long
toList() toSet()	Creates an arbitrary type of list or set	List Set
toCollection(Supplier s)	Creates a Collection of the specified type	Collection

Collector	Description	Return value when passed to collect
toMap(Function k, Function v) toMap(Function k, Function v, BinaryOperator m) toMap(Function k, Function v, BinaryOperator m, Supplier s)	Creates a map using functions to map the keys, values, an optional merge function, and an optional map type supplier	Map

Collecting Using Basic Collectors

Luckily, many of these collectors work in the same way. Let's look at an example.

```
var ohMy = Stream.of("lions", "tigers", "bears");
String result = ohMy.collect(Collectors.joining(", "));
System.out.println(result); // lions, tigers, bears
```

Notice how the predefined collectors are in the Collectors class rather than the Collector interface. This is a common theme, which you saw with Collection versus Collections. In fact, you'll see this pattern again in Chapter 9, "NIO.2," when working with Paths and Path, and other related types.

We pass the predefined joining() collector to the collect() method. All elements of the stream are then merged into a String with the specified delimiter between each element. It is important to pass the Collector to the collect method. It exists to help collect elements. A Collector doesn't do anything on its own.

Let's try another one. What is the average length of the three animal names?

```
var ohMy = Stream.of("lions", "tigers", "bears");
Double result = ohMy.collect(Collectors.averagingInt(String::length));
System.out.println(result); // 5.333333333333333
```

The pattern is the same. We pass a collector to collect(), and it performs the average for us. This time, we needed to pass a function to tell the collector what to average. We used a method reference, which returns an int upon execution. With primitive streams, the result of an average was always a double, regardless of what type is being averaged. For collectors, it is a Double since those need an Object.

Often, you'll find yourself interacting with code that was written without streams. This means that it will expect a Collection type rather than a Stream type. No problem. You can still express yourself using a Stream and then convert to a Collection at the end, for example:

```
var ohMy = Stream.of("lions", "tigers", "bears");
TreeSet<String> result = ohMy
```

```
 .filter(s -> s.startsWith("t"))
 .collect(Collectors.toCollection(TreeSet::new));
System.out.println(result); // [tigers]
```

This time we have all three parts of the stream pipeline. `Stream.of()` is the source for the stream. The intermediate operation is `filter()`. Finally, the terminal operation is `collect()`, which creates a `TreeSet`. If we didn't care which implementation of `Set` we got, we could have written `Collectors.toSet()` instead.

At this point, you should be able to use all of the `Collectors` in Table 4.13 except `groupingBy()`, `mapping()`, `partitioningBy()`, and `toMap()`.

Collecting into Maps

Code using `Collectors` involving maps can get quite long. We will build it up slowly. Make sure that you understand each example before going on to the next one. Let's start with a straightforward example to create a map from a stream.

```
var ohMy = Stream.of("lions", "tigers", "bears");
Map<String, Integer> map = ohMy.collect(
    Collectors.toMap(s -> s, String::length));
System.out.println(map); // {lions=5, bears=5, tigers=6}
```

When creating a map, you need to specify two functions. The first function tells the collector how to create the key. In our example, we use the provided `String` as the key. The second function tells the collector how to create the value. In our example, we use the length of the `String` as the value.

 Returning the same value passed into a lambda is a common operation, so Java provides a method for it. You can rewrite `s -> s` as `Function.identity()`. It is not shorter and may or may not be clearer, so use your judgment on whether to use it.

Now we want to do the reverse and map the length of the animal name to the name itself. Our first incorrect attempt is shown here:

```
var ohMy = Stream.of("lions", "tigers", "bears");
Map<Integer, String> map = ohMy.collect(Collectors.toMap(
    String::length,
    k -> k)); // BAD
```

Running this gives an exception similar to the following:

```
Exception in thread "main"
    java.lang.IllegalStateException: Duplicate key 5
```

What's wrong? Two of the animal names are the same length. We didn't tell Java what to do. Should the collector choose the first one it encounters? The last one it encounters? Concatenate the two? Since the collector has no idea what to do, it "solves" the problem by throwing an exception and making it our problem. How thoughtful. Let's suppose that our requirement is to create a comma-separated `String` with the animal names. We could write this:

```
var ohMy = Stream.of("lions", "tigers", "bears");
Map<Integer, String> map = ohMy.collect(Collectors.toMap(
   String::length,
   k -> k,
   (s1, s2) -> s1 + "," + s2));
System.out.println(map);          // {5=lions,bears, 6=tigers}
System.out.println(map.getClass()); // class java.util.HashMap
```

It so happens that the `Map` returned is a `HashMap`. This behavior is not guaranteed. Suppose that we want to mandate that the code return a `TreeMap` instead. No problem. We would just add a constructor reference as a parameter.

```
var ohMy = Stream.of("lions", "tigers", "bears");
TreeMap<Integer, String> map = ohMy.collect(Collectors.toMap(
   String::length,
   k -> k,
   (s1, s2) -> s1 + "," + s2,
   TreeMap::new));
System.out.println(map); //          // {5=lions,bears, 6=tigers}
System.out.println(map.getClass()); // class java.util.TreeMap
```

This time we got the type that we specified. With us so far? This code is long but not particularly complicated. We did promise you that the code would be long!

Collecting Using Grouping, Partitioning, and Mapping

Great job getting this far. The exam creators like asking about `groupingBy()` and `partitioningBy()`, so make sure you understand these sections very well. Now suppose that we want to get groups of names by their length. We can do that by saying that we want to group by length.

```
var ohMy = Stream.of("lions", "tigers", "bears");
Map<Integer, List<String>> map = ohMy.collect(
   Collectors.groupingBy(String::length));
System.out.println(map);     // {5=[lions, bears], 6=[tigers]}
```

The `groupingBy()` collector tells `collect()` that it should group all of the elements of the stream into a `Map`. The function determines the keys in the `Map`. Each value in the `Map` is a `List` of all entries that match that key.

Note that the function you call in groupingBy() cannot return null. It does
not allow null keys.

Suppose that we don't want a List as the value in the map and prefer a Set instead. No
problem. There's another method signature that lets us pass a *downstream collector*. This is
a second collector that does something special with the values.

```
var ohMy = Stream.of("lions", "tigers", "bears");
Map<Integer, Set<String>> map = ohMy.collect(
    Collectors.groupingBy(
        String::length,
        Collectors.toSet()));
System.out.println(map);     // {5=[lions, bears], 6=[tigers]}
```

We can even change the type of Map returned through yet another parameter.

```
var ohMy = Stream.of("lions", "tigers", "bears");
TreeMap<Integer, Set<String>> map = ohMy.collect(
    Collectors.groupingBy(
        String::length,
        TreeMap::new,
        Collectors.toSet()));
System.out.println(map); // {5=[lions, bears], 6=[tigers]}
```

This is very flexible. What if we want to change the type of Map returned but leave the
type of values alone as a List? There isn't a method for this specifically because it is easy
enough to write with the existing ones.

```
var ohMy = Stream.of("lions", "tigers", "bears");
TreeMap<Integer, List<String>> map = ohMy.collect(
    Collectors.groupingBy(
        String::length,
        TreeMap::new,
        Collectors.toList()));
System.out.println(map);
```

Partitioning is a special case of grouping. With partitioning, there are only two possible
groups—true and false. *Partitioning* is like splitting a list into two parts.

Suppose that we are making a sign to put outside each animal's exhibit. We have two
sizes of signs. One can accommodate names with five or fewer characters. The other is
needed for longer names. We can partition the list according to which sign we need.

```
var ohMy = Stream.of("lions", "tigers", "bears");
Map<Boolean, List<String>> map = ohMy.collect(
    Collectors.partitioningBy(s -> s.length() <= 5));
System.out.println(map);     // {false=[tigers], true=[lions, bears]}
```

Here we passed a `Predicate` with the logic for which group each animal name belongs in. Now suppose that we've figured out how to use a different font, and seven characters can now fit on the smaller sign. No worries. We just change the `Predicate`.

```
var ohMy = Stream.of("lions", "tigers", "bears");
Map<Boolean, List<String>> map = ohMy.collect(
    Collectors.partitioningBy(s -> s.length() <= 7));
System.out.println(map);    // {false=[], true=[lions, tigers, bears]}
```

Notice that there are still two keys in the map—one for each boolean value. It so happens that one of the values is an empty list, but it is still there. As with `groupingBy()`, we can change the type of `List` to something else.

```
var ohMy = Stream.of("lions", "tigers", "bears");
Map<Boolean, Set<String>> map = ohMy.collect(
    Collectors.partitioningBy(
        s -> s.length() <= 7,
        Collectors.toSet()));
System.out.println(map);    // {false=[], true=[lions, tigers, bears]}
```

Unlike `groupingBy()`, we cannot change the type of `Map` that gets returned. However, there are only two keys in the map, so does it really matter which Map type we use?

Instead of using the downstream collector to specify the type, we can use any of the collectors that we've already shown. For example, we can group by the length of the animal name to see how many of each length we have.

```
var ohMy = Stream.of("lions", "tigers", "bears");
Map<Integer, Long> map = ohMy.collect(
    Collectors.groupingBy(
        String::length,
        Collectors.counting()));
System.out.println(map);    // {5=2, 6=1}
```

Debugging Complicated Generics

When working with `collect()`, there are often many levels of generics, making compiler errors unreadable. Here are three useful techniques for dealing with this situation:

- Start over with a simple statement and keep adding to it. By making one tiny change at a time, you will know which code introduced the error.

- Extract parts of the statement into separate statements. For example, try writing `Collectors.groupingBy(String::length, Collectors.counting());`. If it compiles, you know that the problem lies elsewhere. If it doesn't compile, you have a much shorter statement to troubleshoot.

- Use generic wildcards for the return type of the final statement; for example, `Map<?, ?>`. If that change alone allows the code to compile, you'll know that the problem lies with the return type not being what you expect.

Finally, there is a `mapping()` collector that lets us go down a level and add another collector. Suppose that we wanted to get the first letter of the first animal alphabetically of each length. Why? Perhaps for random sampling. The examples on this part of the exam are fairly contrived as well. We'd write the following:

```
var ohMy = Stream.of("lions", "tigers", "bears");
Map<Integer, Optional<Character>> map = ohMy.collect(
    Collectors.groupingBy(
        String::length,
        Collectors.mapping(
            s -> s.charAt(0),
            Collectors.minBy((a, b) -> a -b))));
System.out.println(map);    // {5=Optional[b], 6=Optional[t]}
```

We aren't going to tell you that this code is easy to read. We will tell you that it is the most complicated thing you need to understand for the exam. Comparing it to the previous example, you can see that we replaced `counting()` with `mapping()`. It so happens that `mapping()` takes two parameters: the function for the value and how to group it further.

You might see collectors used with a `static` import to make the code shorter. The exam might even use `var` for the return value and less indentation than we used. This means that you might see something like this:

```
var ohMy = Stream.of("lions", "tigers", "bears");
var map = ohMy.collect(groupingBy(String::length,
  mapping(s -> s.charAt(0), minBy((a, b) -> a -b))));
System.out.println(map);    // {5=Optional[b], 6=Optional[t]}
```

The code does the same thing as in the previous example. This means that it is important to recognize the collector names because you might not have the `Collectors` class name to call your attention to it.

 There is one more collector called `reducing()`. You don't need to know it for the exam. It is a general reduction in case all of the previous collectors don't meet your needs.

Summary

A functional interface has a single abstract method. You must know the functional interfaces.

- `Supplier<T>` with method: `T get()`
- `Consumer<T>` with method: `void accept(T t)`
- `BiConsumer<T, U>` with method: `void accept(T t, U u)`

- `Predicate<T>` with method: `boolean test(T t)`
- `BiPredicate<T, U>` with method: `boolean test(T t, U u)`
- `Function<T, R>` with method: `R apply(T t)`
- `BiFunction<T, U, R>` with method: `R apply(T t, U u)`
- `UnaryOperator<T>` with method: `T apply(T t)`
- `BinaryOperator<T>` with method: `T apply(T t1, T t2)`

An `Optional<T>` can be empty or store a value. You can check whether it contains a value with `isPresent()` and `get()` the value inside. You can return a different value with `orElse(T t)` or throw an exception with `orElseThrow()`. There are even three methods that take functional interfaces as parameters: `ifPresent(Consumer c)`, `orElseGet(Supplier s)`, and `orElseThrow(Supplier s)`. There are three optional types for primitives: `OptionalDouble`, `OptionalInt`, and `OptionalLong`. These have the methods `getAsDouble()`, `getAsInt()`, and `getAsLong()`, respectively.

A stream pipeline has three parts. The source is required, and it creates the data in the stream. There can be zero or more intermediate operations, which aren't executed until the terminal operation runs. The first stream class we covered was `Stream<T>`, which takes a generic argument T. The `Stream<T>` class includes many useful intermediate operations including `filter()`, `map()`, `flatMap()`, and `sorted()`. Examples of terminal operations include `allMatch()`, `count()`, and `forEach()`.

Besides the `Stream<T>` class, there are three primitive streams: `DoubleStream`, `IntStream`, and `LongStream`. In addition to the usual `Stream<T>` methods, `IntStream` and `LongStream` have `range()` and `rangeClosed()`. The call `range(1, 10)` on `IntStream` and `LongStream` creates a stream of the primitives from 1 to 9. By contrast, `rangeClosed(1, 10)` creates a stream of the primitives from 1 to 10. The primitive streams have math operations including `average()`, `max()`, and `sum()`. They also have `summaryStatistics()` to get many statistics in one call. There are also functional interfaces specific to streams. Except for `BooleanSupplier`, they are all for double, int, and long primitives as well.

You can use a `Collector` to transform a stream into a traditional collection. You can even group fields to create a complex map in one line. Partitioning works the same way as grouping, except that the keys are always `true` and `false`. A partitioned map always has two keys even if the value is empty for the key.

You should review the tables in the chapter. While there's a lot of tables, many share common patterns, making it easier to remember them. You absolutely must memorize Table 4.1. You should memorize Table 4.8 and Table 4.9 but be able to spot incompatibilities, such as type differences, if you can't memorize these two. Finally, remember that streams are lazily evaluated. They take lambdas or method references as parameters, which execute later when the method is run.

Exam Essentials

Identify the correct functional interface given the number of parameters, return type, and method name—and vice versa.   The most common functional interfaces are Supplier, Consumer, Function, and Predicate. There are also binary versions and primitive versions of many of these methods.

Write code that uses *Optional*.   Creating an Optional uses Optional.empty() or Optional.of(). Retrieval frequently uses isPresent() and get(). Alternatively, there are the functional ifPresent() and orElseGet() methods.

Recognize which operations cause a stream pipeline to execute.   Intermediate operations do not run until the terminal operation is encountered. If no terminal operation is in the pipeline, a Stream is returned but not executed. Examples of terminal operations include collect(), forEach(), min(), and reduce().

Determine which terminal operations are reductions.   Reductions use all elements of the stream in determining the result. The reductions that you need to know are collect(), count(), max(), min(), and reduce(). A mutable reduction collects into the same object as it goes. The collect() method is a mutable reduction.

Write code for common intermediate operations.   The filter() method returns a Stream<T> filtering on a Predicate<T>. The map() method returns a Stream transforming each element of type T to another type R through a Function <T,R>. The flatMap() method flattens nested streams into a single level and removes empty streams.

Compare primitive streams to *Stream<T>*.   Primitive streams are useful for performing common operations on numeric types including statistics like average(), sum(), etc. There are three primitive stream classes: DoubleStream, IntStream, and LongStream. There are also three primitive Optional classes: OptionalDouble, OptionalInt, and OptionalLong. Aside from BooleanSupplier, they all involve the double, int, or long primitives.

Convert primitive stream types to other primitive stream types. Normally when mapping, you just call the *map()* method.   When changing the class used for the stream, a different method is needed. To convert to Stream, you use mapToObj(). To convert to DoubleStream, you use mapToDouble(). To convert to IntStream, you use mapToInt(). To convert to LongStream, you use mapToLong().

Use *peek()* to inspect the stream.   The peek() method is an intermediate operation often used for debugging purposes. It executes a lambda or method reference on the input and passes that same input through the pipeline to the next operator. It is useful for printing out what passes through a certain point in a stream.

Search a stream.   The findFirst() and findAny() methods return a single element from a stream in an Optional. The anyMatch(), allMatch(), and noneMatch() methods return a boolean. Be careful, because these three can hang if called on an infinite stream with some data. All of these methods are terminal operations.

Sort a stream.   The sorted() method is an intermediate operation that sorts a stream. There are two versions: the signature with zero parameters that sorts using the natural sort order, and the signature with one parameter that sorts using that Comparator as the sort order.

Compare *groupingBy()* and *partitioningBy()*.   The groupingBy() method is a terminal operation that creates a Map. The keys and return types are determined by the parameters you pass. The values in the Map are a Collection for all the entries that map to that key. The partitioningBy() method also returns a Map. This time, the keys are true and false. The values are again a Collection of matches. If there are no matches for that boolean, the Collection is empty.

Review Questions

The answers to the chapter review questions can be found in Appendix B.

1. What could be the output of the following?

```
var stream = Stream.iterate("", (s) -> s + "1");
System.out.println(stream.limit(2).map(x -> x + "2"));
```

  A. 12112

  B. 212

  C. 212112

  D. java.util.stream.ReferencePipeline$3@4517d9a3

  E. The code does not compile.

  F. An exception is thrown.

  G. The code hangs.

2. What could be the output of the following?

```
Predicate<String> predicate = s -> s.startsWith("g");
var stream1 = Stream.generate(() -> "growl!");
var stream2 = Stream.generate(() -> "growl!");
var b1 = stream1.anyMatch(predicate);
var b2 = stream2.allMatch(predicate);
System.out.println(b1 + " " + b2);
```

  A. true false

  B. true true

  C. java.util.stream.ReferencePipeline$3@4517d9a3

  D. The code does not compile.

  E. An exception is thrown.

  F. The code hangs.

3. What could be the output of the following?

```
Predicate<String> predicate = s -> s.length() > 3;
var stream = Stream.iterate("-",
    s -> ! s.isEmpty(), (s) -> s + s);
var b1 = stream.noneMatch(predicate);
var b2 = stream.anyMatch(predicate);
System.out.println(b1 + " " + b2);
```

A. `false false`

B. `false true`

C. `java.util.stream.ReferencePipeline$3@4517d9a3`

D. The code does not compile.

E. An exception is thrown.

F. The code hangs.

4. Which are true statements about terminal operations in a stream that runs successfully? (Choose all that apply.)

A. At most, one terminal operation can exist in a stream pipeline.

B. Terminal operations are a required part of the stream pipeline in order to get a result.

C. Terminal operations have `Stream` as the return type.

D. The `peek()` method is an example of a terminal operation.

E. The referenced `Stream` may be used after calling a terminal operation.

5. Which of the following sets `result` to `8.0`? (Choose all that apply.)

A.

```
double result = LongStream.of(6L, 8L, 10L)
    .mapToInt(x -> (int) x)
    .collect(Collectors.groupingBy(x -> x))
    .keySet()
    .stream()
    .collect(Collectors.averagingInt(x -> x));
```

B.

```
double result = LongStream.of(6L, 8L, 10L)
    .mapToInt(x -> x)
    .boxed()
    .collect(Collectors.groupingBy(x -> x))
    .keySet()
    .stream()
    .collect(Collectors.averagingInt(x -> x));
```

C.

```
double result = LongStream.of(6L, 8L, 10L)
    .mapToInt(x -> (int) x)
    .boxed()
    .collect(Collectors.groupingBy(x -> x))
    .keySet()
    .stream()
    .collect(Collectors.averagingInt(x -> x));
```

D.

```
double result = LongStream.of(6L, 8L, 10L)
    .mapToInt(x -> (int) x)
    .collect(Collectors.groupingBy(x -> x, Collectors.toSet()))
    .keySet()
    .stream()
    .collect(Collectors.averagingInt(x -> x));
```

E.

```
double result = LongStream.of(6L, 8L, 10L)
    .mapToInt(x -> x)
    .boxed()
    .collect(Collectors.groupingBy(x -> x, Collectors.toSet()))
    .keySet()
    .stream()
    .collect(Collectors.averagingInt(x -> x));
```

F.

```
double result = LongStream.of(6L, 8L, 10L)
    .mapToInt(x -> (int) x)
    .boxed()
    .collect(Collectors.groupingBy(x -> x, Collectors.toSet()))
    .keySet()
    .stream()
    .collect(Collectors.averagingInt(x -> x));
```

6. Which of the following can fill in the blank so that the code prints out `false`? (Choose all that apply.)

```
var s = Stream.generate(() -> "meow");
var match = s._____(String::isEmpty);
System.out.println(match);
```

- **A.** allMatch
- **B.** anyMatch
- **C.** findAny
- **D.** findFirst
- **E.** noneMatch
- **F.** None of the above

7. We have a method that returns a sorted list without changing the original. Which of the following can replace the method implementation to do the same with streams?

```
private static List<String> sort(List<String> list) {
    var copy = new ArrayList<String>(list);
    Collections.sort(copy, (a, b) -> b.compareTo(a));
    return copy;
}
```

A.

```
return list.stream()
    .compare((a, b) -> b.compareTo(a))
    .collect(Collectors.toList());
```

B.

```
return list.stream()
    .compare((a, b) -> b.compareTo(a))
    .sort();
```

C.

```
return list.stream()
    .compareTo((a, b) -> b.compareTo(a))
    .collect(Collectors.toList());
```

D.

```
return list.stream()
    .compareTo((a, b) -> b.compareTo(a))
    .sort();
```

E.

```
return list.stream()
    .sorted((a, b) -> b.compareTo(a))
    .collect();
```

F.

```
return list.stream()
    .sorted((a, b) -> b.compareTo(a))
    .collect(Collectors.toList());
```

8. Which of the following are true given this declaration? (Choose all that apply.)
```
var is = IntStream.empty();
```

A. `is.average()` returns the type `int`.

B. `is.average()` returns the type `OptionalInt`.

C. `is.findAny()` returns the type `int`.

D. `is.findAny()` returns the type `OptionalInt`.

E. `is.sum()` returns the type `int`.

F. `is.sum()` returns the type `OptionalInt`.

9. Which of the following can we add after line 6 for the code to run without error and not produce any output? (Choose all that apply.)

```
4: var stream = LongStream.of(1, 2, 3);
5: var opt = stream.map(n -> n * 10)
6:     .filter(n -> n < 5).findFirst();
```

A.

```
if (opt.isPresent())
    System.out.println(opt.get());
```

B.

```
if (opt.isPresent())
    System.out.println(opt.getAsLong());
```

C.

```
opt.ifPresent(System.out.println);
```

D.

```
opt.ifPresent(System.out::println);
```

E. None of these; the code does not compile.

F. None of these; line 5 throws an exception at runtime.

10. Given the four statements (L, M, N, O), select and order the ones that would complete the expression and cause the code to output 10 lines. (Choose all that apply.)

```
Stream.generate(() -> "1")
    L: .filter(x -> x.length() > 1)
    M: .forEach(System.out::println)
    N: .limit(10)
    O: .peek(System.out::println)
;
```

A. L, N

B. L, N, O

C. L, N, M

D. L, N, M, O

E. L, O, M

F. N, M

G. N, O

11. What changes need to be made together for this code to print the string 12345? (Choose all that apply.)

```
Stream.iterate(1, x -> x++)
    .limit(5).map(x -> x)
    .collect(Collectors.joining());
```

- **A.** Change `Collectors.joining()` to `Collectors.joining(",")`.
- **B.** Change `map(x -> x)` to `map(x -> "" + x)`.
- **C.** Change `x -> x++` to `x -> ++x`.
- **D.** Add `forEach(System.out::print)` after the call to `collect()`.
- **E.** Wrap the entire line in a `System.out.print` statement.
- **F.** None of the above. The code already prints `12345`.

12. Which functional interfaces complete the following code? For line 7, assume m and n are instances of functional interfaces that exist and have the same type as y. (Choose three.)

```
6: _____ x = String::new;
7: _____ y = m.andThen(n);
8: _____ z = a -> a + a;
```

- **A.** `BinaryConsumer<String, String>`
- **B.** `BiConsumer<String, String>`
- **C.** `BinaryFunction<String, String>`
- **D.** `BiFunction<String, String>`
- **E.** `Predicate<String>`
- **F.** `Supplier<String>`
- **G.** `UnaryOperator<String>`
- **H.** `UnaryOperator<String, String>`

13. Which of the following is true?

```
List<Integer> x1 = List.of(1, 2, 3);
List<Integer> x2 = List.of(4, 5, 6);
List<Integer> x3 = List.of();
Stream.of(x1, x2, x3).map(x -> x + 1)
    .flatMap(x -> x.stream())
    .forEach(System.out::print);
```

- **A.** The code compiles and prints 123456.
- **B.** The code compiles and prints 234567.
- **C.** The code compiles but does not print anything.
- **D.** The code compiles but prints stream references.

    E. The code runs infinitely.

    F. The code does not compile.

    G. The code throws an exception.

14. Which of the following is true? (Choose all that apply.)

```
4: Stream<Integer> s = Stream.of(1);
5: IntStream is = s.boxed();
6: DoubleStream ds = s.mapToDouble(x -> x);
7: Stream<Integer> s2 = ds.mapToInt(x -> x);
8: s2.forEach(System.out::print);
```

    A. Line 4 causes a compiler error.

    B. Line 5 causes a compiler error.

    C. Line 6 causes a compiler error.

    D. Line 7 causes a compiler error.

    E. Line 8 causes a compiler error.

    F. The code compiles but throws an exception at runtime.

    G. The code compiles and prints 1.

15. Given the generic type `String`, the `partitioningBy()` collector creates a `Map<Boolean, List<String>>` when passed to `collect()` by default. When a down-stream collector is passed to `partitioningBy()`, which return types can be created? (Choose all that apply.)

    A. `Map<boolean, List<String>>`

    B. `Map<Boolean, List<String>>`

    C. `Map<Boolean, Map<String>>`

    D. `Map<Boolean, Set<String>>`

    E. `Map<Long, TreeSet<String>>`

    F. None of the above

16. Which of the following statements are true about this code? (Choose all that apply.)

```
20: Predicate<String> empty = String::isEmpty;
21: Predicate<String> notEmpty = empty.negate();
22:
23: var result = Stream.generate(() -> "")
24:     .limit(10)
25:     .filter(notEmpty)
26:     .collect(Collectors.groupingBy(k -> k))
27:     .entrySet()
28:     .stream()
29:     .map(Entry::getValue)
```

```
30:    .flatMap(Collection::stream)
31:    .collect(Collectors.partitioningBy(notEmpty));
32: System.out.println(result);
```

A. It outputs: {}

B. It outputs: {false=[], true=[]}

C. If we changed line 31 from partitioningBy(notEmpty) to groupingBy(n -> n), it would output: {}

D. If we changed line 31 from partitioningBy(notEmpty) to groupingBy(n -> n), it would output: {false=[], true=[]}

E. The code does not compile.

F. The code compiles but does not terminate at runtime.

17. Which of the following is equivalent to this code? (Choose all that apply.)

```
UnaryOperator<Integer> u = x -> x * x;
```

A. BiFunction<Integer> f = x -> x*x;

B. BiFunction<Integer, Integer> f = x -> x*x;

C. BinaryOperator<Integer, Integer> f = x -> x*x;

D. Function<Integer> f = x -> x*x;

E. Function<Integer, Integer> f = x -> x*x;

F. None of the above

18. What is the result of the following?

```
var s = DoubleStream.of(1.2, 2.4);
s.peek(System.out::println).filter(x -> x > 2).count();
```

A. 1

B. 2

C. 2.4

D. 1.2 and 2.4

E. There is no output.

F. The code does not compile.

G. An exception is thrown.

19. What does the following code output?

```
Function<Integer, Integer> s = a -> a + 4;
Function<Integer, Integer> t = a -> a * 3;
Function<Integer, Integer> c = s.compose(t);
System.out.println(c.apply(1));
```

A. 7

B. 15

    C.   The code does not compile because of the data types in the lambda expressions.

    D.   The code does not compile because of the `compose()` call.

    E.   The code does not compile for another reason.

20. Which of the following functional interfaces contain an abstract method that returns a primitive value? (Choose all that apply.)

    A.   `BooleanSupplier`

    B.   `CharSupplier`

    C.   `DoubleSupplier`

    D.   `FloatSupplier`

    E.   `IntSupplier`

    F.   `StringSupplier`

21. What is the simplest way of rewriting this code?

```
List<Integer> x = IntStream.range(1, 6)
    .mapToObj(i -> i)
    .collect(Collectors.toList());
x.forEach(System.out::println);
```

    A.

```
IntStream.range(1, 6);
```

    B.

```
IntStream.range(1, 6)
    .forEach(System.out::println);
```

    C.

```
IntStream.range(1, 6)
    .mapToObj(i -> i)
    .forEach(System.out::println);
```

    D.   None of the above is equivalent.

    E.   The provided code does not compile.

22. Which of the following throw an exception when an `Optional` is empty? (Choose all that apply.)

    A.   `opt.orElse("");`

    B.   `opt.orElseGet(() -> "");`

    C.   `opt.orElseThrow();`

    D.   `opt.orElseThrow(() -> throw new Exception());`

    E.   `opt.orElseThrow(RuntimeException::new);`

    F.   `opt.get();`

    G.   `opt.get("");`

Chapter

5

Exceptions, Assertions, and Localization

OCP EXAM OBJECTIVES COVERED IN THIS CHAPTER:

✓ **Exception Handling and Assertions**

- Use the try-with-resources construct
- Create and use custom exception classes
- Test invariants by using assertions

✓ **Localization**

- Use the Locale class
- Use resource bundles
- Format messages, dates, and numbers with Java

This chapter is about creating applications that adapt to change. What happens if a user enters invalid data on a web page, or our connection to a database goes down in the middle of a sale? How do we ensure rules about our data are enforced? Finally, how do we build applications that can support multiple languages or geographic regions?

In this chapter, we will discuss these problems and solutions to them using exceptions, assertions, and localization. One way to make sure your applications respond to change is to build in support early on. For example, supporting localization doesn't mean you actually need to support multiple languages right away. It just means your application can be more easily adapted in the future. By the end of this chapter, we hope we've provided structure for designing applications that better adapt to change.

Reviewing Exceptions

An *exception* is Java's way of saying, "I give up. I don't know what to do right now. You deal with it." When you write a method, you can either deal with the exception or make it the calling code's problem. In this section, we cover the fundamentals of exceptions.

If you've recently studied for the 1Z0-815 exam, then you can probably skip this section and go straight to "Creating Custom Exceptions." This section is meant only for review.

Handling Exceptions

A *try statement* is used to handle exceptions. It consists of a try clause, zero or more *catch clauses* to handle the exceptions that are thrown, and an optional *finally clause*, which runs regardless of whether an exception is thrown. Figure 5.1 shows the syntax of a try statement.

A traditional try statement must have at least one of the following: a catch block or a finally block. It can have more than one catch block, including multi-catch blocks, but at most one finally block.

Swallowing an exception is when you handle it with an empty catch block. When presenting a topic, we often do this to keep things simple. Please, *never do this in practice!* Oftentimes, it is added by developers who do not want to handle or declare an exception properly and can lead to bugs in production code.

FIGURE 5.1   The syntax of a try statement

```
try {

    // Protected code

} catch (IOException e) {
                              Exception identifier
    // Handler for IOException

} catch (ArithmeticException | IllegalArgumentException e) {
                                                              Exception identifier
    // Multi-catch handler          Catch either of
                                     these exceptions.
} finally {

    // Always runs after try/catch blocks are finished

}
```

You can also create a *try-with-resources* statement to handle exceptions. A try-with-resources statement looks a lot like a `try` statement, except that it includes a list of resources inside a set of parentheses, (). These resources are automatically closed in the reverse order that they are declared at the conclusion of the `try` clause. The syntax of the try-with-resources statement is presented in Figure 5.2.

Like a regular `try` statement, a try-with-resources statement can include optional `catch` and `finally` blocks. Unlike a `try` statement, though, neither is required. We'll cover try-with-resources statements in more detail in this chapter.

FIGURE 5.2   The syntax of a try-with-resources statement

```
                                                      Required semicolon
                     Resources                        between resources

        try (var in = new FileInputStream("data.txt");
             var out = new FileOutputStream("output.txt");) {

            // Protected code
                                                      Optional semicolon

        } catch (IOException  e) {
Resources are
closed here in       // Exception handler              Optional catch and
reverse order                                          finally clauses
        } finally {

            // finally block

        }
```

Did you notice we used var for the resource type? While var is not required, it is convenient when working with streams, database objects, and especially generics, whose declarations can be lengthy.

> While presenting try-with-resources statements, we include a number of examples that use I/O stream classes that we'll be covering later in this book. For this chapter, you can assume these resources are declared correctly. For example, you can assume the previous code snippet correctly creates FileInputStream and FileOutputStream objects. If you see a try-with-resources statement with an I/O stream on the exam, though, it could be testing either topic.

Distinguishing between *throw* and *throws*

By now, you should know the difference between throw and throws. The throw keyword means an exception is actually being thrown, while the throws keyword indicates that the method merely has the potential to throw that exception. The following example uses both:

```
10: public String getDataFromDatabase() throws SQLException {
11:     throw new UnsupportedOperationException();
12: }
```

Line 10 declares that the method might or might not throw a SQLException. Since this is a checked exception, the caller needs to handle or declare it. Line 11 actually does throw an UnsupportedOperationException. Since this is a runtime exception, it does not need to be declared on line 10.

Examining Exception Categories

In Java, all exceptions inherit from Throwable, although in practice, the only ones you should be handling or declaring extend from the Exception class. Figure 5.3 reviews the hierarchy of the top-level exception classes.

To begin with, a *checked exception* must be handled or declared by the application code where it is thrown. The *handle or declare rule* dictates that a checked exception must be either caught in a catch block or thrown to the caller by including it in the method declaration.

The ZooMaintenance class shows an example of a method that handles an exception, and one that declares an exception.

```
public class ZooMaintenance {
    public void open() {
        try {
            throw new Exception();
        } catch (Exception e) {
```

```
        // Handles exception
    }
  }

  public void close() throws Exception {  // Declares exceptions
    throw new Exception();
  }
}
```

FIGURE 5.3   Categories of exceptions

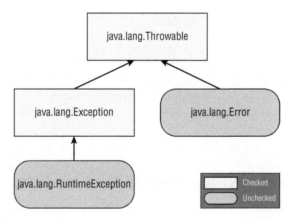

In Java, all exceptions that inherit Exception but not RuntimeException are considered checked exceptions.

On the other hand, an *unchecked exception* does not need to be handled or declared. Unchecked exceptions are often referred to as runtime exceptions, although in Java unchecked exceptions include any class that inherits RuntimeException or Error. An Error is fatal, and it is considered a poor practice to catch it.

For the exam, you need to memorize some common exception classes. You also need to know whether they are checked or unchecked exceptions. Table 5.1 lists the unchecked exceptions that inherit RuntimeException that you should be familiar with for the exam.

TABLE 5.1   Unchecked exceptions

ArithmeticException	ArrayIndexOutOfBoundsException
ArrayStoreException	ClassCastException
IllegalArgumentException	IllegalStateException
MissingResourceException	NullPointerException
NumberFormatException	UnsupportedOperationException

Table 5.2 presents the checked exceptions you should also be familiar with.

TABLE 5.2 Checked exceptions

FileNotFoundException	IOException
NotSerializableException	ParseException
SQLException	

Inheriting Exception Classes

When evaluating catch blocks, the inheritance of the exception types can be important. For the exam, you should know that NumberFormatException inherits from IllegalArgumentException. You should also know that FileNotFoundException and NotSerializableException both inherit from IOException.

This comes up often in multi-catch expressions. For example, why does the following not compile?

```
try {
   throw new IOException();
} catch (IOException | FileNotFoundException e) {} // DOES NOT COMPILE
```

Since FileNotFoundException is a subclass of IOException, listing both in a multi-catch expression is redundant, resulting in a compilation error.

Ordering of exceptions in consecutive catch blocks matters too. Do you understand why the following does not compile?

```
try {
   throw new IOException();
} catch (IOException e) {
} catch (FileNotFoundException e) {} // DOES NOT COMPILE
```

For the exam, remember that trying to catch a more specific exception (after already catching a broader exception) results in unreachable code and a compiler error.

If you're a bit rusty on exceptions or any of this material is new to you, then you may want to review your previous study materials. The rest of this book assumes you know the basics of exception handling.

Creating Custom Exceptions

Java provides many exception classes out of the box. Sometimes, you want to write a method with a more specialized type of exception. You can create your own exception class to do this.

Declaring Exception Classes

When creating your own exception, you need to decide whether it should be a checked or unchecked exception. While you can extend any exception class, it is most common to extend Exception (for checked) or RuntimeException (for unchecked).

Creating your own exception class is really easy. Can you figure out whether the exceptions are checked or unchecked in this example?

```
1: class CannotSwimException extends Exception {}
2: class DangerInTheWater extends RuntimeException {}
3: class SharkInTheWaterException extends DangerInTheWater {}
4: class Dolphin {
5:     public void swim() throws CannotSwimException {
6:         // logic here
7:     }
8: }
```

On line 1, we have a checked exception because it extends directly from Exception. Not being able to swim is pretty bad when we are trying to swim, so we want to force callers to deal with this situation. Line 2 declares an unchecked exception because it extends directly from RuntimeException. On line 3, we have another unchecked exception because it extends indirectly from RuntimeException. It is pretty unlikely that there will be a shark in the water. We might even be swimming in a pool where the odds of a shark are 0 percent! We don't want to force the caller to deal with everything that might remotely happen, so we leave this as an unchecked exception.

The method on lines 5–7 declares that it might throw the checked CannotSwimException. The method implementation could be written to actually throw it or not. The method implementation could also be written to throw a SharkInTheWaterException, an ArrayIndexOutOfBoundsException, or any other runtime exception.

Adding Custom Constructors

These one-liner exception declarations are pretty useful, especially on the exam where they need to communicate quickly whether an exception is checked or unchecked. Let's see how to pass more information in your exception.

The following example shows the three most common constructors defined by the Exception class:

```
public class CannotSwimException extends Exception {
    public CannotSwimException() {
        super();  // Optional, compiler will insert automatically
    }
    public CannotSwimException(Exception e) {
        super(e);
    }
    public CannotSwimException(String message) {
        super(message);
    }
}
```

The first constructor is the default constructor with no parameters. The second constructor shows how to wrap another exception inside yours. The third constructor shows how to pass a custom error message.

 Remember from your 1Z0-815 studies that the default no-argument constructor is provided automatically if you don't write any constructors of your own.

In these examples, our constructors and parent constructors took the same parameters, but this is certainly not required. For example, the following constructor takes an Exception and calls the parent constructor that takes a String:

```
public CannotSwimException(Exception e) {
    super("Cannot swim because: " + e.toString());
}
```

Using a different constructor allows you to provide more information about what went wrong. For example, let's say we have a main() method with the following line:

```
15: public static void main(String[] unused) throws Exception {
16:     throw new CannotSwimException();
17: }
```

The output for this method is as follows:

```
Exception in thread "main" CannotSwimException
    at CannotSwimException.main(CannotSwimException.java:16)
```

The JVM gives us just the exception and its location. Useful, but we could get more. Now, let's change the main() method to include some text, as shown here:

```
15: public static void main(String[] unused) throws Exception {
16:     throw new CannotSwimException("broken fin");
17: }
```

The output of this new main() method is as follows:

```
Exception in thread "main" CannotSwimException: broken fin
    at CannotSwimException.main(CannotSwimException.java:16)
```

This time we see the message text in the result. You might want to provide more information about the exception depending on the problem.

We can even pass another exception, if there is an underlying cause for the exception. Take a look at this version of our main() method:

```
15: public static void main(String[] unused) throws Exception {
16:     throw new CannotSwimException(
17:         new FileNotFoundException("Cannot find shark file"));
18: }
```

This would yield the longest output so far:

```
Exception in thread "main" CannotSwimException:
    java.io.FileNotFoundException: Cannot find shark file
    at CannotSwimException.main(CannotSwimException.java:16)
Caused by: java.io.FileNotFoundException: Cannot find shark file
    ... 1 more
```

Printing Stack Traces

The error messages that we've been showing are called *stack traces*. A stack trace shows the exception along with the method calls it took to get there. The JVM automatically prints a stack trace when an exception is thrown that is not handled by the program.

You can also print the stack trace on your own. The advantage is that you can read or log information from the stack trace and then continue to handle or even rethrow it.

```
try {
    throw new CannotSwimException();
} catch (CannotSwimException e) {
    e.printStackTrace();
}
```

Automating Resource Management

As previously described, a try-with-resources statement ensures that any resources declared in the `try` clause are automatically closed at the conclusion of the `try` block. This feature is also known as *automatic resource management*, because Java automatically takes care of closing the resources for you.

For the exam, a *resource* is typically a file or a database that requires some kind of stream or connection to read or write data. In Chapter 8, "I/O," Chapter 9, "NIO.2," and Chapter 10, "JDBC," you'll create numerous resources that will need to be closed when you are finished with them. In Chapter 11, "Security," we'll discuss how failure to close resources can lead to resource leaks that could make your program more vulnerable to attack.

Resource Management vs. Garbage Collection

Java has great built-in support for garbage collection. When you are finished with an object, it will automatically (over time) reclaim the memory associated with it.

The same is not true for resource management without a try-with-resources statement. If an object connected to a resource is not closed, then the connection could remain open. In fact, it may interfere with Java's ability to garbage collect the object.

To eliminate this problem, it is recommended that you close resources in the same block of code that opens them. By using a try-with-resources statement to open all your resources, this happens automatically.

Constructing Try-With-Resources Statements

What types of resources can be used with a try-with-resources statement? The first rule you should know is: *try-with-resources statements require resources that implement the AutoCloseable interface.* For example, the following does not compile as `String` does not implement the AutoCloseable interface:

```
try (String reptile = "lizard") {
}
```

Inheriting `AutoCloseable` requires implementing a compatible `close()` method.

```
interface AutoCloseable {
   public void close() throws Exception;
}
```

From your studies of method overriding, this means that the implemented version of close() can choose to throw Exception or a subclass, or not throw any exceptions at all.

In Chapter 8 and Chapter 9, you will encounter resources that implement Closeable, rather than AutoCloseable. Since Closeable extends AutoCloseable, they are both supported in try-with-resources statements. The only difference between the two is that Closeable's close() method declares IOException, while AutoCloseable's close() method declares Exception.

Let's define our own custom resource class for use in a try-with-resources statement.

```java
public class MyFileReader implements AutoCloseable {
    private String tag;
    public MyFileReader(String tag) { this.tag = tag;}

    @Override public void close() {
        System.out.println("Closed: "+tag);
    }
}
```

The following code snippet makes use of our custom reader class:

```java
try (var bookReader = new MyFileReader("monkey")) {
    System.out.println("Try Block");
} finally {
    System.out.println("Finally Block");
}
```

The code prints the following at runtime:

```
Try Block
Closed: monkey
Finally Block
```

As you can see, the resources are closed at the end of the try statement, before any catch or finally blocks are executed. Behind the scenes, the JVM calls the close() method inside a hidden finally block, which we can refer to as the *implicit* finally block. The finally block that the programmer declared can be referred to as the *explicit* finally block.

In a try-with-resources statement, you need to remember that the resource will be closed at the completion of the try block, before any declared catch or finally blocks execute.

The second rule you should be familiar with is: *a try-with-resources statement can include multiple resources, which are closed in the reverse order in which they are declared.* Resources are terminated by a semicolon (;), with the last one being optional.

Consider the following code snippet:

```
try (var bookReader = new MyFileReader("1");
    var movieReader = new MyFileReader("2");
    var tvReader = new MyFileReader("3");) {
  System.out.println("Try Block");
} finally {
  System.out.println("Finally Block"); ·
}
```

When executed, this code prints the following:

```
Try Block
Closed: 3
Closed: 2
Closed: 1
Finally Block
```

Real World Scenario

Why You Should Be Using try-with-resources Statements

If you have been working with files and databases and have never used try-with-resources before, you've definitely been missing out. For example, consider this code sample, which does not use automatic resource management:

```
11: public void copyData(Path path1, Path path2) throws Exception {
12:     BufferedReader in = null;
13:     BufferedWriter out = null;
14:     try {
15:         in = Files.newBufferedReader(path1);
16:         out = Files.newBufferedWriter(path2);
17:         out.write(in.readLine());
18:     } finally {
19:         if (out != null) {
20:             out.close();
21:         }
22:         if (in != null) {
23:             in.close();
```

```
24:       }
25:    }
26: }
```

Switching to the try-with-resources syntax, we can replace it with the following, much shorter implementation:

```
11: public void copyData(Path path1, Path path2) throws Exception {
12:    try (var in = Files.newBufferedReader(path1);
13:         var out = Files.newBufferedWriter(path2)) {
14:       out.write(in.readLine());
15:    }
16: }
```

Excluding the method declaration, that's 14 lines of code to do something that can be done in 4 lines of code. In fact, the first version even contains a bug! If out.close() throws an exception on line 20, the in resource will never be closed. The close() statements would each need to be wrapped in a try/catch block to ensure the resources were properly closed.

The final rule you should know is: *resources declared within a try-with-resources statement are in scope only within the try block.*

This is another way to remember that the resources are closed before any catch or finally blocks are executed, as the resources are no longer available. Do you see why lines 6 and 8 don't compile in this example?

```
3: try (Scanner s = new Scanner(System.in)) {
4:    s.nextLine();
5: } catch(Exception e) {
6:    s.nextInt(); // DOES NOT COMPILE
7: } finally {
8:    s.nextInt(); // DOES NOT COMPILE
9: }
```

The problem is that Scanner has gone out of scope at the end of the try clause. Lines 6 and 8 do not have access to it. This is actually a nice feature. You can't accidentally use an object that has been closed.

Resources do not need to be declared inside a try-with-resources statement, though, as we will see in the next section.

Learning the New Effectively Final Feature

Starting with Java 9, it is possible to use resources declared prior to the try-with-resources statement, provided they are marked final or effectively final. The syntax is just to use the resource name in place of the resource declaration, separated by a semicolon (;).

```
11: public void relax() {
12:     final var bookReader = new MyFileReader("4");
13:     MyFileReader movieReader = new MyFileReader("5");
14:     try (bookReader;
15:         var tvReader = new MyFileReader("6");
16:         movieReader) {
17:       System.out.println("Try Block");
18:     } finally {
19:       System.out.println("Finally Block");
20:     }
21: }
```

Let's take this one line at a time. Line 12 declares a final variable bookReader, while line 13 declares an effectively final variable movieReader. Both of these resources can be used in a try-with-resources statement. We know movieReader is effectively final because it is a local variable that is assigned a value only once. Remember, the test for effectively final is that if we insert the final keyword when the variable is declared, the code still compiles.

Lines 14 and 16 use the new syntax to declare resources in a try-with-resources statement, using just the variable name and separating the resources with a semicolon (;). Line 15 uses the normal syntax for declaring a new resource within the try clause.

On execution, the code prints the following:

```
Try Block
Closed: 5
Closed: 6
Closed: 4
Finally Block
```

If you come across a question on the exam that uses a try-with-resources statement with a variable not declared in the try clause, make sure it is effectively final. For example, the following does not compile:

```
31: var writer = Files.newBufferedWriter(path);
32: try(writer) {  // DOES NOT COMPILE
33:     writer.append("Welcome to the zoo!");
34: }
35: writer = null;
```

The writer variable is reassigned on line 35, resulting in the compiler not considering it effectively final. Since it is not an effectively final variable, it cannot be used in a try-with-resources statement on line 32.

The other place the exam might try to trick you is accessing a resource after it has been closed. Consider the following:

```
41: var writer = Files.newBufferedWriter(path);
42: writer.append("This write is permitted but a really bad idea!");
```

```
43: try(writer) {
44:    writer.append("Welcome to the zoo!");
45: }
46: writer.append("This write will fail!");   // IOException
```

This code compiles but throws an exception on line 46 with the message `Stream closed`. While it was possible to write to the resource before the try-with-resources statement, it is not afterward.

Take Care When Using Resources Declared before try-with-resources Statements

On line 42 of the previous code sample, we used `writer` before the try-with-resources statement. While this is allowed, it's a really bad idea. What happens if line 42 throws an exception? In this case, the resource declared on line 41 will *never* be closed! What about the following code snippet?

```
51: var reader = Files.newBufferedReader(path1);
52: var writer = Files.newBufferedWriter(path2);   // Don't do this!
53: try (reader; writer) {}
```

It has the same problem. If line 52 throws an exception, such as the file cannot be found, then the resource declared on line 51 will never be closed. We recommend you use this new syntax sparingly or with only one resource at a time. For example, if line 52 was removed, then the resource created on line 51 wouldn't have an opportunity to throw an exception before entering the automatic resource management block.

Understanding Suppressed Exceptions

What happens if the `close()` method throws an exception? Let's try an illustrative example:

```
public class TurkeyCage implements AutoCloseable {
   public void close() {
      System.out.println("Close gate");
   }
   public static void main(String[] args) {
      try (var t = new TurkeyCage()) {
         System.out.println("Put turkeys in");
      }
   }
}
```

If the TurkeyCage doesn't close, the turkeys could all escape. Clearly, we need to handle such a condition. We already know that the resources are closed before any programmer-coded catch blocks are run. This means we can catch the exception thrown by close() if we want. Alternatively, we can allow the caller to deal with it.

Let's expand our example with a new JammedTurkeyCage implementation, shown here:

```
1:   public class JammedTurkeyCage implements AutoCloseable {
2:       public void close() throws IllegalStateException {
3:           throw new IllegalStateException("Cage door does not close");
4:       }
5:       public static void main(String[] args) {
6:           try (JammedTurkeyCage t = new JammedTurkeyCage()) {
7:               System.out.println("Put turkeys in");
8:           } catch (IllegalStateException e) {
9:               System.out.println("Caught: " + e.getMessage());
10:          }
11:      }
12: }
```

The close() method is automatically called by try-with-resources. It throws an exception, which is caught by our catch block and prints the following:

```
Caught: Cage door does not close
```

This seems reasonable enough. What happens if the try block also throws an exception? When multiple exceptions are thrown, all but the first are called *suppressed exceptions*. The idea is that Java treats the first exception as the primary one and tacks on any that come up while automatically closing.

What do you think the following implementation of our main() method outputs?

```
5:       public static void main(String[] args) {
6:           try (JammedTurkeyCage t = new JammedTurkeyCage()) {
7:               throw new IllegalStateException("Turkeys ran off");
8:           } catch (IllegalStateException e) {
9:               System.out.println("Caught: " + e.getMessage());
10:              for (Throwable t: e.getSuppressed())
11:                  System.out.println("Suppressed: "+t.getMessage());
12:          }
13:      }
```

Line 7 throws the primary exception. At this point, the try clause ends, and Java automatically calls the close() method. Line 3 of JammedTurkeyCage throws an IllegalStateException, which is added as a suppressed exception. Then line 8 catches the primary exception. Line 9 prints the message for the primary exception. Lines 10–11 iterate through any suppressed exceptions and print them. The program prints the following:

```
Caught: Turkeys ran off
Suppressed: Cage door does not close
```

Keep in mind that the catch block looks for matches on the primary exception. What do you think this code prints?

```
5:      public static void main(String[] args) {
6:          try (JammedTurkeyCage t = new JammedTurkeyCage()) {
7:              throw new RuntimeException("Turkeys ran off");
8:          } catch (IllegalStateException e) {
9:              System.out.println("caught: " + e.getMessage());
10:         }
11:     }
```

Line 7 again throws the primary exception. Java calls the close() method and adds a suppressed exception. Line 8 would catch the IllegalStateException. However, we don't have one of those. The primary exception is a RuntimeException. Since this does not match the catch clause, the exception is thrown to the caller. Eventually the main() method would output something like the following:

```
Exception in thread "main" java.lang.RuntimeException: Turkeys ran off
    at JammedTurkeyCage.main(JammedTurkeyCage.java:7)
    Suppressed: java.lang.IllegalStateException:
            Cage door does not close
        at JammedTurkeyCage.close(JammedTurkeyCage.java:3)
        at JammedTurkeyCage.main(JammedTurkeyCage.java:8)
```

Java remembers the suppressed exceptions that go with a primary exception even if we don't handle them in the code.

> If more than two resources throw an exception, the first one to be thrown becomes the primary exception, with the rest being grouped as suppressed exceptions. And since resources are closed in reverse order in which they are declared, the primary exception would be on the last declared resource that throws an exception.

Keep in mind that suppressed exceptions apply only to exceptions thrown in the try clause. The following example does not throw a suppressed exception:

```
5:      public static void main(String[] args) {
6:          try (JammedTurkeyCage t = new JammedTurkeyCage()) {
7:              throw new IllegalStateException("Turkeys ran off");
8:          } finally {
9:              throw new RuntimeException("and we couldn't find them");
10:         }
11:     }
```

Line 7 throws an exception. Then Java tries to close the resource and adds a suppressed exception to it. Now we have a problem. The finally block runs after all this. Since line 9 also throws an exception, the previous exception from line 7 is lost, with the code printing the following:

```
Exception in thread "main" java.lang.RuntimeException:
    and we couldn't find them
    at JammedTurkeyCage.main(JammedTurkeyCage.java:9)
```

This has always been and continues to be bad programming practice. We don't want to lose exceptions! Although out of scope for the exam, the reason for this has to do with backward compatibility. Automatic resource management was added in Java 7, and this behavior existed before this feature was added.

Declaring Assertions

An *assertion* is a boolean expression that you place at a point in your code where you expect something to be true. An *assert statement* contains this statement along with an optional message.

An assertion allows for detecting defects in the code. You can turn on assertions for testing and debugging while leaving them off when your program is in production.

Why assert something when you know it is true? It is true only when everything is working properly. If the program has a defect, it might not actually be true. Detecting this earlier in the process lets you know something is wrong.

In the following sections, we cover the syntax for using an assertion, how to turn assertions on/off, and some common uses of assertions.

 Real World Scenario

Assertions vs. Unit Tests

Most developers are more familiar with unit test frameworks, such as JUnit, than with assertions. While there are some similarities, assertions are commonly used to verify the internal state of a program, while unit tests are most frequently used to verify behavior.

Additionally, unit test frameworks tend to be fully featured with lots of options and tools available. While you need to know assertions for the exam, you are far better off writing unit tests when programming professionally.

Validating Data with the *assert* Statement

The syntax for an assert statement has two forms, shown in Figure 5.4.

FIGURE 5.4   The syntax of assert statements

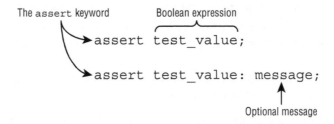

When assertions are enabled and the boolean expression evaluates to false, then an AssertionError will be thrown at runtime. Since programs aren't supposed to catch an Error, this means that assertion failures are fatal and end the program!

> Since Java 1.4, assert is a keyword. That means it can't be used as an identifier at compile time, even if assertions will be disabled at runtime. Keep an eye out for questions on the exam that use it as anything other than a statement.

Assertions may include optional parentheses and a message. For example, each of the following is valid:

```
assert 1 == age;
assert(2 == height);
assert 100.0 == length : "Problem with length";
assert ("Cecelia".equals(name)): "Failed to verify user data";
```

When provided, the error message will be sent to the AssertionError constructor. It is commonly a String, although it can be any value.

Recognizing Assertion Syntax Errors

While the preceding examples demonstrate the appropriate syntax, the exam may try to trick you with invalid syntax. See whether you can determine why the following do not compile:

```
assert(1);
assert x -> true;
assert 1==2 ? "Accept" : "Error";
assert.test(5 > age);
```

The first three statements do not compile because they expect a boolean value. The last statement does not compile because the syntax is invalid.

The three possible outcomes of an assert statement are as follows:

- If assertions are disabled, Java skips the assertion and goes on in the code.

- If assertions are enabled and the boolean expression is true, then our assertion has been validated and nothing happens. The program continues to execute in its normal manner.

- If assertions are enabled and the boolean expression is false, then our assertion is invalid and an AssertionError is thrown.

Presuming assertions are enabled, an assertion is a shorter way of writing the following:

```
if (!boolean_expression) throw new AssertionError(error_message);
```

Let's try an example. Consider the following:

```
1: public class Party {
2:     public static void main(String[] args) {
3:         int numGuests = -5;
4:         assert numGuests > 0;
5:         System.out.println(numGuests);
6:     }
7: }
```

We can enable assertions by executing it using the single-file source-code command, as shown here:

```
java -ea Party.java
```

Uh-oh, we made a typo in our Party class. We intended for there to be five guests and not negative five guests. The assertion on line 4 detects this problem. Java throws the AssertionError at this point. Line 5 never runs since an error was thrown.

The program ends with a stack trace similar to this:

```
Exception in thread "main" java.lang.AssertionError
    at asserts.Assertions.main(Assertions.java:4)
```

If we run the same program using the command line java Party, we get a different result. The program prints –5. Now, in this example, it is pretty obvious what the problem is since the program is only seven lines. In a more complicated program, knowing the state of affairs is more useful.

Enabling Assertions

By default, assert statements are ignored by the JVM at runtime. To enable assertions, use the -enableassertions flag on the command line.

```
java -enableassertions Rectangle
```

You can also use the shortcut -ea flag.

```
java -ea Rectangle
```

Using the -enableassertions or -ea flag without any arguments enables assertions in all classes (except system classes). You can also enable assertions for a specific class or package. For example, the following command enables assertions only for classes in the com.demos package and any subpackages:

```
java -ea:com.demos... my.programs.Main
```

The ellipsis (...) means any class in the specified package or subpackages. You can also enable assertions for a specific class.

```
java -ea:com.demos.TestColors my.programs.Main
```

Enabling assertions is an important aspect of using them, because if assertions are not enabled, assert statements are ignored at runtime. Keep an eye out for questions that contain an assert statement where assertions are not enabled.

Disabling Assertions

Sometimes you want to enable assertions for the entire application but disable it for select packages or classes. Java offers the -disableassertions or -da flag for just such an occasion. The following command enables assertions for the com.demos package but disables assertions for the TestColors class:

```
java -ea:com.demos... -da:com.demos.TestColors my.programs.Main
```

For the exam, make sure you understand how to use the -ea and -da flags in conjunction with each other.

By default, all assertions are disabled. Then, those items marked with -ea are enabled. Finally, all of the remaining items marked with -da are disabled.

Applying Assertions

Table 5.3 list some of the common uses of assertions. You won't be asked to identify the type of assertion on the exam. This is just to give you some ideas of how they can be used.

TABLE 5.3   Assertion applications

Usage	Description
Internal invariants	Assert that a value is within a certain constraint, such as `assert x < 0`.
Class invariants	Assert the validity of an object's state. Class invariants are typically `private` methods within the class that return a boolean.
Control flow invariants	Assert that a line of code you assume is unreachable is never reached.
Pre-conditions	Assert that certain conditions are met before a method is invoked.
Post-conditions	Assert that certain conditions are met after a method executes successfully.

Writing Assertions Correctly

One of the most important rules you should remember from this section is: *assertions should never alter outcomes*. This is especially true because assertions can, should, and probably will be turned off in a production environment.

For example, the following assertion is not a good design because it alters the value of a variable:

```
int x = 10;
assert ++x > 10; // Not a good design!
```

When assertions are turned on, x is incremented to 11; but when assertions are turned off, the value of x is 10. This is not a good use of assertions because the outcome of the code will be different depending on whether assertions are turned on.

Assertions are used for debugging purposes, allowing you to verify that something that you think is true during the coding phase is actually true at runtime.

Working with Dates and Times

The older Java 8 certification exams required you to know a lot about the Date and Time API. This included knowing many of the various date/time classes and their various methods, how to specify amounts of time with the `Period` and `Duration` classes, and even how to resolve values across time zones with daylight savings.

For the Java 11 exam, none of those topics is in scope, although strangely enough, you still need to know how to format dates. This just means if you see a date/time on the exam, you aren't being tested about it. Before we learn how to format dates, let's learn what they are and how to create them.

Creating Dates and Times

In the real world, we usually talk about dates and times as relative to our current location. For example, "I'll call you at 11 a.m. on Friday morning." You probably use date and time independently, like this: "The package will arrive by Friday" or "We're going to the movies at 7:15 p.m." Last but not least, you might also use a more absolute time when planning a meeting across a time zone, such as "Everyone in Seattle and Philadelphia will join the call at 10:45 EST."

Understanding Date and Time Types

Java includes numerous classes to model the examples in the previous paragraph. These types are listed in Table 5.4.

TABLE 5.4   Date and time types

Class	Description	Example
java.time.LocalDate	Date with day, month, year	Birth date
java.time.LocalTime	Time of day	Midnight
java.time.LocalDateTime	Day and time with no time zone	10 a.m. next Monday
java.time.ZonedDateTime	Date and time with a specific time zone	9 a.m. EST on 2/20/2021

Each of these types contains a `static` method called now() that allows you to get the current value.

```
System.out.println(LocalDate.now());
System.out.println(LocalTime.now());
System.out.println(LocalDateTime.now());
System.out.println(ZonedDateTime.now());
```

Your output is going to depend on the date/time when you run it and where you live, although it should resemble the following:

```
2020-10-14
12:45:20.854
2020-10-14T12:45:20.854
2020-10-14T12:45:20.854-04:00[America/New_York]
```

The first line contains only a date and no time. The second line contains only a time and no date. The time displays hours, minutes, seconds, and fractional seconds. The third line contains both a date and a time. Java uses T to separate the date and time when converting LocalDateTime to a String. Finally, the fourth line adds the time zone offset and time zone. New York is four time zones away from Greenwich mean time (GMT) for half of the year due to daylight savings time.

Using the *of()* Methods

We can create some date and time values using the of() methods in each class.

```
LocalDate date1 = LocalDate.of(2020, Month.OCTOBER, 20);
LocalDate date2 = LocalDate.of(2020, 10, 20);
```

Both pass in the year, month, and date. Although it is good to use the Month constants (to make the code easier to read), you can pass the int number of the month directly.

While programmers often count from zero, working with dates is one of the few times where it is expected for you to count from 1, just like in the real world.

When creating a time, you can choose how detailed you want to be. You can specify just the hour and minute, or you can include the number of seconds. You can even include nanoseconds if you want to be very precise (a nanosecond is a billionth of a second).

```
LocalTime time1 = LocalTime.of(6, 15);              // hour and minute
LocalTime time2 = LocalTime.of(6, 15, 30);          // + seconds
LocalTime time3 = LocalTime.of(6, 15, 30, 200);  // + nanoseconds
```

These three times are all different but within a minute of each other. You can combine dates and times in multiple ways.

```
var dt1 = LocalDateTime.of(2020, Month.OCTOBER, 20, 6, 15, 30);
```

```
LocalDate date = LocalDate.of(2020, Month.OCTOBER, 20);
LocalTime time = LocalTime.of(6, 15);
var dt2 = LocalDateTime.of(date, time);
```

The dt1 example shows how you can specify all of the information about the LocalDateTime right in the same line. The dt2 example shows how you can create LocalDate and LocalTime objects separately and then combine them to create a LocalDateTime object.

Real World Scenario

The Factory Pattern

Did you notice that we did not use a constructor in any of these examples? Rather than use a constructor, creation of these objects is delegated to a `static` factory method. The *factory pattern*, or factory method pattern, is a creational design pattern in which a factory class is used to provide instances of an object, rather than instantiating them directly. Oftentimes, factory methods return instances that are subtypes of the interface or class you are expecting.

We will be using the factory pattern throughout this book (and even later in this chapter!). In some cases, using a constructor may even be prohibited. For example, you cannot call new `LocalDate()` since all of the constructors in this class are `private`.

Formatting Dates and Times

The date and time classes support many methods to get data out of them.

```
LocalDate date = LocalDate.of(2020, Month.OCTOBER, 20);
System.out.println(date.getDayOfWeek());   // TUESDAY
System.out.println(date.getMonth());       // OCTOBER
System.out.println(date.getYear());        // 2020
System.out.println(date.getDayOfYear());   // 294
```

Java provides a class called `DateTimeFormatter` to display standard formats.

```
LocalDate date = LocalDate.of(2020, Month.OCTOBER, 20);
LocalTime time = LocalTime.of(11, 12, 34);
LocalDateTime dt = LocalDateTime.of(date, time);

System.out.println(date.format(DateTimeFormatter.ISO_LOCAL_DATE));
System.out.println(time.format(DateTimeFormatter.ISO_LOCAL_TIME));
System.out.println(dt.format(DateTimeFormatter.ISO_LOCAL_DATE_TIME));
```

The code snippet prints the following:

```
2020-10-20
11:12:34
2020-10-20T11:12:34
```

The DateTimeFormatter will throw an exception if it encounters an incompatible type. For example, each of the following will produce an exception at runtime since it attempts to format a date with a time value, and vice versa:

```
System.out.println(date.format(DateTimeFormatter.ISO_LOCAL_TIME));
System.out.println(time.format(DateTimeFormatter.ISO_LOCAL_DATE));
```

If you don't want to use one of the predefined formats, DateTimeFormatter supports a custom format using a date format String.

```
var f = DateTimeFormatter.ofPattern("MMMM dd, yyyy 'at' hh:mm");
System.out.println(dt.format(f));  // October 20, 2020 at 11:12
```

Let's break this down a bit. Java assigns each letter or symbol a specific date/time part. For example, M is used for month, while y is used for year. And case matters! Using m instead of M means it will return the minute of the hour, not the month of the year.

What about the number of symbols? The number often dictates the format of the date/time part. Using M by itself outputs the minimum number of characters for a month, such as 1 for January, while using MM always outputs two digits, such as 01. Furthermore, using MMM prints the three-letter abbreviation, such as Jul for July, while MMMM prints the full month name.

The *Date* and *SimpleDateFormat* Classes

When Java introduced the Date and Time API in Java 8, many developers switched to the new classes, such as DateTimeFormatter. The exam may include questions with the older date/time classes. For example, the previous code snippet could be written using the java.util.Date and java.text.SimpleDateFormat classes.

```
DateFormat s = new SimpleDateFormat("MMMM dd, yyyy 'at' hh:mm");
System.out.println(s.format(new Date()));  // October 20, 2020 at 06:15
```

As we said earlier, if you see dates or times on the exam, regardless of whether they are using the old or new APIs, you are not being tested on them. You only need to know how to format them. For the exam, the rules for defining a custom DateTimeFormatter and SimpleDateFormat symbols are the same.

Learning the Standard Date/Time Symbols

For the exam, you should be familiar enough with the various symbols that you can look at a date/time String and have a good idea of what the output will be. Table 5.5 includes the symbols you should be familiar with for the exam.

TABLE 5.5   Common date/time symbols

Symbol	Meaning	Examples
y	Year	20, 2020
M	Month	1, 01, Jan, January
d	Day	5, 05
h	Hour	9, 09
m	Minute	45
s	Second	52
a	a.m./p.m.	AM, PM
z	Time Zone Name	Eastern Standard Time, EST
Z	Time Zone Offset	−0400

Let's try some examples. What do you think the following prints?

```
var dt = LocalDateTime.of(2020, Month.OCTOBER, 20, 6, 15, 30);

var formatter1 = DateTimeFormatter.ofPattern("MM/dd/yyyy hh:mm:ss");
System.out.println(dt.format(formatter1));

var formatter2 = DateTimeFormatter.ofPattern("MM_yyyy_-_dd");
System.out.println(dt.format(formatter2));

var formatter3 = DateTimeFormatter.ofPattern("h:mm z");
System.out.println(dt.format(formatter3));
```

The output is as follows:

```
10/20/2020 06:15:30
10_2020_-_20
Exception in thread "main" java.time.DateTimeException:
   Unable to extract ZoneId from temporal 2020-10-20T06:15:30
```

The first example prints the date, with the month before the day, followed by the time. The second example prints the date in a weird format with extra characters that are just displayed as part of the output.

The third example throws an exception at runtime because the underlying LocalDateTime does not have a time zone specified. If ZonedDateTime was used instead, then the code would have completed successfully and printed something like 06:15 EDT, depending on the time zone.

As you saw in the previous example, you need to make sure the format String is compatible with the underlying date/time type. Table 5.6 shows which symbols you can use with each of the date/time objects.

TABLE 5.6   Supported date/time symbols

Symbol	LocalDate	LocalTime	LocalDateTime	ZonedDateTime
y	√		√	√
M	√		√	√
d	√		√	√
h		√	√	√
m		√	√	√
s		√	√	√
a		√	√	√
z				√
Z				√

Make sure you know which symbols are compatible with which date/time types. For example, trying to format a month for a LocalTime or an hour for a LocalDate will result in a runtime exception.

Selecting a *format()* Method

The date/time classes contain a format() method that will take a formatter, while the formatter classes contain a format() method that will take a date/time value. The result is that either of the following is acceptable:

```
var dateTime = LocalDateTime.of(2020, Month.OCTOBER, 20, 6, 15, 30);
var formatter = DateTimeFormatter.ofPattern("MM/dd/yyyy hh:mm:ss");
```

```
System.out.println(dateTime.format(formatter)); // 10/20/2020 06:15:30
System.out.println(formatter.format(dateTime)); // 10/20/2020 06:15:30
```

These statements print the same value at runtime. Which syntax you use is up to you.

Adding Custom Text Values

What if you want your format to include some custom text values? If you just type it as part of the format String, the formatter will interpret each character as a date/time symbol. In the best case, it will display weird data based on extra symbols you enter. In the worst case, it will throw an exception because the characters contain invalid symbols. Neither is desirable!

One way to address this would be to break the formatter up into multiple smaller formatters and then concatenate the results.

```
var dt = LocalDateTime.of(2020, Month.OCTOBER, 20, 6, 15, 30);


var f1 = DateTimeFormatter.ofPattern("MMMM dd, yyyy ");
var f2 = DateTimeFormatter.ofPattern(" hh:mm");
System.out.println(dt.format(f1) + "at" + dt.format(f2));
```

This prints October 20, 2020 at 06:15 at runtime.

While this works, it could become difficult if there are a lot of text values and date symbols intermixed. Luckily, Java includes a much simpler solution. You can *escape* the text by surrounding it with a pair of single quotes ('). Escaping text instructs the formatter to ignore the values inside the single quotes and just insert them as part of the final value. We saw this earlier with the 'at' inserted into the formatter.

```
var f = DateTimeFormatter.ofPattern("MMMM dd, yyyy 'at' hh:mm");
System.out.println(dt.format(f));  // October 20, 2020 at 06:15
```

But what if you need to display a single quote in the output too? Welcome to the fun of escaping characters! Java supports this by putting two single quotes next to each other.

We conclude our discussion of date formatting with some various examples of formats and their output that rely on text values, shown here:

```
var g1 = DateTimeFormatter.ofPattern("MMMM dd', Party''s at' hh:mm");
System.out.println(dt.format(g1)); // October 20, Party's at 06:15


var g2 = DateTimeFormatter.ofPattern("'System format, hh:mm: 'hh:mm");
System.out.println(dt.format(g2)); // System format, hh:mm: 06:15


var g3 = DateTimeFormatter.ofPattern("'NEW! 'yyyy', yay!'");
System.out.println(dt.format(g3)); // NEW! 2020, yay!
```

Without escaping the text values with single quotes, an exception will be thrown at run-time if the text cannot be interpreted as a date/time symbol.

```
DateTimeFormatter.ofPattern("The time is hh:mm");  // Exception thrown
```

This line throws an exception since T is an unknown symbol. The exam might also present you with an incomplete escape sequence.

```
DateTimeFormatter.ofPattern("'Time is: hh:mm: ");  // Exception thrown
```

Failure to terminate an escape sequence will trigger an exception at runtime.

Supporting Internationalization and Localization

Many applications need to work in different countries and with different languages. For example, consider the sentence "The zoo is holding a special event on 4/1/15 to look at animal behaviors." When is the event? In the United States, it is on April 1. However, a British reader would interpret this as January 4. A British reader might also wonder why we didn't write "behaviours." If we are making a website or program that will be used in multiple countries, we want to use the correct language and formatting.

Internationalization is the process of designing your program so it can be adapted. This involves placing strings in a properties file and ensuring the proper data formatters are used. *Localization* means actually supporting multiple locales or geographic regions. You can think of a locale as being like a language and country pairing. Localization includes translating strings to different languages. It also includes outputting dates and numbers in the correct format for that locale.

Initially, your program does not need to support multiple locales. The key is to future-proof your application by using these techniques. This way, when your product becomes successful, you can add support for new languages or regions without rewriting everything.

In this section, we will look at how to define a locale and use it to format dates, numbers, and strings.

Picking a Locale

While Oracle defines a locale as "a specific geographical, political, or cultural region," you'll only see languages and countries on the exam. Oracle certainly isn't going to delve into political regions that are not countries. That's too controversial for an exam!

The `Locale` class is in the `java.util` package. The first useful `Locale` to find is the user's current locale. Try running the following code on your computer:

```
Locale locale = Locale.getDefault();
System.out.println(locale);
```

When we run it, it prints en_US. It might be different for you. This default output tells us that our computers are using English and are sitting in the United States.

Notice the format. First comes the lowercase language code. The language is always required. Then comes an underscore followed by the uppercase country code. The country is optional. Figure 5.5 shows the two formats for `Locale` objects that you are expected to remember.

FIGURE 5.5   Locale formats

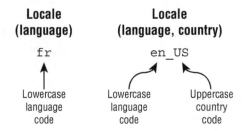

As practice, make sure that you understand why each of these `Locale` identifiers is invalid:

```
US     // Cannot have country without language
enUS   // Missing underscore
US_en  // The country and language are reversed
EN     // Language must be lowercase
```

The corrected versions are en and en_US.

You do not need to memorize language or country codes. The exam will let you know about any that are being used. You do need to recognize valid and invalid formats. Pay attention to uppercase/lowercase and the underscore. For example, if you see a locale expressed as es_CO, then you should know that the language is es and the country is CO, even if you didn't know they represent Spanish and Colombia, respectively.

As a developer, you often need to write code that selects a locale other than the default one. There are three common ways of doing this. The first is to use the built-in constants in the `Locale` class, available for some common locales.

```
System.out.println(Locale.GERMAN);  // de
System.out.println(Locale.GERMANY); // de_DE
```

The first example selects the German language, which is spoken in many countries, including Austria (de_AT) and Liechtenstein (de_LI). The second example selects both German the language and Germany the country. While these examples may look similar, they are not the same. Only one includes a country code.

The second way of selecting a Locale is to use the constructors to create a new object. You can pass just a language, or both a language and country:

```
System.out.println(new Locale("fr"));        // fr
System.out.println(new Locale("hi", "IN")); // hi_IN
```

The first is the language French, and the second is Hindi in India. Again, you don't need to memorize the codes. There is another constructor that lets you be even more specific about the locale. Luckily, providing a variant value is not on the exam.

Java will let you create a Locale with an invalid language or country, such as xx_XX. However, it will not match the Locale that you want to use, and your program will not behave as expected.

There's a third way to create a Locale that is more flexible. The builder design pattern lets you set all of the properties that you care about and then build it at the end. This means that you can specify the properties in any order. The following two Locale values both represent en_US:

```
Locale l1 = new Locale.Builder()
   .setLanguage("en")
   .setRegion("US")
   .build();

Locale l2 = new Locale.Builder()
   .setRegion("US")
   .setLanguage("en")
   .build();
```

 Real World Scenario

The Builder Pattern

Another design pattern commonly used in Java APIs is the builder pattern. The *builder pattern* is a creational pattern in which the task of setting the properties to create an object and the actual creation of the object are distinct steps.

In Java, it is often implemented with an instance of a static nested class. Since the builder and the target class tend to be tightly coupled, it makes sense for them to be defined within the same class.

Once all of the properties to create the object are specified, a `build()` method is then called that returns an instance of the desired object. It is commonly used to construct immutable objects with a lot of parameters since an immutable object is created only at the end of a method chain.

When testing a program, you might need to use a `Locale` other than the default of your computer.

```
System.out.println(Locale.getDefault()); // en_US
Locale locale = new Locale("fr");
Locale.setDefault(locale);              // change the default
System.out.println(Locale.getDefault()); // fr
```

Try it, and don't worry—the `Locale` changes for only that one Java program. It does not change any settings on your computer. It does not even change future executions of the same program.

> The exam may use `setDefault()` because it can't make assumptions about where you are located. In practice, we rarely write code to change a user's default locale.

Localizing Numbers

It might surprise you that formatting or parsing currency and number values can change depending on your locale. For example, in the United States, the dollar sign is prepended before the value along with a decimal point for values less than one dollar, such as $2.15. In Germany, though, the euro symbol is appended to the value along with a comma for values less than one euro, such as 2,15 €.

Luckily, the `java.text` package includes classes to save the day. The following sections cover how to format numbers, currency, and dates based on the locale.

The first step to formatting or parsing data is the same: obtain an instance of a `NumberFormat`. Table 5.7 shows the available factory methods.

TABLE 5.7 Factory methods to get a `NumberFormat`

Description	Using default `Locale` **and a specified** `Locale`
A general-purpose formatter	`NumberFormat.getInstance()` `NumberFormat.getInstance(locale)`
Same as `getInstance`	`NumberFormat.getNumberInstance()` `NumberFormat.getNumberInstance(locale)`
For formatting monetary amounts	`NumberFormat.getCurrencyInstance()` `NumberFormat.getCurrencyInstance(locale)`

TABLE 5.7   Factory methods to get a `NumberFormat` *(continued)*

Description	Using default `Locale` and a specified `Locale`
For formatting percentages	`NumberFormat.getPercentInstance()` `NumberFormat.getPercentInstance(locale)`
Rounds decimal values before displaying	`NumberFormat.getIntegerInstance()` `NumberFormat.getIntegerInstance(locale)`

Once you have the `NumberFormat` instance, you can call `format()` to turn a number into a `String`, or you can use `parse()` to turn a `String` into a number.

The format classes are not thread-safe. Do not store them in instance variables or `static` variables. You'll learn more about thread safety in Chapter 7, "Concurrency."

Formatting Numbers

When we format data, we convert it from a structured object or primitive value into a `String`. The `NumberFormat.format()` method formats the given number based on the locale associated with the `NumberFormat` object.

Let's go back to our zoo for a minute. For marketing literature, we want to share the average monthly number of visitors to the San Diego Zoo. The following shows printing out the same number in three different locales:

```
int attendeesPerYear = 3_200_000;
int attendeesPerMonth = attendeesPerYear / 12;

var us = NumberFormat.getInstance(Locale.US);
System.out.println(us.format(attendeesPerMonth));

var gr = NumberFormat.getInstance(Locale.GERMANY);
System.out.println(gr.format(attendeesPerMonth));

var ca = NumberFormat.getInstance(Locale.CANADA_FRENCH);
System.out.println(ca.format(attendeesPerMonth));
```

The output looks like this:

```
266,666
266.666
266 666
```

This shows how our U.S., German, and French Canadian guests can all see the same information in the number format they are accustomed to using. In practice, we would just call `NumberFormat.getInstance()` and rely on the user's default locale to format the output.

Formatting currency works the same way.

```
double price = 48;
var myLocale = NumberFormat.getCurrencyInstance();
System.out.println(myLocale.format(price));
```

When run with the default locale of en_US for the United States, it outputs $48.00. On the other hand, when run with the default locale of en_GB for Great Britain, it outputs £48.00.

In the real world, use `int` or `BigDecimal` for money and not `double`. Doing math on amounts with `double` is dangerous because the values are stored as floating-point numbers. Your boss won't appreciate it if you lose pennies or fractions of pennies during transactions!

Parsing Numbers

When we parse data, we convert it from a `String` to a structured object or primitive value. The `NumberFormat.parse()` method accomplishes this and takes the locale into consideration.

For example, if the locale is the English/United States (en_US) and the number contains commas, the commas are treated as formatting symbols. If the locale relates to a country or language that uses commas as a decimal separator, the comma is treated as a decimal point.

The `parse()` method, found in various types, declares a checked exception `ParseException` that must be handled or declared in the method in which they are called.

Let's look at an example. The following code parses a discounted ticket price with different locales. The `parse()` method actually throws a checked `ParseException`, so make sure to handle or declare it in your own code.

```
String s = "40.45";

var en = NumberFormat.getInstance(Locale.US);
System.out.println(en.parse(s));  // 40.45

var fr = NumberFormat.getInstance(Locale.FRANCE);
System.out.println(fr.parse(s));  // 40
```

In the United States, a dot (.) is part of a number, and the number is parsed how you might expect. France does not use a decimal point to separate numbers. Java parses it as a formatting character, and it stops looking at the rest of the number. The lesson is to make sure that you parse using the right locale!

The parse() method is also used for parsing currency. For example, we can read in the zoo's monthly income from ticket sales.

```
String income = "$92,807.99";
var cf = NumberFormat.getCurrencyInstance();
double value = (Double) cf.parse(income);
System.out.println(value); // 92807.99
```

The currency string "$92,807.99" contains a dollar sign and a comma. The parse method strips out the characters and converts the value to a number. The return value of parse is a Number object. Number is the parent class of all the java.lang wrapper classes, so the return value can be cast to its appropriate data type. The Number is cast to a Double and then automatically unboxed into a double.

Writing a Custom Number Formatter

Like you saw earlier when working with dates, you can also create your own number format strings using the DecimalFormat class, which extends NumberFormat. When creating a DecimalFormat object, you use a constructor rather than a factory method. You pass the pattern that you would like to use. The patterns can get complex, but you need to know only about two formatting characters, shown in Table 5.8.

TABLE 5.8   DecimalFormat symbols

Symbol	Meaning	Examples
#	Omit the position if no digit exists for it.	$2.2
0	Put a 0 in the position if no digit exists for it.	$002.20

These examples should help illuminate how these symbols work:

```
12: double d = 1234567.467;
13: NumberFormat f1 = new DecimalFormat("###,###,###.0");
14: System.out.println(f1.format(d));  // 1,234,567.5
15:
```

```
16: NumberFormat f2 = new DecimalFormat("000,000,000.00000");
17: System.out.println(f2.format(d));  // 001,234,567.46700
18:
19: NumberFormat f3 = new DecimalFormat("$#,###,###.##");
20: System.out.println(f3.format(d));  // $1,234,567.47
```

Line 14 displays the digits in the number, rounding to the nearest 10th after the decimal. The extra positions to the left are left off because we used #. Line 17 adds leading and trailing zeros to make the output the desired length. Line 20 shows prefixing a nonformatting character ($ sign) along with rounding because fewer digits are printed than available.

Localizing Dates

Like numbers, date formats can vary by locale. Table 5.9 shows methods used to retrieve an instance of a `DateTimeFormatter` using the default locale.

TABLE 5.9   Factory methods to get a `DateTimeFormatter`

Description	Using default `Locale`
For formatting dates	`DateTimeFormatter.ofLocalizedDate(dateStyle)`
For formatting times	`DateTimeFormatter.ofLocalizedTime(timeStyle)`
For formatting dates and times	`DateTimeFormatter.ofLocalizedDateTime(dateStyle, timeStyle)`
	`DateTimeFormatter.ofLocalizedDateTime(dateTimeStyle)`

Each method in the table takes a `FormatStyle` parameter, with possible values SHORT, MEDIUM, LONG, and FULL. For the exam, you are not required to know the format of each of these styles.

What if you need a formatter for a specific locale? Easy enough—just append `withLocale(locale)` to the method call.

Let's put it all together. Take a look at the following code snippet, which relies on a static import for the `java.time.format.FormatStyle.SHORT` value:

```
public static void print(DateTimeFormatter dtf,
    LocalDateTime dateTime, Locale locale) {
  System.out.println(dtf.format(dateTime) + ", "
    + dtf.withLocale(locale).format(dateTime));
}
```

```
public static void main(String[] args) {
   Locale.setDefault(new Locale("en", "US"));
   var italy = new Locale("it", "IT");
   var dt = LocalDateTime.of(2020, Month.OCTOBER, 20, 15, 12, 34);

   // 10/20/20, 20/10/20
   print(DateTimeFormatter.ofLocalizedDate(SHORT),dt,italy);

   // 3:12 PM, 15:12
   print(DateTimeFormatter.ofLocalizedTime(SHORT),dt,italy);

   // 10/20/20, 3:12 PM, 20/10/20, 15:12
   print(DateTimeFormatter.ofLocalizedDateTime(SHORT,SHORT),dt,italy);
}
```

First, we establish en_US as the default locale, with it_IT as the requested locale. We then output each value using the two locales. As you can see, applying a locale has a big impact on the built-in date and time formatters.

Specifying a Locale Category

When you call Locale.setDefault() with a locale, several display and formatting options are internally selected. If you require finer-grained control of the default locale, Java actually subdivides the underlying formatting options into distinct categories, with the Locale.Category enum.

The Locale.Category enum is a nested element in Locale, which supports distinct locales for displaying and formatting data. For the exam, you should be familiar with the two enum values in Table 5.10.

TABLE 5.10 Locale.Category values

Value	Description
DISPLAY	Category used for displaying data about the locale
FORMAT	Category used for formatting dates, numbers, or currencies

When you call `Locale.setDefault()` with a locale, both the `DISPLAY` and `FORMAT` are set together. Let's take a look at an example:

```
10: public static void printCurrency(Locale locale, double money) {
11:     System.out.println(
12:         NumberFormat.getCurrencyInstance().format(money)
13:         + ", " + locale.getDisplayLanguage());
14: }
15: public static void main(String[] args) {
16:     var spain = new Locale("es", "ES");
17:     var money = 1.23;
18:
19:     // Print with default locale
20:     Locale.setDefault(new Locale("en", "US"));
21:     printCurrency(spain, money);   // $1.23, Spanish
22:
23:     // Print with default locale and selected locale display
24:     Locale.setDefault(Category.DISPLAY, spain);
25:     printCurrency(spain, money);   // $1.23, español
26:
27:     // Print with default locale and selected locale format
28:     Locale.setDefault(Category.FORMAT, spain);
29:     printCurrency(spain, money);   // 1,23 €, español
30: }
```

The code prints the same data three times. First, it prints the language of the `spain` and `money` variables using the locale en_US. Then, it prints it using the `DISPLAY` category of es_ES, while the `FORMAT` category remains en_US. Finally, it prints the data using both categories set to es_ES.

For the exam, you do not need to memorize the various display and formatting options for each category. You just need to know that you can set parts of the locale independently. You should also know that calling `Locale.setDefault(us)` after the previous code snippet will change both locale categories to en_US.

Loading Properties with Resource Bundles

Up until now, we've kept all of the text strings displayed to our users as part of the program inside the classes that use them. Localization requires externalizing them to elsewhere.

A *resource bundle* contains the locale-specific objects to be used by a program. It is like a map with keys and values. The resource bundle is commonly stored in a properties file. A *properties file* is a text file in a specific format with key/value pairs.

> For the exam, you only need to know about resource bundles that are created from properties files. That said, you can also create a resource bundle from a class by extending ResourceBundle. One advantage of this approach is that it allows you to specify values using a method or in formats other than String, such as other numeric primitives, objects, or lists.

Our zoo program has been successful. We are now getting requests to use it at three more zoos! We already have support for U.S.-based zoos. We now need to add Zoo de La Palmyre in France, the Greater Vancouver Zoo in English-speaking Canada, and Zoo de Granby in French-speaking Canada.

We immediately realize that we are going to need to internationalize our program. Resource bundles will be quite helpful. They will let us easily translate our application to multiple locales or even support multiple locales at once. It will also be easy to add more locales later if we get zoos in even more countries interested. We thought about which locales we need to support, and we came up with four.

```
Locale us            = new Locale("en", "US");
Locale france        = new Locale("fr", "FR");
Locale englishCanada = new Locale("en", "CA");
Locale frenchCanada  = new Locale("fr", "CA");
```

In the next sections, we will create a resource bundle using properties files. A *properties file* is a text file that contains a list of key/value pairs. It is conceptually similar to a Map<String,String>, with each line representing a different key/value. The key and value are separated by an equal sign (=) or colon (:). To keep things simple, we use an equal sign throughout this chapter. We will also look at how Java determines which resource bundle to use.

Creating a Resource Bundle

We're going to update our application to support the four locales listed previously. Luckily, Java doesn't require us to create four different resource bundles. If we don't have a country-specific resource bundle, Java will use a language-specific one. It's a bit more involved than this, but let's start with a simple example.

For now, we need English and French properties files for our Zoo resource bundle. First, create two properties files.

Zoo_en.properties
```
hello=Hello
open=The zoo is open
```

Zoo_fr.properties
```
hello=Bonjour
open=Le zoo est ouvert
```

The filenames match the name of our resource bundle, Zoo. They are then followed by an underscore (_), target locale, and .properties file extension. We can write our very first program that uses a resource bundle to print this information.

```
10: public static void printWelcomeMessage(Locale locale) {
11:     var rb = ResourceBundle.getBundle("Zoo", locale);
12:     System.out.println(rb.getString("hello")
13:         + ", " + rb.getString("open"));
14: }
15: public static void main(String[] args) {
16:     var us = new Locale("en", "US");
17:     var france = new Locale("fr", "FR");
18:     printWelcomeMessage(us);     // Hello, The zoo is open
19:     printWelcomeMessage(france); // Bonjour, Le zoo est ouvert
20: }
```

Lines 16–17 create the two locales that we want to test, but the method on lines 10–14 does the actual work. Line 11 calls a factory method on ResourceBundle to get the right resource bundle. Lines 12 and 13 retrieve the right string from the resource bundle and print the results.

Remember we said you'd see the factory pattern again in this chapter? It will be used a lot in this book, so it helps to be familiar with it.

Since a resource bundle contains key/value pairs, you can even loop through them to list all of the pairs. The ResourceBundle class provides a keySet() method to get a set of all keys.

```
var us = new Locale("en", "US");
ResourceBundle rb = ResourceBundle.getBundle("Zoo", us);
rb.keySet().stream()
    .map(k -> k + ": " + rb.getString(k))
    .forEach(System.out::println);
```

This example goes through all of the keys. It maps each key to a String with both the key and the value before printing everything.

```
hello: Hello
open: The zoo is open
```

Picking a Resource Bundle

There are two methods for obtaining a resource bundle that you should be familiar with for the exam.

```
ResourceBundle.getBundle("name");
ResourceBundle.getBundle("name", locale);
```

The first one uses the default locale. You are likely to use this one in programs that you write. Either the exam tells you what to assume as the default locale or it uses the second approach.

Java handles the logic of picking the best available resource bundle for a given key. It tries to find the most specific value. Table 5.11 shows what Java goes through when asked for resource bundle Zoo with the locale new `Locale("fr", "FR")` when the default locale is U.S. English.

TABLE 5.11   Picking a resource bundle for French/France with default locale English/US

Step	Looks for file	Reason
1	Zoo_fr_FR.properties	The requested locale
2	Zoo_fr.properties	The language we requested with no country
3	Zoo_en_US.properties	The default locale
4	Zoo_en.properties	The default locale's language with no country

Step	Looks for file	Reason
5	Zoo.properties	No locale at all—the default bundle
6	If still not found, throw MissingResourceException.	No locale or default bundle available

As another way of remembering the order of Table 5.11, learn these steps:

1. Look for the resource bundle for the requested locale, followed by the one for the default locale.

2. For each locale, check language/country, followed by just the language.

3. Use the default resource bundle if no matching locale can be found.

 As we mentioned earlier, Java supports resource bundles from Java classes and properties alike. When Java is searching for a matching resource bundle, it will first check for a resource bundle file with the matching class name. For the exam, you just need to know how to work with properties files.

Let's see if you understand Table 5.11. What is the maximum number of files that Java would need to consider to find the appropriate resource bundle with the following code?

```
Locale.setDefault(new Locale("hi"));
ResourceBundle rb = ResourceBundle.getBundle("Zoo", new Locale("en"));
```

The answer is three. They are listed here:

1. Zoo_en.properties
2. Zoo_hi.properties
3. Zoo.properties

The requested locale is en, so we start with that. Since the en locale does not contain a country, we move on to the default locale, hi. Again, there's no country, so we end with the default bundle.

Selecting Resource Bundle Values

Got all that? Good—because there is a twist. The steps that we've discussed so far are for finding the matching resource bundle to use as a base. Java isn't required to get all of the keys from the same resource bundle. It can get them from any parent of the matching resource bundle. A parent resource bundle in the hierarchy just removes components of the name until it gets to the top. Table 5.12 shows how to do this.

TABLE 5.12   Selecting resource bundle properties

Matching resource bundle	Properties files keys can come from
Zoo_fr_FR	Zoo_fr_FR.properties Zoo_fr.properties Zoo.properties

Once a resource bundle has been selected, only properties along a single hierarchy will be used. Contrast this behavior with Table 5.11, in which the default en_US resource bundle is used if no other resource bundles are available.

What does this mean exactly? Assume the requested locale is fr_FR and the default is en_US. The JVM will provide data from an en_US *only if there is no matching fr_FR or fr resource bundles*. If it finds a fr_FR or fr resource bundle, then only those bundles, along with the default bundle, will be used.

Let's put all of this together and print some information about our zoos. We have a number of properties files this time.

Zoo.properties
```
name=Vancouver Zoo
```

Zoo_en.properties
```
hello=Hello
open=is open
```

Zoo_en_US.properties
```
name=The Zoo
```

Zoo_en_CA.properties
```
visitors=Canada visitors
```

Suppose that we have a visitor from Quebec (which has a default locale of French Canada) who has asked the program to provide information in English. What do you think this outputs?

```
11: Locale.setDefault(new Locale("en", "US"));
12: Locale locale = new Locale("en", "CA");
13: ResourceBundle rb = ResourceBundle.getBundle("Zoo", locale);
14: System.out.print(rb.getString("hello"));
15: System.out.print(". ");
```

```
16: System.out.print(rb.getString("name"));
17: System.out.print(" ");
18: System.out.print(rb.getString("open"));
19: System.out.print(" ");
20: System.out.print(rb.getString("visitors"));
```

The program prints the following:

```
Hello. Vancouver Zoo is open Canada visitors
```

The default locale is en_US, and the requested locale is en_CA. First, Java goes through the available resource bundles to find a match. It finds one right away with Zoo_en_CA.properties. This means the default locale of en_US is irrelevant.

Line 14 doesn't find a match for the key hello in Zoo_en_CA.properties, so it goes up the hierarchy to Zoo_en.properties. Line 16 doesn't find a match for name in either of the first two properties files, so it has to go all the way to the top of the hierarchy to Zoo.properties. Line 18 has the same experience as line 14, using Zoo_en.properties. Finally, line 20 has an easier job of it and finds a matching key in Zoo_en_CA.properties.

In this example, only three properties files were used: Zoo_en_CA.properties, Zoo_en.properties, and Zoo.properties. Even when the property wasn't found in en_CA or en resource bundles, the program preferred using Zoo.properties (the default resource bundle) rather than Zoo_en_US.properties (the default locale).

What if a property is not found in any resource bundle? Then, an exception is thrown. For example, attempting to call rb.getString("close") in the previous program results in a MissingResourceException at runtime.

Formatting Messages

Often, we just want to output the text data from a resource bundle, but sometimes you want to format that data with parameters. In real programs, it is common to substitute variables in the middle of a resource bundle String. The convention is to use a number inside braces such as {0}, {1}, etc. The number indicates the order in which the parameters will be passed. Although resource bundles don't support this directly, the MessageFormat class does.

For example, suppose that we had this property defined:

```
helloByName=Hello, {0} and {1}
```

In Java, we can read in the value normally. After that, we can run it through the MessageFormat class to substitute the parameters. The second parameter to format() is a vararg, allowing you to specify any number of input values.

Given a resource bundle rb:

```
String format = rb.getString("helloByName");
System.out.print(MessageFormat.format(format, "Tammy", "Henry"));
```

that would then print the following:

```
Hello, Tammy and Henry
```

Using the *Properties* Class

When working with the ResourceBundle class, you may also come across the
Properties class. It functions like the HashMap class that you learned about in Chapter 3,
"Generics and Collections," except that it uses String values for the keys and values. Let's
create one and set some values.

```java
import java.util.Properties;
public class ZooOptions {
   public static void main(String[] args) {
      var props = new Properties();
      props.setProperty("name", "Our zoo");
      props.setProperty("open", "10am");
   }
}
```

The Properties class is commonly used in handling values that may not exist.

```java
System.out.println(props.getProperty("camel"));          // null
System.out.println(props.getProperty("camel", "Bob"));   // Bob
```

If a key were passed that actually existed, both statements would have printed it. This is
commonly referred to as providing a default, or backup value, for a missing key.

The Properties class also includes a get() method, but only getProperty() allows for a
default value. For example, the following call is invalid since get() takes only a single
parameter:

```java
props.get("open");                                       // 10am


props.get("open", "The zoo will be open soon");  // DOES NOT COMPILE
```

Using the Property Methods

A Properties object isn't just similar to a Map; it actually inherits Map<Object,Object>.
Despite this, you should use the getProperty() and setProperty() methods when
working with a Properties object, rather than the get()/put() methods. Besides supporting default values, it also ensures you don't add data to the Properties object that
cannot be read.

```java
var props = new Properties();
props.put("tigerAge", "4");
```

```
props.put("lionAge", 5);
System.out.println(props.getProperty("tigerAge"));  // 4
System.out.println(props.getProperty("lionAge"));   // null
```

Since a Properties object works only with String values, trying to read a numeric value returns null. Don't worry, you don't have to know this behavior for the exam. The point is to avoid using the get/put() methods when working with Properties objects.

Summary

This chapter covered a wide variety of topics centered around building applications that respond well to change. We started our discussion with exception handling. Exceptions can be divided into two categories: checked and unchecked. In Java, checked exceptions inherit Exception but not RuntimeException and must be handled or declared. Unchecked exceptions inherit RuntimeException or Error and do not need to be handled or declared. It is considered a poor practice to catch an Error.

You can create your own checked or unchecked exceptions by extending Exception or RuntimeException, respectively. You can also define custom constructors and messages for your exceptions, which will show up in stack traces.

Automatic resource management can be enabled by using a try-with-resources statement to ensure the resources are properly closed. Resources are closed at the conclusion of the try block, in the reverse order in which they are declared. A suppressed exception occurs when more than one exception is thrown, often as part of a finally block or try-with-resources close() operation. The first exception to be encountered will be the primary exception, with the additional exceptions being suppressed. New in Java 9 is the ability to use existing resources in a try-with-resources statement.

An assertion is a boolean expression placed at a particular point in your code where you think something should always be true. A failed assertion throws an AssertionError. Assertions should not change the state of any variables. You saw how to use the -ea and -enableassertions flags to turn on assertions and how the -disableassertions and -da flags can selectively disable assertions for particular classes or packages.

You can create a Locale class with a required lowercase language code and optional uppercase country code. For example, en and en_US are locales for English and U.S. English, respectively. For the exam, you do not need to know how to create dates, but you do need to know how to format them, along with numbers, using a locale. You also need to know how to create custom date and number formatters.

A ResourceBundle allows specifying key/value pairs in a properties file. Java goes through candidate resource bundles from the most specific to the most general to find a match. If no matches are found for the requested locale, Java switches to the default locale and then finally the default resource bundle. Once a matching resource bundle is found, Java looks only in the hierarchy of that resource bundle to select values.

By applying the principles you learned about in this chapter to your own projects, you can build applications that last longer, with built-in support for whatever unexpected events may arise.

Exam Essentials

Be able to create custom exception classes.   A new checked exception class can be created by extending Exception, while an unchecked exception class can be created by extending RuntimeException. You can create numerous constructors that call matching parent constructors, with similar arguments. This provides greater control over the exception handling and messages reported in stack traces.

Perform automatic resource management with try-with-resources statements.   A try-with-resources statement supports classes that inherit the AutoCloseable interface. It automatically closes resources in the reverse order in which they are declared. A try-with-resources statement, as well as a try statement with a finally block, may generate multiple exceptions. The first becomes the primary exception, and the rest are suppressed exceptions.

Apply try-with-resources to existing resources.   A try-with-resources statement can use resources declared before the start of the statement, provided they are final or effectively final. They are closed following the execution of the try-with-resources body.

Know how to write assert statements and enable assertions.   Assertions are implemented with the assert keyword, a boolean condition, and an optional message. Assertions are disabled by default. Watch for a question that uses assertions but does not enable them, or a question that tests your knowledge of how assertions are enabled or selectively disabled from the command line.

Identify valid locale strings.   Know that the language code is lowercase and mandatory, while the country code is uppercase and optional. Be able to select a locale using a built-in constant, constructor, or builder class.

Format dates, numbers, and messages.   Be able to format dates, numbers, and messages into various String formats. Also, know how to define a custom date or number formatter using symbols, including how to escape literal values. For messages, you should also be familiar with using the MessageFormat and Properties classes.

Determine which resource bundle Java will use to look up a key.   Be able to create resource bundles for a set of locales using properties files. Know the search order that Java uses to select a resource bundle and how the default locale and default resource bundle are considered. Once a resource bundle is found, recognize the hierarchy used to select values.

Review Questions

The answers to the chapter review questions can be found in Appendix B.

1. Which of the following classes contain at least one compiler error? (Choose all that apply.)

```
class Danger extends RuntimeException {
   public Danger(String message) {
      super();
   }
   public Danger(int value) {
      super((String) null);
   }
}
class Catastrophe extends Exception {
   public Catastrophe(Throwable c) throws RuntimeException {
      super(new Exception());
      c.printStackTrace();
   }
}
class Emergency extends Danger {
   public Emergency() {}
   public Emergency(String message) {
      super(message);
   }
}
```

   A. Danger
   B. Catastrophe
   C. Emergency
   D. All of these classes compile correctly.
   E. The answer cannot be determined from the information given.

2. Which of the following are common types to localize? (Choose all that apply.)
   A. Dates
   B. Lambda expressions
   C. Class names
   D. Currency
   E. Numbers
   F. Variable names

3. What is the output of the following code?

```java
import java.io.*;
public class EntertainmentCenter {
    static class TV implements AutoCloseable {
        public void close() {
            System.out.print("D");
    } }
    static class MediaStreamer implements Closeable {
        public void close() {
            System.out.print("W");
    } }
    public static void main(String[] args) {
        var w = new MediaStreamer();
        try {
            TV d = new TV(); w;
        }
        {
            System.out.print("T");
        } catch (Exception e) {
            System.out.print("E");
        } finally {
            System.out.print("F");
        }
    }
}
```

- **A.** TWF
- **B.** TWDF
- **C.** TWDEF
- **D.** TWF followed by an exception.
- **E.** TWDF followed by an exception.
- **F.** TWEF followed by an exception.
- **G.** The code does not compile.

4. Which statement about the following class is correct?

```java
1: class Problem extends Exception {
2:     public Problem() {}
3: }
4: class YesProblem extends Problem {}
5: public class MyDatabase {
```

```
6:        public static void connectToDatabase() throw Problem {
7:            throws new YesProblem();
8:        }
9:        public static void main(String[] c) throw Exception {
10:           connectToDatabase();
11:       }
12: }
```

A. The code compiles and prints a stack trace for YesProblem at runtime.

B. The code compiles and prints a stack trace for Problem at runtime.

C. The code does not compile because Problem defines a constructor.

D. The code does not compile because YesProblem does not define a constructor.

E. The code does not compile but would if Problem and YesProblem were switched on lines 6 and 7.

F. None of the above

5. What is the output of the following code?

```
LocalDate date = LocalDate.parse("2020-04-30",
    DateTimeFormatter.ISO_LOCAL_DATE_TIME);
System.out.println(date.getYear() + " "
    + date.getMonth() + " "+ date.getDayOfMonth());
```

A. 2020 APRIL 2

B. 2020 APRIL 30

C. 2020 MAY 2

D. The code does not compile.

E. A runtime exception is thrown.

6. Assume that all of the files mentioned in the answer choices exist and define the same keys. Which one will be used to find the key in line 8?

```
6: Locale.setDefault(new Locale("en", "US"));
7: var b = ResourceBundle.getBundle("Dolphins");
8: System.out.println(b.getString("name"));
```

A. Dolphins.properties

B. Dolphins_US.properties

C. Dolphins_en.properties

D. Whales.properties

E. Whales_en_US.properties

F. The code does not compile.

7. For what value of `pattern` will the following print `<005.21> <008.49> <1,234.0>`?

```
String pattern = "_____";
var message = DoubleStream.of(5.21, 8.49, 1234)
    .mapToObj(v -> new DecimalFormat(pattern).format(v))
    .collect(Collectors.joining("> <"));
System.out.println("<"+message+">");
```

- **A.** `##.#`
- **B.** `0,000.0#`
- **C.** `#,###.0`
- **D.** `#,###,000.0#`
- **E.** The code does not compile regardless of what is placed in the blank.
- **F.** None of the above

8. Which of the following prints OhNo with the assertion failure when the number `magic` is positive? (Choose all that apply.)

- **A.** `assert magic < 0: "OhNo";`
- **B.** `assert magic < 0, "OhNo";`
- **C.** `assert magic < 0 ("OhNo");`
- **D.** `assert(magic < 0): "OhNo";`
- **E.** `assert(magic < 0, "OhNo");`

9. Which of the following exceptions must be handled or declared in the method in which they are thrown? (Choose all that apply.)

```
class Apple extends RuntimeException{}
class Orange extends Exception{}
class Banana extends Error{}
class Pear extends Apple{}
class Tomato extends Orange{}
class Peach extends Banana{}
```

- **A.** Apple
- **B.** Orange
- **C.** Banana
- **D.** Pear
- **E.** Tomato
- **F.** Peach

10. Which of the following changes when made independently would make this code compile? (Choose all that apply.)

```
1:   import java.io.*;
2:   public class StuckTurkeyCage implements AutoCloseable {
3:       public void close() throws IOException {
4:           throw new FileNotFoundException("Cage not closed");
5:       }
6:       public static void main(String[] args) {
7:           try (StuckTurkeyCage t = new StuckTurkeyCage()) {
8:               System.out.println("put turkeys in");
9:           }
10:   } }
```

A. Remove throws IOException from the declaration on line 3.

B. Add throws Exception to the declaration on line 6.

C. Change line 9 to } catch (Exception e) {}.

D. Change line 9 to } finally {}.

E. The code compiles as is.

F. None of the above

11. What is the result of running java EnterPark bird.java sing with the following code?

```
public class EnterPark extends Exception {
   public EnterPark(String message) {
      super();
   }
   private static void checkInput(String[] v) {
      if (v.length <= 3)
         assert(false) : "Invalid input";
   }
   public static void main(String... args) {
      checkInput(args);
      System.out.println(args[0] + args[1] + args[2]);
   }
}
```

A. birdsing

B. The assert statement throws an AssertionError.

C. The code throws an ArrayIndexOutOfBoundsException.

D. The code compiles and runs successfully, but there is no output.

E. The code does not compile.

12. Which of the following are true statements about exception handling in Java? (Choose all that apply.)

A. A traditional `try` statement without a `catch` block requires a `finally` block.

B. A traditional `try` statement without a `finally` block requires a `catch` block.

C. A traditional `try` statement with only one statement can omit the {}.

D. A try-with-resources statement without a `catch` block requires a `finally` block.

E. A try-with-resources statement without a `finally` block requires a `catch` block.

F. A try-with-resources statement with only one statement can omit the {}.

13. Which of the following, when inserted independently in the blank, use locale parameters that are properly formatted? (Choose all that apply.)

```java
import java.util.Locale;
public class ReadMap implements AutoCloseable {
    private Locale locale;
    private boolean closed = false;
    void check() {
        assert !closed;
    }
    @Override public void close() {
        check();
        System.out.println("Folding map");
        locale = null;
        closed = true;
    }
    public void open() {
        check();
        this.locale = _____;
    }
    public void use() {
        // Implementation omitted
    }
}
```

A. `new Locale("xM");`

B. `new Locale("MQ", "ks");`

C. `new Locale("qw");`

    D. `new Locale("wp", "VW");`

    E. `Locale.create("zp");`

    F. `Locale.create("FF");`

    G. The code does not compile regardless of what is placed in the blank.

14. Which of the following is true when creating your own exception class?

    A. One or more constructors must be coded.

    B. Only custom checked exception classes may be created.

    C. Only custom unchecked exception classes may be created.

    D. Custom `Error` classes may be created.

    E. The `toString()` method must be coded.

    F. None of the above

15. Which of the following can be inserted into the blank to allow the code to compile and run without throwing an exception? (Choose all that apply.)

```
var f = DateTimeFormatter.ofPattern("hh o'clock");
System.out.println(f.format(_____.now()));
```

    A. `ZonedDateTime`

    B. `LocalDate`

    C. `LocalDateTime`

    D. `LocalTime`

    E. The code does not compile regardless of what is placed in the blank.

    F. None of the above

16. Which of the following command lines cause this program to produce an error when executed? (Choose all that apply.)

```
public class On {
    public static void main(String[] args) {
        String s = null;
        int check = 10;
        assert s != null : check++;
    }
}
```

    A. `java -da On`

    B. `java -ea On`

    C. `java -da -ea:On On`

    D. `java -ea -da:On On`

    E. The code does not compile.

17. Which of the following statements about resource bundles are correct? (Choose all that apply.)

A. All keys must be in the same resource bundle to be used.

B. A resource bundle is loaded by calling the new `ResourceBundle()` constructor.

C. Resource bundle values are always read using the `Properties` class.

D. Changing the default locale lasts for only a single run of the program.

E. If a resource bundle for a specific locale is requested, then the resource bundle for the default locale will not be used.

F. It is possible to use a resource bundle for a locale without specifying a default locale.

18. What is the output of the following code?

```
import java.io.*;
public class FamilyCar {
    static class Door implements AutoCloseable {
        public void close() {
            System.out.print("D");
    } }
    static class Window implements Closeable {
        public void close() {
            System.out.print("W");
            throw new RuntimeException();
    } }
    public static void main(String[] args) {
        var d = new Door();
        try (d; var w = new Window()) {
            System.out.print("T");
        } catch (Exception e) {
            System.out.print("E");
        } finally {
            System.out.print("F");
        }
} } }
```

A. TWF

B. TWDF

C. TWDEF

D. TWF followed by an exception.

E. TWDF followed by an exception.

F. TWEF followed by an exception.

G. The code does not compile.

19. Suppose that we have the following three properties files and code. Which bundles are used on lines 8 and 9, respectively?

Dolphins.properties
```
name=The Dolphin
age=0
```

Dolphins_en.properties
```
name=Dolly
age=4
```

Dolphins_fr.properties
```
name=Dolly
```

```
5: var fr = new Locale("fr");
6: Locale.setDefault(new Locale("en", "US"));
7: var b = ResourceBundle.getBundle("Dolphins", fr);
8: b.getString("name");
9: b.getString("age");
```

A. Dolphins.properties and Dolphins.properties

B. Dolphins.properties and Dolphins_en.properties

C. Dolphins_en.properties and Dolphins_en.properties

D. Dolphins_fr.properties and Dolphins.properties

E. Dolphins_fr.properties and Dolphins_en.properties

F. The code does not compile.

G. None of the above

20. Fill in the blanks: When formatting text data, the _____ class supports parametrized String values, while the _____ class has built-in support for missing values.

A. TextFormat, Properties

B. MessageFormat, Properties

C. Properties, Formatter

D. StringFormat, Properties

E. Properties, TextFormat

F. Properties, TextHandler

G. None of the above

21. Which changes, when made independently, allow the following program to compile? (Choose all that apply.)

```
1: public class AhChoo {
2:     static class SneezeException extends Exception {}
3:     static class SniffleException extends SneezeException {}
4:     public static void main(String[] args) {
5:         try {
6:             throw new SneezeException();
7:         } catch (SneezeException | SniffleException e) {
8:         } finally {}
9:     } }
```

A. Add throws `SneezeException` to the declaration on line 4.

B. Add throws `Throwable` to the declaration on line 4.

C. Change line 7 to `} catch (SneezeException e) {`.

D. Change line 7 to `} catch (SniffleException e) {`.

E. Remove line 7.

F. The code compiles correctly as is.

G. None of the above

22. What is the output of the following code?

```
LocalDateTime ldt = LocalDateTime.of(2020, 5, 10, 11, 22, 33);
var f = DateTimeFormatter.ofLocalizedTime(FormatStyle.SHORT);
System.out.println(ldt.format(f));
```

A. `3/7/19 11:22 AM`

B. `5/10/20 11:22 AM`

C. `3/7/19`

D. `5/10/20`

E. `11:22 AM`

F. The code does not compile.

G. A runtime exception is thrown.

23. Fill in the blank: A class that implements _____ may be in a try-with-resources statement. (Choose all that apply.)

A. `AutoCloseable`

B. `Resource`

C. `Exception`

D. `AutomaticResource`

E. `Closeable`

F. `RuntimeException`

G. `Serializable`

24. What is the output of the following method if props contains
{veggies=brontosaurus, meat=velociraptor}?

```
    private static void print(Properties props) {
        System.out.println(props.get("veggies", "none")
            + " " + props.get("omni", "none"));
    }
```

A. brontosaurus none

B. brontosaurus null

C. none none

D. none null

E. The code does not compile.

F. A runtime exception is thrown.

25. What is the output of the following program?

```
    public class SnowStorm {
        static class WalkToSchool implements AutoCloseable {
            public void close() {
                throw new RuntimeException("flurry");
            }
        }
        public static void main(String[] args) {
            WalkToSchool walk1 = new WalkToSchool();
            try (walk1; WalkToSchool walk2 = new WalkToSchool()) {
                throw new RuntimeException("blizzard");
            } catch(Exception e) {
                System.out.println(e.getMessage()
                    + " " + e.getSuppressed().length);
            }
            walk1 = null;
        }
    }
```

A. blizzard 0

B. blizzard 1

C. blizzard 2

D. flurry 0

E. flurry 1

F. flurry 2

G. None of the above

26. Which of the following are true of the code? (Choose all that apply.)

```
4: private int addPlusOne(int a, int b) {
5:    boolean assert = false;
6:    assert a++ > 0;
7:    assert b > 0;
8:    return a + b;
9: }
```

A. Line 5 does not compile.

B. Lines 6 and 7 do not compile because they are missing the `String` message.

C. Lines 6 and 7 do not compile because they are missing parentheses.

D. Line 6 is an appropriate use of an assertion.

E. Line 7 is an appropriate use of an assertion.

27. What is the output of the following program?

```
import java.text.NumberFormat;
import java.util.Locale;
import java.util.Locale.Category;
public class Wallet {
    private double money;
    // Assume getters/setters/constructors provided

    private String openWallet() {
        Locale.setDefault(Category.DISPLAY,
            new Locale.Builder().setRegion("us"));
        Locale.setDefault(Category.FORMAT,
            new Locale.Builder().setLanguage("en"));
        return NumberFormat.getCurrencyInstance(Locale.GERMANY)
            .format(money);
    }
    public void printBalance() {
        System.out.println(openWallet());
    }
    public static void main(String... unused) {
        new Wallet(2.4).printBalance();
    }
}
```

A. 2,40 €

B. $2.40

C. 2.4

D. The output cannot be determined without knowing the locale of the system where it will be run.

E. The code does not compile.

F. None of the above

Chapter

6

Modular Applications

OCP EXAM OBJECTIVES COVERED IN THIS CHAPTER:

✓ **Migration to a Modular Application**

- Migrate the application developed using a Java version prior to SE 9 to SE 11 including top-down and bottom-up migration, splitting a Java SE 8 application into modules for migration

- Use jdeps to determine dependencies and identify ways to address the cyclic dependencies

✓ **Services in a Modular Application**

- Describe the components of Services including directives

- Design a service type, load services using ServiceLoader, check for dependencies of the services including consumer and provider modules

If you took the 1Z0-815 exam, you learned the basics of modules. If not, read Appendix A, "The Upgrade Exam," before reading this chapter. That will bring you up to speed. Luckily, you don't have to memorize as many command-line options for the 1Z0-815 exam.

This chapter covers strategies for migrating an application to use modules, running a partially modularized application, and dealing with dependencies. We then move on to discuss services and service locators.

You aren't required to create modules by hand or memorize as many commands to compile and run modules on the 1Z0-816 exam. We still include them in the chapter so you can study and follow along. Feel free to use the files we've already set up in the GitHub repo linked to from www.selikoff.net/ocp11-2.

Reviewing Module Directives

Since you are expected to know highlights of the module-info.java file for the 1Z0-816, we have included the relevant parts here as a reference. If anything in Table 6.1 is unclear or unfamiliar, please stop and read Appendix A before continuing in this chapter.

TABLE 6.1 Common module directives

Derivative	Description
exports <package>	Allows all modules to access the package
exports <package> to <module>	Allows a specific module to access the package
requires <module>	Indicates module is dependent on another module
requires transitive <module>	Indicates the module and that all modules that use this module are dependent on another module
uses <interface>	Indicates that a module uses a service
provides <interface> with <class>	Indicates that a module provides an implementation of a service

If you don't have any experience with uses or provides, don't worry—they will be covered in this chapter.

Comparing Types of Modules

The modules you learned about for the 1Z0-815 exam (or in Appendix A) are called *named modules*. There are two other types of modules: automatic modules and unnamed modules. In this section, we describe these three types of modules. On the exam, you will need to be able to compare them.

Classpath vs. Module Path

Before we get started, a brief reminder that the Java runtime is capable of using class and interface types from both the classpath and the module path, although the rules for each are a bit different. An application can access any type in the classpath that is exposed via standard Java access modifiers, such as a public class.

On the other hand, public types in the module path are not automatically available. While Java access modifiers must still be used, the type must also be in a package that is exported by the module in which it is defined. In addition, the module making use of the type must contain a dependency on the module.

Named Modules

A *named module* is one containing a module-info file. To review, this file appears in the root of the JAR alongside one or more packages. Unless otherwise specified, a module is a named module. Named modules appear on the module path rather than the classpath. You'll learn what happens if a JAR containing a module-info file is on the classpath. For now, just know it is not considered a named module because it is not on the module path.

As a way of remembering this, a named module has the name inside the module-info file and is on the module path. Figure 6.1 shows the contents of a JAR file for a named module. It contains two packages in addition to the module-info.class.

FIGURE 6.1   A named module

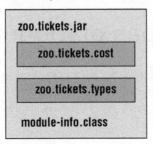

Automatic Modules

An *automatic module* appears on the module path but does not contain a module-info file. It is simply a regular JAR file that is placed on the module path and gets treated as a module.

As a way of remembering this, Java automatically determines the module name. Figure 6.2 shows an automatic module with two packages.

FIGURE 6.2   An automatic module

⊕ **Real World Scenario**

About the Manifest

A JAR file is a zip file with a special directory named META-INF. This directory contains one or more files. The MANIFEST.MF file is always present. The figure shows how the manifest fits into the directory structure of a JAR file.

The manifest contains extra information about the JAR file. For example, it often contains the version of Java used to build the JAR file. For command-line programs, the class with the `main()` method is commonly specified.

Each line in the manifest is a key/value pair separated by a colon. You can think of the manifest as a map of property names and values. The default manifest in Java 11 looks like this:

```
Manifest-Version: 1.0
Created-By: 11.0.2 (Oracle Corporation)
```

The code referencing an automatic module treats it as if there is a `module-info` file present. It automatically exports all packages. It also determines the module name. How does it determine the module name? you ask. Excellent question.

When Java 9 was released, authors of Java libraries were encouraged to declare the name they intended to use for the module in the future. All they had to do was set a property called `Automatic-Module-Name` in the `MANIFEST.MF` file.

Specifying a single property in the manifest allowed library providers to make things easier for applications that wanted to use their library in a modular application. You can think of it as a promise that when the library becomes a named module, it will use the specified module name.

If the JAR file does not specify an automatic module name, Java will still allow you to use it in the module path. In this case, Java will determine the module name for you. We'd say that this happens automatically, but the joke is probably wearing thin by now.

Java determines the automatic module name by basing it off the filename of the JAR file. Let's go over the rules by starting with an example. Suppose we have a JAR file named `holiday-calendar-1.0.0.jar`.

First, Java will remove the extension `.jar` from the name. Then, Java will remove the version from the end of the JAR filename. This is important because we want module names to be consistent. Having a different automatic module name every time you upgraded to a new version would not be good! After all, this would force you to change the module-info file of your nice, clean, modularized application every time you pulled in a later version of the holiday calendar JAR.

Removing the version and extension gives us holiday-calendar. This leaves us with a problem. Dashes (-) are not allowed in module names. Java solves this problem by converting any special characters in the name to dots (.). As a result, the module name is holiday.calendar. Any characters other than letters and numbers are considered special characters in this replacement. Finally, any adjacent dots or leading/trailing dots are removed.

Since that's a number of rules, let's review the algorithm in a list for determining the name of an automatic module.

- If the MANIFEST.MF specifies an Automatic-Module-Name, use that. Otherwise, proceed with the remaining rules.

- Remove the file extension from the JAR name.

- Remove any version information from the end of the name. A version is digits and dots with possible extra information at the end, for example, -1.0.0 or -1.0-RC.

- Replace any remaining characters other than letters and numbers with dots.

- Replace any sequences of dots with a single dot.

- Remove the dot if it is the first or last character of the result.

Table 6.2 shows how to apply these rules to two examples where there is no automatic module name specified in the manifest.

TABLE 6.2   Practicing with automatic module names

#	Description	Example 1	Example 2
1	Beginning JAR name	commons2-x-1.0.0-SNAPSHOT.jar	mod_$-1.0.jar
2	Remove file extension	commons2-x-1.0.0-SNAPSHOT	mod_$-1.0
3	Remove version information	commons2-x	mod_$
4	Replace special characters	commons2.x	mod..
5	Replace sequence of dots	commons2.x	mod.
6	Remove leading/trailing dots (results in the automatic module name)	commons2.x	mod

While the algorithm for creating automatic module names does its best, it can't always come up with a good name. For example, `1.2.0-calendar-1.2.2-good-1.jar` isn't conducive. Luckily such names are rare and out of scope for the exam.

Unnamed Modules

An *unnamed module* appears on the classpath. Like an automatic module, it is a regular JAR. Unlike an automatic module, it is on the classpath rather than the module path. This means an unnamed module is treated like old code and a second-class citizen to modules. Figure 6.3 shows an unnamed module with one package.

FIGURE 6.3   An unnamed module

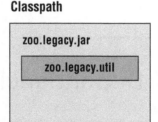

An unnamed module does not usually contain a `module-info` file. If it happens to contain one, that file will be ignored since it is on the classpath.

Unnamed modules do not export any packages to named or automatic modules. The unnamed module can read from any JARs on the classpath or module path. You can think of an unnamed module as code that works the way Java worked before modules. Yes, we know it is confusing to have something that isn't really a module having the word *module* in its name.

Comparing Module Types

You can expect to get questions on the exam comparing the three types of modules. Please study Table 6.3 thoroughly and be prepared to answer questions about these items in any combination. A key point to remember is that code on the classpath can access the module path. By contrast, code on the module path is unable to read from the classpath.

TABLE 6.3   Properties of modules types

Property	Named	Automatic	Unnamed
A _____ module contains a module-info file?	Yes	No	Ignored if present
A _____ module exports which packages to other modules?	Those in the module-info file	All packages	No packages
A _____ module is readable by other modules on the module path?	Yes	Yes	No
A _____ module is readable by other JARs on the classpath?	Yes	Yes	Yes

Analyzing JDK Dependencies

In this part of the chapter, we look at modules that are supplied by the JDK. We also look at the jdeps command for identifying such module dependencies.

Identifying Built-in Modules

Prior to Java 9, developers could use any package in the JDK by merely importing it into the application. This meant the whole JDK had to be available at runtime because a program could potentially need anything. With modules, your application specifies which parts of the JDK it uses. This allows the application to run on a full JDK or a subset.

You might be wondering what happens if you try to run an application that references a package that isn't available in the subset. No worries! The requires directive in the module-info file specifies which modules need to be present at both compile time and runtime. This means they are guaranteed to be available for the application to run.

The most important module to know is java.base. It contains most of the packages you have been learning about for the exam. In fact, it is so important that you don't even have to use the requires directive; it is available to all modular applications. Your module-info.java file will still compile if you explicitly require java.base. However, it is redundant, so it's better to omit it. Table 6.4 lists some common modules and what they contain.

TABLE 6.4 Common modules

Module name	What it contains	Coverage in book
java.base	Collections, Math, IO, NIO.2, Concurrency, etc.	Most of this book
java.desktop	Abstract Windows Toolkit (AWT) and Swing	Not on the exam beyond the module name
java.logging	Logging	Not on the exam beyond the module name
java.sql	JDBC	Chapter 10, "JDBC"
java.xml	Extensible Markup Language (XML)	Not on the exam beyond the module name

The exam creators feel it is important to recognize the names of modules supplied by the JDK. While you don't need to know the names by heart, you do need to be able to pick them out of a lineup.

For the exam, you need to know that module names begin with java for APIs you are likely to use and with jdk for APIs that are specific to the JDK. Table 6.5 lists all the modules that begin with java.

TABLE 6.5 Java modules prefixed with java

java.base	java.naming	java.smartcardio
java.compiler	java.net.http	java.sql
java.datatransfer	java.prefs	java.sql.rowset
java.desktop	java.rmi	java.transaction.xa
java.instrument	java.scripting	java.xml
java.logging	java.se	java.xml.crypto
java.management	java.security.jgss	
java.management.rmi	java.security.sasl	

Table 6.6 lists all the modules that begin with jdk. We recommend reviewing this right before the exam to increase the chances of them sounding familiar. You don't have to memorize them, but you should be able to pick them out of a lineup.

TABLE 6.6   Java modules prefixed with jdk

jdk.accessiblity	jdk.jconsole	jdk.naming.dns
jdk.attach	jdk.jdeps	jdk.naming.rmi
jdk.charsets	jdk.jdi	jdk.net
jdk.compiler	jdk.jdwp.agent	jdk.pack
jdk.crypto.cryptoki	jdk.jfr	jdk.rmic
jdk.crypto.ec	jdk.jlink	jdk.scripting.nashorn
jdk.dynalink	jdk.jshell	jdk.sctp
jdk.editpad	jdk.jsobject	jdk.security.auth
jdk.hotspot.agent	jdk.jstatd	jdk.security.jgss
jdk.httpserver	jdk.localdata	jdk.xml.dom
jdk.jartool	jdk.management	jdk.zipfs
jdk.javadoc	jdk.management.agent	
jdk.jcmd	jdk.management.jfr	

Using *jdeps*

The jdeps command gives you information about dependencies. Luckily, you are not expected to memorize all the options for the 1Z0-816 exam. (If you are taking the 1Z0-817 exam, you *do* need to memorize a lot of module commands, so study Appendix A carefully!)

You are expected to understand how to use jdeps with projects that have not yet been modularized to assist in identifying dependencies and problems. First, we will create a JAR file from this class. If you are following along, feel free to copy the class from the online examples referenced at the beginning of the chapter rather than typing it in.

```
// Animatronic.java
package zoo.dinos;

import java.time.*;
import java.util.*;
import sun.misc.Unsafe;
```

```
public class Animatronic {
   private List<String> names;
   private LocalDate visitDate;

   public Animatronic(List<String> names, LocalDate visitDate) {
      this.names = names;
      this.visitDate = visitDate;
   }
   public void unsafeMethod() {
      Unsafe unsafe = Unsafe.getUnsafe();
   }
}
```

This example is silly. It uses a number of unrelated classes. The Bronx Zoo really did have electronic moving dinosaurs for a while, so at least the idea of having dinosaurs in a zoo isn't beyond the realm of possibility.

Now we can compile this file. You might have noticed there is no `module-info.java` file. That is because we aren't creating a module. We are looking into what dependencies we will need when we do modularize this JAR.

```
javac zoo/dinos/*.java
```

Compiling works, but it gives you some warnings about `Unsafe` being an internal API. Don't worry about those for now—we'll discuss that shortly. (Maybe the dinosaurs went extinct because they did something unsafe.)

Next, we create a JAR file.

```
jar -cvf zoo.dino.jar .
```

We can run the `jdeps` command against this JAR to learn about its dependencies. First, let's run the command without any options. On the first two lines, the command prints the modules that we would need to add with a `requires` directive to migrate to the module system. It also prints a table showing what packages are used and what modules they correspond to.

```
jdeps zoo.dino.jar
```

```
zoo.dino.jar -> java.base
zoo.dino.jar -> jdk.unsupported
   zoo.dinos    -> java.lang      java.base
   zoo.dinos    -> java.time      java.base
   zoo.dinos    -> java.util      java.base
   zoo.dinos    -> sun.misc       JDK internal API (jdk.unsupported)
```

If we run in summary mode, we only see just the first part where `jdeps` lists the modules.

```
jdeps -s zoo.dino.jar

zoo.dino.jar -> java.base
zoo.dino.jar -> jdk.unsupported
```

For a real project, the dependency list could include dozens or even hundreds of packages. It's useful to see the summary of just the modules. This approach also makes it easier to see whether jdk.unsupported is in the list.

 You might have noticed that jdk.unsupported is not in the list of modules you saw in Table 6.6. It's special because it contains internal libraries that developers in previous versions of Java were discouraged from using, although many people ignored this warning. You should not reference it as it may disappear in future versions of Java.

The jdeps command has an option to provide details about these unsupported APIs. The output looks something like this:

```
jdeps --jdk-internals zoo.dino.jar

zoo.dino.jar -> jdk.unsupported
   zoo.dinos.Animatronic  -> sun.misc.Unsafe
      JDK internal API (jdk.unsupported)

Warning: <omitted warning>

JDK Internal API      Suggested Replacement
-----------------     -----------------------

sun.misc.Unsafe       See http://openjdk.java.net/jeps/260
```

The --jdk-internals option lists any classes you are using that call an internal API along with which API. At the end, it provides a table suggesting what you should do about it. If you wrote the code calling the internal API, this message is useful. If not, the message would be useful to the team who did write the code. You, on the other hand, might need to update or replace that JAR file entirely with one that fixes the issue. Note that -jdkinternals is equivalent to --jdk-internals.

 Real World Scenario

About *sun.misc.Unsafe*

Prior to the Java Platform Module System, classes had to be public if you wanted them to be used outside the package. It was reasonable to use the class in JDK code since that is low-level code that is already tightly coupled to the JDK. Since it was needed in multiple packages, the class was made `public`. Sun even named it `Unsafe`, figuring that would prevent anyone from using it outside the JDK.

However, developers are clever and used the class since it was available. A number of widely used open source libraries started using `Unsafe`. While it is quite unlikely that you are using this class in your project directly, it is likely you use an open source library that is using it.

The `jdeps` command allows you to look at these JARs to see whether you will have any problems when Oracle finally prevents the usage of this class. If you find any uses, you can look at whether there is a later version of the JAR that you can upgrade to.

Migrating an Application

All applications developed for Java 8 and earlier were not designed to use the Java Platform Module System because it did not exist yet. Ideally, they were at least designed with projects instead of as a big ball of mud. This section will give you an overview of strategies for migrating an existing application to use modules. We will cover ordering modules, bottom-up migration, top-down migration, and how to split up an existing project.

 **Real World Scenario**

Migrating Your Applications at Work

The exam exists in a pretend universe where there are no open-source dependencies and applications are very small. These scenarios make learning and discussing migration far easier. In the real world, applications have libraries that haven't been updated in 10 or more years, complex dependency graphs, and all sorts of surprises.

Note that you can use all the features of Java 11 without converting your application to modules (except the features in this module chapter, of course!). Please make sure you have a reason for migration and don't think it is required.

This chapter does a great job teaching you what you need to know for the exam. However, it does not adequately prepare you for actually converting real applications to use modules. If you find yourself in that situation, consider reading *The Java Module System* by Nicolai Parlog (Manning Publications, 2019).

Determining the Order

Before we can migrate our application to use modules, we need to know how the packages and libraries in the existing application are structured. Suppose we have a simple application with three JAR files, as shown in Figure 6.4. The dependencies between projects form a graph. Both of the representations in Figure 6.4 are equivalent. The arrows show the dependencies by pointing from the project that will require the dependency to the one that makes it available. In the language of modules, the arrow will go from `requires` to the `exports`.

FIGURE 6.4 Determining the order

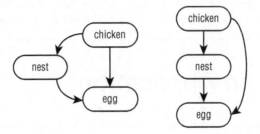

The right side of the diagram makes it easier to identify the top and bottom that top-down and bottom-up migration refer to. Projects that do not have any dependencies are at the bottom. Projects that do have dependencies are at the top.

In this example, there is only one order from top to bottom that honors all the dependencies. Figure 6.5 shows that the order is not always unique. Since two of the projects do not have an arrow between them, either order is allowed when deciding migration order.

FIGURE 6.5 Determining the order when not unique

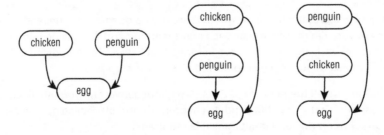

Exploring a Bottom-Up Migration Strategy

The easiest approach to migration is a bottom-up migration. This approach works best when you have the power to convert any JAR files that aren't already modules. For a bottom-up migration, you follow these steps:

1. Pick the lowest-level project that has not yet been migrated. (Remember the way we ordered them by dependencies in the previous section?)

2. Add a `module-info.java` file to that project. Be sure to add any `exports` to expose any package used by higher-level JAR files. Also, add a `requires` directive for any modules it depends on.

3. Move this newly migrated named module from the classpath to the module path.

4. Ensure any projects that have not yet been migrated stay as unnamed modules on the classpath.

5. Repeat with the next-lowest-level project until you are done.

You can see this procedure applied to migrate three projects in Figure 6.6. Notice that each project is converted to a module in turn.

FIGURE 6.6   Bottom-up migration

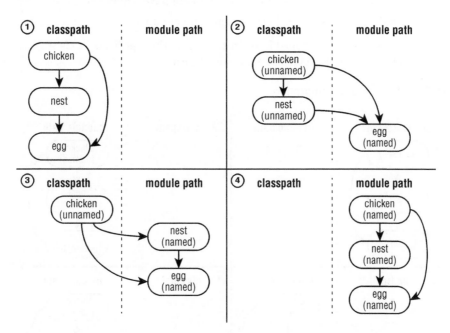

With a bottom-up migration, you are getting the lower-level projects in good shape. This makes it easier to migrate the top-level projects at the end. It also encourages care in what is exposed.

During migration, you have a mix of named modules and unnamed modules. The named modules are the lower-level ones that have been migrated. They are on the module path and not allowed to access any unnamed modules.

The unnamed modules are on the classpath. They can access JAR files on both the classpath and the module path.

Exploring a Top-Down Migration Strategy

A top-down migration strategy is most useful when you don't have control of every JAR file used by your application. For example, suppose another team owns one project. They are just too busy to migrate. You wouldn't want this situation to hold up your entire migration.

For a top-down migration, you follow these steps:

1. Place all projects on the module path.

2. Pick the highest-level project that has not yet been migrated.

3. Add a module-info file to that project to convert the automatic module into a named module. Again, remember to add any exports or requires directives. You can use the automatic module name of other modules when writing the requires directive since most of the projects on the module path do not have names yet.

4. Repeat with the next-lowest-level project until you are done.

You can see this procedure applied in order to migrate three projects in Figure 6.7. Notice that each project is converted to a module in turn.

FIGURE 6.7 Top-down migration

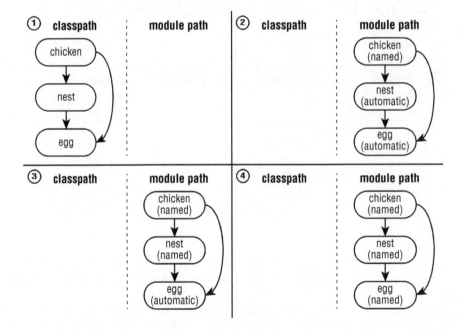

With a top-down migration, you are conceding that all of the lower-level dependencies are not ready but want to make the application itself a module.

During migration, you have a mix of named modules and automatic modules. The named modules are the higher-level ones that have been migrated. They are on the module path and have access to the automatic modules. The automatic modules are also on the module path.

Table 6.7 reviews what you need to know about the two main migration strategies. Make sure you know it well.

TABLE 6.7 Comparing migration strategies

Category	Bottom-Up	Top-Down
A project that depends on all others	Unnamed module on the classpath	Named module on the module path
A project that has no dependencies	Named module on the module path	Automatic module on the module path

Splitting a Big Project into Modules

For the exam, you need to understand the basic process of splitting up a big project into modules. You won't be given a big project, of course. After all, there is only so much space to ask a question. Luckily, the process is the same for a small project.

Suppose you start with an application that has a number of packages. The first step is to break them up into logical groupings and draw the dependencies between them. Figure 6.8 shows an imaginary system's decomposition. Notice that there are seven packages on both the left and right sides. There are fewer modules because some packages share a module.

FIGURE 6.8 First attempt at decomposition

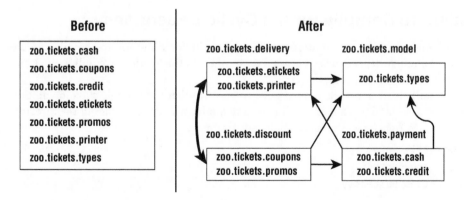

There's a problem with this decomposition. Do you see it? The Java Platform Module System does not allow for *cyclic dependencies*. A cyclic dependency, or *circular dependency*, is when two things directly or indirectly depend on each other. If the `zoo.tickets.delivery` module requires the `zoo.tickets.discount` module, the `zoo.tickets.discount` is not allowed to require the `zoo.tickets.delivery` module.

Now that we all know that the decomposition in Figure 6.8 won't work, what can we do about it? A common technique is to introduce another module. That module contains the code that the other two modules share. Figure 6.9 shows the new modules without any cyclic dependencies. Notice the new module `zoo.tickets.discount`. We created a new package to put in that module. This allows the developers to put the common code in there and break the dependency. No more cyclic dependencies!

FIGURE 6.9   Removing the cyclic dependencies

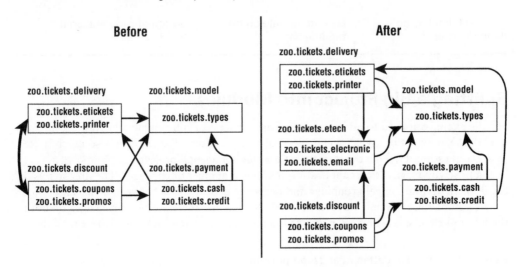

Failing to Compile with a Cyclic Dependency

It is extremely important to understand that Java will not allow you to compile modules that have circular dependencies between each other. In this section, we will look at an example leading to that compiler error.

First, let's create a module named `zoo.butterfly` that has a single class in addition to the `module-info.java` file. If you need a reminder where the files go in the directory structure, see Appendix A or the online code example.

```
// Butterfly.java
package zoo.butterfly;
public class Butterfly {
}
```

```
// module-info.java
module zoo.butterfly {
   exports zoo.butterfly;
}
```

We can compile the butterfly module and create a JAR file in the mods directory named zoo.butterfly.jar. Remember to create a mods directory if one doesn't exist in your folder structure.

```
javac -d butterflyModule
   butterflyModule/zoo/butterfly/Butterfly.java
   butterflyModule/module-info.java

jar -cvf mods/zoo.butterfly.jar -C butterflyModule/ .
```

Now we create a new module, zoo.caterpillar, that depends on the existing zoo.butterfly module. This time, we will create a module with two classes in addition to the module-info.java file.

```
// Caterpillar.java
package zoo.caterpillar;
public class Caterpillar {
}
```

```
// CaterpillarLifecycle.java
package zoo.caterpillar;
import zoo.butterfly.Butterfly;
public interface CaterpillarLifecycle {
   Butterfly emergeCocoon();
}
```

```
// module-info.java
module zoo.caterpillar {
   requires zoo.butterfly;
}
```

Again, we will compile and create a JAR file. This time it is named zoo.caterpillar.jar.

```
javac -p mods -d caterpillarModule
   caterpillarModule/zoo/caterpillar/*.java
   caterpillarModule/module-info.java
jar -cvf mods/zoo.caterpillar.jar -C caterpillarModule/ .
```

At this point, we want to add a method for a butterfly to make caterpillar eggs. We decide to put it in the Butterfly module instead of the CaterpillarLifecycle class to demonstrate a cyclic dependency.

We know this requires adding a dependency, so we do that first. Updating the module-info.java file in the zoo.butterfly module looks like this:

```
module zoo.butterfly {
   exports zoo.butterfly;
   requires zoo.caterpillar;
}
```

We then compile it with the module path mods so zoo.caterpillar is visible:

```
javac -p mods -d butterflyModule
   butterflyModule/zoo/butterfly/Butterfly.java
   butterflyModule/module-info.java
```

The compiler complains about our cyclic dependency.

```
butterflyModule/module-info.java:3: error:
   cyclic dependence involving zoo.caterpillar
      requires zoo.caterpillar;
```

This is one of the advantages of the module system. It prevents you from writing code that has cyclic dependency. Such code won't even compile!

You might be wondering what happens if three modules are involved. Suppose module ballA requires module ballB and ballB requires module ballC. Can module ballC require module ballA? No. This would create a cyclic dependency. Don't believe us? Try drawing it. You can follow your pencil around the circle from ballA to ballB to ballC to ballA to . . . well, you get the idea. There are just too many balls in the air here!

Java will still allow you to have a cyclic dependency between packages within a module. It enforces that you do not have a cyclic dependency between modules.

Creating a Service

In this section, you'll learn how to create a service. A *service* is composed of an interface, any classes the interface references, and a way of looking up implementations of the interface. The implementations are not part of the service.

Services are not new to Java. In fact, the ServiceLoader class was introduced in Java 6. It was used to make applications *extensible*, so you could add functionality without recompiling the whole application. What is new is the integration with modules.

We will be using a tour application in the services section. It has four modules shown in Figure 6.10. In this example, the zoo.tours.api and zoo.tours.reservations models make up the service since they consist of the interface and lookup functionality.

FIGURE 6.10   Modules in the tour application

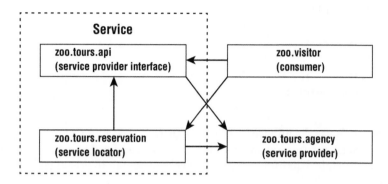

 You aren't required to have four separate modules. We do so to illustrate the concepts. For example, the service provider interface and service locator could be in the same module.

Declaring the Service Provider Interface

First, the zoo.tours.api module defines a Java object called Souvenir. It is considered part of the service because it will be referenced by the interface.

```
// Souvenir.java
package zoo.tours.api;

public class Souvenir {
   private String description;

   public String getDescription() {
      return description;
   }
   public void setDescription(String description) {
      this.description = description;
   }
}
```

Next, the module contains a Java interface type. This interface is called the *service provider interface* because it specifies what behavior our service will have. In this case, it is a simple API with three methods.

```
// Tour.java
package zoo.tours.api;

public interface Tour {
    String name();
    int length();
    Souvenir getSouvenir();
}
```

All three methods use the implicit public modifier, as shown in Chapter 1, "Java Fundamentals." Since we are working with modules, we also need to create a module-info .java file so our module definition exports the package containing the interface.

```
// module-info.java
module zoo.tours.api {
    exports zoo.tours.api;
}
```

Now that we have both files, we can compile and package this module.

```
javac -d serviceProviderInterfaceModule
    serviceProviderInterfaceModule/zoo/tours/api/*.java
    serviceProviderInterfaceModule/module-info.java

jar -cvf mods/zoo.tours.api.jar -C serviceProviderInterfaceModule/ .
```

A service provider "interface" can be an abstract class rather than an actual interface. Since you will only see it as an interface on the exam, we use that term in the book.

To review, the service includes the service provider interface and supporting classes it references. The service also includes the lookup functionality, which we will define next.

Creating a Service Locator

To complete our service, we need a service locator. A *service locator* is able to find any classes that implement a service provider interface.

Luckily, Java provides a ServiceLocator class to help with this task. You pass the service provider interface type to its load() method, and Java will return any implementation services it can find. The following class shows it in action:

```
// TourFinder.java
package zoo.tours.reservations;

import java.util.*;
import zoo.tours.api.*;

public class TourFinder {
```

```java
    public static Tour findSingleTour() {
        ServiceLoader<Tour> loader = ServiceLoader.load(Tour.class);
        for (Tour tour : loader)
            return tour;
        return null;
    }
    public static List<Tour> findAllTours() {
        List<Tour> tours = new ArrayList<>();
        ServiceLoader<Tour> loader = ServiceLoader.load(Tour.class);
        for (Tour tour : loader)
            tours.add(tour);
        return tours;
    }
}
```

As you can see, we provided two lookup methods. The first is a convenience method if you are expecting exactly one Tour to be returned. The other returns a List, which accommodates any number of service providers. At runtime, there may be many service providers (or none) that are found by the service locator.

 The ServiceLoader call is relatively expensive. If you are writing a real application, it is best to cache the result.

Our module definition exports the package with the lookup class TourFinder. It requires the service provider interface package. It also has the uses directive since it will be looking up a service.

```java
// module-info.java
module zoo.tours.reservations {
    exports zoo.tours.reservations;
    requires zoo.tours.api;
    uses zoo.tours.api.Tour;
}
```

Remember that both requires and uses are needed, one for compilation and one for lookup. Finally, we compile and package the module.

```
javac -p mods -d serviceLocatorModule
    serviceLocatorModule/zoo/tours/reservations/*.java
    serviceLocatorModule/module-info.java

jar -cvf mods/zoo.tours.reservations.jar -C serviceLocatorModule/ .
```

Now that we have the interface and lookup logic, we have completed our service.

Invoking from a Consumer

Next up is to call the service locator by a consumer. A *consumer* (or *client*) refers to a module that obtains and uses a service. Once the consumer has acquired a service via the service locator, it is able to invoke the methods provided by the service provider interface.

```
// Tourist.java
package zoo.visitor;

import java.util.*;
import zoo.tours.api.*;
import zoo.tours.reservations.*;

public class Tourist {
   public static void main(String[] args) {
      Tour tour = TourFinder.findSingleTour();
      System.out.println("Single tour: " + tour);

      List<Tour> tours = TourFinder.findAllTours();
      System.out.println("# tours: " + tours.size());
   }
}
```

Our module definition doesn't need to know anything about the implementations since the zoo.tours.reservations module is handling the lookup.

```
// module-info.java
module zoo.visitor {
   requires zoo.tours.api;
   requires zoo.tours.reservations;
}
```

This time, we get to run a program after compiling and packaging.

```
javac -p mods -d consumerModule
   consumerModule/zoo/visitor/*.java
   consumerModule/module-info.java

jar -cvf mods/zoo.visitor.jar -C consumerModule/ .

java -p mods -m zoo.visitor/zoo.visitor.Tourist
```

The program outputs the following:

```
Single tour: null
# tours: 0
```

Well, that makes sense. We haven't written a class that implements the interface yet.

Adding a Service Provider

A *service provider* is the implementation of a service provider interface. As we said earlier, at runtime it is possible to have multiple implementation classes or modules. We will stick to one here for simplicity.

Our service provider is the zoo.tours.agency package because we've outsourced the running of tours to a third party.

```
// TourImpl.java
package zoo.tours.agency;

import zoo.tours.api.*;

public class TourImpl implements Tour {
   public String name() {
      return "Behind the Scenes";
   }
   public int length() {
      return 120;
   }
   public Souvenir getSouvenir() {
      Souvenir gift = new Souvenir();
      gift.setDescription("stuffed animal");
      return gift;
   }
}
```

Again, we need a module-info.java file to create a module.

```
// module-info.java
module zoo.tours.agency {
   requires zoo.tours.api;
   provides zoo.tours.api.Tour with zoo.tours.agency.TourImpl;
}
```

The module declaration requires the module containing the interface as a dependency. We don't export the package that implements the interface since we don't want callers referring to it directly. Instead, we use the provides directive. This allows us to specify that we provide an implementation of the interface with a specific implementation class. The syntax looks like this:

```
provides interfaceName with className;
```

> We have not exported the package containing the implementation. Instead, we have made the implementation available to a service provider using the interface.

Finally, we compile and package it up.

```
javac -p mods -d serviceProviderModule
   serviceProviderModule/zoo/tours/agency/*.java
   serviceProviderModule/module-info.java
jar -cvf mods/zoo.tours.agency.jar -C serviceProviderModule/ .
```

Now comes the cool part. We can run the Java program again.

```
java -p mods -m zoo.visitor/zoo.visitor.Tourist
```

This time we see the following output:

```
Single tour: zoo.tours.agency.TourImpl@1936f0f5
# tours: 1
```

Notice how we didn't recompile the zoo.tours.reservations or zoo.visitor package. The service locator was able to observe that there was now a service provider implementation available and find it for us.

This is useful when you have functionality that changes independently of the rest of the code base. For example, you might have custom reports or logging.

In software development, the concept of separating out different components into stand-alone pieces is referred to as *loose coupling*. One advantage of loosely coupled code is that it can be easily swapped out or replaced with minimal (or zero) changes to code that uses it. Relying on a loosely coupled structure allows service modules to be easily extensible at runtime.

Java allows only one service provider for a service provider interface in a module. If you wanted to offer another tour, you would need to create a separate module.

Merging Service Locator and Consumer

Now that you understand what all four pieces do, let's see if you understand how to merge pieces. We can even use streams from Chapter 4, "Functional Programming," to implement a method that gets all implementation and the length of the shortest and longest tours.

First, let's create a second service provider. Remember the service provider TourImpl is the implementation of the service interface Tour.

```
package zoo.tours.hybrid;

import zoo.tours.api.*;

public class QuickTourImpl implements Tour {
```

```
    public String name() {
        return "Short Tour";
    }
    public int length() {
        return 30;
    }
    public Souvenir getSouvenir() {
        Souvenir gift = new Souvenir();
        gift.setDescription("keychain");
        return gift;
    }
}
```

Before we introduce the lookup code, it is important to be aware of a piece of trickery. There are two methods in ServiceLoader that you need to know for the exam. The declaration is as follows, sans the full implementation:

```
public final class ServiceLoader<S> implements Iterable<S> {

    public static <S> ServiceLoader<S> load(Class<S> service) { ... }

    public Stream<Provider<S>> stream() { ... }

    // Additional methods
}
```

Conveniently, if you call ServiceLoader.load(), it returns an object that you can loop through normally. However, requesting a Stream gives you a different type. The reason for this is that a Stream controls when elements are evaluated. Therefore, a ServiceLoader returns a Stream of Provider objects. You have to call get() to retrieve the value you wanted out of each Provider.

Now we can create the class that merges the service locator and consumer.

```
package zoo.tours.hybrid;

import java.util.*;
import java.util.ServiceLoader.Provider;
import zoo.tours.api.*;

public class TourLengthCheck {

    public static void main(String[] args) {
        OptionalInt max = ServiceLoader.load(Tour.class)
```

```
        .stream()
        .map(Provider::get)
        .mapToInt(Tour::length)
        .max();
    max.ifPresent(System.out::println);

    OptionalInt min = ServiceLoader.load(Tour.class)
        .stream()
        .map(Provider::get)
        .mapToInt(Tour::length)
        .min();
    min.ifPresent(System.out::println);
    }
}
```

As we mentioned, there is an extra method call to use get() to retrieve the value out of the Provider since we are using a Stream.

Now comes the fun part. What directives do you think we need in module-info.java? It turns out we need three.

```
module zoo.tours.hybrid {
    requires zoo.tours.api;
    provides zoo.tours.api.Tour with zoo.tours.hybrid.QuickTourImpl;
    uses zoo.tours.api.Tour;
}
```

We need requires because we depend on the service provider interface. We still need provides so the ServiceLocator can look up the service. Additionally, we still need uses since we are looking up the service interface from another module.

For the last time, let's compile, package, and run.

```
javac -p mods -d multiPurposeModule
    multiPurposeModule/zoo/tours/hybrid/*.java
    multiPurposeModule/module-info.java

jar -cvf mods/zoo.tours.hybrid.jar -C multiPurposeModule/ .

java -p mods -m zoo.tours.hybrid/zoo.tours.hybrid.TourLengthCheck
```

And it works. The output sees both service providers and prints different values for the maximum and minimum tour lengths:

```
120
30
```

Reviewing Services

Table 6.8 summarizes what we've covered in the section about services. We recommend learning what is needed when each artifact is in a separate module really well. That is most likely what you will see on the exam and will ensure you understand the concepts.

TABLE 6.8   Reviewing services

Artifact	Part of the service	Directives required in `module-info.java`
Service provider interface	Yes	`exports`
Service provider	No	`requires` `provides`

Service locator	Yes	`exports`
		`requires`
		`uses`

Consumer	No	`requires`

Summary

There are three types of modules. Named modules contain a `module-info.java` file and are on the module path. They can read only from the module path. Automatic modules are also on the module path but have not yet been modularized. They might have an automatic module name set in the manifest. Unnamed modules are on the classpath.

The `java.base` module is most common and is automatically supplied to all modules as a dependency. You do have to be familiar with the full list of modules provided in the JDK. The `jdeps` command provides a list of dependencies that a JAR needs. It can do so on a summary level or detailed level. Additionally, it can specify information about JDK internal modules and suggest replacements.

The two most common migration strategies are top-down and bottom-up migration. Top-down migration starts migrating the module with the most dependencies and places all other modules on the module path. Bottom-up migration starts migrating a module with no dependencies and moves one module to the module path at a time. Both of these strategies require ensuring you do not have any cyclic dependencies since the Java Platform Module System will not allow cyclic dependencies to compile.

A service consists of the service provider interface and service locator. The service provider interface is the API for the service. One or more modules contain the service provider. These modules contain the implementing classes of the service provider interface. The service locator calls `ServiceLoader` to dynamically get any service providers. It can return the results so you can loop through them or get a stream. Finally, the consumer calls the service provider interface.

Exam Essentials

Identify the three types of modules.   Named modules are JARs that have been modularized. Unnamed modules have not been modularized. Automatic modules are in between. They are on the module path but do not have a `module-info.java` file.

List built-in JDK modules.   The `java.base` module is available to all modules. There are about 20 other modules provided by the JDK that begin with `java.*` and about 30 that begin with `jdk.*`.

Use *jdeps* to list required packages and internal packages.   The `-s` flag gives a summary by only including module names. The `--jdk-internals` (`-jdkinternals`) flag provides additional information about unsupported APIs and suggests replacements.

Explain top-down and bottom-up migration.   A top-down migration places all JARs on the module path, making them automatic modules while migrating from top to bottom. A bottom-up migration leaves all JARs on the classpath, making them unnamed modules while migrating from bottom to top.

Differentiate the four main parts of a service.   A service provider interface declares the interface that a service must implement. The service locator looks up the service, and a consumer calls the service. Finally, a service provider implements the service.

Code directives for use with services.   A service provider implementation must have the `provides` directive to specify what service provider interface it supplies and what class it implements it `with`. The module containing the service locator must have the `uses` directive to specify which service provider implementation it will be looking up.

Review Questions

The answers to the chapter review questions can be found in Appendix B.

1. Which of the following pairs make up a service?

   A. Consumer and service locator

   B. Consumer and service provider interface

   C. Service locator and service provider

   D. Service locator and service provider interface

   E. Service provider and service provider interface

2. A(n) _____ module is on the classpath while a(n) _____ module is on the module path. (Choose all that apply.)

   A. automatic, named

   B. automatic, unnamed

   C. named, automatic

   D. named, unnamed

   E. unnamed, automatic

   F. unnamed, named

   G. None of the above

3. An automatic module name is generated if one is not supplied. Which of the following JAR filename and generated automatic module name pairs are correct? (Choose all that apply.)

   A. `emily-1.0.0.jar` and `emily`

   B. `emily-1.0.0-SNAPSHOT.jar` and `emily`

   C. `emily_the_cat-1.0.0.jar` and `emily_the_cat`

   D. `emily_the_cat-1.0.0.jar` and `emily-the-cat`

   E. `emily.$.jar` and `emily`

   F. `emily.$.jar` and `emily.`

   G. `emily.$.jar` and `emily..`

4. Which of the following statements are true? (Choose all that apply.)

   A. Modules with cyclic dependencies will not compile.

   B. Packages with a cyclic dependency will not compile.

   C. A cyclic dependency always involves exactly two modules.

   D. A cyclic dependency always involves three or more modules.

   E. A cyclic dependency always involves at least two `requires` statements.

   F. An unnamed module can be involved in a cyclic dependency with an automatic module

5. Which module is available to your named module without needing a `requires` directive?

   A. `java.all`

   B. `java.base`

   C. `java.default`

   D. `java.lang`

   E. None of the above

6. Suppose you are creating a service provider that contains the following class. Which line of code needs to be in your `module-info.java`?

```
package dragon;
import magic.*;
public class Dragon implements Magic {
    public String getPower() {
        return "breathe fire";
    }
}
```

   A. `provides dragon.Dragon by magic.Magic;`

   B. `provides dragon.Dragon using magic.Magic;`

   C. `provides dragon.Dragon with magic.Magic;`

   D. `provides magic.Magic by dragon.Dragon;`

   E. `provides magic.Magic using dragon.Dragon;`

   F. `provides magic.Magic with dragon.Dragon;`

7. Which of the following modules is provided by the JDK? (Choose all that apply.)

   A. `java.base;`

   B. `java.desktop;`

   C. `java.logging;`

   D. `java.util;`

   E. `jdk.base;`

   F. `jdk.compiler;`

   G. `jdk.xerces;`

8. Which of the following compiles and is equivalent to this loop?

```
List<Unicorn> all  = new ArrayList<>();
for (Unicorn current : ServiceLoader.load(Unicorn.class))
    all.add(current);
```

A.

```
List<Unicorn> all = ServiceLoader.load(Unicorn.class)
   .getStream()
   .collect(Collectors.toList());
```

B.

```
List<Unicorn> all = ServiceLoader.load(Unicorn.class)
   .stream()
   .collect(Collectors.toList());
```

C.

```
List<Unicorn> all = ServiceLoader.load(Unicorn.class)
   .getStream()
   .map(Provider::get)
   .collect(Collectors.toList());
```

D.

```
List<Unicorn> all = ServiceLoader.load(Unicorn.class)
   .stream()
   .map(Provider::get)
   .collect(Collectors.toList());
```

E.   None of the above

9.   Which command can you run to determine whether you have any code in your JAR file that depends on unsupported internal APIs and suggests an alternative?

A.   `jdeps -internal-jdk`

B.   `jdeps --internaljdk`

C.   `jdeps --internal-jdk`

D.   `jdeps -s`

E.   `jdeps -unsupported`

F.   `jdeps -unsupportedapi`

G.   `jdeps -unsupported-api`

H.   None of the above

10.   For a top-down migration, all modules other than named modules are _____ modules and on the _____ .

A.   automatic, classpath

B.   automatic, module path

C.   unnamed, classpath

D.   unnamed, module path

E.   None of the above

11. Suppose you have separate modules for a service provider interface, service provider, service locator, and consumer. If you add a second service provider module, how many of these modules do you need to recompile?

    A. Zero

    B. One

    C. Two

    D. Three

    E. Four

12. Which of the following modules contains the `java.util` package? (Choose all that apply.)

    A. `java.all;`

    B. `java.base;`

    C. `java.main;`

    D. `java.util;`

    E. None of the above

13. Suppose you have separate modules for a service provider interface, service provider, service locator, and consumer. Which are true about the directives you need to specify? (Choose all that apply.)

    A. The service provider interface must use the `exports` directive.

    B. The service provider interface must use the `provides` directive.

    C. The service provider interface must use the `requires` directive.

    D. The service provider must use the `exports` directive.

    E. The service provider must use the `provides` directive.

    F. The service provider must use the `requires` directive.

14. Suppose you have a project with one package named `magic.wand` and another project with one package named `magic.potion`. These projects have a circular dependency, so you decide to create a third project named `magic.helper`. The `magic.helper` module has the common code containing a package named `magic.util`. For simplicity, let's give each module the same name as the package. Which of the following need to appear in your `module-info` files? (Choose all that apply.)

    A. `exports magic.potion;` in the potion project

    B. `exports magic.util;` in the magic helper project

    C. `exports magic.wand;` in the wand project

    D. `requires magic.util;` in the magic helper project

    E. `requires magic.util;` in the potion project

    F. `requires magic.util;` in the wand project

15. Suppose you have separate modules for a service provider interface, service provider, service locator, and consumer. Which module(s) need to specify a `requires` directive on the service provider?

   A. Service locator

   B. Service provider interface

   C. Consumer

   D. Consumer and service locator

   E. Consumer and service provider

   F. Service locator and service provider interface

   G. Consumer, service locator, and service provider interface

   H. None of the above

16. Which are true statements about a package in a JAR on the classpath containing a `module-info` file? (Choose all that apply.)

   A. It is possible to make it available to all other modules on the classpath.

   B. It is possible to make it available to all other modules on the module path.

   C. It is possible to make it available to exactly one other specific module on the classpath.

   D. It is possible to make it available to exactly one other specific module on the module path.

   E. It is possible to make sure it is not available to any other modules on the classpath.

17. Which are true statements? (Choose all that apply.)

   A. An automatic module exports all packages to named modules.

   B. An automatic module exports only the specified packages to named modules.

   C. An automatic module exports no packages to named modules.

   D. An unnamed module exports only the named packages to named modules.

   E. An unnamed module exports all packages to named modules.

   F. An unnamed module exports no packages to named modules.

18. Suppose you have separate modules for a service provider interface, service provider, service locator, and consumer. Which statements are true about the directives you need to specify? (Choose all that apply.)

   A. The consumer must use the `requires` directive.

   B. The consumer must use the `uses` directive.

   C. The service locator must use the `requires` directive.

   D. The service locator must use the `uses` directive.

19. Which statement is true about the `jdeps` command? (Choose all that apply.)

   A. It can provide information about dependencies on the class level only.

   B. It can provide information about dependencies on the package level only.

   C. It can provide information about dependencies on the class or package level.

   D. It can run only against a named module.

   E. It can run against a regular JAR.

20. Suppose we have a JAR file named `cat-1.2.3-RC1.jar` and `Automatic-Module-Name` in the `MANIFEST.MF` is set to dog. What should an unnamed module referencing this automatic module include in the `module-info.java`?

   A. `requires cat;`

   B. `requires cat.RC;`

   C. `requires cat-RC;`

   D. `requires dog;`

   E. None of the above

Chapter

7

Concurrency

OCP EXAM OBJECTIVES COVERED IN THIS CHAPTER:

✓ **Concurrency**

- Create worker threads using Runnable, Callable and use an ExecutorService to concurrently execute tasks

- Use java.util.concurrent collections and classes including CyclicBarrier and CopyOnWriteArrayList

- Write thread-safe code

- Identify threading problems such as deadlocks and livelocks

✓ **Parallel Streams**

- Develop code that uses parallel streams

- Implement decomposition and reduction with streams

As you will learn in Chapter 8, "I/O," Chapter 9 "NIO.2," and Chapter 10, "JDBC," computers are capable of reading and writing data to external resources. Unfortunately, as compared to CPU operations, these disk/network operations tend to be extremely slow—so slow, in fact, that if your computer's operating system were to stop and wait for every disk or network operation to finish, your computer would appear to freeze or lock up constantly.

Luckily, all modern operating systems support what is known as *multithreaded processing*. The idea behind multithreaded processing is to allow an application or group of applications to execute multiple tasks at the same time. This allows tasks waiting for other resources to give way to other processing requests.

Since its early days, Java has supported multithreaded programming using the Thread class. More recently, the Concurrency API was introduced. It included numerous classes for performing complex thread-based tasks. The idea was simple: managing complex thread interactions is quite difficult for even the most skilled developers; therefore, a set of reusable features was created. The Concurrency API has grown over the years to include numerous classes and frameworks to assist you in developing complex, multithreaded applications. In this chapter, we will introduce you to the concept of threads and provide numerous ways to manage threads using the Concurrency API.

Threads and concurrency tend to be one of the more challenging topics for many programmers to grasp, as problems with threads can be frustrating even for veteran developers to understand. In practice, concurrency issues are among the most difficult problems to diagnose and resolve.

Previous Java certification exams expected you to know details about threads, such as thread life cycles. The 1Z0-816 exam instead covers the basics of threads but focuses more on your knowledge of the Concurrency API. Since we believe that you need to walk before you can run, we provide a basic overview of threads in the first part of this chapter. Be sure you understand the basics of threads both for exam questions and so you better understand the Concurrency API used throughout the rest of the chapter.

Introducing Threads

We begin this chapter by reviewing common terminology associated with threads. A *thread* is the smallest unit of execution that can be scheduled by the operating system. A *process* is a group of associated threads that execute in the same, shared environment. It follows, then, that a *single-threaded process* is one that contains exactly one thread, whereas a *multithreaded process* is one that contains one or more threads.

By *shared environment*, we mean that the threads in the same process share the same memory space and can communicate directly with one another. Refer to Figure 7.1 for an overview of threads and their shared environment within a process.

FIGURE 7.1   Process model

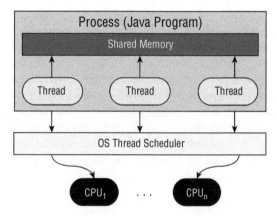

Figure 7.1 shows a single process with three threads. It also shows how they are mapped to an arbitrary number of *n* CPUs available within the system. Keep this diagram in mind when we discuss task schedulers later in this section.

In this chapter, we will talk a lot about tasks and their relationships to threads. A *task* is a single unit of work performed by a thread. Throughout this chapter, a task will commonly be implemented as a lambda expression. A thread can complete multiple independent tasks but only one task at a time.

By shared memory in Figure 7.1, we are generally referring to `static` variables, as well as instance and local variables passed to a thread. Yes, you will finally see how `static` variables can be useful for performing complex, multithreaded tasks! Remember from your 1Z0-815 exam studies that `static` methods and variables are defined on a single class object that all instances share. For example, if one thread updates the value of a `static` object, then this information is immediately available for other threads within the process to read.

Distinguishing Thread Types

It might surprise you that all Java applications, including all of the ones that we have presented in this book, are all multithreaded. Even a simple Java application that prints Hello World to the screen is multithreaded. To help you understand this, we introduce the concepts of system threads and user-defined threads.

A *system thread* is created by the JVM and runs in the background of the application. For example, the garbage collection is managed by a system thread that is created by the JVM and runs in the background, helping to free memory that is no longer in use. For the most part, the execution of system-defined threads is invisible to the application developer. When a system-defined thread encounters a problem and cannot recover, such as running out of memory, it generates a Java Error, as opposed to an Exception.

As discussed in Chapter 5, "Exceptions, Assertions, and Localization," even though it is possible to catch an Error, it is considered a poor practice to do so, since it is rare that an application can recover from a system-level failure.

Alternatively, a *user-defined thread* is one created by the application developer to accomplish a specific task. With the exception of parallel streams presented briefly in Chapter 4, "Functional Programming," all of the applications that we have created up to this point have been multithreaded, but they contained only one user-defined thread, which calls the main() method. For simplicity, we commonly refer to threads that contain only a single user-defined thread as a single-threaded application, since we are often uninterested in the system threads.

Although not required knowledge for the exam, a *daemon thread* is one that will not prevent the JVM from exiting when the program finishes. A Java application terminates when the only threads that are running are daemon threads. For example, if garbage collection is the only thread left running, the JVM will automatically shut down. Both system and user-defined threads can be marked as daemon threads.

Understanding Thread Concurrency

At the start of the chapter, we mentioned that multithreaded processing allows operating systems to execute threads at the same time. The property of executing multiple threads and processes at the same time is referred to as *concurrency*. Of course, with a single-core CPU system, only one task is actually executing at a given time. Even in multicore or multi-CPU systems, there are often far more threads than CPU processors available. How does the system decide what to execute when there are multiple threads available?

Operating systems use a *thread scheduler* to determine which threads should be currently executing, as shown in Figure 7.1. For example, a thread scheduler may employ a *round-robin schedule* in which each available thread receives an equal number of CPU cycles with which to execute, with threads visited in a circular order. If there are 10 available threads, they might each get 100 milliseconds in which to execute, with the process returning to the first thread after the last thread has executed.

When a thread's allotted time is complete but the thread has not finished processing, a context switch occurs. A *context switch* is the process of storing a thread's current state and later restoring the state of the thread to continue execution. Be aware that there is often a cost associated with a context switch by way of lost time saving and reloading a thread's state. Intelligent thread schedules do their best to minimize the number of context switches, while keeping an application running smoothly.

Finally, a thread can interrupt or supersede another thread if it has a higher thread priority than the other thread. A *thread priority* is a numeric value associated with a thread that is taken into consideration by the thread scheduler when determining which threads should currently be executing. In Java, thread priorities are specified as integer values.

 Real World Scenario

The Importance of Thread Scheduling

Even though multicore CPUs are quite common these days, single-core CPUs were the standard in personal computing for many decades. During this time, operating systems developed complex thread-scheduling and context-switching algorithms that allowed users to execute dozens or even hundreds of threads on a single-core CPU system. These scheduling algorithms allowed users to experience the illusion that multiple tasks were being performed at the same time within a single-CPU system. For example, a user could listen to music while writing a paper and receive notifications for new messages.

Since the number of threads requested often far outweighs the number of processors available even in multicore systems, these thread-scheduling algorithms are still employed in operating systems today.

Defining a Task with *Runnable*

As we mentioned in Chapter 4, java.lang.Runnable is a functional interface that takes no arguments and returns no data. The following is the definition of the Runnable interface:

```
@FunctionalInterface public interface Runnable {
    void run();
}
```

The Runnable interface is commonly used to define the task or work a thread will execute, separate from the main application thread. We will be relying on the Runnable interface throughout this chapter, especially when we discuss applying parallel operations to streams.

The following lambda expressions each implement the Runnable interface:

```
Runnable sloth = () -> System.out.println("Hello World");
Runnable snake = () -> {int i=10; i++;};
Runnable beaver = () -> {return;};
Runnable coyote = () -> {};
```

Notice that all of these lambda expressions start with a set of empty parentheses, (). Also, none of the lambda expressions returns a value. The following lambdas, while valid for other functional interfaces, are not compatible with Runnable because they return a value.

```
Runnable capybara = () -> "";                   // DOES NOT COMPILE
Runnable Hippopotamus = () -> 5;                // DOES NOT COMPILE
Runnable emu = () -> {return new Object();};    // DOES NOT COMPILE
```

Creating *Runnable* Classes

Even though Runnable is a functional interface, many classes implement it directly, as shown in the following code:

```
public class CalculateAverage implements Runnable {
    public void run() {
        // Define work here
    }
}
```

It is also useful if you need to pass information to your Runnable object to be used by the run() method, such as in the following constructor:

```
public class CalculateAverages implements Runnable {
    private double[] scores;
    public CalculateAverages(double[] scores) {
        this.scores = scores;
    }
    public void run() {
        // Define work here that uses the scores object
    }
}
```

In this chapter, we focus on creating lambda expressions that implicitly implement the Runnable interface. Just be aware that it is commonly used in class definitions.

Creating a Thread

The simplest way to execute a thread is by using the java.lang.Thread class. Executing a task with Thread is a two-step process. First, you define the Thread with the corresponding task to be done. Then, you start the task by using the Thread.start() method.

As we will discuss later in the chapter, Java does not provide any guarantees about the order in which a thread will be processed once it is started. It may be executed immediately or delayed for a significant amount of time.

 Remember that order of thread execution is not often guaranteed. The exam commonly presents questions in which multiple tasks are started at the same time, and you must determine the result.

Defining the task that a Thread instance will execute can be done two ways in Java:

- Provide a Runnable object or lambda expression to the Thread constructor.
- Create a class that extends Thread and overrides the run() method.

The following are examples of these techniques:

```java
public class PrintData implements Runnable {
   @Override public void run() { // Overrides method in Runnable
      for(int i = 0; i < 3; i++)
         System.out.println("Printing record: "+i);
   }
   public static void main(String[] args) {
      (new Thread(new PrintData())).start();
   }
}

public class ReadInventoryThread extends Thread {
   @Override public void run() { // Overrides method in Thread
      System.out.println("Printing zoo inventory");
   }
   public static void main(String[] args) {
      (new ReadInventoryThread()).start();
   }
}
```

The first example creates a Thread using a Runnable instance, while the second example uses the less common practice of extending the Thread class and overriding the run() method. Anytime you create a Thread instance, make sure that you remember to start the task with the Thread.start() method. This starts the task in a separate operating system thread.

Let's try this. What is the output of the following code snippet using these two classes?

```
2: public static void main(String[] args) {
3:     System.out.println("begin");
4:     (new ReadInventoryThread()).start();
5:     (new Thread(new PrintData())).start();
6:     (new ReadInventoryThread()).start();
7:     System.out.println("end");
8: }
```

The answer is that it is unknown until runtime. The following is just one possible output:

```
begin
Printing zoo inventory
Printing record: 0
end
Printing zoo inventory
Printing record: 1
Printing record: 2
```

This sample uses a total of four threads—the main() user thread and three additional threads created on lines 4–6. Each thread created on these lines is executed as an asynchronous task. By *asynchronous*, we mean that the thread executing the main() method does not wait for the results of each newly created thread before continuing. For example, lines 5 and 6 may be executed before the thread created on line 4 finishes. The opposite of this behavior is a *synchronous* task in which the program waits (or blocks) on line 4 for the thread to finish executing before moving on to the next line. The vast majority of method calls used in this book have been synchronous up until now.

While the order of thread execution once the threads have been started is indeterminate, the order within a single thread is still linear. In particular, the for() loop in PrintData is still ordered. Also, begin appears before end in the main() method.

Calling *run()* Instead of *start()*

Be careful with code that attempts to start a thread by calling run() instead of start(). Calling run() on a Thread or a Runnable does not actually start a new thread. While the following code snippets will compile, none will actually execute a task on a separate thread:

```
System.out.println("begin");
(new ReadInventoryThread()).run();
(new Thread(new PrintData())).run();
(new ReadInventoryThread()).run();
System.out.println("end");
```

> Unlike the previous example, each line of this code will wait until the `run()` method is complete before moving on to the next line. Also unlike the previous program, the output for this code sample will be the same each time it is executed.

In general, you should extend the `Thread` class only under specific circumstances, such as when you are creating your own priority-based thread. In most situations, you should implement the `Runnable` interface rather than extend the `Thread` class.

We conclude our discussion of the `Thread` class here. While previous versions of the exam were quite focused on understanding the difference between extending `Thread` and implementing `Runnable`, the exam now strongly encourages developers to use the Concurrency API.

For the exam, you also do not need to know about other thread-related methods, such as `Object.wait()`, `Object.notify()`, `Thread.join()`, etc. In fact, you should avoid them in general and use the Concurrency API as much as possible. It takes a large amount of skill (and some luck!) to use these methods correctly.

 Real World Scenario

For Interviews, Be Familiar with Thread-Creation Options

Despite that the exam no longer focuses on creating threads by extending the `Thread` class and implementing the `Runnable` interface, it is extremely common when interviewing for a Java development position to be asked to explain the difference between extending the `Thread` class and implementing `Runnable`.

If asked this question, you should answer it accurately. You should also mention that you can now create and manage threads indirectly using an `ExecutorService`, which we will discuss in the next section.

Polling with Sleep

Even though multithreaded programming allows you to execute multiple tasks at the same time, one thread often needs to wait for the results of another thread to proceed. One solution is to use polling. *Polling* is the process of intermittently checking data at some fixed interval. For example, let's say you have a thread that modifies a shared `static counter` value and your `main()` thread is waiting for the thread to increase the value to greater than 100, as shown in the following class:

```
public class CheckResults {
    private static int counter = 0;
    public static void main(String[] args) {
        new Thread(() -> {
            for(int i = 0; i < 500; i++) CheckResults.counter++;
        }).start();
```

```
    while(CheckResults.counter < 100) {
        System.out.println("Not reached yet");
    }
    System.out.println("Reached!");
  }
}
```

How many times does this program print Not reached yet? The answer is, we don't know! It could output zero, ten, or a million times. If our thread scheduler is particularly poor, it could operate infinitely! Using a while() loop to check for data without some kind of delay is considered a bad coding practice as it ties up CPU resources for no reason.

We can improve this result by using the Thread.sleep() method to implement polling. The Thread.sleep() method requests the current thread of execution rest for a specified number of milliseconds. When used inside the body of the main() method, the thread associated with the main() method will pause, while the separate thread will continue to run. Compare the previous implementation with the following one that uses Thread.sleep():

```
public class CheckResults {
    private static int counter = 0;
    public static void main(String[] a) throws InterruptedException {
        new Thread(() -> {
            for(int i = 0; i < 500; i++) CheckResults.counter++;
        }).start();
        while(CheckResults.counter < 100) {
            System.out.println("Not reached yet");
            Thread.sleep(1000); // 1 SECOND
        }
        System.out.println("Reached!");
    }
}
```

In this example, we delay 1,000 milliseconds at the end of the loop, or 1 second. While this may seem like a small amount, we have now prevented a possibly infinite loop from executing and locking up our program. Notice that we also changed the signature of the main() method, since Thread.sleep() throws the checked InterruptedException. Alternatively, we could have wrapped each call to the Thread.sleep() method in a try/catch block.

How many times does the while() loop execute in this revised class? Still unknown! While polling does prevent the CPU from being overwhelmed with a potentially infinite loop, it does not guarantee when the loop will terminate. For example, the separate thread could be losing CPU time to a higher-priority process, resulting in multiple executions of the while() loop before it finishes.

Another issue to be concerned about is the shared counter variable. What if one thread is reading the counter variable while another thread is writing it? The thread reading the shared variable may end up with an invalid or incorrect value. We will discuss these issues in detail in the upcoming section on writing thread-safe code.

Creating Threads with the Concurrency API

Java includes the Concurrency API to handle the complicated work of managing threads for you. The Concurrency API includes the ExecutorService interface, which defines services that create and manage threads for you.

You first obtain an instance of an ExecutorService interface, and then you send the service tasks to be processed. The framework includes numerous useful features, such as thread pooling and scheduling. It is recommended that you use this framework anytime you need to create and execute a separate task, even if you need only a single thread.

Introducing the Single-Thread Executor

Since ExecutorService is an interface, how do you obtain an instance of it? The Concurrency API includes the Executors factory class that can be used to create instances of the ExecutorService object. As you may remember from Chapter 5, the factory pattern is a creational pattern in which the underlying implementation details of the object creation are hidden from us. You will see the factory pattern used again throughout Chapter 9.

Let's start with a simple example using the newSingleThreadExecutor() method to obtain an ExecutorService instance and the execute() method to perform asynchronous tasks.

```java
import java.util.concurrent.*;
public class ZooInfo {
   public static void main(String[] args) {
      ExecutorService service = null;
      Runnable task1 = () ->
         System.out.println("Printing zoo inventory");
      Runnable task2 = () -> {for(int i = 0; i < 3; i++)
            System.out.println("Printing record: "+i);};
      try {
         service = Executors.newSingleThreadExecutor();
         System.out.println("begin");
         service.execute(task1);
         service.execute(task2);
         service.execute(task1);
         System.out.println("end");
      } finally {
         if(service != null) service.shutdown();
      }
   }
}
```

As you may notice, this is just a rewrite of our earlier `PrintData` and `ReadInventoryThread` classes to use lambda expressions and an `ExecutorService` instance.

In this example, we use the `Executors.newSingleThreadExecutor()` method to create the service. Unlike our earlier example, in which we had three extra threads for newly created tasks, this example uses only one, which means that the threads will order their results. For example, the following is a possible output for this code snippet:

```
begin
Printing zoo inventory
Printing record: 0
Printing record: 1
end
Printing record: 2
Printing zoo inventory
```

With a single-thread executor, results are guaranteed to be executed sequentially. Notice that the end text is output while our thread executor tasks are still running. This is because the `main()` method is still an independent thread from the `ExecutorService`.

Shutting Down a Thread Executor

Once you have finished using a thread executor, it is important that you call the `shutdown()` method. A thread executor creates a non-daemon thread on the first task that is executed, so failing to call `shutdown()` will result in your application never terminating.

The shutdown process for a thread executor involves first rejecting any new tasks submitted to the thread executor while continuing to execute any previously submitted tasks. During this time, calling `isShutdown()` will return `true`, while `isTerminated()` will return `false`. If a new task is submitted to the thread executor while it is shutting down, a `RejectedExecutionException` will be thrown. Once all active tasks have been completed, `isShutdown()` and `isTerminated()` will both return `true`. Figure 7.2 shows the life cycle of an `ExecutorService` object.

FIGURE 7.2   `ExecutorService` life cycle

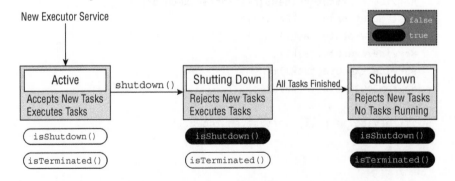

For the exam, you should be aware that shutdown() does not actually stop any tasks that have already been submitted to the thread executor.

What if you want to cancel all running and upcoming tasks? The ExecutorService provides a method called shutdownNow(), which *attempts to stop* all running tasks and discards any that have not been started yet. It is possible to create a thread that will never terminate, so any attempt to interrupt it may be ignored. Lastly, shutdownNow() returns a List<Runnable> of tasks that were submitted to the thread executor but that were never started.

As you learned in Chapter 5, resources such as thread executors should be properly closed to prevent memory leaks. Unfortunately, the ExecutorService interface does not extend the AutoCloseable interface, so you cannot use a try-with-resources statement. You can still use a finally block, as we do throughout this chapter. While not required, it is considered a good practice to do so.

Submitting Tasks

You can submit tasks to an ExecutorService instance multiple ways. The first method we presented, execute(), is inherited from the Executor interface, which the ExecutorService interface extends. The execute() method takes a Runnable lambda expression or instance and completes the task asynchronously. Because the return type of the method is void, it does not tell us anything about the result of the task. It is considered a "fire-and-forget" method, as once it is submitted, the results are not directly available to the calling thread.

Fortunately, the writers of Java added submit() methods to the ExecutorService interface, which, like execute(), can be used to complete tasks asynchronously. Unlike execute(), though, submit() returns a Future instance that can be used to determine whether the task is complete. It can also be used to return a generic result object after the task has been completed.

Table 7.1 shows the five methods, including execute() and two submit() methods, which you should know for the exam. Don't worry if you haven't seen Future or Callable before; we will discuss them in detail shortly.

In practice, using the submit() method is quite similar to using the execute() method, except that the submit() method returns a Future instance that can be used to determine whether the task has completed execution.

TABLE 7.1 ExecutorService methods

Method name	Description
`void execute(Runnable command)`	Executes a Runnable task at some point in the future
`Future<?> submit(Runnable task)`	Executes a Runnable task at some point in the future and returns a Future representing the task
`<T> Future<T> submit(Callable<T> task)`	Executes a Callable task at some point in the future and returns a Future representing the pending results of the task
`<T> List<Future<T>> invokeAll(Collection<? extends Callable<T>> tasks) throws InterruptedException`	Executes the given tasks and waits for all tasks to complete. Returns a List of Future instances, in the same order they were in the original collection
`<T> T invokeAny(Collection<? extends Callable<T>> tasks) throws InterruptedException, ExecutionException`	Executes the given tasks and waits for at least one to complete. Returns a Future instance for a complete task and cancels any unfinished tasks

---

Submitting Tasks: *execute()* vs. *submit()*

As you might have noticed, the execute() and submit() methods are nearly identical when applied to Runnable expressions. The submit() method has the obvious advantage of doing the same thing execute() does, but with a return object that can be used to track the result. Because of this advantage and the fact that execute() does not support Callable expressions, we tend to prefer submit() over execute(), even if you don't store the Future reference. Therefore, we use submit() in the majority of the examples in this chapter.

For the exam, you need to be familiar with both execute() and submit(), but in your own code we recommend submit() over execute() whenever possible.

Waiting for Results

How do we know when a task submitted to an ExecutorService is complete? As mentioned in the previous section, the submit() method returns a java.util.concurrent.Future<V> instance that can be used to determine this result.

```
Future<?> future = service.submit(() -> System.out.println("Hello"));
```

The Future type is actually an interface. For the exam, you don't need to know any of the classes that implement Future, just that a Future instance is returned by various API methods. Table 7.2 includes useful methods for determining the state of a task.

TABLE 7.2   Future methods

Method name	Description
boolean isDone()	Returns true if the task was completed, threw an exception, or was cancelled
boolean isCancelled()	Returns true if the task was cancelled before it completed normally
boolean cancel(boolean mayInterruptIfRunning)	Attempts to cancel execution of the task and returns true if it was successfully cancelled or false if it could not be cancelled or is complete
V get()	Retrieves the result of a task, waiting endlessly if it is not yet available
V get(long timeout, TimeUnit unit)	Retrieves the result of a task, waiting the specified amount of time. If the result is not ready by the time the timeout is reached, a checked TimeoutException will be thrown.

The following is an updated version of our earlier polling example CheckResults class, which uses a Future instance to wait for the results:

```
import java.util.concurrent.*;
public class CheckResults {
   private static int counter = 0;
   public static void main(String[] unused) throws Exception {
      ExecutorService service = null;
      try {
         service = Executors.newSingleThreadExecutor();
         Future<?> result = service.submit(() -> {
            for(int i = 0; i < 500; i++) CheckResults.counter++;
         });
         result.get(10, TimeUnit.SECONDS);
         System.out.println("Reached!");
      } catch (TimeoutException e) {
         System.out.println("Not reached in time");
      } finally {
         if(service != null) service.shutdown();
} } }
```

This example is similar to our earlier polling implementation, but it does not use the Thread class directly. In part, this is the essence of the Concurrency API: to do complex things with threads without having to manage threads directly. It also waits at most 10 seconds, throwing a TimeoutException on the call to result.get() if the task is not done.

What is the return value of this task? As Future<V> is a generic interface, the type V is determined by the return type of the Runnable method. Since the return type of Runnable.run() is void, the get() method always returns null when working with Runnable expressions.

The Future.get() method can take an optional value and enum type java.util.concurrent.TimeUnit. We present the full list of TimeUnit values in Table 7.3 in increasing order of duration. Numerous methods in the Concurrency API use the TimeUnit enum.

TABLE 7.3 TimeUnit values

Enum name	Description
TimeUnit.NANOSECONDS	Time in one-billionth of a second (1/1,000,000,000)
TimeUnit.MICROSECONDS	Time in one-millionth of a second (1/1,000,000)
TimeUnit.MILLISECONDS	Time in one-thousandth of a second (1/1,000)
TimeUnit.SECONDS	Time in seconds
TimeUnit.MINUTES	Time in minutes
TimeUnit.HOURS	Time in hours
TimeUnit.DAYS	Time in days

Introducing *Callable*

The java.util.concurrent.Callable functional interface is similar to Runnable except that its call() method returns a value and can throw a checked exception. The following is the definition of the Callable interface:

```
@FunctionalInterface public interface Callable<V> {
    V call() throws Exception;
}
```

The Callable interface is often preferable over Runnable, since it allows more details to be retrieved easily from the task after it is completed. That said, we use both interfaces throughout this chapter, as they are interchangeable in situations where the lambda does not throw an exception and there is no return type. Luckily, the ExecutorService includes an overloaded version of the submit() method that takes a Callable object and returns a generic Future<T> instance.

Unlike Runnable, in which the get() methods always return null, the get() methods on a Future instance return the matching generic type (which could also be a null value).

Let's take a look at an example using Callable.

```
import java.util.concurrent.*;
public class AddData {
    public static void main(String[] args) throws Exception {
        ExecutorService service = null;
        try {
            service = Executors.newSingleThreadExecutor();
            Future<Integer> result = service.submit(() -> 30 + 11);
            System.out.println(result.get());    // 41
        } finally {
            if(service != null) service.shutdown();
        }
    }
}
```

The results could have also been obtained using Runnable and some shared, possibly static, object, although this solution that relies on Callable is a lot simpler and easier to follow.

Waiting for All Tasks to Finish

After submitting a set of tasks to a thread executor, it is common to wait for the results. As you saw in the previous sections, one solution is to call get() on each Future object returned by the submit() method. If we don't need the results of the tasks and are finished using our thread executor, there is a simpler approach.

First, we shut down the thread executor using the shutdown() method. Next, we use the awaitTermination() method available for all thread executors. The method waits the specified time to complete all tasks, returning sooner if all tasks finish or an InterruptedException is detected. You can see an example of this in the following code snippet:

```
ExecutorService service = null;
try {
    service = Executors.newSingleThreadExecutor();
    // Add tasks to the thread executor
    ...
```

```
} finally {
   if(service != null) service.shutdown();
}
if(service != null) {
   service.awaitTermination(1, TimeUnit.MINUTES);

   // Check whether all tasks are finished
   if(service.isTerminated()) System.out.println("Finished!");
   else System.out.println("At least one task is still running");
}
```

In this example, we submit a number of tasks to the thread executor and then shut down the thread executor and wait up to one minute for the results. Notice that we can call isTerminated() after the awaitTermination() method finishes to confirm that all tasks are actually finished.

 If awaitTermination() is called before shutdown() within the same thread, then that thread will wait the full timeout value sent with awaitTermination().

Submitting Task Collections

The last two methods listed in Table 7.2 that you should know for the exam are invokeAll() and invokeAny(). Both of these methods execute synchronously and take a Collection of tasks. Remember that by synchronous, we mean that unlike the other methods used to submit tasks to a thread executor, these methods will wait until the results are available before returning control to the enclosing program.

The invokeAll() method executes all tasks in a provided collection and returns a List of ordered Future instances, with one Future instance corresponding to each submitted task, in the order they were in the original collection.

```
20: ExecutorService service = ...
21: System.out.println("begin");
22: Callable<String> task = () -> "result";
23: List<Future<String>> list = service.invokeAll(
24:    List.of(task, task, task));
25: for (Future<String> future : list) {
26:    System.out.println(future.get());
27: }
28: System.out.println("end");
```

In this example, the JVM waits on line 23 for all tasks to finish before moving on to line 25. Unlike our earlier examples, this means that end will always be printed last. Also, even though future.isDone() returns true for each element in the returned List, a task could have completed normally or thrown an exception.

On the other hand, the invokeAny() method executes a collection of tasks and returns the result of one of the tasks that successfully completes execution, cancelling all unfinished tasks. While the first task to finish is often returned, this behavior is not guaranteed, as any completed task can be returned by this method.

```
20: ExecutorService service = ...
21: System.out.println("begin");
22: Callable<String> task = () -> "result";
23: String data = service.invokeAny(List.of(task, task, task));
24: System.out.println(data);
25: System.out.println("end");
```

As before, the JVM waits on line 23 for a completed task before moving on to the next line. The other tasks that did not complete are cancelled.

For the exam, remember that the invokeAll() method will wait indefinitely until all tasks are complete, while the invokeAny() method will wait indefinitely until at least one task completes. The ExecutorService interface also includes overloaded versions of invokeAll() and invokeAny() that take a timeout value and TimeUnit parameter.

Scheduling Tasks

Oftentimes in Java, we need to schedule a task to happen at some future time. We might even need to schedule the task to happen repeatedly, at some set interval. For example, imagine that we want to check the supply of food for zoo animals once an hour and fill it as needed. The ScheduledExecutorService, which is a subinterface of ExecutorService, can be used for just such a task.

Like ExecutorService, we obtain an instance of ScheduledExecutorService using a factory method in the Executors class, as shown in the following snippet:

```
ScheduledExecutorService service
    = Executors.newSingleThreadScheduledExecutor();
```

We could store an instance of ScheduledExecutorService in an ExecutorService variable, although doing so would mean we'd have to cast the object to call any scheduled methods.

Refer to Table 7.4 for our summary of ScheduledExecutorService methods.

TABLE 7.4   ScheduledExecutorService methods

Method Name	Description
schedule(Callable<V> callable, long delay, TimeUnit unit)	Creates and executes a Callable task after the given delay
schedule(Runnable command, long delay, TimeUnit unit)	Creates and executes a Runnable task after the given delay
scheduleAtFixedRate(Runnable command, long initialDelay, long period, TimeUnit unit)	Creates and executes a Runnable task after the given initial delay, creating a new task every period value that passes
scheduleWithFixedDelay(Runnable command, long initialDelay, long delay, TimeUnit unit)	Creates and executes a Runnable task after the given initial delay and subsequently with the given delay between the termination of one execution and the commencement of the next

In practice, these methods are among the most convenient in the Concurrency API, as they perform relatively complex tasks with a single line of code. The delay and period parameters rely on the TimeUnit argument to determine the format of the value, such as seconds or milliseconds.

The first two schedule() methods in Table 7.4 take a Callable or Runnable, respectively; perform the task after some delay; and return a ScheduledFuture instance. The ScheduledFuture interface is identical to the Future interface, except that it includes a getDelay() method that returns the remaining delay. The following uses the schedule() method with Callable and Runnable tasks:

```
ScheduledExecutorService service
    = Executors.newSingleThreadScheduledExecutor();
Runnable task1 = () -> System.out.println("Hello Zoo");
Callable<String> task2 = () -> "Monkey";
ScheduledFuture<?> r1 = service.schedule(task1, 10, TimeUnit.SECONDS);
ScheduledFuture<?> r2 = service.schedule(task2, 8,  TimeUnit.MINUTES);
```

The first task is scheduled 10 seconds in the future, whereas the second task is scheduled 8 minutes in the future.

While these tasks are scheduled in the future, the actual execution may be delayed. For example, there may be no threads available to perform the task, at which point they will just wait in the queue. Also, if the ScheduledExecutorService is shut down by the time the scheduled task execution time is reached, then these tasks will be discarded.

Each of the `ScheduledExecutorService` methods is important and has real-world applications. For example, you can use the `schedule()` command to check on the state of processing a task and send out notifications if it is not finished or even call `schedule()` again to delay processing.

The last two methods in Table 7.4 might be a little confusing if you have not seen them before. Conceptually, they are similar as they both perform the same task repeatedly, after completing some initial delay. The difference is related to the timing of the process and when the next task starts.

The `scheduleAtFixedRate()` method creates a new task and submits it to the executor every period, regardless of whether the previous task finished. The following example executes a `Runnable` task every minute, following an initial five-minute delay:

```
service.scheduleAtFixedRate(command, 5, 1, TimeUnit.MINUTES);
```

The `scheduleAtFixedRate()` method is useful for tasks that need to be run at specific intervals, such as checking the health of the animals once a day. Even if it takes two hours to examine an animal on Monday, this doesn't mean that Tuesday's exam should start any later in the day.

Bad things can happen with `scheduleAtFixedRate()` if each task consistently takes longer to run than the execution interval. Imagine your boss came by your desk every minute and dropped off a piece of paper. Now imagine it took you five minutes to read each piece of paper. Before long, you would be drowning in piles of paper. This is how an executor feels. Given enough time, the program would submit more tasks to the executor service than could fit in memory, causing the program to crash.

On the other hand, the `scheduleWithFixedDelay()` method creates a new task only after the previous task has finished. For example, if a task runs at 12:00 and takes five minutes to finish, with a period between executions of two minutes, then the next task will start at 12:07.

```
service.scheduleWithFixedDelay(command, 0, 2, TimeUnit.MINUTES);
```

The `scheduleWithFixedDelay()` is useful for processes that you want to happen repeatedly but whose specific time is unimportant. For example, imagine that we have a zoo cafeteria worker who periodically restocks the salad bar throughout the day. The process can take 20 minutes or more, since it requires the worker to haul a large number of items from the back room. Once the worker has filled the salad bar with fresh food, he doesn't need to check at some specific time, just after enough time has passed for it to become low on stock again.

If you are familiar with creating Cron jobs in Linux to schedule tasks, then you should know that `scheduleAtFixedRate()` is the closest built-in Java equivalent.

Increasing Concurrency with Pools

All of our examples up until now have been with single-thread executors, which, while interesting, weren't particularly useful. After all, the name of this chapter is "Concurrency," and you can't do a lot of that with a single-thread executor!

We now present three additional factory methods in the Executors class that act on a pool of threads, rather than on a single thread. A *thread pool* is a group of pre-instantiated reusable threads that are available to perform a set of arbitrary tasks. Table 7.5 includes our two previous single-thread executor methods, along with the new ones that you should know for the exam.

TABLE 7.5   Executors factory methods

Method	Description
ExecutorService newSingleThreadExecutor()	Creates a single-threaded executor that uses a single worker thread operating off an unbounded queue. Results are processed sequentially in the order in which they are submitted.
ScheduledExecutorService newSingleThreadScheduledExecutor()	Creates a single-threaded executor that can schedule commands to run after a given delay or to execute periodically
ExecutorService newCachedThreadPool()	Creates a thread pool that creates new threads as needed but will reuse previously constructed threads when they are available
ExecutorService newFixedThreadPool(int)	Creates a thread pool that reuses a fixed number of threads operating off a shared unbounded queue
ScheduledExecutorService newScheduledThreadPool(int)	Creates a thread pool that can schedule commands to run after a given delay or to execute periodically

As shown in Table 7.5, these methods return the same instance types, ExecutorService and ScheduledExecutorService, that we used earlier in this chapter. In other words, all of our previous examples are compatible with these new pooled-thread executors!

The difference between a single-thread and a pooled-thread executor is what happens when a task is already running. While a single-thread executor will wait for a thread to become available before running the next task, a pooled-thread executor can execute the next task concurrently. If the pool runs out of available threads, the task will be queued by the thread executor and wait to be completed.

The newFixedThreadPool() takes a number of threads and allocates them all upon creation. As long as our number of tasks is less than our number of threads, all tasks will be executed concurrently. If at any point the number of tasks exceeds the number of threads in the pool, they will wait in a similar manner as you saw with a single-thread executor. In fact, calling newFixedThreadPool() with a value of 1 is equivalent to calling newSingleThreadExecutor().

The newCachedThreadPool() method will create a thread pool of unbounded size, allocating a new thread anytime one is required or all existing threads are busy. This is commonly used for pools that require executing many short-lived asynchronous tasks. For long-lived processes, usage of this executor is strongly discouraged, as it could grow to encompass a large number of threads over the application life cycle.

The newScheduledThreadPool() is identical to the newFixedThreadPool() method, except that it returns an instance of ScheduledExecutorService and is therefore compatible with scheduling tasks.

Real World Scenario

Choosing a Pool Size

In practice, choosing an appropriate pool size requires some thought. In general, you want at least a handful more threads than you think you will ever possibly need. On the other hand, you don't want to choose so many threads that your application uses up too many resources or too much CPU processing power. Oftentimes, the number of CPUs available is used to determine the thread pool size using this command:

```
Runtime.getRuntime().availableProcessors()
```

It is a common practice to allocate threads based on the number of CPUs.

Writing Thread-Safe Code

Thread-safety is the property of an object that guarantees safe execution by multiple threads at the same time. Since threads run in a shared environment and memory space, how do we prevent two threads from interfering with each other? We must organize access to data so that we don't end up with invalid or unexpected results.

In this part of the chapter, we show how to use a variety of techniques to protect data including: atomic classes, synchronized blocks, the Lock framework, and cyclic barriers.

Understanding Thread-Safety

Imagine that our zoo has a program to count sheep, preferably one that won't put the zoo workers to sleep! Each zoo worker runs out to a field, adds a new sheep to the flock, counts the total number of sheep, and runs back to us to report the results. We present the following code to represent this conceptually, choosing a thread pool size so that all tasks can be run concurrently:

```
import java.util.concurrent.*;
public class SheepManager {
    private int sheepCount = 0;
    private void incrementAndReport() {
        System.out.print((++sheepCount)+" ");
    }
    public static void main(String[] args) {
        ExecutorService service = null;
        try {
            service = Executors.newFixedThreadPool(20);
            SheepManager manager = new SheepManager();
            for(int i = 0; i < 10; i++)
                service.submit(() -> manager.incrementAndReport());
        } finally {
            if(service != null) service.shutdown();
        }
    }
}
```

What does this program output? You might think it will output numbers from 1 to 10, in order, but that is far from guaranteed. It may output in a different order. Worse yet, it may print some numbers twice and not print some numbers at all! The following are all possible outputs of this program:

```
1 2 3 4 5 6 7 8 9 10
1 9 8 7 3 6 6 2 4 5
1 8 7 3 2 6 5 4 2 9
```

So, what went wrong? In this example, we use the pre-increment (++) operator to update the sheepCount variable. A problem occurs when two threads both execute the right side of the expression, reading the "old" value before either thread writes the "new" value of the variable. The two assignments become redundant; they both assign the same new value, with one thread overwriting the results of the other. Figure 7.3 demonstrates this problem with two threads, assuming that sheepCount has a starting value of 1.

You can see in Figure 7.3 that both threads read and write the same values, causing one of the two ++sheepCount operations to be lost. Therefore, the increment operator ++ is not thread-safe. As you will see later in this chapter, the unexpected result of two tasks executing at the same time is referred to as a *race condition*.

Conceptually, the idea here is that some zoo workers may run faster on their way to the field but more slowly on their way back and report late. Other workers may get to the field last but somehow be the first ones back to report the results.

FIGURE 7.3   Lack of thread synchronization

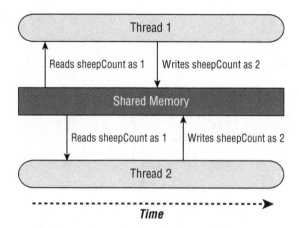

Protecting Data with Atomic Classes

One way to improve our sheep counting example is to use the java.util.concurrent.atomic package. As with many of the classes in the Concurrency API, these classes exist to make your life easier.

In our first SheepManager sample output, the same values were printed twice, with the highest counter being 9 instead of 10. As we demonstrated in the previous section, the increment operator ++ is not thread-safe. Furthermore, the reason that it is not thread-safe is that the operation is not atomic, carrying out two tasks, read and write, that can be interrupted by other threads.

Atomic is the property of an operation to be carried out as a single unit of execution without any interference by another thread. A thread-safe atomic version of the increment operator would be one that performed the read and write of the variable as a single operation, not allowing any other threads to access the variable during the operation. Figure 7.4 shows the result of making the sheepCount variable atomic.

Figure 7.4 resembles our earlier Figure 7.3, except that reading and writing the data is atomic with regard to the sheepCount variable. Any thread trying to access the sheepCount variable while an atomic operation is in process will have to wait until the atomic operation on the variable is complete. Conceptually, this is like setting a rule for our zoo workers that there can be only one employee in the field at a time, although they may not each report their result in order.

Since accessing primitives and references in Java is common in shared environments, the Concurrency API includes numerous useful classes that are conceptually the same as our primitive classes but that support atomic operations. Table 7.6 lists the atomic classes with which you should be familiar for the exam.

FIGURE 7.4 Thread synchronization using atomic operations

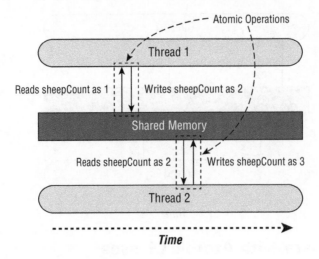

TABLE 7.6 Atomic classes

Class Name	Description
AtomicBoolean	A boolean value that may be updated atomically
AtomicInteger	An int value that may be updated atomically
AtomicLong	A long value that may be updated atomically

How do we use an atomic class? Each class includes numerous methods that are equivalent to many of the primitive built-in operators that we use on primitives, such as the assignment operator (=) and the increment operators (++). We describe the common atomic methods that you should know for the exam in Table 7.7.

In the following example, we update our `SheepManager` class with an `AtomicInteger`:

```
private AtomicInteger sheepCount = new AtomicInteger(0);
private void incrementAndReport() {
   System.out.print(sheepCount.incrementAndGet()+" ");
}
```

How does this implementation differ from our previous examples? When we run this modification, we get varying output, such as the following:

```
2 3 1 4 5 6 7 8 9 10
1 4 3 2 5 6 7 8 9 10
1 4 3 5 6 2 7 8 10 9
```

Unlike our previous sample output, the numbers 1 through 10 will always be printed, although the order is still not guaranteed. Don't worry, we'll address that issue shortly. The key in this section is that using the atomic classes ensures that the data is consistent between workers and that no values are lost due to concurrent modifications.

TABLE 7.7   Common atomic methods

Method name	Description
get()	Retrieves the current value
set()	Sets the given value, equivalent to the assignment = operator
getAndSet()	Atomically sets the new value and returns the old value
incrementAndGet()	For numeric classes, atomic pre-increment operation equivalent to ++value
getAndIncrement()	For numeric classes, atomic post-increment operation equivalent to value++
decrementAndGet()	For numeric classes, atomic pre-decrement operation equivalent to --value
getAndDecrement()	For numeric classes, atomic post-decrement operation equivalent to value--

Improving Access with Synchronized Blocks

While atomic classes are great at protecting single variables, they aren't particularly useful if you need to execute a series of commands or call a method. How do we improve the results so that each worker is able to increment and report the results in order? The most common technique is to use a monitor, also called a *lock*, to synchronize access. A *monitor* is a structure that supports *mutual exclusion*, which is the property that at most one thread is executing a particular segment of code at a given time.

In Java, any Object can be used as a monitor, along with the synchronized keyword, as shown in the following example:

```
SheepManager manager = new SheepManager();
synchronized(manager) {
    // Work to be completed by one thread at a time
}
```

This example is referred to as a *synchronized block*. Each thread that arrives will first check if any threads are in the block. In this manner, a thread "acquires the lock" for the monitor. If the lock is available, a single thread will enter the block, acquiring the lock and preventing all other threads from entering. While the first thread is executing the block, all threads that arrive will attempt to acquire the same lock and wait for the first thread to finish. Once a thread finishes executing the block, it will release the lock, allowing one of the waiting threads to proceed.

To synchronize access across multiple threads, each thread must have access to the same `Object`. For example, synchronizing on different objects would not actually order the results.

Let's revisit our `SheepManager` example and see whether we can improve the results so that each worker increments and outputs the counter in order. Let's say that we replaced our `for()` loop with the following implementation:

```
for(int i = 0; i < 10; i++) {
    synchronized(manager) {
        service.submit(() -> manager.incrementAndReport());
    }
}
```

Does this solution fix the problem? No, it does not! Can you spot the problem? We've synchronized the *creation* of the threads but not the *execution* of the threads. In this example, each thread would be created one at a time, but they may all still execute and perform their work at the same time, resulting in the same type of output that you saw earlier. Diagnosing and resolving threading problems is often one of the most difficult tasks in any programming language.

We now present a corrected version of the `SheepManager` class, which does order the workers.

```
import java.util.concurrent.*;
public class SheepManager {
    private int sheepCount = 0;
    private void incrementAndReport() {
        synchronized(this) {
            System.out.print((++sheepCount)+" ");
        }
    }
    public static void main(String[] args) {
        ExecutorService service = null;
        try {
            service = Executors.newFixedThreadPool(20);
            var manager = new SheepManager();
            for(int i = 0; i < 10; i++)
```

```
            service.submit(() -> manager.incrementAndReport());
        } finally {
            if(service != null) service.shutdown();
        }
    }
}
```

When this code executes, it will consistently output the following:

1 2 3 4 5 6 7 8 9 10

Although all threads are still created and executed at the same time, they each wait at the synchronized block for the worker to increment and report the result before entering. In this manner, each zoo worker waits for the previous zoo worker to come back before running out on the field. While it's random which zoo worker will run out next, it is guaranteed that there will be at most one on the field and that the results will be reported in order.

We could have synchronized on any object, so long as it was the same object. For example, the following code snippet would have also worked:

```
private final Object herd = new Object();
private void incrementAndReport() {
    synchronized(herd) {
        System.out.print((++sheepCount)+" ");
    }
}
```

Although we didn't need to make the herd variable final, doing so ensures that it is not reassigned after threads start using it.

We could have used an atomic variable along with the synchronized block in this example, although it is unnecessary. Since synchronized blocks allow only one thread to enter, we're not gaining any improvement by using an atomic variable if the only time that we access the variable is within a synchronized block.

Synchronizing on Methods

In the previous example, we established our monitor using synchronized(this) around the body of the method. Java actually provides a more convenient compiler enhancement for doing so. We can add the synchronized modifier to any instance method to synchronize automatically on the object itself. For example, the following two method definitions are equivalent:

```
private void incrementAndReport() {
    synchronized(this) {
        System.out.print((++sheepCount)+" ");
    }
}
```

```
private synchronized void incrementAndReport() {
   System.out.print((++sheepCount)+" ");
}
```

The first uses a synchronized block, whereas the second uses the synchronized method modifier. Which you use is completely up to you.

We can also apply the synchronized modifier to static methods. What object is used as the monitor when we synchronize on a static method? The class object, of course! For example, the following two methods are equivalent for static synchronization inside our SheepManager class:

```
public static void printDaysWork() {
   synchronized(SheepManager.class) {
      System.out.print("Finished work");
   }
}
public static synchronized void printDaysWork() {
   System.out.print("Finished work");
}
```

As before, the first uses a synchronized block, with the second example using the synchronized modifier. You can use static synchronization if you need to order thread access across all instances, rather than a single instance.

Avoid Synchronization Whenever Possible

Correctly using the synchronized keyword can be quite challenging, especially if the data you are trying to protect is available to dozens of methods. Even when the data is protected, though, the performance cost for using it can be high.

In this chapter, we present many classes within the Concurrency API that are a lot easier to use and more performant than synchronization. Some you have seen already, like the atomic classes, and others we'll be covering shortly, including the Lock framework, concurrent collections, and cyclic barriers.

While you may not be familiar with all of the classes in the Concurrency API, you should study them carefully if you are writing a lot of multithreaded applications. They contain a wealth of methods that manage complex processes for you in a thread-safe and performant manner.

Understanding the *Lock* Framework

A synchronized block supports only a limited set of functionality. For example, what if we want to check whether a lock is available and, if it is not, perform some other task? Furthermore, if the lock is never available and we synchronize on it, we might hang forever.

The Concurrency API includes the Lock interface that is conceptually similar to using the synchronized keyword, but with a lot more bells and whistles. Instead of synchronizing on any Object, though, we can "lock" only on an object that implements the Lock interface.

Applying a *ReentrantLock* Interface

Using the Lock interface is pretty easy. When you need to protect a piece of code from multithreaded processing, create an instance of Lock that all threads have access to. Each thread then calls lock() before it enters the protected code and calls unlock() before it exits the protected code.

For contrast, the following shows two implementations, one with a synchronized block and one with a Lock instance. As we'll see in the next section, the Lock solution has a number of features not available to the synchronized block.

```
// Implementation #1 with a synchronized block
Object object = new Object();
synchronized(object) {
   // Protected code
}


// Implementation #2 with a Lock
Lock lock = new ReentrantLock();
try {
   lock.lock();
   // Protected code
} finally {
   lock.unlock();
}
```

While certainly not required, it is a good practice to use a try/finally block with Lock instances. This ensures any acquired locks are properly released.

These two implementations are conceptually equivalent. The ReentrantLock class is a simple monitor that implements the Lock interface and supports mutual exclusion. In other words, at most one thread is allowed to hold a lock at any given time.

The ReentrantLock class ensures that once a thread has called lock() and obtained the lock, all other threads that call lock() will wait until the first thread calls unlock(). As far as which thread gets the lock next, that depends on the parameters used to create the Lock object.

The ReentrantLock class contains a constructor that can be used to send a boolean "fairness" parameter. If set to true, then the lock will usually be granted to each thread in the order it was requested. It is false by default when using the no-argument constructor. In practice, you should enable fairness only when ordering is absolutely required, as it could lead to a significant slowdown.

Besides always making sure to release a lock, you also need to make sure that you only release a lock that you actually have. If you attempt to release a lock that you do not have, you will get an exception at runtime.

```
Lock lock = new ReentrantLock();
lock.unlock();  // IllegalMonitorStateException
```

The Lock interface includes four methods that you should know for the exam, as listed in Table 7.8.

TABLE 7.8 Lock methods

Method	Description
void lock()	Requests a lock and blocks until lock is acquired
void unlock()	Releases a lock
boolean tryLock()	Requests a lock and returns immediately. Returns a boolean indicating whether the lock was successfully acquired
boolean tryLock(long,TimeUnit)	Requests a lock and blocks up to the specified time until lock is required. Returns a boolean indicating whether the lock was successfully acquired

Attempting to Acquire a Lock

While the ReentrantLock class allows you to wait for a lock, it so far suffers from the same problem as a synchronized block. A thread could end up waiting forever to obtain a lock. Luckily, Table 7.8 includes two additional methods that make the Lock interface a lot safer to use than a synchronized block.

For convenience, we'll be using the following printMessage() method for the code in this section:

```
public static void printMessage(Lock lock) {
    try {
        lock.lock();
    } finally {
```

```
      lock.unlock();
   }
}
```

tryLock()

The tryLock() method will attempt to acquire a lock and immediately return a boolean result indicating whether the lock was obtained. Unlike the lock() method, it does not wait if another thread already holds the lock. It returns immediately, regardless of whether or not a lock is available.

The following is a sample implementation using the tryLock() method:

```
Lock lock = new ReentrantLock();
new Thread(() -> printMessage(lock)).start();
if(lock.tryLock()) {
   try {
      System.out.println("Lock obtained, entering protected code");
   } finally {
      lock.unlock();
   }
} else {
   System.out.println("Unable to acquire lock, doing something else");
}
```

When you run this code, it could produce either message, depending on the order of execution. A fun exercise is to insert some Thread.sleep() delays into this snippet to encourage a particular message to be displayed.

Like lock(), the tryLock() method should be used with a try/finally block. Fortunately, you need to release the lock only if it was successfully acquired.

It is imperative that your program always checks the return value of the tryLock() method. It tells your program whether the lock needs to be released later.

tryLock(long,TimeUnit)

The Lock interface includes an overloaded version of tryLock(long,TimeUnit) that acts like a hybrid of lock() and tryLock(). Like the other two methods, if a lock is available, then it will immediately return with it. If a lock is unavailable, though, it will wait up to the specified time limit for the lock.

The following code snippet uses the overloaded version of tryLock(long,TimeUnit):

```
Lock lock = new ReentrantLock();
new Thread(() -> printMessage(lock)).start();
```

```
if(lock.tryLock(10,TimeUnit.SECONDS)) {
   try {
      System.out.println("Lock obtained, entering protected code");
   } finally {
      lock.unlock();
   }
} else {
   System.out.println("Unable to acquire lock, doing something else");
}
```

The code is the same as before, except this time one of the threads waits up to 10 seconds to acquire the lock.

Duplicate Lock Requests

The ReentrantLock class maintains a counter of the number of times a lock has been given to a thread. To release the lock for other threads to use, unlock() must be called the same number of times the lock was granted. The following code snippet contains an error. Can you spot it?

```
Lock lock = new ReentrantLock();
if(lock.tryLock()) {
   try {
      lock.lock();
      System.out.println("Lock obtained, entering protected code");
   } finally {
      lock.unlock();
   }
}
```

The thread obtains the lock twice but releases it only once. You can verify this by spawning a new thread after this code runs that attempts to obtain a lock. The following prints false:

```
new Thread(() -> System.out.print(lock.tryLock())).start();
```

It is critical that you release a lock the same number of times it is acquired. For calls with tryLock(), you need to call unlock() only if the method returned true.

Reviewing the *Lock* Framework

To review, the ReentrantLock class supports the same features as a synchronized block, while adding a number of improvements.

- Ability to request a lock without blocking
- Ability to request a lock while blocking for a specified amount of time
- A lock can be created with a fairness property, in which the lock is granted to threads in the order it was requested.

The Concurrency API includes other lock-based classes, although ReentrantLock is the only one you need to know for the exam.

 While not on the exam, ReentrantReadWriteLock is a really useful class. It includes separate locks for reading and writing data and is useful on data structures where reads are far more common than writes. For example, if you have a thousand threads reading data but only one thread writing data, this class can help you maximize concurrent access.

Orchestrating Tasks with a *CyclicBarrier*

We started thread-safety discussing protecting individual variables and then moved on to blocks of code and locks. We complete our discussion of thread-safety by discussing how to orchestrate complex tasks across many things.

Our zoo workers are back, and this time they are cleaning pens. Imagine that there is a lion pen that needs to be emptied, cleaned, and then filled back up with the lions. To complete the task, we have assigned four zoo workers. Obviously, we don't want to start cleaning the cage while a lion is roaming in it, lest we end up losing a zoo worker! Furthermore, we don't want to let the lions back into the pen while it is still being cleaned.

We could have all of the work completed by a single worker, but this would be slow and ignore the fact that we have three zoo workers standing by to help. A better solution would be to have all four zoo employees work concurrently, pausing between the end of one set of tasks and the start of the next.

To coordinate these tasks, we can use the CyclicBarrier class. For now, let's start with a code sample without a CyclicBarrier.

```
import java.util.concurrent.*;
public class LionPenManager {
    private void removeLions() {System.out.println("Removing lions");}
    private void cleanPen() {System.out.println("Cleaning the pen");}
    private void addLions() {System.out.println("Adding lions");}
    public void performTask() {
        removeLions();
        cleanPen();
        addLions();
    }
    public static void main(String[] args) {
        ExecutorService service = null;
        try {
            service = Executors.newFixedThreadPool(4);
            var manager = new LionPenManager();
```

```
        for (int i = 0; i < 4; i++)
            service.submit(() -> manager.performTask());
    } finally {
        if (service != null) service.shutdown();
    }
  }
}
```

The following is sample output based on this implementation:

```
Removing lions
Removing lions
Cleaning the pen
Adding lions
Removing lions
Cleaning the pen
Adding lions
Removing lions
Cleaning the pen
Adding lions
Cleaning the pen
Adding lions
```

Although within a single thread the results are ordered, among multiple workers the output is entirely random. We see that some lions are still being removed while the cage is being cleaned, and other lions are added before the cleaning process is finished. In our conceptual example, this would be quite chaotic and would not lead to a very clean cage.

We can improve these results by using the CyclicBarrier class. The CyclicBarrier takes in its constructors a limit value, indicating the number of threads to wait for. As each thread finishes, it calls the await() method on the cyclic barrier. Once the specified number of threads have each called await(), the barrier is released, and all threads can continue.

The following is a reimplementation of our LionPenManager class that uses CyclicBarrier objects to coordinate access:

```
import java.util.concurrent.*;
public class LionPenManager {
    private void removeLions() {System.out.println("Removing lions");}
    private void cleanPen() {System.out.println("Cleaning the pen");}
    private void addLions() {System.out.println("Adding lions");}
    public void performTask(CyclicBarrier c1, CyclicBarrier c2) {
        try {
            removeLions();
            c1.await();
            cleanPen();
```

```
            c2.await();
            addLions();
        } catch (InterruptedException | BrokenBarrierException e) {
            // Handle checked exceptions here
        }
    }
    public static void main(String[] args) {
        ExecutorService service = null;
        try {
            service = Executors.newFixedThreadPool(4);
            var manager = new LionPenManager();
            var c1 = new CyclicBarrier(4);
            var c2 = new CyclicBarrier(4,
                () -> System.out.println("*** Pen Cleaned!"));
            for (int i = 0; i < 4; i++)
                service.submit(() -> manager.performTask(c1, c2));
        } finally {
            if (service != null) service.shutdown();
        }
    }
}
```

In this example, we have updated performTask() to use CyclicBarrier objects. Like synchronizing on the same object, coordinating a task with a CyclicBarrier requires the object to be static or passed to the thread performing the task. We also add a try/catch block in the performTask() method, as the await() method throws multiple checked exceptions.

The following is sample output based on this revised implementation of our LionPenManager class:

```
Removing lions
Removing lions
Removing lions
Removing lions
Cleaning the pen
Cleaning the pen
Cleaning the pen
Cleaning the pen
*** Pen Cleaned!
Adding lions
Adding lions
Adding lions
Adding lions
```

As you can see, all of the results are now organized. Removing the lions all happens in one step, as does cleaning the pen and adding the lions back in. In this example, we used two different constructors for our `CyclicBarrier` objects, the latter of which called a `Runnable` method upon completion.

Thread Pool Size and Cyclic Barrier Limit

If you are using a thread pool, make sure that you set the number of available threads to be at least as large as your `CyclicBarrier` limit value. For example, what if we changed the code in the previous example to allocate only two threads, such as in the following snippet?

```
ExecutorService service = Executors.newFixedThreadPool(2);
```

In this case, the code will hang indefinitely. The barrier would never be reached as the only threads available in the pool are stuck waiting for the barrier to be complete. This would result in a deadlock, which will be discussed shortly.

The `CyclicBarrier` class allows us to perform complex, multithreaded tasks, while all threads stop and wait at logical barriers. This solution is superior to a single-threaded solution, as the individual tasks, such as removing the lions, can be completed in parallel by all four zoo workers.

There is a slight loss in performance to be expected from using a `CyclicBarrier`. For example, one worker may be incredibly slow at removing lions, resulting in the other three workers waiting for him to finish. Since we can't start cleaning the pen while it is full of lions, though, this solution is about as concurrent as we can make it.

Reusing *CyclicBarrier*

After a `CyclicBarrier` is broken, all threads are released, and the number of threads waiting on the `CyclicBarrier` goes back to zero. At this point, the `CyclicBarrier` may be used again for a new set of waiting threads. For example, if our `CyclicBarrier` limit is 5 and we have 15 threads that call `await()`, then the `CyclicBarrier` will be activated a total of three times.

Using Concurrent Collections

Besides managing threads, the Concurrency API includes interfaces and classes that help you coordinate access to collections shared by multiple tasks. By collections, we are of course referring to the Java Collections Framework that we introduced in Chapter 3,

"Generics and Collections." In this section, we will demonstrate many of the concurrent classes available to you when using the Concurrency API.

Understanding Memory Consistency Errors

The purpose of the concurrent collection classes is to solve common memory consistency errors. A *memory consistency error* occurs when two threads have inconsistent views of what should be the same data. Conceptually, we want writes on one thread to be available to another thread if it accesses the concurrent collection after the write has occurred.

When two threads try to modify the same nonconcurrent collection, the JVM may throw a ConcurrentModificationException at runtime. In fact, it can happen with a single thread. Take a look at the following code snippet:

```
var foodData = new HashMap<String, Integer>();
foodData.put("penguin", 1);
foodData.put("flamingo", 2);
for(String key: foodData.keySet())
   foodData.remove(key);
```

This snippet will throw a ConcurrentModificationException during the second iteration of the loop, since the iterator on keySet() is not properly updated after the first element is removed. Changing the first line to use a ConcurrentHashMap will prevent the code from throwing an exception at runtime.

```
var foodData = new ConcurrentHashMap<String, Integer>();
foodData.put("penguin", 1);
foodData.put("flamingo", 2);
for(String key: foodData.keySet())
   foodData.remove(key);
```

Although we don't usually modify a loop variable, this example highlights the fact that the ConcurrentHashMap is ordering read/write access such that all access to the class is consistent. In this code snippet, the iterator created by keySet() is updated as soon as an object is removed from the Map.

The concurrent classes were created to help avoid common issues in which multiple threads are adding and removing objects from the same collections. At any given instance, all threads should have the same consistent view of the structure of the collection.

Working with Concurrent Classes

You should use a concurrent collection class anytime that you are going to have multiple threads modify a collections object outside a synchronized block or method, even if you don't expect a concurrency problem. On the other hand, immutable or read-only objects can be accessed by any number of threads without a concurrent collection.

Immutable objects can be accessed by any number of threads and do not require synchronization. By definition, they do not change, so there is no chance of a memory consistency error.

In the same way that we instantiate an ArrayList object but pass around a List reference, it is considered a good practice to instantiate a concurrent collection but pass it around using a nonconcurrent interface whenever possible. In some cases, the callers may need to know that it is a concurrent collection so that a concurrent interface or class is appropriate, but for the majority of circumstances, that distinction is not necessary.

Table 7.9 lists the common concurrent classes with which you should be familiar for the exam.

TABLE 7.9 Concurrent collection classes

Class name	Java Collections Framework interfaces	Elements ordered?	Sorted?	Blocking?
ConcurrentHashMap	ConcurrentMap	No	No	No
ConcurrentLinkedQueue	Queue	Yes	No	No
ConcurrentSkipListMap	ConcurrentMap SortedMap NavigableMap	Yes	Yes	No
ConcurrentSkipListSet	SortedSet NavigableSet	Yes	Yes	No
CopyOnWriteArrayList	List	Yes	No	No
CopyOnWriteArraySet	Set	No	No	No
LinkedBlockingQueue	BlockingQueue	Yes	No	Yes

Based on your knowledge of collections from Chapter 3, classes like ConcurrentHashMap and ConcurrentLinkedQueue should be quite easy for you to learn. Take a look at the following code samples:

```
Map<String,Integer> map = new ConcurrentHashMap<>();
map.put("zebra", 52);
map.put("elephant", 10);
System.out.println(map.get("elephant"));  // 10
```

```
Queue<Integer> queue = new ConcurrentLinkedQueue<>();
queue.offer(31);
System.out.println(queue.peek());   // 31
System.out.println(queue.poll());   // 31
```

Like we often did in Chapter 3, we use an interface reference for the variable type of the newly created object and use it the same way as we would a nonconcurrent object. The difference is that these objects are safe to pass to multiple threads.

All of these classes implement multiple interfaces. For example, ConcurrentHashMap implements Map and ConcurrentMap. When declaring methods that take a concurrent collection, it is up to you to determine the appropriate method parameter type. For example, a method signature may require a ConcurrentMap reference to ensure that an object passed to it is properly supported in a multithreaded environment.

Understanding *SkipList* Collections

The SkipList classes, ConcurrentSkipListSet and ConcurrentSkipListMap, are concurrent versions of their sorted counterparts, TreeSet and TreeMap, respectively. They maintain their elements or keys in the natural ordering of their elements. In this manner, using them is the same as the code that you worked with in Chapter 3.

```
Set<String> gardenAnimals = new ConcurrentSkipListSet<>();
gardenAnimals.add("rabbit");
gardenAnimals.add("gopher");
System.out.println(gardenAnimals.stream()
   .collect(Collectors.joining(",")));   // gopher,rabbit


Map<String, String> rainForestAnimalDiet
   = new ConcurrentSkipListMap<>();
rainForestAnimalDiet.put("koala", "bamboo");
rainForestAnimalDiet.entrySet()
   .stream()
   .forEach((e) -> System.out.println(
      e.getKey() + "-" + e.getValue()));  // koala-bamboo
```

When you see SkipList or SkipSet on the exam, just think "sorted" concurrent collections, and the rest should follow naturally.

Understanding *CopyOnWrite* Collections

Table 7.9 included two classes, CopyOnWriteArrayList and CopyOnWriteArraySet, that behave a little differently than the other concurrent examples that you have seen. These classes copy all of their elements to a new underlying structure anytime an element is added, modified, or removed from the collection. By a *modified* element, we mean that the reference in the collection is changed. Modifying the actual contents of objects within the collection will not cause a new structure to be allocated.

Although the data is copied to a new underlying structure, our reference to the Collection object does not change. This is particularly useful in multithreaded environments that need to iterate the collection. Any iterator established prior to a modification will not see the changes, but instead it will iterate over the original elements prior to the modification.

Let's take a look at how this works with an example. Does the following program terminate? If so, how many times does the loop execute?

```
List<Integer> favNumbers =
    new CopyOnWriteArrayList<>(List.of(4,3,42));
for(var n: favNumbers) {
    System.out.print(n + " ");
    favNumbers.add(9);
}
System.out.println();
System.out.println("Size: " + favNumbers.size());
```

When executed as part of a program, this code snippet outputs the following:

```
4 3 42
Size: 6
```

Despite adding elements to the array while iterating over it, the for loop only iterated on the ones created when the loop started. Alternatively, if we had used a regular ArrayList object, a ConcurrentModificationException would have been thrown at runtime. With either class, though, we avoid entering an infinite loop in which elements are constantly added to the array as we iterate over them.

The CopyOnWrite classes are similar to the immutable object pattern that you saw in Chapter 1, "Java Fundamentals," as a new underlying structure is created every time the collection is modified. Unlike a true immutable object, though, the reference to the object stays the same even while the underlying data is changed.

The CopyOnWriteArraySet is used just like a HashSet and has similar properties as the CopyOnWriteArrayList class.

```
Set<Character> favLetters =
    new CopyOnWriteArraySet<>(List.of('a','t'));
for(char c: favLetters) {
    System.out.print(c+" ");
    favLetters.add('s');
}
System.out.println();
System.out.println("Size: "+ favLetters.size());
```

This code snippet prints:

```
a t
Size: 3
```

The CopyOnWrite classes can use a lot of memory, since a new collection structure needs be allocated anytime the collection is modified. They are commonly used in multi-threaded environment situations where reads are far more common than writes.

Revisiting Deleting While Looping

In Chapter 3, we showed an example where deleting from an ArrayList while iterating over it triggered a ConcurrentModificationException. Here we present a version that does work using CopyOnWriteArrayList:

```
List<String> birds = new CopyOnWriteArrayList<>();
birds.add("hawk");
birds.add("hawk");
birds.add("hawk");

for (String bird : birds)
    birds.remove(bird);
System.out.print(birds.size()); // 0
```

As mentioned, though, CopyOnWrite classes can use a lot of memory. Another approach is to use the ArrayList class with an iterator, as shown here:

```
    var iterator = birds.iterator();
    while(iterator.hasNext()) {
        iterator.next();
        iterator.remove();
    }
    System.out.print(birds.size());  // 0
```

Understanding Blocking Queues

The final collection class in Table 7.9 that you should know for the exam is the LinkedBlockingQueue, which implements the BlockingQueue interface. The BlockingQueue is just like a regular Queue, except that it includes methods that will wait a specific amount of time to complete an operation.

Since BlockingQueue inherits all of the methods from Queue, we skip the inherited methods you learned in Chapter 3 and present the new methods in Table 7.10.

TABLE 7.10   BlockingQueue waiting methods

Method name	Description
offer(E e, long timeout, TimeUnit unit)	Adds an item to the queue, waiting the specified time and returning false if the time elapses before space is available
poll(long timeout, TimeUnit unit)	Retrieves and removes an item from the queue, waiting the specified time and returning null if the time elapses before the item is available

The implementation class LinkedBlockingQueue, as the name implies, maintains a linked list between elements. The following sample is using a LinkedBlockingQueue to wait for the results of some of the operations. The methods in Table 7.10 can each throw a checked InterruptedException, as they can be interrupted before they finish waiting for a result; therefore, they must be properly caught.

```
try {
   var blockingQueue = new LinkedBlockingQueue<Integer>();
   blockingQueue.offer(39);
   blockingQueue.offer(3, 4, TimeUnit.SECONDS);
   System.out.println(blockingQueue.poll());
   System.out.println(blockingQueue.poll(10, TimeUnit.MILLISECONDS));
} catch (InterruptedException e) {
   // Handle interruption
}
```

This code snippet prints the following:

```
39
3
```

As shown in this example, since LinkedBlockingQueue implements both Queue and BlockingQueue, we can use methods available to both, such as those that don't take any wait arguments.

Obtaining Synchronized Collections

Besides the concurrent collection classes that we have covered, the Concurrency API also includes methods for obtaining synchronized versions of existing nonconcurrent collection objects. These synchronized methods are defined in the Collections class. They operate on the inputted collection and return a reference that is the same type as the underlying collection. We list these methods in Table 7.11.

TABLE 7.11   Synchronized collections methods

`synchronizedCollection(Collection<T> c)`

`synchronizedList(List<T> list)`

`synchronizedMap(Map<K,V> m)`

`synchronizedNavigableMap(NavigableMap<K,V> m)`

`synchronizedNavigableSet(NavigableSet<T> s)`

`synchronizedSet(Set<T> s)`

`synchronizedSortedMap(SortedMap<K,V> m)`

`synchronizedSortedSet(SortedSet<T> s)`

When should you use these methods? If you know at the time of creation that your object requires synchronization, then you should use one of the concurrent collection classes listed in Table 7.9. On the other hand, if you are given an existing collection that is not a concurrent class and need to access it among multiple threads, you can wrap it using the methods in Table 7.11.

Unlike the concurrent collections, the synchronized collections also throw an exception if they are modified within an iterator by a single thread. For example, take a look at the following modification of our earlier example:

```
var foodData = new HashMap<String, Object>();
foodData.put("penguin", 1);
foodData.put("flamingo", 2);
var synFoodData = Collections.synchronizedMap(foodData);
for(String key: synFoodData.keySet())
   synFoodData.remove(key);
```

This loop throws a ConcurrentModificationException, whereas our example that used ConcurrentHashMap did not. Other than iterating over the collection, the objects returned by the methods in Table 7.11 are safe from memory consistency errors and can be used among multiple threads.

Identifying Threading Problems

A threading problem can occur in multithreaded applications when two or more threads interact in an unexpected and undesirable way. For example, two threads may block each other from accessing a particular segment of code.

The Concurrency API was created to help eliminate potential threading issues common to all developers. As you have seen, the Concurrency API creates threads and manages complex thread interactions for you, often in just a few lines of code.

Although the Concurrency API reduces the potential for threading issues, it does not eliminate it. In practice, finding and identifying threading issues within an application is often one of the most difficult tasks a developer can undertake.

Understanding Liveness

As you have seen in this chapter, many thread operations can be performed independently, but some require coordination. For example, synchronizing on a method requires all threads that call the method to wait for other threads to finish before continuing. You also saw earlier in the chapter that threads in a CyclicBarrier will each wait for the barrier limit to be reached before continuing.

What happens to the application while all of these threads are waiting? In many cases, the waiting is ephemeral, and the user has very little idea that any delay has occurred. In other cases, though, the waiting may be extremely long, perhaps infinite.

Liveness is the ability of an application to be able to execute in a timely manner. Liveness problems, then, are those in which the application becomes unresponsive or in some kind of "stuck" state. For the exam, there are three types of liveness issues with which you should be familiar: deadlock, starvation, and livelock.

Deadlock

Deadlock occurs when two or more threads are blocked forever, each waiting on the other. We can illustrate this principle with the following example. Imagine that our zoo has two foxes: Foxy and Tails. Foxy likes to eat first and then drink water, while Tails likes to drink water first and then eat. Furthermore, neither animal likes to share, and they will finish their meal only if they have exclusive access to both food and water.

The zookeeper places the food on one side of the environment and the water on the other side. Although our foxes are fast, it still takes them 100 milliseconds to run from one side of the environment to the other.

What happens if Foxy gets the food first and Tails gets the water first? The following application models this behavior:

```
import java.util.concurrent.*;
class Food {}
class Water {}
public class Fox {
    public void eatAndDrink(Food food, Water water) {
        synchronized(food) {
            System.out.println("Got Food!");
            move();
            synchronized(water) {
```

```
            System.out.println("Got Water!");
        }
    }
}
public void drinkAndEat(Food food, Water water) {
    synchronized(water) {
        System.out.println("Got Water!");
        move();
        synchronized(food) {
            System.out.println("Got Food!");
        }
    }
}
public void move() {
    try {
        Thread.sleep(100);
    } catch (InterruptedException e) {
        // Handle exception
    }
}
public static void main(String[] args) {
    // Create participants and resources
    Fox foxy = new Fox();
    Fox tails = new Fox();
    Food food = new Food();
    Water water = new Water();
    // Process data
    ExecutorService service = null;
    try {
        service = Executors.newScheduledThreadPool(10);
        service.submit(() -> foxy.eatAndDrink(food,water));
        service.submit(() -> tails.drinkAndEat(food,water));
    } finally {
        if(service != null) service.shutdown();
    }
}
}
```

In this example, Foxy obtains the food and then moves to the other side of the environment to obtain the water. Unfortunately, Tails already drank the water and is waiting for the food to become available. The result is that our program outputs the following, and it hangs indefinitely:

```
Got Food!
Got Water!
```

This example is considered a deadlock because both participants are permanently blocked, waiting on resources that will never become available.

Preventing Deadlocks

How do you fix a deadlock once it has occurred? The answer is that you can't in most situations. On the other hand, there are numerous strategies to help prevent deadlocks from ever happening in the first place. One common strategy to avoid deadlocks is for all threads to order their resource requests. For example, if both foxes have a rule that they need to obtain food before water, then the previous deadlock scenario will not happen again. Once one of the foxes obtained food, the second fox would wait, leaving the water resource available.

There are some advanced techniques that try to detect and resolve a deadlock in real time, but they are often quite difficult to implement and have limited success in practice. In fact, many operating systems ignore the problem altogether and pretend that deadlocks never happen.

Starvation

Starvation occurs when a single thread is perpetually denied access to a shared resource or lock. The thread is still active, but it is unable to complete its work as a result of other threads constantly taking the resource that they are trying to access.

In our fox example, imagine that we have a pack of very hungry, very competitive foxes in our environment. Every time Foxy stands up to go get food, one of the other foxes sees her and rushes to eat before her. Foxy is free to roam around the enclosure, take a nap, and howl for a zookeeper but is never able to obtain access to the food. In this example, Foxy literally and figuratively experiences starvation. It's a good thing that this is just a theoretical example!

Livelock

Livelock occurs when two or more threads are conceptually blocked forever, although they are each still active and trying to complete their task. Livelock is a special case of resource starvation in which two or more threads actively try to acquire a set of locks, are unable to do so, and restart part of the process.

Livelock is often a result of two threads trying to resolve a deadlock. Returning to our fox example, imagine that Foxy and Tails are both holding their food and water resources, respectively. They each realize that they cannot finish their meal in this state, so they both let go of their food and water, run to opposite side of the environment, and pick up the other resource. Now Foxy has the water, Tails has the food, and neither is able to finish their meal!

If Foxy and Tails continue this process forever, it is referred to as livelock. Both Foxy and Tails are active, running back and forth across their area, but neither is able to finish their meal. Foxy and Tails are executing a form of failed deadlock recovery. Each fox notices that they are potentially entering a deadlock state and responds by releasing all of its locked resources. Unfortunately, the lock and unlock process is cyclical, and the two foxes are conceptually deadlocked.

In practice, livelock is often a difficult issue to detect. Threads in a livelock state appear active and able to respond to requests, even when they are in fact stuck in an endless cycle.

Managing Race Conditions

A *race condition* is an undesirable result that occurs when two tasks, which should be completed sequentially, are completed at the same time. We encountered examples of race conditions earlier in the chapter when we introduced synchronization.

While Figure 7.3 shows a classical thread-based example of a race condition, we now provide a more illustrative example. Imagine two zoo patrons, Olivia and Sophia, are signing up for an account on the zoo's new visitor website. Both of them want to use the same username, ZooFan, and they each send requests to create the account at the same time, as shown in Figure 7.5.

What result does the web server return when both users attempt to create an account with the same username in Figure 7.5?

FIGURE 7.5   Race condition on user creation

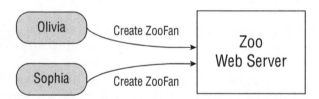

Possible Outcomes for This Race Condition

- Both users are able to create accounts with username ZooFan.

- Both users are unable to create an account with username ZooFan, returning an error message to both users.

- One user is able to create the account with the username ZooFan, while the other user receives an error message.

Which of these results is most desirable when designing our web server? The first possibility, in which both users are able to create an account with the same username, could cause serious problems and break numerous invariants in the system. Assuming that the username is required to log into the website, how do they both log in with the same username and different passwords? In this case, the website cannot tell them apart. This is the worst possible outcome to this race condition, as it causes significant and potentially unrecoverable data problems.

What about the second scenario? If both users are unable to create the account, both will receive error messages and be told to try again. In this scenario, the data is protected since no two accounts with the same username exist in the system. The users are free to try again with the same username, ZooFan, since no one has been granted access to it. Although this might seem like a form of livelock, there is a subtle difference. When the users try to create their account again, the chances of them hitting a race condition tend to diminish. For example, if one user submits their request a few seconds before the other, they might avoid another race condition entirely by the system informing the second user that the account name is already in use.

The third scenario, in which one user obtains the account while the other does not, is often considered the best solution to this type of race condition. Like the second situation, we preserve data integrity, but unlike the second situation, at least one user is able to move forward on the first request, avoiding additional race condition scenarios. Also unlike the previous scenario, we can provide the user who didn't win the race with a clearer error message because we are now sure that the account username is no longer available in the system.

For the third scenario, which of the two users should gain access to the account? For race conditions, it often doesn't matter as long as only one player "wins" the race. A common practice is to choose whichever thread made the request first, whenever possible.

For the exam, you should understand that race conditions lead to invalid data if they are not properly handled. Even the solution where both participants fail to proceed is preferable to one in which invalid data is permitted to enter the system.

Race conditions tend to appear in highly concurrent applications. As a software system grows and more users are added, they tend to appear more frequently. One solution is to use a monitor to synchronize on the relevant overlapping task. In the previous example, the relevant task is the method that determines whether an account username is in use and reserves it in the system if it is available.

Working with Parallel Streams

One of the most powerful features of the Stream API is built-in concurrency support. Up until now, all of the streams with which you have worked have been serial streams. A *serial stream* is a stream in which the results are ordered, with only one entry being processed at a time.

A *parallel stream* is a stream that is capable of processing results concurrently, using multiple threads. For example, you can use a parallel stream and the map() operation to operate concurrently on the elements in the stream, vastly improving performance over processing a single element at a time.

Using a parallel stream can change not only the performance of your application but also the expected results. As you shall see, some operations also require special handling to be able to be processed in a parallel manner.

The number of threads available in a parallel stream is proportional to the number of available CPUs in your environment.

Creating Parallel Streams

The Stream API was designed to make creating parallel streams quite easy. For the exam, you should be familiar with the two ways of creating a parallel stream.

Calling *parallel()* on an Existing Stream

The first way to create a parallel stream is from an existing stream. You just call parallel() on an existing stream to convert it to one that supports multithreaded processing, as shown in the following code:

```
Stream<Integer> s1 = List.of(1,2).stream();
Stream<Integer> s2 = s1.parallel();
```

Be aware that parallel() is an intermediate operation that operates on the original stream. For example, applying a terminal operation to s2 also makes s1 unavailable for further use.

Calling *parallelStream()* on a *Collection* Object

The second way to create a parallel stream is from a Java Collection class. The Collection interface includes a method parallelStream() that can be called on any collection and returns a parallel stream. The following creates the parallel stream directly from the List object:

```
Stream<Integer> s3 = List.of(1,2).parallelStream();
```

We will use both parallel() and parallelStream() throughout this section.

The Stream interface includes a method isParallel() that can be used to test if the instance of a stream supports parallel processing. Some operations on streams preserve the parallel attribute, while others do not. For example, the Stream.concat(Stream s1, Stream s2) is parallel if either s1 or s2 is parallel. On the other hand, flatMap() creates a new stream that is not parallel by default, regardless of whether the underlying elements were parallel.

Performing a Parallel Decomposition

As you may have noticed, creating the parallel stream is the easy part. The interesting part comes in performing a parallel decomposition. A *parallel decomposition* is the process of taking a task, breaking it up into smaller pieces that can be performed concurrently, and then reassembling the results. The more concurrent a decomposition, the greater the performance improvement of using parallel streams.

Let's try it. For starters, let's define a reusable function that "does work" just by waiting for five seconds.

```
private static int doWork(int input) {
   try {
      Thread.sleep(5000);
   } catch (InterruptedException e) {}
   return input;
}
```

We can pretend that in a real application this might be calling a database or reading a file. Now let's use this method with a serial stream.

```
long start = System.currentTimeMillis();
List.of(1,2,3,4,5)
   .stream()
   .map(w -> doWork(w))
   .forEach(s -> System.out.print(s + " "));

System.out.println();
var timeTaken = (System.currentTimeMillis()-start)/1000;
System.out.println("Time: "+timeTaken+" seconds");
```

What do you think this code will output when executed as part of a main() method? Let's take a look.

```
1 2 3 4 5
Time: 25 seconds
```

As you might expect, the results are ordered and predictable because we are using a serial stream. It also took around 25 seconds to process all five results, one at a time. What happens if we use a parallel stream, though?

```
long start = System.currentTimeMillis();
List.of(1,2,3,4,5)
   .parallelStream()
   .map(w -> doWork(w))
   .forEach(s -> System.out.print(s + " "));
```

```
System.out.println();
var timeTaken = (System.currentTimeMillis()-start)/1000;
System.out.println("Time: "+timeTaken+" seconds");
```

With a parallel stream, the `map()` and `forEach()` operations are applied concurrently. The following is sample output:

```
3 2 1 5 4
Time: 5 seconds
```

As you can see, the results are no longer ordered or predictable. The `map()` and `forEach()` operations on a parallel stream are equivalent to submitting multiple `Runnable` lambda expressions to a pooled thread executor and then waiting for the results.

What about the time required? In this case, our system had enough CPUs for all of the tasks to be run concurrently. If you ran this same code on a computer with fewer processors, it might output 10 seconds, 15 seconds, or some other value. The key is that we've written our code to take advantage of parallel processing when available, so our job is done.

Ordering *forEach* Results

The Stream API includes an alternate version of the `forEach()` operation called `forEachOrdered()`, which forces a parallel stream to process the results in order at the cost of performance. For example, take a look at the following code snippet:

```
List.of(5,2,1,4,3)
    .parallelStream()
    .map(w -> doWork(w))
    .forEachOrdered(s -> System.out.print(s + " "));
```

Like our starting example, this outputs the results in the order that they are defined in the stream:

```
5 2 1 4 3
Time: 5 seconds
```

With this change, the `forEachOrdered()` operation forces our stream into a single-threaded process. While we've lost some of the performance gains of using a parallel stream, our `map()` operation is still able to take advantage of the parallel stream and perform a parallel decomposition in 5 seconds instead of 25 seconds.

Processing Parallel Reductions

Besides possibly improving performance and modifying the order of operations, using parallel streams can impact how you write your application. Reduction operations on parallel streams are referred to as *parallel reductions*. The results for parallel reductions can be different from what you expect when working with serial streams.

Performing Order-Based Tasks

Since order is not guaranteed with parallel streams, methods such as findAny() on parallel streams may result in unexpected behavior. Let's take a look at the results of findAny() applied to a serial stream.

```
System.out.print(List.of(1,2,3,4,5,6)
    .stream()
    .findAny().get());
```

This code frequently outputs the first value in the serial stream, 1, although this is not guaranteed. The findAny() method is free to select any element on either serial or parallel streams.

With a parallel stream, the JVM can create any number of threads to process the stream. When you call findAny() on a parallel stream, the JVM selects the first thread to finish the task and retrieves its data.

```
System.out.print(List.of(1,2,3,4,5,6)
    .parallelStream()
    .findAny().get());
```

The result is that the output could be 4, 1, or really any value in the stream. You can see that with parallel streams, the results of findAny() are not as predictable.

Any stream operation that is based on order, including findFirst(), limit(), or skip(), may actually perform more slowly in a parallel environment. This is a result of a parallel processing task being forced to coordinate all of its threads in a synchronized-like fashion.

On the plus side, the results of ordered operations on a parallel stream will be consistent with a serial stream. For example, calling skip(5).limit(2).findFirst() will return the same result on ordered serial and parallel streams.

 **Real World Scenario**

Creating Unordered Streams

All of the streams with which you have been working are considered ordered by default. It is possible to create an unordered stream from an ordered stream, similar to how you create a parallel stream from a serial stream:

```
List.of(1,2,3,4,5,6).stream().unordered();
```

This method does not actually reorder the elements; it just tells the JVM that if an order-based stream operation is applied, the order can be ignored. For example, calling `skip(5)` on an unordered stream will skip any 5 elements, not the first 5 required on an ordered stream.

For serial streams, using an unordered version has no effect, but on parallel streams, the results can greatly improve performance.

```
List.of(1,2,3,4,5,6).stream().unordered().parallel();
```

Even though unordered streams will not be on the exam, if you are developing applications with parallel streams, you should know when to apply an unordered stream to improve performance.

Combining Results with *reduce()*

As you learned in Chapter 4, the stream operation `reduce()` combines a stream into a single object. Recall that the first parameter to the `reduce()` method is called the *identity*, the second parameter is called the *accumulator*, and the third parameter is called the *combiner*. The following is the signature for the method:

```
<U> U reduce(U identity,
    BiFunction<U,? super T,U> accumulator,
    BinaryOperator<U> combiner)
```

We can concatenate a list of char values, using the `reduce()` method, as shown in the following example:

```
System.out.println(List.of('w', 'o', 'l', 'f')
    .parallelStream()
    .reduce("",
        (s1,c) -> s1 + c,
        (s2,s3) -> s2 + s3));  // wolf
```

The naming of the variables in this stream example is not accidental. We used c for char, whereas s1, s2, and s3 are String values.

On parallel streams, the `reduce()` method works by applying the reduction to pairs of elements within the stream to create intermediate values and then combining those intermediate values to produce a final result. Put another way, in a serial stream, wolf is built one character at a time. In a parallel stream, the intermediate values wo and lf are created and then combined.

With parallel streams, we now have to be concerned about order. What if the elements of a string are combined in the wrong order to produce wlfo or flwo? The Stream

API prevents this problem, while still allowing streams to be processed in parallel, as long as you follow one simple rule: make sure that the accumulator and combiner work regardless of the order they are called in. For example, if we add numbers, we can do so in any order.

> While the requirements for the input arguments to the reduce() method hold true for both serial and parallel streams, you may not have noticed any problems in serial streams because the result was always ordered. With parallel streams, though, order is no longer guaranteed, and any argument that violates these rules is much more likely to produce side effects or unpredictable results.

Let's take a look at an example using a problematic accumulator. In particular, order matters when subtracting numbers; therefore, the following code can output different values depending on whether you use a serial or parallel stream. We can omit a combiner parameter in these examples, as the accumulator can be used when the intermediate data types are the same.

```
System.out.println(List.of(1,2,3,4,5,6)
   .parallelStream()
   .reduce(0, (a,b) -> (a - b)));   // PROBLEMATIC ACCUMULATOR
```

It may output –21, 3, or some other value.

You can see other problems if we use an identity parameter that is not truly an identity value. For example, what do you expect the following code to output?

```
System.out.println(List.of("w","o","l","f")
   .parallelStream()
   .reduce("X", String::concat));   // XwXoXlXf
```

On a serial stream, it prints Xwolf, but on a parallel stream the result is XwXoXlXf. As part of the parallel process, the identity is applied to multiple elements in the stream, resulting in very unexpected data.

Selecting a *reduce()* Method

Although the one- and two-argument versions of reduce() do support parallel processing, it is recommended that you use the three-argument version of reduce() when working with parallel streams. Providing an explicit combiner method allows the JVM to partition the operations in the stream more efficiently.

Combining Results with *collect()*

Like reduce(), the Stream API includes a three-argument version of collect() that takes *accumulator* and *combiner* operators, along with a *supplier* operator instead of an identity.

```
<R> R collect(Supplier<R> supplier,
    BiConsumer<R, ? super T> accumulator,
    BiConsumer<R, R> combiner)
```

Also, like reduce(), the accumulator and combiner operations must be able to process results in any order. In this manner, the three-argument version of collect() can be performed as a parallel reduction, as shown in the following example:

```
Stream<String> stream = Stream.of("w", "o", "l", "f").parallel();
SortedSet<String> set = stream.collect(ConcurrentSkipListSet::new,
    Set::add,
    Set::addAll);
System.out.println(set);  // [f, l, o, w]
```

Recall that elements in a ConcurrentSkipListSet are sorted according to their natural ordering. You should use a concurrent collection to combine the results, ensuring that the results of concurrent threads do not cause a ConcurrentModificationException.

Performing parallel reductions with a collector requires additional considerations. For example, if the collection into which you are inserting is an ordered data set, such as a List, then the elements in the resulting collection must be in the same order, regardless of whether you use a serial or parallel stream. This may reduce performance, though, as some operations are unable to be completed in parallel.

Performing a Parallel Reduction on a *Collector*

While we covered the Collector interface in Chapter 4, we didn't go into detail about its properties. Every Collector instance defines a characteristics() method that returns a set of Collector.Characteristics attributes. When using a Collector to perform a parallel reduction, a number of properties must hold true. Otherwise, the collect() operation will execute in a single-threaded fashion.

Requirements for Parallel Reduction with *collect()*

- The stream is parallel.
- The parameter of the collect() operation has the Characteristics.CONCURRENT characteristic.
- Either the stream is unordered or the collector has the characteristic Characteristics.UNORDERED.

For example, while Collectors.toSet() does have the UNORDERED characteristic, it does not have the CONCURRENT characteristic. Therefore, the following is not a parallel reduction even with a parallel stream:

```
stream.collect(Collectors.toSet());  // Not a parallel reduction
```

The Collectors class includes two sets of static methods for retrieving collectors, toConcurrentMap() and groupingByConcurrent(), that are both UNORDERED and CONCURRENT. These methods produce Collector instances capable of performing parallel reductions efficiently. Like their nonconcurrent counterparts, there are overloaded versions that take additional arguments.

Here is a rewrite of an example from Chapter 4 to use a parallel stream and parallel reduction:

```
Stream<String> ohMy = Stream.of("lions","tigers","bears").parallel();
ConcurrentMap<Integer, String> map = ohMy
   .collect(Collectors.toConcurrentMap(String::length,
      k -> k,
      (s1, s2) -> s1 + "," + s2));
System.out.println(map); // {5=lions,bears, 6=tigers}
System.out.println(map.getClass());  // java.util.concurrent.ConcurrentHashMap
```

We use a ConcurrentMap reference, although the actual class returned is likely ConcurrentHashMap. The particular class is not guaranteed; it will just be a class that implements the interface ConcurrentMap.

Finally, we can rewrite our groupingBy() example from Chapter 4 to use a parallel stream and parallel reduction.

```
var ohMy = Stream.of("lions","tigers","bears").parallel();
ConcurrentMap<Integer, List<String>> map = ohMy.collect(
   Collectors.groupingByConcurrent(String::length));
System.out.println(map); // {5=[lions, bears], 6=[tigers]}
```

As before, the returned object can be assigned a ConcurrentMap reference.

Encouraging Parallel Processing

Guaranteeing that a particular stream will perform reductions in parallel, as opposed to single-threaded, is often difficult in practice. For example, the one-argument reduce() operation on a parallel stream may perform concurrently even when there is no explicit combiner argument. Alternatively, you may expect some collectors to perform well on a parallel stream, resorting to single-threaded processing at runtime.

The key to applying parallel reductions is to encourage the JVM to take advantage of the parallel structures, such as using a groupingByConcurrent() collector on a parallel stream rather than a groupingBy() collector. By encouraging the JVM to take advantage of the parallel processing, we get the best possible performance at runtime.

Avoiding Stateful Operations

Side effects can appear in parallel streams if your lambda expressions are stateful. A *stateful lambda expression* is one whose result depends on any state that might change during the execution of a pipeline. On the other hand, a *stateless lambda expression* is one whose result does not depend on any state that might change during the execution of a pipeline.

Let's try an example. Imagine we require a method that keeps only even numbers in a stream and adds them to a list. Also, we want ordering of the numbers in the stream and list to be consistent. The following addValues() method accomplishes this:

```java
public List<Integer> addValues(IntStream source) {
    var data = Collections.synchronizedList(new ArrayList<Integer>());
    source.filter(s -> s % 2 == 0)
        .forEach(i -> { data.add(i); });   // STATEFUL: DON'T DO THIS!
    return data;
}
```

Let's say this method is executed with the following stream:

```java
var list = addValues(IntStream.range(1, 11));
System.out.println(list);
```

Then, the output would be as follows:

```
[2, 4, 6, 8, 10]
```

But what if someone else wrote an implementation that passed our method a parallel stream?

```java
var list = addValues(IntStream.range(1, 11).parallel());
System.out.println(list);
```

With a parallel stream, the order of the output becomes random.

```
[6, 8, 10, 2, 4]
```

The problem is that our lambda expression is stateful and modifies a list that is outside our stream. We could use forEachOrdered() to add elements to the list, but that forces the parallel stream to be serial, potentially losing concurrency enhancements. While these stream operations in our example are quite simple, imagine using them alongside numerous intermediate operations.

We can fix this solution by rewriting our stream operation to no longer have a stateful lambda expression.

```java
public static List<Integer> addValues(IntStream source) {
    return source.filter(s -> s % 2 == 0)
        .boxed()
        .collect(Collectors.toList());
}
```

This method processes the stream and then collects all the results into a new list. It produces the same result on both serial and parallel streams.

```
[2, 4, 6, 8, 10]
```

This implementation removes the stateful operation and relies on the collector to assemble the elements. We could also use a concurrent collector to parallelize the building of the list. The goal is to write our code to allow for parallel processing and let the JVM handle the rest.

It is strongly recommended that you avoid stateful operations when using parallel streams, so as to remove any potential data side effects. In fact, they should be avoided in serial streams since doing so limits the code's ability to someday take advantage of parallelization.

Summary

This chapter introduced you to threads and showed you how to process tasks in parallel using the Concurrency API. The work that a thread performs can be expressed as lambda expressions or instances of Runnable or Callable.

For the exam, you should know how to concurrently execute tasks using ExecutorService. You should also know which ExecutorService instances are available, including scheduled and pooled services.

Thread-safety is about protecting data from being corrupted by multiple threads modifying it at the same time. Java offers many tools to keep data safe including atomic classes, synchronized methods/blocks, the Lock framework, and CyclicBarrier. The Concurrency API also includes numerous collections classes that handle multithreaded access for you. For the exam, you should also be familiar with the concurrent collections including the CopyOnWriteArrayList class, which creates a new underlying structure anytime the list is modified.

When processing tasks concurrently, a variety of potential threading issues can arise. Deadlock, starvation, and livelock can result in programs that appear stuck, while race conditions can result in unpredictable data. For the exam, you need to know only the basic theory behind these concepts. In professional software development, however, finding and resolving such problems is often quite challenging.

Finally, we discussed parallel streams and showed you how to use them to perform parallel decompositions and reductions. Parallel streams can greatly improve the performance of your application. They can also cause unexpected results since the results are no longer ordered. Remember to avoid stateful lambda expressions, especially when working with parallel streams.

Exam Essentials

Create concurrent tasks with a thread executor service using *Runnable* and *Callable*.
An ExecutorService creates and manages a single thread or a pool of threads. Instances
of Runnable and Callable can both be submitted to a thread executor and will be
completed using the available threads in the service. Callable differs from Runnable
in that Callable returns a generic data type and can throw a checked exception.
A ScheduledExecutorService can be used to schedule tasks at a fixed rate or a fixed
interval between executions.

Be able to apply the atomic classes.   An atomic operation is one that occurs without interference by another thread. The Concurrency API includes a set of atomic classes that are
similar to the primitive classes, except that they ensure that operations on them are performed atomically.

Be able to write thread-safe code.   Thread-safety is about protecting shared data
from concurrent access. A monitor can be used to ensure that only one thread processes
a particular section of code at a time. In Java, monitors can be implemented with a
synchronized block or method or using an instance of Lock. ReentrantLock has a
number of advantages over using a synchronized block including the ability to check
whether a lock is available without blocking on it, as well as supporting fair acquisi-
tion of locks. To achieve synchronization, two threads must synchronize on the same
shared object.

Manage a process with a *CyclicBarrier*.   The CyclicBarrier class can be used to force a
set of threads to wait until they are at a certain stage of execution before continuing.

Be able to use the concurrent collection classes.   The Concurrency API includes numerous
collection classes that include built-in support for multithreaded processing, such as
ConcurrentHashMap. It also includes a class CopyOnWriteArrayList that creates a copy
of its underlying list structure every time it is modified and is useful in highly concurrent
environments.

Identify potential threading problems.   Deadlock, starvation, and livelock are three
threading problems that can occur and result in threads never completing their task.
Deadlock occurs when two or more threads are blocked forever. Starvation occurs when
a single thread is perpetually denied access to a shared resource. Livelock is a form of
starvation where two or more threads are active but conceptually blocked forever. Finally,
race conditions occur when two threads execute at the same time, resulting in an unexpected outcome.

Understand the impact of using parallel streams.   The Stream API allows for easy
creation of parallel streams. Using a parallel stream can cause unexpected results, since the
order of operations may no longer be predictable. Some operations, such as reduce() and
collect(), require special consideration to achieve optimal performance when applied to a
parallel stream.

Review Questions

The answers to the chapter review questions can be found in Appendix B.

1. Given an instance of a `Stream` s and a `Collection` c, which are valid ways of creating a parallel stream? (Choose all that apply.)

    A. `new ParallelStream(s)`

    B. `c.parallel()`

    C. `s.parallelStream()`

    D. `c.parallelStream()`

    E. `new ParallelStream(c)`

    F. `s.parallel()`

2. Given that the sum of the numbers from 1 (inclusive) to 10 (exclusive) is 45, what are the possible results of executing the following program? (Choose all that apply.)

    ```
    import java.util.concurrent.locks.*;
    import java.util.stream.*;
    public class Bank {
        private Lock vault = new ReentrantLock();
        private int total = 0;
        public void deposit(int value) {
            try {
                vault.tryLock();
                total += value;
            } finally {
                vault.unlock();
            }
        }
        public static void main(String[] unused) {
            var bank = new Bank();
            IntStream.range(1, 10).parallel()
                .forEach(s -> bank.deposit(s));
            System.out.println(bank.total);
        } }
    ```

    A. 45 is printed.

    B. A number less than 45 is printed.

    C. A number greater than 45 is printed.

    D. An exception is thrown.

    E. None of the above, as the code does not compile

3. Which of the following statements about the `Callable` `call()` and `Runnable` `run()` methods are correct? (Choose all that apply.)

    A. Both can throw unchecked exceptions.

    B. `Callable` takes a generic method argument.

    C. `Callable` can throw a checked exception.

    D. Both can be implemented with lambda expressions.

    E. `Runnable` returns a generic type.

    F. `Callable` returns a generic type.

    G. Both methods return `void`.

4. Which lines need to be changed to make the code compile? (Choose all that apply.)

```
ExecutorService service =    // w1
    Executors.newSingleThreadScheduledExecutor();
service.scheduleWithFixedDelay(() -> {
    System.out.println("Open Zoo");
    return null;    // w2
}, 0, 1, TimeUnit.MINUTES);
var result = service.submit(() ->    // w3
    System.out.println("Wake Staff"));
System.out.println(result.get());    // w4
```

    A. It compiles and runs without issue.

    B. Line w1

    C. Line w2

    D. Line w3

    E. Line w4

    F. It compiles but throws an exception at runtime.

    G. None of the above

5. What statement about the following code is true?

```
var value1 = new AtomicLong(0);
final long[] value2 = {0};
IntStream.iterate(1, i -> 1).limit(100).parallel()
    .forEach(i -> value1.incrementAndGet());
IntStream.iterate(1, i -> 1).limit(100).parallel()
    .forEach(i -> ++value2[0]);
System.out.println(value1+" "+value2[0]);
```

    A. It outputs 100 100.

    B. It outputs 100 99.

C. The output cannot be determined ahead of time.

D. The code does not compile.

E. It compiles but throws an exception at runtime.

F. It compiles but enters an infinite loop at runtime.

G. None of the above

6. Which statements about the following code are correct? (Choose all that apply.)

```java
public static void main(String[] args) throws Exception {
    var data = List.of(2,5,1,9,8);
    data.stream().parallel()
        .mapToInt(s -> s)
        .peek(System.out::println)
        .forEachOrdered(System.out::println);
}
```

A. The peek() method will print the entries in the order: 1 2 5 8 9.

B. The peek() method will print the entries in the order: 2 5 1 9 8.

C. The peek() method will print the entries in an order that cannot be determined ahead of time.

D. The forEachOrdered() method will print the entries in the order: 1 2 5 8 9.

E. The forEachOrdered() method will print the entries in the order: 2 5 1 9 8.

F. The forEachOrdered() method will print the entries in an order that cannot be determined ahead of time.

G. The code does not compile.

7. Fill in the blanks:_____ occur(s) when two or more threads are blocked forever but both appear active. _____ occur(s) when two or more threads try to complete a related task at the same time, resulting in invalid or unexpected data.

A. Livelock, Deadlock

B. Deadlock, Starvation

C. Race conditions, Deadlock

D. Livelock, Race conditions

E. Starvation, Race conditions

F. Deadlock, Livelock

8. Assuming this class is accessed by only a single thread at a time, what is the result of calling the countIceCreamFlavors() method?

```java
import java.util.stream.LongStream;
public class Flavors {
    private static int counter;
    public static void countIceCreamFlavors()  {
```

```
            counter = 0;
            Runnable task = () -> counter++;
            LongStream.range(1, 500)
                .forEach(m -> new Thread(task).run());
            System.out.println(counter);
        }
    }
```

A. The method consistently prints 499.

B. The method consistently prints 500.

C. The method compiles and prints a value, but that value cannot be determined ahead of time.

D. The method does not compile.

E. The method compiles but throws an exception at runtime.

F. None of the above

9. Which happens when a new task is submitted to an ExecutorService, in which there are no threads available?

A. The executor throws an exception when the task is submitted.

B. The executor discards the task without completing it.

C. The executor adds the task to an internal queue and completes when there is an available thread.

D. The thread submitting the task waits on the submit call until a thread is available before continuing.

E. The executor creates a new temporary thread to complete the task.

10. What is the result of executing the following code snippet?

```
List<Integer> lions = new ArrayList<>(List.of(1,2,3));
List<Integer> tigers = new CopyOnWriteArrayList<>(lions);
Set<Integer> bears = new ConcurrentSkipListSet<>();
bears.addAll(lions);
for(Integer item: tigers) tigers.add(4); // x1
for(Integer item: bears) bears.add(5); // x2
System.out.println(lions.size() + " " + tigers.size()
    + " " + bears.size());
```

A. It outputs 3 6 4.

B. It outputs 6 6 6.

C. It outputs 6 3 4.

D. The code does not compile.

E. It compiles but throws an exception at runtime on line x1.

F. It compiles but throws an exception at runtime on line x2.

G. It compiles but enters an infinite loop at runtime.

11. What statements about the following code are true? (Choose all that apply.)

```
Integer i1 = List.of(1, 2, 3, 4, 5).stream().findAny().get();
synchronized(i1) { // y1
    Integer i2 = List.of(6, 7, 8, 9, 10)
        .parallelStream()
        .sorted()
        .findAny().get(); // y2
    System.out.println(i1 + " " + i2);
}
```

A. The first value printed is always 1.

B. The second value printed is always 6.

C. The code will not compile because of line y1.

D. The code will not compile because of line y2.

E. The code compiles but throws an exception at runtime.

F. The output cannot be determined ahead of time.

G. It compiles but waits forever at runtime.

12. Assuming `takeNap()` is a method that takes five seconds to execute without throwing an exception, what is the expected result of executing the following code snippet?

```
ExecutorService service = null;
try {
    service = Executors.newFixedThreadPool(4);
    service.execute(() -> takeNap());
    service.execute(() -> takeNap());
    service.execute(() -> takeNap());
} finally {
    if (service != null) service.shutdown();
}
service.awaitTermination(2, TimeUnit.SECONDS);
System.out.println("DONE!");
```

A. It will immediately print DONE!.

B. It will pause for 2 seconds and then print DONE!.

C. It will pause for 5 seconds and then print DONE!.

D. It will pause for 15 seconds and then print DONE!.

E. It will throw an exception at runtime.

F. None of the above, as the code does not compile

13. What statements about the following code are true? (Choose all that apply.)

```
System.out.print(List.of("duck","flamingo","pelican")
    .parallelStream().parallel()    // q1
    .reduce(0,
        (c1, c2) -> c1.length() + c2.length(),    // q2
        (s1, s2) -> s1 + s2));    // q3
```

    A. It compiles and runs without issue, outputting the total length of all strings in the stream.

    B. The code will not compile because of line q1.

    C. The code will not compile because of line q2.

    D. The code will not compile because of line q3.

    E. It compiles but throws an exception at runtime.

    F. None of the above

14. What statements about the following code snippet are true? (Choose all that apply.)

```
Object o1 = new Object();
Object o2 = new Object();
var service = Executors.newFixedThreadPool(2);
var f1 = service.submit(() -> {
    synchronized (o1) {
        synchronized (o2) { System.out.print("Tortoise"); }
    }
});
var f2 = service.submit(() -> {
    synchronized (o2) {
        synchronized (o1) { System.out.print("Hare"); }
    }
});
f1.get();
f2.get();
```

    A. The code will always output `Tortoise` followed by `Hare`.

    B. The code will always output `Hare` followed by `Tortoise`.

    C. If the code does output anything, the order cannot be determined.

    D. The code does not compile.

    E. The code compiles but may produce a deadlock at runtime.

    F. The code compiles but may produce a livelock at runtime.

    G. It compiles but throws an exception at runtime.

15. Which statement about the following code snippet is correct?

```
2: var cats = Stream.of("leopard", "lynx", "ocelot", "puma")
3:    .parallel();
4: var bears = Stream.of("panda","grizzly","polar").parallel();
5: var data = Stream.of(cats,bears).flatMap(s -> s)
6:    .collect(Collectors.groupingByConcurrent(
7:       s -> !s.startsWith("p")));
8: System.out.println(data.get(false).size()
9:    + " " + data.get(true).size());
```

A. It outputs 3 4.

B. It outputs 4 3.

C. The code will not compile because of line 6.

D. The code will not compile because of line 7.

E. The code will not compile because of line 8.

F. It compiles but throws an exception at runtime.

16. Which statements about methods in ReentrantLock are correct? (Choose all that apply.)

A. The lock() method will attempt to acquire a lock without waiting indefinitely for it.

B. The testLock() method will attempt to acquire a lock without waiting indefinitely for it.

C. The attemptLock() method will attempt to acquire a lock without waiting indefinitely for it.

D. By default, a ReentrantLock fairly releases to each thread, in the order that it was requested.

E. Calling the unlock() method once will release a resource so that other threads can obtain the lock.

F. None of the above

17. What is the result of calling the following method?

```
3: public void addAndPrintItems(BlockingQueue<Integer> queue) {
4:    queue.offer(103);
5:    queue.offer(20, 1, TimeUnit.SECONDS);
6:    queue.offer(85, 7, TimeUnit.HOURS);
7:    System.out.print(queue.poll(200, TimeUnit.NANOSECONDS));
8:    System.out.print(" " + queue.poll(1, TimeUnit.MINUTES));
9: }
```

A. It outputs 20 85.

B. It outputs 103 20.

C. It outputs 20 103.

D. The code will not compile.

E. It compiles but throws an exception at runtime.

F. The output cannot be determined ahead of time.

G. None of the above

18. Which of the following are valid `Callable` expressions? (Choose all that apply.)

   A. `a -> {return 10;}`

   B. `() -> {String s = "";}`

   C. `() -> 5`

   D. `() -> {return null}`

   E. `() -> "The" + "Zoo"`

   F. `(int count) -> count+1`

   G. `() -> {System.out.println("Giraffe"); return 10;}`

19. What is the result of executing the following application? (Choose all that apply.)

    ```
    import java.util.concurrent.*;
    import java.util.stream.*;
    public class PrintConstants {
        public static void main(String[] args) {
            var s = Executors.newScheduledThreadPool(10);
            DoubleStream.of(3.14159,2.71828)    // b1
                .forEach(c -> s.submit(  // b2
                    () -> System.out.println(10*c)));    // b3
            s.execute(() -> System.out.println("Printed"));    // b4
        }
    }
    ```

   A. It compiles and outputs the two numbers, followed by `Printed`.

   B. The code will not compile because of line b1.

   C. The code will not compile because of line b2.

   D. The code will not compile because of line b3.

   E. The code will not compile because of line b4.

   F. It compiles, but the output cannot be determined ahead of time.

   G. It compiles but throws an exception at runtime.

   H. It compiles but waits forever at runtime.

20. What is the result of executing the following program? (Choose all that apply.)

    ```
    import java.util.*;
    import java.util.concurrent.*;
    import java.util.stream.*;
    ```

```
public class PrintCounter {
    static int count = 0;
    public static void main(String[] args) throws
                        InterruptedException, ExecutionException {
        ExecutorService service = null;
        try {
            service = Executors.newSingleThreadExecutor();
            var r = new ArrayList<Future<?>>();
            IntStream.iterate(0,i -> i+1).limit(5).forEach(
                i -> r.add(service.execute(() -> {count++;})) // n1
            );
            for(Future<?> result : r) {
                System.out.print(result.get()+" "); // n2
            }
        } finally {
            if(service != null) service.shutdown();
        } } }
```

A. It prints 0 1 2 3 4.

B. It prints 1 2 3 4 5.

C. It prints null null null null null.

D. It hangs indefinitely at runtime.

E. The output cannot be determined.

F. The code will not compile because of line n1.

G. The code will not compile because of line n2.

21. Given the following code snippet and blank lines on p1 and p2, which values guarantee 1 is printed at runtime? (Choose all that apply.)

```
var data = List.of(List.of(1,2),
    List.of(3,4),
    List.of(5,6));
data. _____  // p1
    .flatMap(s -> s.stream())
    . _____  // p2
    .ifPresent(System.out::print);
```

A. stream() on line p1, findFirst() on line p2.

B. stream() on line p1, findAny() on line p2.

C. parallelStream() in line p1, findAny() on line p2.

D. parallelStream() in line p1, findFirst() on line p2.

E. The code does not compile regardless of what is inserted into the blank.

F. None of the above

22. Assuming 100 milliseconds is enough time for the tasks submitted to the service executor to complete, what is the result of executing the following method? (Choose all that apply.)

```java
private AtomicInteger s1 = new AtomicInteger(0); // w1
private int s2 = 0;

private void countSheep() throws InterruptedException {
    ExecutorService service = null;
    try {
        service = Executors.newSingleThreadExecutor(); // w2
        for (int i = 0; i < 100; i++)
            service.execute(() -> {
                s1.getAndIncrement(); s2++; }); // w3
        Thread.sleep(100);
        System.out.println(s1 + " " + s2);
    } finally {
        if(service != null) service.shutdown();
    }
}
```

A. The method consistently prints 100 99.

B. The method consistently prints 100 100.

C. The output cannot be determined ahead of time.

D. The code will not compile because of line w1.

E. The code will not compile because of line w2.

F. The code will not compile because of line w3.

G. It compiles but throws an exception at runtime.

23. What is the result of executing the following application? (Choose all that apply.)

```java
import java.util.concurrent.*;
import java.util.stream.*;
public class StockRoomTracker {
    public static void await(CyclicBarrier cb) { // j1
        try { cb.await(); } catch (Exception e) {}
    }
    public static void main(String[] args) {
        var cb = new CyclicBarrier(10,
            () -> System.out.println("Stock Room Full!")); // j2
```

```
        IntStream.iterate(1, i -> 1).limit(9).parallel()
            .forEach(i -> await(cb)); // j3
    }
}
```

A. It outputs Stock Room Full!

B. The code will not compile because of line j1.

C. The code will not compile because of line j2.

D. The code will not compile because of line j3.

E. It compiles but throws an exception at runtime.

F. It compiles but waits forever at runtime.

24. What statements about the following class definition are true? (Choose all that apply.)

```
public class TicketManager {
    private int tickets;
    private static TicketManager instance;
    private TicketManager() {}
    static synchronized TicketManager getInstance() {      // k1
        if (instance==null) instance = new TicketManager(); // k2
        return instance;
    }

    public int getTicketCount() { return tickets; }
    public void addTickets(int value) {tickets += value;}  // k3
    public void sellTickets(int value) {
        synchronized (this) { // k4
            tickets -= value;
        }
    }
}
```

A. It compiles without issue.

B. The code will not compile because of line k2.

C. The code will not compile because of line k3.

D. The locks acquired on k1 and k4 are on the same object.

E. The class correctly protects the tickets data from race conditions.

F. At most one instance of TicketManager will be created in an application that uses this class.

25. Which of the following properties of concurrency are true? (Choose all that apply.)

   A. By itself, concurrency does not guarantee which task will be completed first.

   B. Concurrency always improves the performance of an application.

   C. A computer with a single-processor CPU does not benefit from concurrency.

   D. Applications with many resource-heavy tasks tend to benefit more from concurrency than ones with CPU-intensive tasks.

   E. Concurrent tasks do not share the same memory.

26. Assuming an implementation of the `performCount()` method is provided prior to runtime, which of the following are possible results of executing the following application? (Choose all that apply.)

```java
import java.util.*;
import java.util.concurrent.*;
public class CountZooAnimals {
    public static void performCount(int animal) {
        // IMPLEMENTATION OMITTED
    }
    public static void printResults(Future<?> f) {
        try {
            System.out.println(f.get(1, TimeUnit.DAYS)); // o1
        } catch (Exception e) {
            System.out.println("Exception!");
        }
    }
    public static void main(String[] args) throws Exception {
        ExecutorService s = null;
        final var r = new ArrayList<Future<?>>();
        try {
            s = Executors.newSingleThreadExecutor();
            for(int i = 0; i < 10; i++) {
                final int animal = i;
                r.add(s.submit(() -> performCount(animal))); // o2
            }
            r.forEach(f -> printResults(f));
        } finally {
            if(s != null) s.shutdown();
        } } }
```

A. It outputs a number 10 times.

B. It outputs a Boolean value 10 times.

C. It outputs a null value 10 times.

D. It outputs Exception! 10 times.

E. It hangs indefinitely at runtime.

F. The code will not compile because of line o1.

G. The code will not compile because of line o2.

Chapter

8

I/O

OCP EXAM OBJECTIVES COVERED IN THIS CHAPTER:

✓ **I/O (Fundamentals and NIO2)**

- Read data from and write console and file data using I/O Streams

- Use I/O Streams to read and write files

- Read and write objects by using serialization

What can Java applications do outside the scope of managing objects and attributes in memory? How can they save data so that information is not lost every time the program is terminated? They use files, of course! You can design code that writes the current state of an application to a file every time the application is closed and then reloads the data when the application is executed the next time. In this manner, information is preserved between program executions.

This chapter focuses on using the `java.io` API to interact with files and streams. We start by describing how files and directories are organized within a file system and show how to access them with the `java.io.File` class. We then show how to read and write file data with the stream classes. We conclude this chapter by discussing ways of reading user input at runtime using the `Console` class.

In Chapter 9, "NIO.2," we will revisit the discussion of files and directories and show how Java provides more powerful techniques for managing files.

> When we refer to streams in this chapter, we are referring to the I/O streams found in the `java.io` API (unless otherwise specified). I/O streams are completely unrelated to the streams you saw in Chapter 4, "Functional Programming." We agree that the naming can be a bit confusing!

Understanding Files and Directories

We begin this chapter by reviewing what a file and directory are within a file system. We also present the `java.io.File` class and demonstrate how to use it to read and write file information.

Conceptualizing the File System

We start with the basics. Data is stored on persistent storage devices, such as hard disk drives and memory cards. A *file* is a record within the storage device that holds data. Files are organized into hierarchies using directories. A *directory* is a location that can contain files as well as other directories. When working with directories in Java, we often treat them like files. In fact, we use many of the same classes to operate on files and directories. For example, a file and directory both can be renamed with the same Java method.

To interact with files, we need to connect to the file system. The *file system* is in charge of reading and writing data within a computer. Different operating systems use different file systems to manage their data. For example, Windows-based systems use a different file system than Unix-based ones. For the exam, you just need to know how to issue commands using the Java APIs. The JVM will automatically connect to the local file system, allowing you to perform the same operations across multiple platforms.

Next, the *root directory* is the topmost directory in the file system, from which all files and directories inherit. In Windows, it is denoted with a drive name such as c:\, while on Linux it is denoted with a single forward slash, /.

Finally, a *path* is a String representation of a file or directory within a file system. Each file system defines its own path separator character that is used between directory entries. The value to the left of a separator is the parent of the value to the right of the separator. For example, the path value /user/home/zoo.txt means that the file zoo.txt is inside the home directory, with the home directory inside the user directory. You will see that paths can be absolute or relative later in this chapter.

We show how a directory and file system is organized in a hierarchical manner in Figure 8.1.

FIGURE 8.1 Directory and file hierarchy

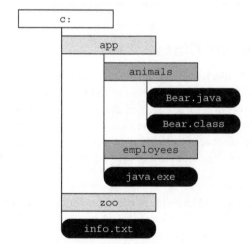

This diagram shows the root directory, c:, as containing two directories, app and zoo, along with the file info.txt. Within the app directory, there are two more folders, animals and employees, along with the file java.exe. Finally, the animals directory contains two files, Bear.java and Bear.class.

Storing Data as Bytes

Data is stored in a file system (and memory) as a 0 or 1, called a *bit*. Since it's really hard for humans to read/write data that is just 0s and 1s, they are grouped into a set of 8 bits, called a *byte*.

What about the Java byte primitive type? As you'll see later when we get to I/O streams, values are often read or written streams using byte values and arrays.

 Real World Scenario

The ASCII Characters

Using a little arithmetic (2^8), we see a byte can be set in one of 256 possible permutations. These 256 values form the alphabet for our computer system to be able to type characters like a, #, and 7.

Historically, the 256 characters are referred to as ASCII characters, based on the encoding standard that defined them. Given all of the languages and emojis available today, 256 characters is actually pretty limiting. Many newer standards have been developed that rely on additional bytes to display characters.

Introducing the *File* Class

The first class that we will discuss is one of the most commonly used in the java.io API: the java.io.File class. The File class is used to read information about existing files and directories, list the contents of a directory, and create/delete files and directories.

An instance of a File class represents the path to a particular file or directory on the file system. The File class cannot read or write data within a file, although it can be passed as a reference to many stream classes to read or write data, as you will see in the next section.

    Remember, a File instance can represent a file or a directory.

Creating a File Object

A File object often is initialized with a String containing either an absolute or relative path to the file or directory within the file system. The *absolute path* of a file or directory is the full path from the root directory to the file or directory, including all subdirectories that contain the file or directory. Alternatively, the *relative path* of a file or directory is the path from the current working directory to the file or directory. For example, the following is an absolute path to the stripes.txt file:

```
/home/tiger/data/stripes.txt
```

The following is a relative path to the same file, assuming the user's current directory is set to /home/tiger:

```
data/stripes.txt
```

Different operating systems vary in their format of pathnames. For example, Unix-based systems use the forward slash, /, for paths, whereas Windows-based systems use the backslash, \, character. That said, many programming languages and file systems support both types of slashes when writing path statements. For convenience, Java offers two options to retrieve the local separator character: a system property and a static variable defined in the File class. Both of the following examples will output the separator character for the current environment:

```
System.out.println(System.getProperty("file.separator"));
System.out.println(java.io.File.separator);
```

The following code creates a File object and determines whether the path it references exists within the file system:

```
var zooFile1 = new File("/home/tiger/data/stripes.txt");
System.out.println(zooFile1.exists());   // true if the file exists
```

This example provides the absolute path to a file and outputs true or false, depending on whether the file exists. There are three File constructors you should know for the exam.

```
public File(String pathname)
```

```
public File(File parent, String child)
```

```
public File(String parent, String child)
```

The first one creates a File from a String path. The other two constructors are used to create a File from a parent and child path, such as the following:

```
File zooFile2 = new File("/home/tiger", "data/stripes.txt");
```

```
File parent = new File("/home/tiger");
File zooFile3 = new File(parent, "data/stripes.txt");
```

In this example, we create two new File instances that are equivalent to our earlier zooFile1 instance. If the parent instance is null, then it would be skipped, and the method would revert to the single String constructor.

The *File* Object vs. the Actual File

When working with an instance of the File class, keep in mind that it only represents a path to a file. Unless operated upon, it is not connected to an actual file within the file system.

For example, you can create a new `File` object to test whether a file exists within the system. You can then call various methods to read file properties within the file system. There are also methods to modify the name or location of a file, as well as delete it.

The JVM and underlying file system will read or modify the file using the methods you call on the `File` class. If you try to operate on a file that does not exist or you do not have access to, some `File` methods will throw an exception. Other methods will return `false` if the file does not exist or the operation cannot be performed.

Working with a *File* Object

The `File` class contains numerous useful methods for interacting with files and directories within the file system. We present the most commonly used ones in Table 8.1. Although this table may seem like a lot of methods to learn, many of them are self-explanatory.

TABLE 8.1   Commonly used `java.io.File` methods

Method Name	Description
`boolean delete()`	Deletes the file or directory and returns `true` only if successful. If this instance denotes a directory, then the directory must be empty in order to be deleted.
`boolean exists()`	Checks if a file exists
`String getAbsolutePath()`	Retrieves the absolute name of the file or directory within the file system
`String getName()`	Retrieves the name of the file or directory.
`String getParent()`	Retrieves the parent directory that the path is contained in or `null` if there is none
`boolean isDirectory()`	Checks if a `File` reference is a directory within the file system
`boolean isFile()`	Checks if a `File` reference is a file within the file system
`long lastModified()`	Returns the number of milliseconds since the epoch (number of milliseconds since 12 a.m. UTC on January 1, 1970) when the file was last modified
`long length()`	Retrieves the number of bytes in the file
`File[] listFiles()`	Retrieves a list of files within a directory
`boolean mkdir()`	Creates the directory named by this path

Method Name	Description
boolean mkdirs()	Creates the directory named by this path including any nonexistent parent directories
boolean renameTo(File dest)	Renames the file or directory denoted by this path to dest and returns true only if successful

The following is a sample program that given a file path outputs information about the file or directory, such as whether it exists, what files are contained within it, and so forth:

```
var file = new File("c:\\data\\zoo.txt");
System.out.println("File Exists: " + file.exists());
if (file.exists()) {
   System.out.println("Absolute Path: " + file.getAbsolutePath());
   System.out.println("Is Directory: " + file.isDirectory());
   System.out.println("Parent Path: " + file.getParent());
   if (file.isFile()) {
      System.out.println("Size: " + file.length());
      System.out.println("Last Modified: " + file.lastModified());
   } else {
      for (File subfile : file.listFiles()) {
         System.out.println("   " + subfile.getName());
      }
   }
}
```

If the path provided did not point to a file, it would output the following:

```
File Exists: false
```

If the path provided pointed to a valid file, it would output something similar to the following:

```
File Exists: true
Absolute Path: c:\data\zoo.txt
Is Directory: false
Parent Path: c:\data
Size: 12382
Last Modified: 1606860000000
```

Finally, if the path provided pointed to a valid directory, such as c:\data, it would output something similar to the following:

```
File Exists: true
Absolute Path: c:\data
Is Directory: true
Parent Path: c:\
    employees.txt
    zoo.txt
    zoo-backup.txt
```

In these examples, you see that the output of an I/O-based program is completely dependent on the directories and files available at runtime in the underlying file system.

On the exam, you might get paths that look like files but are directories, or vice versa. For example, /data/zoo.txt could be a file or a directory, even though it has a file extension. Don't assume it is either unless the question tells you it is!

In the previous example, we used two backslashes (\\) in the path String, such as c:\\data\\zoo.txt. When the compiler sees a \\ inside a String expression, it interprets it as a single \ value.

Introducing I/O Streams

Now that we have the basics out of the way, let's move on to I/O streams, which are far more interesting. In this section, we will show you how to use I/O streams to read and write data. The "I/O" refers to the nature of how data is accessed, either by reading the data from a resource (input) or by writing the data to a resource (output).

Understanding I/O Stream Fundamentals

The contents of a file may be accessed or written via a *stream*, which is a list of data elements presented sequentially. Streams should be conceptually thought of as a long, nearly never-ending "stream of water" with data presented one "wave" at a time.

We demonstrate this principle in Figure 8.2. The stream is so large that once we start reading it, we have no idea where the beginning or the end is. We just have a pointer to our current position in the stream and read data one block at a time.

Each type of stream segments data into a "wave" or "block" in a particular way. For example, some stream classes read or write data as individual bytes. Other stream classes read or write individual characters or strings of characters. On top of that, some stream classes read or write larger groups of bytes or characters at a time, specifically those with the word Buffered in their name.

FIGURE 8.2   Visual representation of a stream

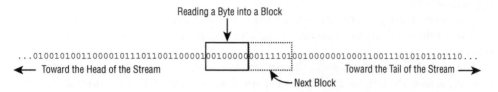

All Java I/O Streams Use Bytes

Although the java.io API is full of streams that handle characters, strings, groups of bytes, and so on, nearly all are built on top of reading or writing an individual byte or an array of bytes at a time. The reason higher-level streams exist is for convenience, as well as performance.

For example, writing a file one byte at a time is time-consuming and slow in practice because the round-trip between the Java application and the file system is relatively expensive. By utilizing a BufferedOutputStream, the Java application can write a large chunk of bytes at a time, reducing the round-trips and drastically improving performance.

Although streams are commonly used with file I/O, they are more generally used to handle the reading/writing of any sequential data source. For example, you might construct a Java application that submits data to a website using an output stream and reads the result via an input stream.

I/O Streams Can Be Big

When writing code where you don't know what the stream size will be at runtime, it may be helpful to visualize a stream as being so large that all of the data contained in it could not possibly fit into memory. For example, a 1 terabyte file could not be stored entirely in memory by most computer systems (at the time this book is being written). The file can still be read and written by a program with very little memory, since the stream allows the application to focus on only a small portion of the overall stream at any given time.

Learning I/O Stream Nomenclature

The java.io API provides numerous classes for creating, accessing, and manipulating streams—so many that it tends to overwhelm many new Java developers. Stay calm!

We will review the major differences between each stream class and show you how to distinguish between them.

Even if you come across a particular stream on the exam that you do not recognize, often the name of the stream gives you enough information to understand exactly what it does.

The goal of this section is to familiarize you with common terminology and naming conventions used with streams. Don't worry if you don't recognize the particular stream class names used in this section or their function; we'll be covering each in detail in the next part of the chapter.

Byte Streams vs. Character Streams

The java.io API defines two sets of stream classes for reading and writing streams: byte streams and character streams. We will use both types of streams throughout this chapter.

Differences between Byte and Character Streams

- Byte streams read/write binary data (0s and 1s) and have class names that end in InputStream or OutputStream.

- Character streams read/write text data and have class names that end in Reader or Writer.

The API frequently includes similar classes for both byte and character streams, such as FileInputStream and FileReader. The difference between the two classes is based on how the bytes of the stream are read or written.

It is important to remember that even though character streams do not contain the word Stream in their class name, they are still I/O streams. The use of Reader/Writer in the name is just to distinguish them from byte streams.

Throughout the chapter, we will refer to both InputStream and Reader as *input streams*, and we will refer to both OutputStream and Writer as *output streams*.

The byte streams are primarily used to work with binary data, such as an image or executable file, while character streams are used to work with text files. Since the byte stream classes can write all types of binary data, including strings, it follows that the character stream classes aren't strictly necessary. There are advantages, though, to using the character stream classes, as they are specifically focused on managing character and string data. For example, you can use a Writer class to output a String value to a file without necessarily having to worry about the underlying character encoding of the file.

The *character encoding* determines how characters are encoded and stored in bytes in a stream and later read back or decoded as characters. Although this may sound simple, Java supports a wide variety of character encodings, ranging from ones that may use one byte for Latin characters, UTF-8 and ASCII for example, to using two or more bytes per character, such as UTF-16. For the exam, you don't need to memorize the character encodings, but you should be familiar with the names if you come across them on the exam.

Character Encoding in Java

In Java, the character encoding can be specified using the Charset class by passing a name value to the static Charset.forName() method, such as in the following examples:

```
Charset usAsciiCharset = Charset.forName("US-ASCII");
Charset utf8Charset = Charset.forName("UTF-8");
Charset utf16Charset = Charset.forName("UTF-16");
```

Java supports numerous character encodings, each specified by a different standard name value.

For character encoding, just remember that using a character stream is better for working with text data than a byte stream. The character stream classes were created for convenience, and you should certainly take advantage of them when possible.

Input vs. Output Streams

Most InputStream stream classes have a corresponding OutputStream class, and vice versa. For example, the FileOutputStream class writes data that can be read by a FileInputStream. If you understand the features of a particular Input or Output stream class, you should naturally know what its complementary class does.

It follows, then, that most Reader classes have a corresponding Writer class. For example, the FileWriter class writes data that can be read by a FileReader.

There are exceptions to this rule. For the exam, you should know that PrintWriter has no accompanying PrintReader class. Likewise, the PrintStream is an OutputStream that has no corresponding InputStream class. It also does not have Output in its name. We will discuss these classes later this chapter.

Low-Level vs. High-Level Streams

Another way that you can familiarize yourself with the java.io API is by segmenting streams into low-level and high-level streams.

A *low-level stream* connects directly with the source of the data, such as a file, an array, or a String. Low-level streams process the raw data or resource and are accessed in a direct and unfiltered manner. For example, a FileInputStream is a class that reads file data one byte at a time.

Alternatively, a *high-level stream* is built on top of another stream using wrapping. *Wrapping* is the process by which an instance is passed to the constructor of another class, and operations on the resulting instance are filtered and applied to the original instance. For example, take a look at the FileReader and BufferedReader objects in the following sample code:

```
try (var br = new BufferedReader(new FileReader("zoo-data.txt"))) {
    System.out.println(br.readLine());
}
```

In this example, `FileReader` is the low-level stream reader, whereas `BufferedReader` is the high-level stream that takes a `FileReader` as input. Many operations on the high-level stream pass through as operations to the underlying low-level stream, such as `read()` or `close()`. Other operations override or add new functionality to the low-level stream methods. The high-level stream may add new methods, such as `readLine()`, as well as performance enhancements for reading and filtering the low-level data.

High-level streams can take other high-level streams as input. For example, although the following code might seem a little odd at first, the style of wrapping a stream is quite common in practice:

```
try (var ois = new ObjectInputStream(
     new BufferedInputStream(
        new FileInputStream("zoo-data.txt")))) {
  System.out.print(ois.readObject());
}
```

In this example, `FileInputStream` is the low-level stream that interacts directly with the file, which is wrapped by a high-level `BufferedInputStream` to improve performance. Finally, the entire object is wrapped by a high-level `ObjectInputStream`, which allows us to interpret the data as a Java object.

For the exam, the only low-level stream classes you need to be familiar with are the ones that operate on files. The rest of the nonabstract stream classes are all high-level streams.

 Real World Scenario

Use Buffered Streams When Working with Files

As briefly mentioned, `Buffered` classes read or write data in groups, rather than a single byte or character at a time. The performance gain from using a `Buffered` class to access a low-level file stream cannot be overstated. Unless you are doing something very specialized in your application, you should always wrap a file stream with a `Buffered` class in practice.

One of the reasons that `Buffered` streams tend to perform so well in practice is that many file systems are optimized for sequential disk access. The more sequential bytes you read at a time, the fewer round-trips between the Java process and the file system, improving the access of your application. For example, accessing 1,600 sequential bytes is a lot faster than accessing 1,600 bytes spread across the hard drive.

Stream Base Classes

The java.io library defines four abstract classes that are the parents of all stream classes defined within the API: InputStream, OutputStream, Reader, and Writer.

The constructors of high-level streams often take a reference to the abstract class. For example, BufferedWriter takes a Writer object as input, which allows it to take any subclass of Writer.

One common area where the exam likes to play tricks on you is mixing and matching stream classes that are not compatible with each other. For example, take a look at each of the following examples and see whether you can determine why they do not compile:

```
new BufferedInputStream(new FileReader("z.txt"));   // DOES NOT COMPILE
new BufferedWriter(new FileOutputStream("z.txt"));  // DOES NOT COMPILE
new ObjectInputStream(
    new FileOutputStream("z.txt"));                 // DOES NOT COMPILE
new BufferedInputStream(new InputStream());         // DOES NOT COMPILE
```

The first two examples do not compile because they mix Reader/Writer classes with InputStream/OutputStream classes, respectively. The third example does not compile because we are mixing an OutputStream with an InputStream. Although it is possible to read data from an InputStream and write it to an OutputStream, wrapping the stream is not the way to do so. As you will see later in this chapter, the data must be copied over, often iteratively. Finally, the last example does not compile because InputStream is an abstract class, and therefore you cannot create an instance of it.

Decoding I/O Class Names

Pay close attention to the name of the I/O class on the exam, as decoding it often gives you context clues as to what the class does. For example, without needing to look it up, it should be clear that FileReader is a class that reads data from a file as characters or strings. Furthermore, ObjectOutputStream sounds like a class that writes object data to a byte stream.

Review of **java.io** Class Name Properties

- A class with the word InputStream or OutputStream in its name is used for reading or writing binary or byte data, respectively.

- A class with the word Reader or Writer in its name is used for reading or writing character or string data, respectively.

- Most, but not all, input classes have a corresponding output class.

- A low-level stream connects directly with the source of the data.

- A high-level stream is built on top of another stream using wrapping.
- A class with `Buffered` in its name reads or writes data in groups of bytes or characters and often improves performance in sequential file systems.
- With a few exceptions, you only wrap a stream with another stream if they share the same abstract parent.

For the last rule, we'll cover some of those exceptions (like wrapping an `OutputStream` with a `PrintWriter`) later in the chapter.

Table 8.2 lists the abstract base classes that all I/O streams inherited from.

TABLE 8.2   The java.io abstract stream base classes

Class Name	Description
InputStream	Abstract class for all input byte streams
OutputStream	Abstract class for all output byte streams
Reader	Abstract class for all input character streams
Writer	Abstract class for all output character streams

Table 8.3 lists the concrete I/O streams that you should be familiar with for the exam. Note that most of the information about each stream, such as whether it is an input or output stream or whether it accesses data using bytes or characters, can be decoded by the name alone.

TABLE 8.3   The java.io concrete stream classes

Class Name	Low/High Level	Description
FileInputStream	Low	Reads file data as bytes
FileOutputStream	Low	Writes file data as bytes
FileReader	Low	Reads file data as characters
FileWriter	Low	Writes file data as characters
BufferedInputStream	High	Reads byte data from an existing InputStream in a buffered manner, which improves efficiency and performance
BufferedOutputStream	High	Writes byte data to an existing OutputStream in a buffered manner, which improves efficiency and performance

Class Name	Low/High Level	Description
`BufferedReader`	High	Reads character data from an existing `Reader` in a buffered manner, which improves efficiency and performance
`BufferedWriter`	High	Writes character data to an existing `Writer` in a buffered manner, which improves efficiency and performance
`ObjectInputStream`	High	Deserializes primitive Java data types and graphs of Java objects from an existing `InputStream`
`ObjectOutputStream`	High	Serializes primitive Java data types and graphs of Java objects to an existing `OutputStream`
`PrintStream`	High	Writes formatted representations of Java objects to a binary stream
`PrintWriter`	High	Writes formatted representations of Java objects to a character stream

Keep Table 8.2 and Table 8.3 handy throughout this chapter. We will discuss these in more detail including examples of each.

Common I/O Stream Operations

While there are a lot of stream classes, many share a lot of the same operations. In this section, we'll review the common methods among various stream classes. In the next section, we'll cover specific stream classes.

Reading and Writing Data

I/O streams are all about reading/writing data, so it shouldn't be a surprise that the most important methods are `read()` and `write()`. Both `InputStream` and `Reader` declare the following method to read byte data from a stream:

```
// InputStream and Reader
public int read() throws IOException
```

Likewise, `OutputStream` and `Writer` both define the following method to write a byte to the stream:

```
// OutputStream and Writer
public void write(int b) throws IOException
```

Hold on. We said we are reading and writing bytes, so why do the methods use `int` instead of `byte`? Remember, the `byte` data type has a range of 256 characters. They needed an extra value to indicate the end of a stream. The authors of Java decided to use a larger data type, `int`, so that special values like –1 would indicate the end of a stream. The output stream classes use `int` as well, to be consistent with the input stream classes.

 Other stream classes you will learn about in this chapter throw exceptions to denote the end of the stream rather than a special value like –1.

The following `copyStream()` methods show an example of reading all of the values of an `InputStream` and `Reader` and writing them to an `OutputStream` and `Writer`, respectively. In both examples, –1 is used to indicate the end of the stream.

```
void copyStream(InputStream in, OutputStream out) throws IOException {
    int b;
    while ((b = in.read()) != -1) {
        out.write(b);
    }
}

void copyStream(Reader in, Writer out) throws IOException {
    int b;
    while ((b = in.read()) != -1) {
        out.write(b);
    }
}
```

 Most I/O stream methods declare a checked `IOException`. File or network resources that a stream relies on can disappear at any time, and our programs need be able to readily adapt to these outages.

The byte stream classes also include overloaded methods for reading and writing multiple bytes at a time.

```
// InputStream
public int read(byte[] b) throws IOException
public int read(byte[] b, int offset, int length) throws IOException
```

```
// OutputStream
public void write(byte[] b) throws IOException
public void write(byte[] b, int offset, int length) throws IOException
```

The offset and length are applied to the array itself. For example, an offset of 5 and length of 3 indicates that the stream should read up to 3 bytes of data and put them into the array starting with position 5.

There are equivalent methods for the character stream classes that use char instead of byte.

```
// Reader
public int read(char[] c) throws IOException
public int read(char[] c, int offset, int length) throws IOException
```

```
// Writer
public void write(char[] c) throws IOException
public void write(char[] c, int offset, int length) throws IOException
```

We'll see examples of these methods later in the chapter.

Closing the Stream

All I/O streams include a method to release any resources within the stream when it is no longer needed.

```
// All I/O stream classes
public void close() throws IOException
```

Since streams are considered resources, it is imperative that all I/O streams be closed after they are used lest they lead to resource leaks. Since all I/O streams implement Closeable, the best way to do this is with a try-with-resources statement, which you saw in Chapter 5, "Exceptions, Assertions, and Localization."

```
try (var fis = new FileInputStream("zoo-data.txt")) {
   System.out.print(fis.read());
}
```

In many file systems, failing to close a file properly could leave it locked by the operating system such that no other processes could read/write to it until the program is terminated. Throughout this chapter, we will close stream resources using the try-with-resources syntax since this is the preferred way of closing resources in Java. We will also use var to shorten the declarations, since these statements can get quite long!

What about if you need to pass a stream to a method? That's fine, but the stream should be closed in the method that created it.

```
public void printData(InputStream is) throws IOException {
   int b;
```

```
    while ((b = is.read()) != -1) {
        System.out.print(b);
    }
}

public void readFile(String fileName) throws IOException {
    try (var fis = new FileInputStream(fileName)) {
        printData(fis);
    }
}
```

In this example, the stream is created and closed in the readFile() method, with the printData() processing the contents.

Closing Wrapped Streams

When working with a wrapped stream, you only need to use close() on the topmost object. Doing so will close the underlying streams. The following example is valid and will result in three separate close() method calls but is unnecessary:

```
try (var fis = new FileOutputStream("zoo-banner.txt"); // Unnecessary
     var bis = new BufferedOutputStream(fis);
     var ois = new ObjectOutputStream(bis)) {
    ois.writeObject("Hello");
}
```

Instead, we can rely on the ObjectOutputStream to close the BufferedOutputStream and FileOutputStream. The following will call only one close() method instead of three:

```
try (var ois = new ObjectOutputStream(
        new BufferedOutputStream(
            new FileOutputStream("zoo-banner.txt")))) {
    ois.writeObject("Hello");
}
```

Manipulating Input Streams

All input stream classes include the following methods to manipulate the order in which data is read from a stream:

```
// InputStream and Reader
public boolean markSupported()
```

```
public void void mark(int readLimit)
```

```
public void reset() throws IOException
```

```
public long skip(long n) throws IOException
```

The mark() and reset() methods return a stream to an earlier position. Before calling either of these methods, you should call the markSupported() method, which returns true only if mark() is supported. The skip() method is pretty simple; it basically reads data from the stream and discards the contents.

Not all input stream classes support mark() and reset(). Make sure to call markSupported() on the stream before calling these methods or an exception will be thrown at runtime.

mark() and *reset()*

Assume that we have an InputStream instance whose next values are LION. Consider the following code snippet:

```
public void readData(InputStream is) throws IOException {
    System.out.print((char) is.read());      // L
    if (is.markSupported()) {
        is.mark(100);   // Marks up to 100 bytes
        System.out.print((char) is.read());  // I
        System.out.print((char) is.read());  // O
        is.reset();     // Resets stream to position before I
    }
    System.out.print((char) is.read());      // I
    System.out.print((char) is.read());      // O
    System.out.print((char) is.read());      // N
}
```

The code snippet will output LIOION if mark() is supported, and LION otherwise. It's a good practice to organize your read() operations so that the stream ends up at the same position regardless of whether mark() is supported.

What about the value of 100 we passed to the mark() method? This value is called the readLimit. It instructs the stream that we expect to call reset() after at most 100 bytes. If our program calls reset() after reading more than 100 bytes from calling mark(100), then it may throw an exception, depending on the stream class.

In actuality, mark() and reset() are not really putting the data back into the stream but storing the data in a temporary buffer in memory to be read again. Therefore, you should not call the mark() operation with too large a value, as this could take up a lot of memory.

skip()

Assume that we have an InputStream instance whose next values are TIGERS. Consider the following code snippet:

```
System.out.print ((char)is.read()); // T
is.skip(2);  // Skips I and G
is.read();   // Reads E but doesn't output it
System.out.print((char)is.read());  // R
System.out.print((char)is.read());  // S
```

This code prints TRS at runtime. We skipped two characters, I and G. We also read E but didn't store it anywhere, so it behaved like calling skip(1).

The return parameter of skip() tells us how many values were actually skipped. For example, if we are near the end of the stream and call skip(1000), the return value might be 20, indicating the end of the stream was reached after 20 values were skipped. Using the return value of skip() is important if you need to keep track of where you are in a stream and how many bytes have been processed.

Flushing Output Streams

When data is written to an output stream, the underlying operating system does not guarantee that the data will make it to the file system immediately. In many operating systems, the data may be cached in memory, with a write occurring only after a temporary cache is filled or after some amount of time has passed.

If the data is cached in memory and the application terminates unexpectedly, the data would be lost, because it was never written to the file system. To address this, all output stream classes provide a flush() method, which requests that all accumulated data be written immediately to disk.

```
// OutputStream and Writer
public void flush() throws IOException
```

In the following sample, 1,000 characters are written to a file stream. The calls to flush() ensure that data is sent to the hard drive at least once every 100 characters. The JVM or operating system is free to send the data more frequently.

```
try (var fos = new FileOutputStream(fileName)) {
   for(int i=0; i<1000; i++) {
      fos.write('a');
      if(i % 100 == 0) {
         fos.flush();
      }
   }
}
```

The flush() method helps reduce the amount of data lost if the application terminates unexpectedly. It is not without cost, though. Each time it is used, it may cause a noticeable delay in the application, especially for large files. Unless the data that you are writing is extremely critical, the flush() method should be used only intermittently. For example, it should not necessarily be called after every write.

You also do not need to call the flush() method when you have finished writing data, since the close() method will automatically do this.

Reviewing Common I/O Stream Methods

Table 8.4 reviews the common stream methods you should know for this chapter. For the read() and write() methods that take primitive arrays, the method parameter type depends on the stream type. Byte streams ending in InputStream/OutputStream use byte[], while character streams ending in Reader/Writer use char[].

TABLE 8.4   Common I/O stream methods

Stream Class	Method Name	Description
All streams	void close()	Closes stream and releases resources
All input streams	int read()	Reads a single byte or returns −1 if no bytes were available
InputStream Reader	int read(byte[] b) int read(char[] c)	Reads values into a buffer. Returns number of bytes read
InputStream Reader	int read(byte[] b, int offset, int length) int read(char[] c, int offset, int length)	Reads up to length values into a buffer starting from position offset. Returns number of bytes read
All output streams	void write(int)	Writes a single byte
OutputStream Writer	void write(byte[] b) void write(char[] c)	Writes an array of values into the stream
OutputStream Writer	void write(byte[] b, int offset, int length) void write(char[] c, int offset, int length)	Writes length values from an array into the stream, starting with an offset index

TABLE 8.4   Common I/O stream methods *(continued)*

Stream Class	Method Name	Description
All input streams	boolean markSupported()	Returns true if the stream class supports mark()
All input streams	mark(int readLimit)	Marks the current position in the stream
All input streams	void reset()	Attempts to reset the stream to the mark() position
All input streams	long skip(long n)	Reads and discards a specified number of characters
All output streams	void flush()	Flushes buffered data through the stream

Remember that input and output streams can refer to both byte and character streams throughout this chapter.

Working with I/O Stream Classes

Now that we've reviewed the types of streams and their properties, it's time to jump in and work with concrete I/O stream classes. Some of the techniques for accessing streams may seem a bit new to you, but as you will see, they are similar among different stream classes.

The I/O stream classes include numerous overloaded constructors and methods. Hundreds in fact. Don't panic! In this section, we present the most common constructors and methods that you should be familiar with for the exam.

Reading and Writing Binary Data

The first stream classes that we are going to discuss in detail are the most basic file stream classes, FileInputStream and FileOutputStream. They are used to read bytes from a file or write bytes to a file, respectively. These classes connect to a file using the following constructors:

```
public FileInputStream(File file) throws FileNotFoundException
public FileInputStream(String name) throws FileNotFoundException
```

```
public FileOutputStream(File file) throws FileNotFoundException
public FileOutputStream(String name) throws FileNotFoundException
```

> If you need to append to an existing file, there's a constructor for that. The
> FileOutputStream class includes overloaded constructors that take a
> boolean append flag. When set to true, the output stream will append to
> the end of a file if it already exists. This is useful for writing to the end of log
> files, for example.

The following code uses FileInputStream and FileOutputStream to copy a file. It's nearly the same as our previous copyStream() method, except that it operates specifically on files.

```
void copyFile(File src, File dest) throws IOException {
    try (var in = new FileInputStream(src);
        var out = new FileOutputStream(dest)) {
      int b;
      while ((b = in.read()) != -1) {
         out.write(b);
      }
    }
}
```

If the source file does not exist, a FileNotFoundException, which inherits IOException, will be thrown. If the destination file already exists, this implementation will overwrite it, since the append flag was not sent. The copy() method copies one byte at a time until it reads a value of –1.

Buffering Binary Data

While our copyFile() method is valid, it tends to perform poorly on large files. As discussed earlier, that's because there is a cost associated with each round-trip to the file system. We can easily enhance our implementation using BufferedInputStream and BufferedOutputStream. As high-level streams, these classes include constructors that take other streams as input.

```
public BufferedInputStream(InputStream in)
public BufferedOutputStream(OutputStream out)
```

Why Use the *Buffered* Classes?

Since the read/write methods that use byte[] exist in InputStream/OutputStream, why use the Buffered classes at all? In particular, we could have rewritten our earlier copyFile() method to use byte[] without introducing the Buffered classes. Put simply, the Buffered classes contain a number of performance improvements for managing data in memory.

For example, the BufferedInputStream class is capable of retrieving and storing in memory more data than you might request with a single read(byte[]) call. For successive calls to the read(byte[]) method with a small byte array, using the Buffered classes would be faster in a wide variety of situations, since the data can be returned directly from memory without going to the file system.

The following shows how to apply these streams:

```java
void copyFileWithBuffer(File src, File dest) throws IOException {
    try (var in = new BufferedInputStream(
            new FileInputStream(src));
        var out = new BufferedOutputStream(
            new FileOutputStream(dest))) {
        var buffer = new byte[1024];
        int lengthRead;
        while ((lengthRead = in.read(buffer)) > 0) {
            out.write(buffer, 0, lengthRead);
            out.flush();
        }
    }
}
```

Instead of reading the data one byte at a time, we read and write up to 1024 bytes at a time. The return value lengthRead is critical for determining whether we are at the end of the stream and knowing how many bytes we should write into our output stream. We also added a flush() command at the end of the loop to ensure data is written to disk between each iteration.

Unless our file happens to be a multiple of 1024 bytes, the last iteration of the while loop will write some value less than 1024 bytes. For example, if the buffer size is 1,024 bytes and the file size is 1,054 bytes, then the last read will be only 30 bytes. If we had ignored this return value and instead wrote 1,024 bytes, then 994 bytes from the previous loop would be written to the end of the file.

Real World Scenario

Choosing a Buffer Size

Given the way computers organize data, it is often appropriate to choose a buffer size that is a power of 2, such as 1,024. Performance tuning often involves determining what buffer size is most appropriate for your application.

What buffer size should you use? Any buffer size that is a power of 2 from 1,024 to 65,536 is a good choice in practice. Keep in mind, the biggest performance gain you'll see is from moving from nonbuffered access to buffered access. Once you are using a buffered stream, you're less likely to see a huge performance difference between a buffer size of 1,024 and 2,048, for example.

Reading and Writing Character Data

The `FileReader` and `FileWriter` classes, along with their associated buffer classes, are among the most convenient I/O classes because of their built-in support for text data. They include constructors that take the same input as the binary file classes.

```
public FileReader(File file) throws FileNotFoundException
public FileReader(String name) throws FileNotFoundException

public FileWriter(File file) throws FileNotFoundException
public FileWriter(String name) throws FileNotFoundException
```

The following is an example of using these classes to copy a text file:

```
void copyTextFile(File src, File dest) throws IOException {
    try (var reader = new FileReader(src);
        var writer = new FileWriter(dest)) {
        int b;
        while ((b = reader.read()) != -1) {
            writer.write(b);
        }
    }
}
```

Wait a second, this looks identical to our `copyFile()` method with byte stream! Since we're copying one character at a time, rather than one byte, it is.

The `FileReader` class doesn't contain any new methods you haven't seen before. The `FileWriter` inherits a method from the `Writer` class that allows it to write `String` values.

```
// Writer
public void write(String str) throws IOException
```

For example, the following is supported in `FileWriter` but not `FileOutputStream`:

```
writer.write("Hello World");
```

We'll see even more enhancements for character streams next.

Buffering Character Data

Like we saw with byte streams, Java includes high-level buffered character streams that improve performance. The constructors take existing `Reader` and `Writer` instances as input.

```
public BufferedReader(Reader in)

public BufferedWriter(Writer out)
```

They add two new methods, `readLine()` and `newLine()`, that are particularly useful when working with `String` values.

```
// BufferedReader
public String readLine() throws IOException

// BufferedWriter
public void newLine() throws IOException
```

Putting it all together, the following shows how to copy a file, one line at a time:

```
void copyTextFileWithBuffer(File src, File dest) throws IOException {
    try (var reader = new BufferedReader(new FileReader(src));
        var writer = new BufferedWriter(new FileWriter(dest))) {
        String s;
        while ((s = reader.readLine()) != null) {
            writer.write(s);
            writer.newLine();
        }
    }
}
```

In this example, each loop iteration corresponds to reading and writing a line of a file. Assuming the length of the lines in the file are reasonably sized, this implementation will perform well.

There are some important distinctions between this method and our earlier `copyFileWithBuffer()` method that worked with byte streams. First, instead of a buffer array, we are using a `String` to store the data read during each loop iteration. By storing the data temporarily as a `String`, we can manipulate it as we would any `String` value. For example, we can call `replaceAll()` or `toUpperCase()` to create new values.

Next, we are checking for the end of the stream with a null value instead of -1. Finally, we are inserting a newLine() on every iteration of the loop. This is because readLine() strips out the line break character. Without the call to newLine(), the copied file would have all of its line breaks removed.

 In the next chapter, we'll show you how to use NIO.2 to read the lines of a file in a single command. We'll even show you how to process the lines of a file using the functional programming streams that you worked with in Chapter 4.

Serializing Data

Throughout this book, we have been managing our data model using classes, so it makes sense that we would want to save these objects between program executions. Data about our zoo animal's health wouldn't be particularly useful if it had to be entered every time the program runs!

You can certainly use the I/O stream classes you've learned about so far to store text and binary data, but you still have to figure out how to put the data in the stream and then decode it later. There are various file formats like XML and CSV you can standardize to, but oftentimes you have to build the translation yourself.

Luckily, we can use serialization to solve the problem of how to convert objects to/from a stream. *Serialization* is the process of converting an in-memory object to a byte stream. Likewise, *deserialization* is the process of converting from a byte stream into an object. Serialization often involves writing an object to a stored or transmittable format, while deserialization is the reciprocal process.

Figure 8.3 shows a visual representation of serializing and deserializing a Giraffe object to and from a giraffe.txt file.

FIGURE 8.3   Serialization process

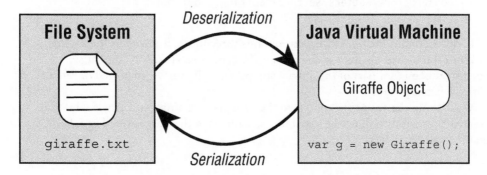

In this section, we will show you how Java provides built-in mechanisms for serializing and deserializing streams of objects directly to and from disk, respectively.

Applying the *Serializable* Interface

To serialize an object using the I/O API, the object must implement the java.io.Serializable interface. The Serializable interface is a marker interface, similar to the marker annotations you learned about in Chapter 2, "Annotations." By marker interface, it means the interface does not have any methods. Any class can implement the Serializable interface since there are no required methods to implement.

Since Serializable is a marker interface with no abstract members, why not just apply it to every class? Generally speaking, you should only mark data-oriented classes serializable. Process-oriented classes, such as the I/O streams discussed in this chapter, or the Thread instances you learned about in Chapter 7, "Concurrency," are often poor candidates for serialization, as the internal state of those classes tends to be ephemeral or short-lived.

The purpose of using the Serializable interface is to inform any process attempting to serialize the object that you have taken the proper steps to make the object serializable. All Java primitives and many of the built-in Java classes that you have worked with throughout this book are Serializable. For example, this class can be serialized:

```
import java.io.Serializable;
public class Gorilla implements Serializable {
    private static final long serialVersionUID = 1L;
    private String name;
    private int age;
    private Boolean friendly;
    private transient String favoriteFood;

    // Constructors/Getters/Setters/toString() omitted
}
```

In this example, the Gorilla class contains three instance members (name, age, friendly) that will be saved to a stream if the class is serialized. Note that since Serializable is not part of the java.lang package, it must be imported or referenced with the package name.

What about the favoriteFood field that is marked transient? Any field that is marked transient will not be saved to a stream when the class is serialized. We'll discuss that in more detail next.

Real World Scenario

Maintaining a *serialVersionUID*

It's a good practice to declare a static serialVersionUID variable in every class that implements Serializable. The version is stored with each object as part of serialization. Then, every time the class structure changes, this value is updated or incremented.

Perhaps our Gorilla class receives a new instance member Double banana, or maybe the age field is renamed. The idea is a class could have been serialized with an older version of the class and deserialized with a newer version of the class.

The serialVersionUID helps inform the JVM that the stored data may not match the new class definition. If an older version of the class is encountered during deserialization, a java.io.InvalidClassException may be thrown. Alternatively, some APIs support converting data between versions.

Marking Data *transient*

Oftentimes, the transient modifier is used for sensitive data of the class, like a password. You'll learn more about this topic in Chapter 11, "Security." There are other objects it does not make sense to serialize, like the state of an in-memory Thread. If the object is part of a serializable object, we just mark it transient to ignore these select instance members.

What happens to data marked transient on deserialization? It reverts to its default Java values, such as 0.0 for double, or null for an object. We'll see examples of this shortly when we present the object stream classes.

 Marking static fields transient has little effect on serialization. Other than the serialVersionUID, only the instance members of a class are serialized.

Ensuring a Class Is *Serializable*

Since Serializable is a marker interface, you might think there are no rules to using it. Not quite! Any process attempting to serialize an object will throw a NotSerializableException if the class does not implement the Serializable interface properly.

How to Make a Class Serializable

- The class must be marked Serializable.
- Every instance member of the class is serializable, marked transient, or has a null value at the time of serialization.

Be careful with the second rule. For a class to be serializable, we must apply the second rule recursively. Do you see why the following `Cat` class is not serializable?

```
public class Cat implements Serializable {
   private Tail tail = new Tail();
}


public class Tail implements Serializable {
   private Fur fur = new Fur();
}


public class Fur {}
```

`Cat` contains an instance of `Tail`, and both of those classes are marked `Serializable`, so no problems there. Unfortunately, `Tail` contains an instance of `Fur` that is not marked `Serializable`.

Either of the following changes fixes the problem and allows `Cat` to be serialized:

```
public class Tail implements Serializable {
   private transient Fur fur = new Fur();
}


public class Fur implements Serializable {}
```

We could also make our `tail` or `fur` instance members `null`, although this would make `Cat` serializable only for particular instances, rather than all instances.

Storing Data with *ObjectOutputStream* and *ObjectInputStream*

The `ObjectInputStream` class is used to deserialize an object from a stream, while the `ObjectOutputStream` is used to serialize an object to a stream. They are high-level streams that operate on existing streams.

```
public ObjectInputStream(InputStream in) throws IOException


public ObjectOutputStream(OutputStream out) throws IOException
```

While both of these classes contain a number of methods for built-in data types like primitives, the two methods you need to know for the exam are the ones related to working with objects.

```
// ObjectInputStream
public Object readObject() throws IOException, ClassNotFoundException


// ObjectOutputStream
public void writeObject(Object obj) throws IOException
```

We now provide a sample method that serializes a List of Gorilla objects to a file.

```
void saveToFile(List<Gorilla> gorillas, File dataFile)
      throws IOException {
   try (var out = new ObjectOutputStream(
         new BufferedOutputStream(
            new FileOutputStream(dataFile)))) {
      for (Gorilla gorilla : gorillas)
         out.writeObject(gorilla);
   }
}
```

Pretty easy, right? Notice we start with a file stream, wrap it in a buffered stream to improve performance, and then wrap that with an object stream. Serializing the data is as simple as passing it to writeObject().

Once the data is stored in a file, we can deserialize it using the following method:

```
List<Gorilla> readFromFile(File dataFile) throws IOException,
      ClassNotFoundException {
   var gorillas = new ArrayList<Gorilla>();
   try (var in = new ObjectInputStream(
         new BufferedInputStream(
            new FileInputStream(dataFile)))) {
      while (true) {
         var object = in.readObject();
         if (object instanceof Gorilla)
            gorillas.add((Gorilla) object);
      }
   } catch (EOFException e) {
      // File end reached
   }
   return gorillas;
}
```

Ah, not as simple as our save method, was it? When calling readObject(), null and -1 do not have any special meaning, as someone might have serialized objects with those values. Unlike our earlier techniques for reading methods from an input stream, we need to use an infinite loop to process the data, which throws an EOFException when the end of the stream is reached.

> If your program happens to know the number of objects in the stream, then you can call readObject() a fixed number of times, rather than using an infinite loop.

Since the return type of readObject() is Object, we need an explicit cast to obtain access to our Gorilla properties. Notice that readObject() declares a checked ClassNotFoundException since the class might not be available on deserialization.

The following code snippet shows how to call the serialization methods:

```
var gorillas = new ArrayList<Gorilla>();
gorillas.add(new Gorilla("Grodd", 5, false));
gorillas.add(new Gorilla("Ishmael", 8, true));
File dataFile = new File("gorilla.data");

saveToFile(gorillas, dataFile);
var gorillasFromDisk = readFromFile(dataFile);
System.out.print(gorillasFromDisk);
```

Assuming the toString() method was properly overridden in the Gorilla class, this prints the following at runtime:

```
[[name=Grodd, age=5, friendly=false],
 [name=Ishmael, age=8, friendly=true]]
```

> ObjectInputStream inherits an available() method from InputStream that you might think can be used to check for the end of the stream rather than throwing an EOFException. Unfortunately, this only tells you the number of blocks that can be read without blocking another thread. In other words, it can return 0 even if there are more bytes to be read.

Understanding the Deserialization Creation Process

For the exam, you need to understand how a deserialized object is created. When you deserialize an object, *the constructor of the serialized class, along with any instance initializers, is not called when the object is created.* Java will call the no-arg constructor of the first nonserializable parent class it can find in the class hierarchy. In our Gorilla example, this would just be the no-arg constructor of Object.

As we stated earlier, any static or transient fields are ignored. Values that are not provided will be given their default Java value, such as null for String, or 0 for int values.

Let's take a look at a new Chimpanzee class. This time we do list the constructors to illustrate that none of them is used on deserialization.

```
import java.io.Serializable;
public class Chimpanzee implements Serializable {
    private static final long serialVersionUID = 2L;
    private transient String name;
    private transient int age = 10;
```

```
    private static char type = 'C';
    { this.age = 14; }

    public Chimpanzee() {
        this.name = "Unknown";
        this.age = 12;
        this.type = 'Q';
    }

    public Chimpanzee(String name, int age, char type) {
        this.name = name;
        this.age = age;
        this.type = type;
    }

    // Getters/Setters/toString() omitted
}
```

Assuming we rewrite our previous serialization and deserialization methods to process a Chimpanzee object instead of a Gorilla object, what do you think the following prints?

```
var chimpanzees = new ArrayList<Chimpanzee>();
chimpanzees.add(new Chimpanzee("Ham", 2, 'A'));
chimpanzees.add(new Chimpanzee("Enos", 4, 'B'));
File dataFile = new File("chimpanzee.data");

saveToFile(chimpanzees, dataFile);
var chimpanzeesFromDisk = readFromFile(dataFile);
System.out.println(chimpanzeesFromDisk);
```

Think about it. Go on, we'll wait.

Ready for the answer? Well, for starters, none of the instance members would be serialized to a file. The name and age variables are both marked transient, while the type variable is static. We purposely accessed the type variable using this to see whether you were paying attention.

Upon deserialization, none of the constructors in Chimpanzee is called. Even the no-arg constructor that sets the values [name=Unknown,age=12,type=Q] is ignored. The instance initializer that sets age to 14 is also not executed.

In this case, the name variable is initialized to null since that's the default value for String in Java. Likewise, the age variable is initialized to 0. The program prints the following, assuming the toString() method is implemented:

```
[[name=null,age=0,type=B],
 [name=null,age=0,type=B]]
```

What about the type variable? Since it's static, it will actually display whatever value was set last. If the data is serialized and deserialized within the same execution, then it will display B, since that was the last Chimpanzee we created. On the other hand, if the program performs the deserialization and print on startup, then it will print C, since that is the value the class is initialized with.

For the exam, make sure you understand that the constructor and any instance initializations defined in the serialized class are ignored during the deserialization process. Java only calls the constructor of the first non-serializable parent class in the class hierarchy. In Chapter 11, we will go even deeper into serialization and show you how to write methods to customize the serialization process.

 Real World Scenario

Other Serialization APIs

In this chapter, we focus on serialization using the I/O streams, such as ObjectInputStream and ObjectOutputStream. While not part of the exam, you should be aware there are many other (often more popular) APIs for serializing Java objects. For example, there are APIs to serialize data to JSON or encrypted data files.

While these APIs might not use I/O stream classes, many make use of the built-in Serializable interface and transient modifier. Some of these APIs also include annotations to customize the serialization and deserialization of objects, such as what to do when values are missing or need to be translated.

Printing Data

PrintStream and PrintWriter are high-level output print streams classes that are useful for writing text data to a stream. We cover these classes together, because they include many of the same methods. Just remember that one operates on an OutputStream and the other a Writer.

The print stream classes have the distinction of being the only I/O stream classes we cover that do not have corresponding input stream classes. And unlike other OutputStream classes, PrintStream does not have Output in its name.

The print stream classes include the following constructors:

```
public PrintStream(OutputStream out)
```

```
public PrintWriter(Writer out)
```

For convenience, these classes also include constructors that automatically wrap the print stream around a low-level file stream class, such as `FileOutputStream` and `FileWriter`.

```
public PrintStream(File file) throws FileNotFoundException
public PrintStream(String fileName) throws FileNotFoundException

public PrintWriter(File file) throws FileNotFoundException
public PrintWriter(String fileName) throws FileNotFoundException
```

Furthermore, the `PrintWriter` class even has a constructor that takes an `OutputStream` as input. This is one of the few exceptions in which we can mix a byte and character stream.

```
public PrintWriter(OutputStream out)
```

 It may surprise you that you've been regularly using a `PrintStream` throughout this book. Both `System.out` and `System.err` are `PrintStream` objects. Likewise, `System.in`, often useful for reading user input, is an `InputStream`. We'll be covering all three of these objects in the next part of this chapter on user interactions.

Besides the inherited `write()` methods, the print stream classes include numerous methods for writing data including `print()`, `println()`, and `format()`. Unlike the majority of the other streams we've covered, the methods in the print stream classes do not throw any checked exceptions. If they did, you would have been required to catch a checked exception anytime you called `System.out.print()`! The stream classes do provide a method, `checkError()`, that can be used to check for an error after a write.

When working with `String` data, you should use a `Writer`, so our examples in this part of the chapter use `PrintWriter`. Just be aware that many of these examples can be easily rewritten to use a `PrintStream`.

print()

The most basic of the print-based methods is `print()`. The print stream classes include numerous overloaded versions of `print()`, which take everything from primitives and `String` values, to objects. Under the covers, these methods often just perform `String.valueOf()` on the argument and call the underlying stream's `write()` method to add it to the stream. For example, the following sets of print/write code are equivalent:

```
try (PrintWriter out = new PrintWriter("zoo.log")) {
   out.write(String.valueOf(5));   // Writer method
   out.print(5);                    // PrintWriter method
```

```
    var a = new Chimpanzee();
    out.write(a==null ? "null": a.toString()); // Writer method
    out.print(a);                              // PrintWriter method
}
```

println()

The next methods available in the PrintStream and PrintWriter classes are the println() methods, which are virtually identical to the print() methods, except that they also print a line break after the String value is written. These print stream classes also include a no-argument version of println(), which just prints a single line break.

The println() methods are especially helpful, as the line break character is dependent on the operating system. For example, in some systems a line feed symbol, \n, signifies a line break, whereas other systems use a carriage return symbol followed by a line feed symbol, \r\n, to signify a line break. Like the file.separator property, the line.separator value is available from two places, as a Java system property and via a static method.

```
System.getProperty("line.separator");
System.lineSeparator();
```

format()

In Chapter 5, you learned a lot about formatting messages, dates, and numbers to various locales. Each print stream class includes a format() method, which includes an overloaded version that takes a Locale.

```
// PrintStream
public PrintStream format(String format, Object args...)
public PrintStream format(Locale loc, String format, Object args...)


// PrintWriter
public PrintWriter format(String format, Object args...)
public PrintWriter format(Locale loc, String format, Object args...)
```

For convenience (as well as to make C developers feel at home), Java includes printf() methods, which function identically to the format() methods. The only thing you need to know about these methods is that they are interchangeable with format().

The method parameters are used to construct a formatted String in a single method call, rather than via a lot of format and concatenation operations. They return a reference to the instance they are called on so that operations can be chained together.

As an example, the following two `format()` calls print the same text:

```
String name = "Lindsey";
int orderId = 5;

// Both print: Hello Lindsey, order 5 is ready
System.out.format("Hello "+name+", order "+orderId+" is ready");
System.out.format("Hello %s, order %d is ready", name, orderId);
```

In the second `format()` operation, the parameters are inserted and formatted via symbols in the order that they are provided in the vararg. Table 8.5 lists the ones you should know for the exam.

TABLE 8.5   Common print stream `format()` symbols

Symbol	Description
%s	Applies to any type, commonly `String` values
%d	Applies to integer values like `int` and `long`
%f	Applies to floating-point values like `float` and `double`
%n	Inserts a line break using the system-dependent line separator

The following example uses all four symbols from Table 8.5:

```
String name = "James";
double score = 90.25;
int total = 100;
System.out.format("%s:%n    Score: %f out of %d", name, score, total);
```

This prints the following:

```
James:
    Score: 90.250000 out of 100
```

Mixing data types may cause exceptions at runtime. For example, the following throws an exception because a floating-point number is used when an integer value is expected:

```
System.out.format("Food: %d tons", 2.0); // IllegalFormatConversionException
```

Using *format()* with *Flags*

Besides supporting symbols, Java also supports optional flags between the % and the symbol character. In the previous example, the floating-point number was printed as 90.250000. By default, %f displays exactly six digits past the decimal. If you want to display only one digit after the decimal, you could use %.1f instead of %f. The format() method relies on rounding, rather than truncating when shortening numbers. For example, 90.250000 will be displayed as 90.3 (not 90.2) when passed to format() with %.1f.

The format() method also supports two additional features. You can specify the total length of output by using a number before the decimal symbol. By default, the method will fill the empty space with blank spaces. You can also fill the empty space with zeros, by placing a single zero before the decimal symbol. The following examples use brackets, [], to show the start/end of the formatted value:

```
var pi = 3.14159265359;
System.out.format("[%f]",pi);      // [3.141593]
System.out.format("[%12.8f]",pi);  // [  3.14159265]
System.out.format("[%012f]",pi);   // [00003.141593]
System.out.format("[%12.2f]",pi);  // [        3.14]
System.out.format("[%.3f]",pi);    // [3.142]
```

The format() method supports a lot of other symbols and flags. You don't need to know any of them for the exam beyond what we've discussed already.

Sample *PrintWriter* Program

Let's put it altogether. The following sample code shows the PrintWriter class in action:

```
File source = new File("zoo.log");
try (var out = new PrintWriter(
   new BufferedWriter(new FileWriter(source)))) {
   out.print("Today's weather is: ");
   out.println("Sunny");
   out.print("Today's temperature at the zoo is: ");
   out.print(1 / 3.0);
   out.println('C');
```

```
    out.format("It has rained %5.2f inches this year %d", 10.2, 2021);
    out.println();
    out.printf("It may rain %s more inches this year", 1.2);
}
```

After the program runs, zoo.log contains the following:

```
Today's weather is: Sunny
Today's temperature at the zoo is: 0.3333333333333333C
It has rained 10.20 inches this year 2021
It may rain 1.2 more inches this year
```

You should pay close attention to the line breaks in the sample. For example, we called println() after our format(), since format() does not automatically insert a line break after the text. One of the most common bugs with printing data in practice is failing to account for line breaks properly.

Review of Stream Classes

We conclude our discussion of stream classes with Figure 8.4. This diagram shows all of the I/O stream classes that you should be familiar with for the exam, with the exception of the filter streams. FilterInputStream and FilterOutputStream are high-level superclasses that filter or transform data. They are rarely used directly.

InputStreamReader and *OutputStreamWriter*

Most of the time, you can't wrap byte and character streams with each other, although as we mentioned, there are exceptions. The InputStreamReader class wraps an InputStream with a Reader, while the OutputStreamWriter class wraps an OutputStream with a Writer.

```
    try (Reader r = new InputStreamReader(System.in);
         Writer w = new OutputStreamWriter(System.out)) {

    }
```

These classes are incredibly convenient and are also unique in that they are the only I/O stream classes to have both InputStream/OutputStream and Reader/Writer in their name.

FIGURE 8.4   Diagram of I/O stream classes

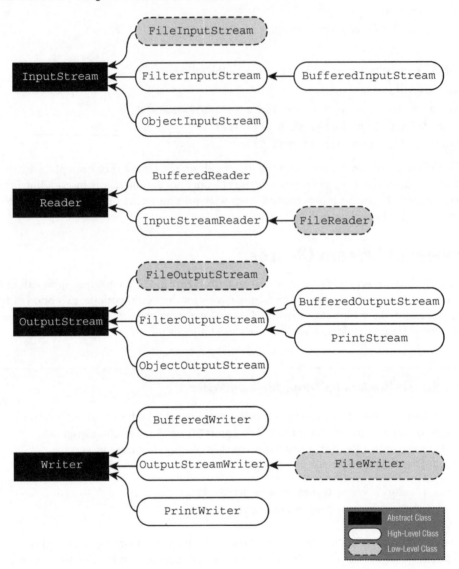

Interacting with Users

The java.io API includes numerous classes for interacting with the user. For example, you might want to write an application that asks a user to log in and prints a success message. This section contains numerous techniques for handling and responding to user input.

Printing Data to the User

Java includes two `PrintStream` instances for providing information to the user: `System.out` and `System.err`. While `System.out` should be old hat to you, `System.err` might be new to you. The syntax for calling and using `System.err` is the same as `System.out` but is used to report errors to the user in a separate stream from the regular output information.

```java
try (var in = new FileInputStream("zoo.txt")) {
    System.out.println("Found file!");
} catch (FileNotFoundException e) {
    System.err.println("File not found!");
}
```

How do they differ in practice? In part, that depends on what is executing the program. For example, if you are running from a command prompt, they will likely print text in the same format. On the other hand, if you are working in an integrated development environment (IDE), they might print the `System.err` text in a different color. Finally, if the code is being run on a server, the `System.err` stream might write to a different log file.

 Real World Scenario

Using Logging APIs

While `System.out` and `System.err` are incredibly useful for debugging stand-alone or simple applications, they are rarely used in professional software development. Most applications rely on a logging service or API.

While there are many logging APIs available, they tend to share a number of similar attributes. First, you create a `static` logging object in each class. Then, you log a message with an appropriate logging level: `debug()`, `info()`, `warn()`, or `error()`. The `debug()` and `info()` methods are useful as they allow developers to log things that aren't errors but may be useful.

The log levels can be enabled as needed at runtime. For example, a server might only output `warn()` and `error()` to keep the logs clean and easy to read. If an administrator notices a lot of errors, then they might enable `debug()` or `info()` logging to help isolate the problem.

Finally, loggers can be enabled for specific classes or packages. While you may be interested in a `debug()` message for a class you write, you are probably not interested in seeing `debug()` messages for every third-party library you are using.

Reading Input as a Stream

The System.in returns an InputStream and is used to retrieve text input from the user. It is commonly wrapped with a BufferedReader via an InputStreamReader to use the readLine() method.

```
var reader = new BufferedReader(new InputStreamReader(System.in));
String userInput = reader.readLine();
System.out.println("You entered: " + userInput);
```

When executed, this application first fetches text from the user until the user presses the Enter key. It then outputs the text the user entered to the screen.

Closing *System* Streams

You might have noticed that we never created or closed System.out, System.err, and System.in when we used them. In fact, these are the only I/O streams in the entire chapter that we did not use a try-with-resources block on!

Because these are static objects, the System streams are shared by the entire application. The JVM creates and opens them for us. They can be used in a try-with-resources statement or by calling close(), although *closing them is not recommended*. Closing the System streams makes them permanently unavailable for all threads in the remainder of the program.

What do you think the following code snippet prints?

```
try (var out = System.out) {}
System.out.println("Hello");
```

Nothing. It prints nothing. Remember, the methods of PrintStream do not throw any checked exceptions and rely on the checkError() to report errors, so they fail silently.

What about this example?

```
try (var err = System.err) {}
System.err.println("Hello");
```

This one also prints nothing. Like System.out, System.err is a PrintStream. Even if it did throw an exception, though, we'd have a hard time seeing it since our stream for reporting errors is closed! Closing System.err is a particularly bad idea, since the stack traces from all exceptions will be hidden.

Finally, what do you think this code snippet does?

```
var reader = new BufferedReader(new InputStreamReader(System.in));
try (reader) {}
String data = reader.readLine();  // IOException
```

It prints an exception at runtime. Unlike the PrintStream class, most InputStream implementations will throw an exception if you try to operate on a closed stream.

Acquiring Input with *Console*

The java.io.Console class is specifically designed to handle user interactions. After all, System.in and System.out are just raw streams, whereas Console is a class with numerous methods centered around user input.

The Console class is a singleton because it is accessible only from a factory method and only one instance of it is created by the JVM. For example, if you come across code on the exam such as the following, it does not compile, since the constructors are all private:

```
Console c = new Console();  // DOES NOT COMPILE
```

The following snippet shows how to obtain a Console and use it to retrieve user input:

```
Console console = System.console();
if (console != null) {
   String userInput = console.readLine();
   console.writer().println("You entered: " + userInput);
} else {
   System.err.println("Console not available");
}
```

The Console object may not be available, depending on where the code is being called. If it is not available, then System.console() returns null. It is imperative that you check for a null value before attempting to use a Console object!

This program first retrieves an instance of the Console and verifies that it is available, outputting a message to System.err if it is not. If it is available, then it retrieves a line of input from the user and prints the result. As you might have noticed, this example is equivalent to our earlier example of reading user input with System.in and System.out.

reader() and *writer()*

The Console class includes access to two streams for reading and writing data.

```
public Reader reader()
```

```
public PrintWriter writer()
```

Accessing these classes is analogous to calling System.in and System.out directly, although they use character streams rather than byte streams. In this manner, they are more appropriate for handling text data.

format()

For printing data with a Console, you can skip calling the writer().format() and output the data directly to the stream in a single call.

```
public Console format(String format, Object... args)
```

The format() method behaves the same as the format() method on the stream classes, formatting and printing a String while applying various arguments. They are so alike, in fact, that there's even an equivalent Console printf() method that does the same thing as format(). We don't want our former C developers to have to learn a new method name!

The following sample code prints information to the user:

```
Console console = System.console();
if (console == null) {
    throw new RuntimeException("Console not available");
} else {
    console.writer().println("Welcome to Our Zoo!");
    console.format("It has %d animals and employs %d people", 391, 25);
    console.writer().println();
    console.printf("The zoo spans %5.1f acres", 128.91);
}
```

Assuming the Console is available at runtime, it prints the following:

```
Welcome to Our Zoo!
It has 391 animals and employs 25 people
The zoo spans 128.9 acres.
```

Using *Console* with a *Locale*

Unlike the print stream classes, Console does not include an overloaded format() method that takes a Locale instance. Instead, Console relies on the system locale. Of course, you could always use a specific Locale by retrieving the Writer object and passing your own Locale instance, such as in the following example:

```
Console console = System.console();
console.writer().format(new Locale("fr", "CA"), "Hello World");
```

readLine() and readPassword()

The Console class includes four methods for retrieving regular text data from the user.

```
public String readLine()
public String readLine(String fmt, Object... args)

public char[] readPassword()
public char[] readPassword(String fmt, Object... args)
```

Like using `System.in` with a `BufferedReader`, the `Console` `readLine()` method reads input until the user presses the Enter key. The overloaded version of `readLine()` displays a formatted message prompt prior to requesting input.

The `readPassword()` methods are similar to the `readLine()` method with two important differences.

- The text the user types is not echoed back and displayed on the screen as they are typing.
- The data is returned as a `char[]` instead of a `String`.

The first feature improves security by not showing the password on the screen if someone happens to be sitting next to you. The second feature involves preventing passwords from entering the `String` pool and will be discussed in Chapter 11.

Reviewing *Console* Methods

The last code sample we present asks the user a series of questions and prints results based on this information using many of various methods we learned in this section:

```
Console console = System.console();
if (console == null) {
    throw new RuntimeException("Console not available");
} else {
    String name = console.readLine("Please enter your name: ");
    console.writer().format("Hi %s", name);
    console.writer().println();

    console.format("What is your address? ");
    String address = console.readLine();

    char[] password = console.readPassword("Enter a password "
        + "between %d and %d characters: ", 5, 10);
    char[] verify = console.readPassword("Enter the password again: ");
    console.printf("Passwords "
        + (Arrays.equals(password, verify) ? "match" : "do not match"));
}
```

Assuming a `Console` is available, the output should resemble the following:

```
Please enter your name: Max
Hi Max
What is your address? Spoonerville
Enter a password between 5 and 10 digits:
Enter the password again:
Passwords match
```

Summary

This chapter is all about using classes in the java.io package. We started off showing you how to operate on files and directories using the java.io.File class.

We then introduced I/O streams and explained how they are used to read or write large quantities of data. While there are a lot of I/O streams, they differ on some key points.

- Byte vs. character streams
- Input vs. output streams
- Low-level vs. high-level streams

Oftentimes, the name of the I/O stream can tell you a lot about what it does.

We visited many of the I/O stream classes that you will need to know for the exam in increasing order of complexity. A common practice is to start with a low-level resource or file stream and wrap it in a buffered stream to improve performance. You can also apply a high-level stream to manipulate the data, such as an object or print stream. We described what it means to be serializable in Java, and we showed you how to use the object stream classes to persist objects directly to and from disk.

We concluded the chapter by showing you how to read input data from the user, using both the system stream objects and the Console class. The Console class has many useful features, such as built-in support for passwords and formatting.

Exam Essentials

Understand files, directories, and streams.   Files are records that store data within a persistent storage device, such as a hard disk drive, that is available after the application has finished executing. Files are organized within a file system in directories, which in turn may contain other directories. The root directory is the topmost directory in a file system.

Be able to use the *java.io.File* class.   A java.io.File instance can be created by passing a path String to the File constructor. The File class includes a number of instance methods for retrieving information about both files and directories. It also includes methods to create/delete files and directories, as well as retrieve a list of files within the directory.

Distinguish between byte and character streams.   Streams are either byte streams or character streams. Byte streams operate on binary data and have names that end with Stream, while character streams operate on text data and have names that end in Reader or Writer.

Distinguish between input and output streams.   Operating on a stream involves either receiving or sending data. The InputStream and Reader classes are the topmost abstract classes that receive data, while the OutputStream and Writer classes are the topmost abstract classes that send data. All I/O output streams covered in this chapter have corresponding input streams, with the exception of `PrintStream` and `PrintWriter`. `PrintStream` is also unique in that it is the only `OutputStream` without the word `Output` in its name.

Distinguish between low-level and high-level streams.   A low-level stream is one that operates directly on the underlying resource, such as a file or network connection. A high-level stream is one that operates on a low-level or other high-level stream to filter data, convert data, or improve performance.

Be able to perform common stream operations.   All streams include a `close()` method, which can be invoked automatically with a try-with-resources statement. Input streams include methods to manipulate the stream including `mark()`, `reset()`, and `skip()`. Remember to call `markSupported()` before using `mark()` and `reset()`, as some streams do not support this operation. Output streams include a `flush()` method to force any buffered data to the underlying resource.

Be able to recognize and know how to use various stream classes.   Besides the four top-level abstract classes, you should be familiar with the file, buffered, print, and object stream classes. You should also know how to wrap a stream with another stream appropriately.

Understand how to use Java serialization.   A class is considered serializable if it implements the `java.io.Serializable` interface and contains instance members that are either serializable or marked `transient`. All Java primitives and the `String` class are serializable. The `ObjectInputStream` and `ObjectOutputStream` classes can be used to read and write a `Serializable` object from and to a stream, respectively.

Be able to interact with the user.   Be able to interact with the user using the system streams (`System.out`, `System.err`, and `System.in`) as well as the `Console` class. The `Console` class includes special methods for formatting data and retrieving complex input such as passwords.

Review Questions

The answers to the chapter review questions can be found in Appendix B.

1. Which class would be best to use to read a binary file into a Java object?

   A. ObjectWriter

   B. ObjectOutputStream

   C. BufferedStream

   D. ObjectReader

   E. FileReader

   F. ObjectInputStream

   G. None of the above

2. Which of the following are methods available on instances of the java.io.File class? (Choose all that apply.)

   A. mv()

   B. createDirectory()

   C. mkdirs()

   D. move()

   E. renameTo()

   F. copy()

   G. mkdir()

3. What is the value of name after the instance of Eagle created in the main() method is serialized and then deserialized?

```java
import java.io.Serializable;
class Bird {
    protected transient String name;
    public void setName(String name) { this.name = name; }
    public String getName() { return name; }
    public Bird() {
        this.name = "Matt";
    }
}
public class Eagle extends Bird implements Serializable {
    { this.name = "Olivia"; }
    public Eagle() {
        this.name = "Bridget";
```

```
        }
        public static void main(String[] args) {
            var e = new Eagle();
            e.name = "Adeline";
        }
    }
```

- **A.** Adeline
- **B.** Matt
- **C.** Olivia
- **D.** Bridget
- **E.** null
- **F.** The code does not compile.
- **G.** The code compiles but throws an exception at runtime.

4. Which classes will allow the following to compile? (Choose all that apply.)

```
        var is = new BufferedInputStream(new FileInputStream("z.txt"));
        InputStream wrapper = new _____(is);
        try (wrapper) {}
```

- **A.** BufferedInputStream
- **B.** FileInputStream
- **C.** BufferedWriter
- **D.** ObjectInputStream
- **E.** ObjectOutputStream
- **F.** BufferedReader
- **G.** None of the above, as the first line does not compile.

5. Which of the following are true? (Choose all that apply.)
- **A.** System.console() will throw an IOException if a Console is not available.
- **B.** System.console() will return null if a Console is not available.
- **C.** A new Console object is created every time System.console() is called.
- **D.** Console can be used only for writing output, not reading input.
- **E.** Console includes a format() method to write data to the console's output stream.
- **F.** Console includes a println() method to write data to the console's output stream.

6. Which statements about closing I/O streams are correct? (Choose all that apply.)
- **A.** InputStream and Reader instances are the only I/O streams that should be closed after use.
- **B.** OutputStream and Writer instances are the only I/O streams that should be closed after use.

C. InputStream/OutputStream and Reader/Writer all should be closed after use.

D. A traditional `try` statement can be used to close an I/O stream.

E. A try-with-resources can be used to close an I/O stream.

F. None of the above.

7. Assume that `in` is a valid stream whose next bytes are XYZABC. What is the result of calling the following method on the stream, using a `count` value of 3?

```
public static String pullBytes(InputStream in, int count)
        throws IOException {
    in.mark(count);
    var sb = new StringBuilder();
    for(int i=0; i<count; i++)
        sb.append((char)in.read());
    in.reset();
    in.skip(1);
    sb.append((char)in.read());
    return sb.toString();
}
```

A. It will return a `String` value of XYZ.

B. It will return a `String` value of XYZA.

C. It will return a `String` value of XYZX.

D. It will return a `String` value of XYZY.

E. The code does not compile.

F. The code compiles but throws an exception at runtime.

G. The result cannot be determined with the information given.

8. Which of the following are true statements about serialization in Java? (Choose all that apply.)

A. Deserialization involves converting data into Java objects.

B. Serialization involves converting data into Java objects.

C. All nonthread classes should be marked `Serializable`.

D. The `Serializable` interface requires implementing `serialize()` and `deserialize()` methods.

E. `Serializable` is a functional interface.

F. The `readObject()` method of `ObjectInputStream` may throw a `ClassNotFoundException` even if the return object is not cast to a specific type.

9. Assuming / is the root directory within the file system, which of the following are true statements? (Choose all that apply.)

A. /home/parrot is an absolute path.

B. /home/parrot is a directory.

   C. /home/parrot is a relative path.

   D. new File("/home") will throw an exception if /home does not exist.

   E. new File("/home").delete() throws an exception if /home does not exist.

10. What are the requirements for a class that you want to serialize to a stream? (Choose all that apply.)

   A. The class must be marked final.

   B. The class must extend the Serializable class.

   C. The class must declare a static serialVersionUID variable.

   D. All static members of the class must be marked transient.

   E. The class must implement the Serializable interface.

   F. All instance members of the class must be serializable or marked transient.

11. Given a directory /storage full of multiple files and directories, what is the result of executing the deleteTree("/storage") method on it?

```
public static void deleteTree(File file) {
    if(!file.isFile())                    // f1
        for(File entry: file.listFiles())  // f2
            deleteTree(entry);
    else file.delete();
}
```

   A. It will delete only the empty directories.

   B. It will delete the entire directory tree including the /storage directory itself.

   C. It will delete all files within the directory tree.

   D. The code will not compile because of line f1.

   E. The code will not compile because of line f2.

   F. None of the above

12. What are possible results of executing the following code? (Choose all that apply.)

```
public static void main(String[] args) {
    String line;
    var c = System.console();
    Writer w = c.writer();
    try (w) {
        if ((line = c.readLine("Enter your name: ")) != null)
            w.append(line);
        w.flush();
    }
}
```

A. The code runs but nothing is printed.

B. The code prints what was entered by the user.

C. An `ArrayIndexOutOfBoundsException` is thrown.

D. A `NullPointerException` is thrown.

E. None of the above, as the code does not compile

13. Suppose that the absolute path /weather/winter/snow.dat represents a file that exists within the file system. Which of the following lines of code creates an object that represents the file? (Choose all that apply.)

A.   `new File("/weather", "winter", "snow.dat")`

B.   `new File("/weather/winter/snow.dat")`

C.   `new File("/weather/winter", new File("snow.dat"))`

D.   `new File("weather", "/winter/snow.dat")`

E.   `new File(new File("/weather/winter"), "snow.dat")`

F. None of the above

14. Which of the following are built-in streams in Java? (Choose all that apply.)

A. `System.err`

B. `System.error`

C. `System.in`

D. `System.input`

E. `System.out`

F. `System.output`

15. Which of the following are not `java.io` classes? (Choose all that apply.)

A. `BufferedReader`

B. `BufferedWriter`

C. `FileReader`

D. `FileWriter`

E. `PrintReader`

F. `PrintWriter`

16. Assuming zoo-data.txt exists and is not empty, what statements about the following method are correct? (Choose all that apply.)

```java
private void echo() throws IOException {
    var o = new FileWriter("new-zoo.txt");
    try (var f = new FileReader("zoo-data.txt");
        var b = new BufferedReader(f); o) {
      o.write(b.readLine());
    }
    o.write("");
}
```

A. When run, the method creates a new file with one line of text in it.

B. When run, the method creates a new file with two lines of text in it.

C. When run, the method creates a new file with the same number of lines as the original file.

D. The method compiles but will produce an exception at runtime.

E. The method does not compile.

F. The method uses byte stream classes.

17. Assume `reader` is a valid stream that supports `mark()` and whose next characters are PEACOCKS. What is the expected output of the following code snippet?

```
var sb = new StringBuilder();
sb.append((char)reader.read());
reader.mark(10);
for(int i=0; i<2; i++) {
    sb.append((char)reader.read());
    reader.skip(2);
}
reader.reset();
reader.skip(0);
sb.append((char)reader.read());
System.out.println(sb.toString());
```

A. PEAE

B. PEOA

C. PEOE

D. PEOS

E. The code does not compile.

F. The code compiles but throws an exception at runtime.

G. The result cannot be determined with the information given.

18. Suppose that you need to write data that consists of int, double, boolean, and String values to a file that maintains the data types of the original data. You also want the data to be performant on large files. Which three `java.io` stream classes can be chained together to best achieve this result? (Choose three.)

A. `FileWriter`

B. `FileOutputStream`

C. `BufferedOutputStream`

D. `ObjectOutputStream`

E. `DirectoryOutputStream`

F. `PrintWriter`

G. `PrintStream`

19. Given the following method, which statements are correct? (Choose all that apply.)

```
public void copyFile(File file1, File file2) throws Exception {
    var reader = new InputStreamReader(
        new FileInputStream(file1));
    try (var writer = new FileWriter(file2)) {
        char[] buffer = new char[10];
        while(reader.read(buffer) != -1) {
            writer.write(buffer);
            // n1
        }
    }
}
```

A. The code does not compile because reader is not a Buffered stream.

B. The code does not compile because writer is not a Buffered stream.

C. The code compiles and correctly copies the data between some files.

D. The code compiles and correctly copies the data between all files.

E. If we check file2 on line n1 within the file system after five iterations of the while loop, it may be empty.

F. If we check file2 on line n1 within the file system after five iterations, it will contain exactly 50 characters.

G. This method contains a resource leak.

20. Which values when inserted into the blank independently would allow the code to compile? (Choose all that apply.)

```
Console console = System.console();
String color = console.readLine("Favorite color? ");
console._____("Your favorite color is %s", color);
```

A. reader().print

B. reader().println

C. format

D. writer().print

E. writer().println

F. None of the above

21. What are some reasons to use a character stream, such as Reader/Writer, over a byte stream, such as InputStream/OutputStream? (Choose all that apply.)

A. More convenient code syntax when working with String data

B. Improved performance

C. Automatic character encoding

D. Built-in serialization and deserialization

E. Character streams are high-level streams.

F. Multithreading support

22. Which of the following fields will be null after an instance of the class created on line 15 is serialized and then deserialized using ObjectOutputStream and ObjectInputStream? (Choose all that apply.)

```
1:  import java.io.Serializable;
2:  import java.util.List;
3:  public class Zebra implements Serializable {
4:      private transient String name = "George";
5:      private static String birthPlace = "Africa";
6:      private transient Integer age;
7:      List<Zebra> friends = new java.util.ArrayList<>();
8:      private Object stripes = new Object();
9:      { age = 10;}
10:     public Zebra() {
11:         this.name = "Sophia";
12:     }
13:     static Zebra writeAndRead(Zebra z) {
14:         // Implementation omitted
15:     }
16:     public static void main(String[] args) {
17:         var zebra = new Zebra();
18:         zebra = writeAndRead(zebra);
19:     } }
```

A. name

B. stripes

C. age

D. friends

E. birthPlace

F. The code does not compile.

G. The code compiles but throws an exception at runtime.

Chapter

9

NIO.2

OCP EXAM OBJECTIVES COVERED IN THIS CHAPTER:

✓ **I/O (Fundamentals and NIO2)**

- Use the Path interface to operate on file and directory paths
- Use the Files class to check, delete, copy or move a file or directory
- Use the Stream API with Files

In Chapter 8, "I/O," we presented the `java.io` API and discussed how to use it to interact with files and streams. In this chapter, we focus on the `java.nio` version 2 API, or NIO.2 for short, to interact with files. NIO.2 is an acronym that stands for the second version of the Non-blocking Input/Output API, and it is sometimes referred to as the "New I/O."

In this chapter, we will show how NIO.2 allows us to do a lot more with files and directories than the original `java.io` API. We'll also show you how to apply the Streams API to perform complex file and directory operations. We'll conclude this chapter by showing the various ways file attributes can be read and written using NIO.2.

While Chapter 8 focused on I/O streams, we're back to using streams to refer to the Streams API that you learned about in Chapter 4, "Functional Programming." For clarity, we'll use the phrase *I/O streams* to discuss the ones found in `java.io` from this point on.

Introducing NIO.2

At its core, NIO.2 is a replacement for the legacy `java.io.File` class you learned about in Chapter 8. The goal of the API is to provide a more intuitive, more feature-rich API for working with files and directories.

By *legacy*, we mean that the preferred approach for working with files and directories with newer software applications is to use NIO.2, rather than `java.io.File`. As you'll soon see, the NIO.2 provides many features and performance improvements than the legacy class supported.

What About NIO?

This chapter focuses on NIO.2, not NIO. Java includes an NIO library that uses buffers and channels, in place of I/O streams. The NIO API was never popular, so much so that nothing from the original version of NIO will be on the OCP exam. Many Java developers continue to use I/O streams to manipulate byte streams, rather than NIO.

People sometimes refer to NIO.2 as just NIO, although for clarity and to distinguish it from the first version of NIO, we will refer to it as NIO.2 throughout the chapter.

Introducing *Path*

The cornerstone of NIO.2 is the `java.nio.file.Path` interface. A `Path` instance represents a hierarchical path on the storage system to a file or directory. You can think of a `Path` as the NIO.2 replacement for the `java.io.File` class, although how you use it is a bit different.

Before we get into that, let's talk about what's similar between these two implementations. Both `java.io.File` and `Path` objects may refer to an absolute path or relative path within the file system. In addition, both may refer to a file or a directory. As we did in Chapter 8 and continue to do in this chapter, we treat an instance that points to a directory as a file since it is stored in the file system with similar properties. For example, we can rename a file or directory with the same commands in both APIs.

Now for something completely different. Unlike the `java.io.File` class, the `Path` interface contains support for symbolic links. A *symbolic link* is a special file within a file system that serves as a reference or pointer to another file or directory. Figure 9.1 shows a symbolic link from `/zoo/favorite` to `/zoo/cats/lion`.

FIGURE 9.1   File system with a symbolic link

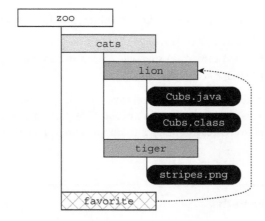

In Figure 9.1, the `lion` folder and its elements can be accessed directly or via the symbolic link. For example, the following paths reference the same file:

/zoo/cats/lion/Cubs.java
/zoo/favorite/Cubs.java

In general, symbolic links are transparent to the user, as the operating system takes care of resolving the reference to the actual file. NIO.2 includes full support for creating, detecting, and navigating symbolic links within the file system.

Creating Paths

Since Path is an interface, we can't create an instance directly. After all, interfaces don't have constructors! Java provides a number of classes and methods that you can use to obtain Path objects, which we will review in this section.

 You might wonder, why is Path an interface? When a Path is created, the JVM returns a file system–specific implementation, such as a Windows or Unix Path class. In the vast majority of circumstances, we want to perform the same operations on the Path, regardless of the file system. By providing Path as an interface using the factory pattern, we avoid having to write complex or custom code for each type of file system.

Obtaining a *Path* with the *Path* Interface

The simplest and most straightforward way to obtain a Path object is to use the static factory method defined within the Path interface.

```
// Path factory method
public static Path of(String first, String... more)
```

It's easy to create Path instances from String values, as shown here:

```
Path path1 = Path.of("pandas/cuddly.png");
Path path2 = Path.of("c:\\zooinfo\\November\\employees.txt");
Path path3 = Path.of("/home/zoodirectory");
```

The first example creates a reference to a relative path in the current working directory. The second example creates a reference to an absolute file path in a Windows-based system. The third example creates a reference to an absolute directory path in a Linux or Mac-based system.

Absolute vs. Relative Paths

Determining whether a path is relative or absolute is actually file-system dependent. To match the exam, we adopt the following conventions:

- If a path starts with a forward slash (/), it is absolute, with / as the root directory. Examples: /bird/parrot.png and /bird/../data/./info

- If a path starts with a drive letter (c:), it is absolute, with the drive letter as the root directory. Examples: `c:/bird/parrot.png` and `d:/bird/../data/./info`

- Otherwise, it is a relative path. Examples: `bird/parrot.png` and `bird/../data/./info`

If you're not familiar with path symbols like . and .., don't worry! We'll be covering them in this chapter.

The `Path.of()` method also includes a varargs to pass additional path elements. The values will be combined and automatically separated by the operating system–dependent file separator you learned about in Chapter 8.

```
Path path1 = Path.of("pandas", "cuddly.png");
Path path2 = Path.of("c:", "zooinfo", "November", "employees.txt");
Path path3 = Path.of("/", "home", "zoodirectory");
```

These examples are just rewrites of our previous set of `Path` examples, using the parameter list of `String` values instead of a single `String` value. The advantage of the varargs is that it is more robust, as it inserts the proper operating system path separator for you.

Obtaining a *Path* with the *Paths* Class

The `Path.of()` method is actually new to Java 11. Another way to obtain a `Path` instance is from the `java.nio.file.Paths` factory class. Note the s at the end of the `Paths` class to distinguish it from the `Path` interface.

```
// Paths factory method
public static Path get(String first, String... more)
```

Rewriting our previous examples is easy.

```
Path path1 = Paths.get("pandas/cuddly.png");
Path path2 = Paths.get("c:\\zooinfo\\November\\employees.txt");
Path path3 = Paths.get("/", "home", "zoodirectory");
```

Since `Paths.get()` is older, the exam is likely to have both. We'll use both `Path.of()` and `Paths.get()` interchangeably in this chapter.

Obtaining a *Path* with a *URI* Class

Another way to construct a `Path` using the `Paths` class is with a URI value. A *uniform resource identifier* (URI) is a string of characters that identify a resource. It begins with a schema that indicates the resource type, followed by a path value. Examples of schema values include `file://` for local file systems, and `http://`, `https://`, and `ftp://` for remote file systems.

The java.net.URI class is used to create URI values.

```
// URI Constructor
public URI(String str) throws URISyntaxException
```

Java includes multiple methods to convert between Path and URI objects.

```
// URI to Path, using Path factory method
public static Path of(URI uri)
```

```
// URI to Path, using Paths factory method
public static Path get(URI uri)
```

```
// Path to URI, using Path instance method
public URI toURI()
```

The following examples all reference the same file:

```
URI a = new URI("file://icecream.txt");
Path b = Path.of(a);
Path c = Paths.get(a);
URI d = b.toUri();
```

Some of these examples may actually throw an IllegalArgumentException at runtime, as some systems require URIs to be absolute. The URI class does have an isAbsolute() method, although this refers to whether the URI has a schema, not the file location.

Other URI Connection Types

A URI can be used for a web page or FTP connection.

```
Path path5 = Paths.get(new URI("http://www.wiley.com"));
Path path6 = Paths.get(new URI("ftp://username:secret@ftp.example.com"));
```

For the exam, you do not need to know the syntax of these types of URIs, but you should be aware they exist.

Obtaining a *Path* from the *FileSystem* Class

NIO.2 makes extensive use of creating objects with factory classes. As you saw already, the Paths class creates instances of the Path interface. Likewise, the FileSystems class creates instances of the abstract FileSystem class.

```
// FileSystems factory method
public static FileSystem getDefault()
```

The `FileSystem` class includes methods for working with the file system directly. In fact, both `Paths.get()` and `Path.of()` are actually shortcuts for this `FileSystem` method:

```
// FileSystem instance method
public Path getPath(String first, String... more)
```

Let's rewrite our three earlier examples one more time to show you how to obtain a `Path` instance "the long way."

```
Path path1 = FileSystems.getDefault().getPath("pandas/cuddly.png");
Path path2 = FileSystems.getDefault()
   .getPath("c:\\zooinfo\\November\\employees.txt");
Path path3 = FileSystems.getDefault().getPath("/home/zoodirectory");
```

 Real World Scenario

Connecting to Remote File Systems

While most of the time we want access to a `Path` object that is within the local file system, the `FileSystems` class does give us the freedom to connect to a remote file system, as follows:

```
// FileSystems factory method
public static FileSystem getFileSystem(URI uri)
```

The following shows how such a method can be used:

```
FileSystem fileSystem = FileSystems.getFileSystem(
   new URI("http://www.selikoff.net"));
Path path = fileSystem.getPath("duck.txt");
```

This code is useful when we need to construct `Path` objects frequently for a remote file system. NIO.2 gives us the power to connect to both local and remote file systems, which is a major improvement over the legacy `java.io.File` class.

Obtaining a *Path* from the *java.io.File* Class

Last but not least, we can obtain `Path` instances using the legacy `java.io.File` class. In fact, we can also obtain a `java.io.File` object from a `Path` instance.

```
// Path to File, using Path instance method
public default File toFile()
```

```
// File to Path, using java.io.File instance method
public Path toPath()
```

These methods are available for convenience and also to help facilitate integration between older and newer APIs. The following shows examples of each:

```
File file = new File("husky.png");
Path path = file.toPath();
File backToFile = path.toFile();
```

When working with newer applications, though, you should rely on NIO.2's Path interface as it contains a lot more features.

Reviewing NIO.2 Relationships

By now, you should realize that NIO.2 makes extensive use of the factory pattern. You should become comfortable with this paradigm. Many of your interactions with NIO.2 will require two types: an abstract class or interface and a factory or helper class. Figure 9.2 shows the relationships among NIO.2 classes, as well as select java.io and java.net classes.

FIGURE 9.2 NIO.2 class and interface relationships

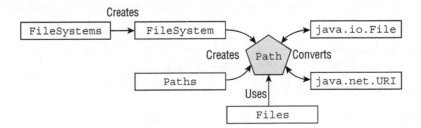

Review Figure 9.2 carefully. When working with NIO.2, keep an eye on whether the class name is singular or plural. The classes with plural names include methods to create or operate on class/interface instances with singular names. Remember, a Path can also be created from the Path interface, using the static factory of() method.

Included in Figure 9.2 is the class java.nio.file.Files, which we'll cover later in the chapter. For now, you just need to know that it is a helper or utility class that operates primarily on Path instances to read or modify actual files and directories.

> The java.io.File is the I/O class you worked with in Chapter 8, while Files is an NIO.2 helper class. Files operates on Path instances, not java.io.File instances. We know this is confusing, but they are from completely different APIs! For clarity, we often write out the full name of the java.io.File class in this chapter.

Understanding Common NIO.2 Features

Throughout this chapter, we introduce numerous methods you should know for the exam. Before getting into the specifics of each method, we present many of these common features in this section so you are not surprised when you see them.

Applying Path Symbols

Absolute and relative paths can contain path symbols. A *path symbol* is a reserved series of characters that have special meaning within some file systems. For the exam, there are two path symbols you need to know, as listed in Table 9.1.

TABLE 9.1   File system symbols

Symbol	Description
.	A reference to the current directory
..	A reference to the parent of the current directory

We illuminate using path symbols in Figure 9.3.

FIGURE 9.3   Relative paths using path symbols

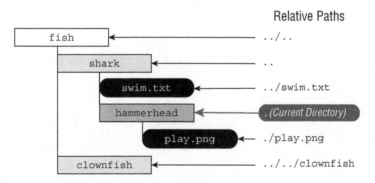

In Figure 9.3, the current directory is /fish/shark/hammerhead. In this case, ../swim.txt refers to the file swim.txt in the parent of the current directory. Likewise, ./play.png refers to play.png in the current directory. These symbols can also be combined for greater effect. For example, ../../clownfish refers to the directory that is two directories up from the current directory.

Sometimes you'll see path symbols that are redundant or unnecessary. For example, the absolute path /fish/shark/hammerhead/.././swim.txt can be simplified to /fish/shark/swim.txt. We'll see how to handle these redundancies later in the chapter when we cover normalize().

Providing Optional Arguments

Many of the methods in this chapter include a varargs that takes an optional list of values. Table 9.2 presents the arguments you should be familiar with for the exam.

TABLE 9.2   Common NIO.2 method arguments

Enum type	Interface inherited	Enum value	Details
LinkOption	CopyOption OpenOption	NOFOLLOW_LINKS	Do not follow symbolic links.
StandardCopyOption	CopyOption	ATOMIC_MOVE	Move file as atomic file system operation.
		COPY_ ATTRIBUTES	Copy existing attributes to new file.
		REPLACE_ EXISTING	Overwrite file if it already exists.
StandardOpenOption	OpenOption	APPEND	If file is already open for write, then append to the end.
		CREATE	Create a new file if it does not exist.
		CREATE_NEW	Create a new file only if it does not exist, fail otherwise.
		READ	Open for read access.
		TRUNCATE_ EXISTING	If file is already open for write, then erase file and append to beginning.
		WRITE	Open for write access.
FileVisitOption	N/A	FOLLOW_LINKS	Follow symbolic links.

With the exceptions of Files.copy() and Files.move() (which we'll cover later), we won't discuss these varargs parameters each time we present a method. The behavior of them should be straightforward, though. For example, can you figure out what the following call to Files.exists() with the LinkOption does in the following code snippet?

```
Path path = Paths.get("schedule.xml");
boolean exists = Files.exists(path, LinkOption.NOFOLLOW_LINKS);
```

The Files.exists() simply checks whether a file exists. If the parameter is a symbolic link, though, then the method checks whether the target of the symbolic link exists instead. Providing LinkOption.NOFOLLOW_LINKS means the default behavior will be overridden, and the method will check whether the symbolic link itself exists.

Note that some of the enums in Table 9.2 inherit an interface. That means some methods accept a variety of enums types. For example, the Files.move() method takes a CopyOption vararg so it can take enums of different types.

```
void copy(Path source, Path target) throws IOException {
    Files.move(source, target,
        LinkOption.NOFOLLOW_LINKS,
        StandardCopyOption.ATOMIC_MOVE);
}
```

Many of the NIO.2 methods use a varargs for passing options, even when there is only one enum value available. The advantage of this approach, as opposed to say just passing a boolean argument, is future-proofing. These method signatures are insulated from changes in the Java language down the road when future options are available.

Handling Methods That Declare *IOException*

Many of the methods presented in this chapter declare IOException. Common causes of a method throwing this exception include the following:

- Loss of communication to underlying file system.

- File or directory exists but cannot be accessed or modified.

- File exists but cannot be overwritten.

- File or directory is required but does not exist.

In general, methods that operate on abstract Path values, such as those in the Path interface or Paths class, often do not throw any checked exceptions. On the other hand, methods that operate or change files and directories, such as those in the Files class, often declare IOException.

There are exceptions to this rule, as we will see. For example, the method Files.exists() does not declare IOException. If it did throw an exception when the file did not exist, then it would never be able to return false!

Interacting with Paths

Now that we've covered the basics of NIO.2, you might ask, what can we do with it? Short answer: a lot. NIO.2 provides a *rich plethora* of methods and classes that operate on Path objects—far more than were available in the java.io API. In this section, we present the Path methods you should know for the exam, organized by related functionality.

Just like String values, Path instances are immutable. In the following example, the Path operation on the second line is lost since p is immutable:

```
Path p = Path.of("whale");
p.resolve("krill");
System.out.println(p);  // whale
```

Many of the methods available in the Path interface transform the path value in some way and return a new Path object, allowing the methods to be chained. We demonstrate chaining in the following example, the details of which we'll discuss in this section of the chapter:

```
Path.of("/zoo/../home").getParent().normalize().toAbsolutePath();
```

> If you start to feel overwhelmed by the number of methods available in the Path interface, just remember: the function of many of them can be inferred by their method name. For example, what do you think the Path method getParent() does? It returns the parent directory of a Path. Not so difficult, was it?

Many of the code snippets in this part of the chapter can be run without the paths they reference actually existing. The JVM communicates with the file system to determine the path components or the parent directory of a file, without requiring the file to actually exist. As rule of thumb, if the method declares an IOException, then it *usually* requires the paths it operates on to exist.

Viewing the Path with *toString()*, *getNameCount()*, and *getName()*

The Path interface contains three methods to retrieve basic information about the path representation.

```
public String toString()
```

```
public int getNameCount()
```

```
public Path getName(int index)
```

The first method, toString(), returns a String representation of the entire path. In fact, it is the only method in the Path interface to return a String. Many of the other methods in the Path interface return Path instances.

The getNameCount() and getName() methods are often used in conjunction to retrieve the number of elements in the path and a reference to each element, respectively. These two methods do not include the root directory as part of the path.

```java
Path path = Paths.get("/land/hippo/harry.happy");
System.out.println("The Path Name is: " + path);
for(int i=0; i<path.getNameCount(); i++) {
    System.out.println("   Element " + i + " is: " + path.getName(i));
}
```

Notice we didn't call toString() explicitly on the second line. Remember, Java calls toString() on any Object as part of string concatenation. We'll be using this feature throughout the examples in this chapter.

The code prints the following:

```
The Path Name is: /land/hippo/harry.happy
   Element 0 is: land
   Element 1 is: hippo
   Element 2 is: harry.happy
```

Even though this is an absolute path, the root element is not included in the list of names. As we said, these methods do not consider the root as part of the path.

```java
var p = Path.of("/");
System.out.print(p.getNameCount()); // 0
System.out.print(p.getName(0));     // IllegalArgumentException
```

Notice that if you try to call getName() with an invalid index, it will throw an exception at runtime.

Our examples print / as the file separator character because of the system we are using. Your actual output may vary throughout this chapter.

Creating a New Path with *subpath()*

The Path interface includes a method to select portions of a path.

```java
public Path subpath(int beginIndex, int endIndex)
```

The references are inclusive of the beginIndex, and exclusive of the endIndex. The subpath() method is similar to the previous getName() method, except that subpath() may return multiple path components, whereas getName() returns only one. Both return Path instances, though.

The following code snippet shows how subpath() works. We also print the elements of the Path using getName() so that you can see how the indices are used.

```
var p = Paths.get("/mammal/omnivore/raccoon.image");
System.out.println("Path is: " + p);
for (int i = 0; i < p.getNameCount(); i++) {
    System.out.println("   Element " + i + " is: " + p.getName(i));
}
System.out.println();
System.out.println("subpath(0,3): " + p.subpath(0, 3));
System.out.println("subpath(1,2): " + p.subpath(1, 2));
System.out.println("subpath(1,3): " + p.subpath(1, 3));
```

The output of this code snippet is the following:

```
Path is: /mammal/omnivore/raccoon.image
   Element 0 is: mammal
   Element 1 is: omnivore
   Element 2 is: raccoon.image

subpath(0,3): mammal/omnivore/raccoon.image
subpath(1,2): omnivore
subpath(1,3): omnivore/raccoon.image
```

Like getNameCount() and getName(), subpath() is 0-indexed and does not include the root. Also like getName(), subpath() throws an exception if invalid indices are provided.

```
var q = p.subpath(0, 4); // IllegalArgumentException
var x = p.subpath(1, 1); // IllegalArgumentException
```

The first example throws an exception at runtime, since the maximum index value allowed is 3. The second example throws an exception since the start and end indexes are the same, leading to an empty path value.

Accessing Path Elements with *getFileName()*, *getParent()*, and *getRoot()*

The Path interface contains numerous methods for retrieving particular elements of a Path, returned as Path objects themselves.

```
public Path getFileName()
```

```
public Path getParent()
```

```
public Path getRoot()
```

The getFileName() returns the Path element of the current file or directory, while getParent() returns the full path of the containing directory. The getParent() returns null if operated on the root path or at the top of a relative path. The getRoot() method returns the root element of the file within the file system, or null if the path is a relative path.

Consider the following method, which prints various Path elements:

```
public void printPathInformation(Path path) {
    System.out.println("Filename is: " + path.getFileName());
    System.out.println("   Root is: " + path.getRoot());
    Path currentParent = path;
    while((currentParent = currentParent.getParent()) != null) {
        System.out.println("   Current parent is: " + currentParent);
    }
}
```

The while loop in the printPathInformation() method continues until getParent() returns null. We apply this method to the following three paths:

```
printPathInformation(Path.of("zoo"));
printPathInformation(Path.of("/zoo/armadillo/shells.txt"));
printPathInformation(Path.of("./armadillo/../shells.txt"));
```

This sample application produces the following output:

```
Filename is: zoo
   Root is: null

Filename is: shells.txt
   Root is: /
   Current parent is: /zoo/armadillo
   Current parent is: /zoo
   Current parent is: /

Filename is: shells.txt
   Root is: null
   Current parent is: ./armadillo/..
   Current parent is: ./armadillo
   Current parent is: .
```

Reviewing the sample output, you can see the difference in the behavior of getRoot() on absolute and relative paths. As you can see in the first and last examples, the getParent() does not traverse relative paths outside the current working directory.

You also see that these methods do not resolve the path symbols and treat them as a distinct part of the path. While most of the methods in this part of the chapter will treat path symbols as part of the path, we will present one shortly that cleans up path symbols.

Checking Path Type with *isAbsolute()* and *toAbsolutePath()*

The Path interface contains two methods for assisting with relative and absolute paths:

```
public boolean isAbsolute()
```

```
public Path toAbsolutePath()
```

The first method, isAbsolute(), returns true if the path the object references is absolute and false if the path the object references is relative. As discussed earlier in this chapter, whether a path is absolute or relative is often file system–dependent, although we, like the exam writers, adopt common conventions for simplicity throughout the book.

The second method, toAbsolutePath(), converts a relative Path object to an absolute Path object by joining it to the current working directory. If the Path object is already absolute, then the method just returns the Path object.

The current working directory can be selected from System.getProperty("user.dir"). This is the value that toAbsolutePath() will use when applied to a relative path.

The following code snippet shows usage of both of these methods when run on a Windows and Linux system, respectively:

```
var path1 = Paths.get("C:\\birds\\egret.txt");
System.out.println("Path1 is Absolute? " + path1.isAbsolute());
System.out.println("Absolute Path1: " + path1.toAbsolutePath());

var path2 = Paths.get("birds/condor.txt");
System.out.println("Path2 is Absolute? " + path2.isAbsolute());
System.out.println("Absolute Path2 " + path2.toAbsolutePath());
```

The output for the code snippet on each respective system is shown in the following sample output. For the second example, assume the current working directory is /home/work.

```
Path1 is Absolute? true
Absolute Path1: C:\birds\egret.txt

Path2 is Absolute? false
Absolute Path2 /home/work/birds/condor.txt
```

Joining Paths with *resolve()*

Suppose you want to concatenate paths in a similar manner as we concatenate strings. The Path interface provides two resolve() methods for doing just that.

```
public Path resolve(Path other)
```

```
public Path resolve(String other)
```

The first method takes a Path parameter, while the overloaded version is a shorthand form of the first that takes a String (and constructs the Path for you). The object on which the resolve() method is invoked becomes the basis of the new Path object, with the input argument being appended onto the Path. Let's see what happens if we apply resolve() to an absolute path and a relative path:

```
Path path1 = Path.of("/cats/../panther");
Path path2 = Path.of("food");
System.out.println(path1.resolve(path2));
```

The code snippet generates the following output:

```
/cats/../panther/food
```

Like the other methods we've seen up to now, resolve() does not clean up path symbols. In this example, the input argument to the resolve() method was a relative path, but what if it had been an absolute path?

```
Path path3 = Path.of("/turkey/food");
System.out.println(path3.resolve("/tiger/cage"));
```

Since the input parameter path3 is an absolute path, the output would be the following:

```
/tiger/cage
```

For the exam, you should be cognizant of mixing absolute and relative paths with the resolve() method. If an absolute path is provided as input to the method, then that is the value that is returned. Simply put, you cannot combine two absolute paths using resolve().

On the exam, when you see Files.resolve(), think concatenation.

Deriving a Path with *relativize()*

The Path interface includes a method for constructing the relative path from one Path to another, often using path symbols.

```
public Path relativize()
```

What do you think the following examples using `relativize()` print?

```
var path1 = Path.of("fish.txt");
var path2 = Path.of("friendly/birds.txt");
System.out.println(path1.relativize(path2));
System.out.println(path2.relativize(path1));
```

The examples print the following:

```
../friendly/birds.txt
../../fish.txt
```

The idea is this: if you are pointed at a path in the file system, what steps would you need to take to reach the other path? For example, to get to `fish.txt` from `friendly/birds.txt`, you need to go up two levels (the file itself counts as one level) and then select `fish.txt`.

If both path values are relative, then the `relativize()` method computes the paths as if they are in the same current working directory. Alternatively, if both path values are absolute, then the method computes the relative path from one absolute location to another, regardless of the current working directory. The following example demonstrates this property when run on a Windows computer:

```
Path path3 = Paths.get("E:\\habitat");
Path path4 = Paths.get("E:\\sanctuary\\raven\\poe.txt");
System.out.println(path3.relativize(path4));
System.out.println(path4.relativize(path3));
```

This code snippet produces the following output:

```
..\sanctuary\raven\poe.txt
..\..\..\habitat
```

The code snippet works even if you do not have an `E:` in your system. Remember, most methods defined in the `Path` interface do not require the path to exist.

The `relativize()` method requires that both paths are absolute or both relative and throws an exception if the types are mixed.

```
Path path1 = Paths.get("/primate/chimpanzee");
Path path2 = Paths.get("bananas.txt");
path1.relativize(path2); // IllegalArgumentException
```

On Windows-based systems, it also requires that if absolute paths are used, then both paths must have the same root directory or drive letter. For example, the following would also throw an `IllegalArgumentException` on a Windows-based system:

```
Path path3 = Paths.get("c:\\primate\\chimpanzee");
Path path4 = Paths.get("d:\\storage\\bananas.txt");
path3.relativize(path4); // IllegalArgumentException
```

Cleaning Up a Path with *normalize()*

So far, we've presented a number of examples that included path symbols that were unnecessary. Luckily, Java provides a method to eliminate unnecessary redundancies in a path.

```
public Path normalize()
```

Remember, the path symbol .. refers to the parent directory, while the path symbol . refers to the current directory. We can apply normalize() to some of our previous paths.

```
var p1 = Path.of("./armadillo/../shells.txt");
System.out.println(p1.normalize()); // shells.txt


var p2 = Path.of("/cats/../panther/food");
System.out.println(p2.normalize()); // /panther/food


var p3 = Path.of("../../fish.txt");
System.out.println(p3.normalize()); // ../../fish.txt
```

The first two examples apply the path symbols to remove the redundancies, but what about the last one? That is as simplified as it can be. The normalize() method does not remove all of the path symbols; only the ones that can be reduced.

The normalize() method also allows us to compare equivalent paths. Consider the following example:

```
var p1 = Paths.get("/pony/../weather.txt");
var p2 = Paths.get("/weather.txt");
System.out.println(p1.equals(p2));                          // false
System.out.println(p1.normalize().equals(p2.normalize())); // true
```

The equals() method returns true if two paths represent the same value. In the first comparison, the path values are different. In the second comparison, the path values have both been reduced to the same normalized value, /weather.txt. This is the primary function of the normalize() method, to allow us to better compare different paths.

Retrieving the File System Path with *toRealPath()*

While working with theoretical paths is useful, sometimes you want to verify the path actually exists within the file system.

```
public Path toRealPath(LinkOption... options) throws IOException
```

This method is similar to normalize(), in that it eliminates any redundant path symbols. It is also similar to toAbsolutePath(), in that it will join the path with the current working directory if the path is relative.

Unlike those two methods, though, toRealPath() will throw an exception if the path does not exist. In addition, it will follow symbolic links, with an optional varargs parameter to ignore them.

Let's say that we have a file system in which we have a symbolic link from /zebra to /horse. What do you think the following will print, given a current working directory of /horse/schedule?

```
System.out.println(Paths.get("/zebra/food.txt").toRealPath());
System.out.println(Paths.get("../../food.txt").toRealPath());
```

The output of both lines is the following:

```
/horse/food.txt
```

In this example, the absolute and relative paths both resolve to the same absolute file, as the symbolic link points to a real file within the file system. We can also use the toRealPath() method to gain access to the current working directory as a Path object.

```
System.out.println(Paths.get(".").toRealPath());
```

Reviewing *Path* Methods

We conclude this section with Table 9.3, which shows the Path methods that you should know for the exam.

TABLE 9.3   *Path* methods

Path of(String, String...)	Path getParent()
URI toURI()	Path getRoot()
File toFile()	boolean isAbsolute()
String toString()	Path toAbsolutePath()
int getNameCount()	Path relativize()
Path getName(int)	Path resolve(Path)
Path subpath(int, int)	Path normalize()
Path getFileName()	Path toRealPath(LinkOption...)

Other than the static method Path.of(), all of the methods in Table 9.3 are instance methods that can be called on any Path instance. In addition, only toRealPath() declares an IOException.

Operating on Files and Directories

Most of the methods we covered in the Path interface operate on theoretical paths, which are not required to exist within the file system. What if you want to rename a directory, copy a file, or read the contents of a file?

Enter the NIO.2 Files class. The Files helper class is capable of interacting with real files and directories within the system. Because of this, most of the methods in this part of the chapter take optional parameters and throw an IOException if the path does not exist. The Files class also replicates numerous methods found in the java.io.File, albeit often with a different name or list of parameters.

Many of the names for the methods in the NIO.2 Files class are a lot more straightforward than what you saw in the java.io.File class. For example, the java.io.File methods renameTo() and mkdir() have been changed to move() and createDirectory(), respectively, in the Files class.

Checking for Existence with *exists()*

The first Files method we present is the simplest. It just checks whether the file exists.

```
public static boolean exists(Path path, LinkOption... options)
```

Let's take a look at some sample code that operates on a features.png file in the /ostrich directory.

```
var b1 = Files.exists(Paths.get("/ostrich/feathers.png"));
System.out.println("Path " + (b1 ? "Exists" : "Missing"));

var b2 = Files.exists(Paths.get("/ostrich"));
System.out.println("Path " + (b2 ? "Exists" : "Missing"));
```

The first example checks whether a file exists, while the second example checks whether a directory exists. This method does not throw an exception if the file does not exist, as doing so would prevent this method from ever returning false at runtime.

Remember, a file and directory may both have extensions. In the last example, the two paths could refer to two files or two directories. Unless the exam tells you whether the path refers to a file or directory, do not assume either.

Testing Uniqueness with *isSameFile()*

Since a path may include path symbols and symbolic links within a file system, it can be difficult to know if two Path instances refer to the same file. Luckily, there's a method for that in the Files class:

```
public static boolean isSameFile(Path path, Path path2)
   throws IOException
```

The method takes two Path objects as input, resolves all path symbols, and follows symbolic links. Despite the name, the method can also be used to determine whether two Path objects refer to the same directory.

While most usages of isSameFile() will trigger an exception if the paths do not exist, there is a special case in which it does not. If the two path objects are equal, in terms of equals(), then the method will just return true without checking whether the file exists.

Assume the file system exists as shown in Figure 9.4 with a symbolic link from /animals/snake to /animals/cobra.

FIGURE 9.4   Comparing file uniqueness

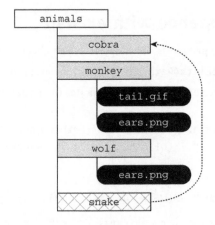

Given the structure defined in Figure 9.4, what does the following output?

```
System.out.println(Files.isSameFile(
   Path.of("/animals/cobra"),
   Path.of("/animals/snake")));
```

```
System.out.println(Files.isSameFile(
    Path.of("/animals/monkey/ears.png"),
    Path.of("/animals/wolf/ears.png")));
```

Since cobra is a symbolic link to snake, the first example outputs true. In the second example, the paths refer to different files, so false is printed.

 This isSameFile() method does not compare the contents of the files. Two files may have identical names, content, and attributes, but if they are in different locations, then this method will return false.

Making Directories with *createDirectory()* and *createDirectories()*

To create a directory, we use these Files methods:

```
public static Path createDirectory(Path dir,
    FileAttribute<?>... attrs) throws IOException
```

```
public static Path createDirectories(Path dir,
    FileAttribute<?>... attrs) throws IOException
```

The createDirectory() will create a directory and throw an exception if it already exists or the paths leading up to the directory do not exist.

The createDirectories() works just like the java.io.File method mkdirs(), in that it creates the target directory along with any nonexistent parent directories leading up to the path. If all of the directories already exist, createDirectories() will simply complete without doing anything. This is useful in situations where you want to ensure a directory exists and create it if it does not.

Both of these methods also accept an optional list of FileAttribute<?> values to apply to the newly created directory or directories. We will discuss file attributes more later in the chapter.

The following shows how to create directories in NIO.2:

```
Files.createDirectory(Path.of("/bison/field"));
Files.createDirectories(Path.of("/bison/field/pasture/green"));
```

The first example creates a new directory, field, in the directory /bison, assuming /bison exists; or else an exception is thrown. Contrast this with the second example, which creates the directory green along with any of the following parent directories if they do not already exist, including bison, field, and pasture.

Copying Files with *copy()*

The NIO.2 Files class provides a method for copying files and directories within the file system.

```
public static Path copy(Path source, Path target,
    CopyOption... options) throws IOException
```

The method copies a file or directory from one location to another using Path objects. The following shows an example of copying a file and a directory:

```
Files.copy(Paths.get("/panda/bamboo.txt"),
    Paths.get("/panda-save/bamboo.txt"));


Files.copy(Paths.get("/turtle"), Paths.get("/turtleCopy"));
```

When directories are copied, the copy is shallow. A *shallow copy* means that the files and subdirectories within the directory are not copied. A *deep copy* means that the entire tree is copied, including all of its content and subdirectories. We'll show how to perform a deep copy of a directory tree using streams later in the chapter.

Copying and Replacing Files

By default, if the target already exists, the copy() method will throw an exception. You can change this behavior by providing the StandardCopyOption enum value REPLACE_EXISTING to the method. The following method call will overwrite the movie.txt file if it already exists:

```
Files.copy(Paths.get("book.txt"), Paths.get("movie.txt"),
    StandardCopyOption.REPLACE_EXISTING);
```

For the exam, you need to know that without the REPLACE_EXISTING option, this method will throw an exception if the file already exists.

Copying Files with I/O Streams

The Files class includes two copy() methods that operate with I/O streams.

```
public static long copy(InputStream in, Path target,
    CopyOption... options) throws IOException
```

```
public static long copy(Path source, OutputStream out)
   throws IOException
```

The first method reads the contents of a stream and writes the output to a file. The second method reads the contents of a file and writes the output to a stream. They are quite convenient if you need to quickly read/write data from/to disk.

The following are examples of each copy() method:

```
try (var is = new FileInputStream("source-data.txt")) {
   // Write stream data to a file
   Files.copy(is, Paths.get("/mammals/wolf.txt"));
}


Files.copy(Paths.get("/fish/clown.xsl"), System.out);
```

While we used FileInputStream in the first example, the streams could have been any valid I/O stream including website connections, in-memory stream resources, and so forth. The second example prints the contents of a file directly to the System.out stream.

Copying Files into a Directory

For the exam, it is important that you understand how the copy() method operates on both files and directories. For example, let's say we have a file, food.txt, and a directory, /enclosure. Both the file and directory exist. What do you think is the result of executing the following process?

```
var file = Paths.get("food.txt");
var directory = Paths.get("/enclosure");
Files.copy(file, directory);
```

If you said it would create a new file at /enclosure/food.txt, then you're way off. It actually throws an exception. The command tries to create a new file, named /enclosure. Since the path /enclosure already exists, an exception is thrown at runtime.

On the other hand, if the directory did not exist, then it would create a new file with the contents of food.txt, but it would be called /enclosure. Remember, we said files may not need to have extensions, and in this example, it matters.

This behavior applies to both the copy() and the move() methods, the latter of which we will be covering next. In case you're curious, the correct way to copy the file into the directory would be to do the following:

```
var file = Paths.get("food.txt");
var directory = Paths.get("/enclosure/food.txt");
Files.copy(file, directory);
```

You also define directory using the resolve() method we saw earlier, which saves you from having to write the filename twice.

```
var directory = Paths.get("/enclosure").resolve(file.getFileName());
```

Moving or Renaming Paths with *move()*

The Files class provides a useful method for moving or renaming files and directories.

```
public static Path move(Path source, Path target,
   CopyOption... options) throws IOException
```

The following is some sample code that uses the move() method:

```
Files.move(Path.of("c:\\zoo"), Path.of("c:\\zoo-new"));
```

```
Files.move(Path.of("c:\\user\\addresses.txt"),
   Path.of("c:\\zoo-new\\addresses2.txt"));
```

The first example renames the zoo directory to a zoo-new directory, keeping all of the original contents from the source directory. The second example moves the addresses.txt file from the directory user to the directory zoo-new, and it renames it to addresses2.txt.

Similarities between *move()* and *copy()*

Like copy(), move() requires REPLACE_EXISTING to overwrite the target if it exists, else it will throw an exception. Also like copy(), move() will not put a file in a directory if the source is a file and the target is a directory. Instead, it will create a new file with the name of the directory.

Performing an Atomic Move

Another enum value that you need to know for the exam when working with the move() method is the StandardCopyOption value ATOMIC_MOVE.

```
Files.move(Path.of("mouse.txt"), Path.of("gerbil.txt"),
   StandardCopyOption.ATOMIC_MOVE);
```

You may remember the atomic property from Chapter 7, "Concurrency," and the principle of an atomic move is similar. An atomic move is one in which a file is moved within the file system as a single indivisible operation. Put another way, any process monitoring the file system never sees an incomplete or partially written file. If the file system does not support this feature, an AtomicMoveNotSupportedException will be thrown.

Note that while ATOMIC_MOVE is available as a member of the StandardCopyOption type, it will likely throw an exception if passed to a copy() method.

Deleting a File with *delete()* and *deleteIfExists()*

The Files class includes two methods that delete a file or empty directory within the file system.

```
public static void delete(Path path) throws IOException
```

```
public static boolean deleteIfExists(Path path) throws IOException
```

To delete a directory, it must be empty. Both of these methods throw an exception if operated on a nonempty directory. In addition, if the path is a symbolic link, then the symbolic link will be deleted, not the path that the symbolic link points to.

The methods differ on how they handle a path that does not exist. The delete() method throws an exception if the path does not exist, while the deleteIfExists() method returns true if the delete was successful, and false otherwise. Similar to createDirectories(), deleteIfExists() is useful in situations where you want to ensure a path does not exist, and delete it if it does.

Here we provide sample code that performs delete() operations:

```
Files.delete(Paths.get("/vulture/feathers.txt"));
Files.deleteIfExists(Paths.get("/pigeon"));
```

The first example deletes the feathers.txt file in the vulture directory, and it throws a NoSuchFileException if the file or directory does not exist. The second example deletes the pigeon directory, assuming it is empty. If the pigeon directory does not exist, then the second line will not throw an exception.

Reading and Writing Data with *newBufferedReader()* and *newBufferedWriter()*

NIO.2 includes two convenient methods for working with I/O streams.

```
public static BufferedReader newBufferedReader(Path path)
    throws IOException
```

```
public static BufferedWriter newBufferedWriter(Path path,
    OpenOption... options) throws IOException
```

You can wrap I/O stream constructors to produce the same effect, although it's a lot easier to use the factory method.

> There are overloaded versions of these methods that take a Charset. You may remember that we briefly discussed character encoding and Charset in Chapter 8. For this chapter, you just need to know that characters can be encoded in bytes in a variety of ways.

The first method, newBufferedReader(), reads the file specified at the Path location using a BufferedReader object.

```
var path = Path.of("/animals/gopher.txt");
try (var reader = Files.newBufferedReader(path)) {
   String currentLine = null;
   while((currentLine = reader.readLine()) != null)
      System.out.println(currentLine);
}
```

This example reads the lines of the files using a BufferedReader and outputs the contents to the screen. As you shall see shortly, there are other methods that do this without having to use an I/O stream.

The second method, newBufferedWriter(), writes to a file specified at the Path location using a BufferedWriter.

```java
var list = new ArrayList<String>();
list.add("Smokey");
list.add("Yogi");

var path = Path.of("/animals/bear.txt");
try (var writer = Files.newBufferedWriter(path)) {
   for(var line : list) {
      writer.write(line);
      writer.newLine();
   }
}
```

This code snippet creates a new file with two lines of text in it. Did you notice that both of these methods use buffered streams rather than low-level file streams? As we mentioned in Chapter 8, the buffered stream classes are much more performant, especially when working with files.

Reading a File with *readAllLines()*

The Files class includes a convenient method for turning the lines of a file into a List.

```java
public static List<String> readAllLines(Path path) throws IOException
```

The following sample code reads the lines of the file and outputs them to the user:

```java
var path = Path.of("/animals/gopher.txt");
final List<String> lines = Files.readAllLines(path);
lines.forEach(System.out::println);
```

Be aware that the entire file is read when readAllLines() is called, with the resulting List<String> storing all of the contents of the file in memory at once. If the file is significantly large, then you may trigger an OutOfMemoryError trying to load all of it into memory. Later in the chapter, we will revisit this method and present a stream-based NIO.2 method that can operate with a much smaller memory footprint.

Reviewing *Files* Methods

Table 9.4 shows the static methods in the Files class that you should be familiar with for the exam.

TABLE 9.4 *Files* methods

boolean exists(Path, LinkOption...)	Path move(Path, Path, CopyOption...)
boolean isSameFile(Path, Path)	void delete(Path)
Path createDirectory(Path, FileAttribute<?>...)	boolean deleteIfExists(Path)
Path createDirectories(Path, FileAttribute<?>...)	BufferedReader newBufferedReader(Path)
Path copy(Path, Path, CopyOption...)	BufferedWriter newBufferedWriter(Path, OpenOption...)
long copy(InputStream, Path, CopyOption...)	List<String> readAllLines(Path)
long copy(Path, OutputStream)	

All of these methods except `exists()` declare `IOException`.

Managing File Attributes

The `Files` class also provides numerous methods for accessing file and directory metadata, referred to as *file attributes*. A file attribute is data about a file within the system, such as its size and visibility, that is not part of the file contents. In this section, we'll show how to read file attributes individually or as a single streamlined call.

Discovering File Attributes

We begin our discussion by presenting the basic methods for reading file attributes. These methods are usable within any file system although they may have limited meaning in some file systems.

Reading Common Attributes with *isDirectory()*, *isSymbolicLink()*, and *isRegularFile()*

The `Files` class includes three methods for determining type of a `Path`.

```
public static boolean isDirectory(Path path, LinkOption... options)
```

```
public static boolean isSymbolicLink(Path path)
```

```
public static boolean isRegularFile(Path path, LinkOption... options)
```

The isDirectory() and isSymbolicLink() methods should be self-explanatory, although isRegularFile() warrants some discussion. Java defines a *regular file* as one that can contain content, as opposed to a symbolic link, directory, resource, or other non-regular file that may be present in some operating systems. If the symbolic link points to an actual file, Java will perform the check on the target of the symbolic link. In other words, it is possible for isRegularFile() to return true for a symbolic link, as long as the link resolves to a regular file.

Let's take a look at some sample code.

```
System.out.print(Files.isDirectory(Paths.get("/canine/fur.jpg")));
System.out.print(Files.isSymbolicLink(Paths.get("/canine/coyote")));
System.out.print(Files.isRegularFile(Paths.get("/canine/types.txt")));
```

The first example prints true if fur.jpg is a directory or a symbolic link to a directory and false otherwise. The second example prints true if /canine/coyote is a symbolic link, regardless of whether the file or directory it points to exists. The third example prints true if types.txt points to a regular file or alternatively a symbolic link that points to a regular file.

> While most methods in the Files class declare IOException, these three methods do not. They return false if the path does not exist.

Checking File Accessibility with *isHidden()*, *isReadable()*, *isWritable()*, and *isExecutable()*

In many file systems, it is possible to set a boolean attribute to a file that marks it hidden, readable, or executable. The Files class includes methods that expose this information.

```
public static boolean isHidden(Path path) throws IOException
```

```
public static boolean isReadable(Path path)
```

```
public static boolean isWritable(Path path)
```

```
public static boolean isExecutable(Path path)
```

A hidden file can't normally be viewed when listing the contents of a directory. The readable, writable, and executable flags are important in file systems where the filename can be viewed, but the user may not have permission to open the file's contents, modify the file, or run the file as a program, respectively.

Here we present sample usage of each method:

```
System.out.print(Files.isHidden(Paths.get("/walrus.txt")));
System.out.print(Files.isReadable(Paths.get("/seal/baby.png")));
System.out.print(Files.isWritable(Paths.get("dolphin.txt")));
System.out.print(Files.isExecutable(Paths.get("whale.png")));
```

If the walrus.txt exists and is hidden within the file system, then the first example prints true. The second example prints true if the baby.png file exists and its contents are readable. The third example prints true if the dolphin.txt file is able to be modified. Finally, the last example prints true if the file is able to be executed within the operating system. Note that the file extension does not necessarily determine whether a file is executable. For example, an image file that ends in .png could be marked executable in some file systems.

With the exception of isHidden(), these methods do not declare any checked exceptions and return false if the file does not exist.

Reading File Size with *size()*

The Files class includes a method to determine the size of the file in bytes.

```
public static long size(Path path) throws IOException
```

The size returned by this method represents the conceptual size of the data, and this may differ from the actual size on the persistent storage device. The following is a sample call to the size() method:

```
System.out.print(Files.size(Paths.get("/zoo/animals.txt")));
```

The Files.size() method is defined only on files. Calling Files.size() on a directory is undefined, and the result depends on the file system. If you need to determine the size of a directory and its contents, you'll need to walk the directory tree. We'll show you how to do this later in the chapter.

Checking for File Changes with *getLastModifiedTime()*

Most operating systems support tracking a last-modified date/time value with each file. Some applications use this to determine when the file's contents should be read again. In the majority of circumstances, it is a lot faster to check a single file metadata attribute than to reload the entire contents of the file.

The Files class provides the following method to retrieve the last time a file was modified:

```
public static FileTime getLastModifiedTime(Path path,
    LinkOption... options) throws IOException
```

The method returns a FileTime object, which represents a timestamp. For convenience, it has a toMillis() method that returns the epoch time, which is the number of milliseconds since 12 a.m. UTC on January 1, 1970.

The following shows how to print the last modified value for a file as an epoch value:

```
final Path path = Paths.get("/rabbit/food.jpg");
System.out.println(Files.getLastModifiedTime(path).toMillis());
```

Improving Attribute Access

Up until now, we have been accessing individual file attributes with multiple method calls. While this is functionally correct, there is often a cost each time one of these methods is called. Put simply, it is far more efficient to ask the file system for all of the attributes at once rather than performing multiple round-trips to the file system. Furthermore, some attributes are file system–specific and cannot be easily generalized for all file systems.

NIO.2 addresses both of these concerns by allowing you to construct views for various file systems with a single method call. A *view* is a group of related attributes for a particular file system type. That's not to say that the earlier attribute methods that we just finished discussing do not have their uses. If you need to read only one attribute of a file or directory, then requesting a view is unnecessary.

Understanding Attribute and View Types

NIO.2 includes two methods for working with attributes in a single method call: a read-only attributes method and an updatable view method. For each method, you need to provide a file system type object, which tells the NIO.2 method which type of view you are requesting. By updatable view, we mean that we can both read and write attributes with the same object.

Table 9.5 lists the commonly used attributes and view types. For the exam, you only need to know about the basic file attribute types. The other views are for managing operating system–specific information.

TABLE 9.5   The attributes and view types

Attributes interface	View interface	Description
BasicFileAttributes	BasicFileAttributeView	Basic set of attributes supported by all file systems
DosFileAttributes	DosFileAttributeView	Basic set of attributes along with those supported by DOS/Windows-based systems
PosixFileAttributes	PosixFileAttributeView	Basic set of attributes along with those supported by POSIX systems, such as UNIX, Linux, Mac, etc.

Retrieving Attributes with *readAttributes()*

The Files class includes the following method to read attributes of a class in a read-only capacity:

```
public static <A extends BasicFileAttributes> A readAttributes(
   Path path,
   Class<A> type,
   LinkOption... options) throws IOException
```

Applying it requires specifying the Path and BasicFileAttributes.class parameters.

```
var path = Paths.get("/turtles/sea.txt");
BasicFileAttributes data = Files.readAttributes(path,
   BasicFileAttributes.class);

System.out.println("Is a directory? " + data.isDirectory());
System.out.println("Is a regular file? " + data.isRegularFile());
System.out.println("Is a symbolic link? " + data.isSymbolicLink());
System.out.println("Size (in bytes): " + data.size());
System.out.println("Last modified: " + data.lastModifiedTime());
```

The BasicFileAttributes class includes many values with the same name as the attribute methods in the Files class. The advantage of using this method, though, is that all of the attributes are retrieved at once.

Modifying Attributes with *getFileAttributeView()*

The following Files method returns an updatable view:

```
public static <V extends FileAttributeView> V getFileAttributeView(
   Path path,
   Class<V> type,
   LinkOption... options)
```

We can use the updatable view to increment a file's last modified date/time value by 10,000 milliseconds, or 10 seconds.

```
// Read file attributes
var path = Paths.get("/turtles/sea.txt");
BasicFileAttributeView view = Files.getFileAttributeView(path,
   BasicFileAttributeView.class);
BasicFileAttributes attributes = view.readAttributes();

// Modify file last modified time
FileTime lastModifiedTime = FileTime.fromMillis(
   attributes.lastModifiedTime().toMillis() + 10_000);
view.setTimes(lastModifiedTime, null, null);
```

After the updatable view is retrieved, we need to call readAttributes() on the view to obtain the file metadata. From there, we create a new FileTime value and set it using the setTimes() method.

```
// BasicFileAttributeView instance method
public void setTimes(FileTime lastModifiedTime,
    FileTime lastAccessTime, FileTime createTime)
```

This method allows us to pass null for any date/time value that we do not want to modify. In our sample code, only the last modified date/time is changed.

> Not all file attributes can be modified with a view. For example, you cannot set a property that changes a file into a directory. Likewise, you cannot change the size of the object without modifying its contents.

Applying Functional Programming

We saved the best for last! In this part of the chapter, we'll combine everything we've presented so far with functional programming to perform extremely powerful file operations, often with only a few lines of code. The Files class includes some incredibly useful Stream API methods that operate on files, directories, and directory trees.

Listing Directory Contents

Let's start with a simple Stream API method. The following Files method lists the contents of a directory:

```
public static Stream<Path> list(Path dir) throws IOException
```

The Files.list() is similar to the java.io.File method listFiles(), except that it returns a Stream<Path> rather than a File[]. Since streams use lazy evaluation, this means the method will load each path element as needed, rather than the entire directory at once.

Printing the contents of a directory is easy.

```
try (Stream<Path> s = Files.list(Path.of("/home"))) {
    s.forEach(System.out::println);
}
```

Let's do something more interesting, though. Earlier, we presented the Files.copy() method and showed that it only performed a shallow copy of a directory. We can use the Files.list() to perform a deep copy.

```
public void copyPath(Path source, Path target) {
   try {
      Files.copy(source, target);
      if(Files.isDirectory(source))
         try (Stream<Path> s = Files.list(source)) {
            s.forEach(p -> copyPath(p,
               target.resolve(p.getFileName())));
         }
   } catch(IOException e) {
      // Handle exception
   }
}
```

The method first copies the path, whether it be a file or a directory. If it is a directory, then only a shallow copy is performed. Next, it checks whether the path is a directory and, if it is, performs a recursive copy of each of its elements. What if the method comes across a symbolic link? Don't worry, we'll address that topic in the next section. For now, you just need to know the JVM will not follow symbolic links when using this stream method.

Closing the Stream

Did you notice that in the last two code samples, we put our Stream objects inside a try-with-resources method? The NIO.2 stream-based methods open a connection to the file system *that must be properly closed*, else a resource leak could ensue. A resource leak within the file system means the path may be locked from modification long after the process that used it completed.

If you assumed a stream's terminal operation would automatically close the underlying file resources, you'd be wrong. There was a lot of debate about this behavior when it was first presented, but in short, requiring developers to close the stream won out.

On the plus side, not all streams need to be closed, only those that open resources, like the ones found in NIO.2. For instance, you didn't need to close any of the streams you worked with in Chapter 4.

Finally, the exam doesn't always properly close NIO.2 resources. To match the exam, we will sometimes skip closing NIO.2 resources in review and practice questions. Please, in your own code, always use try-with-resources statements with these NIO.2 methods.

Traversing a Directory Tree

While the `Files.list()` method is useful, it traverses the contents of only a single directory. What if we want to visit all of the paths within a directory tree? Before we proceed, we need to review some basic concepts about file systems. When we originally described a directory in Chapter 8, we mentioned that it was organized in a hierarchical manner. For example, a directory can contain files and other directories, which can in turn contain other files and directories. Every record in a file system has exactly one parent, with the exception of the root directory, which sits atop everything.

A file system is commonly visualized as a tree with a single root node and many branches and leaves, as shown in Figure 9.5. In this model, a directory is a branch or internal node, and a file is a leaf node.

FIGURE 9.5   File and directory as a tree structure

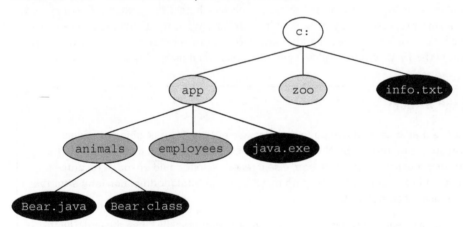

A common task in a file system is to iterate over the descendants of a path, either recording information about them or, more commonly, filtering them for a specific set of files. For example, you may want to search a folder and print a list of all of the .java files. Furthermore, file systems store file records in a hierarchical manner. Generally speaking, if you want to search for a file, you have to start with a parent directory, read its child elements, then read their children, and so on.

Traversing a directory, also referred to as walking a directory tree, is the process by which you start with a parent directory and iterate over all of its descendants until some condition is met or there are no more elements over which to iterate. For example, if we're searching for a single file, we can end the search when the file is found or when we've checked all files and come up empty. The starting path is usually a specific directory; after all, it would be time-consuming to search the entire file system on every request!

Don't Use *DirectoryStream* and *FileVisitor*

While browsing the NIO.2 Javadocs, you may come across methods that use the `DirectoryStream` and `FileVisitor` classes to traverse a directory. These methods predate the existence of the Streams API and were even required knowledge for older Java certification exams. Even worse, despite its name, `DirectoryStream` is not a Stream API class.

The best advice we can give you is to not use them. The newer Stream API–based methods are superior and accomplish the same thing often with much less code.

Selecting a Search Strategy

There are two common strategies associated with walking a directory tree: a depth-first search and a breadth-first search. A *depth-first search* traverses the structure from the root to an arbitrary leaf and then navigates back up toward the root, traversing fully down any paths it skipped along the way. The *search depth* is the distance from the root to current node. To prevent endless searching, Java includes a search depth that is used to limit how many levels (or hops) from the root the search is allowed to go.

Alternatively, a *breadth-first search* starts at the root and processes all elements of each particular depth, before proceeding to the next depth level. The results are ordered by depth, with all nodes at depth 1 read before all nodes at depth 2, and so on. While a breadth-first tends to be balanced and predictable, it also requires more memory since a list of visited nodes must be maintained.

For the exam, you don't have to understand the details of each search strategy that Java employs; you just need to be aware that the NIO.2 Streams API methods use depth-first searching with a depth limit, which can be optionally changed.

Walking a Directory with *walk()*

That's enough background information; let's get to more Steam API methods. The `Files` class includes two methods for walking the directory tree using a depth-first search.

```
public static Stream<Path> walk(Path start,
    FileVisitOption... options) throws IOException
```

```
public static Stream<Path> walk(Path start, int maxDepth,
    FileVisitOption... options) throws IOException
```

Like our other stream methods, `walk()` uses lazy evaluation and evaluates a `Path` only as it gets to it. This means that even if the directory tree includes hundreds or thousands of files, the memory required to process a directory tree is low. The first `walk()` method relies on a default maximum depth of Integer.MAX_VALUE, while the overloaded version allows the user to set a maximum depth. This is useful in cases where the file system might be large and we know the information we are looking for is near the root.

Java uses an int for its maximum depth rather than a long because most file systems do not support path values deeper than what can be stored in an int. In other words, using Integer.MAX_VALUE is effectively like using an infinite value, since you would be hard-pressed to find a stable file system where this limit is exceeded.

Rather than just printing the contents of a directory tree, we can again do something more interesting. The following getPathSize() method walks a directory tree and returns the total size of all the files in the directory:

```java
private long getSize(Path p) {
   try {
      return  Files.size(p);
   } catch (IOException e) {
      // Handle exception
   }
   return 0L;
}

public long getPathSize(Path source) throws IOException {
   try (var s = Files.walk(source)) {
      return s.parallel()
            .filter(p -> !Files.isDirectory(p))
            .mapToLong(this::getSize)
            .sum();
   }
}
```

The getSize() helper method is needed because Files.size() declares IOException, and we'd rather not put a try/catch block inside a lambda expression. We can print the data using the format() method we saw in the previous chapter:

```java
var size = getPathSize(Path.of("/fox/data"));
System.out.format("Total Size: %.2f megabytes", (size/1000000.0));
```

Depending on the directory you run this on, it will print something like this:

```
Total Directory Tree Size: 15.30 megabytes
```

Applying a Depth Limit

Let's say our directory tree was quite deep, so we apply a depth limit by changing one line of code in our getPathSize() method.

```
try (var s = Files.walk(source, 5)) {
```

This new version checks for files only within 5 steps of the starting node. A depth value of 0 indicates the current path itself. Since the method calculates values only on files, you'd have to set a depth limit of at least 1 to get a nonzero result when this method is applied to a directory tree.

Avoiding Circular Paths

Many of our earlier NIO.2 methods traverse symbolic links by default, with a NOFOLLOW_LINKS used to disable this behavior. The walk() method is different in that it does *not* follow symbolic links by default and requires the FOLLOW_LINKS option to be enabled. We can alter our getPathSize() method to enable following symbolic links by adding the FileVisitOption:

```
try (var s = Files.walk(source,
    FileVisitOption.FOLLOW_LINKS)) {
```

When traversing a directory tree, your program needs to be careful of symbolic links if enabled. For example, if our process comes across a symbolic link that points to the root directory of the file system, then every file in the system would be searched!

Worse yet, a symbolic link could lead to a cycle, in which a path is visited repeatedly. A *cycle* is an infinite circular dependency in which an entry in a directory tree points to one of its ancestor directories. Let's say we had a directory tree as shown in Figure 9.6, with the symbolic link /birds/robin/allBirds that points to /birds.

FIGURE 9.6 File system with cycle

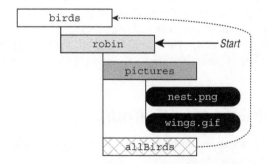

What happens if we try to traverse this tree and follow all symbolic links, starting with /birds/robin? Table 9.6 shows the paths visited after walking a depth of 3. For simplicity, we'll walk the tree in a breadth-first ordering, *although a cycle occurs regardless of the search strategy used.*

TABLE 9.6   Walking a directory with a cycle using breadth-first search

Depth	Path reached
0	/birds/robin
1	/birds/robin/pictures
1	/birds/robin/allBirds ➢ /birds
2	/birds/robin/pictures/nest.png
2	/birds/robin/pictures/nest.gif
2	**/birds/robin/allBirds/robin** **➢ /birds/robin**
3	/birds/robin/allBirds/robin/pictures ➢ /birds/robin/pictures
3	/birds/robin/allBirds/robin/pictures/allBirds ➢ /birds/robin/allBirds ➢ /birds

After walking a distance of 1 from the start, we hit the symbolic link /birds/robin/allBirds and go back to the top of the directory tree /birds. That's OK because we haven't visited /birds yet, so there's no cycle yet!

Unfortunately, at depth 2, we encounter a cycle. We've already visited the /birds/robin directory on our first step, and now we're encountering it again. If the process continues, we'll be doomed to visit the directory over and over again.

Be aware that when the FOLLOW_LINKS option is used, the walk() method will track all of the paths it has visited, throwing a FileSystemLoopException if a path is visited twice.

Searching a Directory with *find()*

In the previous example, we applied a filter to the Stream<Path> object to filter the results, although NIO.2 provides a more convenient method.

```
public static Stream<Path> find(Path start,
    int maxDepth,
    BiPredicate<Path,BasicFileAttributes> matcher,
    FileVisitOption... options) throws IOException
```

The find() method behaves in a similar manner as the walk() method, except that it takes a BiPredicate to filter the data. It also requires a depth limit be set. Like walk(), find() also supports the FOLLOW_LINK option.

The two parameters of the BiPredicate are a Path object and a BasicFileAttributes object, which you saw earlier in the chapter. In this manner, NIO.2 automatically retrieves the basic file information for you, allowing you to write complex lambda expressions that have direct access to this object. We illustrate this with the following example:

```java
Path path = Paths.get("/bigcats");
long minSize = 1_000;
try (var s = Files.find(path, 10,
      (p, a) -> a.isRegularFile()
        && p.toString().endsWith(".java")
        && a.size() > minSize)) {
   s.forEach(System.out::println);
}
```

This example searches a directory tree and prints all .java files with a size of at least 1,000 bytes, using a depth limit of 10. While we could have accomplished this using the walk() method along with a call to readAttributes(), this implementation is a lot shorter and more convenient than those would have been. We also don't have to worry about any methods within the lambda expression declaring a checked exception, as we saw in the getPathSize() example.

Reading a File with *lines()*

Earlier in the chapter, we presented Files.readAllLines() and commented that using it to read a very large file could result in an OutOfMemoryError problem. Luckily, NIO.2 solves this problem with a Stream API method.

```java
public static Stream<String> lines(Path path) throws IOException
```

The contents of the file are read and processed lazily, which means that only a small portion of the file is stored in memory at any given time.

```java
Path path = Paths.get("/fish/sharks.log");
try (var s = Files.lines(path)) {
   s.forEach(System.out::println);
}
```

Taking things one step further, we can leverage other stream methods for a more powerful example.

```java
Path path = Paths.get("/fish/sharks.log");
try (var s = Files.lines(path)) {
   s.filter(f -> f.startsWith("WARN:"))
```

```
    .map(f -> f.substring(5))
    .forEach(System.out::println);
}
```

This sample code searches a log for lines that start with WARN:, outputting the text that follows. Assuming that the input file sharks.log is as follows:

```
INFO:Server starting
DEBUG:Processes available = 10
WARN:No database could be detected
DEBUG:Processes available reset to 0
WARN:Performing manual recovery
INFO:Server successfully started
```

Then, the sample output would be the following:

```
No database could be detected
Performing manual recovery
```

As you can see, functional programming plus NIO.2 gives us the ability to manipulate files in complex ways, often with only a few short expressions.

Files.readAllLines() vs. Files.lines()

For the exam, you need to know the difference between readAllLines() and lines(). Both of these examples compile and run:

```
Files.readAllLines(Paths.get("birds.txt")).forEach(System.out::println);
Files.lines(Paths.get("birds.txt")).forEach(System.out::println);
```

The first line reads the entire file into memory and performs a print operation on the result, while the second line lazily processes each line and prints it as it is read. The advantage of the second code snippet is that it does not require the entire file to be stored in memory at any time.

You should also be aware of when they are mixing incompatible types on the exam. Do you see why the following does not compile?

```
Files.readAllLines(Paths.get("birds.txt"))
    .filter(s -> s.length() > 2)
    .forEach(System.out::println);
```

The readAllLines() method returns a List, not a Stream, so the filter() method is not available.

Comparing Legacy *java.io.File* and NIO.2 Methods

We conclude this chapter with Table 9.7, which shows a comparison between some of the legacy java.io.File methods described in Chapter 8 and the new NIO.2 methods described in this chapter. In this table, file refers to an instance of the java.io.File class, while path and otherPath refer to instances of the NIO.2 Path interface.

TABLE 9.7   Comparison of *java.io.File* and NIO.2 methods

Legacy I/O *File* method	NIO.2 method
file.delete()	Files.delete(path)
file.exists()	Files.exists(path)
file.getAbsolutePath()	path.toAbsolutePath()
file.getName()	path.getFileName()
file.getParent()	path.getParent()
file.isDirectory()	Files.isDirectory(path)
file.isFile()	Files.isRegularFile(path)
file.lastModified()	Files.getLastModifiedTime(path)
file.length()	Files.size(path)
file.listFiles()	Files.list(path)
file.mkdir()	Files.createDirectory(path)
file.mkdirs()	Files.createDirectories(path)
file.renameTo(otherFile)	Files.move(path,otherPath)

Bear in mind that a number of methods and features are available in NIO.2 that are not available in the legacy API, such as support for symbolic links, setting file system–specific attributes, and so on. The NIO.2 is a more developed, much more powerful API than the legacy java.io.File class.

Summary

This chapter introduced NIO.2 for working with files and directories using the Path interface. For the exam, you need to know what the NIO.2 Path interface is and how it differs from the legacy java.io.File class. You should be familiar with how to create and use Path objects, including how to combine or resolve them with other Path objects.

We spent time reviewing various methods available in the Files helper class. As discussed, the name of the function often tells you exactly what it does. We explained that most of these methods are capable of throwing an IOException and many take optional varargs enum values.

We also discussed how NIO.2 provides methods for reading and writing file metadata. NIO.2 includes two methods for retrieving all of the file system attributes for a path in a single call, without numerous round-trips to the operating system. One method requires a read-only attribute type, while the second method requires an updatable view type. It also allows NIO.2 to support operating system–specific file attributes.

Finally, NIO.2 includes Stream API methods that can be used to process files and directories. We discussed methods for listing a directory, walking a directory tree, searching a directory tree, and reading the lines of a file.

Exam Essentials

Understand how to create *Path* objects. An NIO.2 Path instance is an immutable object that is commonly created from the factory method Paths.get() or Path.of(). It can also be created from FileSystem, java.net.URI, or java.io.File instances. The Path interface includes many instance methods for reading and manipulating the abstract path value.

Be able to manipulate *Path* objects. NIO.2 includes numerous methods for viewing, manipulating, and combining Path values. It also includes methods to eliminate redundant or unnecessary path symbols. Most of the methods defined on Path do not declare any checked exceptions and do not require the path to exist within the file system, with the exception of toRealPath().

Be able to operate on files and directories using the *Files* class. The NIO.2 Files helper class includes methods that operate on real files and directories within the file system. For example, it can be used to check whether a file exists, copy/move a file, create a directory, or delete a directory. Most of these methods declare IOException, since the path may not exist, and take a variety of varargs options.

Manage file attributes.   The NIO.2 Files class includes many methods for reading single file attributes, such as its size or whether it is a directory, a symbolic link, hidden, etc. NIO.2 also supports reading all of the attributes in a single call. An attribute type is used to support operating system–specific views. Finally, NIO.2 supports updatable views for modified select attributes.

Be able to operate on directories using functional programming.   NIO.2 includes the Stream API for manipulating directories. The Files.list() method iterates over the contents of a single directory, while the Files.walk() method lazily traverses a directory tree in a depth-first manner. The Files.find() method also traverses a directory but requires a filter to be applied. Both Files.walk() and Files.find() support a search depth limit. Both methods will also throw an exception if they are directed to follow symbolic links and detect a cycle.

Understand the difference between *readAllLines()* and *lines()*.   The Files.readAllLines() method reads all the lines of of a file into memory and returns the result as a List<String>. The Files.lines() method lazily reads the lines of a file, instead returning a functional programming Stream<Path> object. While both methods will correctly read the lines of a file, lines() is considered safer for larger files since it does not require the entire file to be stored in memory.

Review Questions

The answers to the chapter review questions can be found in Appendix B.

1. What is the output of the following code?

```
4: var path = Path.of("/user/./root","../kodiacbear.txt");
5: path.normalize().relativize("/lion");
6: System.out.println(path);
```

   A. ../../lion
   B. /user/kodiacbear.txt
   C. ../user/kodiacbear.txt
   D. /user/./root/../kodiacbear.txt
   E. The code does not compile.
   F. None of the above

2. For which values of path sent to this method would it be possible for the following code to output Success? (Choose all that apply.)

```
public void removeBadFile(Path path) {
    if(Files.isDirectory(path))
        System.out.println(Files.deleteIfExists(path)
            ? "Success": "Try Again");
}
```

   A. path refers to a regular file in the file system.
   B. path refers to a symbolic link in the file system.
   C. path refers to an empty directory in the file system.
   D. path refers to a directory with content in the file system.
   E. path does not refer to a record that exists within the file system.
   F. The code does not compile.

3. What is the result of executing the following code? (Choose all that apply.)

```
4: var p = Paths.get("sloth.schedule");
5: var a = Files.readAttributes(p, BasicFileAttributes.class);
6: Files.mkdir(p.resolve(".backup"));
7: if(a.size()>0 && a.isDirectory()) {
8:     a.setTimes(null,null,null);
9: }
```

A. It compiles and runs without issue.

B. The code will not compile because of line 5.

C. The code will not compile because of line 6.

D. The code will not compile because of line 7.

E. The code will not compile because of line 8.

F. None of the above

4. If the current working directory is /user/home, then what is the output of the following code?

```
var p = Paths.get("/zoo/animals/bear/koala/food.txt");
System.out.print(p.subpath(1,3).getName(1).toAbsolutePath());
```

A. bear

B. animals

C. /user/home/bear

D. /user/home/animals

E. /user/home/food.txt

F. The code does not compile.

G. The code compiles but throws an exception at runtime.

5. Assume /kang exists as a symbolic link to the directory /mammal/kangaroo within the file system. Which of the following statements are correct about this code snippet? (Choose all that apply.)

```
var path = Paths.get("/kang");
if(Files.isDirectory(path) && Files.isSymbolicLink(path))
    Files.createDirectory(path.resolve("joey"));
```

A. A new directory will always be created.

B. A new directory may be created.

C. If the code creates a directory, it will be reachable at /kang/joey.

D. If the code creates a directory, it will be reachable at /mammal/joey.

E. The code does not compile.

F. The code will compile but always throws an exception at runtime.

6. Assume that the directory /animals exists and is empty. What is the result of executing the following code?

```
Path path = Path.of("/animals");
try (var z = Files.walk(path)) {
    boolean b = z
        .filter((p,a) -> a.isDirectory() && !path.equals(p)) // x
        .findFirst().isPresent();  // y
    System.out.print(b ? "No Sub": "Has Sub");
}
```

A. It prints No Sub.

B. It prints Has Sub.

C. The code will not compile because of line x.

D. The code will not compile because of line y.

E. The output cannot be determined.

F. It produces an infinite loop at runtime.

7. If the current working directory is /zoo and the path /zoo/turkey does not exist, then what is the result of executing the following code? (Choose all that apply.)

```
Path path = Paths.get("turkey");
if(Files.isSameFile(path,Paths.get("/zoo/turkey"))) // z1
    Files.createDirectories(path.resolve("info"));     // z2
```

A. The code compiles and runs without issue, but it does not create any directories.

B. The directory /zoo/turkey is created.

C. The directory /zoo/turkey/info is created.

D. The code will not compile because of line z1.

E. The code will not compile because of line z2.

F. It compiles but throws an exception at runtime.

8. Which of the following correctly create Path instances? (Choose all that apply.)

A. new Path("jaguar.txt")

B. FileSystems.getDefault() .getPath("puma.txt")

C. Path.get("cats","lynx.txt")

D. new java.io.File("tiger.txt").toPath()

E. new FileSystem().getPath("lion")

F. Paths.getPath("ocelot.txt")

G. Path.of(Path.of(".").toUri())

9. What is the output of the following code?

```
var path1 = Path.of("/pets/../cat.txt");
var path2 = Paths.get("./dog.txt");
System.out.println(path1.resolve(path2));
System.out.println(path2.resolve(path1));
```

A. /cats.txt
  /dog.txt

B. /cats.txt/dog.txt
  /cat.txt

C. /pets/../cat.txt/./dog.txt
  /pets/../cat.txt

D. /pets/../cat.txt/./dog.txt
  ./dog.txt/pets/../cat.txt

E. None of the above

10. What are some advantages of using `Files.lines()` over `Files.readAllLines()`? (Choose all that apply.)

A. It is often faster.

B. It can be run with little memory available.

C. It can be chained with functional programming methods like `filter()` and `map()` directly.

D. It does not modify the contents of the file.

E. It ensures the file is not read-locked by the file system.

F. There are no differences, because one method is a pointer to the other.

11. Assume `monkey.txt` is a file that exists in the current working directory. Which statements about the following code snippet are correct? (Choose all that apply.)

```
Files.move(Path.of("monkey.txt"), Paths.get("/animals"),
    StandardCopyOption.ATOMIC_MOVE,
    LinkOption.NOFOLLOW_LINKS);
```

A. If /animals/monkey.txt exists, then it will be overwritten at runtime.

B. If /animals exists as an empty directory, then /animals/monkey.txt will be the new location of the file.

C. If monkey.txt is a symbolic link, then the file it points to will be moved at runtime.

D. If the move is successful and another process is monitoring the file system, then it will not see an incomplete file at runtime.

E. The code will always throw an exception at runtime.

F. None of the above

12. What are some advantages of NIO.2 over the legacy `java.io.File` class for working with files? (Choose three.)

A. NIO.2 supports file system–dependent attributes.

B. NIO.2 includes a method to list the contents of a directory.

C. NIO.2 includes a method to traverse a directory tree.

D. NIO.2 includes a method to delete an entire directory tree.

E. NIO.2 includes methods that are aware of symbolic links.

F. NIO.2 supports sending emails.

13. For the `copy()` method shown here, assume that the source exists as a regular file and that the target does not. What is the result of the following code?

```
var p1 = Path.of(".","/","goat.txt").normalize(); // k1
var p2 = Path.of("mule.png");
Files.copy(p1, p2, StandardCopyOption.COPY_ATTRIBUTES); //k2
System.out.println(Files.isSameFile(p1, p2));
```

A. It will output `false`.

B. It will output `true`.

C. It does not compile because of line k1.

D. It does not compile because of line k2.

E. None of the above

14. Assume /monkeys exists as a directory containing multiple files, symbolic links, and sub-directories. Which statement about the following code is correct?

```
var f = Path.of("/monkeys");
try (var m =
        Files.find(f, 0, (p,a) -> a.isSymbolicLink()))) { // y1
    m.map(s -> s.toString())
        .collect(Collectors.toList())
        .stream()
        .filter(s -> s.toString().endsWith(".txt")) // y2
        .forEach(System.out::println);
}
```

A. It will print all symbolic links in the directory tree ending in `.txt`.

B. It will print the target of all symbolic links in the directory ending in `.txt`.

C. It will print nothing.

D. It does not compile because of line y1.

E. It does not compile because of line y2.

F. It compiles but throws an exception at runtime.

15. Which NIO.2 method is most similar to the legacy `java.io.File` method `listFiles`?

A. `Path.listFiles()`

B. `Files.dir()`

C. `Files.ls()`

D. `Files.files()`

E. `Files.list()`

F. `Files.walk()`

16. What are some advantages of using NIO.2's `Files.readAttributes()` method rather than reading attributes individually from a file? (Choose all that apply.)

A. It can be used on both files and directories.

B. For reading a single attribute, it is often more performant.

C. It allows you to read symbolic links.

D. It makes fewer round-trips to the file system.

E. It can be used to access file system–dependent attributes.

F. For reading multiple attributes, it is often more performant.

17. Assuming the /fox/food-schedule.csv file exists with the specified contents, what is the expected output of calling printData() on it?

/fox/food-schedule.csv

```
6am,Breakfast
9am,SecondBreakfast
12pm,Lunch
6pm,Dinner
```

```
void printData(Path path) throws IOException {
    Files.readAllLines(path) // r1
        .flatMap(p -> Stream.of(p.split(","))) // r2
        .map(q -> q.toUpperCase())  // r3
        .forEach(System.out::println);
}
```

- **A.** The code will not compile because of line r1.
- **B.** The code will not compile because of line r2.
- **C.** The code will not compile because of line r3.
- **D.** It throws an exception at runtime.
- **E.** It does not print anything at runtime.
- **F.** None of the above

18. What are some possible results of executing the following code? (Choose all that apply.)

```
var x = Path.of("/animals/fluffy/..");
Files.walk(x.toRealPath().getParent()) // u1
    .map(p -> p.toAbsolutePath().toString()) // u2
    .filter(s -> s.endsWith(".java")) // u3
    .collect(Collectors.toList())
    .forEach(System.out::println);
```

- **A.** It prints some files in the root directory.
- **B.** It prints all files in the root directory.
- **C.** FileSystemLoopException is thrown at runtime.
- **D.** Another exception is thrown at runtime.
- **E.** The code will not compile because of line u1.
- **F.** The code will not compile because of line u2.

19. Assuming the directories and files referenced exist and are not symbolic links, what is the result of executing the following code?

```
var p1 = Path.of("/lizard",".")
    .resolve(Path.of("walking.txt"));
var p2 = new File("/lizard/././actions/../walking.txt")
    .toPath();
System.out.print(Files.isSameFile(p1,p2));
System.out.print(" ");
System.out.print(p1.equals(p2));
System.out.print(" ");
System.out.print(p1.normalize().equals(p2.normalize()));
```

- **A.** true true true
- **B.** false false false
- **C.** false true false
- **D.** true false true
- **E.** true false false
- **F.** The code does not compile.

20. Assuming the current directory is /seals/harp/food, what is the result of executing the following code?

```
final Path path = Paths.get(".").normalize();
int count = 0;
for(int i=0; i<path.getNameCount(); ++i) {
   count++;
}
System.out.println(count);
```

- **A.** 0
- **B.** 1
- **C.** 2
- **D.** 3
- **E.** 4
- **F.** The code compiles but throws an exception at runtime.

21. Assume the source instance passed to the following method represents a file that exists. Also, assume /flip/sounds.txt exists as a file prior to executing this method. When this method is executed, which statement correctly copies the file to the path specified by /flip/sounds.txt?

```
void copyIntoFlipDirectory(Path source) throws IOException {
    var dolphinDir = Path.of("/flip");
    dolphinDir = Files.createDirectories(dolphinDir);
    var n = Paths.get("sounds.txt");
    _____;
}
```

A. Files.copy(source, dolphinDir)

B. Files.copy(source, dolphinDir.resolve(n),
   StandardCopyOption.REPLACE_EXISTING)

C. Files.copy(source, dolphinDir, StandardCopyOption.REPLACE_EXISTING)

D. Files.copy(source, dolphinDir.resolve(n))

E. The method does not compile, regardless of what is placed in the blank.

F. The method compiles but throws an exception at runtime, regardless of what is placed in the blank.

22. Assuming the path referenced by m exists as a file, which statements about the following method are correct? (Choose all that apply.)

```
void duplicateFile(Path m, Path x) throws Exception {
    var r = Files.newBufferedReader(m);
    var w = Files.newBufferedWriter(x,
        StandardOpenOption.APPEND);
    String currentLine = null;
    while ((currentLine = r.readLine()) != null)
        w.write(currentLine);
}
```

A. If the path referenced by x does not exist, then it correctly copies the file.

B. If the path referenced by x does not exist, then a new file will be created.

C. If the path referenced x does not exist, then an exception will be thrown at runtime.

D. If the path referenced x exists, then an exception will be thrown at runtime.

E. The method contains a resource leak.

F. The method does not compile.

JDBC

THE OCP EXAM TOPICS COVERED IN THIS CHAPTER INCLUDE THE FOLLOWING:

✓ **Database Applications with JDBC**

- Connect to databases using JDBC URLs and DriverManager

- Use PreparedStatement to perform CRUD operations

- Use PreparedStatement and CallableStatement APIs to perform database operations

JDBC stands for Java Database Connectivity. This chapter will introduce you to the basics of accessing databases from Java. We will cover the key interfaces for how to connect, perform queries, and process the results.

If you are new to JDBC, note that this chapter covers only the basics of JDBC and working with databases. What we cover is enough for the exam. To be ready to use JDBC on the job, we recommend that you read books on SQL along with Java and databases. For example, you might try *SQL for Dummies,* 9th edition, Allen G. Taylor (Wiley, 2018) and *Practical Database Programming with Java,* Ying Bai (Wiley-IEEE Press, 2011).

For Experienced Developers

If you are an experienced developer and know JDBC well, you can skip the "Introducing Relational Databases and SQL" section. Read the rest of this chapter carefully, though. We found that the exam covers some topics that developers don't use in practice, in particular these topics:

- You probably set up the URL once for a project for a specific database. Often, developers just copy and paste it from somewhere else. For the exam, you actually have to understand this rather than relying on looking it up.

- You are likely using a DataSource. For the exam, you have to remember or relearn how DriverManager works.

Introducing Relational Databases and SQL

Data is information. A piece of data is one fact, such as your first name. A *database* is an organized collection of data. In the real world, a file cabinet is a type of database. It has file folders, each of which contains pieces of paper. The file folders are organized in some way, often alphabetically. Each piece of paper is like a piece of data. Similarly, the folders on your computer are like a database. The folders provide organization, and each file is a piece of data.

A *relational database* is a database that is organized into *tables*, which consist of rows and columns. You can think of a table as a spreadsheet. There are two main ways to access a relational database from Java.

- *Java Database Connectivity Language (JDBC)*: Accesses data as rows and columns. JDBC is the API covered in this chapter.

- *Java Persistence API (JPA)*: Accesses data through Java objects using a concept called *object-relational mapping* (ORM). The idea is that you don't have to write as much code, and you get your data in Java objects. JPA is not on the exam, and therefore it is not covered in this chapter.

A relational database is accessed through Structured Query Language (*SQL*). SQL is a programming language used to interact with database records. JDBC works by sending a SQL command to the database and then processing the response.

In addition to relational databases, there is another type of database called a *NoSQL database*. This is for databases that store their data in a format other than tables, such as key/value, document stores, and graph-based databases. NoSQL is out of scope for the exam as well.

In the following sections, we introduce a small relational database that we will be using for the examples in this chapter and present the SQL to access it. We will also cover some vocabulary that you need to know.

Picking Database Software

In all of the other chapters of this book, you need to write code and try lots of examples. This chapter is different. It's still nice to try the examples, but you can probably get the JDBC questions correct on the exam from just reading this chapter and mastering the review questions.

In this book we will be using Derby (http://db.apache.org/derby) for most of the examples. It is a small in-memory database. In fact, you need only one JAR file to run it. While the download is really easy, we've still provided instructions on what to do. They are linked from the book page.

www.selikoff.net/ocp11-2

There are also stand-alone databases that you can choose from if you want to install a full-fledged database. We like MySQL (www.mysql.com) or PostgreSQL (www.postgresql.org), both of which are open source and have been around for more than 20 years.

While the major databases all have many similarities, they do have important differences and advanced features. Choosing the correct database for use in your job is an important decision that you need to spend much time researching. For the exam, any database is fine for practice.

There are plenty of tutorials for installing and getting started with any of these. It's beyond the scope of the book and the exam to set up a database, but feel free to ask questions in the database/JDBC section of CodeRanch. You might even get an answer from the authors.

Identifying the Structure of a Relational Database

Our sample database has two tables. One has a row for each species that is in our zoo. The other has a row for each animal. These two relate to each other because an animal belongs to a species. These relationships are why this type of database is called a *relational database*. Figure 10.1 shows the structure of our database.

FIGURE 10.1   Tables in our relational database

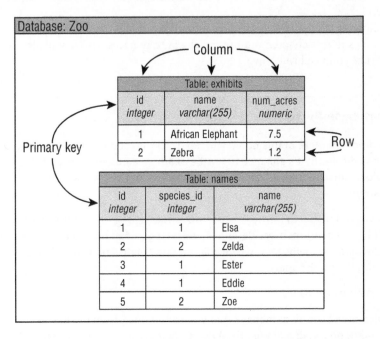

As you can see in Figure 10.1, we have two tables. One is named exhibits, and the other is named names. Each table has a *primary key*, which gives us a unique way to reference each row. After all, two animals might have the same name, but they can't have the same ID. You don't need to know about keys for the exam. We mention it to give you a bit of context. In our example, it so happens that the primary key is only one column. In some situations, it is a combination of columns called a *compound key*. For example, a student identifier and year might be a compound key.

There are two rows and three columns in the exhibits table and five rows and three columns in the names table. You do need to know about rows and columns for the exam.

The Code to Set Up the Database

We provide a program to download, install, and set up Derby to run the examples in this chapter. You don't have to understand it for the exam. Parts of SQL called database definition language (DDL) and database manipulation language (DML) are used to do so. Don't worry—knowing how to read or write SQL is not on the exam!

Before running the following code, you need to add a .jar file to your classpath. Add <PATH TO DERBY>/derby.jar to your classpath. Just make sure to replace <PATH TO DERBY> with the actual path on your file system. You run the program like this:

```
java -cp "<path_to_derby>/derby.jar" SetupDerbyDatabase.java
```

You can also find the code along with more details about setup here:

www.selikoff.net/ocp11-2

For now, you don't need to understand any of the code on the website. It is just to get you set up. In a nutshell, it connects to the database and creates two tables. Then it loads data into those tables. By the end of this chapter, you should understand how to create a Connection and PreparedStatement in this manner.

Writing Basic SQL Statements

The most important thing that you need to know about SQL for the exam is that there are four types of statements for working with the data in tables. They are referred to as CRUD (Create, Read, Update, Delete). The SQL keywords don't match the acronym, so pay attention to the SQL keyword of each in Table 10.1.

TABLE 10.1 CRUD operations

Operation	SQL Keyword	Description
Create	INSERT	Adds a new row to the table
Read	SELECT	Retrieves data from the table
Update	UPDATE	Changes zero or more rows in the table
Delete	DELETE	Removes zero or more rows from the table

That's it. You are not expected to determine whether SQL statements are correct. You are not expected to spot syntax errors in SQL statements. You are not expected to write SQL statements. Notice a theme?

If you already know SQL, you can skip to the section on JDBC. We are covering the basics so that newer developers know what is going on, at least at a high level. We promise there is nothing else in this section on SQL that you need to know. In fact, you probably know a lot that isn't covered here. As far as the exam is concerned, joining two tables is a concept that doesn't exist!

Unlike Java, SQL keywords are case insensitive. This means select, SELECT, and Select are all equivalent. Many people use uppercase for the database keywords so that they stand out. It's also common practice to use *snake case* (underscores to separate "words") in column names. We follow these conventions. Note that in some databases, table and column names may be case sensitive.

Like Java primitive types, SQL has a number of data types. Most are self-explanatory, like INTEGER. There's also DECIMAL, which functions a lot like a double in Java. The strangest one is VARCHAR, standing for "variable character," which is like a String in Java. The *variable* part means that the database should use only as much space as it needs to store the value.

Now it's time to write some code. The INSERT statement is usually used to create one new row in a table; here's an example:

```
INSERT INTO exhibits
VALUES (3, 'Asian Elephant', 7.5);
```

If there are two rows in the table before this command is run successfully, then there are three afterward. The INSERT statement lists the values that we want to insert. By default, it uses the same order in which the columns were defined. String data is enclosed in single quotes.

The SELECT statement reads data from the table.

```
SELECT *
FROM exhibits
WHERE ID = 3;
```

The WHERE clause is optional. If you omit it, the contents of the entire table are returned. The * indicates to return all of the columns in the order in which they were defined. Alternatively, you can list the columns that you want returned.

```
SELECT name, num_acres
FROM exhibits
WHERE id = 3;
```

It is preferable to list the column names for clarity. It also helps in case the table changes in the database.

You can also get information about the whole result without returning individual rows using special SQL functions.

```
SELECT COUNT(*), SUM(num_acres)
FROM exhibits;
```

This query tells us how many species we have and how much space we need for them. It returns only one row since it is combining information. Even if there are no rows in the table, the query returns one row that contains zero as the answer.

The UPDATE statement changes zero or more rows in the database.

```
UPDATE exhibits
SET num_acres = num_acres + .5
WHERE name = 'Asian Elephant';
```

Again, the WHERE clause is optional. If it is omitted, all rows in the table will be updated. The UPDATE statement always specifies the table to update and the column to update.

The DELETE statement deletes one or more rows in the database.

```
DELETE FROM exhibits
WHERE name = 'Asian Elephant';
```

And yet again, the WHERE clause is optional. If it is omitted, the entire table will be emptied. So be careful!

All of the SQL shown in this section is common across databases. For more advanced SQL, there is variation across databases.

Introducing the Interfaces of JDBC

For the exam you need to know five key interfaces of JDBC. The interfaces are declared in the JDK. This is just like all of the other interfaces and classes that you've seen in this book. For example, in Chapter 3, "Generics and Collections," you worked with the interface List and the concrete class ArrayList.

With JDBC, the concrete classes come from the JDBC driver. Each database has a different JAR file with these classes. For example, PostgreSQL's JAR is called something like postgresql-9.4-1201.jdbc4.jar. MySQL's JAR is called something like mysql-connector-java-5.1.36.jar. The exact name depends on the vendor and version of the driver JAR.

This driver JAR contains an implementation of these key interfaces along with a number of other interfaces. The key is that the provided implementations know how to communicate with a database. There are also different types of drivers; luckily, you don't need to know about this for the exam.

Figure 10.2 shows the five key interfaces that you need to know. It also shows that the implementation is provided by an imaginary Foo driver JAR. They cleverly stick the name Foo in all classes.

FIGURE 10.2 Key JDBC interfaces

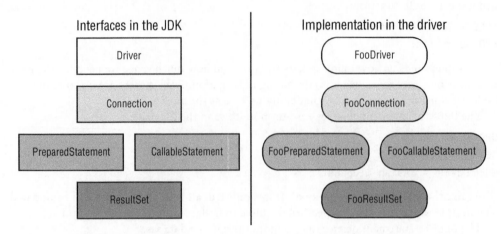

You've probably noticed that we didn't tell you what the implementing classes are called in any real database. The main point is that you shouldn't know. With JDBC, you use only the interfaces in your code and never the implementation classes directly. In fact, they might not even be public classes.

What do these five interfaces do? On a very high level, we have the following:

- `Driver`: Establishes a connection to the database
- `Connection`: Sends commands to a database
- `PreparedStatement`: Executes a SQL query
- `CallableStatement`: Executes commands stored in the database
- `ResultSet`: Reads results of a query

All database interfaces are in the package `java.sql`, so we will often omit the imports.

In this next example, we show you what JDBC code looks like end to end. If you are new to JDBC, just notice that three of the five interfaces are in the code. If you are experienced, remember that the exam uses `DriverManager` instead of `DataSource`.

```
public class MyFirstDatabaseConnection {
    public static void main(String[] args) throws SQLException {
        String url = "jdbc:derby:zoo";
        try (Connection conn = DriverManager.getConnection(url);
            PreparedStatement ps = conn.prepareStatement(
                "SELECT name FROM animal");
            ResultSet rs = ps.executeQuery()) {
            while (rs.next())
                System.out.println(rs.getString(1));
        }
    }
}
```

If the URL were using our imaginary Foo driver, DriverManager would return an instance of FooConnection. Calling prepareStatement() would then return an instance of FooPreparedStatement, and calling executeQuery() would return an instance of FooResultSet. Since the URL uses derby instead, it returns the implementations that derby has provided for these interfaces. You don't need to know their names. In the rest of the chapter, we will explain how to use all five of the interfaces and go into more detail about what they do. By the end of the chapter, you'll be writing code like this yourself.

Compiling with Modules

Almost all the packages on the exam are in the java.base module. As you may recall from your 1Z0-815 studies, this module is included automatically when you run your application as a module.

By contrast, the JDBC classes are all in the module java.sql. They are also in the package java.sql. The names are the same, so it should be easy to remember. When working with SQL, you need the java.sql module and import java.sql.*.

We recommend separating your studies for JDBC and modules. You can use the classpath when working with JDBC and reserve your practice with the module path for when you are studying modules.

That said, if you do want to use JDBC code with modules, remember to update your module-info file to include the following:

```
requires java.sql;
```

Connecting to a Database

The first step in doing anything with a database is connecting to it. First, we will show you how to build the JDBC URL. Then, we will show you how to use it to get a Connection to the database.

Building a JDBC URL

To access a website, you need to know the URL of the website. To access your email, you need to know your username and password. JDBC is no different. To access a database, you need to know this information about it.

Unlike web URLs, a JDBC URL has a variety of formats. They have three parts in common, as shown in Figure 10.3. The first piece is always the same. It is the protocol jdbc. The second part is the *subprotocol*, which is the name of the database such as derby, mysql, or postgres. The third part is the *subname*, which is a database-specific format. Colons (:) separate the three parts.

FIGURE 10.3 The JDBC URL format

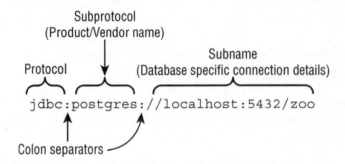

The subname typically contains information about the database such as the location and/or name of the database. The syntax varies. You need to know about the three main parts. You don't need to memorize the subname formats. Phew! You've already seen one such URL.

jdbc:derby:zoo

Notice the three parts. It starts with jdbc and then comes the subprotocol derby, and it ends with the subname, which is the database name. The location is not required, because Derby is an in-memory database.

Other examples of subname are shown here:

jdbc:postgresql://**localhost/zoo**
jdbc:oracle:thin:**@123.123.123.123:1521:zoo**
jdbc:mysql://**localhost:3306**
jdbc:mysql://**localhost:3306/zoo?profileSQL=true**

You can see that each of these JDBC URLs begins with jdbc, followed by a colon, and then followed by the vendor/product name. After that it varies. Notice how all of them include the location of the database, which are localhost, 123.123.123.123:1521, and localhost:3306. Also, notice that the port is optional when using the default location.

To make sure you get this, do you see what is wrong with each of the following?

jdbc:postgresql://local/zoo
jdbc:mysql://123456/zoo
jdbc;oracle;thin;/localhost/zoo

The first one uses local instead of localhost. The literal localhost is a specially defined name. You can't just make up a name. Granted, it is possible for our database server to be named *local*, but the exam won't have you assume names. If the database server has a special name, the question will let you know it. The second one says that the location of the database is 123456. This doesn't make sense. A location can be localhost or an IP address or a domain name. It can't be any random number. The third one is no good because it uses semicolons (;) instead of colons (:).

Getting a Database *Connection*

There are two main ways to get a Connection: DriverManager or DataSource. DriverManager is the one covered on the exam. Do not use a DriverManager in code someone is paying you to write. A DataSource has more features than DriverManager. For example, it can pool connections or store the database connection information outside the application.

 Real World Scenario

Using a *DataSource*

In real applications, you should use a DataSource rather than DriverManager to get a Connection. For one thing, there's no reason why you should have to know the database password. It's far better if the database team or another team can set up a data source that you can reference.

Another reason is that a DataSource maintains a connection pool so that you can keep reusing the same connection rather than needing to get a new one each time. Even the Javadoc says DataSource is preferred over DriverManager. But DriverManager is in the exam objectives, so you still have to know it.

The DriverManager class is in the JDK, as it is an API that comes with Java. It uses the factory pattern, which means that you call a static method to get a Connection, rather than calling a constructor. The factory pattern means that you can get any implementation of the interface when calling the method. The good news is that the method has an easy-to-remember name—getConnection().

To get a Connection from the Derby database, you write the following:

```java
import java.sql.*;
public class TestConnect {
    public static void main(String[] args) throws SQLException {
        Connection conn =
            DriverManager.getConnection("jdbc:derby:zoo");
        System.out.println(conn);
    }
}
```

Running this example as java TestConnect.java will give you an error that looks like this:

```
Exception in thread "main" java.sql.SQLException:
No suitable driver found for jdbc:derby:zoo
    at java.sql/java.sql.DriverManager.getConnection(
        DriverManager.java:702)
    at java.sql/java.sql.DriverManager.getConnection(
        DriverManager.java:251)
    at connection.TestConnect.main(TestConnect.java:9)
```

Seeing SQLException means "something went wrong when connecting to or accessing the database." You will need to recognize when a SQLException is thrown, but not the exact message. As you learned in Chapter 5, "Exceptions, Assertions, and Localization," SQLException is a checked exception.

 If code snippets aren't in a method, you can assume they are in a context where checked exceptions are handled or declared.

In this case, we didn't tell Java where to find the database driver JAR file. Remember that the implementation class for Connection is found inside a driver JAR.

We try this again by adding the classpath with the following:

```
java -cp "<path_to_derby>/derby.jar" TestConnect.java
```

Remember to substitute the location of where the Derby JAR is located.

 Notice that we are using single-file source-code execution rather than compiling the code first. This allows us to use a simpler classpath since it has only one element.

This time the program runs successfully and prints something like the following:

```
org.apache.derby.impl.jdbc.EmbedConnection40@1372082959
(XID = 156), (SESSIONID = 1), (DATABASE = zoo), (DRDAID = null)
```

The details of the output aren't important. Just notice that the class is not Connection. It is a vendor implementation of Connection.

There is also a signature that takes a username and password.

```
import java.sql.*;
public class TestExternal {
    public static void main(String[] args) throws SQLException {
        Connection conn = DriverManager.getConnection(
            "jdbc:postgresql://localhost:5432/ocp-book",
            "username",
```

```
        "Password20182");
      System.out.println(conn);
   }
}
```

Notice the three parameters that are passed to getConnection(). The first is the JDBC URL that you learned about in the previous section. The second is the username for accessing the database, and the third is the password for accessing the database. It should go without saying that our password is not Password20182. Also, don't put your password in real code. It's a horrible practice. Always load it from some kind of configuration, ideally one that keeps the stored value encrypted.

If you were to run this with the Postgres driver JAR, it would print something like this:

```
org.postgresql.jdbc4.Jdbc4Connection@eed1f14
```

Again, notice that it is a driver-specific implementation class. You can tell from the package name. Since the package is org.postgresql.jdbc4, it is part of the PostgreSQL driver.

Unless the exam specifies a command line, you can assume that the correct JDBC driver JAR is in the classpath. The exam creators explicitly ask about the driver JAR if they want you to think about it.

The nice thing about the factory pattern is that it takes care of the logic of creating a class for you. You don't need to know the name of the class that implements Connection, and you don't need to know how it is created. You are probably a bit curious, though.

DriverManager looks through any drivers it can find to see whether they can handle the JDBC URL. If so, it creates a Connection using that Driver. If not, it gives up and throws a SQLException.

 Real World Scenario

Using *Class.forName()*

You might see Class.forName() in code. It was required with older drivers (that were designed for older versions of JDBC) before getting a Connection. It looks like this:

```
public static void main(String[] args)
   throws SQLException, ClassNotFoundException {

   Class.forName("org.postgresql.Driver");
   Connection conn = DriverManager.getConnection(
      "jdbc:postgresql://localhost:5432/ocp-book",
      "username",
      "password");
}
```

Class.forName() loads a class before it is used. With newer drivers, Class.forName() is no longer required.

Working with a *PreparedStatement*

In Java, you have a choice of working with a `Statement`, `PreparedStatement`, or `CallableStatement`. The latter two are subinterfaces of `Statement`, as shown in Figure 10.4.

FIGURE 10.4   Types of statements

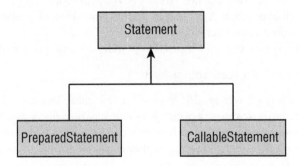

Later in the chapter, you'll learn about using `CallableStatement` for queries that are inside the database. In this section, we will be looking at `PreparedStatement`.

What about `Statement` you ask? It is an interface that both `PreparedStatement` and `CallableStatement` extend. A `Statement` and `PreparedStatement` are similar to each other, except that a `PreparedStatement` takes parameters, while a `Statement` does not. A `Statement` just executes whatever SQL query you give it.

While it is possible to run SQL directly with `Statement`, you shouldn't. `PreparedStatement` is far superior for the following reasons:

- **Performance**: In most programs, you run similar queries multiple times. A `PreparedStatement` figures out a plan to run the SQL well and remembers it.

- **Security**: As you will see in Chapter 11, "Security," you are protected against an attack called SQL injection when using a `PreparedStatement` correctly.

- **Readability**: It's nice not to have to deal with string concatenation in building a query string with lots of parameters.

- **Future use:** Even if your query is being run only once or doesn't have any parameters, you should still use a `PreparedStatement`. That way future editors of the code won't add a variable and have to remember to change to `PreparedStatement` then.

Using the `Statement` interface is also no longer in scope for the JDBC exam, so we do not cover it in this book. In the following sections, we will cover obtaining a `PreparedStatement`, executing one, working with parameters, and running multiple updates.

Obtaining a *PreparedStatement*

To run SQL, you need to tell a PreparedStatement about it. Getting a PreparedStatement from a Connection is easy.

```
try (PreparedStatement ps = conn.prepareStatement(
   "SELECT * FROM exhibits")) {
   // work with ps
}
```

An instance of a PreparedStatement represents a SQL statement that you want to run using the Connection. It does not actually execute the query yet! We'll get to that shortly.

Passing a SQL statement when creating the object is mandatory. You might see a trick on the exam.

```
try (var ps = conn.prepareStatement()) { // DOES NOT COMPILE
}
```

The previous example does not compile, because SQL is not supplied at the time a PreparedStatement is requested. We also used var in this example. We will write JDBC code both using var and the actual class names to get you used to both approaches.

There are overloaded signatures that allow you to specify a ResultSet type and concurrency mode. On the exam, you only need to know how to use the default options, which processes the results in order.

Executing a *PreparedStatement*

Now that we have a PreparedStatement, we can run the SQL statement. The way you run SQL varies depending on what kind of SQL statement it is. Remember that you aren't expected to be able to read SQL, but you do need to know what the first keyword means.

Modifying Data with *executeUpdate()*

Let's start out with statements that change the data in a table. That would be SQL statements that begin with DELETE, INSERT, or UPDATE. They typically use a method called executeUpdate(). The name is a little tricky because the SQL UPDATE statement is not the only statement that uses this method.

The method takes the SQL statement to run as a parameter. It returns the number of rows that were inserted, deleted, or changed. Here's an example of all three update types:

```
10: var insertSql = "INSERT INTO exhibits VALUES(10, 'Deer', 3)";
11: var updateSql = "UPDATE exhibits SET name = '' " +
12:    "WHERE name = 'None'";
13: var deleteSql = "DELETE FROM exhibits WHERE id = 10";
14:
15: try (var ps = conn.prepareStatement(insertSql)) {
16:    int result = ps.executeUpdate();
```

```
17:     System.out.println(result); // 1
18: }
19:
20: try (var ps = conn.prepareStatement(updateSql)) {
21:     int result = ps.executeUpdate();
22:     System.out.println(result); // 0
23: }
24:
25: try (var ps = conn.prepareStatement(deleteSql)) {
26:     int result = ps.executeUpdate();
27:     System.out.println(result); // 1
28: }
```

For the exam, you don't need to read SQL. The question will tell you how many rows are affected if you need to know. Notice how each distinct SQL statement needs its own prepareStatement() call.

Line 15 creates the insert statement, and line 16 runs that statement to insert one row. The result is 1 because one row was affected. Line 20 creates the update statement, and line 21 checks the whole table for matching records to update. Since no records match, the result is 0. Line 25 creates the delete statement, and line 26 deletes the row created on line 16. Again, one row is affected, so the result is 1.

Reading Data with *executeQuery()*

Next, let's look at a SQL statement that begins with SELECT. This time, we use the executeQuery() method.

```
30: var sql = "SELECT * FROM exhibits";
31: try (var ps = conn.prepareStatement(sql);
32:     ResultSet rs = ps.executeQuery() ) {
33:
34:     // work with rs
35: }
```

On line 31, we create a PreparedStatement for our SELECT query. On line 32, we actually run it. Since we are running a query to get a result, the return type is ResultSet. In the next section, we will show you how to process the ResultSet.

Processing Data with *execute()*

There's a third method called execute() that can run either a query or an update. It returns a boolean so that we know whether there is a ResultSet. That way, we can call the proper method to get more detail. The pattern looks like this:

```
boolean isResultSet = ps.execute();
if (isResultSet) {
    try (ResultSet rs = ps.getResultSet()) {
```

```
      System.out.println("ran a query");
   }
} else {
   int result = ps.getUpdateCount();
   System.out.println("ran an update");
}
```

If the PreparedStatement refers to sql that is a SELECT, the boolean is true and we can get the ResultSet. If it is not a SELECT, we can get the number of rows updated.

What do you think happens if we use the wrong method for a SQL statement? Let's take a look.

```
var sql = "SELECT * FROM names";
try (var conn = DriverManager.getConnection("jdbc:derby:zoo");
   var ps = conn.prepareStatement(sql)) {

   var result = ps.executeUpdate();
}
```

This throws a SQLException similar to the following:

```
Statement.executeUpdate() cannot be called with a statement
that returns a ResultSet.
```

We can't get a compiler error since the SQL is a String. We can get an exception, though, and we do. We also get a SQLException when using executeQuery() with SQL that changes the database.

```
Statement.executeQuery() cannot be called with a statement
that returns a row count.
```

Again, we get an exception because the driver can't translate the query into the expected return type.

Reviewing *PreparedStatement* Methods

To review, make sure that you know Table 10.2 and Table 10.3 well. Table 10.2 shows which SQL statements can be run by each of the three key methods on PreparedStatement.

TABLE 10.2   SQL runnable by the execute method

Method	DELETE	INSERT	SELECT	UPDATE
ps.execute()	Yes	Yes	Yes	Yes
ps.executeQuery()	No	No	Yes	No
ps.executeUpdate()	Yes	Yes	No	Yes

Table 10.3 shows what is returned by each method.

TABLE 10.3   Return types of execute methods

Method	Return type	What is returned for SELECT	What is returned for DELETE/INSERT/UPDATE
ps.execute()	boolean	true	false
ps.executeQuery()	ResultSet	The rows and columns returned	n/a
ps.executeUpdate()	int	n/a	Number of rows added/changed/removed

Working with Parameters

Suppose our zoo acquires a new elephant and we want to register it in our names table. We've already learned enough to do this.

```
public static void register(Connection conn) throws SQLException {
   var sql = "INSERT INTO names VALUES(6, 1, 'Edith')";

   try (var ps = conn.prepareStatement(sql)) {
      ps.executeUpdate();
   }
}
```

However, everything is hard-coded. We want to be able to pass in the values as parameters. However, we don't want the caller of this method to need to write SQL or know the exact details of our database.

Luckily, a PreparedStatement allows us to set parameters. Instead of specifying the three values in the SQL, we can use a question mark (?) instead. A *bind variable* is a placeholder that lets you specify the actual values at runtime. A bind variable is like a parameter, and you will see bind variables referenced as both variables and parameters. We can rewrite our SQL statement using bind variables.

```
String sql = "INSERT INTO names VALUES(?, ?, ?)";
```

Bind variables make the SQL easier to read since you no longer need to use quotes around String values in the SQL. Now we can pass the parameters to the method itself.

```
14: public static void register(Connection conn, int key,
15:    int type, String name) throws SQLException {
16:
```

```
17:    String sql = "INSERT INTO names VALUES(?, ?, ?)";
18:
19:    try (PreparedStatement ps = conn.prepareStatement(sql)) {
20:        ps.setInt(1, key);
21:        ps.setString(3, name);
22:        ps.setInt(2, type);
23:        ps.executeUpdate();
24:    }
25: }
```

Line 19 creates a `PreparedStatement` using our SQL that contains three bind variables. Lines 20, 21, and 22 set those variables. You can think of the bind variables as a list of parameters where each one gets set in turn. Notice how the bind variables can be set in any order. Line 23 actually executes the query and runs the update.

Notice how the bind variables are counted starting with 1 rather than 0. This is really important, so we will repeat it.

Remember that JDBC starts counting columns with 1 rather than 0. A common exam (and interview) question tests that you know this!

In the previous example, we set the parameters out of order. That's perfectly fine. The rule is only that they are each set before the query is executed. Let's see what happens if you don't set all the bind variables.

```
var sql = "INSERT INTO names VALUES(?, ?, ?)";
try (var ps = conn.prepareStatement(sql)) {
    ps.setInt(1, key);
    ps.setInt(2, type);
    // missing the set for parameter number 3
    ps.executeUpdate();
}
```

The code compiles, and you get a `SQLException`. The message may vary based on your database driver.

```
At least one parameter to the current statement is uninitialized.
```

What about if you try to set more values than you have as bind variables?

```
var sql = "INSERT INTO names VALUES(?, ?)";
try (var ps = conn.prepareStatement(sql)) {
    ps.setInt(1, key);
    ps.setInt(2, type);
    ps.setString(3, name);
    ps.executeUpdate();
}
```

Again, you get a SQLException, this time with a different message. On Derby, that message was as follows:

```
The number of values assigned is not the same as the
number of specified or implied columns.
```

Table 10.4 shows the methods you need to know for the exam to set bind variables. The ones that you need to know for the exam are easy to remember since they are called set, followed by the name of the type you are getting. There are many others, like dates, that are out of scope for the exam.

TABLE 10.4 PreparedStatement methods

Method name	Parameter type	Example database type
setBoolean	Boolean	BOOLEAN
setDouble	Double	DOUBLE
setInt	Int	INTEGER
setLong	Long	BIGINT
setObject	Object	Any type
setString	String	CHAR, VARCHAR

The first column shows the method name, and the second column shows the type that Java uses. The third column shows the type name that could be in the database. There is some variation by databases, so check your specific database documentation. You need to know only the first two columns for the exam.

Notice the setObject() method works with any Java type. If you pass a primitive, it will be autoboxed into a wrapper type. That means we can rewrite our example as follows:

```
String sql = "INSERT INTO names VALUES(?, ?, ?)";
try (PreparedStatement ps = conn.prepareStatement(sql)) {
    ps.setObject(1, key);
    ps.setObject(2, type);
    ps.setObject(3, name);
    ps.executeUpdate();
}
```

Java will handle the type conversion for you. It is still better to call the more specific setter methods since that will give you a compile-time error if you pass the wrong type instead of a runtime error.

Real World Scenario

Compile vs. Runtime Error When Executing

The following code is incorrect. Do you see why?

```
ps.setObject(1, key);
ps.setObject(2, type);
ps.setObject(3, name);
ps.executeUpdate(sql);   // INCORRECT
```

The problem is that the last line passes a SQL statement. With a PreparedStatement, we pass the SQL in when creating the object.

More interesting is that this does not result in a compiler error. Remember that PreparedStatement extends Statement. The Statement interface does accept a SQL statement at the time of execution, so the code compiles. Running this code gives SQLException. The text varies by database.

Updating Multiple Times

Suppose we get two new elephants and want to add both. We can use the same PreparedStatement object.

```
var sql = "INSERT INTO names VALUES(?, ?, ?)";

try (var ps = conn.prepareStatement(sql)) {

    ps.setInt(1, 20);
    ps.setInt(2, 1);
    ps.setString(3, "Ester");
    ps.executeUpdate();

    ps.setInt(1, 21);
    ps.setString(3, "Elias");
    ps.executeUpdate();
}
```

Note that we set all three parameters when adding Ester, but only two for Elias. The PreparedStatement is smart enough to remember the parameters that were already set and retain them. You only have to set the ones that are different.

Real World Scenario

Batching Statements

JDBC supports batching so you can run multiple statements in fewer trips to the database. Often the database is located on a different machine than the Java code runs on. Saving trips to the database saves time because network calls can be expensive. For example, if you need to insert 1,000 records into the database, then inserting them as a single network call (as opposed to 1,000 network calls) is usually *a lot* faster.

You don't need to know the addBatch() and executeBatch() methods for the exam, but they are useful in practice.

```java
public static void register(Connection conn, int firstKey,
    int type, String... names) throws SQLException {

    var sql = "INSERT INTO names VALUES(?, ?, ?)";
    var nextIndex = firstKey;

    try (var ps = conn.prepareStatement(sql)) {
        ps.setInt(2, type);

        for(var name: names) {
            ps.setInt(1, nextIndex);
            ps.setString(3, name);
            ps.addBatch();

            nextIndex++;
        }
        int[] result = ps.executeBatch();
        System.out.println(Arrays.toString(result));
    }
}
```

Now we call this method with two names:

```java
register(conn, 100, 1,  "Elias", "Ester");
```

The output shows the array has two elements since there are two different items in the batch. Each one added one row in the database.

```
[1, 1]
```

When using batching, you should call executeBatch() at a set interval, such as every 10,000 records (rather than after ten million). Waiting too long to send the batch to the database could produce operations that are so large that they freeze the client (or even worse the database!).

Getting Data from a *ResultSet*

A database isn't useful if you can't get your data. We will start by showing you how to go through a ResultSet. Then we will go through the different methods to get columns by type.

Reading a *ResultSet*

When working with a ResultSet, most of the time you will write a loop to look at each row. The code looks like this:

```
20: String sql = "SELECT id, name FROM exhibits";
21: Map<Integer, String> idToNameMap = new HashMap<>();
22:
23: try (var ps = conn.prepareStatement(sql);
24:     ResultSet rs = ps.executeQuery()) {
25:
26:     while (rs.next()) {
27:         int id = rs.getInt("id");
28:         String name = rs.getString("name");
29:         idToNameMap.put(id, name);
30:     }
31:     System.out.println(idToNameMap);
32: }
```

It outputs this:

```
{1=African Elephant, 2=Zebra}
```

There are a few things to notice here. First, we use the executeQuery() method on line 24, since we want to have a ResultSet returned. On line 26, we loop through the results. Each time through the loop represents one row in the ResultSet. Lines 27 and 28 show you the best way to get the columns for a given row.

A ResultSet has a *cursor*, which points to the current location in the data. Figure 10.5 shows the position as we loop through.

FIGURE 10.5   The ResultSet cursor

	Table: exhibits		
	id *integer*	name *varchar(255)*	num_acres *numeric*
1	African Elephant	7.5	
2	Zebra	1.2	

Initial position ───▶

rs.next() true ───▶

rs.next() true ───▶

rs.next() false ───▶

At line 24, the cursor starts out pointing to the location before the first row in the ResultSet. On the first loop iteration, rs.next() returns true, and the cursor moves to point to the first row of data. On the second loop iteration, rs.next() returns true again, and the cursor moves to point to the second row of data. The next call to rs.next() returns false. The cursor advances past the end of the data. The false signifies that there is no more data available to get.

We did say the "best way." There is another way to access the columns. You can use an index instead of a column name. The column name is better because it is clearer what is going on when reading the code. It also allows you to change the SQL to reorder the columns.

> On the exam, either you will be told the names of the columns in a table or you can assume that they are correct. Similarly, you can assume that all SQL is correct.

Rewriting this same example with column numbers looks like the following:

```
20: String sql = "SELECT id, name FROM exhibits";
21: Map<Integer, String> idToNameMap = new HashMap<>();
22:
23: try (var ps = conn.prepareStatement(sql);
24:     ResultSet rs = ps.executeQuery()) {
25:
26:     while (rs.next()) {
27:         int id = rs.getInt(1);
28:         String name = rs.getString(2);
29:         idToNameMap.put(id, name);
30:     }
31:     System.out.println(idToNameMap);
32: }
```

This time, you can see the column positions on lines 27 and 28. Notice how the columns are counted starting with 1 rather than 0. Just like with a PreparedStatement, JDBC starts counting at 1 in a ResultSet.

Sometimes you want to get only one row from the table. Maybe you need only one piece of data. Or maybe the SQL is just returning the number of rows in the table. When you want only one row, you use an `if` statement rather than a `while` loop.

```
var sql = "SELECT count(*) FROM exhibits";

try (var ps = conn.prepareStatement(sql);
   var rs = ps.executeQuery()) {

   if (rs.next()) {
      int count = rs.getInt(1);
      System.out.println(count);
   }
}
```

It is important to check that `rs.next()` returns `true` before trying to call a getter on the `ResultSet`. If a query didn't return any rows, it would throw a `SQLException`, so the `if` statement checks that it is safe to call. Alternatively, you can use the column name.

```
var sql = "SELECT count(*) AS count FROM exhibits";

try (var ps = conn.prepareStatement(sql);
   var rs = ps.executeQuery()) {

   if (rs.next()) {
      var count = rs.getInt("count");
      System.out.println(count);
   }
}
```

Let's try to read a column that does not exist.

```
var sql = "SELECT count(*) AS count FROM exhibits";

try (var ps = conn.prepareStatement(sql);
   var rs = ps.executeQuery()) {

   if (rs.next()) {
      var count = rs.getInt("total");
      System.out.println(count);
   }
}
```

This throws a SQLException with a message like this:

```
Column 'total' not found.
```

Attempting to access a column name or index that does not exist throws a SQLException, as does getting data from a ResultSet when it isn't pointing at a valid row. You need to be able to recognize such code. Here are a few examples to watch out for. Do you see what is wrong here when no rows match?

```
var sql = "SELECT * FROM exhibits where name='Not in table'";

try (var ps = conn.prepareStatement(sql);
   var rs = ps.executeQuery()) {


   rs.next();
   rs.getInt(1); // SQLException
}
```

Calling rs.next() works. It returns false. However, calling a getter afterward does throw a SQLException because the result set cursor does not point to a valid position. If there actually were a match returned, this code would have worked. Do you see what is wrong with the following?

```
var sql = "SELECT count(*) FROM exhibits";

try (var ps = conn.prepareStatement(sql);
   var rs = ps.executeQuery()) {


   rs.getInt(1); // SQLException
}
```

Not calling rs.next() at all is a problem. The result set cursor is still pointing to a location before the first row, so the getter has nothing to point to. How about this one?

```
var sql = "SELECT count(*) FROM exhibits";

try (var ps = conn.prepareStatement(sql);
   var rs = ps.executeQuery()) {

   if (rs.next())
      rs.getInt(0); // SQLException
}
```

Since column indexes begin with 1, there is no column 0 to point to and a SQLException is thrown. Let's try one more example. What is wrong with this one?

```
var sql = "SELECT name FROM exhibits";

try (var ps = conn.prepareStatement(sql);
    var rs = ps.executeQuery()) {

    if (rs.next())
    rs.getInt("badColumn"); // SQLException
}
```

Trying to get a column that isn't in the ResultSet is just as bad as an invalid column index, and it also throws a SQLException.

To sum up this section, it is important to remember the following:

- Always use an if statement or while loop when calling rs.next().
- Column indexes begin with 1.

Getting Data for a Column

There are lots of get methods on the ResultSet interface. Table 10.5 shows the get methods that you need to know. These are the getter equivalents of the setters in Table 10.4.

TABLE 10.5 ResultSet get methods

Method name	Return type
getBoolean	boolean
getDouble	double
getInt	int
getLong	long
getObject	Object
getString	String

You might notice that not all of the primitive types are in Table 10.5. There are getByte() and getFloat() methods, but you don't need to know about them for the exam. There is no getChar() method. Luckily, you don't need to remember this. The exam will not try to trick you by using a get method name that doesn't exist for JDBC. Isn't that nice of the exam creators?

The getObject() method can return any type. For a primitive, it uses the wrapper class. Let's look at the following example:

```
16: var sql = "SELECT id, name FROM exhibits";
17: try (var ps = conn.prepareStatement(sql);
18:     var rs = ps.executeQuery()) {
19:
20:     while (rs.next()) {
21:         Object idField = rs.getObject("id");
22:         Object nameField = rs.getObject("name");
23:         if (idField instanceof Integer) {
24:             int id = (Integer) idField;
25:             System.out.println(id);
26:         }
27:         if (nameField instanceof String) {
28:             String name = (String) nameField;
29:             System.out.println(name);
30:         }
31:     }
32: }
```

Lines 21 and 22 get the column as whatever type of Object is most appropriate. Lines 23–26 show you how to confirm that the type is Integer before casting and unboxing it into an int. Lines 27–30 show you how to confirm that the type is String and cast it as well. You probably won't use getObject() when writing code for a job, but it is good to know about it for the exam.

Using Bind Variables

We've been creating the PreparedStatement and ResultSet in the same try-with-resources statement. This doesn't work if you have bind variables because they need to be set in between. Luckily, we can nest try-with-resources to handle this. This code prints out the ID for any exhibits matching a given name:

```
30: var sql = "SELECT id FROM exhibits WHERE name = ?";
31:
32: try (var ps = conn.prepareStatement(sql)) {
33:     ps.setString(1, "Zebra");
34:
```

```
35:    try (var rs = ps.executeQuery()) {
36:       while (rs.next()) {
37:          int id = rs.getInt("id");
38:          System.out.println(id);
39:       }
40:    }
41: }
```

Pay attention to the flow here. First, we create the `PreparedStatement` on line 32. Then we set the bind variable on line 33. It is only after these are both done that we have a nested try-with-resources on line 35 to create the `ResultSet`.

Calling a *CallableStatement*

Sometimes you want your SQL to be directly in the database instead of packaged with your Java code. This is particularly useful when you have many queries and they are complex. A *stored procedure* is code that is compiled in advance and stored in the database. Stored procedures are commonly written in a database-specific variant of SQL, which varies among database software providers.

Using a stored procedure reduces network round-trips. It also allows database experts to own that part of the code. However, stored procedures are database-specific and introduce complexity of maintaining your application. On the exam, you need to know how to call a stored procedure but not decide when to use one.

You don't need to know how to read or write a stored procedure for the exam. Therefore, we have not included any in the book. If you want to try the examples, the setup procedure and source code is linked from here:

www.selikoff.net/ocp11-2

> You do not need to learn anything database specific for the exam. Since studying stored procedures can be quite complicated, we recommend limiting your studying on CallableStatement to what is in this book.

We will be using four stored procedures in this section. Table 10.6 summarizes what you need to know about them. In the real world, none of these would be good implementations since they aren't complex enough to warrant being stored procedures. As you can see in the table, stored procedures allow parameters to be for input only, output only, or both.

In the next four sections, we will look at how to call each of these stored procedures.

TABLE 10.6   Sample stored procedures

Name	Parameter name	Parameter type	Description
read_e_names()	n/a	n/a	Returns all rows in the names table that have a name beginning with an E
read_names_by_letter()	prefix	IN	Returns all rows in the names table that have a name beginning with the specified parameter
magic_number()	Num	OUT	Returns the number 42
double_number()	Num	INOUT	Multiplies the parameter by two and returns that number

Calling a Procedure without Parameters

Our read_e_names() stored procedure doesn't take any parameters. It does return a ResultSet. Since we worked with a ResultSet in the PreparedStatement section, here we can focus on how the stored procedure is called.

```
12: String sql = "{call read_e_names()}";
13: try (CallableStatement cs = conn.prepareCall(sql);
14:     ResultSet rs = cs.executeQuery()) {
15:
16:     while (rs.next()) {
17:         System.out.println(rs.getString(3));
18:     }
19: }
```

Line 12 introduces a new bit of syntax. A stored procedure is called by putting the word call and the procedure name in braces ({}).

Line 13 creates a CallableStatement object. When we created a PreparedStatement, we used the prepareStatement() method. Here, we use the prepareCall() method instead.

Lines 14–18 should look familiar. They are the standard logic we have been using to get a ResultSet and loop through it. This stored procedure returns the underlying table, so the columns are the same.

Passing an *IN* Parameter

A stored procedure that always returns the same thing is only somewhat useful. We've created a new version of that stored procedure that is more generic. The read_names_by_letter() stored procedure takes a parameter for the prefix or first letter of the stored procedure. An IN parameter is used for input.

There are two differences in calling it compared to our previous stored procedure.

```
25: var sql = "{call read_names_by_letter(?)}";
26: try (var cs = conn.prepareCall(sql)) {
27:     cs.setString("prefix", "Z");
28:
29:     try (var rs = cs.executeQuery()) {
30:         while (rs.next()) {
31:             System.out.println(rs.getString(3));
32:         }
33:     }
34: }
```

On line 25, we have to pass a ? to show we have a parameter. This should be familiar from bind variables with a PreparedStatement.

On line 27, we set the value of that parameter. Unlike with PreparedStatement, we can use either the parameter number (starting with 1) or the parameter name. That means these two statements are equivalent:

```
cs.setString(1, "Z");
cs.setString("prefix", "Z");
```

Returning an *OUT* Parameter

In our previous examples, we returned a ResultSet. Some stored procedures return other information. Luckily, stored procedures can have OUT parameters for output. The magic_number() stored procedure sets its OUT parameter to 42. There are a few differences here:

```
40: var sql = "{?= call magic_number(?) }";
41: try (var cs = conn.prepareCall(sql)) {
42:     cs.registerOutParameter(1, Types.INTEGER);
43:     cs.execute();
44:     System.out.println(cs.getInt("num"));
45: }
```

On line 40, we included two special characters (?=) to specify that the stored procedure has an output value. This is optional since we have the OUT parameter, but it does aid in readability.

On line 42, we register the OUT parameter. This is important. It allows JDBC to retrieve the value on line 44. Remember to always call `registerOutParameter()` for each OUT or INOUT parameter (which we will cover next).

On line 43, we call `execute()` instead of `executeQuery()` since we are not returning a ResultSet from our stored procedure.

Database-Specific Behavior

Some databases are lenient about certain things this chapter says are required. For example, some databases allow you to omit the following:

- Braces ({})

- Bind variable (?) if it is an OUT parameter

- Call to `registerOutParameter()`

For the exam, you need to answer according to the full requirements, which are described in this book. For example, you should answer exam questions as if braces are required.

Working with an *INOUT* Parameter

Finally, it is possible to use the same parameter for both input and output. As you read this code, see whether you can spot which lines are required for the IN part and which are required for the OUT part.

```
50: var sql = "{call double_number(?)}";
51: try (var cs = conn.prepareCall(sql)) {
52:     cs.setInt(1, 8);
53:     cs.registerOutParameter(1, Types.INTEGER);
54:     cs.execute();
55:     System.out.println(cs.getInt("num"));
56: }
```

For an IN parameter, line 50 is required since it passes the parameter. Similarly, line 52 is required since it sets the parameter. For an OUT parameter, line 53 is required to register the parameter. Line 54 uses `execute()` again because we are not returning a ResultSet.

Remember that an INOUT parameter acts as both an IN parameter and an OUT parameter, so it has all the requirements of both.

Comparing Callable Statement Parameters

Table 10.7 reviews the different types of parameters. You need to know this well for the exam.

TABLE 10.7   Stored procedure parameter types

	IN	OUT	INOUT
Used for input	Yes	No	Yes
Used for output	No	Yes	Yes
Must set parameter value	Yes	No	Yes
Must call `registerOutParameter()`	No	Yes	Yes
Can include ?=	No	Yes	Yes

Closing Database Resources

As you saw in Chapter 8, "I/O," and Chapter 9, "NIO.2," it is important to close resources when you are finished with them. This is true for JDBC as well. JDBC resources, such as a Connection, are expensive to create. Not closing them creates a *resource leak* that will eventually slow down your program.

Throughout the chapter, we've been using the try-with-resources syntax from Chapter 5. The resources need to be closed in a specific order. The ResultSet is closed first, followed by the PreparedStatement (or CallableStatement) and then the Connection.

While it is a good habit to close all three resources, it isn't strictly necessary. Closing a JDBC resource should close any resources that it created. In particular, the following are true:

- Closing a Connection also closes PreparedStatement (or CallableStatement) and ResultSet.

- Closing a PreparedStatement (or CallableStatement) also closes the ResultSet.

It is important to close resources in the right order. This avoids both resource leaks and exceptions.

Writing a Resource Leak

In Chapter 5, you learned that it is possible to declare a type before a try-with-resources statement. Do you see why this method is bad?

```
40: public void bad() throws SQLException {
41:     var url = "jdbc:derby:zoo";
42:     var sql = "SELECT not_a_column FROM names";
```

```
43:     var conn = DriverManager.getConnection(url);
44:     var ps = conn.prepareStatement(sql);
45:     var rs = ps.executeQuery();
46:
47:     try (conn; ps; rs) {
48:         while (rs.next())
49:             System.out.println(rs.getString(1));
50:     }
51: }
```

Suppose an exception is thrown on line 45. The try-with-resources block is never entered, so we don't benefit from automatic resource closing. That means this code has a resource leak if it fails. Do not write code like this.

There's another way to close a `ResultSet`. JDBC automatically closes a `ResultSet` when you run another SQL statement from the same `Statement`. This could be a `PreparedStatement` or a `CallableStatement`. How many resources are closed in this code?

```
14: var url = "jdbc:derby:zoo";
15: var sql = "SELECT count(*) FROM names where id = ?";
16: try (var conn = DriverManager.getConnection(url);
17:     var ps = conn.prepareStatement(sql)) {
18:
19:     ps.setInt(1, 1);
20:
21:     var rs1 = ps.executeQuery();
22:     while (rs1.next()) {
23:         System.out.println("Count: " + rs1.getInt(1));
24:     }
25:
26:     ps.setInt(1, 2);
27:
28:     var rs2 = ps.executeQuery();
29:     while (rs2.next()) {
30:         System.out.println("Count: " + rs2.getInt(1));
31:     }
32:     rs2.close();
33: }
```

The correct answer is four. On line 28, rs1 is closed because the same PreparedStatement runs another query. On line 32, rs2 is closed in the method call. Then the try-with-resources statement runs and closes the PreparedSatement and Connection objects.

 Real World Scenario

Dealing with Exceptions

In most of this chapter, we've lived in a perfect world. Sure, we mentioned that a checked SQLException might be thrown by any JDBC method—but we never actually caught it. We just declared it and let the caller deal with it. Now let's catch the exception.

```
var sql = "SELECT not_a_column FROM names";
var url = "jdbc:derby:zoo";
try (var conn = DriverManager.getConnection(url);
    var ps = conn.prepareStatement(sql);
    var rs = ps.executeQuery()) {

    while (rs.next())
        System.out.println(rs.getString(1));
} catch (SQLException e) {
    System.out.println(e.getMessage());
    System.out.println(e.getSQLState());
    System.out.println(e.getErrorCode());
}
```

The output looks like this:

```
Column 'NOT_A_COLUMN' is either not in any table ...
42X04
30000
```

Each of these methods gives you a different piece of information. The getMessage() method returns a human-readable message as to what went wrong. We've only included the beginning of it here. The getSQLState() method returns a code as to what went wrong. You can Google the name of your database and the SQL state to get more information about the error. By comparison, getErrorCode() is a database-specific code. On this database, it doesn't do anything.

Summary

There are four key SQL statements you should know for the exam, one for each of the CRUD operations: create (INSERT) a new row, read (SELECT) data, update (UPDATE) one or more rows, and delete (DELETE) one or more rows.

For the exam, you should be familiar with five JDBC interfaces: Driver, Connection, PreparedStatement, CallableStatement, and ResultSet. The interfaces are part of the Java API. A database-specific JAR file provides the implementations.

To connect to a database, you need the JDBC URL. A JDBC URL has three parts separated by colons. The first part is jdbc. The second part is the name of the vendor/product. The third part varies by database, but it includes the location and/or name of the database. The location is either localhost or an IP address followed by an optional port.

The DriverManager class provides a factory method called getConnection() to get a Connection implementation. You create a PreparedStatement or CallableStatement using prepareStatement() and prepareCall(), respectively. A PreparedStatement is used when the SQL is specified in your application, and a CallableStatement is used when the SQL is in the database. A PreparedStatement allows you to set the values of bind variables. A CallableStatement also allows you to set IN, OUT, and INOUT parameters.

When running a SELECT SQL statement, the executeQuery() method returns a ResultSet. When running a DELETE, INSERT, or UPDATE SQL statement, the executeUpdate() method returns the number of rows that were affected. There is also an execute() method that returns a boolean to indicate whether the statement was a query.

You call rs.next() from an if statement or while loop to advance the cursor position. To get data from a column, call a method like getString(1) or getString("a"). Column indexes begin with 1, not 0. In addition to getting a String or primitive, you can call getObject() to get any type.

It is important to close JDBC resources when finished with them to avoid leaking resources. Closing a Connection automatically closes the Statement and ResultSet objects. Closing a Statement automatically closes the ResultSet object. Also, running another SQL statement closes the previous ResultSet object from that Statement.

Exam Essentials

Name the core five JDBC interfaces that you need to know for the exam and where they are defined.   The five key interfaces are Driver, Connection, PreparedStatement, CallableStatement, and ResultSet. The interfaces are part of the core Java APIs. The implementations are part of a database driver JAR file.

Identify correct and incorrect JDBC URLs. A JDBC URL starts with jdbc:, and it is followed by the vendor/product name. Next comes another colon and then a database-specific connection string. This database-specific string includes the location, such as localhost or an IP address with an optional port. It may also contain the name of the database.

Describe how to get a *Connection* using *DriverManager*. After including the driver JAR in the classpath, call DriverManager.getConnection(url) or DriverManager.getConnection(url, username, password) to get a driver-specific Connection implementation class.

Run queries using a *PreparedStatement*. When using a PreparedStatement, the SQL contains question marks (?) for the parameters or bind variables. This SQL is passed at the time the PreparedStatement is created, not when it is run. You must call a setter for each of these with the proper value before executing the query.

Run queries using a *CallableStatement*. When using a CallableStatement, the SQL looks like { call my_proc(?)}. If you are returning a value, {?= call my_proc(?)} is also permitted. You must set any parameter values before executing the query. Additionally, you must call registerOutParameter() for any OUT or INOUT parameters.

Choose which method to run given a SQL statement. For a SELECT SQL statement, use executeQuery() or execute(). For other SQL statements, use executeUpdate() or execute().

Loop through a *ResultSet*. Before trying to get data from a ResultSet, you call rs.next() inside an if statement or while loop. This ensures that the cursor is in a valid position. To get data from a column, call a method like getString(1) or getString("a"). Remember that column indexes begin with 1.

Identify when a resource should be closed. If you're closing all three resources, the ResultSet must be closed first, followed by the PreparedStatement, CallableStatement, and then followed by the Connection.

Review Questions

The answers to the chapter review questions can be found in Appendix B.

1. Which interfaces or classes are in a database-specific JAR file? (Choose all that apply.)

    A. `Driver`

    B. `Driver`'s implementation

    C. `DriverManager`

    D. `DriverManager`'s implementation

    E. `PreparedStatement`

    F. `PreparedStatement`'s implementation

2. Which are required parts of a JDBC URL? (Choose all that apply.)

    A. Connection parameters

    B. IP address of database

    C. jdbc

    D. Password

    E. Port

    F. Vendor-specific string

3. Which of the following is a valid JDBC URL?

    A. `jdbc:sybase:localhost:1234/db`

    B. `jdbc::sybase::localhost::/db`

    C. `jdbc::sybase:localhost::1234/db`

    D. `sybase:localhost:1234/db`

    E. `sybase::localhost::/db`

    F. `sybase::localhost::1234/db`

4. Which of the options can fill in the blank to make the code compile and run without error? (Choose all that apply.)

    ```
    var sql = "UPDATE habitat WHERE environment = ?";
    try (var ps = conn.prepareStatement(sql)) {


        _____


        ps.executeUpdate();
    }
    ```

A. ps.setString(0, "snow");

B. ps.setString(1, "snow");

C. ps.setString("environment", "snow");

D. ps.setString(1, "snow"); ps.setString(1, "snow");

E. ps.setString(1, "snow"); ps.setString(2, "snow");

F. ps.setString("environment", "snow");
       ps.setString("environment", "snow");

5. Suppose that you have a table named animal with two rows. What is the result of the following code?

```
 6:  var conn = new Connection(url, userName, password);
 7:  var ps = conn.prepareStatement(
 8:      "SELECT  count(*) FROM animal");
 9:  var rs = ps.executeQuery();
10: if (rs.next()) System.out.println(rs.getInt(1));
```

A. 0

B. 2

C. There is a compiler error on line 6.

D. There is a compiler error on line 10.

E. There is a compiler error on another line.

F. A runtime exception is thrown.

6. Which of the options can fill in the blanks in order to make the code compile?

```
boolean bool = ps._____();
int num = ps._____();
ResultSet rs = ps._____();
```

A. execute, executeQuery, executeUpdate

B. execute, executeUpdate, executeQuery

C. executeQuery, execute, executeUpdate

D. executeQuery, executeUpdate, execute

E. executeUpdate, execute, executeQuery

F. executeUpdate, executeQuery, execute

7. Which of the following are words in the CRUD acronym? (Choose all that apply.)

A. Create

B. Delete

C. Disable

D. Relate

E. Read

F. Upgrade

8. Suppose that the table `animal` has five rows and the following SQL statement updates all of them. What is the result of this code?

```
public static void main(String[] args) throws SQLException {
    var sql = "UPDATE names SET name = 'Animal'";
    try (var conn = DriverManager.getConnection("jdbc:derby:zoo");
        var ps = conn.prepareStatement(sql)) {

        var result = ps.executeUpdate();
        System.out.println(result);
    }
}
```

A. 0

B. 1

C. 5

D. The code does not compile.

E. A `SQLException` is thrown.

F. A different exception is thrown.

9. Suppose `learn()` is a stored procedure that takes one `IN` parameter. What is wrong with the following code? (Choose all that apply.)

```
18: var sql = "call learn()";
19: try (var cs = conn.prepareCall(sql)) {
20:     cs.setString(1, "java");
21:     try (var rs = cs.executeQuery()) {
22:         while (rs.next()) {
23:             System.out.println(rs.getString(3));
24:         }
25:     }
26: }
```

A. Line 18 is missing braces.

B. Line 18 is missing a ?.

C. Line 19 is not allowed to use var.

D. Line 20 does not compile.

E. Line 22 does not compile.

F. Something else is wrong with the code.

G. None of the above. This code is correct.

10. Suppose that the table enrichment has three rows with the animals bat, rat, and snake. How many lines does this code print?

```
var sql = "SELECT toy FROM enrichment WHERE animal = ?";
try (var ps = conn.prepareStatement(sql)) {
    ps.setString(1, "bat");

    try (var rs = ps.executeQuery(sql)) {
        while (rs.next())
            System.out.println(rs.getString(1));
    }
}
```

A. 0

B. 1

C. 3

D. The code does not compile.

E. A SQLException is thrown.

F. A different exception is thrown.

11. Suppose that the table food has five rows and this SQL statement updates all of them. What is the result of this code?

```
public static void main(String[] args) {
    var sql = "UPDATE food SET amount = amount + 1";
    try (var conn = DriverManager.getConnection("jdbc:derby:zoo");
        var ps = conn.prepareStatement(sql)) {

        var result = ps.executeUpdate();
        System.out.println(result);
    }
}
```

A. 0

B. 1

C. 5

D. The code does not compile.

E. A SQLException is thrown.

F. A different exception is thrown.

12. Suppose we have a JDBC program that calls a stored procedure, which returns a set of results. Which is the correct order in which to close database resources for this call?

   A. Connection, ResultSet, CallableStatement

   B. Connection, CallableStatement, ResultSet

   C. ResultSet, Connection, CallableStatement

   D. ResultSet, CallableStatement, Connection

   E. CallableStatement, Connection, ResultSet

   F. CallableStatement, ResultSet, Connection

13. Suppose that the table counts has five rows with the numbers 1 to 5. How many lines does this code print?

```
var sql = "SELECT num FROM counts WHERE num > ?";
try (var ps = conn.prepareStatement(sql)) {
   ps.setInt(1, 3);

   try (var rs = ps.executeQuery()) {
      while (rs.next())
         System.out.println(rs.getObject(1));
   }

   ps.setInt(1, 100);

   try (var rs = ps.executeQuery()) {
      while (rs.next())
         System.out.println(rs.getObject(1));
   }
}
```

   A. 0

   B. 1

   C. 2

   D. 4

   E. The code does not compile.

   F. The code throws an exception.

14. Which of the following can fill in the blank correctly? (Choose all that apply.)

```
var rs = ps.executeQuery();
if (rs.next()) {

    _____;

}
```

A. `String s = rs.getString(0)`

B. `String s = rs.getString(1)`

C. `String s = rs.getObject(0)`

D. `String s = rs.getObject(1)`

E. `Object s = rs.getObject(0)`

F. `Object s = rs.getObject(1)`

15. Suppose `learn()` is a stored procedure that takes one IN parameter and one OUT parameter. What is wrong with the following code? (Choose all that apply.)

```
18: var sql = "{?= call learn(?)}";
19: try (var cs = conn.prepareCall(sql)) {
20:     cs.setInt(1, 8);
21:     cs.execute();
22:     System.out.println(cs.getInt(1));
23: }
```

A. Line 18 does not call the stored procedure properly.

B. The parameter value is not set for input.

C. The parameter is not registered for output.

D. The code does not compile.

E. Something else is wrong with the code.

F. None of the above. This code is correct.

16. Which of the following can fill in the blank? (Choose all that apply.)

```
var sql = "_____";
try (var ps = conn.prepareStatement(sql)) {
    ps.setObject(3, "red");
    ps.setInt(2, 8);
    ps.setString(1, "ball");
    ps.executeUpdate();
}
```

A. `{ call insert_toys(?, ?) }`
B. `{ call insert_toys(?, ?, ?) }`
C. `{ call insert_toys(?, ?, ?, ?) }`
D. `INSERT INTO toys VALUES (?, ?)`
E. `INSERT INTO toys VALUES (?, ?, ?)`
F. `INSERT INTO toys VALUES (?, ?, ?, ?)`

17. Suppose that the table `counts` has five rows with the numbers 1 to 5. How many lines does this code print?

```
var sql = "SELECT num FROM counts WHERE num > ?";
try (var ps = conn.prepareStatement(sql)) {
   ps.setInt(1, 3);

   try (var rs = ps.executeQuery()) {
      while (rs.next())
         System.out.println(rs.getObject(1));
   }

   try (var rs = ps.executeQuery()) {
      while (rs.next())
         System.out.println(rs.getObject(1));
   }
}
```

A. 0
B. 1
C. 2
D. 4
E. The code does not compile.
F. The code throws an exception.

18. There are currently 100 rows in the table `species` before inserting a new row. What is the output of the following code?

```
String insert = "INSERT INTO species VALUES (3, 'Ant', .05)";
String select = "SELECT count(*) FROM species";
try (var ps = conn.prepareStatement(insert)) {
   ps.executeUpdate();
}
try (var ps = conn.prepareStatement(select)) {
   var rs = ps.executeQuery();
   System.out.println(rs.getInt(1));
}
```

A. 100

B. 101

C. The code does not compile.

D. A SQLException is thrown.

E. A different exception is thrown.

19. Which of the options can fill in the blank to make the code compile and run without error? (Choose all that apply.)

```
var sql = "UPDATE habitat WHERE environment = ?";
try (var ps = conn.prepareCall(sql)) {


    _____


    ps.executeUpdate();
}
```

A. `ps.setString(0, "snow");`

B. `ps.setString(1, "snow");`

C. `ps.setString("environment", "snow");`

D. The code does not compile.

E. The code throws an exception at runtime.

20. Which of the following could be true of the following code? (Choose all that apply.)

```
var sql = "{call transform(?)}";
try (var cs = conn.prepareCall(sql)) {
    cs.registerOutParameter(1, Types.INTEGER);
    cs.execute();
    System.out.println(cs.getInt(1));
}
```

A. The stored procedure can declare an IN or INOUT parameter.

B. The stored procedure can declare an INOUT or OUT parameter.

C. The stored procedure must declare an IN parameter.

D. The stored procedure must declare an INOUT parameter.

E. The stored procedure must declare an OUT parameter.

21. Which is the first line containing a compiler error?

```
25: String url = "jdbc:derby:zoo";
26: try (var conn = DriverManager.getConnection(url);
27:     var ps = conn.prepareStatement();
28:     var rs = ps.executeQuery("SELECT * FROM swings")) {
29:     while (rs.next()) {
30:         System.out.println(rs.getInteger(1));
31:     }
32: }
```

- **A.** Line 26
- **B.** Line 27
- **C.** Line 28
- **D.** Line 29
- **E.** Line 30
- **F.** None of the above

Chapter

11

Security

OCP EXAM OBJECTIVES COVERED IN THIS CHAPTER:

✓ **Secure Coding in Java SE Application**

- Prevent Denial of Service in Java applications

- Secure confidential information in Java application

- Implement Data integrity guidelines- injections and inclusion and input validation

- Prevent external attack of the code by limiting Accessibility and Extensibility, properly handling input validation, and mutability

- Securely constructing sensitive objects

- Secure Serialization and Deserialization

It's hard to read the news without hearing about a data breach. As developers, it is our job to write secure code that can stand up to attack. In this chapter, you will learn the basics of writing secure code in stand-alone Java applications.

We will learn how Hacker Harry tries to do bad things and Security Sienna protects her application. By the end of the chapter, you should be able to protect an application from Harry just as well as Sienna.

The exam only covers Java SE (Standard Edition) applications. It does not cover web applications or any other advanced Java.

Designing a Secure Object

Java provides us with many tools to protect the objects that we create. In this section, we will look at access control, extensibility, validation, and creating immutable objects. All of these techniques can protect your objects from Hacker Harry.

Limiting Accessibility

Hacker Harry heard that the zoo uses combination locks for the animals' enclosures. He would very much like to get all the combinations.

Let's start with a terrible implementation.

```
package animals.security;
public class ComboLocks {
    public Map<String, String> combos;
}
```

This is terrible because the `combos` object has `public` access. This is also poor encapsulation. A key security principle is to limit access as much as possible. Think of it as "need to know" for objects. This is called the *principle of least privilege*.

When studying for the 1Z0-815 exam, you learned about the four levels of access control. It would be better to make the `combos` object `private` and write a method to provide the necessary functionality.

```
package animals.security;
public class ComboLocks {
```

```
    private Map<String, String> combos;

    public boolean isComboValid(String animal, String combo) {
        var correctCombo = combos.get(animal);
        return combo.equals(correctCombo);
    }
}
```

This is far better; we don't expose the combinations map to any classes outside the ComboLocks class. For example, package-private is better than public, and private is better than package-private.

Remember, one good practice to thwart Hacker Harry and his cronies is to limit accessibility by making instance variables private or package-private, whenever possible. If your application is using modules, you can do even better by only exporting the security packages to the specific modules that should have access. Here's an example:

```
exports animals.security to zoo.staff;
```

In this example, only the zoo.staff module can access the public classes in the animals.security package.

Restricting Extensibility

Suppose you are working on a class that uses ComboLocks.

```
public class GrasshopperCage {
    public static void openLock(ComboLocks comboLocks, String combo) {
        if (comboLocks.isComboValid("grasshopper", combo))
            System.out.println("Open!");
    }
}
```

Ideally, the first variable passed to this method is an instance of the ComboLocks class. However, Hacker Harry is hard at work and has created this subclass of ComboLocks.

```
public class EvilComboLocks extends ComboLocks {
    public boolean isComboValid(String animal, String combo) {
        var valid = super.isComboValid(animal, combo);
        if (valid) {
            // email the password to Hacker Harry
        }
        return valid;
    }
}
```

This is great. Hacker Harry can check whether the password is valid and email himself all the valid passwords. Mayhem ensues! Luckily, there is an easy way to prevent this problem. Marking a sensitive class as final prevents any subclasses.

```java
public final class ComboLocks {
    private Map<String, String> combos;

    // instantiate combos object

    public boolean isComboValid(String animal, String combo) {
        var correctCombo = combos.get(animal);
        return combo.equals(correctCombo);
    }
}
```

Hacker Harry can't create his evil class, and users of the GrasshopperCage have the assurance that only the expected ComboLocks class can make an appearance.

Creating Immutable Objects

As you might remember from Chapter 1, "Java Fundamentals," an immutable object is one that cannot change state after it is created. Immutable objects are helpful when writing secure code because you don't have to worry about the values changing. They also simplify code when dealing with concurrency.

We worked with some immutable objects in the book. The String class used throughout the book is immutable. In Chapter 3, "Generics and Collections," you used List.of(), Set.of(), and Map.of(). All three of these methods return immutable types.

Although there are a variety of techniques for writing an immutable class, you should be familiar with a common strategy for making a class immutable.

1. Mark the class as final.

2. Mark all the instance variables private.

3. Don't define any setter methods and make fields final.

4. Don't allow referenced mutable objects to be modified.

5. Use a constructor to set all properties of the object, making a copy if needed.

The first rule prevents anyone from creating a mutable subclass. You might notice this is the same technique we used to restrict extensibility. The second rule provides good encapsulation. The third rule ensures that callers and the class itself don't make changes to the instance variables.

The fourth rule is subtler. Basically, it means you shouldn't expose a getter method for a mutable object. For example, can you see why the following is not an immutable object?

```java
1:  import java.util.*;
2:
3:  public final class Animal {
```

```
4:      private final ArrayList<String> favoriteFoods;
5:
6:      public Animal() {
7:          this.favoriteFoods = new ArrayList<String>();
8:          this.favoriteFoods.add("Apples");
9:      }
10:     public List<String> getFavoriteFoods() {
11:         return favoriteFoods;
12:     }
13: }
```

We carefully followed the first three rules, but unfortunately, Hacker Harry can modify our data by calling getFavoriteFoods().clear() or add a food to the list that our animal doesn't like. It's not an immutable object if we can change it contents! If we don't have a getter for the favoriteFoods object, how do callers access it? Simple, by using delegate methods to read the data, as shown in the following:

```
1:  import java.util.*;
2:
3:  public final class Animal {
4:      private final ArrayList<String> favoriteFoods;
5:
6:      public Animal() {
7:          this.favoriteFoods = new ArrayList<String>();
8:          this.favoriteFoods.add("Apples");
9:      }
10:     public int getFavoriteFoodsCount() {
11:         return favoriteFoods.size();
12:     }
13:     public String getFavoriteFoodsElement(int index) {
14:         return favoriteFoods.get(index);
15:     }
16: }
```

In this improved version, the data is still available. However, it is a true immutable object because the mutable variable cannot be modified by the caller. Another option is to create a copy of the favoriteFoods object and return the copy anytime it is requested, so the original remains safe.

```
10:     public ArrayList<String> getFavoriteFoods() {
11:         return new ArrayList<String>(this.favoriteFoods);
12:     }
```

Of course, changes in the copy won't be reflected in the original, but at least the original is protected from external changes. In the next section, we'll see there is another way to copy an object if the class implements a certain interface.

So, what's this about the last rule for creating immutable objects? Let's say we want to allow the user to provide the favoriteFoods data, so we implement the following:

```
1:  import java.util.*;
2:
3:  public final class Animal {
4:      private final ArrayList<String> favoriteFoods;
5:
6:      public Animal(ArrayList<String> favoriteFoods) {
7:          if(favoriteFoods == null)
8:              throw new RuntimeException("favoriteFoods is required");
9:          this.favoriteFoods = favoriteFoods;
10:     }
11:     public int getFavoriteFoodsCount() {
12:         return favoriteFoods.size();
13:     }
14:     public String getFavoriteFoodsElement(int index) {
15:         return favoriteFoods.get(index);
16:     }
17: }
```

To ensure that favoriteFoods is not null, we validate it in the constructor and throw an exception if it is not provided. Hacker Harry is tricky, though. He decides to send us a favoriteFood object but keep his own secret reference to it, which he can modify directly.

```
void modifyNotSoImmutableObject() {
    var favorites = new ArrayList<String>();
    favorites.add("Apples");
    var animal = new Animal(favorites);
    System.out.print(animal.getFavoriteFoodsCount());
    favorites.clear();
    System.out.print(animal.getFavoriteFoodsCount());
}
```

This method prints 1, followed by 0. Whoops! It seems like Animal is not immutable anymore, since its contents can change after it is created. The solution is to use a *copy constructor* to make a copy of the list object containing the same elements.

```
6:      public Animal(List<String> favoriteFoods) {
7:          if(favoriteFoods == null)
8:              throw new RuntimeException("favoriteFoods is required");
9:          this.favoriteFoods = new ArrayList<String>(favoriteFoods);
10:     }
```

The copy operation is called a *defensive copy* because the copy is being made in case other code does something unexpected. It's the same idea as defensive driving. Security Sienna has to be safe because she can't control what others do. With this approach, Hacker Harry is defeated. He can modify the original `favoriteFoods` all he wants, but it doesn't change the `Animal` object's contents.

Cloning Objects

Java has a `Cloneable` interface that you can implement if you want classes to be able to call the `clone()` method on your object. This helps with making defensive copies.

The `ArrayList` class does just that, which means there's another way to write the statement on line 9.

```
9: this.favoriteFoods = (ArrayList) favoriteFoods.clone();
```

The `clone()` method makes a copy of an object. Let's give it a try by changing line 3 of the previous example to the following:

```
public final class Animal implements Cloneable {
```

Now we can write a method within the `Animal` class:"

```
public static void main(String... args) throws Exception {
    ArrayList<String> food = new ArrayList<>();
    food.add("grass");
    Animal sheep = new Animal(food);
    Animal clone = (Animal) sheep.clone();
    System.out.println(sheep == clone);
    System.out.println(sheep.favoriteFoods == clone.favoriteFoods);
}
```

This code outputs the following:

```
false
true
```

By default, the `clone()` method makes a *shallow copy* of the data, which means only the top-level object references and primitives are copied. No new objects from within the cloned object are created. For example, if the object contains a reference to an `ArrayList`, a shallow copy contains a reference to that same `ArrayList`. Changes to the `ArrayList` in one object will be visible in the other since it is the same object.

By contrast, you can write an implementation that does a *deep copy* and clones the objects inside. A deep copy does make a new `ArrayList` object. Changes to the cloned object do not affect the original.

```
public Animal clone() {
    ArrayList<String> listClone = (ArrayList) favoriteFoods.clone();
    return new Animal(listClone);
}
```

Now the main() method prints false twice because the ArrayList is also cloned.

You might have noticed that the clone() method is declared in the Object class. The default implementation throws an exception that tells you the Object didn't implement Cloneable. If the class implements Cloneable, you can call clone(). Classes that implement Cloneable can also provide a custom implementation of clone(), which is useful when the class wants to make a deep copy. Figure 11.1 reviews how Java decides what to do when clone() is called.

FIGURE 11.1 Cloneable logic

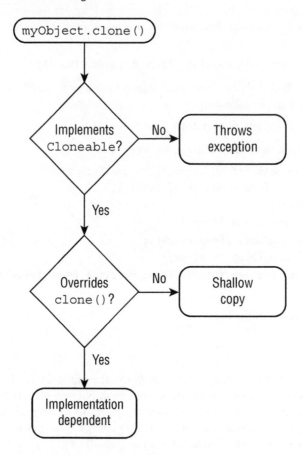

In the last block, implementation-dependent means you should probably check the Javadoc of the overridden clone() method before using it. It may provide a shallow copy, a deep copy, or something else entirely. For example, it may be a shallow copy limited to three levels.

Introducing Injection and Input Validation

Injection is an attack where dangerous input runs in a program as part of a command. For example, user input is often used in database queries or I/O. In this section, we will look at how to protect your code against injection using a `PreparedStatement` and input validation.

An *exploit* is an attack that takes advantage of weak security. Hacker Harry is ready to try to exploit any code he can find. He especially likes untrusted data.

There are many sources of untrusted data. For the exam, you need to be aware of user input, reading from files, and retrieving data from a database. In the real world, any data that did not originate from your program should be considered suspect.

Preventing Injection with a *PreparedStatement*

Our zoo application has a table named `hours` that keeps track of when the zoo is open to the public. Figure 11.2 shows the columns in this table.

FIGURE 11.2   Hours table

hours

day varchar(20)	opens integer	closes integer
sunday	9	6
monday	10	4
tuesday	10	4
wednesday	10	5
thursday	10	4
friday	10	6
saturday	9	6

In the following sections, we will look at two examples that are insecure followed by the proper fix.

Using *Statement*

We wrote a method that uses a `Statement`. In Chapter 10, "JDBC," we didn't use `Statement` because it is often unsafe.

```
public int getOpening(Connection conn, String day)
      throws SQLException {
```

```
    String sql = "SELECT opens FROM hours WHERE day = '" + day +"'";

    try (var stmt = conn.createStatement();
        var rs = stmt.executeQuery(sql)) {
        if (rs.next())
            return rs.getInt("opens");
    }
    return -1;
}
```

Then, we call the code with one of the days in the table.

```
int opening = attack.getOpening(conn, "monday");   // 10
```

This code does what we want. It queries the database and returns the opening time on the requested day. So far, so good. Then Hacker Harry comes along to call the method. He writes this:

```
int evil = attack.getOpening(conn,
    "monday' OR day IS NOT NULL OR day = 'sunday");   // 9
```

This does not return the expected value. It returned 9 when we ran it. Let's take a look at what Hacker Harry tricked our database into doing.

Hacker Harry's parameter results in the following SQL, which we've formatted for readability:

```
SELECT opens FROM hours
    WHERE day = 'monday'
        OR day IS NOT NULL
        OR day = 'sunday'
```

It says to return any rows where day is sunday, monday, or any value that isn't null. Since none of the values in Figure 11.2 is null, this means all the rows are returned. Luckily, the database is kind enough to return the rows in the order they were inserted; our code reads the first row.

Using *PreparedStatement*

Obviously, we have a problem with using Statement, and we call Security Sienna. She reminds us that Statement is insecure because it is vulnerable to SQL injection. As Hacker Harry just showed us an attack, we have to agree.

We switch our code to use PreparedStatement.

```
public int getOpening(Connection conn, String day)
        throws SQLException {
    String sql = "SELECT opens FROM hours WHERE day = '" + day +"'";
    try (var ps = conn.prepareStatement(sql);
```

```
      var rs = ps.executeQuery()) {
      if (rs.next())
         return rs.getInt("opens");
   }
   return -1;
}
```

Hacker Harry runs his code, and the behavior hasn't changed. We haven't fixed the problem! A `PreparedStatement` isn't magic. It gives you the capability to be safe, but only if you use it properly.

Security Sienna shows us that we need to rewrite the SQL statement using bind variables like we did in Chapter 10.

```
public int getOpening(Connection conn, String day)
      throws SQLException {
   String sql = "SELECT opens FROM hours WHERE day = ?";
   try (var ps = conn.prepareStatement(sql)) {
      ps.setString(1, day);
      try (var rs = ps.executeQuery()) {
         if (rs.next())
            return rs.getInt("opens");
      }
   }
   return -1;
}
```

This time, Hacker Harry's code does behave differently.

```
int evil = attack.getOpening(conn,
   "monday' or day is not null or day = 'sunday");  // -1
```

The entire string is matched against the day column. Since there is no match, no rows are returned. This is far better!

If you remember only two things about SQL and security, remember to use a `PreparedStatement` and bind variables.

Little Bobby Tables

SQL injection is often caused by a lack of properly sanitized user input. The author of the popular xkcd.com web comic once asked the question, what would happen if someone's name contained a SQL statement?

"Exploits of a Mom" reproduced with permission from xkcd.com/327/

Oops! Guess the school should have used a `PreparedStatement` and bound each student's name to a variable. If they had, the entire `String` would have been properly escaped and stored in the database.

Some databases, like Derby, prevent such an attack. However, it is important to use a `PreparedStatement` properly to avoid even the possibility of such an attack.

Invalidating Invalid Input with Validation

SQL injection isn't the only type of injection. *Command injection* is another type that uses operating system commands to do something unexpected.

In our example, we will use the `Console` class from Chapter 8, "I/O," and the `Files` class from Chapter 9, "NIO.2." Figure 11.3 shows the directory structure we will be using in the example.

The following code attempts to read the name of a subdirectory of `diets` and print out the names of all the `.txt` files in that directory:

```
Console console = System.console();
String dirName = console.readLine();
Path path = Paths.get("c:/data/diets/" + dirName);
try (Stream<Path> stream = Files.walk(path)) {
   stream.filter(p -> p.toString().endsWith(".txt"))
      .forEach(System.out::println);
}
```

We tested it by typing in `mammals` and got the expected output.

```
c:/data/diets/mammals/Platypus.txt
```

FIGURE 11.3   Directory structure

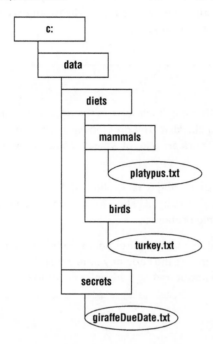

Then Hacker Harry came along and typed .. as the directory name.

```
c:/data/diets/../secrets/giraffeDueDate.txt
c:/data/diets/../diets/mammals/Platypus.txt
c:/data/diets/../diets/birds/turkey.txt
```

Oh, no! Hacker Harry knows we are expecting a baby giraffe just from the filenames. We were not intending for him to see the `secrets` directory.

We decide to chat with Security Sienna about this problem. She suggests we validate the input. We will use a *whitelist* that allows us to specify which values are allowed.

```
Console console = System.console();
String dirName = console.readLine();
if (dirName.equals("mammal") || dirName.equals("birds")) {
   Path path = Paths.get("c:/data/diets/" + dirName);
   try (Stream<Path> stream = Files.walk(path)) {
      stream.filter(p -> p.toString().endsWith(".txt"))
         .forEach(System.out::println);
   }
}
```

This time when Hacker Harry strikes, he doesn't see any output at all. His input did not match the whitelist. When validation fails, you can throw an exception, log a message, or take any other action of your choosing.

Whitelist vs. Blacklist

A *blacklist* is a list of things that aren't allowed. In the previous example, we could have put the dot (.) character on a blacklist. The problem with a blacklist is that you have to be cleverer than the bad guys. There are a lot of ways to cause harm. For example, you can encode characters.

By contrast, the whitelist is specifying what is allowed. You can supply a list of valid characters. Whitelisting is preferable to blacklisting for security because a whitelist doesn't need to foresee every possible problem.

That said, the whitelist solution could require more frequent updates. In the previous example, we would have to update the code any time we added a new animal type. Security decisions are often about trading convenience for lower risk.

Working with Confidential Information

When working on a project, you will often encounter confidential or sensitive data. Sometimes there are even laws that mandate proper handling of data like the Health Insurance Portability and Accountability Act (HIPAA) in the United States. Table 11.1 lists some examples of confidential information.

TABLE 11.1   Types of confidential data

Category	Examples
Login information	• Usernames • Passwords • Hashes of passwords
Banking	• Credit card numbers • Account balances • Credit score
PII (Personal identifiable information)	• Social Security number (or other government ID) • Mother's maiden name • Security questions/answers

In the following sections, we will look at how to secure confidential data in written form and in log files. We will also show you how to limit access.

Guarding Sensitive Data from Output

Security Sienna makes sure confidential information doesn't leak. The first step she takes is to avoid putting confidential information in a `toString()` method. That's just inviting the information to wind up logged somewhere you didn't intend.

She is careful what methods she calls in these sensitive contexts to ensure confidential information doesn't escape. Such sensitive contexts include the following:

- Writing to a log file

- Printing an exception or stack trace

- `System.out` and `System.err` messages

- Writing to data files

Hacker Harry is on the lookout for confidential information in all of these places. Sometimes you have to process sensitive information. It is important to make sure it is being shared only per the requirements.

Protecting Data in Memory

Security Sienna needs to be careful about what is in memory. If her application crashes, it may generate a dump file. That contains values of everything in memory.

When calling the `readPassword()` on `Console`, it returns a `char[]` instead of a `String`. This is safer for two reasons.

- It is not stored as a `String`, so Java won't place it in the `String` pool, where it could exist in memory long after the code that used it is run.

- You can `null` out the value of the array element rather than waiting for the garbage collector to do it.

For example, this code overlays the password characters with the letter x:

```
Console console = System.console();
char[] password = console.readPassword();
Arrays.fill(password, 'x');
```

When the sensitive data cannot be overwritten, it is good practice to set confidential data to `null` when you're done using it. If the data can be garbage collected, you don't have to worry about it being exposed later. Here's an example:

```
LocalDate dateOfBirth = getDateOfBirth();
// use date of birth
dateOfBirth = null;
```

The idea is to have confidential data in memory for as short a time as possible. This gives Hacker Harry less time to make his move.

Limiting File Access

We saw earlier how to prevent command injection by validating requests. Another way is to use a security policy to control what the program can access.

Defense in Depth

It is good to apply multiple techniques to protect your application. This approach is called *defense in depth*. If Hacker Harry gets through one of your defenses, he still doesn't get the valuable information inside. Instead, he is met with another defense.

Validation and using a security policy are good techniques to use together to apply defense in depth.

For the exam, you don't need to know how to write or run a policy. You do need to be able to read one to understand security implications. Luckily, they are fairly self-explanatory. Here's an example of a policy:

```
grant {
    permission java.io.FilePermission
        "C:\\water\\fish.txt",
        "read";
};
```

This policy gives the programmer permission to read, but not update, the fish.txt file. If the program is allowed to read and write the file, we specify the following:

```
grant {
    permission java.io.FilePermission
        "C:\\water\\fish.txt",
        "read, write";
};
```

When looking at a policy, pay attention to whether the policy grants access to more than is needed to run the program. If our application needs to read a file, it should only have read permissions. This is the principle of least privilege we showed you earlier.

Serializing and Deserializing Objects

Imagine we are storing data in an `Employee` record. We want to write this data to a file and read this data back into memory, but we want to do so without writing any potentially sensitive data to disk. From Chapter 8, you should already know how to do this with serialization.

Recall from Chapter 8 that Java skips calling the constructor when deserializing an object. This means it is important not to rely on the constructor for custom validation logic.

Let's define our `Employee` class used throughout this section. Remember, it's important to mark it `Serializable`.

```java
import java.io.*;

public class Employee implements Serializable {
    private String name;
    private int age;

    // Constructors/getters/setters
}
```

In the following sections, we will look at how to make serialization safer by specifying which fields get serialized and the process for controlling serialization itself.

Specifying Which Fields to Serialize

Our zoo has decided that employee age information is sensitive and shouldn't be written to disk. From Chapter 8, you should already know how to do this. Security Sienna reminds us that marking a field as `transient` prevents it from being serialized.

```java
    private transient int age;
```

Alternatively, you can specify fields to be serialized in an array.

```java
private static final ObjectStreamField[] serialPersistentFields =
    { new ObjectStreamField("name", String.class) };
```

You can think of `serialPersistentFields` as the opposite of `transient`. The former is a whitelist of fields that should be serialized, while the latter is a blacklist of fields that should not.

If you go with the array approach, make sure you remember to use the `private`, `static`, and `final` modifiers. Otherwise, the field will be ignored.

Customizing the Serialization Process

Security may demand custom serialization. In our case, we got a new requirement to add the Social Security number to our object. (For our readers outside the United States, a Social Security number is used for reporting your earnings to the government, among other things.) Unlike age, we do need to serialize this information. However, we don't want to store the Social Security number in plain text, so we need to write some custom code.

Take a look at the following implementation that uses writeObject() and readObject() for serialization, which you learned about in Chapter 8. For brevity, we'll use ssn to stand for Social Security number.

```java
import java.io.*;

public class Employee implements Serializable {
    private String name;
    private String ssn;
    private int age;

    // Constructors/getters/setters

    private static final ObjectStreamField[] serialPersistentFields =
        { new ObjectStreamField("name", String.class),
        new ObjectStreamField("ssn", String.class) };

    private static String encrypt(String input) {
        // Implementation omitted
    }
    private static String decrypt(String input) {
        // Implementation omitted
    }

    private void writeObject(ObjectOutputStream s) throws Exception {
        ObjectOutputStream.PutField fields = s.putFields();
        fields.put("name", name);
        fields.put("ssn", encrypt(ssn));
        s.writeFields();
    }
    private void readObject(ObjectInputStream s) throws Exception {
        ObjectInputStream.GetField fields = s.readFields();
        this.name = (String)fields.get("name", null);
        this.ssn = decrypt((String)fields.get("ssn", null));
    }
}
```

This version skips the `age` variable as before, although this time without using the `transient` modifier. It also uses custom read and write methods to securely encrypt/decrypt the Social Security number. Notice the `PutField` and `GetField` classes are used in order to write and read the fields easily.

Suppose we were to update our `writeObject()` method with the `age` variable.

> **`fields.put("age", age);`**

When using serialization, the code would result in an exception.

`java.lang.IllegalArgumentException: no such field age with type int`

This shows the `serialPersistentFields` variable is really being used. Java is preventing us from referencing fields that were not declared to be serializable.

 Real World Scenario

Working with Passwords

In this example, we encrypted and then decrypted the Social Security number to show how to perform custom serialization for security reasons. Some fields are too sensitive even for that. In particular, you should never be able to decrypt a password.

When a password is set for a user, it should be converted to a `String` value using a salt (initial random value) and one-way hashing algorithm. Then, when a user logs in, convert the value they type in using the same algorithm and compare it with the stored value. This allows you to authenticate a user without having to expose their password.

Databases of stored passwords can (and very often do) get stolen. Having them properly encrypted means the attacker can't do much with them, like decrypt them and use them to log in to the system. They also can't use them to log in to other systems in which the user used the same password more than once.

Pre/Post-Serialization Processing

Suppose our zoo employee application is having a problem with duplicate records being created for each employee. They decide that they want to maintain a list of all employees in memory and only create users as needed. Furthermore, each employee's name is guaranteed to be unique. Unlikely in practice we know, but this is a special zoo!

From what you learned about concurrent collections in Chapter 7, "Concurrency," and factory methods, we can accomplish this with a `private` constructor and factory method.

```
import java.io.*;
import java.util.Map;
```

```
import java.util.concurrent.ConcurrentHashMap;

public class Employee implements Serializable {
    ...
    private Employee() {}
    private static Map<String,Employee> pool =
        new ConcurrentHashMap<>();

    public synchronized static Employee getEmployee(String name) {
        if(pool.get(name)==null) {
            var e = new Employee();
            e.name = name;
            pool.put(name, e);
        }
        return pool.get(name);
    }
}
```

This method creates a new Employee if one does not exist. Otherwise, it returns the one stored in the memory pool.

Applying *readResolve()*

Now we want to start reading/writing the employee data to disk, but we have a problem. When someone reads the data from the disk, it deserializes it into a new object, not the one in memory pool. This could result in two users holding different versions of the Employee in memory!

Enter the readResolve() method. When this method is present, it is run *after* the readObject() method and is capable of replacing the reference of the object returned by deserialization.

```
import java.io.*;
import java.util.Map;
import java.util.concurrent.ConcurrentHashMap;

public class Employee implements Serializable {
    ...
    public synchronized Object readResolve()
            throws ObjectStreamException {
        var existingEmployee = pool.get(name);
        if(pool.get(name) == null) {
            // New employee not in memory
            pool.put(name, this);
            return this;
```

```
      } else {
         // Existing user already in memory
         existingEmployee.name = this.name;
         existingEmployee.ssn = this.ssn;
         return existingEmployee;
      }
   }
}
```

If the object is not in memory, it is added to the pool and returned. Otherwise, the version in memory is updated, and its reference is returned.

Notice that we added the synchronized modifier to this method. Java allows any method modifiers (except static) for the readResolve() method including any access modifier. This rule applies to writeReplace(), which is up next.

Applying *writeReplace()*

Now, what if we want to write an Employee record to disk but we don't completely trust the instance we are holding? For example, we want to always write the version of the object in the pool rather than the this instance. By construction, there should be only one version of this object in memory, but for this example let's pretend we're not 100 percent confident of that.

The writeReplace() method is run *before* writeObject() and allows us to replace the object that gets serialized.

```
import java.io.*;
import java.util.Map;
import java.util.concurrent.ConcurrentHashMap;

public class Employee implements Serializable {
   ...
   public Object writeReplace() throws ObjectStreamException {
      var e = pool.get(name);
      return e != null ? e : this;
   }
}
```

This implementation checks whether the object is found in the pool. If it is found in the pool, that version is sent for serialization; otherwise, the current instance is used. We could also update this example to add it to the pool if it is somehow missing.

 If these last few examples seemed a bit contrived, it's because they are. While the exam is likely to test you on these methods, implementing these advanced serialization methods in detail is way beyond the scope of the exam. Besides, transient will probably meet your needs for customizing what gets serialized.

Reviewing Serialization Methods

You've encountered a lot of methods in this chapter. Table 11.2 summarizes the important features of each that you should know for the exam.

TABLE 11.2 Methods for serialization and deserialization

Return type	Method	Parameters	Description
Object	writeReplace()	None	Allows replacement of object *before* serialization
void	writeObject()	ObjectInputStream	Serializes optionally using PutField
void	readObject()	ObjectOutputStream	Deserializes optionally using GetField
Object	readResolve()	None	Allows replacement of object *after* deserialization

We also provide a visualization of the process of writing and reading a record in Figure 11.4.

FIGURE 11.4 Writing and reading an employee

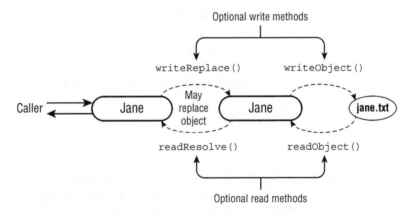

In Figure 11.4, we show how an employee record for Jane is serialized, written to disk, then read from disk, and returned to the caller. We also show that writeReplace() happens before writeObject(), while readResolve() happens after readObject().

Remember that all four of these methods are optional and must be declared in the
Serializable object to be used.

Constructing Sensitive Objects

When constructing sensitive objects, you need to ensure that subclasses can't change the
behavior. Suppose we have a FoodOrder class.

```java
public class FoodOrder {
   private String item;
   private int count;

   public FoodOrder(String item, int count) {
      setItem(item);
      setCount(count);
   }
   public String getItem() { return item; }
   public void setItem(String item) { this.item = item; }
   public int getCount() { return count; }
   public void setCount(int count) { this.count = count; }
}
```

This seems simple enough. It is a Java object with two instance variables and
corresponding getters/setters. We can even write a method that counts how many items are
in our order.

```java
public static int total(List<FoodOrder> orders) {
   return orders.stream()
      .mapToInt(FoodOrder::getCount)
      .sum();
}
```

This method signature pleases Hacker Harry because he can pass in his malicious subclass of FoodOrder. He overrides the getCount() and setCount() methods so that count
is always zero.

```java
public class HarryFoodOrder extends FoodOrder {
   public HarryFoodOrder(String item, int count) {
      super(item, count);
   }
   public int getCount() { return 0; }
   public void setCount(int count) { super.setCount(0); }
}
```

Well, that's not good. Now we can't order any food. Luckily, Security Sienna has three techniques to foil Hacker Harry. Let's take a look at each one. If you need to review the `final` modifier, we covered this in detail in Chapter 1.

Making Methods *final*

Security Sienna points out that we are letting Hacker Harry override sensitive methods. If we make the methods `final`, the subclass can't change the behavior on us.

```
public class FoodOrder {
   private String item;
   private int count;

   public FoodOrder(String item, int count) {
      setItem(item);
      setCount(count);
   }
   public final String getItem() { return item; }
   public final void setItem(String item) { this.item = item; }
   public final int getCount() { return count; }
   public final void setCount(int count) { this.count = count; }
}
```

Now the subclass can't provide different behavior for the get and set methods. In general, you should avoid allowing your constructors to call any methods that a subclass can provide its own implementation for.

Making Classes *final*

Remembering to make methods `final` is extra work. Security Sienna points out that we don't need to allow subclasses at all since everything we need is in `FoodOrder`.

```
public final class FoodOrder {
   private String item;
   private int count;

   public FoodOrder(String item, int count) {
      setItem(item);
      setCount(count);
   }
   public String getItem() { return item; }
   public void setItem(String item) { this.item = item; }
   public int getCount() { return count; }
   public void setCount(int count) { this.count = count; }
}
```

Now Hacker Harry can't create his malicious subclass to begin with!

Making the Constructor *private*

Security Sienna notes that another way of preventing or controlling subclasses is to make the constructor `private`. This technique requires `static` factory methods to obtain the object.

```java
public class FoodOrder {
   private String item;
   private int count;

   private FoodOrder(String item, int count) {
      setItem(item);
      setCount(count);
   }
   public FoodOrder getOrder(String item, int count) {
      return new FoodOrder(item, count);
   }
   public String getItem() { return item; }
   public void setItem(String item) { this.item = item; }
   public int getCount() { return count; }
   public void setCount(int count) { this.count = count; }
}
```

The factory method technique gives you more control over the process of object creation.

 Real World Scenario

How to Protect the Source Code

Since this chapter is about Java SE applications, the person running your program will have access to the code. More specifically, they will have the bytecode (.class) files, typically bundled in a JAR file. With the bytecode, Hacker Harry can decompile your code and get source code. It's not as well written as the code you wrote, but it has equivalent information.

Some people compile their projects with obfuscation tools to try to hide implementation details. *Obfuscation* is the automated process of rewriting source code that purposely makes it more difficult to read. For example, if you try to view JavaScript on a website, entire methods or classes may be on a single line with variable names like aaa, bbb, ccc, and so on. It's harder to know what a method does if it's named gpiomjrqw().

While using an obfuscator makes the decompiled bytecode harder to read and therefore harder to reverse engineer, it doesn't actually provide any security. Remember that security by obscurity will slow down Hacker Harry, but it won't stop him!

Preventing Denial of Service Attacks

A *denial of service* (DoS) attack is when a hacker makes one or more requests with the intent of disrupting legitimate requests. Most denial of service attacks require multiple requests to bring down their targets. Some attacks send a very large request that can even bring down the application in one shot. In this book, we will focus on denial of service attacks.

Unless otherwise specified, a denial of service attack comes from one machine. It may make many requests, but they have the same origin. By contrast, a *distributed denial of service* (DDoS) attack is a denial of service attack that comes from many sources at once. For example, many machines may attack the target. In this section, we will look at some common sources of denial of service issues.

Leaking Resources

One way that Hacker Harry can mount a denial of service attack is to take advantage of poorly written code. This simple method counts the number of lines in a file using NIO.2 methods we saw in Chapter 9:

```
public long countLines(Path path) throws IOException  {
    return Files.lines(path).count();
}
```

Hacker Harry likes this method. He can call it in a loop. Since the method opens a file system resource and never closes it, there is a *resource leak*. After Hacker Harry calls the method enough times, the program crashes because there are no more file handles available.

Luckily, the fix for a resource leak is simple, and it's one you've already seen in Chapter 9. Security Sienna fixes the code by using the try-with-resources statement we saw in Chapter 5, "Exceptions, Assertions, and Localization." Here's an example:

```
public long countLines(Path path) throws IOException  {
    try (var stream = Files.lines(path)) {
        return stream.count();
    }
}
```

Reading Very Large Resources

Another source of a denial of service attacks is very large resources. Suppose we have a simple method that reads a file into memory, does some transformations on it, and writes it to a new file.

```
public void transform(Path in, Path out) throws IOException  {
    var list = Files.readAllLines(in);
```

```
    list.removeIf(s -> s.trim().isBlank());
    Files.write(out, list);
}
```

On a small file, this works just fine. However, on an extremely large file, your program could run out of memory and crash. Hacker Harry strikes again! To prevent this problem, you can check the size of the file before reading it.

Including Potentially Large Resources

An *inclusion* attack is when multiple files or components are embedded within a single file. Any file that you didn't create is suspect. Some types can appear smaller than they really are. For example, some types of images can have a "zip bomb" where the file is heavily compressed on disk. When you try to read it in, the file uses much more space than you thought.

Extensible Markup Language (XML) files can have the same problem. One attack is called the "billion laughs attack" where the file gets expanded exponentially.

The reason these files can become unexpectedly large is that they can include other entities. This means something that is 1 KB can become exponentially larger if it is included enough times.

While handling large files is beyond the scope of the exam, you should understand how and when these issues can come up.

Inclusion attacks are often known for when they include potentially hosted content. For example, imagine you have a web page that includes a script on another website. You don't control the script, but Hacker Harry does. Including scripts from other websites is dangerous regardless of how big they are.

Overflowing Numbers

When checking file size, be careful with an `int` type and loops. Since an `int` has a maximum size, exceeding that size results in integer overflow. Incrementing an `int` at the maximum value results in a negative number, so validation might not work as expected. In this example, we have a requirement to make sure that we can add a line to a file and have the size stay under a million.

```
public static void main(String[] args) {
    System.out.println(enoughRoomToAddLine(100));
    System.out.println(enoughRoomToAddLine(2_000_000));
    System.out.println(enoughRoomToAddLine(Integer.MAX_VALUE));
}
```

```
public static boolean enoughRoomToAddLine(int requestedSize) {
    int maxLength = 1_000_000;
    String newLine = "END OF FILE";

    int newLineSize = newLine.length();
    return requestedSize + newLineSize < maxLength;
}
```

The output of this program is as follows:

```
true
false
true
```

The first true should make sense. We start with a small file and add a short line to it. This is definitely under a million. The second value is false because two million is already over a million even after adding our short line.

Then we get to the final output of true. We start with a giant number that is over a million. Adding a small number to it exceeds the capacity of an int. Java overflows the number into a very negative number. Since all negative numbers are under a million, the validation doesn't do what we want it to.

When accepting numeric input, you need to verify it isn't too large or too small. In this example, the input value requestedSize should have been checked before adding it to newLineSize.

Wasting Data Structures

One advantage of using a HashMap is that you can look up an element quickly by key. Even if the map is extremely large, a lookup is fast as long as there is a good distribution of hashed keys.

Hacker Harry likes assumptions. He creates a class where hashCode() always returns 42 and puts a million of them in your map. Not so fast anymore.

This one is harder to prevent. However, beware of untrusted classes. Code review can help detect the Hacker Harry in your office.

Similarly, beware of code that attempts to create a very large array or other data structure. For example, if you write a method that lets you set the size of an array, Hacker Harry can repeatedly pick a really large array size and quickly exhaust the program's memory. Input validation is your friend. You could limit the size of an array parameter or, better yet, don't allow the size to be set at all.

Real World Scenario

Learning More

This exam covers security as it applies to stand-alone applications. On a real project, you are likely to be using other technologies. Luckily, there are lists of things to watch out for.

Open Web Application Security Project (OWASP) publishes a top 10 list of security issues. Some will sound familiar from this chapter, like injection. Others, like cross-site scripting (XSS), are specific to web applications. XSS involves malicious JavaScript.

If you are deploying to a cloud provider, like Oracle Cloud or AWS, there is even more to be aware of. The Cloud Security Alliance (CSA) also publishes a security list. Theirs is called the Egregious Eleven. This list covers additional worries such as account hijacking.

We've included links to the OWASP Top 10 and Egregious Eleven on our book page.

`http://www.selikoff.net/ocp11-2`

This chapter is just a taste of security. To learn more about security beyond the scope of the exam, please read *Iron-Clad Java,* Jim Manico and August Detlefsen (Oracle Press, 2014).

Summary

When designing a class, think about what it will be used for. This will allow you to choose the most restrictive access modifiers that meet your requirements. It will also help you determine whether subclasses are needed or whether the class should be final. If instances of the class are going to be passed around, it may make sense to make the class immutable so the state is guaranteed not to change.

Injection is an attack where dangerous input can run. SQL injection is prevented using a PreparedStatement with bind variables. Command injection is prevented with input validation and security policies. Whitelisting and the principle of least privilege provide the safest combination.

Confidential information must be handled carefully. It should be carefully dealt with in log files, output, and exception stack traces. Confidential information must also be protected in memory through the proper data structures and object lifecycle.

Object serialization and deserialization needs to be designed with security in mind as well. The transient modifier flags an instance variable as not being eligible for serialization. More granular control can be provided with the serialPersistentFields constant.

It is used to constrain the `writeObject()` method with `PutField` and the `readObject()` method with `GetField`. Finally, the `readResolve()` and `writeReplace()` methods allow you to return a different object or class.

Regardless of whether you are using serialization, objects must take care that the constructor cannot call methods that subclasses can override. Methods that are called from the constructor should be `final`. Making the constructor `private` or the class `final` also meets this requirement.

Finally, applications must protect against denial of service attacks. The most fundamental technique is always using try-with-resources to close resources. Applications should also validate file sizes and input data to ensure data structures are used properly.

Exam Essentials

Identify ways of preventing a denial of service attack. Using a try-with-resources statement for all I/O and JDBC operations prevents resource leaks. Checking the file size when reading a file prevents it from using an unexpected amount of memory. Confirming large data structures are being used effectively can prevent a performance problem.

Protect confidential information in memory. Picking a data structure that minimizes exposure is important. The most common one is using `char[]` for passwords. Additionally, allowing confidential information to be garbage collected as soon as possible reduces the window of exposure.

Compare injection, inclusion, and input validation.   SQL injection and command injection allow an attacker to run expected commands. Inclusion is when one file includes another. Input validation checks for valid or invalid characters from users.

Design secure objects.   Secure objects limit the accessibility of instance variables and methods. They are deliberate about when subclasses are allowed. Often secure objects are immutable and validate any input parameters.

Write serialization and deserializaton code securely.   The `transient` modifier signifies that an instance variable should not be serialized. Alternatively, `serialPersistenceFields` specifies what should be. The `readObject()`, `writeObject()`, `readResolve()`, and `writeReplace()` methods are optional methods that provide further control of the process.

Review Questions

The answers to the chapter review questions can be found in Appendix B.

1. How many requests does it take to have a DDoS attack?

    A. None

    B. One

    C. Two

    D. Many

2. Which of the following is the code an example of? (Choose all that apply.)

    ```java
    public final class Worm {
        private int length;

        public Worm(int length) {
            this.length = length;
        }
        public int getLength() {
            return length;
        }
    }
    ```

    A. Immutability

    B. Input validation

    C. Limiting accessibility

    D. Restricting extensibility

    E. None of the above

3. Which can fill in the blank to make this code compile?

    ```java
    import java.io.*;

    public class AnimalCheckup {
        private String name;
        private int age;

        private static final ObjectStreamField[]
            serialPersistentFields =
            { new ObjectStreamField("name", String.class)};

        private void writeObject(ObjectOutputStream stream)
    ```

```
        throws Exception {

            ObjectOutputStream._____ fields = stream.putFields();
            fields.put("name", name);
            stream.writeFields();
        }
        // readObject method omitted
    }
```

A. `PutField`

B. `PutItem`

C. `PutObject`

D. `UpdateField`

E. `UpdateItem`

F. `UpdateObject`

4. Which of the following can fill in the blank to make a defensive copy of `weights`? (Choose all that apply.)

```
    public class Turkey {
        private ArrayList<Double> weights;
        public Turkey(ArrayList<Double> weights) {
            this.weights = _____;
        }
    }
```

A. `weights`

B. `new ArrayList<>(weights)`

C. `weights.clone()`

D. `(ArrayList) weights.clone()`

E. `weights.copy()`

F. `(ArrayList) weights.copy()`

5. An object has validation code in the constructor. When deserializing an object, the constructor is called with which of the following?

A. `readObject()`

B. `readResolve()`

C. Both

D. Neither

6. Which statements are true about the clone() method? (Choose all that apply.)

   A. Calling clone() on any object will compile.

   B. Calling clone() will compile only if the class implements Cloneable.

   C. If clone() runs without exception, it will always create a deep copy.

   D. If clone() runs without exception, it will always create a shallow copy.

   E. If clone() is not overridden and runs without exception, it will create a deep copy.

   F. If clone() is not overridden and runs without exception, it will create a shallow copy.

7. Which attack could exploit this code?

```
public boolean isValid(String hashedPassword)
    throws SQLException {
    var sql = "SELECT * FROM users WHERE password = ?";
    try (var stmt = conn.prepareStatement(sql)) {
        stmt.setString(1, hashedPassword);
        try (var rs = stmt.executeQuery(sql)) {
            return rs.next();
        }
    }
}
```

   A. Command injection

   B. Confidential data exposure

   C. Denial of service

   D. SQL injection

   E. SQL leak

   F. None of the above

8. You go to the library and want to read a book. Which is true?

```
grant {
    permission java.io.FilePermission
        "/usr/local/library/book.txt",
        "read,write";
};
```

   A. The policy is correct.

   B. The policy is incorrect because file permissions cannot be granted this way.

   C. The policy is incorrect because read should not be included.

   D. The policy is incorrect because the permissions should be separated with semicolons.

   E. The policy is incorrect because write should not be included.

9. Which are true about securing confidential information? (Choose all that apply.)

   A. It is OK to access it in your program.

   B. It is OK to have it in an exception message.

   C. It is OK to put it in a `char[]`.

   D. It is OK to share it with other users.

   E. None of the above

10. Which types of resources do you need to close to help avoid a denial of service? (Choose all that apply.)

    A. Annotations

    B. Exceptions

    C. I/O

    D. JDBC

    E. String

11. Which of the following are considered inclusion attacks? (Choose all that apply.)

    A. Billion laughs attack

    B. Command injection

    C. CSRF

    D. SQL injection

    E. XSS

    F. Zip bomb

12. What is this code an example of?

    ```
    public void validate(String amount) {
        for (var ch : amount.toCharArray())
            if (ch < '0' || ch > '9')
                throw new IllegalArgumentException("invalid");
    }
    ```

    A. Blacklist

    B. Graylist

    C. Orangelist

    D. Whitelist

    E. None of the above

13. Which of the following are true statements about a class `Camel` with a single instance variable `List<String> species`? (Choose all that apply.)

    A. If `Camel` is well encapsulated, then it must have restricted extensibility.

    B. If `Camel` is well encapsulated, then it must be immutable.

C. If Camel has restricted extensibility, then it must have good encapsulation.

D. If Camel has restricted extensibility, then it must be immutable.

E. If Camel is immutable, then it must have good encapsulation.

F. If Camel is immutable, then it must restrict extensibility.

14. Which locations require you to be careful when working with sensitive data to ensure it doesn't leak? (Choose all that apply.)

A. Comments

B. Exception stack traces

C. Log files

D. `System.out`

E. Variable names

F. None of the above

15. What modifiers must be used with the `serialPersistentFields` field in a class? (Choose all that apply.)

A. `final`

B. `private`

C. `protected`

D. `public`

E. `transient`

F. `static`

16. What should your code do when input validation fails? (Choose all that apply.)

A. Call `System.exit()` immediately.

B. Continue execution.

C. Log a message.

D. Throw an exception.

E. None of the above

17. Which techniques can prevent an attacker from creating a top-level subclass that overrides a method called from the constructor? (Choose all that apply.)

A. Adding `final` to the class

B. Adding `final` to the method

C. Adding `transient` to the class

D. Adding `transient` to the method

E. Making the constructor `private`

F. None of the above

18. Which of these attacks is a program trying to prevent when it checks the size of a file?

    A. Denial of service

    B. Inclusion

    C. Injection

    D. None of the above

19. Fill in the blank with the proper method to deserialize an object.

```
public Object _____ throws ObjectStreamException {
    // return an object
}
```

    A. readObject()

    B. readReplace()

    C. readResolve()

    D. writeObject()

    E. writeReplace()

    F. writeResolve()

20. The following code prints true. What is true about the Wombats class implementation of the clone() method?

```
Wombats original = new Wombats();
original.names = new ArrayList<>();
Wombats cloned = (Wombats) original.clone();
System.out.println(original.getNames() == cloned.getNames());
```

    A. It creates a deep copy.

    B. It creates a narrow copy.

    C. It creates a shallow copy.

    D. It creates a wide copy.

Appendix

A

The Upgrade Exam

OCP UPGRADE EXAM OBJECTIVES COVERED IN THIS APPENDIX:

✓ **Local Variable Type Inference**

  ■ Use local variable type inference

  ■ Create and use lambda expressions with local variable type inferred parameters

✓ **Understanding Modules**

  ■ Describe the Modular JDK

  ■ Declare modules and enable access between modules

  ■ Describe how a modular project is compiled and run

This appendix is for anyone taking the 1Z0-817 upgrade exam. Read this appendix before the rest of the book if that's you. This appendix includes topics that were required knowledge for the 1Z0-815 exam, rather than the 1Z0-816 exam, and now show up on the 1Z0-817 exam.

First, we will discuss local variable type inference in detail, aka using var. You need to know this very well. In the rest of the book, we use var for the type in many code examples. In this appendix, we cover the rules in detail so you can be assured you will get these questions correct.

Understanding modules is the second topic we cover and takes up the majority of this appendix. If you've never used modules, they are a completely new way to package and reference Java libraries. This appendix provides a foundation for modules and allows you to understand more advanced topics, such as those discussed in Chapter 6, "Modular Applications."

Much of the material in this appendix was reprinted from Chapter 2, "Java Building Blocks" and Chapter 11, "Modules" of our 1Z0-815 book. We've made the modules' code available online. Since it can be tedious to create the directory structure, this will save you some time. Additionally, the commands need to be exactly right, so we've included those online so you can copy and paste them and compare them with what you typed. Both are available in the resources section of the online test bank and in our 1Z0-815 GitHub repo linked to from
www.selikoff.net/ocp11-2.

Working with Local Variable Type Inference

Starting in Java 10, you have the option of using the keyword var instead of the type for local variables under certain conditions. To use this feature, you just type var instead of the primitive or reference type within a code block. Here's an example:

```java
public void whatTypeAmI() {
    var name = "Hello";
    var size = 7;
}
```

The formal name of this feature is *local variable type inference*. Let's take that apart. First comes *local variable*. This means just what it sounds like. You can use this feature only for local variables. The exam may try to trick you with code like this:

```
public class VarKeyword {
    var tricky = "Hello"; // DOES NOT COMPILE
}
```

Wait a minute! We know the difference between instance and local variables. The variable `tricky` is an instance variable. Local variable type inference works with local variables and not instance variables.

Type Inference of *var*

Now that you understand the local variable part, it is time to go on to what *type inference* means. The good news is that this also means what it sounds like. When you type var, you are instructing the compiler to determine the type for you. The compiler looks at the code on the line of the declaration and uses it to infer the type. Take a look at this example:

```
7:   public void reassignment() {
8:       var number = 7;
9:       number = 4;
10:      number = "five";  // DOES NOT COMPILE
11: }
```

On line 8, the compiler determines that we want an int variable. On line 9, we have no trouble assigning a different int to it. On line 10, Java has a problem. We've asked it to assign a String to an int variable. This is not allowed. It is equivalent to typing this:

```
int number = "five";
```

 If you know a language like JavaScript, you might be expecting var to mean a variable that can take on any type at runtime. In Java, var is still a specific type defined at compile time. It does not change type at runtime.

So, the type of var can't change at runtime, but what about the value? Take a look at the following code snippet:

```
var apples = (short)10;
apples = (byte)5;
apples = 1_000_000;  // DOES NOT COMPILE
```

The first line creates a var named `apples` with a type of short. It then assigns a byte of 5 to it, but did that change the data type of `apples` to byte? Nope! The byte can be automatically promoted to a short, because a byte is small enough that it can fit inside of short. Therefore, the value stored on the second line is a short. In fact, let's rewrite the example showing what the compiler is really doing when it sees the var.

```
short apples = (short)10;
apples = (byte)5;
apples = 1_000_000;  // DOES NOT COMPILE
```

The last line does not compile, as one million is well beyond the limits of short. The compiler treats the value as an int and reports an error indicating it cannot be assigned to apples.

For simplicity when discussing var in the following sections, we are going to assume a variable declaration statement is completed in a single line. For example, you could insert a line break between the variable name and its initialization value, as in the following example:

```
7:  public void breakingDeclaration() {
8:     var silly
9:        = 1;
10: }
```

This example is valid and does compile, but we consider the declaration and initialization of silly to be happening on the same line.

Examples with *var*

Let's go through some more scenarios so the exam doesn't trick you on this topic! Do you think the following code compiles?

```
3:  public void doesThisCompile(boolean check) {
4:     var question;
5:     question = 1;
6:     var answer;
7:     if (check) {
8:        answer = 2;
9:     } else {
10:       answer = 3;
11:    }
12:    System.out.println(answer);
13: }
```

The code does not compile. Remember that for local variable type inference, the compiler looks only at the line with the declaration. Since question and answer are not assigned values on the lines where they are defined, the compiler does not know what to make of them. For this reason, both lines 4 and 6 do not compile.

You might find that strange since both branches of the if/else do assign a value. Alas, it is not on the same line as the declaration, so it does not count for var.

Now we know the initial value needed to determine the type needs to be part of the same statement. Can you figure out why these two statements don't compile?

```
4: public void twoTypes() {
5:    int a, var b = 3;   // DOES NOT COMPILE
6:    var n = null;       // DOES NOT COMPILE
7: }
```

Line 5 wouldn't work even if you replaced var with a real type. All the types declared on a single line must be the same type and share the same declaration. We couldn't write int a, int b = 3; either. Likewise, this is not allowed:

```
5:    var a = 2, b = 3;   // DOES NOT COMPILE
```

In other words, Java does not allow var in multiple variable declarations.

Line 6 is a single line. The compiler is being asked to infer the type of null. This could be any reference type. The only choice the compiler could make is Object. However, that is almost certainly not what the author of the code intended. The designers of Java decided it would be better not to allow var for null than to have to guess at intent.

---

var and null

While a var cannot be initialized with a null value without a type, it can be assigned a null value after it is declared, provided that the underlying data type of the var is an object. Take a look at the following code snippet:

```
13: var n = "myData";
14: n = null;
15: var m = 4;
16: m = null;  // DOES NOT COMPILE
```

Line 14 compiles without issue because n is of type String, which is an object. On the other hand, line 16 does not compile since the type of m is a primitive int, which cannot be assigned a null value.

It might surprise you to learn that a var can be initialized to a null value if the type is specified. The following code with a cast does compile:

```
17: var o = (String) null;
```

Since the type is provided, the compiler can apply type inference and set the type of the var to be String.

Let's try another example. Do you see why this does not compile?

```java
public int addition(var a, var b) {  // DOES NOT COMPILE
   return a + b;
}
```

In this example, a and b are method parameters. These are not local variables. Be on the lookout for var used with constructors, method parameters, or instance variables. Using var in one of these places is a good exam trick to see whether you are paying attention. Remember that var is used only for local variable type inference!

Time for two more examples. Do you think this is legal?

```java
package var;

public class Var {
   public void var() {
      var var = "var";
   }
   public void Var() {
      Var var = new Var();
   }
}
```

Believe it or not, this code does compile. Java is case sensitive, so Var doesn't introduce any conflicts as a class name. Naming a local variable var is legal. Please don't write code that looks like this at your job! But understanding why it works will help get you ready for any tricky exam questions Oracle could throw at you!

There's one last rule you should be aware of. While var is not a reserved word and allowed to be used as an identifier, it is considered a reserved type name. A *reserved type name* means it cannot be used to define a type, such as a class, interface, or enum. For example, the following code snippet does not compile due to the class name:

```java
public class var {  // DOES NOT COMPILE
   public var() {
   }
}
```

It is often inappropriate to use var as the type for every local variable in your code. That just makes the code difficult to understand. If you are ever unsure of whether it is appropriate to use var, there are numerous style guides out there that can help. We recommend the one titled "Style Guidelines for Local Variable Type Inference in Java," which is available at the following location. This resource includes great style suggestions.

   https://openjdk.java.net/projects/amber/LVTIstyle.html

Review of *var* Rules

We complete this section by summarizing all of the various rules for using var in your code. Here's a quick review of the var rules:

1. A var is used as a local variable in a constructor, method, or initializer block.

2. A var cannot be used in constructor parameters, method parameters, instance variables, or class variables.

3. A var is always initialized on the same line (or statement) where it is declared.

4. The value of a var can change but the type cannot.

5. A var cannot be initialized with a null value without a type.

6. A var is not permitted in a multiple-variable declaration.

7. A var is a reserved type name but not a reserved word, meaning it can be used as an identifier except as a class, interface, or enum name.

That's a lot of rules, but ideally most are pretty straightforward. Expect to see var used frequently on the exam and in this book.

 Real World Scenario

var in the Real World

The var keyword is great for exam authors because it makes it easier to write tricky code. When you work on a real project, you want the code to be easy to read.

Once you start having code that looks like the following, it is time to consider using var:

```
PileOfPapersToFileInFilingCabinet pileOfPapersToFile =
    new PileOfPapersToFileInFilingCabinet();
```

You can see how shortening this would be an improvement without losing any information:

```
var pileOfPapersToFile = new PileOfPapersToFileInFilingCabinet();
```

Introducing Modules

When writing code for the exam, you generally see small classes. After all, exam questions have to fit on a single screen! When you work on real programs, they are much bigger. A real project will consist of hundreds or thousands of classes grouped into packages. These packages are grouped into *Java archive (JAR)* files. A JAR is a zip file with some extra information, and the extension is .jar.

In addition to code written by your team, most applications also use code written by others. *Open source* is software with the code supplied and is often free to use. Java has a vibrant open-source software (OSS) community, and those libraries are also supplied as JAR files. For example, there are libraries to read files, connect to a database, and much more.

Some open-source projects even depend on functionality in other open-source projects. For example, Spring is a commonly used framework, and JUnit is a commonly used testing library. To use either, you need to make sure you had compatible versions of all the relevant JARs available at runtime. This complex chain of dependencies and minimum versions is often referred to by the community as *JAR hell*. Hell is an excellent way of describing the wrong version of a class being loaded or even a ClassNotFoundException at runtime.

The *Java Platform Module System* (JPMS) was introduced in Java 9 to group code at a higher level and tries to solve the problems that Java has been plagued with since the beginning. The main purpose of a module is to provide groups of related packages to offer a particular set of functionality to developers. It's like a JAR file except a developer chooses which packages are accessible outside the module. Let's look at what modules are and what problems they are designed to solve.

The Java Platform Module System includes the following:

▪ A format for module JAR files

▪ Partitioning of the JDK into modules

▪ Additional command-line options for Java tools

Exploring a Module

Most of the programs in this book are small. Now imagine we had a whole staff of programmers and were automating the operations of the zoo. There are many things that need to be coded including the interactions with the animals, visitors, the public website, and outreach.

A *module* is a group of one or more packages plus a special file called module-info.java. Figure A.1 lists just a few of the modules a zoo might need. We decided to focus on the animal interactions in our example. The full zoo could easily have a dozen modules. In Figure A.1, notice that there are arrows between many of the modules. These represent *dependencies* where one module relies on code in another. The staff needs to feed the animals to keep their jobs. The line from zoo.staff to zoo.animal.feeding shows the former depends on the latter.

Now let's drill down into one of these modules. Figure A.2 shows what is inside the zoo.animal.talks module. There are three packages with two classes each. (It's a small zoo.) There is also a strange file called module-info.java. This file is required to be inside all modules. We will explain this in more detail later.

FIGURE A.1   Design of a modular system

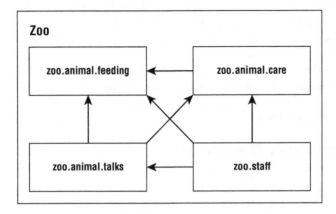

FIGURE A.2   Looking inside a module

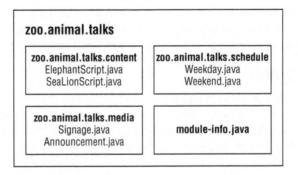

Benefits of Modules

Modules look like another layer of things you need to know in order to program. While using modules is optional, it is important to understand the problems they are designed to solve. Besides, knowing why modules are useful is required for the exam!

Better Access Control

There are four levels of access in a Java class file: private, package-private, protected, and public access. These levels of access control allow you to restrict access to a certain class or package. You could even allow access to subclasses without exposing them to the world.

However, what if we wrote some complex logic that we wanted to restrict to just some packages? For example, we would like the packages in the zoo.animal.talks module to just be available to the packages in the zoo.staff module without making them available to any other code. Our traditional access modifiers cannot handle this scenario.

Developers would resort to hacks like naming a package `zoo.animal.internal`. That didn't work, though, because other developers could still call the "internal" code. There was a class named `sun.misc.Unsafe`, and it got used in places. And that class had `Unsafe` in the name. Clearly, relying on naming conventions was insufficient at preventing developers from calling it in the past.

Modules solve this problem by acting as a fifth level of access control. They can expose packages within the modular JAR to specific other packages. This stronger form of encapsulation really does create internal packages. You'll see how to code it when we talk about the `module-info.java` shortly.

Clearer Dependency Management

It is common for libraries to depend on other libraries. For example, the JUnit 4 testing library depends on the Hamcrest library for matching logic. Developers would have to find this out by reading the documentation or files in the project itself.

If you forgot to include Hamcrest in your classpath, your code would run fine until you used a Hamcrest class. Then it would blow up at runtime with a message about not finding a required class. (We did mention JAR hell, right?)

In a fully modular environment, each of the open-source projects would specify their dependencies in the `module-info.java` file. When launching the program, Java would complain that Hamcrest isn't in the module path, and you'd know right away.

Custom Java Builds

The Java Development Kit (JDK) is larger than 150 MB. Even the Java Runtime Environment (JRE) was pretty big when it was available as a separate download. In the past, Java attempted to solve this with a *compact profile*. The three compact profiles provided a subset of the built-in Java classes so there would be a smaller package for mobile and embedded devices.

However, the compact profiles lacked flexibility. Many packages were included that developers were unlikely to use, such as Java Native Interface (JNI), which is for working with OS-specific programs. At the same time, using other packages like Image I/O required the full JRE.

The Java Platform Module System allows developers to specify what modules they actually need. This makes it possible to create a smaller runtime image that is customized to what the application needs and nothing more. Users can run that image without having Java installed at all.

A tool called `jlink` is used to create this runtime image. Luckily, you only need to know that custom smaller runtimes are possible. How to create them is out of scope for the exam.

In addition to the smaller-scale package, this approach improves security. If you don't use AWT and a security vulnerability is reported for AWT, applications that packaged a runtime image without AWT aren't affected.

Improved Performance

Since Java now knows which modules are required, it only needs to look at those at class loading time. This improves startup time for big programs and requires less memory to run.

While these benefits may not seem significant for the small programs we've been writing, they are far more important for big applications. A web application can easily take a minute to start. Additionally, for some financial applications, every millisecond of performance is important.

Unique Package Enforcement

Another manifestation of JAR hell is when the same package is in two JARs. There are a number of causes of this problem including renaming JARs, clever developers using a package name that is already taken, and having two versions of the same JAR on the classpath.

The Java Platform Module System prevents this scenario. A package is allowed to be supplied by only one module. No more unpleasant surprises about a package at runtime.

 Real World Scenario

Modules for Existing Code

While there are many benefits of using modules, there is also significant work for an existing large application to switch over. In particular, it is common for applications to be on old open-source libraries that do not have module support. The bill for all that technical debt comes due when making the switch to modules.

While not all open source projects have switched over, more than 4,000 have. There's a list of all Java modules on GitHub at

   `https://github.com/sormuras/modules/blob/master/README.md`

Creating and Running a Modular Program

In this section, we will create, build, and run the `zoo.animal.feeding` module. We chose this one to start with because all the other modules depend on it. Figure A.3 shows the design of this module. In addition to the `module-info.java` file, it has one package with one class inside.

FIGURE A.3   Contents of zoo.animal.feeding

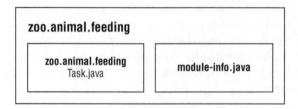

In the next sections, we will create, compile, run, and package the zoo.animal.feeding module.

Creating the Files

First we have a really simple class that prints one line in a main() method. We know, that's not much of an implementation. All those programmers we hired can fill it in with business logic. In this book, we will focus on what you need to know for the exam. So, let's create a simple class.

```java
package zoo.animal.feeding;

public class Task {
   public static void main(String... args) {
      System.out.println("All fed!");
   }
}
```

Next comes the module-info.java file. This is the simplest possible one.

```java
module zoo.animal.feeding {
}
```

There are a few key differences between a module-info file and a regular Java class.

- The module-info file must be in the root directory of your module. Regular Java classes should be in packages.

- The module-info file must use the keyword module instead of class, interface, or enum.

- The module name follows the naming rules for package names. It often includes periods (.) in its name. Regular class and package names are not allowed to have dashes (-). Module names follow the same rule.

That's a lot of rules for the simplest possible file. There will be many more rules when we flesh out this file later in the appendix.

Can a *module-info.java* File Be Empty?

Yes. As a bit of trivia, it was legal to compile any empty file with a .java extension even before modules. The compiler sees there isn't a class in there and exits without creating a .class file.

The next step is to make sure the files are in the right directory structure. Figure A.4 shows the expected directory structure.

FIGURE A.4   Module zoo.animal.feeding directory structure

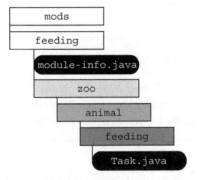

In particular, feeding is the module directory, and the module-info file is directly under it. Just as with a regular JAR file, we also have the zoo.animal.feeding package with one subfolder per portion of the name. The Task class is in the appropriate subfolder for its package.

Also, note that we created a directory called mods at the same level as the module. We will use it for storing the module artifacts a little later in the appendix. This directory can be named anything, but mods is a common name. If you are following along with the online code example, note that the mods directory is not included, because it is empty.

Compiling Our First Module

Before we can run modular code, we need to compile it. Other than the module-path option, this code should look familiar:

```
javac --module-path mods
   -d feeding
   feeding/zoo/animal/feeding/*.java
   feeding/module-info.java
```

> When you're entering commands at the command line, they should be typed all on one line. We use line breaks in the book to make the commands easier to read and study. If you wanted to use multiple lines at the command prompt, the approach varies by operating system. Linux uses a backslash (\) as the line break.

As a review, the –d option specifies the directory to place the class files in. The end of the command is a list of the .java files to compile. You can list the files individually or use a wildcard for all .java files in a subdirectory.

The new part is the module-path. This option indicates the location of any custom module files. In this example, module-path could have been omitted since there are no dependencies. You can think of module-path as replacing the classpath option when you are working on a modular program.

What Happened to the Classpath?

In the past, you would reference JAR files using the classpath option. It had three possible forms: -cp, --class-path, and -classpath. You can still use these options in Java 11. In fact, it is common to do so when writing nonmodular programs.

Just like classpath, you can use an abbreviation in the command. The syntax --module-path and -p are equivalent. That means we could have written many other commands in place of the previous command. The following four commands show the -p option:

```
javac -p mods
   -d feeding
   feeding/zoo/animal/feeding/*.java
   feeding/*.java
```

```
javac -p mods
   -d feeding
   feeding/zoo/animal/feeding/*.java
   feeding/module-info.java
```

```
javac -p mods
   -d feeding
   feeding/zoo/animal/feeding/Task.java
   feeding/module-info.java
```

```
javac -p mods
  -d feeding
  feeding/zoo/animal/feeding/Task.java
  feeding/*.java
```

While you can use whichever you like best, be sure that you can recognize all valid forms for the exam. Table A.1 lists the options you need to know well when compiling modules. There are many more options you can pass to the javac command, but these are the ones you can expect to be tested on.

TABLE A.1 Options you need to know for using modules with javac

Use for	Abbreviation	Long form
Directory for class files	-d <dir>	n/a
Module path	-p <path>	--module-path <path>

 Real World Scenario

Building Modules

Even before modules, it was rare to run javac and java commands manually on a real project. They get long and complicated very quickly. Most developers use a build tool such as Maven or Gradle. These build tools suggest directories to place the class files like target/classes.

With modules, there is even more typing to run these commands by hand. After all, with modules, you are using more directories by definition. This means that it is likely the only time you need to know the syntax of these commands is when you take the exam. The concepts themselves are useful regardless.

Do be sure to memorize the module command syntax. You will be tested on it on the exam. We will be sure to give you lots of practice questions on the syntax to reinforce it.

Running Our First Module

Before we package our module, we should make sure it works by running it. To do that, we need to learn the full syntax. Suppose there is a module named book.module. Inside that module is a package named com.sybex, which has a class named OCP with a main()

method. Figure A.5 shows the syntax for running a module. Pay special attention to the book.module/com.sybex.OCP part. It is important to remember that you specify the module name followed by a slash (/) followed by the fully qualified class name.

FIGURE A.5   Running a module using java

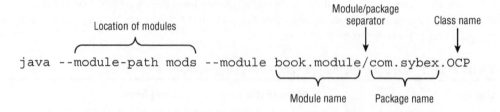

Now that we've seen the syntax, we can write the command to run the Task class in the zoo.animal.feeding package. In the following example, the package name and module name are the same. It is common for the module name to match either the full package name or the beginning of it.

```
java --module-path feeding
   --module zoo.animal.feeding/zoo.animal.feeding.Task
```

Since you already saw that --module-path uses the short form of -p, we bet you won't be surprised to learn there is a short form of --module as well. The short option is -m. That means the following command is equivalent:

```
java -p feeding
   -m zoo.animal.feeding/zoo.animal.feeding.Task
```

In these examples, we used feeding as the module path because that's where we compiled the code. This will change once we package the module and run that.

Table A.2 lists the options you need to know for the java command.

TABLE A.2   Options you need to know for using modules with java

Use for	Abbreviation	Long form
Module name	-m <name>	--module <name>
Module path	-p <path>	--module-path <path>

Packaging Our First Module

A module isn't much use if we can run it only in the folder it was created in. Our next step is to package it. Be sure to create a mods directory before running this command:

```
jar -cvf mods/zoo.animal.feeding.jar -C feeding/ .
```

There's nothing module-specific here. We are packaging everything under the feeding directory and storing it in a JAR file named zoo.animal.feeding.jar under the mods folder. This represents how the module JAR will look to other code that wants to use it.

> It is possible to version your module using the --module-version option. This isn't on the exam but is good to do when you are ready to share your module with others.

Now let's run the program again, but this time using the mods directory instead of the loose classes.

```
java -p mods
    -m zoo.animal.feeding/zoo.animal.feeding.Task
```

You might notice that this command looks identical to the one in the previous section except for the directory. In the previous example, it was feeding. In this one, it is the module path of mods. Since the module path is used, a module JAR is being run.

Figure A.6 shows what the directory structure looks like now that we've compiled and packaged the code.

FIGURE A.6   Module zoo.animal.feeding directory structure with class and jar files

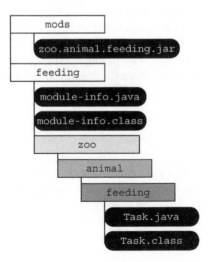

Updating Our Example for Multiple Modules

Now that our zoo.animal.feeding module is solid, we can start thinking about our other modules. As you can see in Figure A.7, all three of the other modules in our system depend on the zoo.animal.feeding module.

FIGURE A.7 Modules depending on zoo.animal.feeding

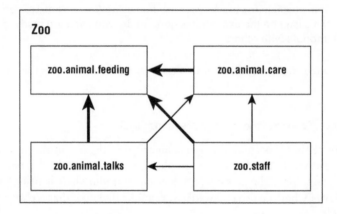

Updating the Feeding Module

Since we will be having our other modules call code in the zoo.animal.feeding package, we need to declare this intent in the module-info file.

The exports keyword is used to indicate that a module intends for those packages to be used by Java code outside the module. As you might expect, without an exports keyword, the module is only available to be run from the command line on its own. In the following example, we export one package:

```
module zoo.animal.feeding {
    exports zoo.animal.feeding;
}
```

Recompiling and repackaging the module will update the module-info inside our zoo.animals.feeding.jar file. These are the same javac and jar commands you ran previously.

```
javac -p mods
    -d feeding
```

```
feeding/zoo/animal/feeding/*.java
feeding/module-info.java
```

```
jar -cvf mods/zoo.animal.feeding.jar -C feeding/ .
```

Creating a Care Module

Next, let's create the zoo.animal.care module. This time, we are going to have two packages. The zoo.animal.care.medical package will have the classes and methods that are intended for use by other modules. The zoo.animal.care.details package is only going to be used by this module. It will not be exported from the module. Think of it as healthcare privacy for the animals.

Figure A.8 shows the contents of this module. Remember that all modules must have a module-info file.

FIGURE A.8   Contents of zoo.animal.care

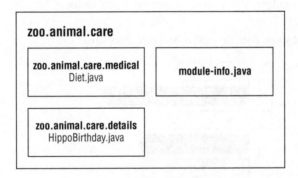

The module contains two basic packages and classes in addition to the module-info.java file.

```
// HippoBirthday.java
package zoo.animal.care.details;
import zoo.animal.feeding.*;
public class HippoBirthday {
    private Task task;
}

// Diet.java
package zoo.animal.care.medical;
public class Diet { }
```

This time the module-info.java file specifies three things.

```
1: module zoo.animal.care {
2:     exports zoo.animal.care.medical;
3:     requires zoo.animal.feeding;
4: }
```

Line 1 specifies the name of the module. Line 2 lists the package we are exporting so it can be used by other modules. So far, this is similar to the zoo.animal.feeding module.

On line 3, we see a new keyword. The requires statement specifies that a module is needed. The zoo.animal.care module depends on the zoo.animal.feeding module.

Next, we need to figure out the directory structure. We will create two packages. The first is zoo.animal.care.details and contains one class named HippoBirthday. The second is zoo.animal.care.medical and contains one class named Diet. Try to draw the directory structure on paper or create it on your computer. If you are trying to run these examples without using the online code, just create classes without variables or methods for everything except the module-info.java files.

Figure A.9 shows the directory structure of this module. Note that module-info.java is in the root of the module. The two packages are underneath it.

FIGURE A.9   Module zoo.animal.care directory structure

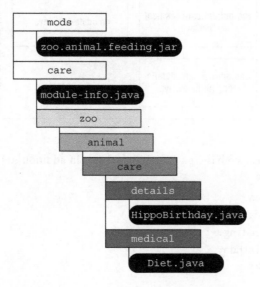

You might have noticed that the packages begin with the same prefix as the module name. This is intentional. You can think of it as if the module name "claims" the matching package and all subpackages.

To review, we now compile and package the module.

```
javac -p mods
   -d care
   care/zoo/animal/care/details/*.java
   care/zoo/animal/care/medical/*.java
   care/module-info.java
```

We compile both packages and the module-info file. In the real world, you'll use a build tool rather than doing this by hand. For the exam, you just list all the packages and/ or files you want to compile.

Order May Matter!

Note that order may matter when compiling a module. Suppose we list the module-info file first when trying to compile.

```
javac -p mods
   -d care
   care/module-info.java
   care/zoo/animal/care/details/*.java
   care/zoo/animal/care/medical/*.java
```

The compiler complains that it doesn't know anything about the package zoo.animal.care.medical.

```
care/module-info.java:3: error: package is empty
   or does not exist: zoo.animal.care.medical
exports zoo.animal.care.medical;
```

A package must have at least one class in it to be exported. Since we haven't yet compiled zoo.animal.care.medical.Diet, the compiler acts as if it doesn't exist. If you get this error message, you can reorder the javac statement. Alternatively, you can compile the packages in a separate javac command, before compiling the module-info file.

Now that we have compiled code, it's time to create the module JAR.

```
jar -cvf mods/zoo.animal.care.jar -C care/ .
```

Creating the Talks Module

So far, we've used only one exports and requires statement in a module. Now you'll learn how to handle exporting multiple packages or requiring multiple modules. In

Figure A.10, observe that the `zoo.animal.talks` module depends on two modules: `zoo
.animal.feeding` and `zoo.animal.care`. This means that there must be two `requires`
statements in the `module-info.java` file.

FIGURE A.10   Dependencies for `zoo.animal.talks`

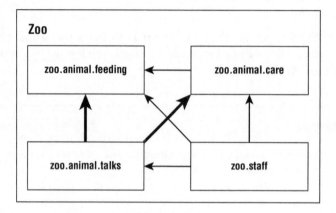

Figure A.11 shows the contents of this module. We are going to export all three packages in this module.

FIGURE A.11   Contents of `zoo.animal.talks`

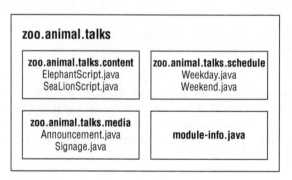

First let's look at the `module-info.java` file for `zoo.animal.talks`.

```
1: module zoo.animal.talks {
2:     exports zoo.animal.talks.content;
3:     exports zoo.animal.talks.media;
4:     exports zoo.animal.talks.schedule;
5:
```

```
6:    requires zoo.animal.feeding;
7:    requires zoo.animal.care;
8: }
```

Line 1 shows the module name. Lines 2–4 allow other modules to reference all three packages. Lines 6–7 specify the two modules that this module depends on.

Then we have the six classes, as shown here:

```
// ElephantScript.java
package zoo.animal.talks.content;
public class ElephantScript { }

// SeaLionScript.java
package zoo.animal.talks.content;
public class SeaLionScript { }

// Announcement.java
package zoo.animal.talks.media;
public class Announcement {
   public static void main(String[] args) {
      System.out.println("We will be having talks");
   }
}

// Signage.java
package zoo.animal.talks.media;
public class Signage { }

// Weekday.java
package zoo.animal.talks.schedule;
public class Weekday { }

// Weekend.java
package zoo.animal.talks.schedule;
public class Weekend {}
```

If you are still following along on your computer, create empty classes in the packages. The following are the commands to compile and build the module:

```
javac -p mods
   -d talks
   talks/zoo/animal/talks/content/*.java
   talks/zoo/animal/talks/media/*.java
```

```
talks/zoo/animal/talks/schedule/*.java
talks/module-info.java
```

```
jar -cvf mods/zoo.animal.talks.jar -C talks/ .
```

Creating the Staff Module

Our final module is `zoo.staff`. Figure A.12 shows there is only one package inside. We will not be exposing this package outside the module.

FIGURE A.12   Contents of `zoo.staff`

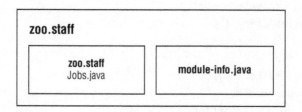

Based on this information, do you know what should go in the `module-info`?

```
module zoo.staff {
    requires zoo.animal.feeding;
    requires zoo.animal.care;
    requires zoo.animal.talks;
}
```

There are three arrows in Figure A.13 pointing from `zoo.staff` to other modules. These represent the three modules that are required. Since no packages are to be exposed from `zoo.staff`, there are no `exports` statements.

FIGURE A.13   Dependencies for `zoo.staff`

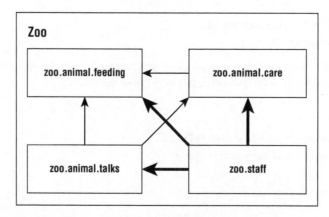

In this module, we have a single class in file Jobs.java.

```
package zoo.staff;
public class Jobs { }
```

For those of you following along on your computer, create an empty class in the package. The following are the commands to compile and build the module:

```
javac -p mods
   -d staff
   staff/zoo/staff/*.java
   staff/module-info.java

jar -cvf mods/zoo.staff.jar -C staff/ .
```

Diving into the *module-info* File

Now that we've successfully created modules, we can talk more about the module-info file. In these sections, we will look at exports, requires, provides, uses, and opens. Now would be a good time to mention that these keywords can appear in any order in the module-info file.

exports

We've already seen how exports *packageName* exports a package to other modules. It's also possible to export a package to a specific module. Suppose the zoo decides that only staff members should have access to the talks. We could update the module declaration as follows:

```
module zoo.animal.talks {
   exports zoo.animal.talks.content to zoo.staff;
   exports zoo.animal.talks.media;
   exports zoo.animal.talks.schedule;

   requires zoo.animal.feeding;
   requires zoo.animal.care;
}
```

From the zoo.staff module, nothing has changed. However, no other modules would be allowed to access that package.

You might have noticed that none of our other modules requires zoo.animal.talks in the first place. However, we don't know what other modules will exist in the future. It is important to consider future use when designing modules. Since we want only one module to have access, we only allow access for that module.

Exported Types

We've been talking about exporting a package. But what does that mean exactly? All public classes, interfaces, and enums are exported. Further, any public and protected fields and methods in those files are visible.

Fields and methods that are private are not visible because they are not accessible outside the class. Similarly, package-private fields and methods are not visible because they are not accessible outside the package.

The exports keyword essentially gives us more levels of access control. Table A.3 lists the full access control options.

TABLE A.3 Access control with modules

Level	Within module code	Outside module
private	Available only within class	No access
default (package-private)	Available only within package	No access
protected	Available only within package or to subclasses	Accessible to subclasses only if exported
public	Available to all classes	Accessible only if package is exported

requires transitive

As you saw earlier, requires *moduleName* specifies that the current module depends on *moduleName*. There's also a requires transitive *moduleName*, which means that any module that requires this module will also depend on *moduleName*.

Well, that was a mouthful. Let's look at an example. Figure A.14 shows the modules with dashed lines for the redundant relationships and solid lines for relationships specified in the module-info. This shows how the module relationships would look if we were to only use transitive dependencies.

For example, zoo.animals.talks depends on zoo.animals.care, which depends on zoo.animals.feeding. That means the arrow between zoo.animals.talks and zoo .animals.feeding no longer appears in Figure A.14.

FIGURE A.14　Transitive dependency version of our modules

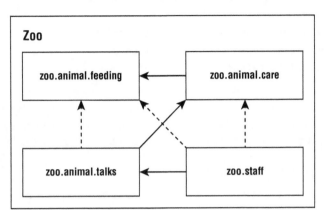

Now let's look at the four module-info files. The first module remains unchanged. We are exporting one package to any packages that use the module.

```
module zoo.animal.feeding {
    exports zoo.animal.feeding;
}
```

The zoo.animal.care module is the first opportunity to improve things. Rather than forcing all remaining modules to explicitly specify zoo.animal.feeding, the code uses requires transitive.

```
module zoo.animal.care {
    exports zoo.animal.care.medical;
    requires transitive zoo.animal.feeding;
}
```

In the zoo.animal.talks module, we make a similar change and don't force other modules to specify zoo.animal.care. We also no longer need to specify zoo.animal.feeding, so that line is commented out.

```
module zoo.animal.talks {
    exports zoo.animal.talks.content to zoo.staff;
    exports zoo.animal.talks.media;
    exports zoo.animal.talks.schedule;

    // no longer needed requires zoo.animal.feeding;
    // no longer needed requires zoo.animal.care;
    requires transitive zoo.animal.care;
}
```

Finally, in the zoo.staff module, we can get rid of two requires statements.

```
module zoo.staff {
    // no longer needed requires zoo.animal.feeding;
    // no longer needed requires zoo.animal.care;
    requires zoo.animal.talks;
}
```

The more modules you have, the more benefits of requires transitive compound. It is also more convenient for the caller. If you were trying to work with this zoo, you could just require zoo.staff and have the remaining dependencies automatically inferred.

Effects of *requires transitive*

Given our newly updated module-info files and using Figure A.14, what is the effect of applying the transitive modifier to the requires statement in our zoo.animal.care module? Applying the transitive modifiers has the following effects:

- Module zoo.animal.talks can optionally declare it requires the zoo.animal.feeding module, but it is not required.

- Module zoo.animal.care cannot be compiled or executed without access to the zoo.animal.feeding module.

- Module zoo.animal.talks cannot be compiled or executed without access to the zoo.animal.feeding module.

These rules hold even if the zoo.animal.care and zoo.animal.talks modules do not explicitly reference any packages in the zoo.animal.feeding module. On the other hand, without the transitive modifier in our module-info file of zoo.animal.care, the other modules would have to explicitly use requires in order to reference any packages in the zoo.animal.feeding module.

Duplicate *requires* Statements

One place the exam might try to trick you is mixing requires and requires transitive together. Can you think of a reason this code doesn't compile?

```
module bad.module {
    requires zoo.animal.talks;
    requires transitive zoo.animal.talks;
}
```

Java doesn't allow you to repeat the same module in a requires clause. It is redundant and most likely an error in coding. Keep in mind that requires transitive is like requires plus some extra behavior.

provides, *uses*, and *opens*

For the remaining three keywords (provides, uses, and opens), we cover just the basics here. They are covered in more detail in Chapter 6.

The provides keyword specifies that a class provides an implementation of a service. For now, you can just think of a service as a fancy interface. To use it, you supply the API and class name that implements the API.

```
provides zoo.staff.ZooApi with zoo.staff.ZooImpl
```

The uses keyword specifies that a module is relying on a service. To code it, you supply the API you want to call.

```
uses zoo.staff.ZooApi
```

Java allows callers to inspect and call code at runtime with a technique called *reflection*. This is a powerful approach that allows calling code that might not be available at compile time. It can even be used to subvert access control! Don't worry—you don't need to know how to write code using reflection for the exam.

Since reflection can be dangerous, the module system requires developers to explicitly allow reflection in the module-info if they want calling modules to be allowed to use it. Here are two examples:

```
opens zoo.animal.talks.schedule;
opens zoo.animal.talks.media to zoo.staff;
```

The first example allows any module using this one to use reflection. The second example gives that privilege only to the zoo.staff package.

Discovering Modules

So far, we've been working with modules that we wrote. Since Java 9, the classes built into the JDK were modularized as well. In this section, we will show you how to use commands to learn about modules.

You do not need to know the output of the commands in this section. You do, however, need to know the syntax of the commands and what they do. We include the output where it facilitates remembering what is going on. But you don't need to memorize that (which frees up more space in your head to memorize command-line options).

The *java* Command

The java command has three module-related options. One describes a module, another lists the available modules, and the third shows the module resolution logic.

It is also possible to add modules, exports, and more at the command line. But please don't. It's confusing and hard to maintain. Note that these flags are available on java, but not all commands are.

Describing a Module

Suppose you are given the zoo.animal.feeding module JAR file and want to know about its module structure. You could "unjar" it and open the module-info file. This would show you that the module exports one package and doesn't require any modules.

```
module zoo.animal.feeding {
    exports zoo.animal.feeding;
}
```

However, there is an easier way. The java command now has an option to describe a module. The following two commands are equivalent:

```
java -p mods
   -d zoo.animal.feeding
```

```
java -p mods
   --describe-module zoo.animal.feeding
```

Each prints information about the module. For example, it might print this:

```
zoo.animal.feeding file:///absolutePath/mods/zoo.animal.feeding.jar
exports zoo.animal.feeding
requires java.base mandated
```

The first line is the module we asked about: zoo.animal.feeding. The second line starts information about the module. In our case, it is the same package exports statement we had in the module-info file.

On the third line, we see requires java.base mandated. Now wait a minute. The module-info file clearly does not specify any modules that zoo.animal.feeding has as dependencies.

The java.base module is special. It is automatically added as a dependency to all modules. This module has frequently used packages like java.util. That's what the mandated is about. You get java.base whether you asked for it or not.

In classes, the java.lang package is automatically imported whether you type it or not. The java.base module works the same way. It is automatically available to all other modules.

More about Describing Modules

You might encounter some surprises when experimenting with --describe-module, so we describe it in a bit more detail here.

As a reminder, the following are the contents of module-info in zoo.animal.care:

```
module zoo.animal.care {
    exports zoo.animal.care.medical to zoo.staff;
    requires transitive zoo.animal.feeding;
}
```

Now we have the command to describe the module and the output:

```
java -p mods -d zoo.animal.care
```

```
zoo.animal.care file:///absolutePath/mods/zoo.animal.care.jar
requires zoo.animal.feeding transitive
requires java.base mandated
qualified exports zoo.animal.care.medical to zoo.staff
contains zoo.animal.care.details
```

The first line of the output is the absolute path of the module file. The two requires lines should look familiar as well. The first is in the module-info, and the other is added to all modules. Next comes something new. The qualified exports is the full name of exporting to a specific module.

Finally, the contains means that there is a package in the module that is not exported at all. This is true. Our module has two packages, and one is available only to code inside the module.

Listing Available Modules

In addition to describing modules, you can use the java command to list the modules that are available. The simplest form lists the modules that are part of the JDK.

```
java --list-modules
```

When we ran it, the output went on for 70 lines and looked like this:

```
java.base@11.0.2
java.compiler@11.0.2
java.datatransfer@11.0.2
```

This is a listing of all the modules that come with Java and their version numbers. You can tell that we were using Java 11.0.2 when testing this example.

More interestingly, you can use this command with custom code. Let's try again with the directory containing our zoo modules:

```
java -p mods --list-modules
```

How many lines do you expect to be in the output this time? There are 74 lines now: the 70 built-in modules plus the four in our zoo system. The custom lines look like this:

```
zoo.animal.care file:///absolutePath/mods/zoo.animal.care.jar
zoo.animal.feeding file:///absolutePath/mods/zoo.animal.feeding.jar
zoo.animal.talks file:///absolutePath/mods/zoo.animal.talks.jar
zoo.staff file:///absolutePath/mods/zoo.staff.jar
```

Since these are custom modules, we get a location on the file system. If the project had a module version number, it would have both the version number and the file system path.

Note that `--list-modules` exits as soon as it prints the observable modules. It does not run the program.

Showing Module Resolution

In case listing the modules didn't give you enough output, you can also use the `--show-module-resolution` option. You can think of it as a way of debugging modules. It spits out a lot of output when the program starts up. Then it runs the program.

```
java --show-module-resolution
  -p feeding
  -m zoo.animal.feeding/zoo.animal.feeding.Task
```

Luckily, you don't need to understand this output. That said, having seen it will make it easier to remember. Here's a snippet of the output:

```
root zoo.animal.feeding file:///absolutePath/feeding/
java.base binds java.desktop jrt:/java.desktop
java.base binds jdk.jartool jrt:/jdk.jartool
...
jdk.security.auth requires java.naming jrt:/java.naming
jdk.security.auth requires java.security.jgss jrt:/java.security.jgss
...
All fed!
```

It starts out by listing the root module. That's the one we are running: `zoo.animal.feeding`. Then it lists many lines of packages included by the mandatory `java.base` module. After a while, it lists modules that have dependencies. Finally, it outputs the result of the program `All fed!`. The total output of this command is 66 lines.

The *jar* Command

Like the java command, the jar command can describe a module. Both of these commands are equivalent:

```
jar -f mods/zoo.animal.feeding.jar -d
jar --file mods/zoo.animal.feeding.jar --describe-module
```

The output is slightly different from when we used the java command to describe the module. With jar, it outputs the following:

```
zoo.animal.feeding jar:file:///absolutePath/mods/
   zoo.animal.feeding.jar/!module-info.class
exports zoo.animal.feeding
requires java.base mandated
```

The JAR version includes the module-info in the filename, which is not a particularly significant difference in the scheme of things. You don't need to know this difference. You do need to know that both commands can describe a module.

The *jdeps* Command

The jdeps command gives you information about dependencies within a module. Unlike describing a module, it looks at the code in addition to the module-info file. This tells you what dependencies are actually used rather than simply declared.

Let's start with a simple example and ask for a summary of the dependencies in zoo .animal.feeding. Both of these commands give the same output, as shown here:

```
jdeps -s mods/zoo.animal.feeding.jar

jdeps -summary mods/zoo.animal.feeding.jar
```

Notice that there is one dash (-) before -summary rather than two. Regardless, the output tells you that there is only one package and it depends on the built-in java.base module.

```
zoo.animal.feeding -> java.base
```

Alternatively, you can call jdeps without the summary option and get the long form:

```
jdeps mods/zoo.animal.feeding.jar
[file:///absolutePath/mods/zoo.animal.feeding.jar]
   requires mandated java.base (@11.0.2)
zoo.animal.feeding -> java.base
   zoo.animal.feeding          -> java.io
      java.base
   zoo.animal.feeding          -> java.lang
      java.base
```

The first part of the output shows the module filename and path. The second part lists the required java.base dependency and version number. This has the high-level summary that matches the previous example.

Finally, the last four lines of the output list the specific packages within the java.base modules that are used by zoo.animal.feeding.

Now, let's look at a more complicated example. This time, we pick a module that depends on zoo.animal.feeding. We need to specify the module path so jdeps knows where to find information about the dependent module. We didn't need to do that before because all dependent modules were built into the JDK.

Following convention, these two commands are equivalent:

```
jdeps -s
   --module-path mods
   mods/zoo.animal.care.jar

jdeps -summary
   --module-path mods
   mods/zoo.animal.care.jar
```

There is not a short form of --module-path in the jdeps command. The output is only two lines:

```
zoo.animal.care -> java.base
zoo.animal.care -> zoo.animal.feeding
```

We can see that the zoo.animal.care module depends on our custom zoo.animal.feeding module along with the built-in java.base.

In case you were worried the output was too short, we can run it in full mode.

```
jdeps --module-path mods
   mods/zoo.animal.care.jar
```

This time we get a lot of output.

```
zoo.animal.care
   [file:///absolutePath/mods/zoo.animal.care.jar]
      requires mandated java.base (@11.0.2)
      requires transitive zoo.animal.feeding
   zoo.animal.care -> java.base
   zoo.animal.care -> zoo.animal.feeding
      zoo.animal.care.details       -> java.lang
         java.base
      zoo.animal.care.details       -> zoo.animal.feeding
         zoo.animal.feeding
      zoo.animal.care.medical       -> java.lang
         java.base
```

As before, there are three sections. The first section is the filename and required dependencies. The second section is the summary showing the two module dependencies with an arrow. The last six lines show the package-level dependencies.

The *jmod* Command

The final command you need to know for the exam is jmod. You might think a JMOD file is a Java module file. Not quite. Oracle recommends using JAR files for most modules. JMOD files are recommended only when you have native libraries or something that can't go inside a JAR file. This is unlikely to affect you in the real world.

The most important thing to remember is that jmod is only for working with the JMOD files. Conveniently, you don't have to memorize the syntax for jmod. Table A.4 lists the common modes.

TABLE A.4   Modes using jmod

Operation	Description
create	Creates a JMOD file
extract	Extracts all files from the JMOD. Works like unzipping
describe	Prints the module details, such as requires
list	Lists all files in the JMOD file
hash	Shows a long string that goes with the file

Reviewing Command-Line Options

Congratulations on reaching the last section of the appendix. This section has a number of tables that cover what you need to know about running command-line options.

Table A.5 shows the command lines you should expect to encounter on the exam.

Since there are so many commands you need to know, we've made a number of tables to review the available options that you need to know for the exam. There are many more options in the documentation. For example, there is a --module option on javac that limits compilation to that module. Luckily, you don't need to know those.

Table A.6 shows the options for javac, Table A.7 shows the options for java, Table A.8 shows the options for jar, and Table A.9 shows the options for jdeps.

TABLE A.5 Comparing command-line operations

Description	Syntax
Compile nonmodular code	**javac -cp** *classpath* -d *directory classesToCompile*
	javac --class-path *classpath* -d *directory classesToCompile*
	javac -classpath *classpath* -d *directory classesToCompile*
Run nonmodular code	**java -cp** *classpath package.className*
	java -classpath *classpath package.className*
	java --class-path *classpath package.className*
Compile a module	**javac -p** *moduleFolderName* -d *directory classesToCompileIncludingModuleInfo*
	javac --module-path *moduleFolderName* -d *directory classesToCompileIncludingModuleInfo*
Run a module	**java -p** *moduleFolderName* **-m** *moduleName/package.className*
	java --module-path *moduleFolderName* **--module** *moduleName/package.className*
Describe a module	**java -p** *moduleFolderName* **-d** *moduleName*
	java --module-path *moduleFolderName* **--describe-module** *moduleName*
	jar --file *jarName* **--describe-module**
	jar -f *jarName* **-d**
List available modules	**java --module-path** *moduleFolderName* **--list-modules**
	java -p *moduleFolderName* **--list-modules**
	java --list-modules
View dependencies	**jdeps -summary --module-path** *moduleFolderName jarName*
	jdeps -s --module-path *moduleFolderName jarName*
Show module resolution	**java --show-module-resolution -p** *moduleFolderName* **-d** *moduleName*
	java --show-module-resolution --module-path *moduleFolderName* **--describe-module** *moduleName*

TABLE A.6 Options you need to know for the exam: `javac`

Option	Description

`-cp <classpath>`
`-classpath <classpath>`
`--class-path <classpath>`
	Location of JARs in a nonmodular program

`-d <dir>`	Directory to place generated class files
`-p <path>` `--module-path <path>`	Location of JARs in a modular program

TABLE A.7 Options you need to know for the exam: `java`

Option	Description

`-cp <classpath>`
`-classpath <classpath>`
`--class-path <classpath>`
	Location of JARs in a nonmodular program

`-p <path>` `--module-path <path>`	Location of JARs in a modular program
`-m <name>` `--module <name>`	Module name to run
`-d` `--describe-module`	Describes the details of a module
`--list-modules`	Lists observable modules without running a program
`--show-module-resolution`	Shows modules when running program

TABLE A.8 Options you need to know for the exam: `jar`

Option	Description
`-c` `--create`	Create a new JAR file
`-v` `--verbose`	Prints details when working with JAR files

TABLE A.8   Options you need to know for the exam: `jar` *(continued)*

Option	Description
`-f` `--file`	JAR filename
`-C`	Directory containing files to be used to create the JAR
`-d` `--describe-module`	Describes the details of a module

TABLE A.9   Options you need to know for the exam: `jdeps`

Option	Description
`--module-path <path>`	Location of JARs in a modular program
`-s` `-summary`	Summarizes output

Summary

In Java, local variable type inference is performed using the `var` keyword for local variables instead of the actual type. When using `var`, the type is set once at compile time and does not change. Local variable type inference can be applied to local variables within a method, constructor, or initializer block. They can also be used for lambda parameters and resource declarations within a try-with-resources statement.

The Java Platform Module System organizes code at a higher level than packages. Each module contains one or more packages and a `module-info` file. Advantages of the Java Platform Module System include better access control, clearer dependency management, custom runtime images, improved performance, and unique package enforcement.

The process of compiling and running modules uses the `--module-path`, also known as `-p`. Running a module uses the `--module` option, also known as `-m`. The class to run is specified in the format `moduleName/packageName.className`.

The `module-info` file supports a number of keywords. The `exports` keyword specifies that a package should be accessible outside the module. It can optionally restrict that export to a specific package. The `requires` keyword is used when a module depends on code in another module. Additionally, requires transitive can be used when all modules that require one module should always require another. The provides and uses keywords are used when sharing and consuming an API. Finally, the opens keyword is used for allowing access via reflection.

Both the java and jar commands can be used to describe the contents of a module. The java command can additionally list available modules and show module resolution. The jdeps command prints information about packages used in addition to module-level information. Finally, the jmod command is used when dealing with files that don't meet the requirements for a JAR.

Exam Essentials

Be able to use *var* correctly.   A var is used for a local variable inside a constructor, a method, or an initializer block. It cannot be used for constructor parameters, method parameters, instance variables, or class variables. A var is initialized on the same line where it is declared, and while it can change value, it cannot change type. A var cannot be initialized with a null value without a type, nor can it be used in multiple variable declarations. Finally, var is not a reserved word in Java and can be used as a variable name.

Identify benefits of the Java Platform Module System.   Be able to identify benefits of the JPMS from a list such as access control, dependency management, custom runtime images, performance, and unique package enforcement. Also be able to differentiate benefits of the JPMS from benefits of Java as a whole. For example, garbage collection is not a benefit of the JPMS.

Use command-line syntax with modules.   Use the command-line options for javac, java, and jar. In particular, understand the module (-m) and module path (-p) options.

Create basic *module-info* files.   Place the module-info.java file in the root directory of the module. Know how to code using exports to expose a package and how to export to a specific module. Also, know how to code using requires and requires transitive to declare a dependency on a package or to share that dependency with any modules using the current module.

Identify advanced *module-info* keywords.   The provides keyword is used when exposing an API. The uses keyword is for consuming an API. The opens keyword is for allowing the use of reflection.

Display information about modules.   The java command can describe a module, list available modules, or show the module resolution. The jar command can describe a module similar to how the java command does. The jdeps command prints details about a module and packages. The jmod command provides various modes for working with JMOD files rather than JAR files.

Review Questions

The answers to the Appendix A review questions can be found in Appendix B.

1. Which of the following code snippets about `var` compile without issue when used in a method? (Choose all that apply.)

    A. `var spring = null;`

    B. `var fall = "leaves";`

    C. `var evening = 2; evening = null;`

    D. `var night = new Object();`

    E. `var day = 1/0;`

    F. `var winter = 12, cold;`

    G. `var fall = 2, autumn = 2;`

    H. `var morning = ""; morning = null;`

2. Which of the following statements about `var` are true? (Choose all that apply.)

    A. A var can be used as a constructor parameter.

    B. The type of var is known at compile time.

    C. A var cannot be used as an instance variable.

    D. A var can be used in a multiple variable assignment statement.

    E. The value of var cannot change at runtime.

    F. The type of var cannot change at runtime.

    G. The word var is a reserved word in Java.

3. Which of the following are valid instance variable declarations? (Choose all that apply.)

    A. `var null = 6_000;`

    B. `var $_ = 6_000;`

    C. `var $2 = 6_000f;`

    D. `var var = 3_0_00.0;`

    E. `var #CONS = 2_000.0;`

    F. `var %C = 6_000_L;`

    G. None of the above

4. Which of the following is an advantage of the Java Platform Module System?

    A. A central repository of all modules

    B. Encapsulating packages

    C. Encapsulating objects

    D. No defined types

    E. Platform independence

5. Which statement is true of the following module?

```
zoo.staff
|---zoo
    |-- staff
        |-- Vet.java
```

A. The directory structure shown is a valid module.

B. The directory structure would be a valid module if module.java were added directly underneath zoo.staff.

C. The directory structure would be a valid module if module.java were added directly underneath zoo.

D. The directory structure would be a valid module if module-info.java were added directly underneath zoo.staff.

E. The directory structure would be a valid module if module-info.java were added directly underneath zoo.

F. None of these changes would make this directory structure a valid module.

6. Suppose module puppy depends on module dog, and module dog depends on module animal. Fill in the blank so that code in module dog can access the animal.behavior package in module animal.

```
module animal {
    _____ animal.behavior;
}
```

A. export

B. exports

C. require

D. requires

E. require transitive

F. requires transitive

G. None of the above

7. Fill in the blanks so this command to run the program is correct:

```
java
    _____ zoo.animal.talks/zoo/animal/talks/Peacocks
    _____ modules
```

A. -d and -m

B. -d and -p

C. -m and -d

D. -m and -p

    E. –p and –d

    F. –p and –m

    G. None of the above

8. Which of the following statements are true in a `module-info.java` file? (Choose all that apply.)

    A. The opens keyword allows the use of reflection.

    B. The opens keyword declares an API is called.

    C. The use keyword allows the use of reflection.

    D. The use keyword declares an API is called.

    E. The uses keyword allows the use of reflection.

    F. The uses keyword declares an API is called.

    G. The file can be empty (zero bytes).

9. What is true of a module containing a file named `module-info.java` with the following contents? (Choose all that apply.)

```
module com.food.supplier {}
```

    A. All packages inside the module are automatically exported.

    B. No packages inside the module are automatically exported.

    C. A main method inside the module can be run.

    D. A main method inside the module cannot be run since the class is not exposed.

    E. The `module-info.java` file contains a compiler error.

    F. The `module-info.java` filename is incorrect.

10. Suppose module `puppy` depends on module `dog` and module `dog` depends on module `animal`. Which two lines allow module `puppy` to access the `animal.behavior` package in module `animal`? (Choose two.)

```
module animal {
    exports animal.behavior;
}
module dog {
    _____ animal;   // line S
}
module puppy {
    _____ dog;      // line T
}
```

    A. require on line S

    B. require on line T

    C. requires on line S

    D. requires on line T

    E. require transitive on line S

    F. require transitive on line T

    G. requires transitive on line S

    H. requires transitive on line T

11. Which commands take a --module-path parameter? (Choose all that apply.)

    A. javac

    B. java

    C. jar

    D. jdeps

    E. jmod

    F. None of the above

12. Which of the following are legal commands to run a modular program? (Choose all that apply.)

    A. java -p x -m x/x

    B. java -p x-x -m x/x

    C. java -p x -m x-x/x

    D. java -p x -m x/x-x

    E. java -p x -m x.x

    F. java -p x.x -m x.x

    G. None of the above

13. Which would best fill in the blank to complete the following code?

```
module _____ {
    exports com.unicorn.horn;
    exports com.unicorn.magic;
}
```

    A. com

    B. com.unicorn

    C. com.unicorn.horn

    D. com.unicorn.magic

    E. The code does not compile.

    F. The code compiles, but none of these would be a good choice.

14. Which are valid modes for the jmod command? (Choose all that apply.)

    A. add

    B. create

    C. `delete`

    D. `describe`

    E. `extract`

    F. `list`

    G. `show`

15. Suppose you have the commands `javac`, `java`, and `jar`. How many of them support a `--show-module-resolution` option?

    A. Zero

    B. One

    C. Two

    D. Three

16. Which are true statements about the following module? (Choose all that apply.)

```
class dragon {
    exports com.dragon.fire;
    exports com.dragon.scales to castle;
}
```

    A. All modules can reference the `com.dragon.fire` package.

    B. All modules can reference the `com.dragon.scales` package.

    C. Only the `castle` module can reference the `com.dragon.fire` package.

    D. Only the `castle` module can reference the `com.dragon.scales` package.

    E. None of the above

17. Which would you expect to see when describing any module?

    A. `requires java.base mandated`

    B. `requires java.core mandated`

    C. `requires java.lang mandated`

    D. `requires mandated java.base`

    E. `requires mandated java.core`

    F. `requires mandated java.lang`

    G. None of the above

18. Which are valid calls to list a summary of the dependencies? (Choose all that apply.)

    A. `jdeps flea.jar`

    B. `jdeps -s flea.jar`

    C. `jdeps -summary flea.jar`

    D. `jdeps --summary flea.jar`

    E. None of the above

19. Which is the first line to contain a compiler error?

```
1: module snake {
2:     exports com.snake.tail;
3:     exports com.snake.fangs to bird;
4:     requires skin;
5:     requires transitive skin;
6: }
```

A. Line 1

B. Line 2

C. Line 3

D. Line 4

E. Line 5

F. The code does not contain any compiler errors.

20. Which of the following would be a legal module name? (Choose all that apply.)

A. com.book

B. com-book

C. com.book$

D. com-book$

E. 4com.book

F. 4com-book

21. What can be created using the Java Platform Module System that could not be created without it? (Choose all that apply.)

A. JAR file

B. JMOD file

C. Smaller runtime images for distribution

D. Operating system–specific bytecode

E. TAR file

F. None of the above

22. Which of the following options does not have a one-character shortcut? (Choose all that apply.)

A. describe-module

B. list-modules

C. module

D. module-path

E. show-module-resolution

F. summary

23. Which of the following are legal commands to run a modular program where n is the module name and c is the class name? (Choose all that apply.)

A. `java -module-path x -m n.c`

B. `java --module-path x -p n.c`

C. `java --module-path x -m n/c`

D. `java --module-path x -p n/c`

E. `java --module-path x -m n c`

F. `java --module-path x -p n c`

G. None of the above

Appendix
B

Answers to Review Questions

Chapter ~~1.~~ 12 Java Fundamentals

1. **A, D.** Instance and `static` variables can be marked `final`, making option A correct. Effectively `final` means a local variable is not marked `final` but whose value does not change after it is set, making option B incorrect. The `final` modifier can be applied to classes, but not interfaces, making option C incorrect. Remember, interfaces are implicitly `abstract`, which is incompatible with `final`. Option D is correct, as the definition of a `final` class is that it cannot be extended. Option E is incorrect, as `final` refers only to the reference to an object, not its contents. Finally, option F is incorrect, as `var` and `final` can be used together.

2. **C.** When an enum contains only a list of values, the semicolon (;) after the list is optional. When an enum contains any other members, such as a constructor or variable, then it is required. Since the code is missing the semicolon, it does not compile, making option C the correct answer. There are no other compilation errors in this code. If the missing semicolon was added, then the program would print 0 1 2 at runtime.

3. **C.** Popcorn is an inner class. Inner classes are only allowed to contain `static` variables that are marked `final`. Since there are no other compilation errors, option C is the only correct answer. If the `final` modifier was added on line 6, then the code would print 10 at runtime. Note that `private` constructors can be used by any methods within the same class.

4. **B, F.** A `default` interface method is always `public`, whether you include the identifier or not, making option B correct and option A incorrect. Interfaces cannot contain `default static` methods, making option C incorrect. Option D is incorrect, as `private` interface methods are not inherited and cannot be marked `abstract`. Option E is incorrect, as a method can't be marked both `protected` and `private`. Finally, interfaces can include both `private` and `private static` methods, making option F correct.

5. **B, D.** Option B is a valid functional interface, one that could be assigned to a `Consumer<Camel>` reference. Notice that the `final` modifier is permitted on variables in the parameter list. Option D is correct, as the exception is being returned as an object and not thrown. This would be compatible with a `BiFunction` that included `RuntimeException` as its return type.

   Option A is incorrect because it mixes `var` and non-`var` parameters. If one argument uses `var`, then they all must use `var`. Option C is invalid because the variable b is used twice. Option E is incorrect, as a `return` statement is permitted only inside braces ({}). Option F is incorrect because the variable declaration requires a semicolon (;) after it. Finally, option G is incorrect. If the type is specified for one argument, then it must be specified for each and every argument.

6. **C, E.** You can reduce code duplication by moving shared code from `default` or `static` methods into a `private` or `private static` method. For this reason, option C is correct. Option E is also correct, as making interface methods `private` means users of the

interface do not have access to them. The rest of the options are not related to private methods, although backward compatibility does apply to default methods.

7. F. When using an enum in a switch statement, the case statement must be made up of the enum values only. If the enum name is used in the case statement value, then the code does not compile. For example, VANILLA is acceptable but Flavors.VANILLA is not. For this reason, the three case statements do not compile, making option F the correct answer. If these three lines were corrected, then the code would compile and produce a NullPointerException at runtime.

8. A, C. A functional interface can contain any number of nonabstract methods including default, private, static, and private static. For this reason, option A is correct, and option D is incorrect. Option B is incorrect, as classes are never considered functional interfaces. A functional interface contains exactly one abstract method, although methods that have matching signatures as public methods in java.lang.Object do not count toward the single method test. For these reasons, option C is correct, and option E is incorrect. Finally, option F is incorrect. While a functional interface can be marked with the @FunctionalInterface annotation, it is not required.

9. G. Trick question—the code does not compile! The Spirit class is marked final, so it cannot be extended. The main() method uses an anonymous inner class that inherits from Spirit, which is not allowed. If Spirit was not marked final, then options C and F would be correct. Option A would print Booo!!!, while options B, D, and E would not compile for various reasons.

10. E. The code OstrichWrangler class is a static nested class; therefore, it cannot access the instance member count. For this reason, line 6 does not compile, and option E is correct. If the static modifier on line 4 was removed, then the class would compile and produce two files: Ostrich.class and Ostrich$OstrichWrangler.class. You don't need to know that $ is the syntax, but you do need to know the number of classes and that OstrichWrangler is not a top-level class.

11. D. In this example, CanWalk and CanRun both implement a default walk() method. The definition of CanSprint extends these two interfaces and therefore won't compile unless the interface overrides both inherited methods. The version of walk() on line 12 is an overload, not an override, since it takes an int value. Since the interface doesn't override the methods, the compiler can't decide which default method to use, leading to a compiler error and making option D the correct answer.

12. C. The functional interface takes two int parameters. The code on line m1 attempts to use them as if one is an Object, resulting in a compiler error and making option C the correct answer. It also tries to return String even though the return data type for the functional interface method is boolean. It is tricky to use types in a lambda when they are implicitly specified. Remember to check the interface for the real type.

13. E, G. For this question, it helps to remember which implicit modifiers the compiler will insert and which it will not. Lines 2 and 3 compile with interface variables assumed to be public, static, and final. Line 4 also compiles, as static methods are assumed to be

public if not otherwise marked. Line 5 does not compile. Non-`static` methods within an interface must be explicitly marked `private` or `default`. Line 6 compiles, with the `public` modifier being added by the compiler. Line 7 does not compile, as interfaces do not have `protected` members. Finally, line 8 compiles, with no modifiers being added by the compiler.

14. E. `Diet` is an inner class, which requires an instance of `Deer` to instantiate. Since the `main()` method is `static`, there is no such instance. Therefore, the `main()` method does not compile, and option E is correct. If a reference to `Deer` were used, such as calling `new Deer().new Diet()`, then the code would compile and print bc at runtime.

15. G. The `isHealthy()` method is marked `abstract` in the enum; therefore, it must be implemented in each enum value declaration. Since only `INSECTS` implements it, the code does not compile, making option G correct. If the code were fixed to implement the `isHealthy()` method in each enum value, then the first three values printed would be `INSECTS`, 1, and `true`, with the fourth being determined by the implementation of `COOKIES.isHealthy()`.

16. A, D, E. A valid functional interface is one that contains a single abstract method, excluding any `public` methods that are already defined in the `java.lang.Object` class. `Transport` and `Boat` are valid functional interfaces, as they each contain a single abstract method: `go()` and `hashCode(String)`, respectively. Since the other methods are part of `Object`, they do not count as abstract methods. `Train` is also a functional interface since it extends `Transport` and does not define any additional abstract methods.

   `Car` is not a functional interface because it is an abstract class. `Locomotive` is not a functional interface because it includes two abstract methods, one of which is inherited. Finally, `Spaceship` is not a valid interface, let alone a functional interface, because a `default` method must provide a body. A quick way to test whether an interface is a functional interface is to apply the `@FunctionalInterface` annotation and check if the code still compiles.

17. A, F. Option A is a valid lambda expression. While `main()` is a `static` method, it can access `age` since it is using a reference to an instance of `Hyena`, which is effectively final in this method. Remember from your 1Z0-815 studies that `var` is a reserved type, not a reserved word, and may be used for variable names. Option F is also correct, with the lambda variable being a reference to a `Hyena` object. The variable is processed using deferred execution in the `testLaugh()` method.

   Options B and E are incorrect; since the local variable `age` is not effectively final, this would lead to a compilation error. Option C would also cause a compilation error, since the expression uses the variable name p, which is already declared within the method. Finally, option D is incorrect, as this is not even a lambda expression.

18. C, D, G. Option C is the correct way to create an instance of an inner class `Cub` using an instance of the outer class `Lion`. The syntax looks weird, but it creates an object of the outer class and then an object of the inner class from it. Options A, B, and E use incorrect syntax for creating an instance of the `Cub` class. Options D and G are the correct way to create an instance of the static nested `Den` class, as it does not require an instance of `Lion`,

while option F uses invalid syntax. Finally, option H is incorrect since it lacks an instance of Lion. If rest() were an instance method instead of a static method, then option H would be correct.

19. D. First off, if a class or interface inherits two interfaces containing default methods with the same signature, then it must override the method with its own implementation. The Penguin class does this correctly, so option E is incorrect. The way to access an inherited default method is by using the syntax Swim.super.perform(), making option D correct. We agree the syntax is bizarre, but you need to learn it. Options A, B, and C are incorrect and result in compiler errors.

20. A, B, C, D. Effectively final refers to local variables whose value is not changed after it is set. For this reason, option A is correct, and options E and F are incorrect. Options B and C are correct, as lambda expressions can access final and effectively final variables. Option D is also correct and is a common test for effectively final variables.

21. B, E. Like classes, interfaces allow instance methods to access static members, but not vice versa. Non-static private, abstract, and default methods are considered instance methods in interfaces. Line 3 does not compile because the static method hunt() cannot access an abstract instance method getName(). Line 6 does not compile because the private static method sneak() cannot access the private instance method roar(). The rest of the lines compile without issue.

22. D, F. Java added default methods primarily for backward compatibility. Using a default method allows you to add a new method to an interface without having to recompile a class that used an older version of the interface. For this reason, option D is correct. Option F is also correct, as default methods in some APIs offer a number of convenient methods to classes that implement the interface. The rest of the options are not related to default methods.

23. C, F. Enums are required to have a semicolon (;) after the list of values if there is anything else in the enum. Don't worry, you won't be expected to track down missing semicolons on the whole exam—only on enum questions. For this reason, line 5 should have a semicolon after it since it is the end of the list of enums, making option F correct. Enum constructors are implicitly private, making option C correct as well. The rest of the enum compiles without issue.

24. E. Option A does not compile because the second statement within the block is missing a semicolon (;) at the end. Option B is an invalid lambda expression because t is defined twice: in the parameter list and within the lambda expression. Options C and D are both missing a return statement and semicolon. Options E and F are both valid lambda expressions, although only option E matches the behavior of the Sloth class. In particular, option F only prints Sleep:, not Sleep: 10.0.

25. B. Zebra.this.x is the correct way to refer to x in the Zebra class. Line 5 defines an abstract local class within a method, while line 11 defines a concrete anonymous class that extends the Stripes class. The code compiles without issue and prints x is 24 at runtime, making option B the correct answer.

Chapter 2: Annotations

1. E. In an annotation, an optional element is specified with the default modifier, followed by a constant value. Required elements are specified by not providing a default value. Therefore, the lack of the default term indicates the element is required. For this reason, option E is correct.

2. D, F. Line 5 does not compile because = is used to assign a default value, rather than the default modifier. Line 7 does not compile because annotation and interface constants are implicitly public and cannot be marked private. The rest of the lines do not contain any compilation errors.

3. B, D, E. The annotations @Target and @Repeatable are specifically designed to be applied to annotations, making options D and E correct. Option B is also correct, as @Deprecated can be applied to almost any declaration. Option A is incorrect because @Override can be applied only to methods. Options C and F are incorrect because they are not the names of built-in annotations.

4. D. Annotations should include metadata (data about data) that is relatively constant, as opposed to attribute data, which is part of the object and can change frequently. The price, sales, inventory, and people who purchased a vehicle could fluctuate often, so using an annotation would be a poor choice. On the other hand, the number of passengers a vehicle is rated for is extra information about the vehicle and unlikely to change once established. Therefore, it is appropriate metadata and best served using an annotation.

5. B, C. Line 4 does not compile because the default value of an element must be a non-null constant expression. Line 5 also does not compile because an element type must be one of the predefined immutable types: a primitive, String, Class, enum, another annotation, or an array of these types. The rest of the lines do not contain any compilation errors.

6. E, G. The annotation declaration includes one required element, making option A incorrect. Options B, C, and D are incorrect because the Driver declaration does not contain an element named value(). If directions() were renamed in Driver to value(), then options B and D would be correct. The correct answers are options E and G. Option E uses the shorthand form in which the array braces ({}) can be dropped if there is only one element. Options C and F are not valid annotation uses, regardless of the annotation declaration. In this question, the @Documented and @Deprecated annotations have no impact on the solution.

7. A, B, C, D, E, F. Annotations can be applied to all of the declarations listed. If there is a type name used, an annotation can be applied.

8. B, F. In this question, Ferocious is the repeatable annotation, while FerociousPack is the containing type annotation. The containing type annotation should contain a single value() element that is an array of the repeatable annotation type. For this reason, option B is correct. Option A would allow FerociousPack to compile, but not Ferocious. Option C is an invalid annotation element type.

The repeatable annotation needs to specify the class name of its containing type annotation, making option F correct. While it is expected for repeatable annotations to contain elements to differentiate its usage, it is not required. For this reason, the usage of @Ferocious is a valid marker annotation on the Lion class, making option G incorrect.

9. D. To use an annotation with a value but not element name, the element must be declared with the name value(), not values(), making option A incorrect. The value() annotation may be required or optional, making option B incorrect. The annotation declaration may contain other elements, provided none is required, making option C incorrect. Option D is correct, as the annotation must not include any other values. Finally, option E is incorrect, as this is not a property of using a value() shorthand.

10. G. Furry is an annotation that can be applied only to types. In Bunny, it is applied to a method; therefore, it does not compile. If the @Target value was changed to ElementType.METHOD (or @Target removed entirely), then the rest of the code would compile without issue. The use of the shorthand notation for specifying a value() of an array is correct.

11. C, D, F. The @SafeVarargs annotation can be applied to a constructor or private, static, or final method that includes a varargs parameter. For these reasons, options C, D, and F are correct. Option A is incorrect, as the compiler cannot actually enforce that the operations are safe. It is up to the developer writing the method to verify that. Option B is incorrect as the annotation can be applied only to methods that cannot be overridden and abstract methods can always be overridden. Finally, option E is incorrect, as it is applied to the declaration, not the parameters.

12. B, C, D. Annotations cannot have constructors, so line 5 does not compile. Annotations can have variables, but they must be declared with a constant value. For this reason, line 6 does not compile. Line 7 does not compile as the element unit is missing parentheses after the element name. Lines 8 compiles and shows how to use annotation type with a default value.

13. A, D. An optional annotation element is one that is declared with a default value that may be optionally replaced when used in an annotation. For these reasons, options A and D are correct.

14. D. The @Retention annotation determines whether annotations are discarded when the code is compiled, at runtime, or not at all. The presence, or absence, of the @Documented annotation determines whether annotations are discarded within generated Javadoc. For these reasons, option D is correct.

15. B. A marker annotation is an annotation with no elements. It may or may not have constant variables, making option B correct. Option E is incorrect as no annotation can be extended.

16. F. The @SafeVarargs annotation does not take a value and can be applied only to methods that cannot be overridden (marked private, static, or final). For these reasons, options A and B produce compilation errors. Option C also does not compile, as this annotation can be applied only to other annotations. Even if you didn't remember that, it's clear it has nothing to do with hiding a compiler warning. Option D does not compile as @SuppressWarnings requires a value. Both options E and F allow the code to compile without error, although only option F will cause a compile without warnings. The unchecked value is required when performing unchecked generic operations.

17. B, E. The @FunctionalInterface marker annotation is used to document that an interface is a valid functional interface that contains exactly one abstract method, making option B correct. It is also useful in determining whether an interface is a valid functional interface, as the compiler will report an error if used incorrectly, making option E correct. The compiler can detect whether an interface is a functional interface even without the annotation, making options A and C incorrect.

18. C, D, E, F. Line 5 and 6 do not compile because Boolean and void are not supported annotation element types. It must be a primitive, String, Class, enum, another annotation, or an array of these types. Line 7 does not compile because annotation elements are implicitly public. Finally, line 8 does not compile because the Strong annotation does not contain a value() element, so the shorthand notation cannot be used. If line 2 were changed from force() to value(), then line 8 would compile. Without the change, though, the compiler error is on line 8. The rest of the lines do not contain any compilation errors, making options C, D, E, and F correct.

19. A, F. The @Override annotation can be applied to a method but will trigger a compiler error if the method signature does not match an inherited method, making option A correct. The annotation @Deprecated can be applied to a method but will not trigger any compiler errors based on the method signature. The annotations @FunctionalInterface, @Repeatable, and @Retention cannot be applied to methods, making these options incorrect. Finally, @SafeVarargs can be applied to a method but will trigger a compiler error if the method does not contain a varargs parameter or is able to be overridden (not marked private, static, or final).

20. D, F. Line 6 contains a compiler error since the element name buoyancy is required in the annotation. If the element were renamed to value() in the annotation declaration, then the element name would be optional. Line 8 also contains a compiler error. While an annotation can be used in a cast operation, it requires a type. If the cast expression was changed to (@Floats boolean), then it would compile. The rest of the code compiles without issue.

21. G. The @Inherited annotation determines whether or not annotations defined in a super type are automatically inherited in a child type. The @Target annotation determines the location or locations an annotation can be applied to. Since this was not an answer choice, option G is correct. Note that ElementType is an enum used by @Target, but it is not an annotation.

22. F. If @SuppressWarnings("deprecation") is applied to a method that is using a deprecated API, then warnings related to the usage will not be shown at compile time, making option F correct. Note that there are no built-in annotations called @Ignore or @IgnoreDeprecated.

23. A. This question, like some questions on the exam, includes extraneous information that you do not need to know to solve it. Therefore, you can assume the reflection code is valid.

That said, this code is not without problems. The default retention policy for all annotations is RetentionPolicy.CLASS if not explicitly stated otherwise. This means the annotation information is discarded at compile time and not available at runtime. For this reason, none of the members will print anything, making option A correct.

If @Retention(RetentionPolicy.RUNTIME) were added to the declaration of Plumber, then the worker member would cause the default annotation value(), Mario, to be printed at runtime, and option B would be the correct answer. Note that foreman would not cause Mario to be printed even with the corrected retention annotation. Setting the value of the annotation is not the same as setting the value of the variable foreman.

24. A, E. The annotation includes only one required element, and it is named value(), so it can be used without an element name provided it is the only value in the annotation. For this reason, option A is correct, and options B and D are incorrect. Since the type of the value() is an array, option B would work if it was changed to @Dance({33, 10}). Option C is incorrect because it attempts to assign a value to fast, which is a constant variable not an element. Option E is correct and is an example of an annotation replacing all of the optional values. Option F is incorrect, as value() is a required element.

25. C. The Javadoc @deprecated annotation should be used, which provides a reason for the deprecation and suggests an alternative. All of the other answers are incorrect, with options A and B having the wrong case too. Those annotations should be written @Repeatable and @Retention since they are Java annotations.

Chapter 3: Generics and Collections

1. B. The answer needs to implement List because the scenario allows duplicates. Since you need a List, you can eliminate options C and D immediately because HashMap is a Map and HashSet is a Set. Option A, Arrays, is trying to distract you. It is a utility class rather than a Collection. An array is not a collection. This leaves you with options B and E. Option B is a better answer than option E because LinkedList is both a List and a Queue, and you just need a regular List.

2. D. The answer needs to implement Map because you are dealing with key/value pairs per the unique id field. You can eliminate options A, C, and E immediately since they are not a Map. ArrayList is a List. HashSet and TreeSet are Sets. Now it is between HashMap and TreeMap. Since the question talks about ordering, you need the TreeMap. Therefore, the answer is option D.

3. C, G. Line 12 creates a List<?>, which means it is treated as if all the elements are of type Object rather than String. Lines 15 and 16 do not compile since they call the String methods isEmpty() and length(), which are not defined on Object. Line 13 creates a List<String> because var uses the type that it deduces from the context. Lines 17 and 18 do compile. However, List.of() creates an immutable list, so both of those lines would throw an UnsupportedOperationException if run. Therefore, options C and G are correct.

4. D. This is a FIFO (first-in, first-out) queue. On line 7, we remove the first element added, which is "hello". On line 8, we look at the new first element ("hi") but don't remove it. On lines 9 and 10, we remove each element in turn until no elements are left, printing hi and ola together. Note that we don't use an `Iterator` to loop through the `LinkedList` to avoid concurrent modification issues. The order in which the elements are stored internally is not part of the API contract.

5. B, F. Option A does not compile because the generic types are not compatible. We could say `HashSet<? extends Number> hs2 = new HashSet<Integer>();`. Option B uses a lower bound, so it allows superclass generic types. Option C does not compile because the diamond operator is allowed only on the right side. Option D does not compile because a `Set` is not a `List`. Option E does not compile because upper bounds are not allowed when instantiating the type. Finally, option F does compile because the upper bound is on the correct side of the =.

6. B. The class compiles and runs without issue. Line 10 gives a compiler warning for not using generics but not a compiler error. Line 4 compiles fine because `toString()` is defined on the `Object` class and is therefore always available to call.

Line 9 creates the `Hello` class with the generic type `String`. It also passes an `int` to the `println()` method, which gets autoboxed into an `Integer`. While the `println()` method takes a generic parameter of type T, it is not the same `<T>` defined for the class on line 1. Instead, it is a different T defined as part of the method declaration on line 5. Therefore, the `String` argument on line 9 applies only to the class. The method can actually take any object as a parameter including autoboxed primitives. Line 10 creates the `Hello` class with the generic type `Object` since no type is specified for that instance. It passes a `boolean` to `println()`, which gets autoboxed into a `Boolean`. The result is that hi-1hola-true is printed, making option B correct.

7. A, D. The code compiles fine. It allows any implementation of `Number` to be added. Lines 5 and 8 succesfully autobox the primitives into an `Integer` and `Long`, respectively. `HashSet` does not guarantee any iteration order, making options A and D correct.

8. B, F. We're looking for a `Comparator` definition that sorts in descending order by `beakLength`. Option A is incorrect because it sorts in ascending order by `beakLength`. Similarly, option C is incorrect because it sorts the `beakLength` in ascending order within those matches that have the same `name`. Option E is incorrect because there is no `thenComparingNumber()` method.

Option B is a correct answer, as it sorts by `beakLength` in descending order. Options D and F are trickier. First notice that we can call either `thenComparing()` or `thenComparingInt()` because the former will simply autobox the `int` into an `Integer`. Then observe what `reversed()` applies to. Option D is incorrect because it sorts by name in ascending order and only reverses the beak length of those with the same name. Option F creates a comparator that sorts by name in ascending order and then by beak size in ascending order. Finally, it reverses the result. This is just what we want, so option F is correct.

9. E. Trick question! The Map interface uses put() rather than add() to add elements to the map. If these examples used put(), the answer would be options A and C. Option B is no good because a long cannot be placed inside a Double without an explicit cast. Option D is no good because a char is not the same thing as a String.

10. A. The array is sorted using MyComparator, which sorts the elements in reverse alphabetical order in a case-insensitive fashion. Normally, numbers sort before letters. This code reverses that by calling the compareTo() method on b instead of a.

11. A. Line 3 uses local variable type inference to create the map. Lines 5 and 7 use autoboxing to convert between the int primitive and the Integer wrapper class. The keys map to their squared value. 1 maps to 1, 2 maps to 4, 3 maps to 9, 4 maps to 16, and so on.

12. A, B, D. The generic type must be Exception or a subclass of Exception since this is an upper bound. Options C and E are wrong because Throwable is a superclass of Exception. Option D uses an odd syntax by explicitly listing the type, but you should be able to recognize it as acceptable.

13. B, E. The showSize() method can take any type of List since it uses an unbounded wildcard. Option A is incorrect because it is a Set and not a List. Option C is incorrect because the wildcard is not allowed to be on the right side of an assignment. Option D is incorrect because the generic types are not compatible.

    Option B is correct because a lower-bounded wildcard allows that same type to be the generic. Option E is correct because Integer is a subclass of Number.

14. C. This question is difficult because it defines both Comparable and Comparator on the same object. The t1 object doesn't specify a Comparator, so it uses the Comparable object's compareTo() method. This sorts by the text instance variable. The t2 object did specify a Comparator when calling the constructor, so it uses the compare() method, which sorts by the int.

15. A. When using binarySearch(), the List must be sorted in the same order that the Comparator uses. Since the binarySearch() method does not specify a Comparator explicitly, the default sort order is used. Only c2 uses that sort order and correctly identifies that the value 2 is at index 0. Therefore, option A is correct. The other two comparators sort in descending order. Therefore, the precondition for binarySearch() is not met, and the result is undefined for those two.

16. B, D, F. The java.lang.Comparable interface is implemented on the object to compare. It specifies the compareTo() method, which takes one parameter. The java.util.Comparator interface specifies the compare() method, which takes two parameters.

17. B, D. Line 1 is a generic class that requires specifying a name for the type. Options A and C are incorrect because no type is specified. While you can use the diamond operator <> and the wildcard ? on variables and parameters, you cannot use them in a class declaration. This means option B is the only correct answer for line 1. Knowing this allows you to fill in line 3. Option E is incorrect because T is not a class and certainly not one compatible with String. Option F is incorrect because a wildcard cannot be specified on the right side when instantiating an object. We're left with the diamond operator, making option D correct.

18. A, B. Y is both a class and a type parameter. This means that within the class Z, when we refer to Y, it uses the type parameter. All of the choices that mention class Y are incorrect because it no longer means the class Y.

19. A, D. A LinkedList implements both List and Queue. The List interface has a method to remove by index. Since this method exists, Java does not autobox to call the other method. Queue has only the remove by object method, so Java does autobox there. Since the number 1 is not in the list, Java does not remove anything for the Queue.

20. E. This question looks like it is about generics, but it's not. It is trying to see whether you noticed that Map does not have a contains() method. It has containsKey() and containsValue() instead. If containsKey() was called, the answer would be false because 123 is an Integer key in the Map, rather than a String.

21. A, E. The key to this question is keeping track of the types. Line 48 is a Map<Integer, Integer>. Line 49 builds a List out of a Set of Entry objects, giving us List<Entry<Integer, Integer>>. This causes a compile error on line 56 since we can't multiply an Entry object by two.

Lines 51 through 54 are all of type List<Integer>. The first three are immutable, and the one on line 54 is mutable. This means line 57 throws an UnsupportedOperationException since we attempt to modify the list. Line 58 would work if we could get to it. Since there is one compiler error and one runtime error, options A and E are correct.

22. B. When using generic types in a method, the generic specification goes before the return type.

23. B, E. Both Comparator and Comparable are functional interfaces. However, Comparable is intended to be used on the object being compared, making option B correct. The removeIf() method allows specifying the lambda to check when removing elements, making option E correct. Option C is incorrect because the remove() method takes an instance of an object to look for in the Collection to remove. Option D is incorrect because removeAll() takes a Collection of objects to look for in the Collection to remove.

24. F. The first two lines correctly create a Set and make a copy of it. Option A is incorrect because forEach takes a Consumer parameter, which requires one parameter. Options B and C are close. The syntax for a lambda is correct. However, s is already defined as a local variable, and therefore the lambda can't redefine it. Options D and E use incorrect syntax for a method reference. Option F is correct.

25. F. The first call to merge() calls the mapping function and adds the two numbers to get 13. It then updates the map. The second call to merge() sees that the map currently has a null value for that key. It does not call the mapping function but instead replaces it with the new value of 3. Therefore, option F is correct.

Chapter 4: Functional Programming

1. D. No terminal operation is called, so the stream never executes. The first line creates an infinite stream reference. If the stream were executed on the second line, it would get the first two elements from that infinite stream, "" and "1", and add an extra character, resulting in "2" and "12", respectively. Since the stream is not executed, the reference is printed instead.

2. F. Both streams created in this code snippet are infinite streams. The variable b1 is set to true since anyMatch() terminates. Even though the stream is infinite, Java finds a match on the first element and stops looking. However, when allMatch() runs, it needs to keep going until the end of the stream since it keeps finding matches. Since all elements continue to match, the program hangs.

3. E. An infinite stream is generated where each element is twice as long as the previous one. While this code uses the three-parameter iterate() method, the condition is never false. The variable b1 is set to false because Java finds an element that matches when it gets to the element of length 4. However, the next line tries to operate on the same stream. Since streams can be used only once, this throws an exception that the "stream has already been operated upon or closed." If two different streams were used, the result would be option B.

4. A, B. Terminal operations are the final step in a stream pipeline. Exactly one is required, because it triggers the execution of the entire stream pipeline. Therefore, options A and B are correct. Option C is true of intermediate operations, rather than terminal operations. Option D is incorrect because peek() is an intermediate operation. Finally, option E is incorrect because once a stream pipeline is run, the Stream is marked invalid.

5. C, F. Yes, we know this question is a lot of reading. Remember to look for the differences between options rather than studying each line. These options all have much in common. All of them start out with a LongStream and attempt to convert it to an IntStream. However, options B and E are incorrect because they do not cast the long to an int, resulting in a compiler error on the mapToInt() calls.

    Next, we hit the second difference. Options A and D are incorrect because they are missing boxed() before the collect() call. Since groupingBy() is creating a Collection, we need a nonprimitive Stream. The final difference is that option F specifies the type of Collection. This is allowed, though, meaning both options C and F are correct.

6. A. Options C and D do not compile because these methods do not take a Predicate parameter and do not return a boolean. When working with streams, it is important to remember the behavior of the underlying functional interfaces. Options B and E are incorrect. While the code compiles, it runs infinitely. The stream has no way to know that a match won't show up later. Option A is correct because it is safe to return false as soon as one element passes through the stream that doesn't match.

7. F. There is no `Stream<T>` method called `compare()` or `compareTo()`, so options A through D can be eliminated. The `sorted()` method is correct to use in a stream pipeline to return a sorted `Stream`. The `collect()` method can be used to turn the stream into a `List`. The `collect()` method requires a collector be selected, making option E incorrect and option F correct.

8. D, E. The `average()` method returns an `OptionalDouble` since averages of any type can result in a fraction. Therefore, options A and B are both incorrect. The `findAny()` method returns an `OptionalInt` because there might not be any elements to find. Therefore, option D is correct. The `sum()` method returns an `int` rather than an `OptionalInt` because the sum of an empty list is zero. Therefore, option E is correct.

9. B, D. Lines 4–6 compile and run without issue, making option F incorrect. Line 4 creates a stream of elements [1, 2, 3]. Line 5 maps the stream to a new stream with values [10, 20, 30]. Line 6 filters out all items not less than 5, which in this case results in an empty stream. For this reason, `findFirst()` returns an empty `Optional`.

Option A does not compile. It would work for a `Stream<T>` object, but we have a `LongStream` and therefore need to call `getAsLong()`. Option C also does not compile, as it is missing the `::` that would make it a method reference. Options B and D both compile and run without error, although neither produces any output at runtime since the stream is empty.

10. F. Only one of the method calls, `forEach()`, is a terminal operation, so any answer in which M is not the last line will not execute the pipeline. This eliminates all but options C, E, and F. Option C is incorrect because `filter()` is called before `limit()`. Since none of the elements of the stream meets the requirement for the `Predicate<String>`, the `filter()` operation will run infinitely, never passing any elements to `limit()`. Option E is incorrect because there is no `limit()` operation, which means that the code would run infinitely. Only option F is correct. It first limits the infinite stream to a finite stream of 10 elements and then prints the result.

11. B, C, E. As written, the code doesn't compile because the `Collectors.joining()` expects to get a `Stream<String>`. Option B fixes this, at which point nothing is output because the collector creates a `String` without outputting the result. Option E fixes this and causes the output to be 11111. Since the post-increment operator is used, the stream contains an infinite number of the character 1. Option C fixes this and causes the stream to contain increasing numbers.

12. B, F, G. We can eliminate four choices right away. Options A and C are there to mislead you; these interfaces don't actually exist. Option D is incorrect because a `BiFunction<T,U,R>` takes three generic arguments, not two. Option E is incorrect because none of the examples returns a `boolean`.

Moving on to the remaining choices, the declaration on line 6 doesn't take any parameters, and it returns a `String`, so a `Supplier<String>` can fill in the blank, making option F correct. Another clue is that it uses a constructor reference, which should scream `Supplier`! This makes option F correct.

The declaration on line 7 requires you to recognize that `Consumer` and `Function`, along with their binary equivalents, have an `andThen()` method. This makes option B correct.

Finally, line 8 takes a single parameter, and it returns the same type, which is a UnaryOperator. Since the types are the same, only one generic parameter is needed, making option G correct.

13. F. If the map() and flatMap() calls were reversed, option B would be correct. In this case, the Stream created from the source is of type Stream<List>. Trying to use the addition operator (+) on a List is not supported in Java. Therefore, the code does not compile, and option F is correct.

14. B, D. Line 4 creates a Stream and uses autoboxing to put the Integer wrapper of 1 inside. Line 5 does not compile because boxed() is available only on primitive streams like IntStream, not Stream<Integer>. Line 6 converts to a double primitive, which works since Integer can be unboxed to a value that can be implicitly cast to a double. Line 7 does not compile for two reasons. First, converting from a double to an int would require an explicit cast. Also, mapToInt() returns an IntStream so the data type of s3 is incorrect. The rest of the lines compile without issue.

15. B, D. Options A and C do not compile, because they are invalid generic declarations. Primitives are not allowed as generics, and Map must have two generic type parameters. Option E is incorrect because partitioning only gives a Boolean key. Options B and D are correct because they return a Map with a Boolean key and a value type that can be customized to any Collection.

16. B, C. First, this mess of code does compile. While this code starts out with an infinite stream on line 23, it does become finite on line 24 thanks to limit(), making option F incorrect. The pipeline preserves only nonempty elements on line 25. Since there aren't any of those, the pipeline is empty. Line 26 converts this to an empty map.

Lines 27 and 28 create a Set with no elements and then another empty stream. Lines 29 and 30 convert the generic type of the Stream to List<String> and then String. Finally, line 31 gives us another Map<Boolean, List<String>>.

The partitioningBy() operation always returns a map with two Boolean keys, even if there are no corresponding values. Therefore, option B is correct if the code is kept as is. By contrast, groupingBy() returns only keys that are actually needed, making option C correct if the code is modified on line 31.

17. E. The question starts with a UnaryOperator<Integer>, which takes one parameter and returns a value of the same type. Therefore, option E is correct, as UnaryOperator actually extends Function. Notice that other options don't even compile because they have the wrong number of generic types for the functional interface provided. You should know that a BiFunction<T,U,R> takes three generic arguments, a BinaryOperator<T> takes one generic argument, and a Function<T,R> takes two generic arguments.

18. D. The terminal operation is count(). Since there is a terminal operation, the intermediate operations run. The peek() operation comes before the filter(), so both numbers are printed. After the filter(), the count() happens to be 1 since one of the numbers is filtered out. However, the result of the stream pipeline isn't stored in a variable or printed, and it is ignored.

19. A. The a.compose(b) method calls the Function parameter b before the reference Function variable a. In this case, that means that we multiply by 3 before adding 4. This gives a result of 7, making option A correct.

20. A, C, E. Java includes support for three primitive streams, along with numerous functional interfaces to go with them: int, double, and long. For this reason, options C and E are correct. There is one exception to this rule. While there is no BooleanStream class, there is a BooleanSupplier functional interface, making option A correct. Java does not include primitive streams or related functional interfaces for other numeric data types, making options B and D incorrect. Option F is incorrect because String is not a primitive, but an object. Only primitives have custom suppliers.

21. B. Both lists and streams have forEach() methods. There is no reason to collect into a list just to loop through it. Option A is incorrect because it does not contain a terminal operation or print anything. Options B and C both work. However, the question asks about the simplest way, which is option B.

22. C, E, F. Options A and B compile and return an empty string without throwing an exception, using a String and Supplier parameter, respectively. Option G does not compile as the get() method does not take a parameter. Options C and F throw a NoSuchElementException. Option E throws a RuntimeException. Option D looks correct but will compile only if the throw is removed. Remember, the orElseThrow() should get a lambda expression or method reference that returns an exception, not one that throws an exception.

Chapter 5: Exceptions, Assertions, and Localization

1. C. Exception and RuntimeException, along with many other exceptions in the Java API, define a no-argument constructor, a constructor that takes a String, and a constructor that takes a Throwable. For this reason, Danger compiles without issue. Catastrophe also compiles without issue. Just creating a new checked exception, without throwing it, does not require it to be handled or declared. Finally, Emergency does not compile. The no-argument constructor in Emergency must explicitly call a parent constructor, since Danger does not define a no-argument constructor.

2. A, D, E. Localization refers to user-facing elements. Dates, currency, and numbers are commonly used in different formats for different countries. Class and variable names, along with lambda expressions, are internal to the application, so there is no need to translate them for users.

3. G. A try-with-resources statement uses parentheses, (), rather than braces, {}, for the try section. This is likely subtler than a question that you'll get on the exam, but it is still important to be on alert for details. If parentheses were used instead of braces, then the code would compile and print TWDF at runtime.

4. F. The code does not compile because the throw and throws keywords are incorrectly used on lines 6, 7, and 9. If the keywords were fixed, then the rest of the code would compile and print a stack track with YesProblem at runtime.

5. E. A LocalDate does not have a time element. Therefore, a Date/Time formatter is not appropriate. The code compiles but throws an exception at runtime. If ISO_LOCAL_DATE was used, then the code would compile and option B would be the correct answer.

6. C. Java will first look for the most specific matches it can find, starting with Dolphins_en_US.properties. Since that is not an answer choice, it drops the country and looks for Dolphins_en.properties, making option C correct. Option B is incorrect because a country without a language is not a valid locale.

7. D. When working with a custom number formatter, the 0 symbol displays the digit as 0, even if it's not present, while the # symbol omits the digit from the start or end of the String if it is not present. Based on the requested output, a String that displays at least three digits before the decimal (including a comma) and at least one after the decimal is required. It should display a second digit after the decimal if one is available. For this reason, option D is the correct answer. In case you are curious, option A displays at most only one value to the right of the decimal, printing <5.2> <8.5> <1234>. Option B is close to the correct answer but always displays four digits to the left of the decimal, printing <0,005.21> <0,008.49> <1,234.0>. Finally, option C is missing the zeros padded to the left of the decimal and optional two values to the right of the decimal, printing <5.2> <8.5> <1,234.0>.

8. A, D. An assertion consists of a boolean expression followed by an optional colon (:) and message. The boolean expression is allowed to be in parentheses, but this is not required. Therefore, options A and D are correct.

9. B, E. An exception that must be handled or declared is a checked exception. A checked exception inherits Exception but not RuntimeException. The entire hierarchy counts, so options B and E are both correct.

10. B, C. The code does not compile, so option E is incorrect. Option A is incorrect because removing the exception from the declaration causes a compilation error on line 4, as FileNotFoundException is a checked exception that must be handled or declared. Option B is correct because the unhandled exception within the main() method becomes declared. Option C is also correct because the exception becomes handled. Option D is incorrect because the exception remains unhandled. Finally, option F is incorrect because the changes for option B or C will allow the code to compile.

11. C. The code compiles fine, so option E is incorrect. The command line has only two arguments, so args.length is 2 and the if statement is true. However, because assertions are not enabled, it does not throw an AssertionError, so option B is incorrect. The println() method attempts to print args[2], which generates an ArrayIndexOutOfBoundsException, so the answer is option C.

12. A, B. A try-with-resources statement does not require a catch or finally block. A traditional try statement requires at least one of the two. Neither statement can be written without a body encased in braces, {}.

13. C, D. The code compiles with the appropriate input, so option G is incorrect. A locale consists of a required lowercase language code and optional uppercase country code. In the `Locale()` constructor, the language code is provided first. For these reasons, options C and D are correct. Options E and F are incorrect because a `Locale` is created using a constructor or `Locale.Builder` class.

14. D. You can create custom checked, unchecked exceptions, and even errors. The default constructor is used if one is not supplied. There is no requirement to implement any specific methods.

15. F. The code compiles, but the first line produces a runtime exception regardless of what is inserted into the blank. When creating a custom formatter, any nonsymbol code must be properly escaped using pairs of single quotes (`'`). In this case, it fails because o is not a symbol. Even if you didn't know o wasn't a symbol, the code contains an unmatched single quote. If the properly escaped value of `"hh' o''clock'"` was used, then the correct answers would be `ZonedDateTime`, `LocalDateTime`, and `LocalTime`. Option B would not be correct because `LocalDate` values do not have an hour part.

16. B, C. The code compiles, so option E is incorrect. While it is a poor practice to modify variables in an assertion statement, it is allowed. To enable assertions, use the flag –ea or –enableassertions. To disable assertions, use the flag –da or –disableassertions. The colon indicates a specific class. Option A is incorrect, as assertions are already disabled by default. Option B is correct because it turns on assertions for all classes (except system classes). Option C is correct because it disables assertions for all classes but then turns them back on for this class. Finally, option D is incorrect as it enables assertions everywhere except the On class.

17. D, F. Option A is incorrect because Java will look at parent bundles if a key is not found in a specified resource bundle. Option B is incorrect because resource bundles are loaded from `static` factory methods. In fact, `ResourceBundle` is an `abstract` class, so calling that constructor is not even possible. Option C is incorrect, as resource bundle values are read from the `ResourceBundle` object directly. Option D is correct because the locale is changed only in memory. Option E is incorrect, as the resource bundle for the default locale may be used if there is no resource bundle for the specified locale (or its locale without a country code). Finally, option F is correct. The JVM will set a default locale automatically, making it possible to use a resource bundle for a locale, even if a locale was not explicitly set.

18. C. After both resources are declared and created in the try-with-resources statement, T is printed as part of the body. Then the try-with-resources completes and closes the resources in reverse order from which they were declared. After W is printed, an exception is thrown. However, the remaining resource still needs to be closed, so D is printed. Once all the resources are closed, the exception is thrown and swallowed in the catch block, causing E to be printed. Last, the `finally` block is run, printing F. Therefore, the answer is TWDEF.

19. D. Java will use `Dolphins_fr.properties` as the matching resource bundle on line 7 because it is an exact match on the language of the requested locale. Line 8 finds a

matching key in this file. Line 9 does not find a match in that file; therefore, it has to look higher up in the hierarchy. Once a bundle is chosen, only resources in that hierarchy are allowed. It cannot use the default locale anymore, but it can use the default resource bundle specified by `Dolphins.properties`.

20. B. The `MessageFormat` class supports parametrized `String` values that take input values, while the `Properties` class supports providing a default value if the property is not set. For this reason, option B is correct.

21. C. The code does not compile because the multi-`catch` on line 7 cannot catch both a superclass and a related subclass. Options A and B do not address this problem, so they are incorrect. Since the `try` body throws `SneezeException`, it can be caught in a `catch` block, making option C correct. Option D allows the `catch` block to compile but causes a compiler error on line 6. Both of the custom exceptions are checked and must be handled or declared in the `main()` method. A `SneezeException` is not a `SniffleException`, so the exception is not handled. Likewise, option E leads to an unhandled exception compiler error on line 6.

22. E. Even though `ldt` has both a date and time, the formatter outputs only time.

23. A, E. Resources must inherit `AutoCloseable` to be used in a try-with-resources block. Since `Closeable`, which is used for I/O classes, extends `AutoCloseable`, both may be used.

24. E. The `Properties` class defines a `get()` method that does not allow for a default value. It also has a `getProperty()` method, which returns the default value if the key is not provided.

25. G. The code does compile because the resource `walk1` is not `final` or effectively final and cannot be used in the declaration of a try-with-resources statement. If the line that set `walk1` to `null` was removed, then the code would compile and print `blizzard 2` at runtime, with the exception inside the `try` block being the primary exception since it is thrown first. Then two suppressed exceptions would be added to it when trying to close the `AutoCloseable` resources.

26. A, E. Line 5 does not compile because `assert` is a keyword, making option A correct. Options B and C are both incorrect because the parentheses and message are both optional. Option D is incorrect because assertions should never alter outcomes, as they may be disabled at runtime. Option E is correct because checking an argument passed from elsewhere in the program is an appropriate use of an assertion.

27. E. The `Locale.Builder` class requires that the `build()` method be called to actually create the `Locale` object. For this reason, the two `Locale.setDefault()` statements do not compile because the input is not a `Locale`, making option E the correct answer. If the proper `build()` calls were added, then the code would compile and print the value for Germany, 2,40 €. As in the exam, though, you did not have to know the format of currency values in a particular locale to answer the question. Note that the default locale category is ignored since an explicit currency locale is selected.

Chapter 6: Modular Applications

1. D. A service consists of the service provider interface and logic to look up implementations using a service locator. This makes option D correct. Make sure you know that the service provider itself is the implementation, which is not considered part of the service.

2. E, F. Automatic modules are on the module path but do not have a `module-info` file. Named modules are on the module path and do have a `module-info`. Unnamed modules are on the classpath. Therefore, options E and F are correct.

3. A, B, E. Any version information at the end of the JAR filename is removed, making options A and B correct. Underscores (`_`) are turned into dots (`.`), making options C and D incorrect. Other special characters like a dollar sign (`$`) are also turned into dots. However, adjacent dots are merged, and leading/trailing dots are removed. Therefore, option E is correct.

4. A, E. A cyclic dependency is when a module graph forms a circle. Option A is correct because the Java Platform Module System does not allow cyclic dependencies between modules. No such restriction exists for packages, making option B incorrect. A cyclic dependency can involve two or more modules that require each other, making option E correct, while options C and D are incorrect. Finally. Option F is incorrect because unnamed modules cannot be referenced from an automatic module.

5. B. Option B is correct because `java.base` is provided by default. It contains the `java.lang` package among others.

6. F. The `provides` directive takes the interface name first and the implementing class name second. The `with` keyword is used. Only option F meets these two criteria, making it the correct answer.

7. A, B, C, F. Option D is incorrect because it is a package name rather than a module name. Option E is incorrect because `java.base` is the module name, not `jdk.base`. Option G is wrong because we made it up. Options A, B, C, and F are correct.

8. D. There is no `getStream()` method on a `ServiceLoader`, making options A and C incorrect. Option B does not compile because the `stream()` method returns a list of `Provider` interfaces and needs to be converted to the `Unicorn` interface we are interested in. Therefore, option D is correct.

9. C. The `jdeps` command has an option `--internal-jdk` that lists any code using unsupported/internal APIs and prints a table with suggested alternatives. This makes option C correct. Option D is incorrect because it does not print out the table with a suggested alternative. Options A, B, E, F, and G are incorrect because those options do not exist.

10. B. A top-down migration strategy first places all JARs on the module path. Then it migrates the top-level module to be a named module, leaving the other modules as automatic modules. Option B is correct as it matches both of those characteristics.

11. A. Since this is a new module, you need to compile the new module. However, none of the existing modules needs to be recompiled, making option A correct. The service locator will see the new service provider simply by having the new service provider on the module path.

12. B. The most commonly used packages are in the `java.base` module, making option B correct.

13. A, E, F. Option A is correct because the service provider interface must specify `exports` for any other modules to reference it. Option F is correct because the service provider needs access to the service provider interface. Option E is also correct because the service provider needs to declare that it provides the service.

14. B, E, F. Since the new project extracts the common code, it must have an `exports` directive for that code, making option B correct. The other two modules do not have to expose anything. They must have a `requires` directive to be able to use the exported code, making options E and F correct.

15. H. This question is tricky. The service provider must have a `uses` directive, but that is on the service provider interface. No modules need to specify `requires` on the service provider since that is the implementation.

16. A. Since the JAR is on the classpath, it is treated as a regular unnamed module even though it has a `module-info` file inside. Remember from learning about top-down migration that modules on the module path are not allowed to refer to the classpath, making options B, and D incorrect. The classpath does not have a facility to restrict packages, making option A correct and options C and E incorrect.

17. A, F. An automatic module exports all packages, making option A correct. An unnamed module is not available to any modules on the module path. Therefore, it doesn't export any packages, and option F is correct.

18. A, C, D. Option A and C are correct because both the consumer and the service locator depend on the service provider interface. Additionally, option D is correct because the service locator must specify that it `uses` the service provider interface to look it up.

19. C, E. The `jdeps` command provides information about the class or package level depending on the options passed, making option C correct. It is frequently used to determine what dependencies you will need when converting to modules. This makes it useful to run against a regular JAR, making option E correct.

20. E. Trick question! An unnamed module doesn't use a `module-info` file. Therefore, option E is correct. An unnamed module can access an automatic module. The unnamed module would simply treat the automatic module as a regular JAR without involving the `module.info` file.

Chapter 7: Concurrency

1. D, F. There is no such class within the Java API called `ParallelStream`, so options A and E are incorrect. The method defined in the `Stream` class to create a parallel stream from an existing stream is `parallel()`; therefore, option F is correct, and option C is incorrect. The method defined in the `Collection` class to create a parallel stream from a collection is `parallelStream()`; therefore, option D is correct, and option B is incorrect.

2. A, D. The `tryLock()` method returns immediately with a value of `false` if the lock cannot be acquired. Unlike `lock()`, it does not wait for a lock to become available. This code fails to check the return value, resulting in the protected code being entered regardless of whether the lock is obtained. In some executions (when `tryLock()` returns `true` on every call), the code will complete successfully and print 45 at runtime, making option A correct. On other executions (when `tryLock()` returns `false` at least once), the `unlock()` method will throw an `IllegalMonitorStateException` at runtime, making option D correct. Option B would be possible if there was no lock at all, although in this case, failure to acquire a lock results in an exception at runtime.

3. A, C, D, F. All methods are capable of throwing unchecked exceptions, so option A is correct. Runnable and `Callable` statements both do not take any arguments, so option B is incorrect. Only `Callable` is capable of throwing checked exceptions, so option C is also correct. Both Runnable and `Callable` are functional interfaces that can be implemented with a lambda expression, so option D is also correct. Finally, Runnable returns `void` and `Callable` returns a generic type, making option F correct and making options E and G incorrect.

4. B, C. The code does not compile, so options A and F are incorrect. The first problem is that although a `ScheduledExecutorService` is created, it is assigned to an `ExecutorService`. The type of the variable on line w1 would have to be updated to `ScheduledExecutorService` for the code to compile, making option B correct. The second problem is that `scheduleWithFixedDelay()` supports only Runnable, not `Callable`, and any attempt to return a value is invalid in a Runnable lambda expression; therefore, line w2 will also not compile, and option C is correct. The rest of the lines compile without issue, so options D and E are incorrect.

5. C. The code compiles and runs without throwing an exception or entering an infinite loop, so options D, E, and F are incorrect. The key here is that the increment operator ++ is not atomic. While the first part of the output will always be 100, the second part is nondeterministic. It could output any value from 1 to 100, because the threads can overwrite each other's work. Therefore, option C is the correct answer, and options A and B are incorrect.

6. C, E. The code compiles, so option G is incorrect. The `peek()` method on a parallel stream will process the elements concurrently, so the order cannot be determined ahead of time, and option C is correct. The `forEachOrdered()` method will process the elements in the order they are stored in the stream, making option E correct. It does not sort the elements, so option D is incorrect.

7. D. Livelock occurs when two or more threads are conceptually blocked forever, although they are each still active and trying to complete their task. A race condition is an undesirable result that occurs when two tasks are completed at the same time, which should have been completed sequentially.

8. A. The method looks like it executes a task concurrently, but it actually runs synchronously. In each iteration of the forEach() loop, the process waits for the run() method to complete before moving on. For this reason, the code is actually thread-safe. It executes a total of 499 times, since the second value of range() excludes the 500. Since the program consistently prints 499 at runtime, option A is correct. Note that if start() had been used instead of run() (or the stream was parallel), then the output would be indeterminate, and option C would have been correct.

9. C. If a task is submitted to a thread executor, and the thread executor does not have any available threads, the call to the task will return immediately with the task being queued internally by the thread executor. For this reason, option C is the correct answer.

10. A. The code compiles without issue, so option D is incorrect. The CopyOnWriteArrrayList class is designed to preserve the original list on iteration, so the first loop will be executed exactly three times and, in the process, will increase the size of tigers to six elements. The ConcurrentSkipListSet class allows modifications, and since it enforces uniqueness of its elements, the value 5 is added only once leading to a total of four elements in bears. Finally, despite using the elements of lions to populate the collections, tigers and bears are not backed by the original list, so the size of lions is 3 throughout this program. For these reasons, the program prints 3 6 4, and option A is correct.

11. F. The code compiles and runs without issue, so options C, D, E, and G are incorrect. There are two important things to notice. First, synchronizing on the first variable doesn't actually impact the results of the code. Second, sorting on a parallel stream does not mean that findAny() will return the first record. The findAny() method will return the value from the first thread that retrieves a record. Therefore, the output is not guaranteed, and option F is correct. Option A looks correct, but even on serial streams, findAny() is free to select any element.

12. B. The code snippet submits three tasks to an ExecutorService, shuts it down, and then waits for the results. The awaitTermination() method waits a specified amount of time for all tasks to complete, and the service to finish shutting down. Since each five-second task is still executing, the awaitTermination() method will return with a value of false after two seconds but not throw an exception. For these reasons, option B is correct.

13. C. The code does not compile, so options A and E are incorrect. The problem here is that c1 is an int and c2 is a String, so the code fails to combine on line q2, since calling length() on an int is not allowed, and option C is correct. The rest of the lines compile without issue. Note that calling parallel() on an already parallel stream is allowed, and it may in fact return the same object.

14. C, E. The code compiles without issue, so option D is incorrect. Since both tasks are submitted to the same thread executor pool, the order cannot be determined, so options A and B are incorrect, and option C is correct. The key here is that the order in which the resources o1 and o2 are synchronized could result in a deadlock. For example, if the first thread gets a lock on o1 and the second thread gets a lock on o2 before either thread can get their second lock, then the code will hang at runtime, making option E correct. The code cannot produce a livelock, since both threads are waiting, so option F is incorrect. Finally, if a deadlock does occur, an exception will not be thrown, so option G is incorrect.

15. A. The code compiles and runs without issue, so options C, D, E, and F are incorrect. The collect() operation groups the animals into those that do and do not start with the letter p. Note that there are four animals that do not start with the letter p and three animals that do. The logical complement operator (!) before the startsWith() method means that results are reversed, so the output is 3 4 and option A is correct, making option B incorrect.

16. F. The lock() method will wait indefinitely for a lock, so option A is incorrect. Options B and C are also incorrect, as the correct method name to attempt to acquire a lock is tryLock(). Option D is incorrect, as fairness is set to false by default and must be enabled by using an overloaded constructor. Finally, option E is incorrect because a thread that holds the lock may have called lock() or tryLock() multiple times. A thread needs to call unlock() once for each call to lock() and tryLock().

17. D. The methods on line 5, 6, 7, and 8 each throw InterruptedException, which is a checked exception; therefore, the method does not compile, and option D is the only correct answer. If InterruptedException was declared in the method signature on line 3, then the answer would be option F, because adding items to the queue may be blocked at runtime. In this case, the queue is passed into the method, so there could be other threads operating on it. Finally, if the operations were not blocked and there were no other operations on the queue, then the output would be 103 20, and the answer would be option B.

18. C, E, G. A Callable lambda expression takes no values and returns a generic type; therefore, options C, E, and G are correct. Options A and F are incorrect because they both take an input parameter. Option B is incorrect because it does not return a value. Option D is not a valid lambda expression, because it is missing a semicolon at the end of the return statement, which is required when inside braces {}.

19. F, H. The application compiles and does not throw an exception, so options B, C, D, E, and G are incorrect. Even though the stream is processed in sequential order, the tasks are submitted to a thread executor, which may complete the tasks in any order. Therefore, the output cannot be determined ahead of time, and option F is correct. Finally, the thread executor is never shut down; therefore, the code will run but it will never terminate, making option H also correct.

20. F. The key to solving this question is to remember that the execute() method returns void, not a Future object. Therefore, line n1 does not compile, and option F is the correct answer. If the submit() method had been used instead of execute(), then option C would have been the correct answer, as the output of the submit(Runnable) task is a Future<?> object that can only return null on its get() method.

21. A, D. The findFirst() method guarantees the first element in the stream will be returned, whether it is serial or parallel, making options A and D correct. While option B may consistently print 1 at runtime, the behavior of findAny() on a serial stream is not guaranteed, so option B is incorrect. Option C is likewise incorrect, with the output being random at runtime. Option E is incorrect because any of the previous options will allow the code to compile.

22. B. The code compiles and runs without issue, so options D, E, F, and G are incorrect. The key aspect to notice in the code is that a single-thread executor is used, meaning that no task will be executed concurrently. Therefore, the results are valid and predictable with 100 100 being the output, and option B is the correct answer. If a pooled thread executor was used with at least two threads, then the sheepCount2++ operations could overwrite each other, making the second value indeterminate at the end of the program. In this case, option C would be the correct answer.

23. F. The code compiles without issue, so options B, C, and D are incorrect. The limit on the cyclic barrier is 10, but the stream can generate only up to 9 threads that reach the barrier; therefore, the limit can never be reached, and option F is the correct answer, making options A and E incorrect. Even if the limit(9) statement was changed to limit(10), the program could still hang since the JVM might not allocate 10 threads to the parallel stream.

24. A, F. The class compiles without issue, so option A is correct, and options B and C are incorrect. Since getInstance() is a static method and sellTickets() is an instance method, lines k1 and k4 synchronize on different objects, making option D incorrect. The class is not thread-safe because the addTickets() method is not synchronized, and option E is incorrect. For example, one thread could call sellTickets() while another thread calls addTickets(). These methods are not synchronized with each other and could cause an invalid number of tickets due to a race condition.

Finally, option F is correct because the getInstance() method is synchronized. Since the constructor is private, this method is the only way to create an instance of TicketManager outside the class. The first thread to enter the method will set the instance variable, and all other threads will use the existing value. This is actually a singleton pattern.

25. A, D. By itself, concurrency does not guarantee which task will be completed first, so option A is correct. Furthermore, applications with numerous resource requests will often be stuck waiting for a resource, which allows other tasks to run. Therefore, they tend to benefit more from concurrency than CPU-intensive tasks, so option D is also correct. Option B is incorrect because concurrency may in fact make an application slower if it is truly single-threaded in nature. Keep in mind that there is a cost associated with allocating additional memory and CPU time to manage the concurrent process. Option C is incorrect because single-processor CPUs have been benefiting from concurrency for decades. Finally, option E is incorrect; there are numerous examples in this chapter of concurrent tasks sharing memory.

26. C, D. The code compiles and runs without issue, so options F and G are incorrect. The return type of performCount() is void, so submit() is interpreted as being applied to a Runnable expression. While submit(Runnable) does return a Future<?>, calling get() on it always returns null. For this reason, options A and B are incorrect, and option C is correct. The performCount() method can also throw a runtime exception, which will then be thrown by the get() call as an ExecutionException; therefore, option D is also a correct answer. Finally, it is also possible for our performCount() to hang indefinitely, such as with a deadlock or infinite loop. Luckily, the call to get() includes a timeout value. While each call to Future.get() can wait up to a day for a result, it will eventually finish, so option E is incorrect.

Chapter 8: I/O

1. F. Since the question asks about putting data into a structured object, the best class would be one that deserializes the data. Therefore, ObjectInputStream is the best choice. ObjectWriter, BufferedStream, and ObjectReader are not I/O stream classes. ObjectOutputStream is an I/O class but is used to serialize data, not deserialize it. FileReader can be used to read text file data and construct an object, but the question asks what would be the best class to use for binary data.

2. C, E, G. The command to move a file or directory using a File is renameTo(), not mv() or move(), making options A and D incorrect, and option E correct. The commands to create a directory using a File are mkdir() and mkdirs(), not createDirectory(), making option B incorrect, and options C and G correct. The mkdirs() differs from mkdir() by creating any missing directories along the path. Finally, option F is incorrect as there is no command to copy a file in the File class. You would need to use an I/O stream to copy the file along with its contents.

3. B. The code compiles and runs without issue, so options F and G are incorrect. The key here is that while Eagle is serializable, its parent class, Bird, is not. Therefore, none of the members of Bird will be serialized. Even if you didn't know that, you should know what happens on deserialization. During deserialization, Java calls the constructor of the first nonserializable parent. In this case, the Bird constructor is called, with name being set to Matt, making option B correct. Note that none of the constructors or instance initializers in Eagle is executed as part of deserialization.

4. A, D. The code will compile if the correct classes are used, so option G is incorrect. Remember, a try-with-resources statement can use resources declared before the start of the statement. The reference type of wrapper is InputStream, so we need a class that inherits InputStream. We can eliminate BufferedWriter, ObjectOutputStream, and BufferedReader since their names do not end in InputStream. Next, we see the class must take another stream as input, so we need to choose the remaining streams that are high-level streams. BufferedInputStream is a high-level stream, so option A is correct. Even though the instance is already a BufferedInputStream, there's no rule that it can't be wrapped multiple times by a high-level stream. Option B is incorrect, as FileInputStream operates on a file, not another stream. Finally, option D is correct—an ObjectInputStream is a high-level stream that operates on other streams.

5. B, E. The JVM creates one instance of the `Console` object as a singleton, making option C incorrect. If the console is unavailable, `System.console()` will return `null`, making option B correct. The method cannot throw an `IOException` because it is not declared as a checked exception. Therefore, option A is incorrect. Option D is incorrect, as a `Console` can be used for both reading and writing data. The `Console` class includes a `format()` method to write data to the output stream, making option E correct. Since there is no `println()` method, as `writer()` must be called first, option F is incorrect.

6. C, D, E. All I/O streams should be closed after use or a resource leak might ensue, making option C correct. While a try-with-resources statement is the preferred way to close an I/O stream, it can be closed with a traditional `try` statement that uses a `finally` block. For this reason, both options D and E are correct.

7. G. Not all I/O streams support the `mark()` operation; therefore, without calling `markSupported()` on the stream, the result is unknown until runtime. If the stream does support the `mark()` operation, then the result would be XYZY, and option D would be correct. The `reset()` operation puts the stream back in the position before the `mark()` was called, and `skip(1)` will skip X. If the stream does not support the `mark()` operation, a run-time exception would likely be thrown, and option F would be correct. Since you don't know if the input stream supports the `mark()` operation, option G is the only correct choice.

8. A, F. In Java, serialization is the process of turning an object to a stream, while deserial-ization is the process of turning that stream back into an object. For this reason, option A is correct, and option B is incorrect. Option C is incorrect, because many nonthread classes are not marked `Serializable` for various reasons. The `Serializable` interface is a marker interface that does not contain any abstract methods, making options D and E incorrect. Finally, option F is correct, because `readObject()` declares the `ClassNotFoundException` even if the class is not cast to a specific type.

9. A. Paths that begin with the root directory are absolute paths, so option A is correct, and option C is incorrect. Option B is incorrect because the path could be a file or directory within the file system. There is no rule that files have to end with a file extension. Option D is incorrect, as it is possible to create a `File` reference to files and directories that do not exist. Option E is also incorrect. The `delete()` method returns `false` if the file or directory cannot be deleted.

10. E, F. For a class to be serialized, it must implement the `Serializable` interface and con-tain instance members that are serializable or marked `transient`. For these reasons, options E and F are correct. Marking a class `final` does not impact its ability to be serial-ized, so option A is incorrect. Option B is incorrect, as `Serializable` is an interface, not a class. Option C is incorrect. While it is a good practice for a serializable class to include a `static serialVersionUID` variable, it is not required. Finally, option D is incorrect as `static` members of the class are ignored on serialization already.

11. C. The code compiles, so options D and E are incorrect. The method looks like it will delete a directory tree but contains a bug. It never deletes any directories, only files. The result of executing this program is that it will delete all files within a directory tree, but none of the directories. For this reason, option C is correct.

12. E. The code does not compile, as the `Writer` methods `append()` and `flush()` both throw an `IOException` that must be handled or declared. Even without those lines of code, the try-with-resources statement itself must be handled or declared, since the `close()` method throws a checked `IOException` exception. For this reason, option E is correct. If the `main()` method was corrected to declare `IOException`, then the code would compile. If the `Console` was not available, it would throw a `NullPointerException` on the call to `c.writer()`; otherwise, it would print whatever the user typed in. For these reasons, options B and D would be correct.

13. B, E. Option A does not compile, as there is no `File` constructor that takes three parameters. Option B is correct and is the proper way to create a `File` instance with a single `String` parameter. Option C is incorrect, as there is no constructor that takes a `String` followed by a `File`. There is a constructor that takes a `File` followed by a `String`, making option E correct. Option D is incorrect because the first parameter is missing a slash (`/`) to indicate it is an absolute path. Since it's a relative path, it is correct only when the user's current directory is the root directory.

14. A, C, E. The `System` class has three streams: `in` is for input, `err` is for error, and `out` is for output. Therefore, options A, C, and E are correct. The others do not exist.

15. E. `PrintStream` and `PrintWriter` are the only I/O classes that you need to know that don't have a complementary `InputStream` or `Reader` class, so option E is correct.

16. A, D. The method compiles, so option E is incorrect. The method creates a `new-zoo.txt` file and copies the first line from `zoo-data.txt` into it, making option A correct. The try-with-resources statement closes all of declared resources including the `FileWriter` `o`. For this reason, the `Writer` is closed when the last `o.write()` is called, resulting in an `IOException` at runtime and making option D correct. Option F is incorrect because this implementation uses the character stream classes, which inherit from `Reader` or `Writer`.

17. C. The code compiles without issue. Since we're told the `Reader` supports `mark()`, the code also runs without throwing an exception. P is added to the `StringBuilder` first. Next, the position in the stream is marked before E. The E is added to the `StringBuilder`, with AC being skipped, then the O is added to the `StringBuilder`, with CK being skipped. The stream is then `reset()` to the position before the E. The call to `skip(0)` doesn't do anything since there are no characters to skip, so E is added onto the `StringBuilder` in the next `read()` call. The value PEOE is printed, and option C is correct.

18. B, C, D. Since you need to write primitives and `String` values, the `OutputStream` classes are appropriate. Therefore, you can eliminate options A and F since they use `Writer` classes. Next, `DirectoryOutputStream` is not a `java.io` class, so option E is incorrect. The data should be written to the file directly using the `FileOutputStream` class, buffered with the `BufferedOutputStream` class, and automatically serialized with the `ObjectOutputStream` class, so options B, C, and D are correct. `PrintStream` is an `OutputStream`, so it could be used to format the data. Unfortunately, since everything is converted to a `String`, the underlying data type information would be lost. For this reason, option G is incorrect.

19. C, E, G. First, the method does compile, so options A and B are incorrect. Methods to read/write byte[] values exist in the abstract parent of all I/O stream classes. This implementation is not correct, though, as the return value of read(buffer) is not used properly. It will only correctly copy files whose character count is a multiple of 10, making option C correct and option D incorrect. Option E is also correct as the data may not have made it to disk yet. Option F would be correct if the flush() method was called after every write. Finally, option G is correct as the reader stream is never closed.

20. C. Console includes a format() method that takes a String along with a list of arguments and writes it directly to the output stream, making option C correct. Options A and B are incorrect, as reader() returns a Reader, which does not define any print methods. Options D and E would be correct if the line was just a String. Since neither of those methods take additional arguments, they are incorrect.

21. A, C. Character stream classes often include built-in convenience methods for working with String data, so option A is correct. They also handle character encoding automatically, so option C is also correct. The rest of the statements are irrelevant or incorrect and are not properties of all character streams.

22. G. The code compiles, so option F is incorrect. To be serializable, a class must implement the Serializable interface, which Zebra does. It must also contain instance members that either are marked transient or are serializable. The instance member stripes is of type Object, which is not serializable. If Object implemented Serializable, then all objects would be serializable by default, defeating the purpose of having the Serializable interface. Therefore, the Zebra class is not serializable, with the program throwing an exception at runtime if serialized and making option G correct. If stripes were removed from the class, then options A and C would be the correct answers, as name and age are both marked transient.

Chapter 9: NIO.2

1. E. The relativize() method takes a Path value, not a String. For this reason, line 5 does not compile, and option E is correct. If line 5 was corrected to use a Path value, then the code would compile, but it would print the value of the Path created on line 4. Since Path is immutable, the operations on line 5 are not saved anywhere. For this reason, option D would be correct. Finally, if the value on line 5 was assigned to path and printed on line 6, then option A would be correct.

2. F. The code does not compile, as Files.deleteIfExists() declares the checked IOException that must be handled or declared. Remember, most Files methods declare IOException, especially the ones that modify a file or directory. For this reason, option F is correct. If the method was corrected to declare the appropriate exceptions, then option C would be correct. Option B would also be correct, if the method were provided a symbolic link that pointed to an empty directory. Options A and E would not print anything, as Files.isDirectory() returns false for both. Finally, option D would throw a DirectoryNotEmptyException at runtime.

3. C, E. The method to create a directory in the `Files` class is `createDirectory()`, not `mkdir()`. For this reason, line 6 does not compile, and option C is correct. In addition, the `setTimes()` method is available only on `BasicFileAttributeView`, not the read-only `BasicFileAttributes`, so line 8 will also not compile, making option E correct.

4. C. First, the code compiles and runs without issue, so options F and G are incorrect. Let's take this one step at a time. First, the `subpath()` method is applied to the absolute path, which returns the relative path `animals/bear`. Next, the `getName()` method is applied to the relative path, and since this is indexed from zero, it returns the relative path `bear`. Finally, the `toAbsolutePath()` method is applied to the relative path `bear`, resulting in the current directory `/user/home` being incorporated into the path. The final output is the absolute path `/user/home/bear`, making option C correct.

5. B, C. The code snippet will attempt to create a directory if the target of the symbolic link exists and is a directory. If the directory already exists, though, it will throw an exception. For this reason, option A is incorrect, and option B is correct. It will be created in `/mammal/kangaroo/joey`, and also reachable at `/kang/joey` because of the symbolic link, making option C correct.

6. C. The `filter()` operation applied to a `Stream<Path>` takes only one parameter, not two, so the code does not compile, and option C is correct. If the code was rewritten to use the `Files.find()` method with the `BiPredicate` as input (along with a `maxDepth` value), then the output would be option B, `Has  Sub`, since the directory is given to be empty. For fun, we reversed the expected output of the ternary operation.

7. F. The code compiles without issue, so options D and E are incorrect. The method `Files.isSameFile()` first checks to see whether the `Path` values are the same in terms of `equals()`. Since the first path is relative and the second path is absolute, this comparison will return `false`, forcing `isSameFile()` to check for the existence of both paths in the file system. Since we know `/zoo/turkey` does not exist, a `NoSuchFileException` is thrown, and option F is the correct answer. Options A, B, and C are incorrect since an exception is thrown at runtime.

8. B, D, G. Options A and E are incorrect because `Path` and `FileSystem`, respectively, are abstract types that should be instantiated using a factory method. Option C is incorrect because the `static` method in the `Path` interface is `of()`, not `get()`. Option F is incorrect because the `static` method in the `Paths` class is `get()`, not `getPath()`. Options B and D are correct ways to obtain a `Path` instance. Option G is also correct, as there is an overloaded `static` method in `Path` that takes a URI instead of a `String`.

9. C. The code compiles and runs without issue, so option E is incorrect. For this question, you have to remember two things. First, the `resolve()` method does not normalize any path symbols, so options A and B are not correct. Second, calling `resolve()` with an absolute path as a parameter returns the absolute path, so option C is correct, and option D is incorrect.

10. B, C. The methods are not the same, because `Files.lines()` returns a `Stream<String>` and `Files.readAllLines()` returns a `List<String>`, so option F is incorrect. Option A is incorrect, because performance is not often the reason to prefer one to the other. `Files.lines()` processes each line via lazy evaluation, while `Files.readAllLines()` reads the entire file into memory all at once. For this reason, `Files.lines()` works better on large files with limited memory available, and option B is correct. Although a `List` can be converted to a stream, this requires an extra step; therefore, option C is correct since the resulting object can be chained directly to a stream. Finally, options D and E are incorrect because they are true for both methods.

11. D. The target path of the file after the `move()` operation is `/animals`, not `/animals/monkey.txt`, so options A and B are both incorrect. Option B will actually throw an exception at runtime since `/animals` already exists and is a directory. Next, the `NOFOLLOW_LINKS` option means that if the source is a symbolic link, the link itself and not the target will be copied at runtime, so option C is also incorrect. The option `ATOMIC_MOVE` means that any process monitoring the file system will not see an incomplete file during the move, so option D is correct. Option E is incorrect, since there are circumstances in which the operation would be allowed. In particular, if `/animals` did not exist then the operation would complete successfully.

12. A, C, E. Options A, C, and E are all properties of NIO.2 and are good reasons to use it over the `java.io.File` class. Option B is incorrect, as both `java.io.File` and NIO.2 include a method to list the contents of a directory. Option D is also incorrect as both APIs can delete only empty directories, not a directory tree. Finally, option F is incorrect, as sending email messages is not a feature of either API.

13. A. The code compiles and runs without issue, so options C, D, and E are incorrect. Even though the file is copied with attributes preserved, the file is considered a separate file, so the output is `false`, making option A correct and option B incorrect. Remember, `isSameFile()` returns `true` only if the files pointed to in the file system are the same, without regard to the file contents.

14. C. The code compiles and runs without issue, so options D, E, and F are incorrect. The most important thing to notice is that the depth parameter specified as the second argument to `find()` is 0, meaning the only record that will be searched is the top-level directory. Since we know that the top directory is a directory and not a symbolic link, no other paths will be visited, and nothing will be printed. For these reasons, option C is the correct answer.

15. E. The `java.io.File` method `listFiles()` retrieves the members of the current directory without traversing any subdirectories. Option E is correct, as `Files.list()` returns a `Stream<Path>` of a single directory. `Files.walk()` is close, but it iterates over the entire directory tree, not just a single directory. The rest of the methods do not exist.

16. D, E, F. Whether a path is a symbolic link, file, or directory is not relevant, so options A and C are incorrect. Using a view to read multiple attributes leads to fewer round-trips between the process and the file system and better performance, so options D and F are correct. For reading single attributes, there is little or no expected gain, so option B is incorrect. Finally, views can be used to access file system–specific attributes that are not available in `Files` methods; therefore, option E is correct.

17. B. The `readAllLines()` method returns a `List`, not a `Stream`. Therefore, the call to `flatMap()` is invalid, and option B is correct. If the `Files.lines()` method were instead used, it would print the contents of the file one capitalized word at a time, with commas removed.

18. A, D. The code compiles without issue, so options E and F are incorrect. The `toRealPath()` method will simplify the path to `/animals` and throw an exception if it does not exist, making option D correct. If the path does exist, calling `getParent()` on it returns the root directory. Walking the root directory with the filter expression will print all `.java` files in the root directory (along with all `.java` files in the directory tree), making option A correct. Option B is incorrect because it will skip files and directories that do not end in the `.java` extension. Option C is also incorrect as `Files.walk()` does not follow symbolic links by default. Only if the `FOLLOW_LINKS` option is provided and a cycle is encountered will the exception be thrown.

19. D. The code compiles and runs without issue, so option F is incorrect. If you simplify the redundant path symbols, then p1 and p2 represent the same path, `/lizard/walking.txt`. Therefore, `isSameFile()` returns `true`. The second output is `false`, because `equals()` checks only if the path values are the same, without reducing the path symbols. Finally, the normalized paths are the same, since all extra symbols have been removed, so the last line outputs `true`. For these reasons, option D is correct.

20. B. The `normalize()` method does not convert a relative path into an absolute path; therefore, the path value after the first line is just the current directory symbol. The `for()` loop iterates the name values, but since there is only one entry, the loop terminates after a single iteration. Therefore, option B is correct.

21. B. The method compiles without issue, so option E is incorrect. Option F is also incorrect. Even though `/flip` exists, `createDirectories()` does not throw an exception if the path already exists. If `createDirectory()` were used instead, then option F would be correct. Next, the `copy()` command takes a target that is the path to the new file location, not the directory to be copied into. Therefore, the target path should be `/flip/sounds.txt`, not `/flip`. For this reason, options A and C are incorrect. Since the question says the file already exists, the `REPLACE_EXISTING` option must be specified or an exception will be thrown at runtime, making option B the correct answer.

22. B, E. Option F is incorrect, as the code does compile. The method copies the contents of a file, but it removes all the line breaks. The `while()` loop would need to include a call to `w.newLine()` to correctly copy the file. For this reason, option A is incorrect. Option B is correct, and options C and D are incorrect. The `APPEND` option creates the file if it does not exist; otherwise, it starts writing from the end of the file. Option E is correct because the resources created in the method are not closed or declared inside a try-with-resources statement.

Chapter 10: JDBC

1. **B, F.** The `Driver` and `PreparedStatement` interfaces are part of the JDK, making options A and E incorrect. The concrete `DriverManager` class is also part of the JDK, making options C and D incorrect. Options B and F are correct since the implementation of these interfaces is part of the database-specific driver JAR file.

2. **C, F.** A JDBC URL has three parts. The first part is the string `jdbc`, making option C correct. The second part is the subprotocol. This is the vendor/product name, which isn't an answer choice. The subname is vendor-specific, making option F correct as well.

3. **A.** A JDBC URL has three main parts separated by single colons, making options B, C, E, and F incorrect. The first part is always `jdbc`, making option D incorrect. Therefore, the correct answer is option A. Notice that you can get this right even if you've never heard of the Sybase database before.

4. **B, D.** When setting parameters on a `PreparedStatement`, there are only options that take an index, making options C and F incorrect. The indexing starts with 1, making option A incorrect. This query has only one parameter, so option E is also incorrect. Option B is correct because it simply sets the parameter. Option D is also correct because it sets the parameter and then immediately overwrites it with the same value.

5. **C.** A `Connection` is created using a `static` method on `DriverManager`. It does not use a constructor. Therefore, option C is correct. If the `Connection` was created properly, the answer would be option B.

6. **B.** The first line has a return type of `boolean`, making it an `execute()` call. The second line returns the number of modified rows, making it an `executeUpdate()` call. The third line returns the results of a query, making it an `executeQuery()` call.

7. **A, B, E.** CRUD stands for Create, Read, Update, Delete, making options A, B, and E correct.

8. **C.** This code works as expected. It updates each of the five rows in the table and returns the number of rows updated. Therefore, option C is correct.

9. **A, B.** Option A is one of the answers because you are supposed to use braces ({}) for all SQL in a `CallableStatement`. Option B is the other answer because each parameter should be passed with a question mark (?). The rest of the code is correct. Note that your database might not behave the way that's described here, but you still need to know this syntax for the exam.

10. **E.** The code compiles because `PreparedStatement` extends `Statement` and `Statement` allows passing a `String` in the `executeQuery()` call. While `PreparedStatement` can have bind variables, `Statement` cannot. Since this code uses `executeQuery(sql)` in `Statement`, it fails at runtime. A `SQLException` is thrown, making option E correct.

11. D. JDBC code throws a `SQLException`, which is a checked exception. The code does not handle or declare this exception, and therefore it doesn't compile. Since the code doesn't compile, option D is correct. If the exception were handled or declared, the answer would be option C.

12. D. JDBC resources should be closed in the reverse order from that in which they were opened. The order for opening is `Connection`, `CallableStatement`, and `ResultSet`. The order for closing is `ResultSet`, `CallableStatement`, and `Connection`.

13. C. This code calls the `PreparedStatement` twice. The first time, it gets the numbers greater than 3. Since there are two such numbers, it prints two lines. The second time, it gets the numbers greater than 100. There are no such numbers, so the `ResultSet` is empty. A total of two lines is printed, making option C correct.

14. B, F. In a `ResultSet`, columns are indexed starting with 1, not 0. Therefore, options A, C, and E are incorrect. There are methods to get the column as a `String` or `Object`. However, option D is incorrect because an `Object` cannot be assigned to a `String` without a cast.

15. C. Since an `OUT` parameter is used, the code should call `registerOutParameter()`. Since this is missing, option C is correct.

16. E. First, notice that this code uses a `PreparedStatement`. Options A, B, and C are incorrect because they are for a `CallableStatement`. Next, remember that the number of parameters must be an exact match, making option E correct. Remember that you will not be tested on SQL syntax. When you see a question that appears to be about SQL, think about what it might be trying to test you on.

17. D. This code calls the `PreparedStatement` twice. The first time, it gets the numbers greater than 3. Since there are two such numbers, it prints two lines. Since the parameter is not set between the first and second calls, the second attempt also prints two rows. A total of four lines are printed, making option D correct.

18. D. Before accessing data from a `ResultSet`, the cursor needs to be positioned. The call to `rs.next()` is missing from this code.

19. E. This code should call `prepareStatement()` instead of `prepareCall()` since it not executing a stored procedure. Since we are using `var`, it does compile. Java will happily create a `CallableStatement` for you. Since this compile safety is lost, the code will not cause issues until runtime. At that point, Java will complain that you are trying to execute SQL as if it were a stored procedure, making option E correct.

20. E. Since the code calls `registerOutParameter()`, we know the stored procedure cannot use an `IN` parameter. Further, there is no `setInt()`, so it cannot be an `INOUT` parameter either. Therefore, the stored procedure must use an `OUT` parameter, making option E the answer.

21. B. The `prepareStatement()` method requires SQL be passed in. Since this parameter is omitted, line 27 does not compile, and option B is correct. Line 30 also does not compile as the method should be `getInt()`. However, the question asked about the first compiler error.

Chapter 11: Security

1. D. A distributed denial of service (DDoS) attack requires multiple requests by definition. Even a regular denial of service attack often requires multiple requests. For example, if you forget to close resources, it will take a number of tries for your application to run out of resources. Therefore, option D is correct.

2. A, C, D. Since the class is final, it restricts extensibility, making option D correct. The private variable limits accessibility, making option C correct. Finally, option A is correct. This is an immutable class since it's not possible to change the state after construction. This class does not do any validation, making option B incorrect.

3. A. The PutField class is used with the writeObject() method, making option A correct. There is also a GetField class used with the readObject() method.

4. B, D. Option A is incorrect because it does not make a copy. Options E and F are incorrect because ArrayList does not have a copy() method. Option C is incorrect because the clone() method returns an Object and needs to be cast, so that option does not compile. Options B and D are correct because they copy the ArrayList using the copy constructor and clone() method, respectively.

5. D. When deserializing an object, Java does not call the constructor. Therefore, option D is correct.

6. A, F. The clone() method is declared on the Object class. Option A is correct because it will always compile. However, the call will throw an exception if the class that is being cloned does not implement Cloneable. Assuming this interface is implemented, the default implementation creates a shallow copy, making option F correct. If the class wants to implement a deep copy, it must override the clone() method with a custom implementation.

7. F. This is a trick question—there is no attack. Option E is incorrect because SQL leak is not the name of an attack. Option C is incorrect because the PreparedStatement and ResultSet are closed in a try-with-resources block. While we do not see the Connection closed, we also don't see it opened. The exam allows us to assume code that we can't see is correct. Option D is an incorrect answer because bind variables are being used properly with a PreparedStatement. Options A and B are incorrect because they are not related to the example. Since none of these attacks applies here, option F is correct.

8. E. The policy compiles and uses correct syntax. However, it gives permissions that are too broad. The user needs to be able to read a book, so write permissions should not be granted.

9. A, C. Many programs use confidential information securely, making option A correct. After all, you wouldn't be able to bank online if programs couldn't work with confidential information. It is also OK to put it in certain data structures. A built-in Java API puts a password in a char[], making option C correct. Exposing the information unintentionally is not OK, making option B incorrect. Sharing confidential information with others is definitely not OK, making option D incorrect.

10. C, D. Any resource accessing things outside your program should be closed. Options C and D are correct because I/O and JDBC meet this criteria.

11. A, F. An inclusion attack needs to include something. Options A and F are correct because they are used with XML and ZIP file respectively. Options B and D are incorrect because injection is not an inclusion attack. Options C and E are not inclusion attacks either. In fact, you might not have heard of them. Both are attacks used against web applications. Don't worry if you see something on the exam that you haven't heard of; it isn't a correct answer.

12. D. The validation code checks that each character is between 0 and 9. Since it is comparing to allowed values, this is an example of a whitelist, and option D is correct. If it were the opposite, it would be a blacklist. There is no such thing as a gray or orange list.

13. E, F. Option A is incorrect because good encapsulation requires `private` state rather than declaring the class `final`. Option B is incorrect because the well-encapsulated `Camel` class can have a getter that exposes the `species` variable to be modified. Options C and D are incorrect because a class can be `final` while having `public` variables and be mutable. Option E is correct because methods that expose `species` could change it, which would prevent immutability. Option F is correct because you cannot enforce immutability in a subclass.

14. B, C, D. Any information the user can see requires care. Options B, C, and D are correct for this reason. Comments and variable names are part of the program, not the data it handles, making options A and E incorrect.

15. A, B, F. The `serialPersistentFields` field is used to specify which fields should be used in serialization. It must be declared `private static final`, or it will be ignored. Therefore, options A, B, and F are correct.

16. C, D. The application should log a message or throw an exception, making options C and D correct. It should not immediately terminate the program with `System.exit()` as that does not execute gracefully, making option A incorrect. It also should not ignore the issue, making option B incorrect.

17. A, B, E. Options A and E are correct because they prevent subclasses from being created outside the class definition. Option B is also correct because it prevents overriding the method. Options C and D are incorrect because `transient` is a modifier for variables, not classes or methods.

18. A. Reading an extremely large file is a form of a denial of service attack, making option A correct.

19. C. Options B and F are incorrect because these method names are not used by any serialization or deserialization process. Options A and D are incorrect because the return type for these methods is `void`, not `Object`. Option E is almost correct, as that is a valid method signature, but our question asks for the method used in deserialization, not serialization. Option C is the correct answer.

20. C. A shallow copy does not create copies of the nested objects, making option C correct. Options B and D are incorrect because narrow and wide copies are not terms. Option A is incorrect because a deep copy does copy the nested objects.

Appendix A: The Upgrade Exam

1. B, D, E, H. A var cannot be initialized with a null value, but it can be assigned a null value if the underlying type is not a primitive. For these reasons, option H is correct, but options A and C are incorrect. Options B and D are correct as the underlying types are String and Object, respectively. Option E is correct, as this is a valid numeric expression. You might know that dividing by zero produces a runtime exception, but the question was only about whether or not the code compiled. Finally, options F and G are incorrect as var cannot be used in a multiple variable assignment.

2. B, C, F. A var cannot be used for a constructor or method parameter, nor for an instance or class variable, making option A incorrect and option C correct. The type of var is known at compile time and the type cannot be changed at runtime, although its value can change at runtime. For these reasons, options B and F are correct, and option E is incorrect. Option D is incorrect, as var is not permitted in multiple variable declarations. Finally, option G is incorrect, as var is not a reserved word in Java.

3. G. None of these declarations is a valid instance variable declaration, as var cannot be used with instance variables, only local variables. For this reason, option G is the only correct answer. If the question were changed to be about local variable declarations, though, then the correct answers would be B, C, and D. An identifier must start with a letter, $, or _, so options E and F would be incorrect. Finally, null is a reserved word but var is not, so option A would be incorrect.

4. B. Option B is correct since modules allow you to specify which packages can be called by external code. Options C and E are incorrect because they are provided by Java without the module system. Option A is incorrect because there is not a central repository of modules. Option D is incorrect because Java defines types.

5. D. Modules are required to have a module-info.java file at the root directory of the module. Option D matches this requirement.

6. B. Options A, C, and E are incorrect because they refer to keywords that don't exist. The exports keyword is used when allowing a package to be called by code outside of the module, making option B the correct answer. Notice that options D and F are incorrect because requires uses module names and not package names.

7. G. The -m or --module option is used to specify the module and class name. The -p or -module-path option is used to specify the location of the modules. Option D would be correct if the rest of the command were correct. However, running a program requires specifying the package name with periods (.) instead of slashes. Since the command is incorrect, option G is correct.

8. A, F, G. Options C and D are incorrect because there is no use keyword. Options A and F are correct because opens is for reflection and uses declares an API that consumes a service. Option G is also correct as the file can be completely empty. This is just something you have to memorize.

9. B, C. Packages inside a module are not exported by default, making option B correct and option A incorrect. Exporting is necessary for other code to use the packages; it is not necessary to call the main method at the command line, making option C correct and option D incorrect. The `module-info.java` file has the correct name and compiles, making options E and F incorrect.

10. D, G. Options A, B, E, and F are incorrect because they refer to keywords that don't exist. The `requires transitive` keyword is used when specifying a module to be used by the requesting module and any other modules that use the requesting module. Therefore, `dog` needs to specify the transitive relationship, and option G is correct. The module `puppy` just needs to `require dog`, and it gets the transitive dependencies, making option D correct.

11. A, B, D. Options A and B are correct because the `-p` (`--module-path`) option can be passed when compiling or running a program. Option D is also correct because `jdeps` can use the `--module-path` option when listing dependency information.

12. A, B. The `-p` specifies the module path. This is just a directory, so all of the options have a legal module path. The `-m` specifies the module, which has two parts separated by a slash. Options E and F are incorrect since there is no slash. The first part is the module name. It is separated by periods (.) rather than dashes (-), making option C incorrect. The second part is the package and class name, again separated by periods. The package and class names must be legal Java identifiers. Dashes (-) are not allowed, ruling out option D. This leaves options A and B as the correct answers.

13. B. A module claims the packages underneath it. Therefore, options C and D are not good module names. Either would exclude the other package name. Options A and B both meet the criteria of being a higher-level package. However, option A would claim many other packages including `com.sybex`. This is not a good choice, making option B the correct answer.

14. B, D, E, F. This is another question you just have to memorize. The `jmod` command has five modes you need to be able to list: `create`, `extract`, `describe`, `list`, and `hash`. The `hash` operation is not an answer choice. The other four are making options B, D, E, and F correct.

15. B. The `java` command uses this option to print information when the program loads. You might think `jar` does the same thing since it runs a program too. Alas, this parameter does not exist on `jar`.

16. E. There is a trick here. A module definition uses the keyword `module` rather than `class`. Since the code does not compile, option E is correct. If the code did compile, options A and D would be correct.

17. A. When running `java` with the `-d` option, all the required modules are listed. Additionally, the `java.base` module is listed since it is included automatically. The line ends with `mandated`, making option A correct. The `java.lang` is a trick since that is a package that is imported by default in a class rather than a module.

18. B, C. Option A will run, but it will print details rather than a summary. Options B and C are both valid options for the jdeps command. Remember that -summary uses a single dash (-).

19. E. The module name is valid as are the exports statements. Lines 4 and 5 are tricky because each is valid independently. However, the same module name is not allowed to be used in two requires statements. The second one fails to compile on line 5, making option E the answer.

20. A, C. Module names look a lot like package names. Each segment is separated by a period (.) and uses characters valid in Java identifiers. Since identifiers are not allowed to begin with numbers, options E and F are incorrect. Dashes (-) are not allowed either, ruling out options B and D. That leaves options A and C as the correct answers.

21. B, C. Option A is incorrect because JAR files have always been available regardless of the JPMS. Option D is incorrect because bytecode runs on the JVM and is not operating system–specific by definition. While it is possible to run the tar command, this has nothing to do with Java, making option E incorrect. Option B is one of the correct answers as the jmod command creates a JMOD file. Option C is the other correct answer because smaller runtime images are one of the benefits of the JPMS.

22. B, E. Option A is incorrect because describe-module has the d equivalent. Option C is incorrect because module has the m equivalent. Option D is incorrect because module-path has the p equivalent. Option F is incorrect because summary has the s equivalent. Options B and E are the correct answers because they do not have equivalents.

23. C. The -p option is a shorter form of --module-path. Since the same option cannot be specified twice, options B, D, and F are incorrect. The --module option is an alternate form of -m. The module name and class name are separated with a slash, making option C the answer.

Index

Symbols

<> (diamond) operator, 113–114
:: operator, 108

A

absolute path, 422–423, 478–479
abstract classes, *versus* interfaces, 32
abstract method, 5, 11
add() method, 116
allMatch() method, 197, 199–200
ambiguous type errors, 108
and() method, 186
andThen() method, 186
annotations
  @ symbol, 61
  arrays, of values, passing,
    73–74
  constant variables, 68
  containing type, 80
  creating, 64–69
  in declarations, 69–70
  declaring, 65, 92
    annotation-specific, 74–82
  @Deprecated, 85–86
  @Documented, 78–79
  elements, 61, 92
    abstract, 67–68
    default value, 66–67
    modifiers, 67–68
    optional, 66
    public, 67–68
    required and optional, 71
    specifying, 65
    type, selecting, 67
    value(), 71–73
  @FunctionalInterface, 84–85
  @Inherited, 79
  Javadoc, 78–79
  marker annotations, 64
  metadata and, 60–61, 63
  purpose, 61–63
  relationships and, 62
  @Repeatable, 79–81
  @Retention, 77–78
  rules, 68–69
  @SafeVarargs, 88–89
  shorthand notations, 73–74
  Spring Framework, 63
  @SuppressWarnings, 86–88
  @Target, 74
    default behavior, 82
    ElementType values, 74–76
    TYPE_USE parameter, 76–77
anonymous classes
  defining, 18–20
  lambda expressions and, 20
anyMatch() method, 199–200
application migration
  bottom-up, 322–323
  cyclic dependency, 326–328
  order, 321–322
  splitting big projects, 325–326
  top-down, 324–325
arguments, passing, 160–161
arrays, passing, annotations and, 73–74
ASCII characters, 422
assert keyword, 265
assert statement, 264–265
assertions
  applications, 268
  applying, 267–268
  declaring, 264–268
  disabling, 267
  enabling, 266–267
  syntax errors, 265
  versus unit tests, 264
  writing, 268
asynchronous tasks, threads, 352
attribute data, 60
autoboxing, 111–112
automatic modules, 312–315
automatic resource management, 256

Online Test Bank

Register to gain one year of FREE access after activation to the online interactive test bank to help you study for your OCP Java SE 11 Programmer II certification exam—included with your purchase of this book! All of the chapter review questions in this book and the online only practice exams are included in the online test bank so you can practice in a timed and graded setting.

Register and Access the Online Test Bank

To register your book and get access to the online test bank, follow these steps:

1. Go to bit.ly/SybexTest (this address is case sensitive)!
2. Select your book from the list.
3. Complete the required registration information, including answering the security verification to prove book ownership. You will be emailed a pin code.
4. Follow the directions in the email or go to www.wiley.com/go/sybextestprep.
5. Find your book on that page and click the "Register or Login" link with it. Then enter the pin code you received and click the "Activate PIN" button.
6. On the Create an Account or Login page, enter your username and password, and click Login or, if you don't have an account already, create a new account.
7. At this point, you should be in the test bank site with your new test bank listed at the top of the page. If you do not see it there, please refresh the page or log out and log back in.